INDIA'S GRAND STRATEGY

War and International Politics in South Asia

Series Editor: **Srinath Raghavan**
　　　　　　　Senior Fellow, Centre for Policy Research, New Delhi.

This Series seeks to foster original and rigorous scholarship on the dynamics of war and international politics in South Asia. Following Clausewitz, war is understood as both a political and a social phenomenon which manifests itself in a variety of forms ranging from total wars to armed insurrections. International politics is closely intertwined with it, for war not only plays an important role in the formation of an international order but also a threat to its continued existence. The Series will therefore focus on the international as well as domestic dimensions of war and security in South Asia. Comparative studies with other geographical areas are also of interest.

　　A fundamental premise of this Series is that we cannot do justice to the complexities of war by studying it from any single, privileged academic stand point; the phenomenon is best explained in a multidisciplinary framework. The Series welcomes a wide array of approaches, paradigms and methodologies, and is interested in historical, theoretical, and policy-oriented scholarship. In addition to monographs, the Series will from time to time publish collections of essays.

Also in this Series

Fighting Like a Guerrilla: The Indian Army and Counterinsurgency
Rajesh Rajagopalan
ISBN 978-0-415-45684-5

Indian Foreign Policy in a Unipolar World
Editor: Harsh V. Pant
HB ISBN 978-0-415-48004-8
PB ISBN 978-0-415-84306-5

India's Nuclear Debate: Exceptionalism and the Bomb
Priyanjali Malik
ISBN 978-0-415-56312-3

Interrogating International Relations: India's Strategic Practice and the Return of History
Jayashree Vivekanandan
ISBN 978-0-415-59812-5

INDIA'S GRAND STRATEGY

History, Theory, Cases

Editors

Kanti Bajpai
Saira Basit
V. Krishnappa

Routledge
Taylor & Francis Group
LONDON NEW YORK NEW DELHI

First published 2014 in India
by Routledge
912 Tolstoy House, 15–17 Tolstoy Marg, Connaught Place, New Delhi 110 001

Simultaneously published in the UK
by Routledge
2 Park Square, Milton Park, Abingdon, Oxon OX14 4RN

Routledge is an imprint of the Taylor & Francis Group, an informa business

© 2014 Kanti Bajpai, Saira Basit and V. Krishnappa

Typeset by
Solution Graphics
A-14, Indira Puri, Loni Road
Ghaziabad, Uttar Pradesh 201 102

All rights reserved. No part of this book may be reproduced or utilised in any form or by any electronic, mechanical or other means, now known or hereafter invented, including photocopying and recording, or in any information storage and retrieval system without permission in writing from the publishers.

British Library Cataloguing-in-Publication Data
A catalogue record of this book is available from the British Library

ISBN 978-0-415-73965-8

'Does India have a grand strategy'? is a contentious question, but this volume proves conclusively that a younger generation of Indian scholars respond to it with a vigorous and original 'yes' – even if their answers vary as to what the strategy is and should be. A must-read for those interested in new thinking in the world's most complex and challenged great power.

STEPHEN PHILIP COHEN
Senior Fellow, The India Project, Foreign Policy
Brookings Institution, Washington DC

Here is an up-to-date, serious and thoughtful treatment of a very vital subject for all who care about India. Kanti Bajpai and his fellow editors have put together a valuable collection which will repay reading again and again.

MEGHNAD DESAI
Emeritus Professor of Economics, London School of Economics

As India rises on the world stage, there is growing interest in the sources of its strategic conduct. Bajpai, Basit and Krishnappa map a terrain that has been barely explored. There is no better introduction to understanding India's grand strategy.

C. RAJA MOHAN
Head, Strategic Studies and Distinguished Fellow
Observer Research Foundation, New Delhi

What a magnificent achievement! A decisive refutation of the thesis that India lacks – or has not reflected on – grand strategy. This volume captures Indian thinking about grand strategy in all its nuances and variations. No scholar of Indian national security can afford not to engage it.

ASHLEY J. TELLIS
Senior Associate, Carnegie Endowment for International Peace
Washington DC

India's economic rise at the turn of the century has rekindled interest in India's global role and aspirations. This collection of essays is a valuable introduction to an emerging literature on how India views its rise and what it means for the world.

SANJAYA BARU
Director, Geo-Economics and Strategy
The International Institute for Strategic Studies, London

Contents

Foreword by Arvind Gupta and Sven G. Holtsmark	ix
Acknowledgements	xiii
Introduction: India's Grand Strategic Thought and Practice *Kanti Bajpai, Saira Basit and V. Krishnappa*	1

Part I: Grand Strategy in Indian History

1. 'Grand Strategic Thought' in the Ramayana and Mahabharata *Swarna Rajagopalan*	31
2. Strategy, Legitimacy and the Imperium: Framing the Mughal Strategic Discourse *Jayashree Vivekanandan*	63
3. Liberal Thought and Colonial Military Institutions *Srinath Raghavan*	86

Part II: Grand Strategy in Modern India

4. Indian Grand Strategy: Six Schools of Thought *Kanti Bajpai*	113
5. Nehru's Advocacy of Internationalism and Indian Foreign Policy *S. Kalyanaraman*	151
6. Economic Modernisation and the Growing Influence of Neoliberalism in India's Strategic Thought *N. S. Sisodia*	176
7. An Elephant with a Small 'Footprint': The Realist Roots of India's Strategic Thought and Policies *Bharat Karnad*	200
8. 'Jiski Lathi, Uski Bhains': The Hindu Nationalist View of International Politics *Rahul Sagar*	234

9. Securing India: Gandhian Intuitions 258
   Siddharth Mallavarapu

Part III: Grand Strategy: Core Interests and Vital Peripheries

10. Indian Strategic Culture: The Pakistan Dimension 287
    Ali Ahmed

11. China, in Three Avatars 308
    Tanvi Madan

12. Aberrant Conversationalists: India and the United States Since 1947 360
    Rudra Chaudhuri

13. India, Afghanistan and the 'End Game'? 376
    Shanthie Mariet D'Souza

14. Collateral Damage: Iran in a Reconfigured Indian Grand Strategy 412
    Sarang Shidore

15. Redefining India's Grand Strategy? The Evolving Nature of India's Israel Policy 449
    Nicolas Blarel

16. The Institutional Origins and Determinants of India's Africa Policy 479
    Constantino Xavier

Bibliography 507
About the Editors 565
Notes on Contributors 566
Index 569

Foreword

The economic transformation of India and China in the past two decades has transformed the strategic landscape of both Asia and the world. Asia is fast emerging as a geopolitical and economic pivot. It is now widely believed that the 21st century will witness the consolidation of the economic, political and technological power of Asian states. India, as one of the key Asian states, has the potential to project comprehensive power in the region and help foster a stable environment around its periphery. Skillfully handled, the forward march of India holds immense potential for securing peace and stability in the region and the world.

For these and other reasons, the evolution of Indian democracy and its attitudes towards international issues are of great significance to the world community. Not surprisingly, therefore, India's rise has increased the scholarly interest in studying India's strategic behaviour and its ideational sources. There is an increasing number of publications analysing various aspects of India's security and foreign policy decision making processes. However, India's strategic thought has received only sporadic attention among scholars and commentators. This volume seeks to fill this important gap in the body of literature.

The essays in the volume address the question of whether there is a coherent Indian strategic culture. The contributions taken together encourage us to believe that modern India's foreign policy has shown a high level of consistency in its policies, views and behaviour in spite of the change in governments, ruling parties and circumstances, a fact which indicates the presence of a shared strategic culture. This Indian strategic culture can be linked to four distinct aspirations of what may be called the Indian strategic elite. First, the quest for strategic autonomy and equality of status – a post-colonial state's striving for independent identity and international personality in accordance with its size, civilisational heritage, historical experience and its vision for the post-colonial world order. Second, reconciliation of the national with internationalism – the elite world-views in post-independent India have sought to reconcile what appeared to be two conflicting ideological tendencies in the international system.

Nationalism was seen as a crucial ideological source for energy and vitality of the new nation, at the same time as internationalism was seen both as an antidote to the excesses of parochial nationalism and as an aspirational anchor for the world India wants to bring into being. Third, the quest for co-operative behaviour through peaceful resolution of international conflicts – non-violent means such as dialogue and international law are preferred over military and coercive means. Fourth, the quest for political, social and economic justice for all peoples of the world, especially decolonised nations.

The volume details how elements of contemporary debates and the attitudes of the Indian policy elite can be found in ancient texts such as the Ramayana and the Mahabharata and how they are linked to administrative experience during Mughal rule and elite worldviews during the colonial period. The Indian tradition of strategic thought emphasises the concept of *dharma* – a set of rules that bound the ruler and the ruled alike. Also, Indian concepts of statecraft had strong moral and ethical undertones in contrast to the contemporary realist emphasis on aggregate power and material factors. Even more significant from the point of view of the contemporary world is the Indian concept of *Vasudhaiva Kutumbakam* – the idea of seeing the entire earth as one family. A related concept in Indian strategic thought is *ahimsa* or non-violence, which was the key element in the Indian freedom movement led by Mahatma Gandhi and remains of crucial relevance in the pursuit of peace. The precept of non-alignment or strategic autonomy, which informs Indian foreign policy, can also be traced to the ideas developed in Indian strategic thinking during the national freedom struggle. These ancient and pre-independence Indian concepts are as relevant in our times marked by conflict, fragmentation and avarice as they were in the past.

We are delighted that the collaboration between the Institute for Defence Studies and Analyses (IDSA) and the Institute for Defence Studies (IFS) has borne fruit, not simply in contributing to the academic literature on India, but also by providing a forum for debates among Indians thinking about their country's strategic thought and between Indian and international scholars, among them Norwegians. We are pleased that many of the contributors of this volume are young scholars in the early stages of their academic career. Hopefully, they will keep on enlightening us on important topics and continue to enrich the literature on Indian strategic thought.

We hope this volume will be read by students, academics, policy-makers, and general readers with an interest in Indian security policy. We also hope the ideas in this volume will be taken as points of departure for further debate and studies.

In the end, we would like to specially acknowledge the crucial role of the volume editors, Kanti Bajpai, Saira Basit and V. Krishnappa, in conceptualising, designing and executing this project and the volume with care and dedication.

February 2013

Dr Arvind Gupta
Director General, IDSA, New Delhi
Professor Sven G. Holtsmark
Director, IFS, Oslo

Acknowledgements

This volume is the outcome of bilateral co-operation between the Institute for Defence Studies and Analyses (IDSA), New Delhi, and the Institute for Defence Studies (IFS), Oslo. The four-year co-operation project was sponsored by The Royal Norwegian Embassy in New Delhi and the Norwegian Ministry of Foreign Affairs, Oslo. We would like to acknowledge the contributions of a number of individuals, especially Her Excellency Ambassador Ann Ollestad, Aslak Brun, Lasse Bjørn Johannessen, and Kristin Traavik at the Norwegian Emabassy in New Delhi. The project received encouragement and support from many senior leaders of the Government of Norway. We were fortunate that the current Minister of Foreign Affairs, Espen Barth Eide, and his predecessor Jonas Gahr Støre, took the time to be part of various activities connected with this project. We also thank the former Minister of Defence and Minister of Foreign Affairs Bjørn Tore Godal for agreeing to be a part of our activities. In addition, we would also like to place on record our gratitude to former Minister of State for Defence and the pre-sent minister of Human Resource Development Mallipudi Mangapati Raju Pallam, who took the time to participate in our deliberations in New Delhi.

We received unstinting support and encouragement from the current and former Directors of both IDSA and IFS. This project took shape under the leadership of Narendra S. Sisodia at IDSA and Professor Rolf Tamnes at IFS who gave generous support, encouragement and time. At the same time, we would also like to thank Dr Arvind Gupta and Professor Sven Holtsmark, present directors of the respective institutes, for the continued interest and support they provided for the successful completion of this volume.

The contents of this volume are greatly enriched by the participants of the international seminar held in Oslo in September 2010. We would like to thank all the participants who presented the papers contained in this volume. Particularly, we would like to make a special mention of the contributions made by Naresh Chandra, Meghnad Desai, Admiral Arun Prakash, and Ahmed Rashid.

This volume greatly benefited from their active participation during the seminar. Professor Sunil Khilnani at the King's India Institute has been a source of inspiration and encouragement. He kick-started the programme with a special lecture and followed it up with his time and support in subsequent months. Thanks also to Dr Srinath Raghavan, series editor for making this volume possible. Ms Princy Marin George at IDSA greatly helped in putting together the manuscript. In the end, we would also like to thank our colleagues at IFS and IDSA for all their support, participation and encouragement.

INTRODUCTION
INDIA'S GRAND STRATEGIC THOUGHT AND PRACTICE
Kanti Bajpai, Saira Basit and V. Krishnappa

This book is about India's grand strategy – how Indians think about grand strategy and how India practices grand strategy in its most important security arenas. The term grand strategy is not one that is used very often in referring to the way that India deals with security. Some prefer the appellation 'national security strategy'. We see no harm in that term, yet choose to stay with grand strategy on the argument that it has a historical lineage in strategic thought, going back at least to Basil Liddell Hart's usage. Others argue that India has no coherent way of dealing with security and therefore both words – 'grand' and 'strategy' – are inappropriate. The editors of the volume are sceptical on the grounds that no complex, modern society could be devoid of grand strategic thinking and a more or less coherent set of practices that amount to a grand strategy. Given that India is a rising power and expected to play an increasingly prominent role in the international system, it is vital to understand how Indians think about grand strategy and how they practice it. The essays published here are part of an effort at mapping both grand strategic thought and practice.

Definitions and Concepts

We use the term grand strategy to mean the combination of national resources and capabilities – military, diplomatic, political, economic, cultural and moral – that are deployed in the service of national security. National security has an external and an internal component. Our use of grand strategy refers therefore to both external and internal security. The essays presented here deal mostly with external security. Clearly, however, no country can conceive of national security without also considering internal security. In other work, one of the editors has tried to describe Indian grand strategic thinking with reference to both external and internal security.[1] The more historical essays in our volume – especially those by Rajagopalan, Vivekanandan and Raghavan – transcend the external–internal divide, and to that extent the volume throws light on different conceptions of internal security. Karnad's essay refers explicitly to how India handles internal security, particularly in restive, separatist states.

The word 'security' is an essentially contested concept.[2] There is an alphabet soup of security conceptions – national security, comprehensive security, human security, co-operative security, economic security, environmental security, energy security, amongst others. The term national security might be inclusive of all the others – for who would say that a nation's security should not be more or less comprehensive in scope, that it should not be mindful of individual freedom and safety within its borders (as connoted by human security), that it should not aim for stability and engagement with other nations including military rivals (co-operative security), and that economic, environmental and energy goals will not be key parts of its overall security? Having said that, national security conceptions will vary in time and space – societies will differ amongst themselves in the emphasis they place on the values they wish to protect, the threats they confront and perceive, and the capacities they deploy in protecting key values against threats. Indeed, a society will differ in terms of national security values, threats and capacities not just in relation to other societies but also in comparison to itself at different historical junctures. National security conceptions, in short, are not forever.

At any given time, decision-makers will seek to protect various values. These values will likely include territorial integrity, freedom to make foreign and domestic policy, military stability with one's rivals, a preferred way of political, economic, and cultural life, economic well-being and regime survival. They may hold dear other values as well. The relationship between different values can and

---

[1] Kanti Bajpai, 'Indian Strategic Culture', in Michael R. Chambers, ed., *South Asia in 2020: Future Strategic Balances and Alliances* (Carlisle, Pennsylvania: Strategic Studies Institute, US Army War College, 2003), pp. 245–303.

[2] Arnold Wolfers, 'National Security as an Ambiguous Symbol', *Political Science Quarterly*, 67, 4 (December 1952), pp. 481–502; David Baldwin, 'The Concept of Security', *Review of International Studies*, 23, 1 (1997), pp. 5–26.

will vary. Values are seldom all equally important; some may be more important than others. States may want more of one value and be willing to sacrifice a quantum of other values to protect the primary value. In a world of scarcities, it is implausible that one can hold all values equally dear. As in so many other spheres of social existence, 'satisficing' is probably the best that decision-makers can do. Absolute security – that is, the achievement of all values without limit – is unattainable. Indeed, a leader who seriously advocates absolute security risks leading his or her society astray and putting it at great risk.

The threats to national values, on the other hand, may be multifarious. They may include other states, far or near, big or small; non-state actors of various kinds (separatists, revolutionaries, global terrorists, irredentist groups, mafias, smugglers, pirates, religious organisations, business enterprises); Nature itself (earthquakes, tsunamis, volcanoes, extreme weather, pandemics); and man-made – if unintentional – disasters (global warming, pollution, large-scale industrial accidents).

We can think of insecurity as threats in relation to the capacities to deal with those threats: the stronger the threats and the weaker the capabilities, the greater the insecurity. A society that has a large number of threats to its values but also has strong capacities to deal with them is more secure than one with fewer threats but even weaker capacities. A society will have many capacities for dealing with threats to its values: force, diplomacy, political ideology, economic power (for example, tradeable goods, finance/aid, technology and expertise), popular and classical cultural products, knowledge and intellectual capital, moral arguments and leadership and much more besides. Given that threats are numerous and capacities are limited in a world of scarce resources, decision-makers must make choices about which values are more important and which capacities and resources will be devoted to protecting which values. As noted earlier, security is not absolute. The specific combination of capacities that a nation deploys for its external and internal security describes its grand strategy.

The term 'grand strategy' has been used mostly in connection with the United States after the Second World War, even though its provenance is British.[3] Still, even in the US, it was not a commonly

---

[3] For the original use of the term 'grand strategy' see Basil Liddell Hart, *Strategy*, 2nd rev. edn (Toronto: Meridian, 1991). Hart used the term

used term. Popularisers of the term included Paul Kennedy, Edward Luttwak and Michael Howard, all distinguished scholars with a particular interest in war and peace and military history.[4] George Kennan, in his famous long-telegram, outlined a grand strategy for the US in its confrontation with the Soviet Union, a grand strategy that proved to be remarkably prescient.[5] Grand strategy studies have tended to be of the great powers, past and present. Whereas we would argue that all countries have grand strategy, political scientists and historians have concentrated their attention on the great powers and particularly the US for which there is now a fairly voluminous literature. We safely predict that Chinese grand strategy will be a subject of increasing attention; indeed, it is already filling the pages of journals and books.[6] The focus on the most consequential powers is understandable. It does not and should not however rule out studies of lesser powers. Surely much may be learned by studying grand strategy comparatively and by paying attention to the grand strategies of regional powers, middle powers, small states and so on.

As a rising power, India too will figure in the grand strategy literature in the years to come. Interestingly, four important works, published within the past two years, are grand strategic in scope.

'grand strategy' to refer to the marshalling of a state's resources – military, diplomatic, political, economic, cultural, and moral – for the purposes of war. We would substitute the word 'security' for the word 'war'.

[4] Paul Kennedy, ed., *Grand Strategies in War and Peace* (New Haven: Yale University Press, 1991); Edward Luttwak, *The Grand Strategy of the Byzantine Empire* (Cambridge, Mass.: Belknap Press of Harvard University Press); Edward Luttwak, *The Grand Strategy of the Roman Empire: From the First Century A.D. to the Third Century* (Baltimore, MD: Johns Hopkins University Press, 1979); Edward Luttwak, *The Grand Strategy of the Soviet Union* (New York: St. Martin's, 1984); Michael Howard, *War in European History* (Oxford: Oxford University Press, 1976); Michael Howard, *Grand Strategy*, Vol. 4 (London: The Stationery Office Books, 1972).

[5] See 'The Sources of Soviet Conduct', in George F. Kennan, *American Diplomacy* (Chicago: University of Chicago Press, 1984), pp. 107–28. This is the original Mr. X, 'Long Telegram', that was the basis of containment.

[6] On Chinese grand strategy see, for instance, Michael Swaine and Ashley Tellis, *Interpreting China's Grand Strategy* (Santa Monica, CA.: RAND, 2000); Avery Goldstein, *Rising to the Challenge: China's Grand Strategy and International Security* (Stanford: Stanford University Press, 2005); Wang Jisi, 'China's Search for a Grand Strategy: A Rising Great Power Finds Its Way', *Foreign Affairs*, 90, 2 (March/April 2011), pp. 68–79.

We refer here to Kapil Kak's edited volume, *Comprehensive Security for an Emerging India*, Admiral Raja Menon and Rajiv Kumar's *The Long View from New Delhi: To Define the Indian Grand Strategy for Foreign Policy*, Rajiv Kumar and Santosh Kumar's *In the National Interest: A Strategic Foreign Policy for India*, and Sunil Khilnani et al., *Nonalignment 2.0: A Foreign and Strategic Policy for India in the 21st Century*.[7] A recent edited volume is Krishnappa Venkatshamy and Princy George, *India's National Security Strategy: 2020 Perspectives*. Indians are not terribly comfortable with the term 'grand strategy'.[8] Reactions to the term vary, but they are usually pejorative. A typical reaction is to say that reference to grand strategy in the same breath as India is misleading for several reasons: India has no coherent plan amounting to grand strategy; grand strategy is far too elevated a term for the kind of ad hoc decision making that is India's wont; and India, being a modest and prudential power, does not and should not aspire to anything as ambitious as grand strategy. Interestingly, of the five works cited here, only one explicitly uses the term grand strategy to describe its contents. All three, however, include the words strategy or strategic, suggesting that though they have shied away from the term grand strategy they are nonetheless referring to something like it.

Rationale for the Volume

Why produce a volume on Indian grand strategy? We make five arguments here.

First of all, as we noted at the start of this essay, we see this book as a corrective to the view that India has no grand strategy – that

---

[7] Kapil Kak, ed., *Comprehensive Security for an Emerging India* (New Delhi: Centre for Air Power Studies and Knowledge World Publishers, 2012); Rajiv Kumar and Santosh Kumar, *In the National Interest: A Strategic Foreign Policy for India* (New Delhi: Business Standard Books, 2010); Admiral Raja Menon and Rajiv Kumar, *The Long View From Delhi: To Define the Indian Grand Strategy for Foreign Policy* (New Delhi: Indian Council for Research on International Economic Relations and the Academic Foundation, 2010); Sunil Khilnani, Rajiv Kumar, Pratap Bhanu Mehta, Lt. Gen. (Retd.) Prakash Menon, Nandan Nilekani, Srinath Raghavan, Shyam Saran, and Siddharth Vardarajan, *Non-alignment 2.0: A Foreign and Strategic Policy for India in the 21st Century* (New Delhi: Centre for Policy Research, 2012).

[8] Krishnappa Venkatshamy and Princy George, eds, *Grand Strategy for India: 2020 and Beyond* (New Delhi: Pentagon Publishers, 2012).

it has no coherent, identifiable way of deploying its military, diplomatic, political, economic, cultural and moral resources toward the goals of security. It is also intended to be a corrective to the view that India has no grand strategic thinking. Both views have become a pernicious common sense about India. George K. Tanham's RAND monograph *Indian Strategic Thought: An Interpretive Essay*, published in 1994, reflected both Indian and foreign estimates of India.[9] Tanham spent several months in India interviewing members of India's strategic community and reading about India. He concluded famously:

> Indians have not been great strategic thinkers or developers of strategy, although they have been profound thinkers in many other fields ... (their) view of life as unpredictable did not lead Indians to see the need for strategy and even if they had, they would have been unlikely to proceed because if the future is unknown and unknowable why plan?[10]

K. Subrahmanyam, the doyen of Indian strategic thinking, who more or less agreed with Tanham, frequently bemoaned the lack of strategic thinking amongst Indian leaders, officials, military officers, academics, business people, the media and the attentive public.[11] Subrahmanyam grants that Nehruvian non-alignment was a grand strategy but criticises Indians for not 'thinking through the strategic consequences of non-alignment', so that even this original grand strategy failed to be amplified adequately. It, therefore, could not be applied sensibly to particular situations and to a changing strategic environment. Subrahmanyam's overall point is that Nehru apart, there has been little grand strategic thinking in India. We challenge this view – Subrahmanyam himself was a distinguished thinker who had considerable impact on how Indians thought about security. As the essays published here suggest, there is a respectable body of thinking on grand strategy, and there is an identifiable set of policies that amount to grand strategic practice as well. We believe that

---

[9] George K. Tanham, *Indian Strategic Thought: An Interpretive Essay* (Santa Monica, CA: RAND, 1992).

[10] Cited in K. Subrahmanyam, 'Does India Have a Strategic Perspective?' in K. Subrahmanyam with Arthur Monteiro, *Shedding Shibboleths: India's Evolving Strategic Outlook* (New Delhi: Wordsmiths, 2005), p. 4.

[11] See, for instance, his essay, 'Does India Have a Strategic Perspective?' in Subrahmanyam, *Shedding Shibboleths*, pp. 3–17.

our volume barely scratches the surface in terms of reconstructing the history of Indian grand strategy, both thought and practice, and that there is much more that can be done in depicting Indian grand strategy.

Second, as we also noted at the beginning of this introduction, a rising power is an object of curiosity. Indians as well as foreigners wonder what kind of power India will be.[12] The Indian economy is projected in aggregate economic terms to move up behind Japan into fourth place and likely to become number three by 2030 if not sooner.[13] On the back of sustained economic growth and an enlarging population, India will pass the US to be the second largest economy behind China. While these straight-line projections are open to objection, the fact that India will be one of the top five economies in the world is not seriously in question. How will a more powerful and presumably more confident India behave towards its own citizens, its region (South Asia), its extended neighbourhood (the rest of Asia, the Gulf, the Indian Ocean), and the great powers (China and the US primarily)? The essays here give us clues to these questions.

Third, understanding Indian grand strategy is not just about the future; it is also about the past and present. With a comprehension of Indian grand strategic thought and practice, we may be in a better position to understand what India did in the past and what it is doing in the present and why. The essays published here, we hope, will help readers get a better grasp of various aspects of Indian policies and pronouncements going back not only to Nehruvian days but also more recent times. For instance, to the extent that Indian grand

---

[12] Rahul Sagar's article, 'State of Mind: What Kind of Power Will India Become?', *International Affairs*, 85, 4 (2009), pp. 801–16, is one of the most recent efforts to answer that question. For earlier post-Cold War views, see Tanham, *Indian Strategic Thought*; Stephen P. Cohen, *India: Emerging Power* (Washington DC: The Brookings Institution Press, 2001) and Kanti Bajpai, 'Indian Strategic Culture', amongst others.

[13] On India's becoming the third largest economy, see Arvind Subramanian, *Eclipse: Living in the Shadow of China's Economic Dominance* (New Delhi: Viva Books with the Petersen Institute for International Economics, 2011), p. 87. Subramanian's projection is just one of several that make this prediction. India looks likely to be the third biggest economy by 2030 regardless of whether one estimates in actual dollars or purchasing power parity (PPP) terms.

strategy has been more Neoliberal since 1989 (as noted in the Bajpai and Sisodia essays), its current emphasis on economic interactions with partners as well as adversaries, its tilt towards the US, and its pragmatic stance towards China are more easily understood.

Fourth, we hope that this collection of essays will contribute to debates in India about the relative merits of different grand strategies. Indian grand strategic choices were a matter of debate even during the Nehruvian period: Nehru was challenged within his party (for example by Sardar Patel), by other parties (the Jan Sangh, Swatantra Party and the Communist Party of India) and by the media and public opinion (this was most evident in respect of China from 1959 or so onwards).[14] However, grand strategy was most a subject of debate in the aftermath of the Cold War. The end of the Cold War had been devoutly wished for by India, but its precipitous end shocked Indian policy makers and commentators. In the years following the collapse of communism and the Soviet Union, a fairly rambunctious debate broke out in India over the future of Indian grand strategy. India had, seemingly, come out on the losing side of the Cold War, having tilted over the years towards the Soviet Union and its allies. Worse, India's major rivals – Pakistan and China – had been on the winning side, having worked closely with the US against the Soviet Union. A number of contending perspectives became public. The Indian grand strategy debate was mostly visible in the print media but it also featured behind closed doors in seminar and conference rooms as well as the precincts of the bureaucracy. One of the most fertile periods of debate was in 1994–95 during the negotiations on the Comprehensive Test Ban Treaty in the Conference on Disarmament in Geneva. The nuclear tests of 1998, the Lahore declaration and then the Kargil war with Pakistan in 1999 and the crises with Pakistan in 2001–2 after the terrorist attacks on the Kashmir legislature as well as the Indian Parliament, all provoked further, roiling debate. At any rate, our hope is that this volume will take the policy debate forward and will help proponents of different perspectives refine their arguments in contention with opposing viewpoints. The recent publications on foreign policy, national security and grand strategy noted earlier suggest that another wave of debate has begun, set in motion no doubt by the growth in Indian

---

[14] C. Raja Mohan, *Crossing the Rubicon* (New Delhi: Viking, 2003), p. 34.

power, the astonishing rise of India's great northern neighbour, China and the relative decline of the United States.

Fifth, the writings on grand strategy are not just interesting for their insights into the past, present and future of Indian policy but also for what they reveal about Indian political thought. The arguments of strategists are not just an analytical and prescriptive discourse about India's security; they are also revealing of Indian thinking about the political world. Put differently, grand strategic thought can be deconstructed for much deeper assumptions and ratiocinations about social and political life. There is always an ontological base to the arguments about this or that grand strategy, and these arguments as forms of public reasoning can be taken quite seriously for what they suggest about the nature of Indian thought and about the play of ideology.[15]

Organisation of the Volume

The volume is organised in three sections: 'Grand Strategy in Indian History', 'Grand Strategy in Modern India' and 'Grand Strategy: Core Interests and Vital Peripheries'. The first section contains three essays on the historical context of Indian grand strategic thought and practice. These examine an ancient, epic period of writing (Rajagopalan) featuring two of the great books of Hinduism, the Ramayana and the Mahabharata; a middle period in India's past under the greatest Mughal emperor, Akbar (Vivekanandan); and the early 19th century stirrings of nationalism in which Indian liberals raised their voices against British colonial military institutions (Raghavan). The second section consists of six essays that explore the sources of modern grand strategic thinking and practice (Bajpai, Kalyanaraman, Sisodia, Karnad, Sagar, and Mallavarapu). The third and final section, comprising seven essays (Ahmed, Madan, Chaudhuri, D'Souza, Shidore, Blarel, and Xavier), disentangle debates and policies relating to India's key external interlocutors – Pakistan, China and the US ('core interests') as well as Afghanistan, Iran, Israel, and Africa ('vital peripheries').

---

[15] For the view that one should take public reasoning as discourse seriously for what it reveals ideologically, see Rochana Bajpai, *Debating Difference: Group Rights and Liberal Democracy in India* (New Delhi: Oxford University Press, 2011), pp. 10–16.

Grand Strategy in Indian History

How have Indic states in the subcontinent thought about and practiced grand strategy? What combination of military, diplomatic, political, economic, cultural and moral resources have they deployed for the purposes of security? Before we get to the essays in this section, it is worth saying a word on some obvious omissions in the volume.

A fairly glaring one is Kautilya and his *Arthashastra*, the great Indian book on statecraft.[16] Kautilya's work is often cited as a key instance of Indian strategic thinking, one that ranks with Machiavelli's *The Prince*. Whether it has this status is an open question. Our sense is that it does not do so. While there are certainly some maxims from it that have almost canonical status, it is a text that has largely been caricatured. Understanding of the text is not deep in India. It is most likely taught in the military academies of India, but there is little Indian reflection on it, and the text does not seem to have been deeply internalised by Indian leaders, officials and military officers. Also absent from this volume are essays on the many other classical books of Hindu thought including the Bhagavad Gita, the Vedas, Upanishads, Puranas, the Laws of Manu, the Sutras, Vedantas, and Dharma Shastras, amongst others.[17] Our thinking here again is that whereas these are works of philosophical and cultural importance, it is unclear how salient they are in the study of Indian strategic thought and how well known they are, even subliminally, amongst policy makers. As for the middle period of Indian history, influenced by the arrival of Islam in the Indian subcontinent, this volume once again is deficient. Are there no great texts from this period? Again, we cannot rule this out. Yet it is instructive that few scholars or practitioners of strategy in India would be able to name a single work from this period that influenced Indian statecraft. We must also consider the possibility that the British period in India produced seminal strategic thinking and

---

[16] Kautilya, *Arthashastra*, ed. by L. N. Rangarajan (New Delhi: Penguin, 1992). An early essay on Kautilya is George Modelski, 'Kautilya: Foreign Policy and International System in the Ancient Hindu World', *American Political Science Review*, 58, 3 (September 1964), pp. 549–60.

[17] Bharat Karnad refers to a number of these works in his book, *Nuclear Weapons and Indian Security: The Realist Foundations of Strategy* (New Delhi: Macmillan, 2002), pp. 1–65.

writing that has seeped into the Indian mindset and has stayed on after the departure of the colonial rulers. C. Raja Mohan, the Indian strategic analyst, has argued that Curzon's thinking was influential and that Curzonian geopolitical ideas about the role of India deserve attention.[18] This may well be true, in which case we suggest that an excavation of the British era is also a worthwhile effort in the study of the history of Indian strategy.

It is also worth saying a few words on Indian strategic practice in the *longue durée* of history. Except for the essay by Jayashree Vivekananda, the volume does not contain any reflections on Indian grand strategic practice in history. Even her essay, perforce, is restricted to one period of Mughal history, albeit a crucial one. The many great Indian empires, from the Maurya period onwards, cannot have been without grand strategy, yet we know little of these Indic worlds. How they dealt with internal security, with the semi-independent, independent and often insurgent kingdoms on their peripheries, with neighbouring empires (Afghan, Persian, Central Asia, Chinese, Tibetan, Gorkha, and Burmese, to name just a few) and with the European empires that began to make their appearance in the 15th century is ripe for study from a grand strategy perspective.[19]

Swarna Rajagopalan's chapter on the Ramayana and Mahabharata suggests that the epics, ancient though they are, continue to inform Indian thinking. Implicit in her view is that the narratives, values and arguments in the two epics are deeply embedded in the consciousness of Indians, especially Hindus. For Rajagopalan, paying attention to the epics is instructive for contemporary India. Her reading of the two great books suggests that the rulers of the ancient Indic world were guided by a core set of political values above all focused on the necessity of preserving order against chaos and *dharma* against *adharma*, by a fluid sense of self and other, and by definite rules, strategies and methods in dealing with the internal and external realm (howsoever internal and external may be defined). In the world of the epics, those responsible for securing society were to maintain order and dharma and prevent a return to anarchy, which

---

[18] Mohan, *Crossing the Rubicon*, pp. 204–36.

[19] For the study of international relations and international societies before the modern period including the Indic world, see Barry Buzan and Richard Little, *International Systems in World History: Remaking the Study of International Relations* (Oxford: Oxford University Press, 2000).

meant periodically ridding the world of those who would subvert dharma for their own ends. Differences and battle lines were drawn around dharma and adharma rather than cultural and national identity. The (apparent) absence of a clearly-articulated, meticulously-executed grand strategy in contemporary India may in fact be consistent with traditional Indian political thought which emphasised that while rulers should be guided by norms and principles, these were context-dependent and were never absolute in their application. Rulers above all must preserve order and dharma, and their actions must finally be judged by their success or failure in that regard. Contrary to modern grand strategy, which is obsessed with the cultivation of state power and influence, the protagonists in the Indic world of the epics would have considered evil and deserving of death those rulers who sought to expand their power and influence, for the duty of a ruler was to preserve order and dharma not to conquer and dominate.

Jayashree Vivekanandan's essay suggests that it is not just the ancient epics that influence contemporary grand strategic thought and practice but also the more recent past. Vivekanandan analyses the manner in which the Mughal empire under Akbar, one of the most powerful empires in medieval history, strategised. She notes that while the empire sought to expand, it avoided massive war. War was matched by diplomacy – by varying strategies of material and symbolic accommodation aimed at the regional kingdoms in the 'core' and 'periphery' of the subcontinent. Given the size of the subcontinent and given the militarisation of its society, the empire did not enjoy a monopoly over force. Coercion therefore could not be the only way. Vivekanandan shows that a variety of strategies were used to hold the empire together – the *mansabdari* system to integrate chiefs, clan leaders and aristocrats into the Mughal court; the exhibition of imperial power throughout the realm by having the imperial administration camp in different parts of the empire; the propagation of a secular and ecumenical-minded spiritual order built around the divinity of the emperor himself which sought to be inclusive of Muslim and Hindu beliefs; and an ideology of paternalism and loyalty centred on Akbar. Vivekanandan suggests that ancient India and the Indian epics featured both a Realist tradition of strategy which features the necessity of violence and power but also a moral and symbolic one which emphasised accommodation and justice in the service of stability and order. The Mughals, she seems to suggest, prioritised the latter. Not surprisingly, perhaps, the modern Indian state, drawing on both its ancient and medieval past, has also attempted to rely more on range of accommodative strategies in dealing with internal as well as external rivals.

Srinath Raghavan takes another route to understanding the roots of Indian strategic thought and practice. Raghavan's essay examines the role of the Indian liberals or moderates in the early 20th century who initially, from a political economy perspective, developed a critique of military institutions under the British Raj. The military, in this view, was a drain on India, particularly in so far as it was being used overseas in other parts of the empire. Indian liberals not only debated the economics of the military; they also questioned the strategic need for a large standing army, as the threats to India receded in the early 20th century. Gradually, the liberals developed a quite different critique, namely, that the officers' corps was an alien institution, with no Indians in it. Over the years, the liberals argued successfully for a gradual Indianisation of the military and its training institutions. They also championed the cause of civilian control of the military. Under pressure politically in India and in the shadow of war after 1914, London and the Raj conceded. Raghavan notes that while the liberals lost the argument on the course of the nationalist struggle and indeed also lost a number of battles with the imperial government on military institutions, they provided valuable service to India in the long run, on the Indianisation of the military, the setting up of military training institutions and the nature of civil–military relations. Raghavan's essay is a reminder that Indian strategic thought and practice came not just from the British but also from the Indian liberals whose interventions on military institutions were to be so consequential. Indeed, Raghavan suggests that it is the Indian liberals more than the British who shaped modern India's view of civilian control of the military. His counterfactual is an intriguing one: what if the liberals had won and Indianisation of the officers' corps had proceeded faster? Would the Indian military have fared so poorly against China in 1962?

GRAND STRATEGY IN MODERN INDIA

When we move from the historical to the contemporary, what do these essays tell us about Indian grand strategy? After independence, with the departure of the British, one might have expected an efflorescence of Indian grand strategising. Certainly if one goes by debates in the press and in parliament, there was great liveliness in the discussions on national security. This is hardly surprising since, as a newly-independent country, India had to confront the issues of war and peace, both internal and external.

New Delhi was almost immediately confronted by a series of challenges. With the lapsing of paramountcy, there were over five hundred states to be integrated into the union. In retrospect, this was accomplished with quite amazing rapidity and efficiency except in the case of Junagadh, Hyderabad and Kashmir.[20] The Indian leadership resorted to a modest show of arms in the first two cases but found itself at war in the third case, a war that dragged on for over a year from October 1947 to December 1948. Thereafter, India confronted the possibility of war with Pakistan. A year later, in 1949, Chinese Communist forces had forced the Nationalists out of Mainland China and taken control. By 1950, New Delhi was already deep into discussions with Beijing over the fate of Tibet, and whereas India sought peace and co-operation with its great neighbour to the north, there was no doubt that relations were complex and could become militarised. Internally, apart from the police actions in Junagadh and Hyderabad, the government had to establish law and order throughout the new country, deal with the massive influx of refugees in the wake of partition, confront rising communist forces, and deal with separatism amongst the Naga tribes. Externally, apart from Pakistan and China, there were fears of neo-colonial bullying by the British and the US, subversion by the two communist giants, the Soviet Union and China and the stability of buffer states such as Bhutan and Nepal as well as the borderlands with Burma. There was also the larger balance of power and influence in Asia and the world and the role that India would play in the international system which was rapidly polarising between the Western and the Communist bloc.

At this moment, obviously, Jawaharlal Nehru played an enormous role. So much has been written about the first prime minister –

---

[20] This story has been told in V. P. Menon, *The Transfer of Power in India* (Princeton: Princeton University Press, 1957) and *Integration of the Indian States* (Hyderabad: Orient Longman Ltd., 1997). Menon was constitutional adviser to three British Viceroys and later worked closely with Sardar Patel to bring about the accession and integration of the princely states to independent India.

his ideas and policies – but our sense is that there is a great deal more that could be written about this era, even about Nehru. Srinath Raghavan's *War and Peace in Modern India: A Strategic History of the Nehru Years* indicates how much more there is yet to know about India's first prime minister and his strategic practice.[21] As contemporary historians and political scientists access the Nehruvian archive, we can expect far more work on him. Nehru was however not the only person to have thought strategically about India. During the nationalist period, there were many others who had thought about India's relations with the outside world as well as its internal order including Abul Kalam Azad, Subhas Chandra Bose, Mohandas Karamchand Gandhi, Aurobindo Ghose, M. S. Golwalker, Mohammed Ali Jinnah, Sardar Patel, C. Rajagopalachari, M. N. Roy, Tej Bahadur Sapru, Veer Savarkar, and Rabindranath Tagore, amongst the more prominent political and thought leaders. After independence, there were others that reflected on and wrote about India and the world including the socialist parliamentarian Ram Manohar Lohia, the philosopher and statesman S. Radhakrishnan and, somewhat later, Prime Minister Indira Gandhi, the historian and diplomat K. M. Panikkar, veteran officials G. S. Bajpai, K. P. S. Menon and H. M. Patel, the international relations scholars A. Appadurai and Sisir Gupta, the army generals and strategists D. K. Palit and K. Sundarji, the civil servant and thinker K. Subrahmanyam, and many fine journalists.

Behind the scenes, there were undoubtedly many in political, administrative and diplomatic life who contributed to India's strategic thought and practice. For instance, Indira Gandhi could call on a sophisticated group of policy-makers and thinkers including D. P. Dhar, P. N. Dhar and P. N. Haksar. The long-serving and influential intelligence chiefs B. N. Mullick and R. N. Kao, also undoubtedly served up analysis and recommendations on broader lines of policy to the political leadership.

How can we characterise the grand strategic scene in contemporary India? What is the legacy of the political and thought leaders

---

[21] See Srinath Raghavan, *War and Peace in Modern India: A Strategic History of the Nehru Years* (Ranikhet: Permanent Black, 2010). See also Sunil Khilnani, *The Idea of India* (New Delhi: Penguin India, 1998); Ramachandra Guha, *India After Gandhi: A History of the World's Largest Democracy* (New Delhi: Picador India, 2007).

of the nationalist and post-nationalist period? In his framing essay, Kanti Bajpai suggests that today's India features three major schools and three relatively minor schools of grand strategic thinking, with different but also overlapping views of how to deal with India's major external challenges, namely, Pakistan, China, and the US. The three major schools are Nehruvianism, Neoliberalism and Hyperrealism and the three minor schools are Marxism, Hindu nationalism or Hindutva and Gandhianism. The touchstone of Nehruvian thinking is the internationalist belief in the power of communication and negotiation to deal with security threats. Neoliberals, inspired by market economics and the extraordinary explosion in trade, investment, and the diffusion of technology, put their faith in economics and commerce and a mercantilist approach to external relations. Hyperrealists, by contrast, argue the case for military power, in dealing with rivals. Marxists believe that solidarity amongst the progressive states of the world and a commitment to socialism within India will ensure security. Hindu nationalists see a cohering around a Hindu civilisational core and a more muscular military stance as being the guarantors of India's security. Gandhians, by contrast, argue that security can only be realised in a decentralised, non-violent, and morally true India that spurns industrialisation and Western modernity.

The ensuing essays in this section of the volume explore five of the six schools that Bajpai identifies in greater detail – Nehruvianism, Neoliberalism, Realism, Hindu nationalism, and Gandhianism.

S. Kalyanaraman argues that while Nehru and Nehruvianism are associated with internationalism, the full extent of internationalist ideas and policies have not been explored. Kalyanaraman sees Nehruvian internationalism as marked by five key elements – opposition to colonialism, imperialism and racialism; non-alignment and pan-Asianism; mediation between the great powers; nuclear disarmament; and Panchashila or peaceful coexistence. Together, these defined the larger project of 'non-alignment' which Kalyanaraman argues was neither a means of exploiting bipolarity nor a sophisticated version of the balance of power. Nehruvian internationalism, he suggests, predated bipolarity and had its origins in the Congress Party of the 1920s. Nehru and the Congress sought to reconcile nationalism and internationalism at various points in pre-independence history, especially during the Second World War. After independence, too, they constantly had to protect India's sovereignty and interests and weigh these up against the requirements of international co-operation and more cosmopolitan interests. Kalyanaraman notes that Nehruvian internationalism was gradually abridged – non-alignment was compromised by the tilt to the Soviet Union, pan-Asianism crumbled, and India itself went nuclear. Nevertheless, he concludes, internationalism is alive and well in India and should be a cornerstone of its external policies.

With the end of the Cold War, Nehruvianism has come into question as never before, with various alternatives seeking to replace it as the governing template of grand strategy. Some have argued that the shift from Nehruvianism is a move from idealism to 'pragmatism'; others have suggested it is a move towards 'realism'. C. Raja Mohan has argued the former case, suggesting that Nehruvian idealism was replaced by a much more cold-eyed, calculative view of India's interests and options.[22] Narendra Sisodia concurs in his piece on Neoliberalism. Sisodia suggests that in the wake of the economic crisis of 1991, India adopted a Neoliberal economic policy emphasising the role of the market with a commensurate shift in geopolitical strategy as well. India focused on economic relations even with rivals, tilted to the US strategically, opened out to greater interactions with East and Southeast Asia, the European Union, and China, tried to develop South Asia into a single economic space, and finally went nuclear. Unfortunately, India's Neoliberalism has not improved its security. Sisodia concludes that, at least in three crucial cases, a Neoliberal strategic posture has not helped – with Pakistan, China and South Asia, relations with which continue to be marked by deep mistrust. Moreover, Neoliberalism as a grand strategy faces powerful challenges ahead – economic crisis in the West, worries over growing economic inequality in India and China, contradictions between India's burgeoning relationship with China and its equally strong relationships with the US and Japan, and finally, the attachment of states to 'power politics'. Sisodia also worries that weak economic, social and institutional linkages with its neighbours, Indian domestic politics, the lack of a common threat in southern

---

[22] Mohan, *Crossing the Rubicon*, pp. xi–xxii.

Asia, and an underdeveloped understanding of the limitations posed by complex interdependence between India, Pakistan, China and the smaller South Asian states will hinder co-operation.

If Nehruvianism and Neoliberalism have not solved India's grand strategic problems, can power politics and Realism do better? Bharat Karnad suggests that they can, if Indian leaders apply the tenets of a historical, culturally-derived *realpolitik* going back to the Vedic era. Karnad argues that India's post-independence leaders have got their realpolitik lessons all wrong. They have chosen more often than not to coerce internal enemies and smaller neighbouring states; and they have chosen to bend at the knee before the bigger powers, such as the US and China. New Delhi should, he argues vigorously, have done the exact opposite: it should have used incentives and co-operation to bind the smaller states to India strategically, and it should have built its military strength and allied with others to balance against the big powers. Pakistan and the smaller states in South Asia even now should be drawn into India's orbit against its main rival, China. Furthermore, he notes that India has mistakenly relied on the US to help it against China, going so far as to compromise its nuclear weapons programme in order to propitiate Washington, when it should have been clear to New Delhi that the US, in its competition with China, needs India as much as the other way round. Karnad despairs at what he considers to be muddle-headedness and pusillanimity on India's part.

A fourth perspective on Indian grand strategy is that of Hindu nationalism or Hindutva. Rahul Sagar examines the thinking of two prophet-voices in the Hindutva tradition – Vinayak Savarkar and Madhav Golwalker – who (early in the 20th century) argued a case that is familiar enough to Realists: India should be militarily strong in defence of its security because that is the way of the world. Sagar argues, however, that Hindu nationalists are not identical to Realists. According to Savarkar and Golwalker, while security must be paramount and while nations should do whatever it takes to be secure – the cultivation of alliances and one's own military power, above all – the key is martial spirit and social cohesion based on an exclusionary nationalism. Alliances in the end leave one's security in the hands of possibly capricious and selfish others. And military power, however potent, is only as effective as the spirit that deploys it: where the spirit is weak, the use of military power is ineffective. A martial spirit and social cohesion are therefore vital. An exclusionary nationalism is the basis for both because, as Savarkar claims, '[t]he foe that has nothing in common with us is the foe likely to be most bitterly resisted by us' (quoted in Sagar, Chapter Eight). Sagar notes that in a world where India is beset by stronger powers, the Hindutva view could well gain ground. He concludes that the Hindutva insistence on exclusionary nationalism may bring about exactly the danger that it seeks to combat: weakened domestic cohesion and therefore reduced national power.

If Nehruvianism is on the wane, if Neoliberalism has not delivered on its promise of security, if India seems unable to deploy a culturally-engendered realpolitik with any finesse, and if Hindutva risks bringing on the very danger that it fears, what can Gandhianism offer? Working with Gandhi's own words, Siddharth Mallavarapu suggests that to understand a Gandhian perspective on India's security it is necessary to understand his key philosophical and political concepts – truth, ahimsa, satyagraha and swaraj. A society in which these are widely practiced will, in a Gandhian view, be secure. Gandhi does not pretend, however, that practicing them will be easy. Their dissemination and internalisation will be a struggle. Nevertheless, a society without truth, ahimsa, satyagraha and swaraj will fall prey to all the evils of modern Western society: it will be a competitive, expansionary, violent entity that will desecrate nature and seek dominion over others. Gandhi was ambivalent, Mallavarapu shows, about the place of armies and police forces. A society that had not detached itself from violence would, he acknowledged, need to have both institutions. Both external and internal defence might require them. Violence, in any case, was preferable to cowardice. Yet, it is clear that Gandhi, deep down, opposed anything but the most minimal defence. Nuclear weapons were abhorrent to him, representing as they did both the most diabolical weapons as also the most instrumental uses of science and technology. India could be made secure if it perfected the art of non-violent resistance and built a moral, truthful, decentralised, and frugal society. In effect, the Gandhian view of security resides in an emancipation of Indians from Western-style individualism, consumerism, industrialism, and science. An India freed from alien values, Gandhi seems to suggest, would not endanger other societies and would therefore not excite their attention.

Which of these five perspectives or schools of thought is the strongest today? Our sense is that Nehruvianism, Neoliberalism, and Realism are the main contenders in the grand strategic arena. Hindutva thought is close to Realism in its insistence on the centrality of power and violence, and Gandhianism, always a minor stream of thought, is weaker still today, 60 years after the Mahatma's death. Aspects of it in any case have been absorbed into Nehruvianism. After the Cold War, we would argue, Nehruvianism has lost ground in the Indian strategic community, leaving the three major schools more or less equal in their influence.

GRAND STRATEGY: CORE INTERESTS AND VITAL PERIPHERIES

We have described India's core interests in terms of relations with Pakistan, China and the US, and depicted its vital peripheries in terms of Afghanistan, Iran, Israel, and Africa. Our delimiting of core interests in this way is probably not very controversial. We might have included South Asia as a core interest, but clearly the greatest challenges in the region come from Pakistan, not Bangladesh, Bhutan, Nepal, and Sri Lanka. In the peripheries, we might have included East and Southeast Asia, which particularly in terms of economic opportunities is increasingly vital. Fortunately for India, the region is not a threat. Chinese influence in East and Southeast Asia is of concern, and India has done more to counter China than is often realised. There is any case, a growing body of work on India's policies towards the region.[23] On the other hand, there is not a great deal on India's relations with Afghanistan, Iran, Israel, and Africa, all of which define an extended western flank for India.

At the core of India's concerns historically has been Pakistan. Ali Ahmed argues that at least in respect of Pakistan, India has been more assertive than at any time in the past. This assertive strategic

---

[23] For instance, see David Brewster, 'Indian Strategic Thinking about East Asia', *Journal of Strategic Studies*, 34, 6 (December 2011), pp. 825–52; Walter C. Ladwig, 'Delhi's Pacific Ambition: Naval Power, "Look East," and India's Emerging Influence in the Asia-Pacific', *Asian Security*, 5, 2 (2009), pp. 87–113.

posture, in his judgment, has proven counter-productive: it has created a security challenge for Pakistan, to which Islamabad has responded by unleashing a sub-conventional proxy war against India. Those in India who bemoan the lack of strategic culture/thinking, according to Ahmed, are Realists or cultural nationalists who want India to be more aggressive against Pakistan. Ahmed argues that this greater assertiveness can be traced back to the Indira Doctrine in the 1980s and has culminated in a posture of near-compellence. Pakistan's growing military strength and particularly its nuclear weapons, its alliance-like relations with the US and China, and its proxy war to counter India's power have heightened regional insecurity. This has resulted in a vicious circle between the two countries: Pakistan's response, particularly its sub-conventional war against India, has encouraged India to consider the launching of punitive strikes against Islamabad. The resulting 'Cold Start' doctrine of the Indian Army could in turn cause Pakistan to adopt more risky conventional and nuclear strategies. Ahmed argues that Realists have unwittingly given greater space to cultural nationalists in India who, for domestic political purposes, want to demonise Pakistan and India's Muslim minority. Instead of compellence, India could adopt a strategic doctrine of defensive realism and a military doctrine of defensive deterrence. Ahmed detects greater elements of pragmatism towards Pakistan in the United Progressive Alliance (UPA) government's handling of the relationship and would like to see this to be the core of Indian policy.

Tanvi Madan's essay on how the Indian strategic community views China suggests that India is quite divided on grand strategy. Where Ahmed sees the growing influence of Realists and cultural nationalists, Madan concludes that the liberals and pragmatists are in the ascendant, at least if we judge by actual Indian policy. Madan's excavation of Indian views of China delineates three broad perspectives or schools of thought: optimists, pessimists and pragmatists (reminiscent of Bajpai's Nehruvians, Hyperrealists and Neoliberals in grand strategy). Madan unpacks the three 'prisms' through which India–China relations are perceived by looking at the general beliefs and arguments of each school, their interpretation of past events, and their view of a number of substantive issues that affect the relationship (territory, Sino-Pakistani relations, bilateral rivalry in other regions, and so on). Madan then describes the policy prescriptions that flow from the diagnoses of the three schools. Optimists argue for greater communication, conciliation and co-operation with China over a range of issues; pessimists urge India to balance Chinese power, to exploit China's weaknesses (as in Tibet or with its neighbours), and to contain China geopolitically in league with others; and pragmatists want India to co-operate where possible and contain where necessary. As for the future, Madan concludes that while pragmatism dominates policy a complex mix of domestic, regional, international, political, economic, and social factors will determine which way India–China relations unfold in the years ahead.

If India's posture on Pakistan is a mix of aggression and pragmatism and if the government's attitude to China is a largely pragmatic one, what about the other key strategic relationship, with the US? Rudra Chaudhuri argues that few would disagree that India's relationship with the United States has been transformed. Yet, it is not clear what this transformation actually means for India, the US and issues such as international terrorism. Despite the momentous changes in India's approach to the US, and in turn, successive American administrations – both Republican and Democrat – to India, key questions remain underexplored: how exactly has India changed, and how do Indian elites view the relationship? Chaudhuri's essay focuses on three cases: the Korean War in 1950, the Iraq War in 2003, and present-day Afghanistan. He argues that the two countries, despite their disagreements going back to 1950, have been 'aberrant conversationalists' – seemingly doomed to disagree on key matters, to make their disagreement known, and, at the same time, to continue the discussion in search of common ground. Since the early 1980s, a measure of pragmatism entered the strategic calculations of both countries, and this has continued to the present. Chaudhuri shows that in all three cases there have been elements of convergence on ends and means, but there have also been differences. India in particular is quite happy to maintain a distance from US policies and to be formally non-aligned. Its policies in Afghanistan show that such a policy has its benefits.

Shanthie Mariet D'Souza's essay takes off from where Chaudhuri ends, namely, Indian policy in Afghanistan, its origins, development, successes, and limitations. D'Souza shows that India's role in the reconstruction of post-9/11 Afghanistan has generated a fairly intense policy debate within the Indian strategic community and in the press. As a rising power with a desire to extend its influence beyond its neighbourhood, India's interest have centred on supporting the establishment of a democratic and pluralistic government in Kabul, creating the economic, and social conditions in which extremism and terrorism are reduced, and helping connect Afghanistan as a land bridge that will benefits the entire region economically. To achieve these objectives, India has adopted a soft power approach consisting of civilian capacity building, developmental aid, revival of India's cultural and historical linkages with Afghanistan, and working for the trade and energy integration of the war-ravaged country with South and Central Asia. This role, well received by most Afghans, has important lessons for the international community for the long-term stabilisation of Afghanistan. However, as the discourse on the endgame gains momentum and the possibility of a Western exit from Afghanistan looms ever larger, whether India's interests can be defended and its role in Afghanistan can be sustained or even expanded is a subject of growing importance in New Delhi. Some think that this is impossible without an Indian military presence in Afghanistan, others think that an Indian troop presence is impossible, and yet others think that India can reach out to Pashtuns and even Taliban sympathisers to sustain India's current role.

One of India's partners in opposition to a Talibanised Afghanistan was and is Iran. However, India's relations with Iran are marked by ambivalence: on the one hand, Iran is seen as a check and balance against Pakistan and Wahhabi Islamic forces as well as a crucial source of energy; on the other hand, its internal regime, statements on India's Kashmir policy, and nuclear plans worry New Delhi. Sarang Shidore's essay analyses the India–Iran relationship in the post-Cold War period. In his view, India and Iran were traditionally built around a convergence of interests on energy and security. The idea of an India–Pakistan–Iran (IPI) pipeline and growing strategic ties pointed to the logic of an even deeper partnership in the late 1990s and early 2000s. Instead, relations reversed course starting in 2005, and more recently have taken an even sharper turn for the worse. According to Shidore, standard Neorealist analyses do not adequately explain why India did not pursue a more balanced strategy in relation to Iran, as other states have done. Mindful of the US's distaste for Iran and in the eagerness to close out the nuclear deal with Washington, New Delhi voted against Iran in the International Atomic Energy Agency (IAEA) on Tehran's nuclear programme, cautioned Iran publicly over proliferation, and shifted its stance on the IPI. Shidore argues that India's evolving strategic culture in the past decade provides a more complete explanation of why this happened. This evolution took place in the context of a shift in Indian state identity caused by domestic and diasporic factors. Shidore's reading of the State, media and scholarly discourse on India's external relations suggests that the powerful Indian middle class, which increasingly identifies with the US, and which emphasises liberal democracy in its construction of self and other, tilted Indian policy on Iran towards US preferences.

What explains the change in India's Israel policy? Why did India shun Israel from the 1950s through the 1980s and then launch into a strategic partnership with it from 1991 onwards? In September 1950, after two years of intense debate, Indian Prime Minister Jawaharlal Nehru decided to recognise the newly-created state of Israel while deferring the establishment of full diplomatic relations. It was not however until January 1992 that India became the last major non-Arab and non-Islamic state to establish full and normal diplomatic relations with Israel. What was the strategic thinking behind the foreign policy decisions taken in 1950 and 1992 to first recognise and then, over 40 years later, to finally establish full diplomatic relations with Israel? Nicholas Blarel argues that New Delhi's Israel policy can be understood in the light of more general orientations that have historically guided India's strategic behaviour: security (both internal and external), foreign policy autonomy, and economic development. In 1950, India decided that the quest for security, autonomy and development necessitated a very limited relationship with Israel. In 1992, it chose exactly the opposite: a fuller relationship with Israel now fitted its security, foreign policy, and economic objectives. India's decisions in both cases were hardheaded and rational and, arguably, successful. Blarel suggests that while this is so, the puzzling part of the story is the period of the 1970s and 1980s, when ignoring Israel seemed to bring India few if any gains, particularly in respect of security and foreign policy autonomy. Blarel's analysis is supportive of the view, which the earlier essays on relations with Pakistan, China, the US, Afghanistan, and Iran echo, namely, that New Delhi changed orientations after the Cold War and that the change of direction has been 'pragmatic' for the most part. Pakistan is a partial exception, if Ahmed's arguments are correct, but even he notes that under the Manmohan Singh government Indian policy has been far more measured.

Finally, has Indian policy towards Africa been more energetic and pragmatic than in the past? Constantino Xavier's answer is yes, especially in the 2000s and particularly after the first India–Africa summit in 2008, but India's African involvement still lacks sufficient direction and drive. To say 'Indian policy towards Africa', according to Xavier, is to overstate the different initiatives that have been taken, which do not quite add up to an overall, integrated, long-term plan to further Indian interests in the continent. His study of Indian policy making on Africa suggests that there are numerous stakeholders including most prominently the Ministry of External Affairs, and while these are increasingly being drawn into a coherent community, the Africa group in India still lacks sufficient intellectual capital and unity of purpose. Xavier's essay suggests that there is a striking absence of sophisticated and clear thinking about where Africa fits into India's external policies, and there is an absence of integrated action – in short, there is not much of a grand strategic feel to India's Africa policy. While it is clear enough that Indian interests in African today are primarily economic, that is by no means the sum total of Indian policy towards the continent. Having said that, it is unclear what Indian policy is about – economic gain, balancing China, building peace and security, lining up diplomatic support for India's UN Security Council bid, and so on. For some, this is a virtue, since it allows India to be more flexible and to avoid the accusation that it sees Africa through a selfish, grand strategic lens. If India is different from China in being less calculative and overbearing, so much the better, is the view of India's Africanists. Xavier questions whether a series of largely ad hoc policies can suffice and whether or not India's Africanists are simply making a virtue out of necessity.

Conclusion

What does this volume tell us? We highlight the following conclusions.

First of all, India has a rich heritage to draw on in conceptualising grand strategy. The essays by Rajagopalan, Vivekanandan and Raghavan introduce us to that heritage and give us some glimpses into the resources of the past. Clearly, though, there is much more to do in respect of unearthing the past and tracing through its links to the present.

Second, contrary to the rather gloomy view that India is absent grand strategic thinking, we would contend that there is a lively milieu. The various perspectives, schools of thought, or strategic approaches that feature in the Indian debate are not unique. Other countries can surely gesture at rather similar divisions of strategic opinion and argumentation. Even Hindu nationalism or Hindutva is not particularly unique – its ontology and modes of reasoning would be quite familiar in many parts of the world. Gandhianism probably is the most original of the various schools of thought. In saying this, we do not imply that Gandhian thought was altogether indigenous or native. Clearly, Gandhi drew on a range of thinking, from different traditions, including Western.

Third, Indian thought and practice today, in respect of its core interests and vital peripheries (as denoted here), is marked by a constant balancing and equilibrating. Indian policy towards Pakistan tilts towards aggressiveness and then tilts back towards moderation. China is seen as a threat but policy towards it combines military strength, on the one hand, and negotiations, trade, and solidarity, on the other hand. The US appears as a quasi-ally in the balance of power game with China and in the confronting of terrorism but is held at arms' length diplomatically and militarily as part of a new non-alignment. New Delhi supports the war on terrorism in Afghanistan and urges the West to stay as long as possible, yet refuses to put boots on the ground itself, insists on following its own development-led policy towards that troubled country, and begins to reach out to the Taliban. Iran is a rich source of energy, a check against Pakistan, and an ally on Afghanistan. At the same time, New Delhi frowns at its nuclear ambitions and votes with the US in the IAEA. Indian hostility or unease at cohabiting strategically with Israel has been replaced by a deep defence, counter-terror, and economic relationship. However, India continues to back the formation of a Palestinian state and to accord Palestine a UN seat. Finally, India seemingly is back in Africa, after a retreat in the 1990s. Its interests are commercial and economic, and grand strategic in a larger sense, but New Delhi's return has been cautious, mindful of not giving offence, and remains ad hoc. Is this supposedly pragmatic middle way caused by confusion in strategic thinking? Is it, by contrast, a rational response to the great complexities that India, like so many other states, confronts in these quite different relationships and arenas – a form of hedging? Or is it determined by an increasingly ramified domestic policy-making space in which politicians, bureaucracies, businesses, the media, and various non-state actors haul and pull New Delhi in different directions? One thing is certain in terms of a research agenda: we need many more fine-honed and fine-grained analyses of Indian policy that seek to answer such questions.

Fourth, India over the past two decades has 'stepped out' internationally in a way that it had not done since the 1950s when Nehru was at the helm. Its strategic debates are more public and vigorous than at any time since Nehru. It has begun to look well beyond its own region in terms of its interests, role, and influence. With key interlocutors, especially Pakistan, China and the US, it is far more engaged than it was from the early 1960s to the late 1990s. And with Afghanistan, Iran, Israel, and Africa, and of course with the rest of Asia, it has much deeper links now – strategic, diplomatic, political, economic, and cultural – than at any other time since independence. While our volume does not deal with India's presence in multilateral fora, clearly it is a far more salient one. New Delhi is 'at the table' in many more arenas and institutions – the list in Asia and the Indian Ocean area alone is a long one. India is heard with more attention in the UN, International Monetary Fund (IMF) and World Bank, and a host of other organisations. Its membership in the G-20 is a sign that it is expected to play a greater part in world affairs. In short, India is well placed to help shape international order to an unprecedented degree.

Finally, we suggest that Indian grand strategy has to be understood with an eye to domestic politics. Anyone interested in laying bare Indian grand strategic thought is implicitly saying that ideas and concepts within a country are influential on actual grand strategic practice, that the internal intellectual environment has an impact on security policy. International structure – the distribution of power in the international system as well as the dominant ideas and norms in international society — affect grand strategic choices, to be sure; but so does domestic structure. In the final section of the volume, we saw in every chapter that domestic politics sets limits on and creates opportunities for grand strategic practice. This is not terribly surprising: how can external policy ever be divorced from internal policy? Yet, we are just beginning in India to trace the effects of the domestic on the international. Here too, we would suggest, is a research agenda for the future.

Part I
Grand Strategy in Indian History

1
'GRAND STRATEGIC THOUGHT' IN THE RAMAYANA AND MAHABHARATA

Swarna Rajagopalan

Most Indians inherit a rudimentary knowledge of the Ramayana and Mahabharata stories as part of their cultural DNA. Multiple literary versions thrive, as do oral narrations, at least as numerous as have been Indians themselves through history. Indian politics too uses the vocabulary of the epics – from *ramarajya*, to describe an ideal polity, to *Kurukshetra*, to metaphorically describe battlefields in electoral and ideological contexts – as well as stories and characters from the epics feature in polemics and analyses. The significance of the epics extends to all spheres of social life in India, particularly statecraft, since the protagonists were born into princely families and their alienation and accession to power were central elements of the plots of both epics. It is both interesting and useful, therefore, to ask: What was India's 'grand strategic thinking' as revealed in the epics? In answering this question, this chapter explores several related ideas in the context of the Ramayana and the Mahabharata to illuminate the values, worldview and codes of their characters.

Grand Strategic Thought and the Indian Epics: Analytical Challenges

What is grand strategic thought? A simple working definition is surprisingly elusive, in spite of tomes being published on strategy, strategic culture and national strategy. The search for one leads in many directions.[1] The architects of this project define grand strategy

---

[1] See Raymond Aron, 'The Evolution of Modern Strategic Thought', *Adelphi Series*, 9, 54 (1969), pp. 1–17; Kanti Bajpai, 'Indian Strategic Culture',

as the combination of resources a government uses – military, diplomatic, economic, cultural, and political – to achieve the ends of security, however the latter is defined by that society. In the absence of a suitable working definition of 'grand strategic thought', this chapter will use the following definition: 'Grand strategic thought' refers to the ideas and assumptions drawn from a broader base of values, experiences and preferences that inform a state's policies, choices, resource use and approach to the world outside in its quest for security.

Concepts and ideas are particular to time and space. Can one take a concept that is the product of a particular historical moment and cultural context to an entirely different time – even mythical time – and space?

Most of the discussion of strategic thought begins with Clausewitz, who belonged to the age of the French Revolution, the Napoleonic wars and the Congress of Vienna. Nation-states in Europe at that time were redefining their boundaries and consolidating their jurisdictions. This situation is similar to that of Asia and Africa in the second half of the 20th century, when modern nation-states came into being in these continents. 'Strategic' is applied most often to national armies, 'strategic culture' is bound by national borders, and 'grand strategic thought' refers to the achievement of state objectives. It is hard to apply these conceptual terms to the mythical age of the epics. In the epics, there are no modern nation-states and there is no well-mapped global cartographic imagination. Both the epics revolve around *dharma*, the politics of family and the politics of honour; and conflict has more to do with restitution of rights than

---

in Michael R. Chambers, ed., *South Asia in 2020: Future Strategic Balances and Alliances* (Carlisle, PA: Strategic Studies Institute, United States Army War College, 2002), pp. 245–304; J. Boone Bartholomees, Jr., 'A Survey of Strategic Thought', in *U.S. Army War College Guide to National Security Policy and Strategy* (Carlisle, PA: Strategic Studies Institute, United States Army War College, 2004), pp. 79–100; Colin S. Gray, 'Strategic Culture as Context: The First Generation of Theory Strikes Back', *Review of International Studies*, 25, 1 (January 2004), pp. 49–69; Jeffrey S. Lantis, 'Strategic Culture and National Security Policy', *International Studies Review*, 4, 3 (Autumn 2002), pp. 87–113; Ben D. Mor, 'Public Diplo-macy in Grand Strategy', *Foreign Policy Analysis*, 2 (2006), pp. 157–76.

conquest or domination alone. The quest for suzerainty takes a ritual rather than a purely military form.[2]

It is also difficult to find an equivalent phrase for 'strategic thought', one that holds true across time, space and language. 'Security' is one example; but the debate on the meaning of 'security' has lent enough clarity to the multiple but valid understandings of the term so that it is possible to operationalise its meaning if not find and use its exact translation in Indian languages.[3]

Finally, there is the question of whether the ideas of 'strategy' and 'grand strategic thought' are at all relevant to a globalised world of constant flows – of people, information, money, goods and weapons – that have eroded state monopolies on all three dimensions of order, welfare and legitimacy. Who will make and enforce strategy, for what ends and, indeed, against whom or what?

Ironically, this last issue is what still makes the topic of this chapter interesting. Today's world, in many ways, resembles the world of the epics more than it does the classical Westphalian world on which strategic studies are predicated. The nature and power of the state is as variable today as it was in the polities described in the Ramayana or the Mahabharata, depending on the ruling elite and the first or one among many institutions and collectives, which are becoming as important as they were in the epics. People wandered between polities, then as now. Today, lines between communities are blurred (which they have always been), but in the world of the epics, the lines were blurred between species too – which may also resemble our growing ecological consciousness. The ability to

---

[2] It is interesting that while scholars in security studies – a field Richard K. Betts identifies as the 'rubric encompassing strategic thought' – have tried to expand the scope of the field; they have not considered the fact that its key concepts might need to be recast in terms of non-Western values and epistemologies. Civilisational diversity is only relevant as a source of conflict, and relativism seems to apply most to sources of insecurity that impinge on personal and political freedoms. See Richard K. Betts, 'Should Strategic Studies Survive?', *World Politics*, 50, 1 (1997), p. 9 (pp. 7–33).

[3] See Swarna Rajagopalan, 'Securing Rama's World', in Swarna Rajagopalan, ed., *Security and South Asia: Ideas, Institutions and Initiatives* (New Delhi: Routledge, 2006), pp. 24–53. Also, see Swarna Rajagopalan, 'Reconciliation in the Indian Epics', *Peace Prints, South Asian Journal of Peacebuilding*, 1, 1 (Spring 2008). Available at http://www.wiscomp.org/pp-v1/Swarna_Rajagopalan.pdf, accessed on May 16, 2012.

communicate across the globe existed then as well because the epics were predicated on a bounded universe, but technology has enabled that today and in some ways our world is as small or as large as that of the Ramayana and the Mahabharata. We are as closely linked as the world of the Mahabharata where the war between cousins drew the world into its ambit. Finally, although prevailing moral standards are arguably lower in today's world, there is a growing consensus on norms and demand for an enforceable morality in politics and government that resonates across contemporary and mythical universes.

The Epics: A Brief Introduction

The Ramayana and the Mahabharata are the two major pan-Indian epics, alive in as many versions as there have been Indians and recounted in daily life, teaching and celebration, through every narrative and art form. Protagonists in both the epics are from the warrior/ruler caste and, therefore, statecraft, politics and conflict form a significant, even central, thread of both narratives although interpersonal factors move the stories forward. This makes the epics an important resource for the study of Indian political ideas, and their continuing relevance is reflected in the use of tropes like ramarajya in contemporary politics.[4]

THE RAMAYANA

Dasharatha of Ayodhya was childless but, through the performance of a ritual, was blessed with four incomparable and virtuous sons. From an early age, the best of teachers came their way and they learnt both how to use weapons and, more importantly, why and when to use them – to defend the good and the righteous. Even as youth, they were sent to the peripheries of their kingdom to offer protection to ascetics for the completion of important rituals. On the way back to Ayodhya, Rama won the hand of Sita, the princess of Mithila, in a competition to find her a suitor. His brothers also married Sita's cousins.

As Rama stepped out of his student life into that of a householder, it was deemed appropriate to formally anoint him the heir-apparent.

---

[4] Brief profiles of the dramatis personae of the two epics are given in a chapter-end appendix.

The politics of Dasharatha's polygamous household decided otherwise. Rama was exiled in fulfillment of a long-forgotten promise and Dasharatha's second son (by another wife) took his place. Rama, Sita and his brother Lakshmana left for the forest; Rama, in order to keep his father's word, Lakshmana, to serve his older brother and Sita, to stay with her husband. Their forest sojourn was idyllic, and they spent time with forest-dwelling sages and ascetics. Their exile did not absolve them of their duty to protect, and they found many occasions to use the arms they carried with them.

A chance encounter altered the tenor of their exile and set the stage for the dramatic culmination both of the epic and, in some versions, the purpose of Rama's life. Shoorpanakha, who was the sister of the king of Lanka, saw Rama in the forest and propositioned him. Rama and Lakshmana toyed with her, sending her back and forth between them, each suggesting the other as more suitable for her. Stung, furious, Shoorpanakha considered Sita to be the reason for her rejection and went on to attack her, whereupon the brothers severed her nose and ears (and in the classic Tamil version, her breasts as well) as retribution. Disfigured and insulted, Shoorpanakha urged her brother, Ravana, to avenge her humiliation. Hostilities came to a head with Sita's abduction by Ravana. She was held captive in a grove while being alternately threatened and entreated to submit to his advances.

The next trajectory of Rama and Lakshmana's journey was southward, in search of Sita. En route, they befriended and allied with a community of *vanara*s (forest-dwellers, commonly depicted as monkeys). One of them, Hanuman, located Sita and tried to negotiate her release, but was insulted and his tail was set on fire. He then used that to burn down Lanka. The vanaras formed Rama's army and they marched south together. The bridge to Lanka was built with the help of animals and birds, who came to serve the righteous prince.

The next chapter is actually called *Yuddha Kanda* or 'War Chapter'. When all diplomatic missions failed, Ravana's brother defected and sought protection in Rama's camp. For 10 days, the two sides warred, incurring heavy losses. Finally, Rama's army won and Ravana was killed. Sita was put through an ordeal of fire to test her chastity before she could return to Rama's side. By this time, the period of exile had ended too, and Rama returned to Ayodhya where his brother had been his regent.

There is a post-script to this story, a later addition infamous for Sita's return to exile. We are told that Ayodhya under Rama's rule enjoyed a utopian idyll, made possible by his perfect adherence to dharma. On hearing that one of his subjects had cast aspersions on his wife's fidelity during her captivity in Lanka and, by extension, on his ability to place righteousness above his affections, Rama exiled Sita although she was pregnant. In this version, the epic ends with his reunion with his sons, while Sita chooses to leave him rather than prove her chastity all over again.

The standard, some would say original, version of the Ramayana is the one recorded by Valmiki though other versions too have been influential in the linguistic regions to which they belonged – such as the Tamil Ramayana by Kambar, the Bengali Ramayana by Krittibasa or the Hindi *Ramcharitmanas* by Tulsidas. Details of the story vary, but the main elements of the plot remain the same and if there are small shifts in perspective, the characters remain more or less the same. This paper draws primarily on the Valmiki Ramayana, in its best-selling translation by the Gita Press.[5]

The Mahabharata

The Mahabharata is a far more complex story than the Ramayana, encompassing many other stories (including that of Rama) and containing cross-references to virtually all of India's mythological heritage. At its core, it is the story of Bharata's dynasty and of the internecine rivalry that brought virtually the entire subcontinent to war. The summary in this section cannot do justice to the richness of the epic, which is not merely a single text but an entire tradition in itself.

---

[5] In-text citations from these two epics only are used in the chapter. For the Ramayana, the two-volume translation of the texts used: *Srimad Valmiki Ramayana*, 2 vols (Gorakhpur: Gita Press, 1969, 6th edn 2001). The first volume contains four books of the text (*Balakandam, Ayodhyakandam, Aranyakandam* and *Kishkindhakandam*) and the second volume contains three (*Sundarakandam, Yuddhakandam* and *Uttarakandam*). The style for in-text references from the text is: SVR (for Srimad Valmiki Ramayanam), 1 or 2 to indicate the volume, the abbreviated name of the book (Bala, Ayodhya, Aranya, Kishkindha, Sundara, Yuddha and Uttara), canto number: verse number, page number in that volume. The full source citation appears in the chapter-end references.

As the story unfolds, succession to the Kuru throne is complicated in every generation for one reason or another, starting with Yayati who gave the bulk of his kingdom to the one son who would trade his youth for Yayati's premature ageing. Shantanu promised Satyavati that the sons she bore him would succeed him, and not his first-born. The latter gave up his claim to the throne out of deference to his father's promise, and also promised not to marry and have children of his own. Bheeshma, as he came to be known, found wives for his brothers and supervised the raising of the children they begot. The elder son, Dhritarashtra, was blind and unable to rule. So, the younger son, Pandu, inherited the throne out of turn, although he was too feeble to live a full life, and eventually was succeeded by Dhritarashtra himself. Dhritarashtra had a 100 sons and Pandu had five.

Raised together, but with the knowledge of their competing claims to the throne, the 100 Kaurava brothers and the five Pandava brothers were taken, in the main plot of the epic, through multiple cycles of schemes, narrow escapes, exiles and fake reconciliations before the great Mahabharata war took place. The war was preceded by diplomatic efforts, as wars often are. However, direct talks and all efforts at mediation failed. At the end of the 18 days of war, all 100 Kauravas were dead as were their allies, cousins and many in the succeeding generation. It was in the period after the war, that the eldest Pandava brother Yudhishthira received explicit instruction in statecraft from the dying family elder and statesman Bheeshma. But the story does not end with the war. How the Pandavas ruled and how they shook off the grief caused by this fratricidal conflict to establish their suzerainty over the 'world' of the Mahabharata is also part of the story, as is their abdication of the throne in favour of their only surviving grandchild, Parikshit.

The character of Krishna is central to the epic, although his own story is peripheral to it. He is cousin to both sets of princes, playmate, mentor, teacher, strategist and, when needed, divine incarnation. Incidents in the Mahabharata acquire a didactic quality when he intervenes or comments on them.

There are several versions of the Mahabharata too, and, as befits such a complex story, there is variation between them. The authoritative critical edition of the text is the one prepared by the

Bhandarkar Oriental Research Institute, Pune, but this chapter uses another classic translation by Kisari Mohan Ganguli.[6]

Searching the Epics for Strategic Insights

It should be noted that by and large, people writing about the political ideas in the epics more or less bypass the Ramayana and focus on two sections of the Mahabharata, the *Shanti Parva* and the *Anushasan Parva*. These two sections constitute the death-bed advice about governance and dharma that Bheeshma imparts to Yudhishthira who has won the war but lost heart. These are the most explicitly educational portions of the epics. Rich as they are, the problem with focusing on the didactic sections is their irrelevance to the most common way in which Indians come to learn the epics: oral narration. Typically, the long treatises are not part of the story that is told, with the rare exception of a discursive session that might draw on a few extracts. Therefore, if the argument for examining the epics is that everyone is aware of the stories and their lessons, then the Shanti and Anushasan Parvas are the least useful portions for our purpose – hardly anyone is likely to know their content.[7]

---

[6] The 18 books (*parvas*) of the Mahabharata were translated by Kisari Mohan Ganguli and published in four volumes between 1883 and 1896. Following is the style of in-text citation of references from the text: KMG (Kisari Mohan Ganguli); 1, 2, 3 or 4 to indicate the volume; the name of the parva (*Adi, Sabha, Vana, Virata, Udyoga, Bheeshma, Drona, Karna, Shalya, Sauptika, Stri, Shanti, Anushasan, Ashvamedhika, Ashramavasika, Mausala, Mahaprasthanika,* and *Svargarohana*); the page number in that parva in this edition. The full source citation is included in the references at the end of this chapter.

[7] Although the works of three Western authors have become influential in the literature on Indian strategic ideas, their reading and research are limited to the purpose of finding in Indian thought and traditions things they have already defined in Western terms. Adda Bozeman's 1960 book has an India section, which is the weakest in her global survey of cultural interactions across time and space. Her work is important mainly because she pioneered the study of history and culture as a pre-requisite for diplomatic practice. George Tanham's 1992 RAND study has a populist appeal given its identification of factors influencing Indian thought and its outlining of paradoxes in contemporary Indian thinking, but it is not particularly scholarly Stephen Rosen's 1996 book explored civil–military relations in

Here, the working definition of grand strategic thought adopted at the beginning of this chapter is interpreted in terms of two broad themes – values and instruments for creating security – which we explore in the stories with the aim to offer an idea of the perspectives and values Indians in the epics brought to their interaction with the world.

VALUES

Incidents and interactions in the epics reflect three core values: dharma, the fear of anarchy and a valourisation of diversity, and the very fluid definition of the self.

Dharma

The core value in the epics – one that is common to most Indian traditions – is dharma. Dharma is both the ideological foundation and the purpose of the political community, which is intended to end the state of anarchy and restore and protect dharma. Interestingly, dharma itself is, to a great extent, mutable according to time, individual and circumstances, rather than being a rigid, moral stance. Indeed, sometimes, dharma requires actions that are morally ambivalent, as the epics tell us.

There are at least three dimensions of dharma in the context of politics. The first is the dimension of social order. *Varnashramadharma* is a concrete social manifestation of this dimension: the idea that every social station/social group has a particular social function and that every stage of life brings certain duties. In his advice to Rama, Narada describes the centrality of varnashramadharma to the passing of the ages. As the practice of austerities spreads from one *varna* to the other, morality declines and the passing of the ages marks this decline. (SVR 2, Uttara 74: pp. 879–80) Varna is the referent of

---

India and China, placing early India in a much larger context, concluding that caste is the main explanatory factor for Indian thinking about matters strategic and diplomatic. All of them interpret India primarily in social and cultural terms, with caste being the single most important factor in their reading. See Adda Bozeman, *Politics and Culture in International History* (Princeton, NJ: Princeton University Press, 1960); George K. Tanham, *Indian Strategic Thought: An Interpretive Essay* (Santa Monica, CA: RAND, 1992); Stephen Peter Rosen, *Societies and Military Power: India and Its Armies* (Ithaca, NY: Cornell University Press, 1996).

most discussions about duties and responsibilities. *Brahmana*s must observe austerities and perform penances and rituals for the good of the world. *Kshatriya*s must protect them and others in the society. Right from the first book of the Ramayana, when sage Vishvamitra asks Dasharatha to send his young sons to guard the site of his penance, to the *Bhagavad Gita* itself, the idea that birth within a varna comes with sacrosanct social responsibility is reiterated through events and anecdotes in the epics.

The second dimension of dharma is at the individual level. What constitutes a particular individual's dharma and what choices s/he makes in relation to that dharma? When that choice is *adharmik* (contrary to dharma), it is the king's/state's duty and the kshatriya's prerogative to punish the person making the choice. For the individual, this dharma is in large part a function of her/his relationships. Dharma, here, constitutes appropriate conduct for an individual in his/her relationships, be it as father, son, husband, mother, daughter, wife or any other family relationships that have always been an important part of Indian life. Rama's decision to honour his father's promise to his stepmother, is his dharma as a son; Sita's to walk with him in the forest, her interpretation of her dharma as a wife.

This dharma is also the dharma of contract and promise. Yudhishthira, in accepting the invitation to gamble with his cousins, tacitly accepted the consequences of the game's outcome. Therefore, although the provocation was extreme, he felt honour-bound to accept the terms of exile offered to him and his family and to abide by them. Time and again, his friends exhorted him to fight – right from the early years of exile and also once towards the end. But to Yudhishthira that would have been a travesty of dharma. Rama's setting a high standard for personal adherence to dharma in the Ramayana finds mention in the Mahabharata, in Yudhishthira's frequent references to an exiled prince of Ayodhya from an earlier age.

The individual might also choose the dharma of right and wrong above relationships or contract. Vibheeshana does this when he walks out on his brother to take Rama's side, as does Yuyutsu, one of Duryodhana's brothers. But the epic narrative is set in motion largely by the adharmik consequences of the way an individual interprets her/his dharma; for instance, Kaikeyi's manoeuvres, in the Ramayana, to place her own son Bharata on the throne of Ayodhya.

The dharma of the king and the ruling class in general is to prevent a collapse of the social order and to punish individual adharmik choices that have harmful social consequences. In the epics though, individual infringements can also be punished by divine intervention, the curses of sages and ascetics, or even the aggrieved party.

The point here is that if there is something whose value creates a strategic interest for the polities of the epics, then it is dharma. Dharma is the referent object as well the value that gives legitimacy to the political elite.

The Fear of Anarchy

Why is dharma so important? In Indian political thought, dharma is a bulwark against chaos, which is the most dreaded socio-political condition. In the *Shanti Parva*, Bheeshma describes the origin of kingship to Yudhishthira: 'A kingdom in which anarchy prevails becomes weak and is soon afflicted by robbers. In kingdoms torn by anarchy, righteousness cannot dwell. The inhabitants devour one another. An anarchy is the worst possible of states' (KMG 3, Shanti 67: 147–48). The people then made a compact: 'He who becomes harsh in speech, or violent in temper, he who seduces or abducts other people's wives or robs the wealth that belongs to others, should be cast off by us' (KMG 3, Shanti 67: 148). They then approached Brahma to appoint a king from among them and made a pact with the king that absolved him of the sin of their individual transgressions. That was the first king, Manu, and since his time, as Bheeshma stresses in his death-bed discourse to his great-nephew, the most important duty of the king has been the protection of dharma and those who live within the fold of varnashramadharma. The primary orientation of the polity is, thus, inward, not outward.

The great fear that animated thinking about governance was that of *matsyanyaya*, the evocative Indian description of anarchy, wherein the big fish would eat the small fish. Dharma stood between society and matsyanyaya, and dharma was underpinned by a king whose personal dharma was impeccable and who could use *danda*, punishment, to ensure compliance. In our time, matsyanyaya takes many forms: unregulated globalisation without a safety net and international webs of money, political support and weapons that underpin terrorist networks, for instance. When the state is unable to ensure everyday physical security and welfare, at least to assure survival, the social order crumbles. Today's fear of failed states is a reflection of the old fear of matsyanyaya.

In today's context, dharma may be reinterpreted as a preference for norm-based interactions. Multilateral fora like the United Nations and its agencies; global conferences and summits; and negotiated treaties articulate and/or reflect this preference. The ideal is that everyone should share a core set of values and agree to live by them. In the epics, this ideal went along with the right of the collective to punish gross transgressions. In our age, this right is circumscribed, ironically, by other norms protecting the internal sovereignty of the state. Dharmik campaigns in the epics, however, were limited to ousting the person(s) responsible for transgressions and there was no room for regime change and nation-building activities at the end of the war.

The Self, Other and Diversity

Defining 'the world outside' is actually where our challenges begin, because it begins with defining the self. The Ramayana and the Mahabharata are set in ages (*tretayuga* and *dvaaparayuga*) where worlds and species intermingled freely and there lived beings whose lives straddled these ages, and whose prodigious memories blurred the borders of time as well. Many beings are able to change form to satisfy purpose and passion. Glimpses and reminders of past lives also surface through the course of the epics. So, where does the self stop and the 'other' begin?

In neither epic are protagonists merely what they seem to be. Rama, the hero of the Ramayana, is not who he thinks he is. In most versions of the epic, we are privy to Rama's secret, but in spite of occasional revelations, he lives and acts as a human prince devoted to dharma. In the Mahabharata, Krishna's divinity is acknowledged everywhere, but the Pandava princes also have divine fathers, and Arjuna's bond with Krishna transcends lives. The essence of Vishnu is in all four sons of Dasharatha.

Family ties further blur the separation between the individual self and others. Not only are particular family units as close as to be considered one person, but marriage, in its many variations, contributes to this. Draupadi is won by Arjuna in a contest to find her the best suitor, but she becomes the wife of all five Pandava brothers. Rather than becoming the source of rivalry between them, she binds them together, and her public humiliation and unrelenting anger thereafter keep them focused on the purpose of their birth – the war that will end the age. Arjuna consorts with a water-serpent princess (Uloopi) who bears a son. Bheema marries a *rakshasi*, Hidimbi who too bears him a mighty son. One of Krishna's chief wives is Jambavati, princess of the black bears. The god of wind and an *apsara*, reborn as a monkey, are the natural parents of Hanuman. Ravana's harem has women from every species around the world. His own parentage is mixed – he is descended from Brahma himself but is a rakshasa. It is as if even genetics observes no difference between species.

In the wonderfully liberal world of the epics, marriage does not preclude the embrace of natural children from other dalliances. The Pandavas are, in fact, not Pandavas, but more correctly, *Kaunteya*s, sons of Kunti; Pandu's wives Kunti and Madri call on *deva*s to sire their children, when Pandu cannot. In fact, parentage is the thread that causes the tangled web of the Mahabharata. The author of the Mahabharata, Vyasa, is the natural child of the woman who marries into the Kuru dynasty. When her own sons die without children, she calls him to father children with her two daughters-in-law, and he also fathers the child of their maid. Thus, none of the key players in this war over dynastic succession is naturally born to a member of the dynasty. In the Ramayana, Sita herself is furrow-born – an abandoned girl-child found in the earth by her foster father.

Moving fluidly back and forth between ages, lives, worlds, species, forms and races, even when the people of the epics speak of their country and kingdom, it does not have the bricks, mortar and barbed wire connotation of our times. The great war in the Mahabharata is fought over the right to inherit a kingdom, but that territory is not the point at all is illustrated in the last-minute offer made by the eldest Pandava prince: Five villages in return for peace. Four of these are associated with particularly happy or humiliating moments in their lives (Kushasthala, Vrikasthala, Makandi and Varanavata); they are not contiguous or necessarily important places. The choice of the fifth is left to the Kauravas. It is the recognition of the Pandavas' birthright and punishment for the Kauravas' wrongdoing that is at the heart of the war (KMG 2, Udyoga 31: 55–56).

In the Ramayana, there are many moments when the story of a particular land is narrated. But land, identity and polity are seldom closely identified, except, perhaps, in the Uttarakandam story of Lanka being created especially for rakshasas to live in. Moreover, there is nothing permanent about any such association. Lanka is occupied for a time by Vaishravana, a deva, and then reclaimed for rakshasas.

The free interaction between peoples and other species, and the lament that a decline in this mobility was a mark of the passing of ages suggests that the epics appear to value diversity. Migration was freer in the epics than it is now, and the reality that people were and could be mobile is recognised. Anxiety about migration, in these stories, was the anxiety that immigrants or hosts might not follow the same idea of dharma, not that they were different. In our time, debates everywhere about identity, citizenship and mobility relate to this value.

Adherence to dharma is the line that demarcates the self from the other. Dharma can be interpreted conservatively as upholding the social order and its mores. It can also be interpreted broadly to mean doing what is right: speaking the truth, showing compassion and keeping one's word. Across ages, in the Indian context, dharma survives when everyone does their part. Age, social status and caste, and indeed 'race' (that is, devas, asuras, rakshasas, vanaras, etc.), have a place and a part to play in preserving dharma and keeping the world as it should be.

Dharma is ultimately individual, just as the journey of each soul is individual. The dharmik or adharmik behaviour of the individual may have a social context and consequences for the community or world, but the choice to adhere to dharma or to depart from it, is individual. The dharma of the king is the dharma of the individual who is the king. Arjuna's dharma, at the centre of the Bhagavad Gita discourse in the Mahabharata, lies at the intersection of his kshatriya identity and his relationships. The choice is his, whether or not to fight. In the Ramayana, Ravana makes the choice to fight for Sita. Adharmik behaviour is his choice; it is not his nature or, necessarily, the nature of his people. Plenty of his advisors warn him that his choice is folly, but he chooses to disregard the welfare of his people.

The epics accept that individuals can be on both sides of the line of dharma, depending on the context. Rama and Krishna, divinity incarnate in different ages, epitomise this. Both are incarnate for a purpose; the first is dimly conscious of this, the second seems to be fully aware. In popular renditions, Krishna almost manipulates circumstances and individuals in order to make the war inevitable.

When a fantastic court is built for the Pandavas in the wilderness that they have been given as theirs to rule, he gently, slyly suggests a family gathering so that their cousins and rivals may visit and be jealous. He rightly anticipates that jealousy and covetousness will set in motion the events that will lead, years later, to the war that he must preside over.[8] Rama is considered *maryada purushottama*, the perfect man, though three of his actions remain contentious: his killing of Vali from a hiding-place; Sita's exile in response to public opinion and his killing of a *shudra* (a member of the fourth varna, associated mainly with occupations involving work done with one's own hands) for performing austerities. The Valmiki version of the epic offers a defence for all three actions; however, the epics being living traditions, each narrator approaches the dharmik dilemma afresh and each audience applies the dharma of its own time and place to these actions.

Individuals pay for singular transgressions of dharma, but these usually have an end-point. Apsaras and *gandharva*s (semi-divine beings) are often banished to earth in human, rakshasa, *yaksha* (nature spirits*)* or animal forms for a certain period of time. Usually their encounter with Rama, Krishna or another being whose dharma is perfect, offers the opportunity for redemption. The line of dharma does not 'other' these random offenders. It does seal the fate of those who persist in adharmik acts. The 'other' in the epics is the person who chooses the path of adharma rather than the person who acts once or twice in a way that violates dharma or whose occasional actions have ethical ambivalence.

Ravana and the Kauravas are villains for this reason alone. And the greatness of the epics lies in the fact that no opportunity is lost in reminding us of the good qualities of the 'bad guys'. Duryodhana's generosity with gifts and alms, his talent for deep friendship and love, his charisma and his valour, are all pointed out, along with the repeated references to the evil he epitomises. Ravana's scholarship, his proficiency in music, his faith, the rigours of his penance and his compelling personality are often preludes to descriptions of his megalomania, his bestialities and his ego. In both instances, the epics present these characters as multifaceted, but in letting one side of their personality dominate the other, these characters choose the

---

[8] See, for example, Ramesh Menon, *The Mahabharata*, Vol. 1 (New Delhi: Rupa, 2004), pp. 387–97.

adharmik path. The door to redemption, to forgiveness and to crossing back over to dharma remain open until the very end.

The friends and allies of the adharmik individual are not presumed to be inherently evil or opposed to dharma. Karna, Duryodhana's friend who learns that he is, in fact, Kunti's first son, chooses the dharma of friendship and loyalty and fights on the Kauravas' side. Shalya, the maternal uncle of the two youngest Pandavas Nakula and Sahadeva, is taken care of and entertained by the Kauravas on his way to meet his nephews. When he finds out that his host is Duryodhana, he repays the debt of that hospitality by fighting for the Kauravas. Ravana's brother Kumbhakarna and his uncle Mareecha both counsel him against abducting and holding Sita captive. However, when it comes to taking sides, they back him up for their own reasons – love in one case, fear in the other. The epic narrative explains their decisions as well. One person's choice of the adharmik path drags others along in its wake.

Two more instances of 'othering', both from the Ramayana, must be mentioned nonetheless. One of the justifications Rama offers Vali for the manner in which Rama shoots him, is that Vali is only an animal and may, therefore, be hunted down even when he does not see the hunter. This appears in a section that follows the one in which we learn about Vali's greatness and Vali's articulate challenge that there was no dharma in the way he was killed. Vali, despite his keen awareness of dharma and intimate interactions with the human world, remains 'but a monkey' (SVR 1, Kishkindha 18: 40, p. 802) In all other instances, the justification for killing is a violation of dharma, but for most animals, there no need for a justification, as this instance suggests.

The second instance, interesting from the point of view of contemporary Indian politics, is the killing of Shambuka. In the perfectly just world of ramarajya, a brahmana arrives at Rama's court carrying the body of his dead son. Rama learns that the cause of this death is the performance by a shudra of austerities reserved for brahmanas. Rama is told that this is adharma and will cause untold misery in his domain. Seeking out the offending hermit, Rama questions him very specifically as to his caste and on receiving an honest answer, beheads him summarily. Thus, caste emerges in this instance as an important form of 'othering', which it has not been in the narrative until then. (SVR 2, Uttara 73–75, pp. 878–83) Caste as an 'othering' factor also features in the Mahabharata, be it in the story of

Ekalavya or the question of Karna and Krishna's caste. In fact, the most impermeable dividing line between the self and the 'other' may be marked by caste, but it is such an interior marking that the question of strategising against those on the other side of the line makes no sense in the context of the epics (even though it might today).

In the Ramayana, as Hanuman and the monkeys look out to the sea, the latter seems to mark the end of their world, but characters in the epics interact with the worlds that thrive beyond their line of vision. The true world 'outside', real othering, happens across the line of adherence to dharmik norms, as we have pointed out.

Oddly, while 'othering' reflects the fluidity of identities and interactions in the epic world, it is just as fluid in today's world. Strategic studies and security decision-makers work on the assumption that state borders are axiomatic and sacrosanct; restriction of mobility is a standard tool used by them. Within states as well, identity politics reinforces mutual alienation. The same individual and community can belong to the state and be alien at the same time.

When states violate present-day dharmik norms, i.e., the regimes and international conventions they have ratified, the international community can only censure them. However, states and coalitions of states have appropriated the right to intervene in the name of collective security and norm enforcement. Within states, the enforcement of dharmik norms is just as hard; the state retains a legal monopoly over legitimate violence, but what is legitimate is relative and other non-state actors also exercise violence. Human rights violations – a major adharmik act in our time – are perpetrated by everyone. If compliance with norms is the dharma of the day, then the line between the self and the other is usually blurred.

Creating Security

In the epic universe, security is first about order and then about upholding dharma. Order, in fact, is what upholds and protects dharma. The ruling class is charged with the work of maintaining order and protecting dharma, as Vishwamitra points out to Dasharatha when he demands that the young princes of Ayodhya be sent with him to protect his sacrifice, and as Krishna suggests to Arjuna, urging him to fight his friends and family. The protection of dharma depends on the appropriate performance of individual duties. For a ruler, the performance of duties comprises three parts. First, rituals of sovereignty establish and renew his legitimacy. Second, a number of policy instruments or approaches are placed at his disposal. Finally, clear protocols on engagement govern his choice and deployment of these instruments. The observance of all of these is also part of his duty as a ruler, and their correct observance, in turn, reinforces the social order.

Rituals of Sovereignty

Sacrifices were the ritual pivot of political authority in early India. Public sacrifices were performed for the general welfare and from the point of view of the kshatriya ruler, they served two purposes. First, they performed a ritual of atonement for the killing that their dharma involved. Second, as occasions for gift-giving, they were moments for forging and consolidating alliances and relationships within the political elite. Finally, they were important foreign relations instruments, underscoring internal sovereignty and establishing the extent of the king's suzerainty. The two sacrifices that feature in the epics are the *Rajasuya* and the *Ashvamedha*.

The Rajasuya is performed by Yudhishthira at a time when Indraprastha, the city of Pandavas, is at the zenith of its glory. The Pandavas have transformed a wilderness into the beautiful and prosperous city of Indraprastha. The creation of a uniquely beautiful *sabha* marks the perfect moment for their king to be recognised by the world. But the intention to perform the sacrifice was not Yudhisthira's. It was Narada, the itinerant sage and Krishna who were instrumental in convincing Yudishthira. Narada comes to Indraprastha directly from Indra's heavenly court where he reports, Pandu does not sit even all these years after his death. The reason for this is that his sons have not yet formalised their paramountcy. While Yudhishthira is upset by this news, he lacks the confidence to perform the Rajasuya. Krishna convinces him and offers him advice on how to bring the last few doubters around. The Rajasuya process involves getting consent (in the form of tributes) from every king in *Bharatavarsha* (as the Indian universe was known in the epic age). In order to do so, hostile kings would have to be confronted and vanquished and reluctant princes would have to be persuaded.

After the festivities, Yudhishthira's cousin Duryodhana enviously describes the tributes offered. Those offering tributes come from every part of the world as known to contemporary Indians – the Himalayan regions, what is now Southwest Asia, the peninsular region, the coasts and also Sri Lanka. They bring with them every possible gift right from special plants and herbs from their regions, to elephants, gold, silk, precious jewels and serving girls and serving men. Yajnasena, the king of Panchala, even gifted the Pandavas his kingdom. Such was the extravagance of the presents that kings coming from as far as the Kailash region in the Himalayas with their special mountain plants; and the Cholas, Pandyas and Singhalas from the south with sandal, gems and gem-studded textiles were not permitted to enter. As they waited patiently at the gates, others were told that 'if they could wait and bring good tribute they could obtain admission' (KMG 1, Sabha 51: 104). Duryodhana tells his father that the attendant princes vied with each other to wait on Yudhishthira and brought him special items for the ritual. The spectacle and the sound of the rare conches used had several princes in a swoon, including Duryodhana. 'And all orders of men, good, indifferent and low, belonging to numberless races, coming from diverse lands made Yudhishthira's habitation the epitome of the world' (KMG 1, Sabha 51: 105). Duryodhana narrates, that performing such a sacrifice gave Yudhishthira such prosperity and status that only two clans did not pay him tribute – the Panchalas whose daughter was his queen and who had gifted him their kingdom, and the Andhaka-Vrishnis, who were Krishna's family and exceptionally close to the Pandavas. Such is the political import of the Rajasuya that it takes Yudhishthira and his brothers from princes who were making the best of a piece of kingdom given to them in charity to suzerains of most of the subcontinent.

A few years after the Rajasuya, the king might perform the *Vajapeya* sacrifice, to renew both his vitality and the fertility of the land. But the culmination of a king's reign is undoubtedly the performance of the Ashvamedha. The ritual is thought to empower the king so much that when Mahabali was about to perform his 100th Ashvamedha, it was time for another *avatara* of Vishnu.

The year-long sacrifice begins in the spring when a horse is set free by the king to roam the world. An army follows the horse on its journey. When the horse crosses a border, the local ruler can either allow the horse to roam unchecked and send gifts for its owner through the army, or stop the horse and fight the accompanying army. But neither allowing the horse through his domain nor stopping the horse and losing the battle is tantamount to losing the throne or kingdom. The defeated king pays tribute, accepts the victor's suzerainty, attends the final sacrifice of the Ashvamedha and continues to rule his kingdom. The Ashvamedha features in both the epics. Yudhishthira and Rama both perform the sacrifice in the post-war phase of their stories.

At the end of the Mahabharata war, Yudhishthira is racked with guilt at the thousands dead. The kingdom is bankrupt and he has lost his family and friends. Vyasa, his grandfather, advises him: '[T]hose that commit sins, can always free themselves through penance, sacrifice and gifts' (KMG 4, Ashvamedhika 3: 3). The Ashvamedha of Yudhishthira 'was distinguished by a profuse abundance of food and wealth and jewels and gems, and oceans of wines of different kinds' (KMG 4, Ashvamedha 89: 155). By the time of its performance, no foes of the Pandavas remained alive and unconquered, and the main result of the *yajna* was to cleanse the king of all his sins. What is the gift that truly cleanses the king? It is the gift of all conquered lands to the brahmanas and we are told, 'unto Vyasa he gave away the Earth' or what he describes as the 'Earth conquered by Arjuna' (KMG 4, Ashvamedhika 89: 153). However, in narrating this story to Yudhishthira's great-grandson, the sage Vaishampayana adds: 'Thou shouldst not, O king, think highly of sacrifice ... Abstention from injury as regards all creatures, contentment, conduct, sincerity, penances, self-restraint, truthfulness, and gifts are each equal in point of merit to sacrifice' (KMG 4, Ashvamedhika 90: 162).

Rama too performs the Ashvamedha sacrifice but what is interesting is that he begins by discussing with his brothers the merits of performing the Rajasuya. Rama tells his brothers: 'Now I want to perform Rajasuya – the outer limit of piety, O brother ... I wish to perform the excellent Rajasuya. Therein (resides) eternal righteousness' (SVR 2, Uttara 83: 3–5, p. 896). Bharata's response, however is:

> O righteous one, in you is established the highest form of righteousness, this entire earth and all fame ... All kings like us, look upon Thee holy one, the lord of worlds as the gods (look upon) Prajapati ... all kings regard you as sons to their fathers, you are the resort of this world and also of beings ... How, O king, you being so, wish to perform the sacrifice (Rajasuya), in which there shall be the destruction of royal families of earth. O King, those men, who on this earth are possessed of valour, all of them, will be destroyed, due to the anger of all. O lion among men, possessed of unparalleled valour, accompanied with merits, it befits to you not to destroy this earth, all indeed are under your sway (SVR 2, Uttara 83: 10–15, pp. 896–97).

Rama accepts this advice and changes his mind, saying: 'That action is not to be undertaken by the wise which causes pain to the worlds' (SVR 2, Uttara 83: 19, p. 897). To this Lakshmana replies: '[T]he great sacrifice Ashwamedha is the purifier of all sins (and) shall be your purifier, (although) difficult (to perform), if you so please' (SVR 2, Uttara 84: 2, p. 898). Lakshmana and Rama recall stories of other miraculous Ashwamedha yajnas – whereby heavens were regained, the killing of a Brahmin was expiated and a king under a curse to transform into a woman became a man again. Rama decides to perform the Ashvamedha himself. In the Ramayana, the culmination of the yajna reunites Rama with the children he has never seen and parts him from Sita forever, marking the beginning of the end of the avatara.

Policy Instruments and Approaches

Classical Indian political thought identifies four expedients (*upaya*) that the ruler can use within and beyond his/her kingdom: *sama* (conciliation), *dana* (gift-giving), *bheda* (dissension) and danda, to which the epics and later texts add *upeksha* (indifference), *maya* (illusion and deceit) and *indrajala* (strategem). The last three are particularly commended to those who wield less power within a dispensation.[9] These expedients could apply within and across polities. All of them are seen in the epics.

Sama includes praise and celebration of commonalities, focusing on the benefits of co-operation, empathy and felicitation.[10] The Mahabharata quintessentially documents the conversation between sincere and insincere sama. As every attempt to kill one or all of the Pandavas fail, the Kauravas and their father welcome the brothers back to Hastinapura with insincere tears of relief and joy. Under the leadership of Yudhishthira, the Pandavas take these interactions at face value. On Yudhishthira's part, especially, every return courtesy is a sincere one, including the final pre-war offer of five villages in the shared interest of averting a fratricidal war. It is important to note that military defeat in the Indian context seldom meant occupation and direct rule; more often, it meant the collection of tributes,

---

[9] V. R. Ramachandra Dikshitar, *War in Ancient India* (New Delhi: Motilal Banarsidass, 1987), pp. 332–36.

[10] Kautilya, *The Arthashastra*, ed. by L. N. Rangarajan (New Delhi: Penguin, 1987), p. 114.

the acknowledgement of the winner's suzerainty, a local changing of the guard and a return to old ways. Conciliation was the preferred, rather default way. Thus, Rama crowns Vibheeshana king rather than accepting the throne of Lanka as a prize for defeating Ravana in battle.

Dana, giving, is an important part of every individual's life. Kshatriyas may atone for the violence that is part of their dharma by giving gifts. At the end of the Mahabharata war, a depressed and grieving Yudhishthira is advised to perform a Rajasuya yajna and give generously. In the policy context, dana includes monetary rewards, special favours, tax exemptions and employment. Duryodhana's impulsive gift of a kingdom to Karna is the beginning of a lifetime generous friendship that ultimately obliges Karna to fight against those he discovers are his brothers. Generous giving is the sign of greatness in a king, and the iconic status of Harishchandra and Karna in Indian mythology attests to this.

Bheda or the sowing of dissension consists in exploiting existing differences within another camp. On the eve of the Mahabharata war, Karna receives two visitors. The first is Krishna, who stops by on his way out after a last-ditch effort to avert war. Krishna chooses this critical moment to reveal Karna's parentage – he is also Kunti's son. Happy and sad, torn, Karna chooses to be on the side of his friend Duryodhana who has supported him in hard times. Later, Kunti comes to him with the same information. He promises her that she will be left with either him or Arjuna. Karna is the most valuable part of the Kaurava army and the one that Yudhishthira worries about. He does not defect, but his promise to Kunti that he will spare his other brothers weakens Kaurava prospects immeasurably.

Danda is the use of punishment or force. Notwithstanding the idealism of the epic polity, danda is the centerpiece of its functions and its powers. So much so, one perspective or even, school of Indian political thought, is called *dandaniti*. The emphasis on danda follows from both the fear of matsyanyaya and from dharma being the rationale for political organisation. The use of danda keeps dharma alive and restrains those with a tendency for wrong-doing.[11] The increasing use of force is a mark of the passing ages.

---

[11] U. N. Ghoshal, *A History of Indian Political Ideas* (London: Oxford University Press, 1959), p. 193.

Upeksha, translated as neutrality or indifference, is not an option in either war. Both Rama's war with Ravana and the Mahabharata war are fought to establish the ascendancy of dharma over adharmik forces. To some extent, Krishna's brother Balarama's decision to go away on a pilgrimage rather than choose between the Pandavas who had dharma on their side, and his favourite student, Duryodhana, reflects upeksha.

Maya or deceit features in both epics. Mareecha, a rakshasa, takes the form of a golden deer to draw Sita's attention and lure Rama away in his pursuit. Ravana takes the form of a mendicant to approach Sita when she is alone. Keechaka is killed by Bheema disguised as Draupadi to end the former's acts of sexual harassment.

Indrajala or stratagem is used liberally by the Kauravas, and two important instances come to mind. First, the Pandavas are sent away to spend time in Varanavata, where Duryodhana has an associate build a palace of lac for them. The idea is that the palace would 'accidentally' catch fire, and the brothers, their mother and wife would burn to cinders, ending their claim to Hastinapura once and for all. This is averted also by stratagem. The Pandavas have a tunnel dug secretly for them, and after setting fire to the palace, escape unhurt. The second stratagem is the infamous game of dice that causes Yudhishthira to gamble everything away, right down to his wife. The dice, literally, are loaded against him from the outset; The dice, literally, are loaded against him from the outset; his opponent, Duryodhana's maternal uncle Shakuni is a master and is said to play with magic dice, and Yudhishthira is known to be a poor player. Yet, honour requires Yudhishthira to accept the invitation to play, as the Kauravas know he would.

The six methods of statecraft called *shadgunyam* are explicitly more outward-looking: *sandhi* (peace), *vigraha* (war), *asana* (waiting for the enemy to strike the first blow), *yana* (attack), *samshraya* (alliance), and *dvaidibhava* (duplicity).[12]

Sandhi refers to open diplomatic activity of the sort that precedes the start of the Mahabharata war, with emissaries going back and forth between the Kaurava court and the Pandava camp. Temporary and permanent alliances and agreements fall under this category.

---

[12] A. L. Basham, *The Wonder That Was India* (Calcutta: Rupa, 1967), p. 125; Dikshitar, *War in Ancient India*, pp. 314–26.

Vigraha includes both open and covert war. Rama's attack on Vali when the latter is engaged in combat with his brother, the planned massacre at Varanavata or the wars that mark the culmination of the epics, are all examples of vigraha. Expediencies and methods are value-neutral; it is the use to which they are put that lends them value.

Asana or restraint is also considered an important method, and Yudhishthira's patient vigil through 13 years of exile might, in fact, be considered an example. He does not lack justification, support or advocates of a quick war to reclaim his lost rights; but he chooses to wait, first because it is the right thing to do and second because it would give them time. Yana refers to a preparedness to march, possibly after a period of asana.

Allies and associates play a critical part in both the Ramayana and the Mahabharata wars. Rama and Lakshmana begin their Lanka campaign long before they locate Sita, but seeking support or *samshraya* from the vanara king, Sugriva. It is with the help of the monkeys and bears of the world, not to mention squirrels and birds, that Rama is able to cross the ocean and face Ravana. Similarly, the period before the Mahabharata war sees both sides send emissaries to secure support from clans and kings all over Bharatavarsha. Duplicity or *dvaidibhava* is appealing because even when allies are needed, it is a way of distancing oneself from the ally while keeping the enemy at a distance.

Rules of Engagement

The world depicted in the epics was a rule-bound universe. Every form of engagement came with a protocol and with shared rules of engagement. In fact, in this world, we might even say that one of the few ways to distinguish between the self and the other is the observance of these procedures and protocols. Through both the epics, we see certain protocols observed.

For instance, in both the epics, there are encounters between the people exiled and hermitages and communities. The former, most often, approached the latter respectfully, often sending one person forward to introduce the group and asking for permission to enter the hermitage/community grounds. The idea that residence anywhere means sharing responsibility is also important; the itinerant kshatriyas take it upon themselves to offer protection to the communities (usually ascetic communities) that they stay with. In one instance, in a community beleaguered by the weekly demands for a victim by a man-eating rakshasa, Baka, Kunti offers her son Bheema as the week's sacrifice. Yes, she knows he would more than match the monster, but as far as the villagers are concerned, she is offering to share their fate as a good guest should.

The most striking instance, however, has to do with the rules of combat. The Mahabharata has a vivid description:

> Then the Kurus, the Pandavas, and the Somakas made certain covenants, and settled the rules, O bull of Bharata's race, regarding the different kinds of combat. Persons equally circumstanced must encounter each other, fighting fairly. And if having fought fairly the combatants withdraw (without fear of molestation), even that would be gratifying to us. Those who engaged in contests of words should be fought against with words. Those that left the ranks should never be slain. A car-warrior should have a car-warrior for his antagonist; he on the neck of an elephant should have a similar combatant for his foe; a horse should be met by a horse, and a foot-soldier, O Bharata, should be met by foot-soldier. Guided by considerations of fitness, willingness, daring and might, one should strike another, giving notice. No one should strike another that is unprepared or panic-struck. One engaged with another, one seeking quarter, one retreating, one whose weapon is rendered unfit, uncased in mail, should never be struck. Car-drivers, animals (yoked to cars or carrying weapons) men engaged in the transport of weapons, players on drums and blowers on conches should never be struck. Having made these covenants, the Kurus, and the Pandavas, and the Somakas wondered, much, gazing at each other. (KMG 2, Bheeshma 1: 2–3)

In addition, combat is generally confined to the hours between sunrise and sunset with each army retiring for rest and the wounded getting medical attention in evening hours. In the Ramayana war, Ravana's most humiliating moment is not the one in which he is fatally wounded, but when Rama sees him tired at the end of a long duel and stops, saying, 'Go home, rest and come back to fight another day'.

There are two things to note here. First, the creation of covenants specifying the rules of engagement is considered important. Second, violation of the covenants is often critical to turning the tide of the battle; that is, they occur in debatable circumstances. Drona is killed by letting him first overhear a white lie that Ashvatthama, his son, is dead. In fact, an elephant by the same name is killed and Yudhishthira utters the only lie of his life when he confirms that Ashvatthama (undertone, the elephant) is dead. A heartbroken Drona is an easy target. Arjuna's son Abhimanyu enters a battle formation based on the wheel, the *chakravyuha*, that he knows how to enter but not to exit; hence, those giving him cover get cut off from him. The young man is trapped and encircled by leading warriors on the Kaurava side who engage him in combat until he loses his chariot and weapons. Then, they kill him. This cold-blooded act provokes the next: Arjuna's oath to kill Jayadratha by sundown or die. As the day goes by and Arjuna is nowhere close to Jayadratha, Krishna engineers a moment's darkness just as it is at sunset to lull Jayadratha into a false sense of security, whereupon Arjuna kills him. Finally, Karna, arguably the epic's tragic hero, is killed by Arjuna in a pre-destined moment and pre-destined way, but the bottom-line for us is that Arjuna shoots him when his chariot is mired in mud and he is unarmed. All the Pandavas' violations are justified in terms of their cause being a dharmik one; so, clearly, the final point to note is that these covenants and norms are not the same as dharma.

Grand Strategic Thought in the Indian Epics

The two epics are oceans of stories, and even a lifetime of knowing them and living with them does not make it easy to grasp their teachings at one go. The didactic passages in the epics emphasise the importance of the king to the polity. The king, through the use of danda, wards off the threat of anarchy. However, dharma must guide the king, in personal and political matters, and the realistic acceptance of the importance of punishment is not a carte blanche. Identity is not defined as we now do, and the lines around the 'self' are fluid, inclusive and dynamic. Dharma is the line that separates the self from the other. Repeated violations of dharma result in 'othering' and battle and conquest are about eliminating the source of these violations. In sum, dharma is the ideological foundation and the purpose of the political community; it is a bulwark against anarchy. It is mutable according to individual, time and circumstance, and it operates at both the individual and the social level.

Classical Indian thinking about the structures and functions of government are reflected in the epics, which discuss the role of the king, the quality of his advisors and also enlist a range of policy instruments available: conciliation, gift, dissension, punishment, neutrality and deceit. Of these, punishment is essential, conciliation preferred and deceit avoidable (except in an emergency). Tactical options are also discussed: peace, war, restraint, preparedness to march, support-building and duplicity. The dharmik way requires rules of engagement but sometimes dharma requires breaking rules. The epics leave open the 'means and ends' debate. The performance of sacrifices served the moral purpose of atonement for killing but they also served to affirm recognition of the king's authority within the kingdom and among other kings. In other words, they were an affirmation of internal sovereignty and external suzerainty. Divinities incarnate as heroes and the purpose of incarnation, not contemporary standards like national interest or ideological hegemony, drive the plot of the epics towards culmination.

The world of the epics is quite unlike the international system upon which ideas about strategy, strategic thought, strategic culture and grand strategic thought are predicated. However, there are some interesting similarities with the world in which we presently live.

People (if not species) interact freely across the world. Where there are physical limits placed by distance and visa regimes, the realms of global capitalism and the Internet facilitate flow of wealth, services and ideas almost as seamlessly. Government is clearly the first among equals rather than primary or sole political actor; this is as in the epic age where pre-eminent as the king was, his authority depended upon the blessings of others and the support of society. There is a growing global consensus on many norms – a new dharma perhaps – from human rights to global warming to gender equality. So what are the insights we can gain from the epics that are pertinent to our time and the broader concern of this volume?

The legacy of the epics bears little resemblance to the realist world that scholars like Morgenthau described; indeed, the protagonists of the epics would have considered rulers who defined national interest in terms of power, evil and deserving to be killed.[13] We might say the following: in the world of the epics, those responsible for securing society were to uphold dharma and prevent a return to anarchy,

---

[13] Hans J. Morgenthau, *Politics among Nations: The Struggle for Power and Peace*, 4th edn (New York: Knopf, 1967).

which meant periodically getting rid of those who subverted dharma for their ends. The lines of difference and the battle lines were drawn around the problem of sustaining dharma.

We are able to trace remnants of this legacy in the Indian context. The Indian penchant for claiming the moral high ground in international relations and the idealism of the Nehruvian era clearly carry traces of the importance given to dharma as the foundation and purpose of political action. The blurring of inside and outside continues, especially in South Asia – the question now is whether foreign policy is now directed towards alien states or kin-states? India's borders may not be porous any more but shared history and culture make the categories of insider and outsider fluid, with the same identity holding different positions at different times. Anxiety about disorder remains, having been reinforced in the years of the drafting of the Constitution by the memories of Partition riots. The resultant Constitution is as much about the use of danda – retaining the colonial penal code, emergency provisions, a centre-led federation and other structures that tend towards centralised control over autonomy – as it is about rajadharma – what the state should do, how its functionaries should be and how to check their power.

The much-lamented absence of carefully articulated, meticulously executed grand strategic thought in Indian foreign policy may in fact be consistent with our own traditional political ethics, as described by our epics. Indeed, there is not much room for it in the traditional worldview where the only justification for violence is to punish those whose behaviour violates the moral and ethical standards of the time. One could even say that those who did have a grand strategic plan to increase their power or to conquer other worlds, were the ones that Rama and Krishna were born to vanquish! In other words, classical grand strategic thinking might be said to have been an abomination from the perspective of the epics. But if the question were to be posed in broader terms, Indian civilisation as read from the epics did have a definite core of political values; a fluid sense of self and the other, leading to a fairly inclusive worldview and definite protocols relating to state action, akin to today's international and constitutional regimes.

Appendix: Dramatis Personae

If the word Trinity might be applied to the Hindu pantheon, Brahma is its Creator, Vishnu preserves Creation, and Shiva (not mentioned in this chapter) is Destroyer.

Narada is an itinerant seer, who travels through time and space to do the work of the gods.

RAMAYANA

Bharata, Rama's other brother, abdicates the throne his mother seeks for him. When Rama is in exile, he crowns Rama's slippers and acts as their regent until Rama's return. His lack of personal ambition is exemplary.

Dasharatha is the king of Ayodhya and the father of Rama, Lakshmana, Bharata and Shatrughna (not mentioned in this chapter).

Hanuman is the son of Anjana and the wind-god Vayu. His physical prowess is more than matched by his intellect and his devotion to Rama is such that a prayer to him is tantamount to a prayer to Rama. As a playful child, Hanuman's powers made him extraordinarily – if innocently – disruptive, so he is made unaware of his true abilities until moments where they are needed.

Kumbhakarna is Ravana's brother. Massive in size and appetite, he spends most of his time asleep, waking briefly to satiate himself.

Lakshmana is Rama's brother and the son of Dasharatha, who follows Rama into exile and it is said that he stays awake the entire 14 years to keep vigil for his brother and sister-in-law.

Mareecha is Ravana's maternal uncle. His first encounter with Rama and Lakshmana is on their first expedition to provide protection to an important ritual that he has been desecrating time and again. He is shot into the distant ocean by Rama, emerging chastised and reformed. Afraid of Ravana's wrath, he transforms himself into a golden deer that Sita desires for a pet and leads Rama away from their hermitage. His last act of loyalty to Ravana is to imitate Rama's voice in a cry for help. Sita then drives Lakshmana out to help his distressed brother who they assume, is in trouble. She thereby becomes vulnerable to Ravana's abduction ploy.

Rama, the protagonist of the Ramayana, is the prince of Ayodhya, incarnation of Vishnu born to kill Ravana and in Indian lore, maryada purushottama or ideal/perfect man.

Ravana, the king of Lanka, is a great scholar and musician, whose piety and penance win him the boon of invincibility against every being save monkey and man. The promise of invincibility unleashes Ravana's ambition and arrogance, and in turn these terrorise the world and threaten dharma. This is why Vishnu is incarnated as a man, and is supported by monkeys in the campaign against Ravana.

Sambuka is a Shudra whose performance of austerities is held to so disturb the dharmik order that a Brahmin's son dies. He is summarily executed by Rama to restore the order that is considered appropriate for the treta age.

Sita, the furrow-born princess of Mithila, is married to Rama, abducted by Ravana and is the pivot of the Ramayana story.

Shoorpanakha, Ravana's sister, is humiliated by Rama and Lakshmana when she propositions them, and this humiliation is the catalyst for the events that follow.

Sugriva is Vali's brother, king of the Vanaras and Rama's friend.

Vaisravana, a minor god, is granted the right to rule Lanka. He is ousted by rakshasas.

Vali is the king of the Vanaras. He is invincible and one of the few to survive Ravana's rampage. Vali and his brother, Sugriva set off to fight a demon that is terrorising their people, and when Vali enters a cave in pursuit, Sugriva blocks the entrance so the demon cannot escape. But when blood trickles out soon after, Sugriva assumes his brother is dead and after the mourning period, ascends his throne and takes his wife. The furious Vali emerges after a while, reclaims his throne and exiles Sugriva. The rivalry between them is resolved when Sugriva meets and enlists Rama's help. Rama's presence is concealed from Vali who is fighting a duel with his brother, but he shoots the Vanara king nonetheless.

Vibheeshana is Ravana's brother. When Ravana repeatedly rejects his counsel, refusing to return Sita and avert war, Vibheeshana defects and seeks asylum in Rama's camp.

Mahabharata

Krishna is not the protagonist of the Mahabharata, but indubitably its prime mover and shaker. He is Vishnu incarnate as a Yadava prince with the task of assuring that the Mahabharata war takes place.

Arjuna is the fourth of Kunti's sons, the third after her marriage to Pandu. His natural father is Indra, the king of heaven and the god of rain and storms. The epic also refers to him as *Nara* of *Nara-Narayana*, Vishnu's incarnation as twin sages. He is thus inseparable from Vishnu/Krishna. Arjuna's journeys are an important element of the epic narrative, gathering weaponry and allies in their wake.

Baka is a rakshasa with an insatiable appetite who terrorises the town of *Ekachakra*. Bheema volunteers to take food up to him and kills him.

Balarama is Krishna's brother and wrestling coach for the Kauravas and Pandavas. Duryodhana is his favourite student.

- Bheema is the third of Kunti's sons, the second after her marriage to Pandu. His natural father is Vayu, the wind-god, which makes him the half-brother of Hanuman. He is extremely strong and quick to feeling. Of the five brothers, he is most expressive of his devotion to Draupadi.
- Bheeshma, whose name was Devavrata, gives up the right to succeed his father and then stays single so that his children would not grow up to challenge his promise. Bheeshma is the patriarch of the Kuru clan and it is his deathbed discourse to Yudhishthira that makes up the main didactic section of the epic.
- Draupadi is the fire-born daughter of Drupada, the king of Panchala. The purpose of her birth is the destruction of the Kauravas. Arjuna wins her hand in marriage but she is the wife of all the five Pandavas and their chief queen. The fuel that stokes the conflict between the cousins, is the memory of her being summoned to a full court after the fateful game of dice and the Kaurava call to disrobe her there.
- Duryodhana is the eldest Kaurava brother. His resentment and envy of his cousins are the root cause of the events that lead to the great war.
- Harishchandra is an ancestor of Rama, whose generosity and honesty remain a standard for Indians.
- Hidimbi is Bheema's first wife. She is a rakshasi who chances upon the Pandavas when they are resting in a forest where she lives with her brother.
- Jambavati is Krishna's bear-wife and the daughter of Jambavan, the bear-king who fought on Rama's side.
- Karna is the first of Kunti's sons, born when she was a girl. His natural father is Surya, the sun-god, from whom he inherited brilliance. Karna's generosity is legendary in the epic, and he practically gives away his life before the war starts. Karna was raised by a charioteer and his wife, never knowing his real parents till the eve of the war. Therefore, being befriended by Duryodhana and having enjoyed his generosity makes him loyal to the Kauravas till the end.
- Kaunteyas are the sons of Kunti – the five Pandavas and Karna, her first-born.
- Kauravas are the 100 sons of Dhritarashtra, Bheeshma's nephew begotten by Vyasa and his deceased brother's wife, Ambalika.
- Keechaka is the brother-in-law of the king of Virata, where the Pandavas and Draupadi spent their year in disguise.
- Kunti is the wife of Pandu and the mother of Karna, Yudhisthira, Bheema and Arjuna. She is also the paternal aunt of Krishna. As a girl, Kunti is taught a mantra by which she can summon any god to have intercourse with her and give her a son.
- Madri is the second wife of Pandu and the mother of Nakula and Sahadeva (not mentioned in this chapter), the last two Pandavas.

Manu is the first king and lawgiver.

Pandavas are the five sons born to the wives of Pandu, Dhritarashtra's half-brother and Vyasa's son by his deceased brother's other wife, Ambalika. Pandu is cursed that sex will prove fatal to him. So through a mantra known to his first wife, Kunti, he gets his wives (Kunti and Madri) to call upon the gods to give them children. He raises these children as his own and they bear his name.

Parikshit is the grandson of the Pandavas and he succeeds Yudhishthira to the throne of Hastinapura.

Satyavati is a boatman's daughter whose encounter with a sage gives her a son, Vyasa, who is said to have authored the Mahabharata. Later, when her sons die without children, she calls on this son to father her daughter-in-laws' children so the Kuru dynasty can continue.

Shalya is Madri's brother and the Pandavas' uncle. He fights for the Kauravas to repay their hospitality, and is the last commander of their army. Shalya is Karna's charioteer when Karna falls.

Shantanu is a descendant of Yayati (the twelfth generation succeeding Yayati). He was first married to the river Ganga, who bore him eight sons, the last of whom was Devavrata (Bheeshma). After she left him, he met and married Satyavati, whose father imposed the condition that her son would follow Shantanu as king.

Uloopi is a Naga princess who seeks and seduces Arjuna on one of his journeys. She bears him a son, Iravan, who is killed during the Mahabharata war.

Vyasa, or Krishna Dwaipayana, is the grandfather of the warring princes and the author of the Mahabharata, or at least its core sections.

Yajnasena, king of Panchala, is also known as Drupada. He is Draupadi's and Dhrishtadhyumna's father.

Yayati is the forefather of the Kuru and the Yadava clans. He married two rivals who had been friends. Yadu, one of his first wife's sons, founded the Yadava dynasty, in which Krishna was born. Yayati abdicated in favour of his son by his second wife, Puru, who traded his youth with his father's old age so that his father could continue to enjoy worldly pleasures.

Yudhishthira is the second of Kunti's sons, the first after her marriage to Pandu. Therefore, he is the eldest Pandava. His natural father is Yama, the god of death and also the law-giver. From Yama, he inherits his extraordinary devotion to dharma.

2

STRATEGY, LEGITIMACY AND THE IMPERIUM
FRAMING THE MUGHAL STRATEGIC DISCOURSE

Jayashree Vivekanandan*

వ

Mainstream International Relations' (hereafter IR) penchant to debate power within statist frames is well known. But in the din of conformism, a pervasive manifestation of power often overlooked imperialism. Intriguingly, despite being the most enduring political system to have existed in most parts of the world, the empire remains an understudied subject within IR.[1] The focus has primarily been on the Westphalian order and the manner in which relations between sovereign states have evolved since the 17th century. The retrospective interpretation of international history has meant a diminishing interest in time periods more distant from the one

---

* This essay draws upon research conducted for my book, *Interrogating International Relations: India's Strategic Practice and the Return of History* (New Delhi and London: Routledge, 2011).

[1] Within IR literature, the conceptualisation of empire has followed three modes. Empire was seen as a hierarchical political order operating on a large scale which did not amount to absolute territorial control. Empires that dominated the political landscape during the ancient and medieval periods fall within this category, although they did signify the concentration of social power. The 19th and 20th centuries saw the rise of colonial empires that systematised domination through developed state machinery such as improved communication and bureaucratic networks. A distinct feature of modern empires was that nation-states constituted the pivot around which they were built. The third conceptualisation of the term accommodated a broader definition of empires that recognised rule through economic domination without formal territorial control. The political economy of empires was an aspect that was further highlighted and developed by the Marxists. See Martin Shaw, 'Post-Imperial and Quasi-Imperial: State and Empire in the Global Era', *Millennium*, 31, 2 (2002), pp. 329–30.

we live in. Consequently, the ancient and medieval periods appear either irrelevant to or unrepresentative of contemporary concerns within the discipline.

The empire occupies a central position in this essay, both as a theoretical concept in which the internal and the external domains often overlapped, and as an empirical case study of the manner in which strategies were formulated and power was negotiated in history.[2] The notion of empire makes for interesting interpretations of international history since it accommodates a diversity of political experiences, particularly of the non-Western world within its theoretical ambit. It provides us with a creative conceptual tool not only to include differently arranged political orders in our understanding of the historical international system, but also to analyse political control in its dynamic expressions as negotiated power.[3] If history matters, including the contingent forms that political units may take from time to time, then the study of empires in the time span of a country's evolving strategic practice becomes both desirable and necessary. Admittedly, there has been a renewed focus on the historical antecedents of international relations. All critical approaches, despite their divergent interpretations, attempt at offering a social theory of the state. From constructivism and the English School to feminism and post-colonialism, problematising some of the basic premises of IR has become the theoretical touchstone for approaches deviating from mainstream IR theory.

The essay attempts to locate itself within this evolving conversation on the need to historicise strategic studies. The case study chosen in this regard pertains to India, which, despite its long history of strategic planning, paradoxically remains understudied for its

---

[2] Tarak Barkawi and Mark Laffey, 'Retrieving the Imperial: Empire and International Relations', *Millennium*, 31, 1 (2002), pp. 110–13.

[3] The empire as a notion is integrally linked to the conceptual evolution of sovereignty and to the parallel encounters of the West with the rest of the world. Paul Gilroy's book on slavery, *The Black Atlantic: Modernity and Double Consciousness* (Cambridge: Harvard University Press, 1993), brings out the interlinkages between the West and the marginalised slave populations of the Caribbean. It offers an important corrective to the notion that the American and the French revolutions occurred in splendid isolation, whereas Gilroy demonstrates how they were linked to the slave revolts of the Caribbean in the eighteenth and nineteenth centuries (Barkawi and Laffey, 'Retrieving the Imperial', p. 114).

supposedly incoherent strategic approach. The essay focuses on the evolution of India's strategic approach during the medieval period when the Mughal empire steadily expanded under Emperor Akbar from 1556 to 1605. Although Akbar's India is a well-analysed subject of discussion in history, it remains an atypical case study within IR given that the discipline's ceaseless search for essences and core attributes often leads it to the ancient period but seldom to the medieval era.

However, the interested theorist would find this particular phase significant for several reasons. Akbar's reign fell at the cusp of critical transitions that oversaw prolonged periods of intermittent warfare giving way to an extended period of expansion and consolidation spread over nearly three centuries. The empire, which at its peak covered almost the whole of the Indian subcontinent, was the early precursor to the modern Indian state. The fact that much of the Mughal empire did not fragment into numerous nation-states as its contemporaries like the Ottoman and Habsburg empires did, but remained largely integrated within the modern Indian state is a telling testament to the empire's legacy of cohesiveness. The Mughal imperium recognised the political significance of nurturing a composite ruling class and the centrality of debate and integration in building state capacity.[4] Integration and negotiated order, the indispensable attributes of a modern nation-state, were at the core of the Mughal imperial domain, evident in the patronising of religious debates and the mediating of different world views that made the Mughal court an early precursor to the secular state in India.

Mughal Strategic Tradition: The Operative Dimension

The Mughal state held together a population of 100 million, five times that of the Ottomans in 1700.[5] Mughal rule over such a vast and populous landmass assumes importance, more so since the society it ruled over was heavily militarised. Locating the Mughal state

---

[4] Sanjay Subrahmanyam, 'A Tale of Three Empires: Mughals, Ottomans, and Habsburgs in a Comparative Context', *Common Knowledge*, 12, 1 (2006), pp. 90–91.

[5] Barbara Metcalf and Thomas Metcalf, *A Concise History of India* (Cambridge: Cambridge University Press, 2002), p. 1.

within the context of social militarisation reveals the latent power dynamics that influenced the prospects for imperial expansion. The lack of monopoly over force, as we shall see, made the strategy of accommodation appear a more favourable option to the Mughals.

Mughal military history is marked by a singular absence of major battles, despite the fact that the limits of the imperial domain were steadily pushing outwards under Akbar. But for the two battles of Panipat in 1526 and 1556, and the battle of Khanwa in 1527, no wars of comparable proportions occurred during the period of Mughal expansion. Mughal military superiority in the few battles that occurred in the early period often overwhelmed adversaries into submission to avoid taking on the Mughals in open battle.[6] The Mughals leveraged their capacity to project power that was often greater than the actual military capability they were able to deploy, evident from the Mewar king's reluctance to engage Akbar when he entered Chittor with a small force in 1567. There were several factors that mediated the interface of the Mughal state with its regional adversaries and Mughal response strategies sought to institutionalise the means through which the numerous and diffused threats were met.

Akbar's calculus of expansion targeting the northern and north-western territories was not entirely a novel one. Across historical periods, the North Indian plain has remained the predominant seat of political power both in terms of frequency and longevity and it is where empires have fanned out from in all directions.[7] Although the frequency with which pan-Indian powers emerged had declined in the medieval ages as compared to the ancient period, there was a steady consolidation of power under a single political power in the last four centuries beginning with the Mughals. The prospects of establishing a pan-Indian state under the Mughals and later the British was predicated on increased agricultural productivity coupled with better communication systems and enhanced military capabilities, without necessarily spelling the end for smaller regional entities.

---

[6] Douglas Streusand, *The Formation of the Mughal Empire* (New Delhi: Oxford University Press, 1989), pp. 52, 65.

[7] Hermann Kulke and Dietmar Rothermund, *A History of India* (London: Routledge, 1998), p. 9.

The changing political environment held significant strategic implications for India as the highly centralised system of administration prevalent in the ancient period gave way to a more diffused mode of governance among pan-Indian medieval rulers such as the Mughals. The emergence of regional kingdoms signified a definitive shift towards multiple power centres that necessitated a mediated approach to administration. Akbar's policy of accommodation needs to be analysed within this evolving strategic context as an attempt to negotiate an acceptable arrangement with rival regional powers that he could ill-afford to ignore. Within the empire, clear patterns of influence quickly emerged that manifested themselves in material and ideational expressions of power. The areas that lay in proximity to the imperial centre such as the Rajput principalities became the more peaceful core of the empire as a result of Akbar's intensive and consistent accommodationist policies. Peripheral kingdoms in the Deccan, on the other hand, being on the fringes of the Mughal empire, were consequently marginalised from the ambit of accommodation. The relative frequency of wars is indicative of this trend with the core areas experiencing fewer wars as the means of dispute settlement with the Mughals than the periphery, which saw heightened levels of coercion mark their relations with the imperial centre. The power of socialisation clearly yielded attractive benefits for those who were co-opted into the system, but weakened with distance.

Militarisation was not uncommon in medieval societies, yet the scale and density of the armed medieval Indian society was of phenomenal proportions. Levels of social militarisation in India were high, estimated at more than three per cent of the total population, which stood at roughly 135 million in 1600.[8] This vast reservoir

---

[8] A more accurate estimate would be the share of the armed population drawn from the total active male population, which constituted the main resource base for military personnel. Dirk Kolff estimates the military labour force to be roughly 10 per cent of the active male population (*Naukar, Rajput and Sepoy: The Ethnohistory of the Military Labour Market in Hindustan 1450–1850* [Cambridge: Cambridge University Press, 1990], p. 3). No contemporary European society presented such high levels of militarisation. In 1600, military force was a mere 0.4 per cent of the total population in France, 2.5 per cent in Spain and 0.7 per cent in England and Wales (ibid., p. 135).

of military manpower constituted a military labour market chiefly because the participants competed with one another to be employed by the highest bidder. Those offering their services were recruited into regional armies through middlemen such as *zamindar*s.[9] But how does social militarisation become a point of reference for Mughal grand strategy? The sheer vastness of the military labour market implied that power was not always formally centred or organised in regional armies, but diffused and dynamic in its operation. The Mughals had to cope with its formidable proportions, especially since it influenced the effectiveness of their bid to dominate the existing power networks. It is evident that the large masses of armed peasantry and war bands posed a serious challenge to Mughal power, an example of which was the nature of opposition Akbar faced at Chittor. Resistance to the Mughal forces came not only from the Rajputs who numbered 8000 but also from the 40,000-strong peasant army.[10] With violence being an endemic feature of medieval Indian society, the Mughals clearly lacked monopoly over force. As Kolff notes,

> It is clear that Indian agrarian society was to a large extent an armed society, skilled in the use of arms. ... Moreover, the countryside was studded with little forts. ... In such a society, no government, however powerful, could even begin to think of achieving a monopoly on the use of arms. In some respects, the millions of armed men, cultivators and otherwise, that government was supposed to rule over, were its rivals rather than its subjects.[11]

The fairly even distribution of retaliatory power prevented the Mughals from resorting to coercion against their adversaries. Particular regional kingdoms could be defeated by the sheer dint of military superiority, but the source of military power from which these kingdoms drew their might continued to thrive. Although attempts were made at forced migration and deportation of thousands to Central Asia for the slave trade, these measures proved unsustainable in the long run and failed to make any drastic impact on the military labour market. Moreover, the Mughals were well

---

[9] Kolff, *Naukar, Rajput and Sepoy*, p. 7; Jos Gommans, *Mughal Warfare: Indian Frontiers and High Roads to Empire 1500–1700* (London: Routledge, 2002), p. 63.
[10] Ibid., p. 10.
[11] Ibid., p. 7.

aware of the limitations of undertaking counter-measures, as the armed peasantry, which formed a sizeable chunk of the military labour market, constituted the revenue base of the empire. Under these circumstances, the Mughal state had little option but to continue the practice of employing large numbers from the military labour market, a practice similar to that followed by the Delhi Sultanate under the Lodi Afghans. Their coping strategies included tactics such as giving zamindars lucrative positions within the imperial military-administrative structure, despite which the Mughals did not succeed in controlling the vast military labour market and the threat of sedition remained constant.

Akbar sought to counter the potential challenge by the military labour market by devising the *mansabdari* system that went on to constitute the basic administrative structure of the Mughals. Introduced in 1573–74, the mansabdari system became a systematic means of tapping the military potential, otherwise outside state control. The modus operandi was simple: induct chieftains, clan leaders and aristocrats who command considerable status and power into the nobility by giving them ranks in the military-administrative structure. The *mansab* or the rank, which determined the position of the official (*mansabdar*) in the hierarchy, enjoined upon him the responsibility to maintain a required number of mounted retainers for the Mughal army. The system was modified to differentiate between the mansabdar's personal rank (*zat*) and the troopers he was expected to maintain (*sawar*). Since he had to maintain troops at his own expense, his income was calculated on the basis of both, his zat and sawar ranks.

The mansabdari system, structurally hierarchical with the emperor at the apex of the administrative structure, served to establish a clear chain of command that centred political sovereignty in the emperor alone. The Mughal princes were given ranks that placed them in subordination to the emperor, as against the traditional system of collective sovereignty in which they were co-claimants to the throne.[12] The system, which was designed to absorb the maximum possible number of military recruits into the Mughal army, could ill-afford to be insular or exclusionary in its operation. Since the Mughal nobility was not sustained primarily on the heredity principle and allowed for a certain degree of merit, the system ensured optimal absorption

---

[12] Streusand, *Formation of the Mughal Empire*, p. 109.

of warlords and recruits. It enabled the Mughal state to harness the manpower available through various recruitment networks for which a closed nobility system would have been inappropriate.[13] However, while every effort was made by Akbar to draw in warlords to fill the swelling ranks of the Mughal army, he was only too aware of the need to consolidate his position within the empire. The lack of monopoly over force led Akbar to adopt various manipulative strategies including the periodic transfer of mansabdars and the assignment of distant *jagirs* (transferable territorial assignments) to prevent them from developing local power bases.

The Mughal state realised the strategic significance of power projection and gradually developed its ability to project power over great distances. Mobility became a vital state stratagem towards this end towards which the emperors devised ingenious means to stay mobile and tour their domain. Exhibitionism was key and the imperial camp became a veritable showcase of the grandeur of the Mughal court. Although mobile imperial camps were common to the empires of medieval Asia and Western Europe, the wealth and display in the Mughal camp was of a scale that surpassed its European counterparts. The Mughal emperors, more than their Ottoman counterparts, regarded touring their domain as a significant state activity.[14]

The mobile capital was essentially the royal entourage that carefully replicated the imperial hierarchy to the last detail. It was led by the emperor and followed by the princes and nobles according to their respective ranks, with the entourage flanked by 8000 horsemen. The mobile capital was the face of the Mughal empire, the visible manifestation of its power and grandeur. While the camp was a visual phenomenon, with a breadth of over one-and-a-half miles, it was also a functional administrative unit, complete with merchants, accountants, soldiers and artisans. The mobile imperial capital led by the emperor became the veritable seat of

---

[13] Gommans, *Mughal Warfare*, p. 70.

[14] The mobile imperial capital travelled and camped within an annual radius of action of roughly 1200 km from Delhi, touching many power centres around the political centre and resuming contact with local rulers in the process. Gommans calculates that the four Mughal emperors (Akbar, Jahangir, Shah Jahan, and Aurangzeb) spent 35 per cent of their reign in travel (ibid., p. 108).

political power. Strategically, the camp deterritorialised Mughal sovereignty by decoupling its association with the established capital from which the emperor ruled when in residence. By adopting a broader and more dynamic definition of sovereign power, Akbar enhanced the Mughal ability to effectively project power across a wider radius than a permanent capital would have enabled. Given the considerable periods of time that the emperor spent touring his territories, it was imperative that the affairs of the empire were not hindered in the process. Thus, Akbar oversaw and administered from the mobile imperial camp every aspect of the administration that required his attention including the imperial household, the nobility and the treasury.[15] As the entourage perambulated across a wide sweep of the empire, the imperial treasury engaged in brisk trade with local economies, its financial might on full display. The Mughal coinage system, by superseding local monetary systems, helped in standardising monetary transactions across the empire. Further, the imperial camp was a symbolic showcase of the assimilative ethos of the Mughal court. Mobility and co-habitation ensured that sectarian and ethnic identities remained muted and the thick web of internal interactions amongst the nobles and the retainers fostered a liberal and cosmopolitan ethos.[16]

Mughal Strategic Tradition: The Discursive Dimension

Although the political conditions in 16th century India played a decisive role in determining Akbar's grand strategy, the Mughal state was in many ways also responding to the prevailing social milieu. The consciousness that Muslim subjects remained a minority in medieval India while the Muslim political elite ruled over a predominantly Hindu population spawned two parallel traditions in Indo-Islamic thought. The orthodox movement chose to focus on the shared vulnerabilities of Indian Muslims in the early periods and envisaged the king as playing the role of the primary protector of his Muslim subjects. It also yielded the liberal tradition that was

---

[15] J. F. Richards, *Power, Administration and Finance in Mughal India* (Hampshire: Variorum, 1993), p. 136.

[16] Gommans, *Mughal Warfare*, pp. 105–10.

committed to devising means of establishing communal harmony between Hindus and Muslims.[17] The reformist tradition abjured the narrow interpretation of Islam that the orthodox elements propagated and instead accorded a more enabling role to religion in political affairs, calling upon it 'to illustrate its support for the universal human ideals'.[18] The central issue that occupied the advocates of both dispositions was the extent to which the powers and duties of the ruler were to be circumscribed by the strictures of the *Sharia*.[19] Despite sharp differences between the traditions, the debates within Indo-Islamic thought constituted a continuum ranging from staunch orthodoxy to a conciliatory approach to Hindu subjects in the medieval era.[20]

The ensuing polemics on religion, politics and society spawned a rich literature on the subject of state capacity and duties of the ruler towards his subjects. An integral part of the liberal tradition was the *akhlaq* literature, a set of medieval Persian treatises that propounded moral and ethical codes of conduct. The texts, patronised by the Mughals, came to constitute the normative underpinnings of Akbar's grand strategy. The akhlaq literature sought to frame an essentially non-Islamic political discourse within the Islamic terms of debate. Although it consciously drew upon the established and widely accepted grammar of religion (*din*) and the *Sharia*, religious rhetoric was used to support arguments that were vastly different

---

[17] The *Naqshbandi* Sufi Jan-i Janan believed that Hinduism had its own lineage of prophets in Rama and Krishna, whose mission and message were similar to that of Prophet Mohammed. See Yohannan Friedmann, 'Islamic Thought in Relation to the Indian Context', in Richard Eaton, ed., *India's Islamic Traditions: 711–1750* (New Delhi: Oxford University Press, 2003), p. 58.

[18] Friedmann, 'Islamic Thought', p. 52.

[19] Ibid., p. 51; Muzaffar Alam, 'Akhlaqi Norms and Mughal Governance', in Muzaffar Alam et al., eds, *The Making of Indo-Persian Culture: Indian and French Studies* (New Delhi: Manohar, 2000), p. 73.

[20] Al-Biruni (973–1050) offered the initial scholarly perspective on Hinduism and its believers. Al-Biruni believed the association of Hinduism with idolatry to be misplaced, arguing instead that the enlightened sections of both communities attained religious consciousness without resorting to idol worship. Those who did could belong to any religious faith and came to depend on constructed representations of the divine due to their lack of education (Friedmann, 'Islamic Thought', pp. 52–54).

from the classical tradition followed in Islamic law books. The akhlaq body of writings, which envisaged kingship as a responsive and unifying institution, considered the check on the monarchy to be not extraneous to the ruler but inherent to the very nature of his duties. His position and duties were informed by an abiding concern with justice, which served to constrain his powers and inform his policies. Justice was understood in akhlaq literature to imply a dynamic state of harmonious balance in society among contending groups. The entire apparatus of the state and its resources were to be devoted to the pursuit of this secular conception of justice. The *Akhlaq-i Humayuni,* compiled by Ikhtiyar-al-Husaini during Babur's reign, asserts that '[t]he perfection of man ... is impossible to achieve without a peaceful social organisation, where everyone could earn his living by co-operation and helping each other.' Despite its Quranic citations, the treatise does not limit itself to the confines of a narrow religious debate; rather, it strongly advocates a universal approach to issues of justice and peace.[21]

Akbar held the akhlaq treatises in high regard and recognised their intrinsic appeal; he also realised their potential in rendering his position legitimate. On Fazl's advice, he not only listened to the injunctions given in Nasir-al Din Tusi's *Akhlaq-i Nasiri,* but he also ordered his officials to read the text regularly. It is evident that the philosophy of *Akhlaq-i Humayuni* was deeply ingrained in the Mughal approach to politics. As Alam notes: 'The influence of Ikhtiyar al-Husaini's *Akhlaq* is unmistakable on their [Mughals'] religious and political views as well as their actual politics. Babur's descendants in India sought stability, as al-Husaini had desired, by harmonising their political actions with the *akhlaqi* norms of governance'.[22] The liberal discourse centred on the treatises served to foster a moderate and accommodative intellectual climate in Mughal India. The Mughals were attentive to the concerns of the diverse social groups that made up their empire. Indeed, and one of the initiatives Akbar took in this regard was to patronise the official translation of ancient Indian texts. Fazl notes that Akbar's objective when commissioning translations of Sanskrit works into Persian was to smoothen out differences between the two communities through reasoned argument and debate. The akhlaqi emphasis on reason as the path to justice is

---

[21] Alam, 'Akhlaqi Norms', p. 77.
[22] Ibid., p. 84.

amply evident in Fazl's argument that the translations encouraged people to 'refrain from hostility ... seek truth, find out each other's virtues and vices and endeavour to correct themselves'.[23] By patronising translations of Hindu texts, Akbar and his successors were also according importance and recognition to the pre-Islamic phase of Indian history to which these texts belonged.[24] In a sense, the official project 'secularised' the reading of history by expanding its ambit further back in time than an Islamic reading would render.[25]

Royal patronage to the akhlaq tradition extended to commissioning key treatises, one of which was the *Akhlaq-i Jahangiri* by Nur ud-Din Qazi, for whom the principle of justice was the overriding concern in matters of governance. Mughal prince Dara Shukoh (1615–59) arguably the liberal tradition's most committed proponent, considered Hinduism and Islam to be complementary and compatible. Dara asserted that the religious principle of monotheism upheld in all the holy books including the Bible, the Quran and the Vedas point to clear complementarities between the religions. His thesis of grasping the essence of the Quran with the aid of a Hindu scripture was a radical notion that challenged the self-referential nature of Islam.[26] It was this potential for complementarities and mutual learning between the two traditions that the akhlaq literature was primarily concerned with. The Mughals found the liberal tradition especially appealing for both their operative and discursive facets. The treatises not only offered practical injunctions to the emperor on matters of statecraft, but also crucially moulded Mughal disposition towards accommodation and conciliation.

---

[23] Badauni cited in Alam, 'Akhlaqi Norms', p. 85. Badauni offers a counter-narrative to Fazl's portrayal of a liberal and tolerant Mughal regime. Badauni's *Muntakhabut Tawarikh*, compiled before his death in 1615, should be read in the context of his general disapproval of Akbar's eclecticism that amounted to an undermining of Islamic practices in favour of more moderate policies. Badauni, *Muntakhabut Tawarikh*, trans. by George Ranking, Vol. 1 (Patna: Academica Asiatica, 1898, reprinted 1973).

[24] However, the early years of Akbar's reign saw a general sense of intolerance towards the Hindus, a position that he rejected in favour of a more liberal approach in the 1570s, given his growing inclination towards *Sufi* doctrines. See Iqtidar Alam Khan 'Akbar's Personality Traits and World Outlook: A Critical Appraisal', *Social Scientist*, 20, 9–10 (1992), p. 20.

[25] Alam, 'Akhlaqi Norms', p. 85.

[26] Friedmann, 'Islamic Thought', p. 56.

The functioning of the imperial court was predicated on an elaborate set of rituals and court practices, which conditioned the behaviour of the nobles in attendance at the Mughal court and were instrumental in creating a syncretic court culture.[27] The unifying rationale behind this syncretism was Akbar's dynastic ideology, which sought to portray him as the bearer of Divine Light. As the descendent of God, Akbar's knowledge and intrinsic worth was portrayed in self-referential rather than in relative terms and as such, was independent of the positions and interpretations put forward by the religious community. The Divine Light theory elevated the emperor to a position distinct from other claimants to power by hailing him as 'the origin of stability'. Akbar's dynastic ideology marked a radical shift from the appanage system of governance that had threatened the prospects of imperial expansion and consolidation under Babur and Humayun. The system, that entailed the bestowal of lands and titles on close members of the royal family, tended to create multiple power centres in the empire. Under Akbar, sovereignty was centred in the person of the Mughal emperor who became the sole sanctioning authority of appointments and promotions within the nobility.[28] The iterative nature of court practices ensured that overriding loyalty to the emperor became the much-emphasised trait expected of a respectable noble at the Mughal court.

Although a multi-ethnic and multi-religious elite constituted the Mughal aristocracy, the courtly emphasis on loyalty provided them with a 'secular' focal point distinct from their primordial identities. The code of behaviour expected of a loyal aristocrat was personified in the *khanazad*s or nobles attached to the Mughal household

---

[27] The level of integration in the Mughal empire is evident from the fact that by the 17th century, the nobles at the court including the Rajputs spoke Persian (Subrahmanyam, 'A Tale of Three Empires', p. 91).

[28] The nobles were expected to offer their service to him in any of the three modes – personal attendance at the royal court as an expression of submission, participation in war and military campaigns, and the more formal mode of appointments to administrative and military positions. See J. F. Richards, 'Norms of Comportment Among Imperial Mughal Officers', in Barbara Metcalf, ed., *Moral Conduct and Authority: The Place of Adab in South Asian Islam* (London: University of California Press, 1984), p. 257; Iqtidar Husain Siddiqui, *Mughal Relations with the Indian Ruling Elite* (New Delhi: Munshiram Manoharlal, 1983), pp. 210–14.

through familial and hereditary ties. They were to build on an established lineage of loyal service to the ruler through their valour, commitment and ready willingness for sacrifice. Not only did the institution of *khanazadi* entail a constant reiteration and demonstration of these qualities as a sign of personal subordination to the emperor, it also implied imbibing the etiquette and behavioural attributes associated with the Mughal court culture. What was noteworthy about khanazads was that personal loyalty and submission defined their existence; they came to derive their identity from the Mughal emperor, their master and patron. The khanazadi system drew upon Akbar's dynastic ideology; his divine origins made him the undisputed master whom it was a privilege to serve and attend to. In some respects, the institution of imperial discipleship was also based on the notion of the Islamic military slave who personally attended to his master. The domains of the court and the household overlapped to the extent that the distinction between the personal and the political often blurred.[29] Since the khanazadi tradition was grounded in notions of imperial service and martial ethos, it is not surprising that the master-servant relationship was one of the most stable institutions of the Mughal era.

However, syncretic as the court culture may have been, induction into the Mughal nobility did not entail conversion to Islam, 'a phenomenon whose parallel would have been inconceivable under the Habsburgs ... and somewhat difficult under the Ottomans'.[30] Furthermore, Akbar's military campaigns were portrayed as the progressive realisation of the state of *Sulh-i kul* (absolute peace). It was the ideological extension of Akbar's strategy of accommodation that saw conflict as a transient condition rather than as a perpetual state of affairs. In bearing greater affinity to the *Sufi* and *Bhakti* sects than to orthodox Islam or Hinduism, Sulh-i kul appealed to the faculty of reason over blind faith. The operative principle for Fazl is reason, the axiom that prevails as the supreme arbiter of differences in the ideal state of being. The mindless imitation of practices, according to Fazl, led to social strife and signified the absence of

---

[29] This seamless quality of Akbar's authority was in contradistinction to the decision of Philip II of Spain's to institutionalise a clear dichotomy between the public and private domains.

[30] Subrahmanyam, 'A Tale of Three Empires', p. 83.

Sulh-i kul. In a pluralistic setting, reason was to be the unifying force in society, and its pursuit alone could help the emperor achieve a harmonious social balance.

The underlying emphasis on universalism and inclusiveness found expression in yet another discursive aspect of Akbar's grand strategy: his 'ideology of paternalism'. Fazl carefully crafted Akbar's image as the Universal Man along the lines of the Sufi thinker Ibn al-Arabi's conception of the Perfect Man. The universalist connotations of such a portrayal envisaged the emperor as executing a role wider than that defined within Islamic kingship. His elevation of Akbar to an exalted position as 'the emanation of God's light' or the extension of the divine force approximates the status of the king within Hindu kingship. Indeed, Fazl's universalism was not dichotomous in that it was not posited against an outside entity. Instead, it drew from the divinity that he alone was bestowed with.

The Mughal grand strategy drew upon a rich tradition of liberal secular thought that came to inform the imperial policies of Akbar. Although he initiated a number of modes of power projection using both subtle and ostentatious means of asserting his authority, Akbar's policies were couched within a social milieu that emphasised coexistence and the social acceptance of difference. The universalist tenor of the liberal tradition provided the appropriate justification for Akbar to move away from particularistic and religious notions of legitimacy, towards a more secular and personalised interpretation of his authority. Juxtaposing the Mughal empire with its contemporaries helps further highlight its unique ideational foundations and perhaps explains why the powerful Hapsburg and Ottoman empires disintegrated into multiple states in a manner that the Mughal empire did not. The Habsburg empire's preference for homogeneity in institutional practices, coupled with its markedly colonial policy of encouraging settler colonies and resource exploitation, made it an imperial entity that relented little to the plurality of its colonies. The Ottoman empire was distinctly different in this regard for its willingness to compromise and collaborate with local power structures. So were the Mughals, whose policy of creating an integrated ruling class consisting of diverse ethnic and religious backgrounds but united in their loyalty to the emperor became one of the chief factors behind the empire's resilience.

IMPLICATIONS FOR INDIA'S STRATEGIC PRACTICE

Cultural replication and ritual sovereignty were vital processes of state formation in Asian polities, which extended beyond the state's formal institutions. The Western notion of state monopoly of force needs to be problematised since historically Asian polities were akin to intercontinental empires, unlike Europe's nation-states.[31] Mughal power rested firmly on the notion of ritual sovereignty that was high on symbolic content and stressed the centrality of the ruler in maintaining order and stability within the imperial system.[32] The Mughal emperor sought to project himself as a symbolic omnipresent centre to which all elements of sovereignty gravitated and drew their meaning from: his subjects, the land he ruled and the apparatus of the empire. But the empire was more than the sum of its parts; its outward functionality was based on certain core values that were intrinsic to the Mughal ethos. Enculturation in the Mughal court was induced and reinforced through a number of means, ranging from symbolic measures to those that enabled Akbar to extend and exercise control over political matters outside the court.

Akbar's strategy reflected the overriding compulsion to indigenise his power: its sources, its ostensible representations and its actual exercise. His realisation that perceptions of legitimacy required him to 'go native', as it were, in many overt ways was shared by many ambitious rulers in the past. Akbar's image was a careful replication of the medieval Hindu king whose vital function entailed protecting

---

[31] Susanne Rudolph suggests an alternative framework of a custodial state ruling over the various mechanisms of a 'self-regulating' society such as castes, regions and religious communities. Rudolph's model is instructive not only for the comparative frames within which she locates Asian polities such as the Mughal empire, but also for drawing attention to the cultural contexts within which Indian empires learnt to operate. See Susanne Hoeber Rudolph, 'Presidential Address: State Formation in Asia- Prolegomenon to a Comparative Study', *Journal of Asian Studies*, 46, 4 (1987), p. 740.

[32] Rudolph defines 'ritual sovereignty' as,

> [c]ultural activities, symbols, and processes that in the absence of instrumental mechanisms nevertheless create a domain, a realm. Ritual sovereignty has ceremonial, aesthetic, and architectonic aspects as well as historically grounded, genealogically perpetuated elements... These are processes and signs by which a universal monarch is gradually elevated into a species distinct from the more accessible chiefs and kings of tribal confederacies and lineage states (ibid.).

the realm of norms and beliefs. This included deference to the all-important notion of 'balance' personified by the Hindu king, thereby locating the institution of kingship firmly within society rather than above it. The association of Akbar's persona with the sun as the source of light, his daily appearances for the benefit of the gathered public, and his representation as a paternal figure and a spiritual guide to his people were all initiatives that went on to indigenise his authority according to existing traditions.

The preponderance of the military labour market further underlines the need to locate the Mughal state and its military power within the social context. Given that the state exercised limited power over the sources of potential threats, it is not surprising that intelligence gathering was traditionally accorded high priority within Indian political thought. For rulers of large empires, surveillance was a mode of gaining better control over their land and subjects. Information mostly travelled through informal channels facilitated by the movement of soldiers, merchants and pilgrims. Apart from its practical benefits, surveillance also carried symbolic significance since it projected the power of the king. It helped promote the notion that the 'universal king' was omnipresent, aware of all major and minor happenings within his realm and effectively used it to offset his lack of actual control over local affairs.[33]

IMPLICATIONS FOR THE STATE

A long view of a country's strategic past reveals that certain traditions were formulated regarding the manner in which political space was to be organised, controlled and defended. These traditions are best seen as successful and optimal responses to the challenges to state power prevalent at a particular time. In Indian strategic thought, the realist tradition that focussed on the calculated acquisition and exercise of power is juxtaposed with the moralist tradition, which stressed ethical dimensions of power such as peace and justice.[34]

---

[33] Christopher Bayly, 'The Pre-history of "Communalism": Religious Conflict in India, 1700–1860', *Modern Asian Studies*, 19, 2 (1985), p. 13; Kate Brittlebank, *Tipu Sultan's Search for Legitimacy: Islam and Kingship in a Hindu Domain* (New Delhi: Oxford University Press, 1997).

[34] Torkel Brekke, 'Between Prudence and Heroism: Ethics of War in the Hindu Tradition', in Torkel Brekke, ed., *The Ethics of War in Asian Civilisations: A Comparative Perspective* (Abingdon, Oxon: Routledge, 2006), p. 138.

The two traditions trace their lineage to two conflicting notions of the state that are expounded in classical texts. The *nitishastra* texts conceive of the state as a managerial, unitary and bureaucratised entity capable of attaining power (*artha*). Kautilya's 'circle of kings' was one such response, given the fractured political environment he wrote in. A response strategy at variance with Kautilya's calculative king focussed on the just ruler whose primary role was to maintain the rule of *dharma* on which his society was based. In this alternative conception, the basis of kingship is primarily ethical and religious (dharma) supported by a network of personal relationships.[35] The two contending philosophical strains are discernible in the epics and texts down the ages, although the extent to which each succeeded in influencing the strategic practice of kings varied. However, what can be stated in unambiguous terms is that Indians throughout history have not only known how to strategise but have also negotiated and mediated security problems in diverse ways.

The two traditions were in a way responding to the prevailing political climate in ancient India. Political fragmentation was the norm during the ancient and medieval periods, but this did not imply political chaos as is commonly assumed. Indeed, although ancient India was fragmented into multiple kingdoms, the political landscape formed a chequered board on which Kautilya based his well-developed network of alternating relations of alliance and enmity. Sovereignty in ancient India was a nebulous concept that did not entail the clear demarcation of the king's political realm. Since, theoretically, the authority of the king was universal (given that he was seen as the microcosm of the entire cosmos), making a distinction between the internal and the external domains was self-limiting. The logic of the all-encompassing authority of the king extended to the use of force as well. A dualistic understanding of the use of force (of seeing internal violence as sedition and external force as war) was likewise absent in Indian theorisations. Thus, the strategies employed in war against external enemies were similar

---

[35] Burton Stein, 'The State and the Agrarian Order in Medieval South India: A Historiographical Critique', in Burton Stein, ed., *Essays on South India* (Hawaii: The University Press of Hawaii, 1975), pp. 81–82; Mahendra Prasad Singh, 'Indian State: Historical Context and Change', *The Indian Historical Review*, 21, 1–2 (1995).

to those against internal opponents.[36] A tradition that suited the imperatives of a particular time period did not appear appropriate in another, causing it to recede behind a more astute strategy. The interplay of these response strategies is rooted in culture insofar as the language and the metaphors employed belonged to a particular cultural milieu.[37] The cultural tropes and practices resorted to for the legitimisation of power are resonant of a certain way of life unique to that societal context. The nature and profile of that society itself may change over time, and so would the terms in which power is conceived of and exercised. History, in that sense, permits us to conceptualise culture in dynamic terms.

Indian grand strategies of any hue, whether accommodationist, offensive or defensive, sought to undergird the notion of security within the larger normative framework of harmony and stability. Importantly, the ethical underpinning of security resonated well with the image of the king as the keeper of societal values and the balancer of conflicting forces. At the operational level, the wide array of strategies at the disposal of the state was logical, given the diverse and diffuse nature of threats to its security. While none of the prescribed measures were in any way uniquely Indian, a taxonomy that prioritised negotiation, compromise and sedition over the resort to force has endured as an abiding feature of India's strategic practice. This is not to tow the much-favoured culturalist line of argument that Indians are programmed to exhaust options of peaceable co-existence. The claim that political fragmentation was a regressive condition in India that led to chaos can be traced to the normative appeal of the modern state for its absolute control over territory. Fragmented territories with fungible boundaries were the prevalent norm in the ancient and medieval periods, and were hardly unique to India. The strategic traditions directed the king to vanquish and not annihilate his enemies, quite simply because there were too many to engage with in futile and costly endeavours. Leaving the domain of the vanquished ruler undisturbed in return for his submission was an eminently desirable political arrangement. Thus, we see the familiar picture of the king withdrawing to rule from his designated capital after extracting the assurance of recognition and

---

[36] Brekke, 'Between Prudence and Heroism', pp. 120–21.

[37] Valerie Hudson, ed., *Culture and Foreign Policy* (Boulder: Lynne Rienner, 1997), pp. 28–29.

submission from the local ruler.[38] The *modus operandi* was in no way idealistic and politically naïve, but rather practical and well-suited to the conditions that ambitious kings had to deal with.

It is of little surprise that the Indian strategic traditions did not survive in any recognisable and functional form during the colonial period. The two conditions supporting their sustenance, namely the scenario of fragmented polities and the social context that invested political power with symbolic significance, underwent drastic change under colonialism. Territorial space gradually came under centralised control that is characteristic of a modern state. Further, the imperatives of the colonial mission and the attendant process of bureaucratisation caused the British state to consciously distance itself from Indian society.[39] Although recent research reveals the vulnerabilities and dependencies of colonialism that shaped the colonial state in ways it could not avoid, the disruption it caused in strategic affairs was far more definitive.[40]

IMPLICATIONS FOR THE DISCIPLINE

Developing a historically contingent view of strategic practice also brings into question the manner in which notions of culture and national identity are framed within IR. During the last four decades, culture as an explanatory variable has found increasing acceptance within political science. With Jack Snyder's *The Soviet Strategic Culture: Implications for Nuclear Options* published in 1977, the notion of political culture was brought within the ambit of security studies. Part of the new intellectual exercise was to sketch out the 'national character' of countries with the aid of which their behaviour could be explained and, hopefully, predicted. The underlying assumption that every community was identifiable by a set of unique national characteristics yielded an essentialist notion of culture. Following a lull with the end of the Cold War, cultural studies witnessed a revival

---

[38] Rudolph, 'Presidential Address', p. 736.

[39] Alena Alamgir, '"The Learned Brahmen, Who Assists Me": Changing Colonial Relationships in the 18th and 19th Century India', *Journal of Historical Sociology*, 19, 4 (2006), p. 429.

[40] Catherine Hall, ed., *Cultures of Empire: Colonizers in Britain and the Empire in the Nineteenth and Twentieth Centuries* (Manchester: Manchester University Press, 2000); Robert Johnson, *British Imperialism* (Hampshire: Palgrave Macmillan, 2003).

in the 1990s and with that the notion of strategic culture was resurrected.[41] The materialist interpretation was gradually replaced by a culturally contingent approach to security studies, which admitted that states could indeed behave in ways that could not be entirely explained by the rational behaviour argument. However, the fundamental tenets of strategic culture studies are based on its assertion of communities as the repositories of culture. The anti-essentialists offer an alternative reading of culture that stresses the 'processes' of identity formation than a static identity itself. Reeves emphasises the need to move 'beyond the notion that there is a place and obvious space for everything and it can all be bottled, pickled, canned and put on a shelf forever marked "culture"'.[42] Hence, the abiding 'human focus' of culturalists, both in the articulation of culture by notable personalities in the past and its presence as the 'mind-set' aiding and conditioning its people, is hardly surprising. For this very reason, studies of post-colonial societies have to necessarily be overtly cultural to acknowledge and problematise such tropes.[43]

There exists today a growing body of literature that challenges historical and cultural essentialisation within various frames of reference such as the nation, caste, religion and gender.[44] This trend

---

[41] Jeffrey Lantis, 'Strategic Culture and National Security Policy', *International Studies Review*, 4, 3 (2002), pp. 87–113. Strategic culture came to be defined as 'a nation's tradition, values, attitudes, patterns of behaviour, habits, symbols, achievements and particular ways of adapting to the environment and solving problems with respect to the threat or use of force' (Ken Booth, 'The Concept of Strategic Culture Affirmed', in Carl Jacobsen, ed., *Strategic Power USA/USSR* [London: Palgrave Macmillan, 1990], p. 121).

[42] Julie Reeves, *Culture and International Relations: Narratives, Natives and Tourists* (London: Routledge, 2004), p. 85.

[43] Gyanendra Pandey, *Memory, History and the Question of Violence: Reflections on the Reconstruction of Partition* (Calcutta: K. P. Bagchi and Company, 1999), p. 8; Geeta Chowdhry and Sheila Nair, eds, *Power, Postcolonialism and International Relations: Reading Race, Gender and Class* (London: Routledge, 2002), p. 19.

[44] Partha Chatterjee, *Nationalist Thought and the Colonial World* (London: Zed Books, 1986); Nicholas Dirks, 'Castes of Mind', *Representations*, 37 (1992); Prasenjit Duara, 'The Discourse of Civilization and Pan-Asianism', *Journal of World History*, 12, 1 (2001); Christopher Bayly, 'The Pre-history of "Communalism"? Religious Conflict in India, 1700–1860', *Modern Asian Studies*, 19, 2 (1985).

towards problematising received wisdom has been woefully tardy in IR barring a few exceptions.[45] Although certain culturalists like George Tanham and Stephen Rosen appear to base their claims on extensive historical references, this recourse to history has been both selective and anecdotal. For instance, the essence of India was located in the caste structure that supposedly informed its strategic outlook. The rendering of a reductionist and ahistorical interpretation of Indian culture was further reinforced by the claim of India's idealist, other-worldly orientation. Culturalists argue that Indian philosophy reposes faith in the pre-determined course of fate which human agency can do little to alter. Theories of the immutability of caste as a collective identity and the Indian sense of cyclical time that was seen to impede purposeful individual action and rational judgement were among the caricatures that contributed to the image of a passive Indian lacking agency.

This instrumental view of history takes the contemporary connotation of concepts back in time to demonstrate their resilience. It is based on the retrospective positioning of historical events and occurrences in a manner that conveys a sense of continuity with the present.[46] The fallacy often committed by theorists and even historians is to trace a given idea in its developed form back in time. Quentin Skinner refers to this tendency as 'the mythology of doctrines', wherein an idea assumes an identity independent of its evolutionary history.[47] A selective reading of history is then reduced

---

[45] Chowdhury and Nair, eds, *Power, Postcolonialism and International Relations*; Phillip Darby, *The Fiction of Imperialism: Reading between International Relations and Postcolonialism* (London: Cassell, 1998); Niels Brimnes, 'Globalization and Indian Civilization: Questionable Continuities', in Mehdi Mozaffari, ed., *Globalization and Civilizations* (London: Routledge, 2002), pp. 242–63.

[46] This assumption undergirds Kenneth Waltz's claim that the 'texture of international politics remains highly constant [throughout history], patterns recur and events repeat themselves endlessly'. See Kenneth Waltz, *Theory of International Politics* (Reading, Mass.: Addison-Wesley, 1979), p. 66.

[47] Susanne Rudolph similarly cautions against transposing a contemporary concept into a time frame when it did not exist or carry the same connotations. For instance, what could possibly be interpreted as an 'agent' in the *Arthashastra* is instead termed a 'spy', which presupposes the existence of a highly bureaucratised state machinery – a typically modern construct. The choice of terminology is not an innocent one since such interpretations

to 'searching for approximations to the ideal type' and 'pointing out earlier 'anticipations' of later doctrines'.[48] To pluck an idea out of its context is to effectively lose track of its deviations in history. The history of ideas seeks to study ideas in their historical contexts rather than with their modern-day connotations. An exploration of the history of ideas exhorts us to problematise, a task that can be both powerful and disorienting. It also nudges us to re-examine notions of sovereignty, power and identity in different temporal frames and warns us against attributing contemporary meanings to these. Theoretical approaches such as post-colonial studies, historical sociology and constructivism seek to prise open rigid constructions of power. They also challenge the dominance of the Western tradition in political and military thought, against which the lesser traditions appear as partial and momentary interventions. In a Eurocentric framework that has celebrated the West as the seat of scholarship, it is of little surprise that thinkers and strategists from the margins seldom figure. Critical discourses offer us several openings to intervene in the ensuing debate on interdisciplinarity and indicate new directions of research for the study of strategic thought in post-colonial societies such as India.

---

of history assume the existence of oriental despotisms that were able to exercise their absolutist control through an extensive spy network (Rudolph, 'Presidential Address', p. 738).

[48] Quentin Skinner, *Visions of Politics: Regarding Method*, Vol. 1 (Cambridge: Cambridge University Press, 2002), pp. 60–63. Norbert Elias' sociological approach to the study of court society in 17th and 18th century France can be considered a notable work on the history of ideas. For instance, although Elias concedes that 'court society is a social formation whose market-value is low', he firmly believes in the 'subordination of present-day values' to the valuations prevalent during the historical period under focus. See Norbert Elias, *The Court Society*, trans. by Edmund Jephcott (Oxford: Basil Blackwell, 1983), p. 28.

3

LIBERAL THOUGHT AND COLONIAL MILITARY INSTITUTIONS

Srinath Raghavan

Discussions of Indian strategic thought tend to identify a certain set of schools. The labels might differ and the categories overlap, but usually the discussion focuses on Gandhian, Nehruvian, Hindu Nationalist, Realist, and Liberal traditions. The liberal tradition is something of an anomaly in this classification. For, unlike the rest, which are traced back to the colonial period if not earlier, the liberal tradition is implicitly assumed to have begun only in the early 1990s following the opening up of the Indian economy.[1] The liberal tradition, then, actually refers to a variant of recent neoliberal thought and ideas. Such a definition results in a partial and anaemic appreciation of Indian liberal thought on military matters, which has a long intellectual history. Part of the reason for this neglect lies in the fact that the older liberal tradition appears to have little resonance today: unlike the Gandhians, or the Nehruvians, or the Hindu Nationalists, it is not clear who the contemporary heirs are to this tradition. However, this neglect also stems partly from the limited engagement with history by students of Indian strategy.

This chapter examines liberal thought on military institutions in the colonial era. It traces the ideas and policies espoused by a group of liberals starting from the late 19th century until the end of the 1930s. Not all members of this group were contemporaries, but they consciously drew on the thinking of one another – and as such it can be classified as a distinct tradition. The distinguishing characteristic of these liberals was their interest in military institutions as opposed

---

[1] See for instance the discussion of liberals in Rahul Sagar, 'State of Mind: What Kind of Power Will India Become?', *International Affairs*, 85, 4 (2009), pp. 813–16.

to ruminations on large ends and means that characterise the other 'grand strategic' traditions. Precisely for this reason, the tradition should be of interest to us. After all, strategy is a practical activity, and military institutions are central to it.

I have chosen the label 'liberals' (always in lower case) for two reasons. First, all of them identified with and drew upon the liberal constitutional traditions that initially entered India in the early 19th century and subsequently underwent several mutations. Second, this group of liberals cut across party political affiliation. At one point many of them were known as the 'moderates' in the Indian National Congress as opposed to the 'extremists'. Later they formed part of the short-lived 'Swarajist' group within the Congress party. Some prominent liberals like Mohammed Ali Jinnah were part of the Muslim League. The political glue that held them together was their vision of constitutional advancement towards self-rule. In some ways, their interest in obtaining for India a constitutional status akin to that of the other dominions such as Canada and Australia explains their interest in military matters. For indigenous control of the military was a critical marker of dominion status. By the same token, their contemporaries who eschewed the path of constitutional reform and sought to struggle for 'complete independence' paid limited attention to military matters. To the extent that the latter thought about these issues, they believed that once India was independent, military reform could easily be tackled. The liberals, of course, ended up on the losing side of the question of how to move out of British control. But I argue that this failure should not make us oblivious to their immense contribution in re-tooling colonial military institutions. Without these it seems unlikely that any of the other strategic visions on offer for independent India would have at all been practicable.

The Military in Early Liberal Thought

Military issues entered the mainstream of Indian liberalism through the duct of political economy. During the 'moment' of constitutional liberalism during the 1810s and the 1820s, Indian intellectuals had fashioned from a range of sources – British, indigenous, and international – an assortment of political concepts that would constitute the vocabulary – whether in acceptance, opposition or modification – of Indian liberalism throughout the colonial period. Amongst these concepts was the idea of a 'drain of wealth' from the subcontinent. This found its earliest expression in the writings of Rammohan Roy, a pioneering Bengali liberal thinker. Roy implicitly compared British exploitation in Ireland with that in India, and set out arguments that presaged the notion of a 'drain of wealth'.[2] The idea, however, was presented most forcefully and achieved wide currency only after the 1870s. The economic critique of British rule in India was mounted by a group of liberals which included: Dadabhai Naoroji, a successful businessman and politician, Justice M. G. Ranade, R. C. Dutt, retired Indian Civil Service officer and author of the two-volume *Economic History of India* (1902, 1904), and K. T. Telang, a popular writer and political-economist.

This critique, usually referred to as economic nationalism, focused on the poverty created in India by the application of the classic economic theory of free trade. The principal argument was that British colonialism in the later 19th century had abandoned earlier modes of direct exploitation for a more subtle one of exploitation through free trade and foreign capital investment. India had at once been made a supplier of agricultural raw material and food-grain to Britain and a consumer of manufactured goods from Britain. The resultant investment of foreign capital meant that a 'drain of wealth' occurred through the expatriation of profit from India. Calculations of this drain ranged from £ 12 million a year to £ 30 million a year. On average this amounted to at least half of the total revenue income of the British Raj. The result was a direct impoverishment of India and the hampering of indigenous capital formation that was the key to industrialisation and to development.[3]

The drain theory remains a contentious issue among economic historians. From our perspective, its importance lies in the fact that it created a discursive space for the consideration of military issues.

---

[2] C. A. Bayly, 'Rammohan Roy and the Advent of Constitutional Liberalism in India, 180030', in Shruti Kapila, ed., *An Intellectual History for India* (Cambridge: Cambridge University Press, 2010), pp. 18–34. Also see C. A. Bayly, *Recovering Liberties: Indian Thought in the Age of Liberalism and Empire* (Cambridge: Cambridge University Press, 2011).

[3] The standard account is Bipan Chandra, *The Rise and Growth of Economic Nationalism in India* (New Delhi: People's Publishing House, 1966). For the wider intellectual currents shaping these ideas see, Bayly, *Recovering Liberties*.

For the liberals claimed that the military charges were a key component of this drain and that military expenditure was compounding the onerous burden on India. They observed that the Indian army was being deployed in imperial wars all across the globe, especially in Africa and Asia. Together with the Indian frontier wars, these placed rather a heavy burden on Indian finances. There was real force to these arguments. Even in peacetime about 40 per cent of the central government's revenue was spent on the 'Army in India'. In 1900–1, for instance, the government spent nearly three times more on the army than it did on irrigation, famine relief and education. In 1921–22, military expenditure was a whopping 59 per cent of the government's revenue.[4] A corollary to this was the liberals' demand for Indianisation of the administrative services. Indianised services, they argued, would not only reduce the drain of money which was expatriated through the payment of salaries and pensions to British personnel, but would also create a civil service that would be more responsive to India's needs. The argument for Indianisation was soon extended to cover the military as well.

These strands of liberal thinking on military matters are clearly discernible in the resolutions adopted by the Indian National Congress.[5] At its very first session in 1885, the Congress resolved that 'the proposed increase in the military expenditure of the empire is unnecessary and in the existing circumstances of the country, excessive'. The way to curb the spiralling expenditure was 'by retrenchment'. At the second session of the Congress, it was argued that the government should initiate a system of volunteering.[6] Variants of these arguments continued to be advanced by the Indian National Congress in its subsequent meetings. However, the most

---

[4] The figures are from David Omissi, *The Sepoy and the Raj: The Indian Army, 1860–1940* (London: Macmillan, 1994). 'Army in India' was the official term used after 1895 to describe the entire military establishment in India, including British troops. The term 'Indian Army' was applied to units comprising Indian soldiers and officers, while 'British Army in India' referred to units of British Army deployed in India.

[5] Proceedings of 1885 and 1886, File No. 1/1885–1920, All India Congress Committee Papers, Nehru Memorial Museum and Library (NMML), New Delhi.

[6] Ibid.

sophisticated statement of the liberal position came from their most prominent spokesman at the turn of the century, Gopal Krishna Gokhale.

In his annual speeches on the budget before the Imperial Legislative Council, Gokhale developed these arguments at some length.[7] Speaking in 1902, he argued for 'a considerable reduction' of taxation and 'a large increase' in outlay on education and other domestic reforms. How could these objectives be simultaneously achieved? 'My answer is that the only way to attain both objects simultaneously is to reduce the overgrown military expenditure of the country.'[8] In a rhetorical move characteristic of liberal critiques of the government's policies, Gokhale cited its own officials in support of his argument. When the strength of the army was increased in 1885, the law and finance members of the government had pointed out that the existing strength of the army had been sufficient for all purposes of India: defence against external aggression, and maintenance of internal security. Nevertheless, the fear of a conflict with Russia had led to these increases. Yet the fact, as Gokhale pointed out, was that, 'during the last two years over 20,000 troops are engaged outside India in doing the work of the Imperial Government'.[9] If the government was unwilling to reduce the army's strength and 'if the strength maintained is in excess of India's own requirements ... the cost of the excess portion should, as a matter of mere justice, be borne by the Imperial Government.'[10] Dadabhai Naoroji made the same point more trenchantly. Was it, he asked,

> just and worthy of the British name, conscience, and wealth, to burden India with this expenditure? India, impoverished, bleeding, and perishing by England's own drain of its wealth of over 30 millions every year, and thereby afflicted with famine and plague! Is it not cruel in the extreme?[11]

---

[7] Budget Speech 1902 in W. R. Mujawar, ed., *Speeches and Writings of Gopal Krishna Gokhale*, Vol. 1 (New Delhi: Mangalam Publications, 2009), pp. 23–24.
[8] Ibid.
[9] Ibid.
[10] Ibid.
[11] Cited in R. P. Masani, *Dadabhai Naoroji: The Grand Old Man of India* (London: George, Allen & Unwin, 1939), p. 454.

The Widening Critique

In his speech on the 1903 budget, Gokhale restated and amplified these points. His arguments subtly went beyond economic and fiscal considerations and alluded to the military's dominant institutional position in the Raj. Gokhale argued that

> Indian finance is virtually at the mercy of military considerations, and no well-sustained or vigorous effort by the State on an adequate scale for the material advancement or the moral progress of the people is possible while our revenues are liable to be appropriated in an ever-increasing proportion for military purposes.[12]

Military security, he conceded, was undoubtedly a 'paramount consideration'. But he went to argue that military preparedness had 'no definite standard and might absorb whatever resources can be made available for it practically without limit'.[13] Quoting Lord Salisbury, he claimed that military efficiency must be relative and not absolute. It ought to be determined by 'a combined consideration of its needs of defence and the resources that it can fairly devote for the purpose'.[14] In effect, Gokhale was arguing that the military's own assessment of its requirements was being accorded excessive weight in the government's consideration of the matter.

In subsequent years, this line of argument grew sharper. Speaking in 1907, for instance, Gokhale argued that the standpoint of the soldier was only one of several views that needed to be factored in — and a narrow one at that: 'whose principal idea is to raise the efficiency of the Army to as high a state of perfection as possible, and who wants to take for this purpose all the money he can get'.[15] In an artful move to undercut the military's claims of expertise, he said that he would be 'guilty of presumption' if he spoke on technical military matters. 'But there are certain broad questions of policy ... which all men of average intelligence may claim to understand

---

[12] Budget Speech 1903, *Speeches and Writings of Gopal Krishna Gokhale*, Vol. 1, pp. 41–42.

[13] Ibid.

[14] Ibid.

[15] Budget Speech, 1907, *Speeches and Writings of Gopal Krishna Gokhale*, Vol. 1, pp. 144–45.

and discuss.'[16] Gokhale proceeded to argue that with the Japanese triumph over Russia in the war of 1905, the bogey of Russian threat to India had been laid to rest. What was more, Britain and Japan had also entered into an alliance. In these circumstances, 'India may well ask to be relieved now of a part of her present army expenditure'.[17] The analysis of military expenditure thus broadened out to a wider argument about civil–military relations.

This developing liberal critique of the relationship between the government and the army occurred against the backdrop of the grim struggle for power that began in 1904 between the then Viceroy, Lord Curzon, and his Commander-in-Chief, Lord Kitchener.[18] The conflict began as a skirmish but soon escalated to a major battle, involving principle and pride in about equal measure. It quickly reached a point where neither the Viceroy nor the Commander-in-Chief would give in. Ultimately, it led to the resignation and departure of Curzon. If the outcome seems somewhat surprising, we may recall that Lord Kitchener of Khartoum was widely regarded as the 'first hero of the empire' and enjoyed a public standing unrivalled by any general since the Duke of Wellington. Whether he deserved this reputation is a different matter. The bone of contention between them was the role and relative power of the 'Military Member' of the Viceroy's Council. The Military Member was different from the Commander-in-Chief, who was the executive head of the army, responsible for its organisation, training, mobilisation and fighting. But the Commander-in-Chief was also the second-ranking member of Viceroy's Council, the equivalent of a senior cabinet minister. This arrangement gave the military considerable clout in the government; indeed, in such a system the notion of civilian control was rather diluted.

The Military Member, also an army officer, headed the Military Department, which handled the army's finances and administration, and acted as a second military advisor to the Viceroy. As soon as

---

[16] Budget Speech, 1907, *Speeches and Writings of Gopal Krishna Gokhale*, Vol. 1, pp. 144–45.

[17] Ibid.

[18] The following account draws on Stephen P. Cohen, *The Indian Army and its Contribution to the Development of a Nation* (New Delhi: Oxford University Press, 1990), pp. 22–28; David Gilmour, *Curzon: Imperial Statesman 1859–1925* (London: John Murray, 1994), pp. 296–317.

Kitchener took office, he called for abolishing the post of the Military Member and for centralising administrative and command functions in the office of the Commander-in-Chief. He referred to the system as one of 'dual control', which would create problems in time of war. Kitchener especially resented both the power of the Military Member – an officer junior in rank – to criticise his proposals and the Military Member's access to the Viceroy. Curzon initially persuaded Kitchener to work the existing system for a year, before demanding significant changes. Kitchener agreed; but his year was up in three months; and the Commander-in-Chief was back with his demand for doing away with the Military Member. Kitchener also orchestrated a campaign in London, unbeknownst to Curzon, and managed to secure the appointment of a committee to look into this question. As most administrative reform committees, this one proposed a compromise. The post would be retained but with drastically reduced powers; the Military Member would become the Military Supply Member, whose functions would go no further than the title announced. Curzon resisted, and was ultimately forced to resign.

The position of Military Member was abolished in 1905 and the Commander-in-Chief was made directly responsible to the Viceroy's council for administrative as well as command functions – an arrangement continued right until India attained independence in 1947. The arguments advanced by both protagonists are worth examining a bit more closely. Curzon felt that by destroying the position of Military Member, Kitchener sought 'not to disestablish an individual or a department, but to subvert the military authority of the Government of India as a whole, and to substitute for it a military autocracy in the person of the Commander-in-Chief'.[19] The governor of Madras, who was officiating as Viceroy when Curzon was away, also pointed out that the problem was not that the Military Member was issuing orders to a senior officer, the Commander-in-Chief. The Military Member's orders were not his own but that of the Indian government. The question was whether the government 'should retain the power of giving orders to the c-in-c [Commander-in-Chief] or whether the c-in-c should be largely emancipated from that control'.[20] Kitchener, for his part, contemptuously dismissed

---

[19] Cited in Cohen, *The Indian Army*, p. 25.
[20] Cited in Gilmour, *Curzon*, p. 313

Curzon's claims. He declared that he did want to establish an autocracy, but only 'the autocracy exercised in his *own sphere* by every commander of a regiment or a brigade or a division. I desire ... to put an end to the existing divorce between responsibility and control.'[21]

Here was an argument for a separate military sphere which should be beyond the purview of civilian interference – direct or indirect. This argument would resonate well after Curzon and Kitchener had moved on. Interestingly enough, Curzon put his finger on the nub of the problem. As he wrote, 'who would determine when a military question became a general question of policy, or when the storekeeper [his pejorative term for Military Supply Member] was to blossom into the advisor?'[22] The implications that flowed from the manner in which the Curzon–Kitchener spat was resolved troubled the Indian liberals, who believed that the military already had a disproportionate voice in the government. Moreover, the Indians had practically no say in the structuring and working of the system. As Naoroji wrote in August 1905, 'Now that the Curzon–Kitchener fight is over, may I ask: What about the people of India? Where do they come in? They had not the slightest voice whatever in the matter'.[23] The room for the liberals to actually influence the system would only open up after the constitutional reforms following the Great War.

Military expenditure and the related issue of civil–military relations apart, the liberals also questioned the existing structure of the Indian army. Gokhale contrasted the Indian army with those of other European states. The latter maintained a small peacetime army with a system of reserves that enabled the army's size to be increased in short order. Even Japan, he pointed out, had a peace establishment half the size of India's but was capable of mobilising double the number of men than India could. This also implied that, in times of peace, Japan and other European states that adopted this model spent a fraction of what India did. 'Our Army is for all practical purposes a standing army, maintained on a war footing even in times of peace.'[24] This system was financially 'the most wasteful

---

[21] Cited in Cohen, *The Indian Army*, pp. 25–26.
[22] Cited in Gilmour, *Curzon*, p. 326.
[23] Cited in Masani, *Dadabhai Naoroji*, p. 456.
[24] Budget Speech 1903, *Speeches and Writings of Gopal Krishna Gokhale*, pp. 43–45.

conceivable'.²⁵ But 'even as an organisation of national defence, it is radically faulty.'²⁶ Worse still, this system was in place 'while the whole population is disarmed and the process of demartialisation [*sic*] continues apace.'²⁷ The term 'demartialisation' was repeatedly deployed by Gokhale in his analyses. It linked his critique of the Indian military system to another notion that lay at the heart of the republican tradition: the idea of a citizen-soldier.²⁸ Gokhale contended that 'India is about the only country in the civilised world where the people are debarred from the privileges of citizen soldier-ship and from all voluntary participation in the responsibilities of national defence.'²⁹

This argument was the obverse of the liberals' critique of the 'martial races' doctrine that governed recruitment for the Indian army. Related to it was the demand for opening up the officer cadre to Indians. Gokhale suggested that the Indianisation of the officers' corps was not only tied to the issue of 'economic administration' but also to 'the political elevation of the people of India.'³⁰ He tartly observed that 'Everywhere else, the Army and the Navy offer careers to aspiring youths ... These services, for us in this country, practically do not exist.'³¹ These arguments, too, were repeatedly laid out by Gokhale and other liberals. But to little avail.

Until 1917, only British officers could be King's Commissioned Officers (KCOs). Their commission enabled them to command both British and Indian troops. Below the KCOs was a grade of Indian officers known as Viceroy's Commissioned Officers (VCOs), who performed the duties of platoon commanders and provided a crucial link between British officers and Indian sepoys. The VCOs, of course, were not commissioned officers in any real sense. Rather,

---

²⁵ Budget Speech 1903, *Speeches and Writings of Gopal Krishna Gokhale*, pp. 43–45.
²⁶ Ibid.
²⁷ Ibid.
²⁸ For a discussion of this tradition in the West, see Eliot Cohen, *Citizens and Soldiers: The Dilemmas of Military Service* (Ithaca: Cornell University Press, 1985).
²⁹ Budget Speech 1903, *Speeches and Writings of Gopal Krishna Gokhale*, pp. 43–45.
³⁰ Ibid.
³¹ Ibid., p. 58.

they rose from the ranks and their utility lay precisely in the fact that they hailed from the same ethnic community as the rank-and-file. The liberals were not the only ones to call for the entry of Indians to the officer corps. The princes of India were equally keen to secure these positions for the aristocracy. After considerable stone-walling from the imperial authorities, the princes caught the sympathetic ear of Curzon. The Viceroy regarded the Indian princes as the 'only class in India who are bound to us by every tie of self-interest, if not loyalty'.[32] Along with the then Secretary of India, Lord Hamilton, Curzon instituted the Imperial Cadet Corps (ICC). This was a small institution, modelled on public schools, which provided rudimentary military training to 20–30 scions of the Indian princely order. After much discussion, it was decided that the products of the ICC would be used for ceremonial duties (such as forming the Viceroy's Bodyguard in the *durbar* of 1903) and in Imperial Service Troops contingents. The numbers involved were minuscule and the experiment never really took off. Following the outbreak of the Great War in 1914, the ICC was simply folded up.[33] The liberals could hardly be expected to be enthused by such measures. Curzon's assurance that the ICC would be a vehicle for Indianisation of the army, said Gokhale, 'though kept to the ear, has been broken to the heart'.[34] By contrast the proportion of British officers in every Indian battalion was on the rise. 'Such growing distrust of the people', he lamented, 'is to be deplored from every point of view, and not until a policy of greater trust is inaugurated, will the military problem ... be satisfactorily dealt with.'[35]

Military Reform after the Great War

The window of change opened a crack in 1917, when the British government declared that Indians were eligible for the King's commission. The announcement was prompted by several considerations.

---

[32] Cited in Chandar Sundaram, 'Grudging Concessions: The Officer Corps and its Indianization, 1817–1940', in Daniel Marston and Chandar Sundaram, eds, *A Military History of India and South Asia: From the East India Company to the Nuclear Era* (Westport: Praeger Security International, 2007), p. 92.

[33] Ibid., pp. 92–93.

[34] Budget Speech 1906, *Speeches and Writings of Gopal Krishna Gokhale*, pp. 118–19.

[35] Ibid.

First, there was India's enormous contribution to the Allied war effort, amounting to about 1.4 million soldiers of whom 800,000 saw action in Asia, Africa and Europe. Furthermore, the Indian politicians were determined to extract some concessions in return for India's contribution. In his presidential address at the Indian National Congress session of 1915, Satyendra Sinha observed that whilst Indians were actively fighting in various theatres, 'not one of them can receive a commission in His Majesty's army – irrespective of birth, education, or efficiency.'[36] B. G. Tilak, the senior 'extremist' Congress leader, spoke at recruitment rallies urging the youth to volunteer: 'If you want Home Rule be prepared to defend your home.'[37] The link between enlistment and political reform was obvious. Finally, the British officials were keen to curb the rising influence of the nationalists. In 1916, the Indian National Congress and the Muslim League had concluded the Lucknow Pact, forging a short-lived but effective alliance. Their agitation was organised through Tilak's Home Rule League. In the political package aimed at diffusing this united front, Indianisation was also included.

From 1917, 10 seats a year were reserved at the Royal Military College, Sandhurst. But this was only for 'suitable Indians', the category being defined as 'selected representatives of families of fighting classes which have rendered valuable services to the State during the War'.[38] Places were granted mainly to members of the princely order who were not expected to pursue a professional military career and to some senior VCOs and NCOs who would retire before long. An Indian Cadet College was opened at Indore in 1918 to grant temporary wartime commission, but was shut down soon after the war. In 1918 the case for political reform gathered steam, resulting in the Montagu–Chelmsford Report. The report came at a juncture when the outcome of the war hung in the balance. The authors of the Report were keen to cement the loyalty of important Indian groups. As Edwin Montagu, Secretary of State for India, observed, 'it is important to avoid a state of things in India which would not only impair her war effort, but might also place new burdens on the military resources of the Empire.'[39]

---

[36] Cited in Sundaram, 'Grudging Concessions', p. 94.
[37] Cited in Cohen, *The Indian Army*, p. 92.
[38] Cited in Sundaram, 'Grudging Concessions', p. 94.
[39] Ibid.; Also Omissi, *Sepoy and the Raj*, pp. 161–62.

The need to harness Indian military manpower for imperial purposes continued after the war. The Government of India was directed to conduct a review, assuming that the British element need not exceed pre-war levels. However, the size of the Indian component was to be determined keeping in view likely imperial obligations in Persia and the Pacific.[40] In effect, Britain was urging India to be prepared to accept military responsibilities overseas. This was one of the considerations in enacting the Government of India Act of 1919 that gave shape to the principles outlined in the Montagu-Chelmsford Report. The Act created a Legislative Assembly of 145 members and a Council of State of 60 members – a majority of the delegates to both houses being elected rather than appointed. The army was a 'reserved' subject, and its budget could not be voted upon let alone amended. But the Assembly provided a useful forum for Indians – especially the liberals – to turn the spotlight on military issues.

In the meantime, the future of the Indian military was examined by an 'Army in India Committee' led by Lord Esher, comprising senior British civil and military officials, and two Indian members. In its recommendations, the Committee asserted the importance of imperial duties in the consideration of Indian defence requirements. It rejected increased democratic control over the military and proposed buttressing the Commander-in-Chief's position. It also rejected widening the recruitment base beyond the so-called 'martial races' and paid mere lip-service to preparing Indians for Sandhurst.[41] These recommendations drew sharp criticism in the newly-constituted legislative assembly. Indeed, the debate on the Esher Committee Report provided the liberals an opening to push their agenda for military reform. A Select Committee of the legislative assembly was formed to examine the report. The 15-member Select Committee was chaired by Sir Tej Bahadur Sapru, Law Member and a prominent liberal. The conclusions of the Select Committee were tabled as a set of 15 resolutions in the house (in the form of recommendations to the Governor General). The resolutions were moved by Sir P. S. Sivaswamy Aiyer, a leading liberal from Madras with a keen interest

---

[40] Government of India Office, March 22, 1919, L/MIL/3/1118, Asia Pacific & Africa Collections (APAC), British Library, London.

[41] Esher Committee Report, 1919–20, L/MIL/17/5/1762, APAC.

in military matters. The resolutions reflected and built upon the range of concerns voiced by the liberals in the preceding years.

The opening salvo was fired on the burgeoning military expenditure. The resolutions stated that 'the purpose of Army in India must be held to be defence of India against external aggression and the maintenance of internal peace ... Military resources of India should not be developed in a manner suited to imperial necessities.'[42] For any employment in pursuit of the latter, the costs must be borne by the British government as was the case with the other dominions. The resolutions went on to address the related, and in some ways the central structural problem of civil–military relations. The absence of 'a fully responsible government in India' did not warrant a different form of civil–military relations than that prevailing in Britain.[43] To emphasise the 'principle of ultimate supremacy of the civil power' it was essential that the commander-in-chief ceased to be a member of the governor general's executive council.[44] Instead, the portfolio of defence, including supply, should be entrusted to a civilian member of the executive council, assisted by an 'Army Council' comprising the Commander-in-Chief and other senior military officials and civilians too. Besides, the Commander-in-Chief's dealings with his military counterparts in Britain would be open to scrutiny and he would not be allowed to commit the Indian government to 'any pecuniary responsibility or any line of military policy that has not already been the subject of decision by them'.[45]

The resolutions addressed the issue of nationalisation in some detail. They called for broadening the base of military recruitment; for the formation of an adequate territorial force; for the introduction in the Indian Army of a system of short colour service followed by a few years in reserve; and for the reduction of the ratio of British to Indian troops in the Army in India. Furthermore Indians, 'including the educated middle classes', should be eligible to enter commissioned ranks of the army.[46] In nominating candidates for the selection process, non-official Indians should be associated

---

[42] Resolutions on Esher Committee, CID 119-D, CAB 6/4, The National Archives (TNA), London.
[43] Ibid.
[44] Ibid.
[45] Ibid.
[46] Ibid.

with the authorities. The resolutions suggested that to begin with no less than 25 per cent of the total King's Commissions granted each year at Sandhurst should go to Indians. Adequate preliminary training should be provided to Indians prior to their joining Sandhurst. Finally, it was desirable to establish an Indian Military College, along the lines of Sandhurst.[47]

The resolutions were passed by a slim majority, but only after the recommendations had been significantly amended to favour the 'martial races'.[48] The question of reforming the structure of civil–military relations had little traction with the Government of India. The issue of imperial contribution was considered by a sub-committee of the Committee on Imperial Defence in Britain. The sub-committee finessed the matter by arguing that 'the Indian Army cannot be treated as if it were absolutely at the disposal of His Majesty's Government for service outside India'.[49] But the Sivaswamy Aiyer Resolutions did manage to set the terms of the debate on Indianisation.

To follow up on the Esher Report and the Resolutions, a Military Requirements Committee was former under the Commander in Chief, General Rawlinson.[50] Rawlinson was deeply unsympathetic on the issue of nationalisation, but went along with the liberals' demands merely because he was sure that they would be utterly unacceptable to London. He was right. But the British Government also suggested that India create a new Dominion Army (officered by Indians) to exist alongside the Indian Army. The budgetary implications and the anticipated political backlash led New Delhi to resist this idea and advance a new plan. This called for complete Indianisation in three stages of 14 years each. In stage one, 27 units would be Indianised; in stage two, 47; and in stage three, 41. If stage one proved successful, the other two could be done over a reduced period of 30 years. The Committee on Imperial Defence was prepared to allow the Indianisation of only four units. Following

---

[47] Resolutions on Esher Committee, CID 119-D, CAB 6/4, The National Archives (TNA), London.

[48] Gautam Sharma, *Nationalisation of the Indian Army, 1885–1947* (New Delhi: Allied Publishers, 1996), pp. 62–63.

[49] Report of Sub-Committee on Indian Military Requirements, 1922, CID125-D, CAB6/4, TNA.

[50] Military Requirements Committee, 1921, L/MIL/17/5/1773, APAC.

protests from the Viceroy of India, who argued that even the moderate nationalists would be insulted by this number, London agreed to the Indianisation of eight units. Thereafter all King's Commissioned Indian Officers (KCIOs) passing out of Sandhurst would be posted only to these units. This ensured that Indian officers would not command British troops and would remain segregated.[51]

Towards an Indian Sandhurst

As a sop to nationalist opinion, the British had established an Indian Territorial Force in 1920. The force was, however, restricted to 20 battalions totalling 20,000 men – a number that was reached in 1925. A branch of the territorial force called the University Training Corps was set up in Indian colleges towards the same political end. By mid-1923, 52 Indian cadets had been admitted to Sandhurst. But only 14 had passed out and received commissions. This prompted the Government of India to act on one of the Sivaswamy Aiyer resolutions to establish a pre-Sandhurst training institution. The Prince of Wales Royal Indian Military College opened in Dehradun in 1922. The government sought to pass off these measures as serious advances on the road to Indianisation. But the liberal military experts would not be taken in.

Writing in a journal of opinion published from London, Tej Bahadur Sapru observed that the question of defence and nationalisation were the foremost issues agitating the minds of his colleagues.[52] Opponents of according India dominion status trotted out the specious argument that India was incapable of ensuring its own military security. Sapru argued that most of the dominions faced similar problems when they were granted internal autonomy. Moreover, what had the British done to make India self-reliant in matters of defence? The eight units scheme of Indianisation 'cannot be

---

[51] Omissi, *Sepoy and the Raj*, pp. 168–78; Anirudh Deshpande, *British Military Policy in India: Colonial Constraints and Declining Power* (New Delhi: Manohar, 2005), pp. 91–98.

[52] Tej Bahadur Sapru, 'The Problem of India's Aspirations', *The Contemporary Review* (November 1923), reproduced in K. N. Raina and K. V. Gopala Ratnam, eds, *Tej Bahadur Sapru: Profiles and Tributes* (Allahabad: Tej Bahadur Sapru Commemoration Volume Committee, 1972), pp. 195–96.

expected to satisfy the ambition of India'.[53] It might be an improvement from the earlier situation, but it was 'wholly disproportionate' to demands of his countrymen.

> We want to be admitted into every branch of the army. We want every facility for training in military instruction and if the Dehra Dun College has not evoked much interest or enthusiasm, it is, I believe, through the feeling that it is wholly inadequate to the needs of the situation.[54]

Mohammed Ali Jinnah, the liberal leader of the Muslim League, punctured the government's claims with wit and perspicacity. During his intervention on the budget of 1924 in the Assembly, Jinnah held to account the Commander-in-Chief. He observed that a paltry 10 seats had been reserved for Indians (as opposed to the 25 per cent demanded by the liberals) at Sandhurst. The Indian Army he noted currently had 2078 British officers. At this going rate, he asked rhetorically, 'how many centuries will it take to Indianise the Army'.[55] He went on to argue that the system of selection was flawed. He advised the Commander-in-Chief to 'have an Indian Member sitting by your side on that Bench with a sufficient amount of money at his disposal to make the Indian Army a national army as soon as possible.'[56] Echoing the arguments of Gokhale, Jinnah argued that the larger problem was the force structure and utility. To keep military expenditure at a manageable level, two measures were needed. First, the bill for the troops required for imperial purposes should be footed by London. Second, a proper system of short colour service and reserves needed to be introduced. The territorial force was not adequate to the task. The numbers needed were much higher and the men required 'a real, proper training, a training which will enable those men to stand by the side of the Regular Army as a real reserve force'.[57]

---

[53] Sapru, 'The Problem of India's Aspirations', pp. 195–96.
[54] Ibid.
[55] Jinnah's Speech on March 6, 1924 in M. Rafique Afzal, ed., *Selected Speeches and Statements of the Quaid-i-Azam Mohammed Ali* (Lahore: Research Society of Pakistan, 1966), pp. 122–28.
[56] Ibid.
[57] Ibid.

The liberals, for their part, saw the establishment of a military college in India along the lines of Sandhurst as the fastest way to Indianise the officer corps. The Sivaswamy Aiyer resolutions had alluded to the need for such an institution. A similar resolution was adopted in 1923 but the government was in no mood to accept it. In February 1925, a resolution on this demand was introduced yet again by an Indian member, B. Venkatapatiraju. The army secretary sought to scotch the resolution by pointing out that it had already been declined by the government and that the idea was premature. Jinnah intervened in support of the resolution with a withering criticism of the government's stand. Addressing the Commander-in-Chief, he said that Indianisation was 'delayed beyond every reasonable time limit ... You have not made a real, earnest, honest endeavour to enable the people of India to have a proper training in military matters.'[58] He demanded the appointment of a committee 'with comprehensive terms of reference' to look into the issue of establishing an Indian Sandhurst: 'for Heaven's sake at once have a proper body constituted ... and let us have an honest and straightforward scheme which will assure the people of India'.[59] The next day, the Congress leader Motilal Nehru threw his weight behind Jinnah. 'The whole of India ... is solidly in favour of the proposition', he claimed. He urged the government to 'at once proceed to act upon it by taking steps to formulate a scheme with the assistance of some members of this house and of expert advice'.[60] The resolution was adopted by the Assembly.

The government responded by constituting the Indian Sandhurst Committee under the chief of general staff, Sir Andrew Skeen. The Indian component of the committee included Jinnah and Motilal Nehru, some retired VCOs and members of ICC. The Skeen Committee presented its recommendations in November 1926. These ranged well beyond the Committee's terms of reference and proposed a large-scale expansion of Indianisation. It recommended the immediate doubling of places for Indians at Sandhurst from 10 to 20,

---

[58] Jinnah's Speech on February 18, 1925, *Selected Speeches and Statements of the Quaid-i-Azam Mohammed Ali*, pp. 167–72.

[59] Ibid.

[60] Speech on February 19, 1925 in Ravinder Kumar and Hari Dev Sharma, eds, *Selected Works of Motilal Nehru*, Vol. 4 (New Delhi: Vikas Publishing House, 1986), pp. 418–21.

with later progressive increases; the setting up of an Indian Sandhurst by 1933 with an intake of 300 cadets for a three-year course; an increase the intake of the Royal Indian Military College and the setting up of another institution elsewhere in India; abolition of the eight unit scheme in favour of unrestricted Indianisation; the opening up of artillery and air force to KCIOs. If these measures were instituted, the report estimated that by 1952 half of the officer corps in the Indian army would be Indian. The legislative assembly welcomed the report, adopted it in September 1927, and recommended full implementation.

The Government of India was taken aback. After being placed on ice for a year and a half, the report was rejected on the grounds that it exceeded its terms. But realising the need to mollify the Indians, the government held out minor concessions. The number of places in Sandhurst would be increased from 10 to 25, and a small number would be admitted to the artillery and air force colleges in the UK. The increased intake did not mean an expansion of the eight unit scheme. Rather the new officers would be absorbed in the same units replacing the VCOs.[61] The liberals were, of course, deeply disappointed. The announcement, Motilal Nehru told the Assembly, 'leaves me cold'.[62] It meant that the government 'would not contemplate even at a remote date the contingency of India's standing on her own feet.'[63] The term 'Indianisation', he declared, was a misnomer: 'The Army is ours; we have to officer our own Army; there is no question of Indianising there. What we want is to get rid of the Europeanisation of the Army.'[64] Jinnah too pitched in with his characteristically forthright style. Under the arrangement proposed by the government, the utmost intake of Indians would be 37 a year. 'In the first instance, and on Doomsday it will be something more', Jinnah acerbically noted.[65] The 'most objectionable part' of

---

[61] Omissi, *Sepoy and the Raj*, pp. 178–82, Deshpande, *British Military Policy in India*, pp. 99–104, and Sundaram, 'Grudging Concessions', pp. 97–98.

[62] Speech on March 8, 1928 in K. M. Panikkar and A. Pershad, eds, *The Voice of Freedom: Selected Speeches of Pandit Motilal Nehru* (Bombay: Asia Publishing House, 1961), pp. 345–49.

[63] Ibid.

[64] Ibid.

[65] Speech on March 10, 1928, *Selected Speeches and Statements of the Quaid-i-Azam Mohammed Ali Jinnah*, pp. 275–81.

the government's announcement was 'not only the continuance but the extension of the system of eight units.'[66] The entire record, he concluded, did 'no credit to the government.'[67]

By this time, the wider political context was astir. The all-white Statutory Commission appointed by the British government to review the operation of the Indian constitutional system met with a boycott during their sojourn to India. Motilal Nehru began jockeying for a joint Hindu–Muslim constitutional scheme in response to the Simon Commission. At an all-party conference in August 1928, the Motilal Nehru Report was finalised. The effort was, however, rendered futile following Gandhi's refusal to endorse a constitutional struggle for freedom. Yet, the Report reflected the accumulated liberal thinking on military matters (the military sections were mainly drafted by Tej Bahadur Sapru) and advanced recommendations that would have a delayed impact. The Report rejected the position that without an 'Indian' army, India was unfit for dominion status. It stated: 'We have not merely paid for our army, but we have raised our troops ... We have gone further than the colonies have done in the matter of undertaking our defence.' Further, at the present pace adopted by the government, 'it should take at least century before the army will be really Indianised'.[68]

The Report called for statutory obligation on the government to establish military training schools and colleges. It also proposed an overhaul of the existing system of civil–military relations and management of defence policy. It further asked for 'the representation of the army in the legislature by a responsible minister (as opposed to the commander in chief), who will, in actual administration, no doubt be guided by expert advice'. For considering questions of defence policy, the governor general should appoint a 'Committee of Defence' consisting of the prime minister (who would chair the committee), the defence and foreign affairs ministers,

---

[66] Speech on March 10, 1928, *Selected Speeches and Statements of the Quaid-i-Azam Mohammed Ali Jinnah*, pp. 275–81.
[67] Ibid.
[68] All Parties Conference 1928: Report of the Committee Appointed by the Conference to Determine the Principles of the Constitution of India (Allahabad: General Secretary, All India Congress Committee, 1928).

the Commander-in-Chief and other service chiefs, and two other experts.[69]

Following Gandhi's rejection of the Viceroy's offer of dominion status, the latter sought to bring the moderates around in the First Round Table conference of October 1930. Military issues were entrusted to a subcommittee whose Indian members included Sapru and Jinnah among others. During the discussion on Indianisation, Jinnah wanted the subcommittee to discuss specific numbers and determine the pace of Indianisation. British members on the committee suggested only mentioning the need for hastening Indianisation and for creating an Indian Sandhurst. But Jinnah refused to relent. The important question, he insisted, was 'how effect is to be given to the rate or the pace of Indianisation. That is a question that must be discussed by this committee and some principle be laid down.'[70] A 'pious expression of opinion' would simply not do. Eventually a majority on the subcommittee decided that instead laying down a time-table they would recommend immediate steps to increase the rate of Indianisation.[71]

By the time the Round Table Conference concluded it was clear that increased speed of Indianisation could no longer be delayed. For the first time, in 1929, more than 10 Indian candidates qualified for Sandhurst. By 1930, 77 KCIOs had been commissioned in the army. Thus in April 1931, the Viceroy announced the extension of Indianisation from eight units to a full combat division of 15 units. In accordance with the Round Table Conference recommendations, an Indian Military College Committee was set up. Chaired by the Commander-in-Chief, Sir Philip Chetwode, the committee submitted its report in July 1931. The committee included prominent liberals like Sivaswamy Aiyer. Interestingly, Aiyer's work on the committee was supported by Nirad Chaudhuri, an eccentric Bengali of immense erudition who had written a pioneering critique of the martial races theory and who would go on to become a major

---

[69] All Parties Conference 1928: Report of the Committee Appointed by the Conference to Determine the Principles of the Constitution of India (Allahabad: General Secretary, All India Congress Committee, 1928).

[70] Discussion in the Defence Subcommittee on January 7 and January 12, 1931 in M. Rafique Afzal, ed., *Selected Speeches and Statements of the Quaid-i-Azam Mohammed Ali Jinnah*, pp. 359–79.

[71] Ibid.

writer.[72] The committee recommended the establishment of an Indian Military College (IMC), with an annual intake of 60 cadets for a three-year programme. On passing out, they would be called Indian Commissioned Officers (ICOs) not KCIOs. Once the IMC was established, Indian cadets would no longer go to Sandhurst. In the event, the Royal Indian Military Academy was opened in Dehradun in October 1932. But it had an annual intake of only 40 cadets, out of which 15 would be filled by open competition, and the rest were reserved for VCOs and the States' troops.

Through the rest of the decade, Indianisation proceeded at a leisurely pace. As the possibility of war began to loom large, the legislative assembly passed a resolution in September 1938 calling for a committee to recommend ways of increasing Indianisation. By this time the liberals' political standing had shrunk. And the radical wing of the Congress party denounced the government's policy on Indianisation as 'a sham' and called for complete Indianisation in 15 years. By the time committee got working, the Second World War had begun. The war resulted in a massive expansion of the Indian Army, which in turn created more officer posts. On June 17, 1940, the Indian government eventually declared that the ICOs would no longer be restricted to the select Indianised units and would be posted throughout the Indian Army. Indianisation was finally in the offing.[73]

Conclusion

Looking back at the liberals' efforts for reform of Indian military institutions, it is easy to conclude that these were entirely disproportionate to the outcomes achieved. It is tempting to suggest that the liberals were naïve in their faith in the possibility of constitutional reform. This was certainly the view of their more radical contemporaries who believed that the only problem was the existence of the British Raj. Once independence was achieved, military reforms would automatically take place. Writing in 1927, Jawaharlal Nehru

---

[72] On Chaudhuri's role, see Nirad C. Chaudhuri, *Thy Hand Great Anarch!* (London: Chatto Windus, 1987), pp. 319–27.

[73] Omissi, *Sepoy and the Raj*, 184–89; Sundaram, 'Grudging Concessions', pp. 99–100.

derided the 'Skeen Committees and the like making feeble proposals which might result in the course of generations in Indianising a part of the army'.[74] With its tremendous man-power and resources, he believed, India could solve the problem 'within a year or two'.[75] This he thought could be done by promoting non-commissioned officers and taking immediate steps to train more officers – just as Western armies had done during the Great War.[76]

In retrospect it is clear that the liberals were on the losing side of a political argument. But assessments such as those of Jawaharlal Nehru had more than a whiff of wishful thinking to them. For all their failings, it is difficult to deny that the dogged efforts of Naoroji and Gokhale, Aiyer and Motilal Nehru, Sapru and Jinnah, created and nurtured institutions that would prove invaluable to independent India. Without the officers trained at Sandhurst, for instance, independent India would have had Indian officers in junior positions only. Without the Royal Indian Military Academy, the subsequent expansion of the officer corps would have been difficult to pull off. Without the liberals' longstanding plans for restructuring civil–military relations, independent India might have persisted with the skewed pattern inherited from the Raj. It is ironic that the British are given credit for a system of military subordination to civilian authority, whereas it was the liberals who identified the fundamental flaw in the British system and proposed an alternative – one that was eventually adopted by the Indian Republic.

It is an interesting counter-factual exercise to consider what might have happened if the British had acceded to the liberals' proposals for early and speedy Indianisation. After all, one of the crucial problems facing independent India was that in August 1947 the senior-most Indian officer was only a brigadier. This had important consequences in the years ahead; for several officers climbed up the chain of command rather quickly and arguably without adequate preparation for higher direction of war. This told with considerable effect on the quality of advice tendered by the military brass in

---

[74] Nehru's note of September 13, 1927 in S. Gopal, ed., *Selected Works of Jawaharlal Nehru (First Series)*, Vol. 2, (New Delhi: Orient Longman, 1975), p. 358.
[75] Ibid.
[76] Ibid.

dealing with China from the late 1950s onwards.[77] Had the liberals' arguments been heeded, might the upper-reaches of the Indian military have been better prepared to meet the challenge from China? One doesn't have to answer this in the affirmative to acknowledge the importance of the forgotten Indian liberal tradition of military thought.

---

[77] Srinath Raghavan, *War and Peace in Modern India: A Strategic History of the Nehru Years* (Ranikhet: Permanent Black, 2010).

Part II
Grand Strategy in Modern India

4

INDIAN GRAND STRATEGY
SIX SCHOOLS OF THOUGHT

Kanti Bajpai

Do Indians think strategically, and does India have a grand strategy or even aspire to a grand strategy? While it would seem to be a truism that every country must have some conception of how it deploys military, diplomatic, political, economic, and cultural resources for the purposes of security, in the case of India there is a tradition of scepticism. George K. Tanham, the author of a well-known monograph on Indian strategic thought written in the 1990s, and K. Subrahmanyam, India's most famous strategic analyst, hold the view that India lacks systematic thinking about strategic matters and that part of the reason for this is the country's aversion to power.[1] Notwithstanding the scepticism, this essay suggests that Indians do indeed think about grand strategy, even if they don't use the term 'grand strategy' to describe what they are doing, and that at any given time India does have a set of policies that in aggregate amounts to a grand strategy.

The claim here is that Indian grand strategic thinking can be described in terms of three leading 'schools': Nehruvianism, Neoliberalism and Hyperrealism. These schools have come into sharp relief with the end of the Cold War. Their adherents are to be found in the various branches of government – the civil services and armed forces. There are Nehruvians, Neoliberals and Hyper-realists amongst all the political parties. Proponents of the various schools are also to be found in the media, academic life and policy institutes. The terms used to describe the schools are not in common

---

[1] George K. Tanham, *Indian Strategic Thought: An Interpretive Essay* (Santa Monica, CA: RAND, 1992); K. Subrahmanyam, *Shedding Shibboleths: India's Evolving Strategic Outlook* (New Delhi: Wordsmiths, 2005).

parlance and few Indians in the strategic community would, therefore, describe themselves in these terms. Nevertheless, it is the argument of this chapter, building on my own earlier work, that there is a fairly clear division in the strategic elite along the lines of Nehruvianism, Neoliberalism and Hyperrealism, as evidenced by the writings on strategic issues that appear in newspapers, magazines, academic journals, and books. Other scholars including Stephen P. Cohen, Tobias Engelmeier, J. Mohan Malik, Deepa Ollapally, Rajesh Rajagopalan, and Rahul Sagar have also noticed that there are different streams of thought on India's external relations.[2]

In addition, the chapter suggests that it is possible to think about three relatively minor schools of grand strategy based on Marxism, Hindutva (or political Hinduism), and Gandhianism – I say 'based on' because none of the three has been articulated very clearly and in any great depth or specificity in relation to what we are calling grand strategy here, but all three do inspire lines of thinking about how India should deal with its security. The proponents of these schools are not as prominent in the Indian strategic community nor as visible in terms of their writings. Their adherents in government and politics are far fewer. Nonetheless, I would suggest that they have historically had influence in Indian thinking and they continue to evoke interest. Marxism is the reigning ideology of various communist parties in India, and Hindutva is the philosophical bedrock of the second largest national party, the Bharatiya Janata Party (BJP), and associated organisations in the Sangh Parivar (especially the Rashtriya Swayamsevak Sangh or RSS), which in combination represent political Hinduism. Gandhianism has certainly faded in India, since 1947, but the anti-corruption protests of 2011, led by Anna Hazare and his team, with its explicitly Gandhian symbols

---

[2] Stephen P. Cohen, *India: Emerging Power* (New Delhi: Oxford University Press, 2001); Tobias Engelmeier, *Nation-Building and Foreign Policy in India: An Identity-Strategy Conflict* (New Delhi: Cambridge University Press, 2009); J. Mohan Malik, 'Eyeing the Dragon: India's China Debate', *Asia-Pacific Center for Security Studies (APCSS)*, December 2003. Available at http://www.apcss.org/Publications/SAS/ChinaDebate_Malik.pdf, accessed on September 6, 2010; Deepa Ollapally and Rajesh Rajagopalan, 'The Pragmatic Challenge to Indian Foreign Policy', *Washington Quarterly*, 34, 2 (Spring 2011), pp. 145–162; Rahul Sagar, 'State of Mind: What Kind of Power Will India Become?' *International Affairs*, 85, 4 (2009), pp. 804–16.

and discourse, rocked the ruling United Progressive Alliance (UPA) government and the Indian parliament.

If India does have strategic thought, does it also have grand strategy? This question is much less controversial now than it was 10 years ago when the term 'grand strategy' would have evoked puzzlement and some amusement in India and amongst India watchers abroad.[3] With the story of India's rise, it is a far more respectable, less risible question. In recent years, Western experts have expressed a certain degree of impatience over the lack of a coherent, ambitious grand strategy on the part of a rising India.[4] Indians, by contrast, have seen more coherence in Indian policies and are more comfortable with a modest Indian grand strategic posture. In common, though, is the view that the lineaments of a grand strategy are at least visible. It is the contention here that, like virtually any country, India has a grand strategy and in fact has had grand strategy since its independence. Sunil Khilnani's classic *The Idea of India* can be read as a very elegant statement of post-independent India's grand strategy. Ramachandra Guha's more recent *India after Gandhi* also in effect charts the outlines of India's grand strategy.[5]

In an ideal world, there would be a clear, singular relationship between grand strategic thought and grand strategic policy in which policy would reflect a body of ideas about the threats that a country faces and the array of responses to those threats. The real world being far messier, this is seldom the case. Even in the apparently classic case of the United States in the Cold War, the ideas of

---

[3] Recent attempts to delineate a grand strategy for India can be found in Rajiv Kumar and Santosh Kumar, *In the National Interest: A Strategic Foreign Policy for India* (New Delhi: Business Standard Books, 2010); Admiral Raja Menon and Rajiv Kumar, *The Long View From New Delhi: To Define the Indian Grand Strategy for Foreign Policy* (New Delhi: Academic Foundation, 2010); Kapil Kak, ed., *Comprehensive Security for an Emerging India* (New Delhi: Knowledge World, 2010).

[4] Most recently, former Canadian High Commissioner to India, David Malone, has written about India's foreign policy and grand strategy with acuity and sympathy. See David Malone, *Does the Elephant Dance? Contemporary Indian Foreign Policy* (Oxford: Oxford University Press, 2011).

[5] Sunil Khilnani, *The Idea of India* (New Delhi: Penguin India, 1998); Ramachandra Guha, *India After Gandhi: A History of the World's Largest Democracy* (New Delhi: Picador India, 2007).

containment never quite correlated exactly to containment policy in practice. In the case of post-Cold War India, three streams of grand strategic thought have vied for dominance. Two decades later, it is possible to argue that Indian grand strategy *qua* actual policy is fairly clearly inclined towards one of them, Neoliberalism. Nonetheless, all three schools continue to have their supporters, and there remain some fairly sharp disagreements at the level of ideas.

This chapter is organised as follows. First, drawing on my earlier work, it summarises the three leading schools of thought in respect of the major grand strategic challenges facing India – Pakistan, China and the United States. Secondly, it asks whether there are other grand strategic formulations that the earlier paper ignored. In particular, can we speak of a Marxist, Hindutva and Gandhian perspective on grand strategy? Finally, the chapter ends with some thoughts on whether or not, across the six approaches, there are areas of agreement on Indian approaches and policies towards to its security. Broadly, the answer is that there is a convergence on a number of grand strategic orientations and that convergence is in some crucial respects at odds with actual Indian grand strategy in practice today.

Nehruvian, Neoliberal and Hyperrealist Grand Strategic Thought

In order to reconstruct the Nehruvian, Neoliberal and Hyperrealist schools of thought, we need to understand that they both agree and disagree on a fundamental set of assumptions and arguments about (*a*) international life, (*b*) the nature of the adversary, and (*c*) the role of violence/force – what Alastair Iain Johnston in his seminal work on strategic culture has called a 'central paradigm'.[6]

---

[6] See Alastair Iain Johnston, 'Thinking About Strategic Culture', *International Security*, 19, 4 (Spring 1995), pp. 32–64. For Johnston, the central strategic paradigm consists of three parts – the role of war in human affairs, the nature of the adversary and the threat it poses, and the efficacy of the use of force (ibid., pp. 46–47). I have modified his schema somewhat to focus on how a body of strategic thought conceives of international life, the nature of the adversary, and the role of violence/force. This section relies largely on my essay 'Indian Strategic Culture', in Michael R. Chambers, ed., *South Asia in 2020: Future Strategic Balances and Alliances* (Carlisle, Pennsylvania: Strategic Studies Institute, US Army War College, 2003), pp. 245–303.

THE NATURE OF INTERNATIONAL LIFE

First of all, all three schools accept that at the heart of international relations is what International Relations theorists call 'anarchy', the notion that the state being sovereign recognises no higher authority.[7] In the condition of anarchy, with no higher authority that lawfully and rightfully regulates relations between nations, each state is in the end responsible for its own security and well-being. Above all, states strive to protect their territory and autonomy.

Second, the three paradigms recognise that the staples of international relation are interests, power, and violence. States cannot avoid the responsibility of pursuing the national interest, however that is defined. Nor can they be indifferent to the cultivation of power – their own and that of other states. States must in some measure accrue power in a competitive system. Conflict and war are a constant shadow over inter-state relations. While the three paradigms differ on the causes of conflict and war and on the ability of states to control and transcend these forces, all three accept that disputes and large-scale organised violence are a regular feature of international relations.

Third, the three paradigms accept that power comprises both military and economic capabilities, at a minimum. States need both types of capabilities. While they differ on the optimum mix and use of these capabilities, proponents of the three views are in agreement that military and economic strength are vital for security.

Beyond this common base, the three paradigms differ. Fundamental to Nehruvianism is the argument that states and peoples can come to understand each other better and thereby make and sustain peace. Nehruvians accept that in the international system, without a supranational authority, the threat of war to settle disputes and rivalries is in some measure inescapable. States must look after themselves in such a world, in which violence is a regrettable last resort.[8] However, Nehruvians believe that the state of anarchy can be mitigated, if not eventually supervened. International laws and institutions, military restraint, negotiations and compromise,

---

[7] For the notion of anarchy, see Kenneth N. Waltz, *Theory of International Politics* (New York: McGraw Hill, 1979).

[8] Gopal Krishna, 'India and International Order: Retreat from Idealism', in Hedley Bull and Adam Watson, eds, *The Expansion of International Society* (Oxford: Clarendon Press, 1984), pp. 270–71.

co-operation, free intercourse between societies, and regard for the well-being of peoples everywhere and not just one's own citizens, all these can overcome the rigours of the international system.[9] Furthermore, to make preparations for war and a balance of power the central objectives of security and foreign policy is, for Nehruvians, both ruinous and futile: ruinous because arms spending can only impoverish societies materially and create the very conditions that sustain violence and war; futile because, ultimately, balances of power are fragile and do not prevent large-scale violence (as the two world wars so catastrophically demonstrated).[10]

Neoliberals also accept the general characterisation of international relations as a state of war.[11] That coercion plays an important role in such a world is not denied by them. The lure of mutual gain in any interaction is also, however, a powerful conditioning factor amongst states, particularly as they become more interdependent. They often express their distinct view of international relations by comparing the role of military and economic power. According to Neoliberals, states pursue not just military power but also economic well-being. They do so in part because economic strength is ultimately the basis for military power. Economic strength can, in addition, substitute for military power; military domination is one way of achieving one's ends; economic domination is another. For Neoliberals, economic power may be more effective than military power; and military power, with its diversion of finance and capital to non-productive ends, can in fact derogate from economic power.

---

[9] Many of these themes are evident in Nehru's speeches. See, for instance, Nehru's thoughts on the importance of the Commonwealth and United Nations in Jawaharlal Nehru, *India's Foreign Policy: Selected Speeches, September 1946–April 1961* (New Delhi: The Publications Division, Ministry of Information and Broadcasting, Government of India, 1961), pp. 132–81.

[10] On the fragility of the balance of power approach, see Jawaharlal Nehru, *The Discovery of India* (New Delhi: The Jawaharlal Nehru Memorial Fund and Oxford University Press, 1981 [1946]), pp. 536–48.

[11] India's Neoliberals are not the same as neoliberal institutionalists in International Relations Theory (such as Robert Keohane). Indian Neoliberals are no great believers in the positive role of international institutions in fostering co-operation.

Thus, in situations of 'complex interdependence' force is unusable or ineffective.[12]

Most importantly, though, Neoliberals believe that economic well-being is vital for national security in a broader sense. Economically-deprived people cannot be satisfied people, and dissatisfied people cannot be secure.[13] The key question then is: where does economic strength and well-being come from? In the Neoliberal view, it can only come from free market policies. Free market policies at home imply, in addition, free trade abroad. Free trade is a relationship of mutual gain, even if asymmetric gain, and is therefore a factor in the relations between states. Indeed, where Nehruvians see communication and contact as the key to the transformation of international relations, Neoliberals believe that trade and economic interactions can achieve this.[14] Where Nehruvians favour international law, institutions, treaties, and agreements as a way of transcending anarchy, Neoliberals place their faith in self-regarding calculations of the national interest. States act towards each other not so much according to agreed-upon principles and norms of international behaviour but rather guided by the purely instrumental benefits of alternative lines of policy and their watchword is flexibility and pragmatism.

---

[12] See C. Raja Mohan, 'Trade as Strategy: Chinese Lessons', *The Hindu*, August 16, 2001 on how China, in contrast to India, has used trade and economic relations more generally to 'leverage' relations with the US. Also, see Sanjaya Baru, 'Economic Diplomacy', *Seminar*, 461, January 1998, pp. 66–67 on the influence of economics in statecraft. The term 'complex interdependence' originates in Robert O. Keohane and Joseph Nye, *Power and Interdependence*, 4th edn (New York: Longman, 2011).

[13] Sanjaya Baru, 'National Security in An Open Economy', in *Strategic Consequences of India's Economic Performance* (New Delhi: Academic Foundation, 2006), pp. 88–90.

[14] On the importance of economics and the market in strategy, see Shekhar Gupta, 'The Real Battle Will be for the Market', *The Indian Express*, January 13, 2001 Available at http://www.indianexpress.com/ie/daily/20010115/shekhar.htm, accessed on August 31, 2011; Editorial, 'Business, Not Politics', *Indian Express*, January 11, 2001. Available at http://www.indianexpress.com/Storyold/168606/, accessed on August 31, 2011; C. Raja Mohan, 'Trade as Strategy: Chinese Lessons', *The Hindu*, August 16, 2001; Jairam Ramesh, '"Yankee Go Home, But Take Me With You:" Yet Another Perspective on Indo-American Relations', *Economic and Political Weekly*, 34, 50 (December 11, 1999), pp. 3532–34.

Hyperrealists harbour the most pessimistic view of international relations.[15] While Nehruvians and Neoliberals believe that international relations can be transformed – either by means of communication and contact or by free-market economic reforms and the logic of comparative advantage – Hyperrealists see an endless cycle of repetition in interstate interactions. The governing metaphor of Hyperrealists is threat and counter-threat.[16] In the absence of a supranational authority that can tell them how to behave and is capable of enforcing those commands, states are doomed to balance of power, deterrence, and war. Conflict and rivalry between states cannot be transformed into peace and friendship (except temporarily as an alliance against a common foe); they can only be managed by the threat and use of violence.[17]

From this, Hyperrealists conclude that the surest way of achieving peace and stability is through the accumulation of military power and the willingness to use force.[18] Hyperrealists reject the Nehruvian and Neoliberal concern over military spending, arguing that there is no very good evidence that defence derogates from development.[19] Indeed, defence spending may, in the Keynesian sense at least, boost economic growth and development. Hyperrealists, like Neoliberals, are also sceptical about the role of institutions, laws, treaties, and agreements. For Hyperrealists, what counts in international relations is power in the service of national interest; all the rest is illusion. The Neoliberal faith in the power of economics is equally one that Hyperrealists do not share. Hyperrealists invert the relationship between military and economic power. Historically, they argue, military power is more important than, and probably prior to, economic power. A state that can build its military power

---

[15] I use the term 'Hyperrealism' to signify that the proponents of these views value force and unilateral methods much more than a prudential Realism would allow.

[16] Bharat Karnad, 'Introduction', in *Future Imperilled: India's Security in the 1990s and Beyond* (New Delhi: Viking, 1994), p. 2.

[17] Brahma Chellaney, 'Preface', in *Securing India's Future in the New Millennium* (New Delhi: Orient Longman and the Centre for Policy Research, 1999), p. xviii.

[18] Ibid., p. 528.

[19] Ibid., p. 531.

will safeguard its international interests and will build an economy and society that is strong.[20]

THE NATURE OF THE ADVERSARY

If this is the general view that Nehruvians, Neoliberals and Hyper-realists have of international life, and if the problem of war is at the heart of the *problematique* of International Relations, how do adherents of the three schools perceive the adversary or 'Other'?

For Nehruvians, war is a choice that states can and will make. While Nehruvians accept that the international system is anarchic and that states pursue their interests with vigour, violence is not inevitable.[21] Wars, as Nehru affirmed, are made in the minds of men, and therefore it is in the minds of men that war must be eradicated.[22] War is not a natural, inherent activity. It can, therefore, be avoided and, if and when it cannot be avoided, it can at least be limited. The state of war – the fear, expectation, and preparation for war – can be overcome by wise, co-operative policies amongst states.[23]

The adversary, in the Nehruvian view, therefore is not a permanent one. War arises from misperceptions and ideological systems that colour the attitudes of states and societies and spread fear

---

[20] For this kind of view of military and economic power, see Karnad, 'Introduction', p. 2; Chellaney, 'Challenges to India's National Security', pp. 529–34.

[21] Krishna, 'India and International Order', pp. 270–71 on Nehru's use of the term 'anarchy' in the context of international relations. On the pursuit of national interest and the necessity of defence, see Nehru, *India's Foreign Policy*, pp. 45–46.

[22] Here Nehru is echoing the UNESCO Constitution, which begins with the sentence: 'That since wars begin in the minds of men, it is in the minds of men that the defences of peace must be constructed'. See UNESCO Constitution, UNESCO.org. Available at http://portal.unesco.org/en/ev.php-URL_ID=15244&URL_DO=DO_TOPIC&URL_SECTION=201.html, accessed on September 1, 2013.

[23] Nehru, 'Future Taking Shape', in *India's Foreign Policy*, pp. 1–3. This was the historic March 6, 1946 radio broadcast by Nehru on the occasion of the institution of an Interim Government leading up to Indian independence.

and hatred. The adversary either does not comprehend India or is misled about Indian goals and methods. Its leadership may be at fault. Ordinary citizens may support their governments out of ignorance or illusion created by government propaganda. The adversary therefore can become a friend – by means of greater communication and contact with India and Indians, in various informal and formal, inter-state and transnational settings.[24]

Neoliberals, too, admit that war is a possibility between sovereign states. However, it is not the only inherent condition in the international system. Given that societies have different comparative advantages and that there is a global division of labour, states cannot escape the logic of interdependence.[25] Interdependence makes for more pragmatic policies internationally. In their external relations, states worry not just about war but also about trade, investment and technology.[26]

In the Neoliberal imaginary, therefore, adversarial relations are produced by two factors. First, like Nehruvians, Neoliberals hold misunderstanding and miscalculation as being responsible for conflict. If governments and peoples were more clear-headed and weighed up the costs and benefits of alternative courses of action properly, they would see that rivalry and violence are irrational and that the benefits of economic relations untrammelled by quarrels over territory are far greater than anything that may be gained from conflict. Second, military confrontation is fundamentally an old-fashioned condition which cannot be sustained as economic globalisation goes forward. India itself is guilty of seeing its relations with various countries in the old geo-political way because it has not understood the logic and power of globalisation.[27] The adversary,

---

[24] See Muchkund Dubey, 'India's Foreign Policy: Aims and Strategies', in Nancy Jetly, ed., *India's Foreign Policy: Challenges and Prospects* (New Delhi: Vikas, 1999), pp. 23–25 for this kind of view. Dubey notes that Indian attitudes and policies and Indian misperceptions in turn create the conditions for misunderstanding and fear amongst India's neighbours.

[25] Baru, *National Security*, pp. 13–14.

[26] Sanjaya Baru, 'Economic Diplomacy', *Seminar*, 461 (January 1998), p. 67; Sanjaya Baru, 'The Economic Dimensions of India's Foreign Policy', *World Affairs*, 2, 2 (April–June 1998), pp. 90–91.

[27] For this general approach, see Baru, 'Economic Diplomacy', pp. 66–70, Baru, 'Economic Dimensions', pp. 88–103; Baru, *National Security*, pp. 14–17.

in short, is not a fixed and unchanging entity. All states, seen in the correct perspective, represent opportunities, economic opportunities in particular, as much as they represent danger, if only leaders and elites had the wit and wherewithal to comprehend this.

Hyperrealists offer quite different perspectives about the nature of the adversary. For them, war is a constant possibility in an anarchical system and, while it can be destructive and painful, it is also the basis for a state's autonomy and security. War is not therefore an aberration, as Nehruvians and Neoliberals think, but rather a natural tendency of international relations, every bit as likely in the future as in the past. Preparing for war is therefore not warmongering; it is responsible and wise statecraft. War comes when rival states calculate that the other side is either getting too powerful or is weakening.[28]

In the Hyperrealist view, the international system is a lonely place. States have no permanent friends: anyone can be an adversary. The adversary, as much as India, must prepare for war in the service of its interests and survival. Other things being equal, neighbouring states are more likely to be adversaries: conflicts over territory, status, and power are ever-present possibilities in intimate relationships. No amount of communication and contact or economic interaction will transform the relationship because international relations is zero-sum. Only a balance of power can regulate relations with nearby or distant rivals.[29]

THE ROLE OF FORCE

According to Nehruvians, it is communication and contact between governments and peoples rather than force that will end conflict and make India more secure. International organisations and inter-state negotiations are ways of institutionalising communication and contact. The threat or use of force, particularly in a coercive, offensive

---

See also K. Subrahmanyam, 'Asia's Security Concerns in the 21st Century', in Jasjit Singh, ed., *Asian Security Concerns in the 21st Century* (New Delhi: Knowledge World, 1999), p. 12 on globalisation, interdependence and war avoidance.

[28] On the importance of national power or strength, see Brahma Chellaney, 'Preface', in Chellaney, ed., *Securing India's Future in the New Millennium*, p. xviii.

[29] Chellaney, 'Challenges to India's National Security', p. 558.

way, is counterproductive and will generally be reciprocated by the adversary, leaving the basic quarrel unchanged. Both parties can only be weakened and harmed by a relationship built on force. All issues, in the end, are negotiable. India must dispose of enough force to defend itself, but it should not have so much that it makes others fearful. Certainly, force must be absolutely the last resort, even if it is used coercively.[30]

For Neoliberals, force is an outmoded and blunt instrument unsuited to the new world order. States must have enough force to defend themselves, but it is economic power and the capacity to innovate in a global economy that eventually makes societies secure. Force in the service of expansionism is irrelevant. Territorial conquest and control, in a world where capital, information, and even skills flow across national boundaries, is anachronistic. States must be attentive to defence needs, but on the whole India's economic growth and modernisation and its integration into a globalised world economy is its greatest source of strength.[31] India would do better to use its increasing economic power as a way of influencing others than to use force in such a role.[32]

Force, in the Hyperrealist view, is an indispensable instrument in international relations. It is the only means by which states can truly achieve their ends against rivals. States must accept that violence may be necessary in the national interest. Force may be deployed purely defensively, but the best defense is often offense. It may even save lives on both sides. Control of territory is not old fashioned but rather militarily imperative, especially in conflicts with neighbours. In the end, force may have to be used to destroy the adversary's military formations and to control or wrest contested territory. No political or military leadership can responsibly avoid planning for the coercive use of force. Only 'idealists' of various stripes –

---

[30] Nehru, *India's Foreign Policy*, pp. 35, 45–46.

[31] C. Raja Mohan's 'Trade as Strategy', makes the point that integrating with the global economy not only brings prosperity but also status and influence, a point that India should learn from China.

[32] Baru, 'Economic Diplomacy', p. 67 notes that 'economic policy can itself be an instrument of foreign policy if it enables a country to win friends and influence people'.

Nehruvians or Neoliberals – could fool themselves into thinking that a more aggressive posture is always bad.[33]

DEALING WITH PAKISTAN, CHINA AND THE UNITED STATES

What are the implications of these arguments for India's posture towards its greatest grand strategic challenges, namely, Pakistan, China and the United States? I have dealt with this in detail in my earlier articles.[34] Table 4.1 summarises the views of the three schools.

The table requires some explication and commentary. First of all, there are differences but also similarities amongst the three schools. Nehruvians and Neoliberals are far more dovish about Pakistan and China than are Hyperrealists, though for different reasons. Nehruvians see both neighbours as fellow developing countries, as culturally akin, and as victims of imperialism. Neoliberals are less dovish than Nehruvians, but more 'pragmatic' than Hyperrealists because they believe in the power of economics to bring states closer and because they argue that with globalisation the imperatives to co-operate for material gain will eventually trump traditional quarrels over territory and identity. Nehruvians and Hyperrealists share a suspicion of the US, but all three schools recognise that the US must be engaged for the foreseeable future.

Second, only the Nehruvians have much faith in a dogged programme of diplomatic negotiations and treaty-making as a way of regulating relations with India's adversaries. Neoliberals believe that economics will flatten out differences and that diplomacy is little more than a rationalisation of what is more or less inescapable materially. Hyperrealists think that the *ultima ratio* of international relations is military power. Similarly, only the Nehruvians set any store by non-alignment. Neither Neoliberals nor Hyperrealists have much interest in India's traditional relationship with developing countries, except in a strictly tactical sense, that is, in terms of countering China's influence with them, getting their support for India's UN aspirations, and exploiting them for their resources.

---

[33] See Chellaney, 'Challenges to India's National Security', p. 536 on why India needs to adopt a more 'punitive', less 'reactive' posture vis-à-vis Pakistan.

[34] See Bajpai, 'Indian Strategic Culture', pp. 245–303.

Table 4.1: Views of the Three Schools of Thought

Schools of thought	Strategy towards Pakistan	Strategy towards China	Strategy towards the US
Nehruvianism	• Bilateral negotiation and compromise to settle disputes • Treaties and agreements • Trade, tourism, people to people engagement • Defensive posture militarily; minimum nuclear deterrence; CBMs and other agreements on military force • Non-alignment to keep the great powers out of the region	• Bilateral negotiation and compromise to settle disputes • Treaties and agreements • Trade, tourism, people to people engagement • Defensive posture militarily; minimum nuclear deterrence; CBMs and other agreements on military force • Non-alignment to limit antagonism with China • Co-operation with China in Asian affairs; India–Russia–China; Asia for Asians • Joint resistance against the US diplomatically and politically	• Resistance to US hegemony and imperialism • Non-alignment and solidarity with developing countries in multilateral forums • Co-operation with other great and secondary powers against US dominance (IBSA; China and Russia) • Bridging role between US and other great powers; avoid polarisation in international system • Persuade the US to change its policies: don't give up on the US
Neoliberalism	• Nehruvianism is ineffective and inflexible. Trade and other economic instruments and agreements are the key in tying Pakistan into co-operation • Non-alignment is meaningless in a unipolar, globalised world • Great powers should be brought into the region on India's side, particularly the US	• Nehruvianism is ineffective and inflexible. • Trade and economics is the key • Military power sufficient to deter China • Non-alignment is meaningless • Co-operation with China in Asia is likely to be temporary and infructuous except in economics. China is going to move into the Indian Ocean area militarily and into South Asia politically • India–Russia–China as a front against the US: each power has more in common with the US • The US must stay in Asia as offshore balancer and work with India on Indian Ocean security	• Nehruvianism is futile and wrong. • The US and the West are strategically, politically, and culturally India's partners • Embrace a partnership with the US to balance China, and to access trade, investment, technology, military hardware, and emerging technologies

Hyperrealism	• Nehruvianism is wrong. Pakistan will only come to terms when India is militarily overwhelming. Liberals are wrong too. Trade and economics will not bring Pakistan round • Non-alignment is a strategy of the weak. India has to be strong militarily and deny the region to the great powers • Militarily, India should be aggressive and retaliate against sub-conventional warfare by taking the fight to Pakistan	• Liberals are right about Chinese intentions and moves. Nehruvians are wrong • In the short term, India could ally with the US. The US will eventually leave Asia • India has to build conventional and nuclear forces sufficient to deter China • India should build relations with Japan, South Korea, Taiwan, Vietnam to counter China	• All partnerships with the developing world are futile. They don't add anything to Indian power. In fact, they are a liability • US is not a reliable partner and is potentially a threat to India's rise in the long run • India must be an autonomous centre of power, with the full range of military capabilities, including nuclear capabilities, sufficient to deal with threats from Pakistan, China, and the US

Source: Prepared by the author.

Third, all three schools believe that India needs military force including nuclear weapons to ensure its defence. Nehruvians are the most defensive minded, partly with an eye to affordability and internal economy. Neoliberals cast an eye on a rising China and worry that without sophisticated arms from the US and Russia, India will not be able to handle China. They are, therefore, far more enthusiastic about arms purchases from the US, in particular, which has the most advanced systems in the world. Hyperrealists have the most ambitious view of India's force requirements. They would purchase from wherever necessary and dramatically increase domestic capabilities for arms production as well. While Nehruvians and Neoliberals would build a minimum deterrent (100 warheads or less), Hyperrealists think that India should match China and have the full range of nuclear weapons, from tactical to thermonuclear. Nehruvians and Neoliberals regard nuclear warfighting as implausible, but Hyperrealists believe that warfighting is feasible.[35]

Fourth, it is possible to 'reconcile' these divergent strategic views, in a manner of speaking. Thus, when India is relatively weak, Nehruvianism is an appealing posture and might win the grudging approval of Neoliberals and Hyperrealists. As India grows in strength, particularly economic strength, a Neoliberal phase might be attractive and garner support across the Indian strategic community. In an economically strong India, which has risen to third place in the world economy, opinion might well favour a more assertive, Hyperrealist stance.

Marxist, Hindutva, and Gandhian Grand Strategic Thinking

While Nehruvianism, Neoliberalism and Hyperrealism dominate strategic thinking in contemporary India, historically there were alternatives, specifically, Marxism, Hindutva and Gandhianism. These three schools, in the loose sense that the term 'schools' has been used here, have had their 'prophet voices' and adherents, and the first two in particular have had the backing of political parties, namely, the communist parties of India – the Communist Party of India (CPI) and the CPI (Marxist), that is, CPI(M) – and the Bharatiya

---

[35] I have dealt with the differences on nuclear weapons in my article 'Indian Strategic Culture', pp. 245–303.

Janata Party (BJP), respectively. Gandhianism, almost by definition, has not had a party that stands behind its values – Gandhi disdained the idea that his thought would be frozen into a programme for all time and that it would give rise to a political party – but it has had support amongst members of the Congress Party, at least until the 1960s, and in Vinoba Bhave and Jayaprakash Narayan it had two famous public figures after independence who extolled its ideals.

This section sets out the Marxist, Hindutva, and Gandhian view of the nature of international life, the nature of the adversary, and the role of force. What I present here is a first and rather preliminary cut at understanding these alternative grand strategic perspectives. A much more thorough reading of key sources will be required, in particular of Marxist and Hindutva writings, to do the two perspectives greater justice. The corpus of contemporary Gandhian writings on international life and India's external relations is small, but even here more research is required.

THE NATURE OF INTERNATIONAL LIFE

Indian Marxism, Hindutva, and Gandhianism, while quite disparate in their political values and practices, do share some meta-dispositions about the nature of international life. Most strikingly, all three regard the nation-state as a historically contingent form of political organisation. While all three accept that, at this stage in history, the nation–state is the dominant form of political organisation, none of them regard it as the final and exclusive expression of political loyalty and activity. For Marxists, there is, above all, class. Humans exist in classes, and it is the relationship amongst classes that is the dynamic mover and shaper of history. For proponents of political Hinduism, humans live their lives primarily in civilisations which are the bearers of culture, and the most important relationships are between civilisations. For Gandhians, the individual conscience is more important than the nation-state or any other human collective.

All three schools of thought accept that the international system comprises nation-states, that nationalism is more or less inescapable and, more positively, that it constitutes a form of human emancipation. At the same time, all three remain profoundly ambivalent towards nationalism and the nation-state. Marxism has famously had its tensions with nationalism. Indian Marxist thought accepts the existence and importance of nationalism, but at the centre of its politics is the existence of class and class struggle. Thus, the nation-state and the international system are superstructural and in the end determined by class relations in the base. Relations between states are a function of class relations and, in the long run, as socialism and then communism are achieved, nation-states as well as the international system would become largely irrelevant if they are not abolished altogether. The essential relationships would be between capital and labour, leading to revolution, the dictatorship of the proletariat, and, finally, a classless society, in one country after another until communism holds sway all over the world. How the world would be organised in a classless future, according to Marxists, is unknown, since humanity will have undergone such profound change that it is impossible to say what form collective life will take in a global communist future. Broadly, Indian Marxists accepted the Stalinist argument that socialism and communism would have to be consolidated in the Soviet Union and thence spread in stages to the rest of the world: put more abstractly, the struggle between the working class and bourgeoisie is a national one first and foremost.[36] In this sense, Marxists accepted the interim reality of nation-states even as socialism and communism advanced. In the interim, the usual imperatives and practices of international relations would subsist – the competition between states, the insistence on sovereignty, the possibility of war, and the necessity of national armies.

Hindutva also regards nationalism and the nation-state with a degree of ambivalence, though perhaps with a less jaundiced eye than either Marxism or Gandhianism. For political Hinduism, civilisations matter.[37] The relationships between civilisations are primary. Civilisations are in competition, and historically are marked by rise and fall. India is a civilisation-state in that an entire cultural and social world developed and found its highest expression within the boundaries roughly of the modern Indian state. Hindutva

---

[36] On this see, see Prakash Karat, *Politics and Policies: A Marxist Perspective* (Hyderabad: Prajashakti Book House, 2008), p. 295. Karat is General Secretary of the leading Communist Party in India, the CPI(M).

[37] I draw here on the section on Hindutva in my chapter, 'Indian Conceptions of Order and Justice: Nehruvian, Gandhian, Hindutva, and Neo-liberal', in Rosemary Foot, John Lewis Gaddis and Andrew Hurrell, eds, *Order and Justice in International Relations* (Oxford: Oxford University Press, 2003), pp. 236–61.

proponents see Hindu civilisation as having had a great past but as having fallen on hard times, when Hindus fell out amongst themselves and were overwhelmed by other more aggressive civilisations, first Islam and then Western Christianity. States are the repositories and agents of civilisations, and to that extent Hindutva is quite comfortable with a Westphalian international system of nation-states: states uphold and promote their civilisations. Nationalism and the nation-state might therefore be coterminous with civilisations, but not necessarily so. In the end, though, it is civilisations that shape and move history. Hindu civilisation, being superior to others, will eventually lead the world – not through the force of arms but rather through its powers of attraction. Other civilisations will come to acknowledge that Hindu civilisation has answered the most profound questions about human existence and has constructed an order that regulates human relationships better than any other. At that point, India and Indian civilisation will come to dominate the world. In the meantime, in a world of nation-states, India, as the defender of Hindu civilisation, must play the game of international relations adeptly, even ruthlessly.

The Gandhian view of nationalism and nation-states is also quite ambivalent. While Gandhi himself led the nationalist movement and certainly affirmed the necessity of independence from British rule, he saw nationalism and the nation-state embedded within a much larger set of relationships. At the centre of the Gandhian worldview is the individual and his conscience.[38] The individual's values and behaviour are the key to ordering human relationships. Individuals live in families and beyond that in communities, especially small, face-to-face communities such as villages and urban localities, which in turn are embedded in nation-states. States in turn are parts of regions and continents and, in the end, an international system of states. The individual has obligations to each of these collectives, and each of these has obligations to the individual. Individuals must abide by the norms and rules of families, communities, nation-states, and international order until and unless they come into conflict with individual conscience. Truth and non-violence must guide conscience, and it is an individual's right and responsibility to abide by the dictates finally of her conscience, not the norms and rules of the

---

[38] Bajpai, 'Indian Conceptions of Order and Justice', pp. 236–61.

collective. The primacy accorded nationalism and the nation-state that characterises Nehruvianism, Neoliberalism and Hyperrealism are not to be found in Gandhian thought. Gandhians accept that there is a world of nation-states and that in such a world there is contention, violence, and organised force. However, this is only part of human reality and ultimately may be a transitory part, as small, face-to-face communities living a simple, self-reliant life become the true units of human existence, with states and governments being mere formal entities that enclose and protect these small, simple communities.

THE NATURE OF THE ADVERSARY AND THREATS TO SECURITY

If these are the basic views of nationalism and the nation-state held by Marxists, Hindutva proponents, and Gandhians, who are India's adversaries and what are the threats to India?

For Marxists, the primary threat is imperialism. In a capitalist world, where the class structure privileges the bourgeoisie or middle class, the major capitalist states stand at the top of an imperial system. They constitute the agents of capitalism. The leading capitalist state is of course the US, and therefore for Marxists, India's greatest threat is the US. India is embedded in global capitalism which is a transnational system of production and exchange. The primary agent of capitalism is the US. If the conditions of the Indian working class and peasantry are to be improved and if eventually there is to be socialism and communism in India, it can only be if the forces of global capitalism are held at bay.[39] This means limiting the influence and power of the United States. With the end of the Cold War, and the spread of globalisation, Marxists regard the US as an even greater threat than before. During the Cold War, the Soviet Union served as a check against American power and as a bulwark for 'progressive' forces. With the demise of the Soviet Union, in a unipolar world, the threat of US imperialism has been magnified. Marxists see global capitalism, aided and abetted by the US state, as attempting to penetrate the Indian market and influence its internal economic, political, social, and even cultural structures. The US is

---

[39] See, for instance, Karat, *Politics and Policies*, pp. 289–97.

not a military threat to India precisely because, in an open society such as India, the Americans have an array of other means by which to determine the course of Indian decision-making. Elsewhere, in societies which are not so open, the US is prone to use force to get its way – most recently, in Afghanistan and Iraq.[40]

Marxists regard the threat to India from the US as being magnified by internal forces in India that are complicit with the great imperialist. Thus, the ruling class and bourgeoisie are entangled with global capitalism materially as well as culturally and serve the interests of capitalism.[41] In effect, therefore, they are disposed to furthering the interests of the US. Having said this, Marxists do not give up altogether on the Indian ruling class and bourgeoisie. This class can be used to further progressive causes in India and to resist the US abroad.[42] In the end though, it is only the working class that can bring about socialism. The Indian ruling class and bourgeoisie will tend to be a 'comprador' class, serving the interests of global capitalism. For Marxists, the Congress Party and Bharatiya Janata Party (BJP), pre-eminently the parties of the upper and middle classes, are not very different in this regard. The Congress, which once had progressive and nationalist credentials, gradually succumbed to the influence of landed interests and of Indian and foreign capital. The BJP was always, even in its Jan Sangh incarnation, a communal and petty bourgeois party which inclined towards global capital and the US.[43]

Hindutva proponents see the threats to India in terms of three civilisational rivals: the Christian West, the Muslim world, and China.[44] Since the main theoreticians of Hindutva wrote during the colonial period, it may have been politic for them not to identify the West and Western states too prominently as civilisational competitors. However, in the 1990s, there was more explicit reference

---

[40] Karat, *Politics and Policies*, pp. 329–34 on the US' war on terrorism and its interventions in Afghanistan and Iraq.

[41] Ibid., pp. 295–96.

[42] Ibid., p. 298.

[43] Ibid., p. 145 on the Jan Sangh/BJP's attraction to the US.

[44] M. S. Golwalker, *We or Our Nationhood Defined* (Nagpur: Bharat Publications, 1939), pp. 2–3. Golwalker was the second head of the RSS, the right-wing Hindu organisation, from the mid-1950s to the early 1970s, and influenced many of the senior leaders of the Bharatiya Janata Party (BJP).

to Christian civilisation and Western states, in particular the United States, as being a threat to India, perhaps as a greater threat than 'Muslim' Pakistan and China and Chinese civilisation.

While Hindutva proponents refer to civilisational competition and strife, their worries do not seem to be exclusively cultural, at least in respect of Islam and China. In the Hindutva imagination, the threat to India is not only from the values and practices of Islam and China as civilisational entities as it is from the ambitions and machinations of the Pakistani and Chinese states. For the first generation of Hindutva proponents, Pakistan was perhaps the greatest threat to India, with China in second place.[45] By the 1990s, with the coming of globalisation and spread of ideas, investments, and goods from the West, particularly the US, America and the West came to be viewed as perhaps the greater long-term threats.[46]

For Hindutva writers, civilisations or civilisation states are seen as both external adversaries and internal, 'fifth column' enemies. Thus, in the Hindutva telling of Indian history, Islamic armies conquered India in large part by exploiting the differences amongst Hindus. Force and religious conversion helped maintain Muslim hegemony. The material and psychological weakness of Hindus, over hundreds of years of Muslim rule, ensured Islamic rule in India. The coming of British and Western civilisation promised to liberate Hindus from the thrall of Muslim rule, and to this extent the first generation of Hindutva proponents are more positive about the Christian West. As Hindus gradually overcame their lack of confidence, they emancipated themselves from Muslim power. After independence, Muslim Pakistan came to pose an external threat but also an internal one in the sense that, in collusion with Indian Muslims, it worked

---

[45] See M.S. Golwalker, *Bunch of Thoughts*, 3rd edition (Bangalore: Sahitya Sindhu Prakashana, 1996), pp. 289–91 and p. 277 on China and Pakistan, respectively.

[46] On the contemporary period, see the Hindutva-inspired writings of Tarun Vijay, *India Battles to Win* (New Delhi: Rupa, 2009), pp. 205–207, 214–15, 230 where he speaks in rather affectionate tones about China and Pakistan, alluding to civilisational regard between India and China and to an admiration of Indian culture amongst ordinary Pakistanis. He says nothing comparable about the US. Vijay was Editor of the RSS newspaper, *Organiser*, and a frequent television commentator representing the political Right.

to weaken India from within.⁴⁷ Indian secularists, led by Nehru and the Congress Party, by pandering to the Muslims and other minorities and by emphasising differences among Hindus along caste lines, played into the hands of Pakistan.

China appeared as a threat, in the Hindutva imagination, in the early 1960s, in the context of the 1962 war, as an expansionist, ruthless, communist power, bent on conquering Indian lands. Like Pakistan, which uses Indian Muslims as a fifth column, China too is seen as working through internal collaborators, particularly Indian communists and various socialist sympathisers, to advance its interests. Here again, for Hindutva proponents, it is Nehru and the Congress Party, in its apparent gullibility and weakness, and impervious to the ambitions of a powerful and shrewd adversary, that fails to protect Indian interests. With their talk of peace and non-alignment, they fail to see China's cold-blooded plan to humiliate India and to take disputed territory by force.⁴⁸

The Hindutva view of the West has always been ambivalent. On the one hand, the West, along with Islam, conquered India and subjugated Hindus. On the other hand, Western colonialism, particularly British, delivered Hindus from Muslim rule and opened up opportunities for the Hindu majority.⁴⁹ After independence, this ambivalence continued. The West, led by the US, was a potential ally against Pakistan and China. At the same time, for the better part of the Cold War, the US was allied to Pakistan and towards the end of the rivalry with the Soviet Union, was allied to China as well. Here again, it was Nehru and the Congress Party, with their insistence on non-alignment, that failed to build a strong relationship with the US and other Western states. After the Cold War, as the West insisted on the opening of markets and the universalisation of rules of international behaviour and as they crusaded on human rights and non-proliferation, Hindutva commentators began to see the Western powers as posing an economic, cultural, diplomatic, and security threat to India. The fifth column now was Indian

---

⁴⁷ For this argument, see Golwalker, *Bunch of Thoughts*, pp. 298–99.

⁴⁸ Vijay, *India Battles to Win*, p. 210 on how Nehru failed to comprehend the seriousness of China's position on the border quarrel.

⁴⁹ See Golwalker, *Bunch of Thoughts*, on the role of British colonialism in releasing Hindus from Muslim domination.

Christians and Christian missionaries working amongst India's poor and marginalised to convert them and to sow disaffection against the Indian state.[50]

For Gandhians, the greatest threat to India is modernity in the form of industrial civilisation. Industrial civilisation both in its material form and in its dominant values threatens traditional Indian ways of life. It is also hostile to the ideal India that Gandhians would like to build in the future, an India in which the individual lives in balance with family, community, nation, and the world. Industrial civilisation may enrich humans materially, but it is not sustainable on a global scale, and in any case engenders inequalities. More importantly, it impoverishes human relationships and demeans the individual and by extension, collective life. For Gandhians, there is little hope of achieving the ideal society in which truth and non-violence reign in a world in thrall to industrial civilisation. The Western states invented and maintain industrial civilisation, and so they are the greatest threats to traditional and ideal India. Gandhians are not xenophobic and are not anti-western per se – the West was not always an industrial civilisation and historically gave the world many gifts as well; but they are firmly opposed to modern Western civilisation *qua* industrial civilisation. This Western culture, with its emphasis on acquisitiveness, consumerism, and material plenty, is inimical to the simple, robust, egalitarian life that Gandhians extol in which humans live extremely frugally and in which small, intimate communities marked by equality and reciprocity are the norm. Industrial civilisation must therefore be dismantled, and Western societies must change.[51]

For Gandhians, as for Marxists and proponents of political Hinduism, India is threatened as much by its own people as by outsiders. While Gandhians do not look for scapegoats and fifth columns, they do see a form of collusion with external forces. In the Gandhian view, Indians, particularly upper and middle-class Indians, have drifted away from their cultural moorings and acquired the habits and ways of thought of the West. As a result, Indians have

---

[50] For this kind of argument, see Vijay, *India Battles to Win*, pp. 162–63.

[51] On the Gandhian critique of Western modernity and industrialism, see Bhikhu Parekh, *Gandhi: A Very Short Introduction* (Oxford: Oxford University Press, 2001), pp. 78–91.

fallen into the modernity trap, and in this sense are responsible for their own condition. Traditional Indian values and practices are not all good, but modern Indians are in danger from an even bigger danger, namely, industrialism and westernism. If Indians seek to build a modern industrial life on the scale of the West, they will be doomed if they are not enslaved. Independence will be a formal, legal fiction, little else. As a result of colonialism, Indians have become culturally westernised. Collusion arises from cultural and ideological domination, from a deep internalisation of an alien way of life, one that persists even after independence. On this deep structure will be erected political, economic, and social superstructures which will perpetuate an industrial civilisation rather than emancipation.[52]

THE ROLE OF VIOLENCE AND FORCE

If these are the views of Marxists, Hindutva proponents and Gandhians on the basic image of international life and the threats to India, what is their attitude to the role of force and violence in human affairs and international affairs more specifically? Since strategic thinking, including grand strategic thinking, is concerned with the use of force (amongst other resources), it is important to ask how a putative Marxist, Hindutva, or Gandhian grand strategic approach treats the issue of organised violence. Broadly, we will see that they vary in their views of violence and organised violence in particular, with Gandhians being the most hostile, but in the end all three accept that there is a place for violence.

For Marxists, social life is deeply marked by violence – of the ruling classes over the more subaltern. Given the dominance of the ruling class and its proclivity to use violence to maintain its position, only violence by the revolutionary forces led by the working class can dislodge the ruling class. Violence is not the only resource that revolutionary groups will deploy, but there will be moments when it is inescapable. If so, we can see that Indian Marxists are not averse to violence in international life. Countries will have armed forces and must be able to defend themselves. India too must have armed forces and be prepared to defend itself against imperial forces as well enemies closer to home. Marxists are concerned about the drag

---

[52] See Judith M. Brown, ed., *Mahatma Gandhi: The Essential Writings* (Oxford: Oxford University Press, 2008), pp. 67–87 for his general critique of Westernism and industrial civilisation.

on development by excessive defence spending, but they are not intrinsically opposed to India having an adequate defence.[53]

Hindutva proponents are even more acceptant of the use of organised violence. In their worldview, the more powerful civilisations and states will always use whatever means at their disposal, including violence, to maintain their position in the world. This is the lesson that they draw from their reading of civilisational histories including India's. India, in this view, was subjugated by force of arms by Muslims and then Western colonial powers. Hindutva commentators excoriate Indians, beginning with Gandhi, who believe in non-violence. Nor is their attitude to violence one of restraint. Violence has to be used to achieve complete victory over an opponent. In addition, violence can be emancipatory: for a people that has long been subjugated and lost its élan, violence might be therapeutic. Thus, independent India must have armed forces, and it must be prepared to use them in whatever way necessary.[54]

Gandhians, on the face of it, differ from Marxists and Hindutva proponents quite considerably in their deep opposition to violence. Violence is abhorrent to them, and Gandhi himself went to great lengths to defend the practice of non-violence, arguing that non-violent resisters could even face regular armies should they choose to attack India. Gandhi suggested that while the loss of human life would be considerable on the part of the defenders, the attackers would eventually sicken of harming unarmed adversaries and would stop their aggression.[55] If so, India did not require a regular army. In any case, an India that was organised on Gandhian lines would not be an object of aggression in the first place since it would threaten no one.[56] Having said that, Gandhi and Gandhians accept

---

[53] See Karat, *Politics and Policies*, p. 90 on the patriotic duty of Indians to stand behind the fight in Kargil in 1999 against Pakistani intruders and p. 140 on sensitivity to the costs of (nuclear) weapons in relation to the imperatives of economic development.

[54] Golwalker makes these various propositions about the role and necessity of force. See an analysis of Golwalker in my essay, 'Hinduism and Weapons of Mass Destruction: Pacifist, Prudential, and Political', in Sohail Hashmi, ed., *Ethics and Weapons of Mass Destruction* (New York: Cambridge University Press, 2004), pp. 308–20.

[55] Gandhi's argument is noted in Karnad, *Nuclear Weapons and India's Security*, p. 32.

[56] Parekh, *Gandhi*, p. 103.

that violence is preferable to cowardice. Individuals and nations, in defence of their security and honour, could use violence if they had no other means available to them and if they were not trained in the arts of non-violent resistance. Certainly, to do nothing in one's own defence was unacceptable and the mark of a coward.[57] Having said this, Gandhi himself never quite conceded that India needed an army. He seems to have acquiesced in the dispatch of the Indian army to Kashmir in 1947 to defend the state against armed invaders from the Pakistani side and, in the face of Nehru's insistence that India would require a military after independence, Gandhi did not in the end challenge his protégé outright on the issue.[58] Nevertheless, his faith in non-violent resisters as the armies of the long-term future remained intact.

Dealing with Pakistan, China and the US

How then would or do Indian Marxists, Hindutva proponents and Gandhians see Indian grand strategy? How should India deal with the threats to its independence and security? What is their disposition towards Pakistan, China and the United States?

The primary concern of Indian Marxists is the US, but they do offer thoughts on how India can deal with Pakistan and China as well. With respect to Pakistan, their views are not very different from that of the Nehruvians emphasising military vigilance and preparedness plus bilateral negotiations and agreements leading to a final settlement of disputes. Marxists clearly want India to be in a position to defend itself against Pakistan. However, their attitude towards defence, like that of the Nehruvians, is one of sufficiency. Thus, during the Kargil war, they supported India's effort to oust Pakistani forces from India's side of the Line of Control (LOC), but they opposed Indian forces crossing the LOC to widen the war, warning that escalation would only risk intervention by the international community.[59] Marxists also opposed India's going nuclear, arguing that this overturned India's traditional stance on disarmament and made India more vulnerable to low-intensity conflict. While India should keep the nuclear option open, and while it should refuse to

---

[57] Brown, *Mahatma Gandhi*, pp. 198–200.
[58] Karnad, *Nuclear Weapons and India's Security*, pp. 48–52, 60–61.
[59] Karat, *Politics and Policies*, p. 86.

sign the US-sponsored Comprehensive Test Ban Treaty (CTBT), it should not become a nuclear weapons power.[60]

Marxists want India to deal with Pakistan bilaterally, even if there is no 'immediate positive response', and they oppose internationalisation of the Kashmir dispute in the sense of mediation by outside powers or by the UN.[61] They fear that as India grows closer to the US, New Delhi may wittingly or unwittingly allow the Americans to become involved with Kashmir. When the BJP-led NDA government tested nuclear weapons in 1998 and when it turned to the US for diplomatic help during the Kargil war, the Marxist view was that India was in danger of internationalising its dispute with Pakistan and by extension internationalising the issue of Kashmir. Marxists criticised the NDA government for asking the international community to condemn Pakistan's aggression, to impose sanctions on Islamabad, and to stop Pakistani aid during the war on the grounds that this would bring outside powers into regional disputes.[62]

The Marxist attitude towards China is a fraternal one: the two countries can and should be friends. Marxists regard the border dispute as a legacy of imperialism and support India's traditional stance of a negotiated settlement.[63] Their reading of the relationship is that the two countries have more in common than in conflict. They see China's spectacular rise as an opportunity for India, particularly in trade. India can also learn from China, in terms of the state's role in human development, in promoting high rates of growth, and in regulating the economy. Indian Marxists grant that China faces a number of economic and social challenges as a result of its reforms, but in their view India has a lot to learn from Chinese policies.[64] In addition, in an unequal and imperialistic world, in which the US is determined to remain the hegemon, the two countries are potential partners.[65] Marxists have written very little on how the border conflict can be resolved, on what kind of defence posture India should

---

[60] Karat, *Politics and Policies*, p. 155.

[61] Sitaram Yechury, *Socialism in a Changing World* (Hyderabad: Prajashakti Book House, 2008), p. 18. Yechury is a member of the CPI(M) Politburo and a member of the Indian Parliament.

[62] Karat, *Politics and Policies*, pp. 84–85.

[63] Ibid., p. 352 on the need for a negotiated settlement.

[64] Yechury, *Socialism in a Changing World*, pp. 109–24.

[65] Ibid., pp. 19–20.

have against China (conventional and nuclear), on China's various regional relationships in and around South Asia that might work against Indian interests (for example, in Bangladesh, Burma, Nepal, Sri Lanka, or the Indian Ocean region), or on the Pakistan–China relationship. Taking, as they do, a benign view of Chinese motives and of the need for India to avoid conflict with its giant neighbour, there is little by way of engaging these more contentious issues in the relationship.

It is in respect of the US, the primary threat to global and Indian security, that the Marxist perspective is best revealed. From the premise that the US is the greatest imperial power of the age, Indian Marxists derive a series of prescriptions for India. Fundamentally, India itself and in league with other states and social forces must resist US policies and programmes. The US as the leading agent of globalisation must be opposed whenever and wherever possible. Thus, in confronting economic globalisation, progressive social forces – movements in civil society all over the world, communist and socialist parties, trade unions, amongst others – must collaborate to mount protests and to disseminate critiques of capitalism and the role of the US.[66] At the international level, India must work to cooperate with other developing countries, particularly within the Non-Aligned Movement (NAM), to ensure that there is a check on US power. Specifically, India should organise NAM to champion the cause of free trade without protectionism, of technology transfers to poorer nations, and of debt write-offs.[67] Domestically, India must stop the expansion of global finance capital into its economy. To do this, it must reject the dictates of the International Monetary Fund (IMF) to roll back the state. Marxists argue instead that looking at the role of the Chinese state, India and other developing countries should empower the state to increase its regulatory functions, to control financial flows, particularly speculative capital flows that are 'predatory' and cause great instability.[68] Put differently, India must

---

[66] Yechury, *Socialism in a Changing World*, p. 16.

[67] Ibid., p. 79.

[68] Karat, *Politics and Policies*, pp. 293–99 on the role of global finance capital and the need for further state regulation of the flows of capital. See also Yechury, *Socialism in a Changing World*, pp. 109–14 on the important role of the state in economic development.

be internally resilient in order to confront global capitalism and its agents who seek to exploit and dominate the Indian people.

The US must also be resisted in a variety of other sites. Globalisation is not just an economic phenomenon. It is also the spreading of 'universal' norms and practices in respect of other areas of international life, such as the proliferation of weapons of mass destruction, humanitarian intervention, and human rights and democracy. Marxists view these as being sponsored by the US in the interest of its own political and strategic preferences. They are not therefore universal in the sense of having been concluded collectively by free and sovereign nations. Resistance here must take various forms. The US' insistence on the indefinite extension of the Nuclear Non-Proliferation Treaty (NPT) and the CTBT and its refusal to begin the process of nuclear disarmament must be opposed. At the very least, India must not sign the NPT and CTBT.[69] The USs' championing of humanitarian intervention has to be seen in light of its record of intervention – in Yugoslavia, Iraq and Afghanistan – as serving its interests rather than as a cosmopolitan service to the international system.[70] So also, the US's invitation to India to be part of a 'community of democracies' is a stratagem to legitimise American interference in the affairs of sovereign nations and to draw India into a political and strategic partnership.[71]

In sum, Marxists would urge negotiations and a defensive defence posture with Pakistan, economic emulation and engagement with China, and, above all, economic, diplomatic, and political resistance to the US based on solidarity with other developing countries.

Hindutva proponents today are quite divided in their strategic views. There is an older view that is deeply antagonistic to Pakistan and China, but there is also a more contemporary perspective that

---

[69] See Karat, *Politics and Policies*, pp. 155, 166, 343–52 on India not signing the CTBT and NPT; Yechury, *Socialism in a Changing World*, p. 80 on the CPI(M) opposition to the indefinite extension of the NPT.

[70] Yechury in *Socialism in a Changing World*, p. 81 hints at this when he notes that the US 'had hijacked the United Nations for its blatant interference in the internal affairs of third world countries'.

[71] See Karat, *Politics and Policies*, pp. 133–36 on how the US-sponsored 'community of democracies' serves US interests and promotes American interference in other countries' affairs. See also p. 128 on how the US is using the idea to 'co-opt' countries into an association under American leadership.

sees the US with great suspicion and regards Pakistan and China as rivals who can be brought around.[72]

In the case of earlier Hindutva perspectives, Muslim Pakistan and Sinic China are seen as more or less unremitting rivals.[73] To deal with them, India must be strong, particularly militarily, and in the case of Pakistan, must be willing to take the fight to the opponent.[74] If necessary, India should undermine its enemies from within.[75] In any case, it should aim not just for defence but instead for more or less total victory over Pakistan and China.[76] For older Hindutva proponents, India needs to shed its timidity and to become a more muscular society, willing to use force when warranted, with both domestic and external enemies. In short, India needs to change psychologically and be more calculative and assertive.[77]

More contemporary Hindutva proponents take a rather different view. For them, Pakistan and China are tractable, if only India is astute enough to deal with them. The US on the other hand is a domineering power that is not to be trusted. At bottom, these kinds of Hindutva proponents argue a civilisational case. Pakistan and China are seen as having been influenced by, and admiring of, India civilisationally; the US is not.

According to the more contemporary Hindutva group, Pakistan and China have hurt India by promoting subversion internally and by holding Indian territory. They are rivals, and war is not impossible. But their people are well disposed towards India. It is the army and elites of Pakistan and the Communist Party and military in China that are antagonistic to India and that stir up anti-Indian feelings. Ordinary Pakistanis and Chinese are being misled about India but admire Indian civilisation. The Chinese are fascinated even now by Buddhism and Indian popular culture.[78]

---

[72] Swapan Dasgupta, the conservative-minded journalist who is widely regarded as being sympathetic to the BJP and Hindutva view, can be taken as an example of those who are deeply suspicious of Pakistan and China.

[73] Golwalker, *Bunch of Thoughts*, pp. 289–91, on China, and pp. 277, 298–99, 300 on Pakistan.

[74] Ibid., pp. 302, 316–17, 325.

[75] Ibid., pp. 319–22.

[76] Ibid., pp. 303, 325, 341.

[77] Ibid., pp. 262, 271, 277.

[78] Vijay, *India Battles to Win*, pp. 206, 214–16, 253–57.

Relations with these two countries have not been helped by India's tendency to accept US ideas and analyses. India must therefore look at Pakistan and China with Indian and not American eyes.[79] The US has been mischievous in other ways. It has interfered in Pakistan and spoiled its politics. India has a stake in Pakistani democracy, but religious extremism, the military, and the US have not allowed democracy to flourish there.[80] Contemporary Hindutva proponents are particularly positive about China. India's views of China are coloured by the US government and media. Indians need a cold-eyed but not unkindly look at their great northern neighbour. China is 'a threat, but China is also a great friend'.[81] With China, unlike Pakistan, India has only had to fight once.[82] Contemporary China is an economic and military power, and this is a threat to India. In dealing with China, India must be prepared to deal with differences 'firmly but calmly'.[83] It must become an economic and military power in turn if it is to stand up to China. For all its growing power, China has internal weaknesses. India's strength – democracy – is China's weakness. India cannot forsake its strengths to please Beijing. New Delhi should not bow to Chinese pressure on the activities of the Tibetan refugees in India. It must continue to champion the case of Tibetan autonomy within China. New Delhi must also be aware of China's encirclement of India from Pakistan to Southeast Asia. India must break out of this encirclement by maintaining its links with Tibet, cultivating Burma, strengthening its relations with South Asian neighbours, and of course building up its military capabilities.[84] In sum, relations with China can be fraternal based on mutual civilisational respect provided India plays its own hand in dealing with China, refuses to play the US's anti-China game, and cultivates its economic, military, and political strengths.

Contemporary Hindutva proponents have a fairly negative view of the US, as a domineering, interfering power that relentlessly pursues its own interests. Having said this, India's position towards the

---

[79] Vijay, *India Battles to Win*, pp. 204–5, 214, 217–18.
[80] Ibid., pp. 177–80.
[81] Ibid., p. 214.
[82] Ibid.
[83] Ibid., p. 207.
[84] Ibid., p. 235. On the primary importance of building military power, see p. 308.

US should be a fairly neutral one. India should be neither anti- nor pro-US.[85] The US is not a direct military threat and therefore India's policies towards it must be of a different order. India's internal cultural resilience based on the Hindu-ness of Indian society is, for Hindutva proponents, the greatest protection against all threats – internal and external. If India acknowledges its Hindu-ness, it will be internally united and able to resist any hostile powers.

To conclude, contemporary Hindutva proponents argue that India should be internally resilient particularly in a cultural sense, that it should be militarily and economically strong against Pakistan and China but should attempt to use its cultural capital with both to improve relations, and that it should be wary of the US without becoming anti-American.

We can be brief about Gandhian views of India's strategic posture towards Pakistan, China, and the US because there are few if any contemporary writings on India's external relations from this perspective. Essentially, one has to proceed here by extrapolating from the basic arguments of Gandhians about international relations, as sketched in earlier. For Gandhians, the greatest threat to India is from modern industrial civilisation. Clearly, then, of the three powers, it is the US that poses the greatest threat. The US is not a military threat to India, but its propagation of a way of life that is morally corrosive and economically, socially, and physically unsustainable will harm Indians. The US, as it engorges itself materially, will be an imperial power that will threaten the independence of others and will exhaust the planet's resources. Its culture will infect India and other countries and lead them on the path of moral and material collapse. Pakistan and China are not of this culture. They are therefore lesser threats. They are a danger to India's territory, and if they cannot be resisted by means of non-violence, they must be resisted by force of arms. However, India's posture towards them must be purely defensive. The cornerstone of India's approach must be negotiation and principled compromise. Since both Pakistan and China are also in danger from industrial civilisation, they are potential allies of India in resisting the US and other Western powers.

---

[85] Vijay, *India Battles to Win*, p. 210. It captures this rather agnostic view of the US. Interestingly, there is not one approving comment about the US in the entire book. The only exception is Vijay's essay on the election of Barack Obama, pp. 187–89.

The US is not however irredeemable. Unlike the Marxists and Hindutva proponents who draw a hard line in the sand in relation to the US, Gandhians believe that one can convert one's adversary to one's point of view through resistance and persuasion. Thus, Americans can be rid of industrialism if they so choose and draw closer to India and other developing countries.

What can we conclude from this review of three alternative grand strategic orientations? First, while all three are fairly utopian in conceiving of class, civilisation and individual conscience as being the primary units or agents of social and therefore international reality, they accept that in the meantime the existence of nation–states jealous of their territory and sovereignty will exist and that the 'traditional' norms and practices of states will regulate world politics – force, war, diplomacy, balance of power, international law and institutions, and so on. That states will therefore have grand strategies is implicit in this thinking about international life.

Second, in terms of the threats to India, there is variation amongst the three schools, but it is striking that there is convergence on suspicion and fear of the West, particularly the US. Marxists, Hindutva proponents, and Gandhians, for different and sometimes similar reasons see the US and its principal allies as dangers to India. For the Marxists, the US is the principal agent of global capitalism and imperialism that wants to exploit India economically; for Hindutva proponents, it is the strongest power on earth, representing Christian civilisation, and therefore intrinsically alien if not hostile to India and its values and way of life; and for Gandhians, the US is the core of industrial civilisation and of a dead-end modernity that will, if it takes root in India, destroy Indian culture and society.

Third, the three approaches see external forces as combining with internal, Indian groups to undermine India. Thus, Marxists see the US and its allies as well as multinational corporations collaborating with Indian accomplices in government, the media and business to open up the Indian market. Hindutva proponents worry that the West uses Christian missionaries and peddles Christian cultural values through popular culture, academic works and the media to weaken Indian culture. Gandhians worry that industrial civilisational values are being deeply internalised by Indians, that these values embody violence, selfishness and corruption, and that they will hollow India out from within.

Fourth, all three approaches accept that organised violence is a feature of social life and that sometimes violence must be used. Marxists countenance revolutionary violence on the part of the working class against an entrenched and cruel ruling class. Hindutva proponents view violence as justifiable if not positively emancipatory for a repressed and colonised people striving to be free. Gandhians, who are the most opposed to the use of organised violence, concede that violence is preferable to cowardice. Marxists and Hindutva proponents do not oppose states maintaining armies and the use of force to protect people and territory. Gandhians are the most critical of national armies but can comprehend that states will have them until they have trained an army of non-violent resisters.

Fifth, in dealing with the threats to India, the three schools show a striking degree of convergence even if for different reasons. All three are dovish on Pakistan and China even as they recognise the need for a robust defence against aggression. Collaboration and accommodation are possible with both of India's neighbours, and for Marxists and Gandhians in particular, both countries can be allies against the US. While the US is not a military threat, it can and should be resisted, diplomatically, politically and culturally.

Finally, the three approaches are also convergent in respect of a lack of interest in multilateral institutions. There are few, if any, references to the importance of global institution in their writings. For Marxists, the US dominates the international system, and until it does so, multilateral institutions will fundamentally reflect the wishes of American policy makers. In that sense, these institutions are not genuinely multilateral. Hindutva proponents rarely mention global institutions, but one can imagine that their analysis would not be dissimilar. Until India is a part of the UN Security Council as a Permanent Member, it is unlikely that the Hindutva group will be interested in global institutions except to look upon them with suspicion as tools of the powerful. As for Gandhians, they would note Gandhi's scepticism about formal institutions, domestic or international, which represent centralised and large-scale political structures inimical to local self-government and an authentic community life.[86]

---

[86] On Gandhi's scepticism with regard to formal institutions, see Parekh's discussion on Gandhi's attitude to the state (Parekh, *Gandhi*, pp. 99–105). Nalin Anadkat, *International Political Thought of Gandhi, Nehru and Lohia* (New Delhi: Bharatiya Kala Prakashan, 2000), p. 62 notes that for Gandhi

Conclusion

Do the six grand strategic schools described here agree on anything? This survey of grand strategic thinking is suggestive of agreement or convergence, even if for different reasons, on the following:

(*a*) Force and defence: The use of force exists as a norm in the state system, and India must have defence, minimal or otherwise. Only Gandhians oppose a nuclear weapons programme.

(*b*) Defensive defence, minimum nuclear deterrence: Indians are agreed that force should be used defensively and as a last resort and that India's nuclear arsenal should be a minimal one. Hyperrealists are more positive about the use of force and argue for a much bigger nuclear arsenal, and Gandhians are the most opposed to nuclear weapons.

(*c*) Economics and culture matter: Force is not the only means of securing India. Economic and cultural instruments are important. Hyperrealists again are sceptical: in the end, India must be a first-rank military power. Globalisation and market economics are viewed with suspicion, in varying degrees, by everyone except by Neoliberals.

(*d*) Negotiated dispute settlement: Negotiated settlements of disputes are always preferable to the use of force and coercion.

(*e*) International institutions: Multilateral institutions and international institutions in general (including international law) are regarded as being primarily agencies of the most influential powers or as being ineffective, at least in respect of inter-state conflict. Nehruvians historically have disagreed with this view, but today's Nehruvians may not be outside this consensus.

(*f*) Moderation on Pakistan and China: Negotiation and accommodation are the way to deal with Pakistan and China. India should of course be vigilant with respect to both neighbours and defend itself vigorously if attacked. Nehruvians and

---

'customs, conventions, agreements or treaties' were mere 'patchworks for survival'. Gandhi also argued that laws and treaties reflected the wishes of the most powerful and favoured the status quo. Hence, he was not particularly enamoured of the League of Nations or the UN. For this see Anadkat, *International Political Thought*, pp. 73–74.

Marxists see China as a possible friend with no significant quarrels except over the border (which in their view is tractable). Hyperrealists do not agree that Pakistan and China can be dealt with in this way and are particularly wary of a rising China.

(g) Suspicion of the US: There is fear and suspicion of the US, for various reasons. The US should be countered through diplomatic co-operation with other states – the developing countries, middle powers such as South Africa and Brazil, or Russia and China. Yet, engaging and co-operating with the US, where possible, is vital. Even the Marxists recognise this. Neoliberals are the most promotive of a deeper engagement with the US. Only the Hyperrealists are explicit about the possibility of military confrontation with the US. Even they regard this simply as a largely theoretical possibility, in the distant future.

What these points describe is the lowest common denominator of Indian grand strategic thought, what adherents of the various perspectives can more or less agree on. A closer look at the points of agreement suggests that this lowest-common-denominator grand strategy amounts to a prudential, defensive realism.[87] Amongst the six grand strategic approaches, it would seem that Nehruvianism is closest to the consensus described above. Elsewhere, I have suggested that in fact Indian policy over the past decade or more most closely resembles the preferences of the Neoliberals.[88] On the other hand, going by the analysis presented here, at the ideational level there is a greater affinity for Nehruvianism.

Is there a split between the theoreticians of grand strategy and the practitioners? At the very least, we can conclude that if the practice of grand strategy is tilted towards Neoliberalism, it will

---

[87] On the importance of prudence and caution in Indian policy, see Pratap Bhanu Mehta, 'Still Under Nehru's Shadow? The Absence of Foreign Policy Frameworks in India', *India Review*, 8, 3 (July–September, 2009), pp. 209–33 and Srinath Raghavan, *War and Peace in Modern India: A Strategic History of the Nehru Years* (New Delhi: Orient Blackswan, 2010). Raghavan refers to Nehru as a 'liberal realist' (pp. 14–17).

[88] Bajpai, 'Indian Strategic Culture'.

constantly face criticism in India from a strategic community which is suspicious of closeness to the US and of fascination with globalisation and market economics. Neoliberal policies in the long run may not be sustainable, and we should expect course corrections.[89]

---

[89] An influential recent report that has been widely commented upon argues that India must hew to a new form of non-alignment and adopt a measured, balanced approach to the US and China. See Sunil Khilnani, Rajiv Kumar, Pratap Bhanu Mehta, Lt. Gen. (Retd.) Prakash Menon, Nandan Nilekani, Srinath Raghavan, Shyam Saran, and Siddharth Vardarajan, *Non-alignment 2.0: A Foreign and Strategic Policy for India in the Twenty First Century*. A report issued by the Centre for Policy Research, New Delhi. Available at http://www.cprindia.org/workingpapers/3844-nonalignment-20-foreign-and-strategic-policy-india-twenty-first-century, accessed on March 23, 2012. This is suggestive of the course correction noted earlier. Since 2008, there has been a noticeable cooling of relations with the US after the high-point of the nuclear deal. Differences over the deal, policies and approaches to Afghanistan, the treatment of Indian diplomatic personnel and students in the US, the end-user agreement associated with US weapons sales, New Delhi's decision not to shortlist US fighters for its purchase of multi-combat role aircraft (MCRA), India's coolness to the Container Security Initiative (CSI) and other joint military ventures, Indian reluctance to go along with the West on the intervention in Libya and sanctions against Iran – all show that the relationship is beset by a number of points of conflict even though levels of co-operation between the two countries are at an all-time high.

5

NEHRU'S ADVOCACY OF INTERNATIONALISM AND INDIAN FOREIGN POLICY

S. Kalyanaraman

That Jawaharlal Nehru was an internationalist is widely accepted. But the extent to which Nehru's internationalist ideas informed and permeated the foreign policy that he crafted and practised has not been hitherto fully explored. This chapter highlights the internationalist aspect of Nehru's worldview, so as to enable a more comprehensive understanding of Nehru the statesman. Nehru's was, however, not a lone view. Internationalism was, in fact, an integral element of the Indian National Congress' expression of nationalism during the struggle for freedom. Thus, a better understanding of Nehru the statesman also contributes to a greater appreciation of the ideas that shaped and continue to shape India's approach to international affairs.

The chapter's schema is as follows. After providing an overview of Nehru's internationalist foreign policy framework, the first section discusses the origins of Indian internationalism as an integral element of the expression of Indian nationalism from the 1920s. The second section focuses on the dilemma that Indian nationalists faced in terms of reconciling their demand for independence from British imperialism with the internationalist responsibility of opposing Nazism, fascism and militarism and how they sought to reconcile the two particularly in the Quit India Resolution. Section three discusses the pre-independence Indian views on pan-Asianism and Asian unity, which were not only an outcome of opposition to Western colonialism but were also impelled by internationalist aspirations. Section four parses select speeches of Nehru in the run-up to and after independence to demonstrate the internationalist framework that guided Indian foreign policy during the Nehru years. The chapter concludes by highlighting the importance of India continuing to promote international interests even as it sagaciously caters to its security interests.

An Overview of Nehru's Foreign Policy Framework

The essence of internationalism lies in three propositions. One, the world is becoming globalised through economic processes and by the growth of communications. Two, this economic globalisation finds a reflection in political processes in terms of greater interaction and collaboration both between governments and between civil society groups. And three, these processes ought to be encouraged because they promote the 'international interest' in terms of greater understanding, prosperity, peace, freedom, and so on and so forth.[1]

Nehru subscribed to these internationalist propositions. An early indication came in a letter to his daughter Indira, in August 1933, in which he observed that the world had been moving 'towards greater interdependence between nations, a greater internationalism', that 'an enormous and intricate structure of international relations and trade' had developed and that, as a result, the world had become 'one single inseparable whole' with each of its parts influencing others and in turn being influenced by others.[2] From the perspective of the series of letters he had written on world history, he went on to note:

> [I]t is quite impossible now to have a separate history of nations. We have outgrown that stage, and only a single world history, connecting the different threads from all the nations, and seeking to find the real forces that move them, can now be written with any useful purpose.[3]

Flowing from this perspective, Nehru, in subsequent years, repeatedly articulated the aspiration of transforming the system of states

---

[1] For a succinct summary of the idea of internationalism, see Fred Halliday, 'Three Concepts of Internationalism', *International Affairs*, 64, 2 (Spring 1988), p. 188.

[2] Jawaharlal Nehru, *Glimpses of World History* (New Delhi: Oxford University Press, 1982), pp. 946–47.

[3] Ibid., p. 947.

into a just, peaceful and co-operative international order, with states even shedding some limited aspects of their sovereignty in favour of supranational organisations such as the United Nations (UN).[4] In effect, what he aspired to was the ideal of One World, which he began to frequently invoke from the early 1940s. Consequently, the foreign policy that he designed and practised after independence was aimed at nudging the world along in this direction.

Nehru's foreign policy consisted of five elements. The first was opposition to colonialism, imperialism and racialism. In Nehru's view, these needed to be opposed not only because they were unjust and exploitative, but because their very essence was rivalry and competition for the world's resources which fuelled wars and conflicts and power politics in general. Thus, ending imperialism and the conflicts associated with it would automatically bring about a peaceful and co-operative international framework among free nations.

The second element was the concept of non-alignment vis-à-vis the two Cold War blocs. Non-alignment did not merely mean that India would stay aloof from other people's quarrels or avoid foreign entanglements in order to concentrate on the enormous domestic challenges. But built into its very conception was the idea of creating an 'area of peace'[5] between the two rival blocs to ensure that the Cold War did not engulf the entire world and eventually lead to a third world war. Inherent in this position was opposition to all alliances and especially to the spread of superpower alliances in Asia, so that this 'area of peace' was not in any way constricted and superpower rivalries were kept at bay. This desire to preserve Asia, in

---

[4] Indian delegates to the UN Commission that drafted the Universal Declaration of Human Rights sought to make the declaration 'a fundamental law of the United Nations' and to vest the Security Council with authority to investigate human rights violations and enforce their redressal within the UN framework. See Manu Bhagawan, 'A New Hope: India, the United Nations and the Making of the Universal Declaration of Human Rights', *Modern Asian Studies*, 44, 2 (2010), pp. 311–47.

[5] Nehru repeatedly referred to the importance of creating an 'area of peace' in the course of many speeches. For instance, see Jawaharlal Nehru, *India's Foreign Policy: Selected Speeches, September 1946–April 1961* (New Delhi: Publications Division, Ministry of Information and Broadcasting, Government of India, 1961), p. 67.

particular, as an 'area of peace' was underpinned by the ideas associated with pan-Asianism, which had been articulated particularly during the inter-war period. Thus, non-alignment and a collective Asian effort to limit the Cold War would impart the peace impulse into the international situation, which otherwise seemed inexorably headed towards another conflict of global dimensions, this time with the associated horror of nuclear weapons.

The necessity of ensuring that Cold War tensions did not boil over into an open conflict between the superpowers led India to play an active mediatory role when conflicts broke out, particularly in Asia and Africa. This third element of India's foreign policy was clearly evident in its role during the Korean War and in its efforts to prevent the internationalisation of the conflict in Indo-China.

In addition, a key imperative was disarmament, the advocacy of which constituted the fourth element in India's foreign policy. Nehru's emphasis on nuclear disarmament in particular was driven by the belief, which is common to all those who espouse internationalism, that such a step in itself would generate a greater sense of security for the nuclear weapon powers as well as engender a 'climate of peace' for all.[6] A lowering of international tensions would in turn pave the way for turning the Cold War back and evolving a co-operative framework of interstate relations.

One other way to lower tensions and evolve a co-operative international framework was through the adoption of the principle of peaceful co-existence as embodied in the *Panchsheel* principles. This fifth element in India's foreign policy found expression in the 1954 India–China agreement on Tibet and, subsequently, in the Bandung Declaration as well. India contended that the conduct of all interstate relations on the basis of the Panchsheel – respect for each other's territorial integrity and sovereignty, mutual non-aggression, mutual non-interference in internal affairs, equality and mutual benefit in bilateral relations, and the resolve to co-exist peacefully – would lead to the evolution of a peaceful and co-operative international order, which, in turn, would pave the way for the realisation of the ideal of One World.

Together, these five elements made up the framework of India's foreign policy, which came to be identified with the term 'non-alignment'. Underpinning them was the emphasis placed on the

---

[6] Nehru, *India's Foreign Policy*, p. 178.

United Nations and its role in eliminating colonialism and imperialism, in generating a 'climate of peace' by localising conflicts, in nudging the world towards disarmament and nuclear disarmament in particular, and in mediating between parties to international disputes. The principal objective behind all these elements was the fostering of peace and co-operation among free nations, thus engendering the emergence of a normative world order, the One World that Nehru repeatedly invoked in his speeches and statements.

What this perspective implies is that non-alignment cannot be narrowly seen as an expression of nationalist assertion and as a policy that sought to exploit bipolarity for promoting the national interest in terms of preserving sovereignty, completing territorial consolidation and promoting economic development.[7] Nor was non-alignment a sophisticated application of the balance of power to reduce the capability of the two superpowers to influence India's behaviour, by 'threatening to move, and moving, towards the polarities of alignment in either direction' which 'constituted an unacceptable risk' for them.[8] Instead, non-alignment was part and parcel of a larger internationalist policy framework, the various elements of which were designed to make movement towards a One World possible.

The Origins of Indian Internationalism

Internationalism emerged as an integral part of Indian nationalism in the 1920s when the Indian National Congress (hereafter, Congress) first began to systematically think about, and articulate its views on, foreign affairs. This, however, does not mean that the Congress did not take any positions previously on international affairs. In fact, from its very inception, Congress had taken a critical position on colonialism and imperialism. Early Congress leaders had repeatedly condemned Britain and especially its use of the Indian military

---

[7] See, for instance, the argument put forth by Ernest W. Lefever, 'Nehru, Nasser, and Nkrumah on Neutralism', in Laurence W. Martin, ed., *Neutralism and Nonalignment: The New States in World Affairs* (Westport, Connecticut: Greenwood Press Publishers, 1962), pp. 93–120; see in particular, pp. 116–20.

[8] A. P. Rana, *The Imperatives of Nonalignment: Conceptual Study of India's Foreign Policy Strategy in the Nehru Period* (New Delhi: Macmillan, 1976), p. 93; see also pp. 50–56, 92–114.

for imperialist expansion in various parts of Asia. As a corollary, they also consistently expressed their sympathy for and solidarity with colonised peoples everywhere.[9] This sense of solidarity led to the idea of an Asian identity and of Asianism in a nascent form, especially in the wake of Japan's emergence as a modern industrial power and its victory over Russia in 1905, which were seen as heralding the resurgence of Asia.[10] These themes of anti-imperialism and solidarity with colonised peoples as well as the idea of Asianism subsequently became integrated into the larger view of international affairs that the Congress developed from the 1920s onwards.

It was in the 1920s that international co-operation and internationalism emerged as a theme in Congress articulations on foreign affairs. And this coincided with the evolution of its political goal from self-government to complete independence. During the decade, Congress began to complement its nationalist demand for full independence with the internationalist call for 'the elimination of political and economic imperialism everywhere and the co-operation of free nations'.[11] It found inspiration in the triumphs of the Chinese revolutionary forces and saw in them portents for India's own freedom and for the elimination of European imperialism throughout Asia. Congress also began to take greater interest in the progress of other nationalist movements like those in the Dutch East Indies, Indo-China, and in West Asia including Egypt.[12]

Moreover, considering that 'the struggle for freedom was ... common ... against ... imperialism and [that] joint deliberation and, where possible, joint action were desirable', Congress appointed Nehru as its official representative to the Congress of Oppressed

---

[9] For a detailed description of the evolving Congress position on this issue between 1885 and 1918, see Bimla Prasad, *The Origins of Indian Foreign Policy: The Indian National Congress and World Affairs, 1885–1947* (Calcutta: Bookland Private Ltd., 1960), pp. 27–52.

[10] Bipan Chandra et al., *India's Struggle for Independence 1857–1947* (New Delhi: Penguin, 1989), pp. 386–89. According to C. F. Andrews, even remote villagers talked about the victory of a small Asian nation over a big European power; cited in Prasad, *Origins of Indian Foreign Policy*, p. 29.

[11] As early as 1920, Congress had passed a resolution on foreign policy in which it emphasised co-operation with other countries and especially with India's neighbours. See Jawaharlal Nehru, *The Discovery of India* (New Delhi: Penguin, 2004), p. 459.

[12] Nehru, *The Discovery of India*, pp. 460–61.

Nationalities held in Brussels in February 1927.[13] In his speeches and statements at the conference, Nehru expressed 'the deep commitment of Indian nationalism to internationalism' as well as to anti-colonial struggles across the world.[14] In tune with this commitment, Congress affiliated itself with the League against Imperialism and for National Independence, which was founded by the Brussels Conference; and Nehru was elected to the League's Executive Council. But this affiliation lasted only for four years until April 1930 because Congress became disillusioned with the radical turn taken by the League and its criticism of the moderation displayed by Congress leaders.[15] Nehru was expelled from the League in 1931 for his part in the Delhi truce between Congress and the British government in India.[16] Notwithstanding these developments, Congress declared that the Indian struggle for freedom was part of the worldwide struggle against imperialism. It also decided to open a Foreign Department to 'develop contacts with other peoples and movements fighting against imperialism'.[17]

In 1927, Congress also evolved an important policy position on a future war, when the international situation appeared to be drifting towards another major European conflict. This was consequent to a report titled 'A Foreign Policy for India' which Nehru prepared in September that year. In this report, Nehru pointed to England's on-going preparations for war against Russia and contended that if the Congress were to 'patiently wait and do nothing', India would get dragged into this conflict which would be to the obvious benefit of British imperialism. Given that India had no quarrel with Russia but instead admired the latter's revolutionary course, Nehru advocated that India declare its intention to refuse to become a party to any war without its express consent.[18] Congress endorsed this

---

[13] Jawaharlal Nehru, *An Autobiography* (New Delhi: Oxford University Press, 1980), p. 161.

[14] Chandra et al., *India's Struggle for Independence*, p. 391.

[15] T. A. Keenleyside, 'The Inception of Indian Foreign Policy: The Non-Nehru Contribution', *South Asia: Journal of South Asian Studies*, 4, 2 (1981), p. 68.

[16] Nehru, *Autobiography*, p. 164.

[17] Chandra et al., *India's Struggle for Independence*, p. 392.

[18] Sarvepalli Gopal, ed., *Selected Works of Jawaharlal Nehru* [hereafter, SWJN], 1st Series, Volume 2 (New Delhi: Orient Longman, 1972), pp. 348–64.

recommendation and asserted in a resolution passed later that year that the Indian people, who had no quarrel with their neighbours and wished to live in peace with them, had the right to decide whether or not to participate in a war. The resolution further stated that if the British government were to embark upon an imperialist war and seek to involve India in it, then the people of India had a duty to refuse to take part in such a war or to even extend any co-operation.[19] In subsequent years, this principle became 'one of the foundations of Congress policy and ... of Indian policy' in general.[20]

This determination not to participate in an imperialist war was closely tied to the conception of how a free India would conduct its foreign relations. Given its size, resources and potential strength, it was contended that 'India could not be a mere hanger-on of any country or group of nations' and that its 'freedom and growth would make a vital difference to Asia and therefore to the world'.[21] This combination of ideas and principles – anti-imperialism, including a refusal to take part in imperialist wars, and internationalism, including the imperative of international co-operation among anti-colonial movements and among free countries after they become independent – eventually became key pillars of India's foreign policy after independence.

Reconciling Nationalism and Internationalism

As the 1930s unfolded, the European situation changed fundamentally with the rise of fascism and Nazism. These ideologies were anathema to the Congress and it saw in them embodiments of imperialism and racialism against which it was waging a non-violent struggle. To these was added Japanese militarism in Asia. A major war once again appeared imminent although it would be different from the one that Congress had envisaged in the late 1920s. This new state of affairs placed the Congress in a dilemma. As Nehru asked, '[H]ow would we reconcile the two dominant trends of our policy – opposition to British imperialism and opposition to fascism

---

[19] Sarvepalli Gopal, *SWJN*, p. 25.
[20] Nehru, *Discovery of India*, p. 461.
[21] Ibid., p. 464.

and Nazism? How would we bring in line our nationalism and our internationalism?"[22]

Here, it would be pertinent to note that until then none of the Congress leaders including Gandhi and Nehru saw a disjuncture between Indian nationalism and internationalism. In December 1924, during his presidential address to the Congress at Belgaum, Gandhi, the ardent nationalist, had observed that '[t]he better mind of the world desires today not absolutely independent States warring one against another but a federation of friendly inter-dependent States.'[23] Further, writing in *Young India* in September 1925, Gandhi noted that his 'patriotism includes the good of mankind in general' and therefore his 'service of India includes the service of humanity'.[24] This harmony between nationalism and internationalism was also affirmed by Nehru, who noted in his autobiography (written in 1934–35) that those Indians who stood for national independence also stood for internationalism irrespective of whether they were socialists or non-socialists. Moreover, the Congress' demand for independence was not being driven by the desire for 'isolation'. On the contrary, an independent India was 'perfectly willing to surrender part of that independence, in common with other countries, to a real international order.'[25] Here, for the first time, we see the natural outgrowth of Nehru's ideas on internationalism mentioned earlier: of the world moving towards 'greater interdependence', 'a greater internationalism' and becoming 'one single inseparable whole'. Nehru's prescription for such a world was the creation of an international order in which free countries willingly surrender part of their independence for the sake of the common good of humanity.

But this perception of harmony between nationalism and internationalism was severely tested by the imminence of war in Europe between England and Germany. The question before Congress leaders was how to reconcile the nationalist struggle for independence against British imperialism with the internationalist obligation

---

[22] Nehru, *Discovery of India*, pp. 460–61.
[23] *Collected Works of Mahatma Gandhi Online*, Vol. 29, p. 499. Available at http://www.gandhiserve.org/cwmg/VOL029.PDF, accessed on August 30, 2010.
[24] *Collected Works of Mahatma Gandhi Online*, Vol. 32, p. 411. Available at http://www.gandhiserve.org/cwmg/VOL032.PDF, accessed on August 30, 2010.
[25] Nehru, *An Autobiography*, p. 420.

to oppose the vulgar, brutal and racist regime of Nazi Germany? But then arose another question: didn't imperialism also represent the Nazi 'principles and theories of life and the state' although in a 'different garb, and somewhat disguised for the sake of decency'?[26] In which case, would not a war between these two powers be nothing more than another contest between rival imperialisms? These contradictions appeared to make for an absurd choice. When war broke out and the Viceroy declared that India too was at war, the Congress refused to associate the Indian people in the war. It argued that even as war was being waged for democratic freedom, that very freedom was being denied to India. Instead, Congress asked the British government to declare its war aims with respect to democracy, imperialism and the new international order and, in particular, how Britain planned to apply those ideas to India at that present moment. At the same time, in tune with its internationalism, Congress also expressed an interest in a free and democratic India associating itself with 'other free nations for mutual defence against aggression and for economic co-operation' as well as for the establishment of 'a real world order based on freedom and democracy'.[27] It was through such a finessing of the issue that the Congress sought to reconcile its nationalism with its internationalism. Subsequently, it espoused its internationalist ideas to a fuller degree in the Quit India Resolution of August 1942 in which it concretely established the link between Indian nationalism and internationalism.[28]

The Quit India Resolution asserted that ending British rule in India 'is an urgent necessity, both for the sake of India and for the success of the cause of the United Nations'.[29] For, 'the degrading and

---

[26] Nehru, *Discovery of India*, p. 5.

[27] Ibid., p. 472; see also pp. 471–73.

[28] The Quit India Resolution passed by the All India Congress Committee on August 8, 1942 was drafted by Nehru. The Committee had rejected another draft that Gandhi had prepared and chose the version submitted by Nehru. But the fact remains that it was as much 'a part of the Nehruvian vision as it is the Gandhian'. See Bhagawan, 'A New Hope', p. 318.

[29] All quotes here and in the following paragraphs of this sub-section are from the Quit India Resolution. For the full text of the resolution, see 'No. 470: The Quit India Resolution', in Nicholas Mansergh, ed., *Constitutional Relations between Britain and India. The Transfer of Power 1942–7: Vol. II: 'Quit India' 30 April–21 September 1942* (London: Her Majesty's Stationery Office, 1971), pp. 621–24.

enfeebling' British rule is making India less capable of defending itself and of contributing to the cause of world freedom for which the war was being waged. At the same time, Congress attributed the setbacks in the war till then to the Allied policy, which was based not on freedom but on the subjection of colonial countries and the continuation of imperialism. It noted that instead of adding strength, the possession of empire had become 'a burden and a curse'. Hence, it was absolutely necessary to immediately end imperial rule in India, which had become the crux of the question of imperialism in the wake of the successes of the Axis Powers. Ending British rule would immediately lead to India becoming an ally of the 'United Nations' and throwing all its resources against the aggression of the Axis Powers. Independent India's entry into the war would not only materially affect the fortunes of the conflict but would also bring all colonised peoples on to the side of the 'United Nations'. Here, the Resolution also issued the warning that India's freedom must become 'the symbol of and prelude to' the freedom of all other colonised countries of Asia and that no effort must be made to subsequently bring the territories conquered by Japan under the rule of any other Colonial Power.

After laying out these steps that needed to be taken, the Resolution went on to talk about the Congress' vision of the future of the international system. It began by asserting that 'the future peace, security and ordered progress of the world demand a world federation of free nations' and that the modern world's problems cannot be solved on any other basis. It then went on to note that:

> Such a world federation would ensure the freedom of its constituent nations, the prevention of aggression and exploitation by one nation over another, the protection of national minorities, the advancement of all backward areas and peoples, and the pooling of the world's resources for the common good of all. On the establishment of such a world federation, disarmament would be practicable in all countries, national armies, navies and air forces would no longer be necessary, and a world federal defence force would keep the world peace and prevent aggression.[30]

The Resolution then noted that independent India 'would gladly join such a world federation and co-operate on an equal basis with other countries in the solution of international problems'.

---

[30] Mansergh, 'No. 470: The Quit India Resolution', *Constitutional Relations between Britain and India*, pp. 621–24.

Here, in the Quit India Resolution, stands a full expression of Indian internationalism: the emphasis on anti-imperialism, anti-racialism and freedom for all subject peoples particularly in Asia; the idea of free nations joining together to form the UN; the importance of the UN serving as the mainstay of a new international order, and of a world federation that would work for the common good of all humanity; and finally, the ideal of global disarmament. Each of these elements would later become an integral part of independent India's foreign policy.

Pan-Asianism and Asian Solidarity

An integral part of the internationalist vision articulated by the Quit India Resolution was the freedom of all colonised peoples of Asia and the admonition that those countries which had come under Japanese occupation should not later be reverted to their former imperial masters or to any other imperial power. Underpinning this call and the accompanying admonition was the idea of Asian solidarity vis-à-vis European imperialism, which had informed the Congress outlook on international affairs from its inception. During the inter-war years in particular, this sense of solidarity evolved into assertions about a common Asian identity, given the perceived cultural, religious and spiritual similarities among the countries of Asia. This, in turn, led to articulations about the cultural unity of Asia and, in particular, the unity of India and China, as well as about the spirituality of Asia, its higher morality and its pacifist tradition, all culminating in ideas about an Asian political federation.

The affirmation by nationalist Indians of the value of indigenous traditions was part of the reaction against Western colonialism and imperialism.[31] This led them to stigmatise Western materialism and to contrast it with the superiority of Indian and Asian spiritualism. Rabindranath Tagore put forward the idea that Asia, the 'continent of eternal light', was united by 'a common bond of spiritualism' and that it was this spirituality which distinguished Asian civilisation from the materialistic West.[32] Inherent in Tagore's claim was

---

[31] Christophe Jaffrelot, 'India's Look East Policy: An Asianist Strategy in Perspective', *India Review*, 2, 2 (April 2003), p. 36.

[32] Cited in T. A. Keenleyside, 'Nationalist Indian Attitudes Towards Asia: A Troublesome Legacy for Post-Independence Indian Foreign Policy', *Pacific Affairs*, 55, 2 (Summer 1982), p. 211.

the notion of the moral superiority of the spiritual East over the industrialised West, given the Asian tendency to 'bend our heads before all that is humanly great' in contrast to the Western penchant for glorifying what is 'mechanically perfect'.[33] Tagore, in fact, believed that real civilisation was still alive only in Asia since 'the lamp of ancient Greece is extinct ... the power of Rome lies dead and buried ... [while] civilisation, whose basis is society and the spiritual ideal of man, is still a living thing in China and in India.'[34] The civilised countries of Asia, in Tagore's view, shared three essential attributes: spiritual strength, the love of simplicity, and recognition of social obligation, which, together, had provided the foundation in the past for 'the closest tie of friendship' between India and the whole of eastern Asia extending from Burma to Japan.[35]

An important sub-theme of Asian unity was the perceived unity of India and China, the roots of which were seen in the spread of Buddhism from India to China and in the long history of friendly exchanges. This idea received a fillip in the wake of the 1927 joint statement issued by Indian and Chinese delegates to the Brussels conference. The statement noted that India and China had been united 'by the most intimate cultural ties' for more than 3000 years till the advent of British imperialism cut off this 'friendly intercourse' and emphasised the resumption of 'the ancient personal, cultural and political relations'.[36] Nehru, who had helped draft this statement, later averred that these two 'sister nations from the dawn of history, with their long traditions of culture and peaceful development of ideas', had a leading part to play in the evolution of a new international equilibrium.[37] In the 1940s he wrote about how India and China were once again looking towards each other and how modern Indian and Chinese 'pilgrims' are 'bringing their message

---

[33] Keenleyside, 'Nationalist Indian Attitudes Towards Asia', p. 211.

[34] Rabindranath Tagore, *Nationalism* (New Delhi: Penguin, 2009), p. 9.

[35] Ibid., pp. 6–7.

[36] See Nehru's report on the Brussels Congress submitted to the All India Congress Committee, reproduced at Appendix I in Prasad, *Origins of Indian Foreign Policy*, pp. 272–73.

[37] Sarvepalli Gopal, ed., *SWJN*, Volume 8 (New Delhi: Orient Longman, 1976), p. 709.

of cheer and goodwill and creating fresh bonds of a friendship that will endure'.[38]

At the same time, nationalist Indians also stressed India's past cultural and religious links with the countries of South and Southeast Asia. Some scholars even argued that this whole area had once formed a single 'cultural federation' permeated by Indian influence and referred to this region as 'Greater India'.[39] The idea of a 'Greater India' was never officially endorsed by the Congress because of the risk of India being perceived as expansionist. Nehru's own view was that there was a residual 'feeling of respect and friendship' for India in the countries of Southeast Asia, because of its past role as 'a mother country' which had 'nourished them with rich fare from her own treasure-house' and which had left 'its powerful impress' upon them.[40] Indeed, Nehru and others envisaged an important and even influential role for India in Asia. In January 1947, Nehru reminded members of the Indian Constituent Assembly that they not only shouldered the responsibility of the freedom of the Indian people but also 'the responsibility of the leadership of a large part of Asia, the responsibility of being some kind of guide to vast numbers of people all over the world'.[41] Two months later, inaugurating the Asian Relations Conference, he noted that India 'is the natural centre and focal point of the many forces at work in Asia' because of its location at 'the meeting point of Western and Northern and Eastern and South-East Asia', which, in the past, had led to a great deal of economic and cultural flows in all directions.[42]

The larger point to note in all this was the perceived contrast between, on the one hand, the spiritual unity and peaceful intercourse that had marked Asian history, and on the other hand, the hatred, nationalistic rivalry, power politics and imperialism that

---

[38] Nehru, *Discovery of India*, p. 211.

[39] For instance, see Kalidas Nag, *Greater India* (Bombay: The Book Centre Private Ltd., 1960), which contains essays on the history of India's ties with China as well as with South, Southeast and West Asia.

[40] Nehru, *Discovery of India*, p. 212.

[41] Jawaharlal Nehru, 'We Wish for Peace', in *India's Foreign Policy: Selected Speeches, September 1946–April 1961* (New Delhi: Publications Division, Ministry of Information and Broadcasting, Government of India, 1961), p. 12.

[42] Nehru, 'Asia Finds Herself Again', in *India's Foreign Policy*, p. 250.

characterised Europe and the West. Commenting on this contrast, Sarvepalli Radhakrishnan observed that the 'pacific tradition and temperament' of Asian countries served as a 'necessary complement and antidote to the pragmatic nationalism of the West'.[43] But others such as Pandit Krishna Kant Malaviya went to the extent of arguing that the 'only panacea for all the ills of the world' lay in the establishment of the 'domination of the East' because only Asians, with their 'love of peace, spiritualism and goodwill for all can ... bring peace on this earth'.[44]

These views about the cultural and spiritual unity of Asia as well as its pacifist tradition culminated in the idea of an Asian political federation. It was thought that such a federation would, to begin with, strengthen the joint struggle against Western imperialism. Several Congress and non-Congress leaders advocated this idea during the 1920s, including C. R. Das, Mohammad Ali and Sriniwasa Aiyengar.[45] In fact, the 1928 Calcutta session of the Congress had passed a resolution authorising the Working Committee to take steps to organise a meeting of a pan-Asiatic federation in India in the year 1930, though the scheme was later abandoned because of the Congress' immersion in mass civil disobedience.[46]

While Nehru was initially sceptical about Asian unity and the idea of an Asian federation, he came to embrace it later. His reappraisal was based on the understanding that the world, passing as it was through the Second World War, had come to a stage where 'the day of small countries is past' and where 'the day of even big countries standing by themselves is past'.[47] This trend meant that even super powers such as the United States and the Soviet Union, although capable of standing by themselves, were likely to join with other countries or groups. Nehru felt that 'the only intelligent solution' for a conflict-riven planet was 'a world federation of free countries'.[48] However, in the absence of the wisdom or the strength

---

[43] Cited in Keenleyside, 'Nationalist Indian Attitudes towards Asia', p. 211.
[44] Ibid., p. 212.
[45] Prasad, *Origins of Indian Foreign Policy*, p. 72.
[46] Ibid., p. 77.
[47] Sarvepalli Gopal, ed., *SWJN*, Volume 11 (New Delhi: Orient Longman, 1978), p. 191.
[48] Ibid.

to realise this ideal, what was more likely to occur in his view was the coming into being of groupings of nations or large federations. In this regard, he cited the example of the idea then being proposed in Europe that the countries of that continent form a federation or union and in which grouping sometimes the United States and the British Dominions were also included. Nehru also noted that neither China nor India were included as members of the proposed grouping. Moreover, the formation of any such grouping would increase the potential of Western countries to continue to exploit Asia and Africa. Under these circumstances, Nehru argued, it would be ideal to forge an Eastern federation that was not hostile to the West, 'but nevertheless standing on its own feet, self-reliant and joining with all others in favour of world peace and world federation'.[49] Such an eastern federation, in his view, would inevitably include Afghanistan, Burma, Ceylon, China, India, and Nepal. Nehru also thought that Iran and Siam as well as some others could well join this federation, which would constitute 'a powerful combination of free nations joined together for their own good as well as the good of the world.'[50] Elsewhere, Nehru developed this idea further by talking about the formation of an 'Asiatic Federation of Nations'. He proposed that India and China take the initiative in this regard by inviting Afghanistan, Burma, Ceylon, Indonesia, Malaya and Nepal to join the Federation. And he also considered it desirable to include Iran, Iraq and Thailand in such a grouping.[51]

Even Gandhi advocated some kind of an Asian political federation in his address at the Asian Relations Conference in March 1947.[52] All these ideas associated with pan-Asianism – Asian spirituality, common identity, unity, pacifism and political federation – had an impact on how independent India viewed Asia and how in the initial years after independence it sought to rally Asian countries together to promote peace and fashion a normative international order. This is clearly evident in the inaugural speech that Nehru gave at the Asian Relations Conference held in New Delhi. Heralding the re-emergence of Asia as an important factor in international

---

[49] Ibid.
[50] Sarvepalli Gopal, ed., *SWJN*, Volume 11, p. 192.
[51] See B. Shiva Rao, 'The Vicious Circle in India', *Foreign Affairs*, 19, 4 (July 1941), p. 844.
[52] Jaffrelot, 'India's Look East Policy', p. 37.

affairs, he emphasised that Asian countries had assembled together in a spirit of co-operation to further 'the great design of promoting peace and progress all over the world'.[53] The role of Asia in the maintenance of peace was particularly important given that the West had repeatedly driven the world into innumerable wars and conflicts and even now, in the immediate aftermath of a world war and after the birth of the atomic age, was talking about another war. In contrast, the countries of Asia did not have a 'legacy of conflict', though they may have had the odd quarrel with their neighbours.[54] Nehru contended that given that 'the whole spirit and outlook of Asia are peaceful', the continent's emergence would prove to be 'a powerful influence for world peace'.[55] Indeed, there could be no peace in the world unless Asia played its part. The promotion of peace would, in turn, make possible movement towards the ideal of One World, because some sort of a world federation was essential to deal with the pressing problems confronting humanity at large. While there were many obstacles and dangers in the path of achieving this ideal, Nehru concluded that the way forward lay in Asian countries extending full support for the fledgling United Nations and in co-operating together to bring about this One World.[56]

'One World' and Nehru's Foreign Policy

It was this internationalist aspiration to nudge the world towards One World that animated independent India's foreign policy during the Nehru years. In fact, on the eve of the San Francisco meeting of the United Nations, Gandhi released a press statement in which he reiterated the internationalist vision that the Congress had pronounced in the Quit India Resolution – an end to imperialism with the granting of freedom to India, the idea of a world federation of free nations working for the common good of humanity, the role of the United Nations as the mainstay of such an international order

---

[53] Nehru, 'Asia Finds Herself Again', in *India's Foreign Policy*, p. 251.

[54] Nehru explicitly drew this contrast during a speech in the Indian Constituent Assembly in March 1949. See, 'India and Asia', in *India's Foreign Policy*, p. 23.

[55] Nehru, 'Asia Finds Herself Again', in *India's Foreign Policy*, p. 251.

[56] For the full text of the speech, see Nehru, 'Asia Finds Herself Again', in *India's Foreign Policy*, pp. 248–53.

and global disarmament. He concluded by asserting that Indian nationalism 'spells internationalism' and that 'the demand for Indian independence is in no way selfish'.[57]

Nehru reiterated this internationalist vision in the very first statement on foreign policy that he made six days after assuming charge of the interim Government and of the Foreign Affairs portfolio in early September 1946. 'Free India', Nehru clearly stated, 'would work to bring about a "One World," 'a world in which there is the free co-operation of free peoples, and no class or group exploits another'.[58] For this purpose, he called for an end to colonialism, imperialism and racialism because 'peace and freedom are indivisible and the denial of freedom anywhere must endanger freedom everywhere and lead to conflict and war'.[59] In order to build this One World, India, for its part, would not participate in the power politics of the Cold War blocs that had by then begun to emerge. Nehru contended that in the past power politics had led to world wars, and pursuing such policies would in future lead to 'disasters on an even vaster scale'.[60]

Here were clearly laid out two of the principal elements that would make up independent India's foreign policy – anti-imperialism and non-alignment – as part of the larger internationalist vision of a new normative world order. As seen earlier, their roots lay in the ideas that animated Congress during the freedom struggle – solidarity with colonised peoples and refusal to take part in imperialist wars driven by power politics.

Nehru elaborated the other aspects of these two elements in subsequent speeches and statements. He advocated that India should take a lead role in articulating the policy of non-alignment because if it did not do so then other countries including those that were emerging or were soon likely to emerge as free independent states would also be forced to join one of the two blocs. This would mean that there would ultimately be no country left to provide a lead for

---

[57] *Collected Works of Mahatma Gandhi Online*, Vol. 86, pp. 188–91. Available at http://www.gandhiserve.org/cwmg/VOL086.PDF, accessed on July 14, 2010.

[58] Nehru, 'Future Taking Shape', in *India's Foreign Policy*, p. 2.

[59] Ibid.

[60] Ibid.

peace, thus bringing world war closer.[61] What was therefore needed was the establishment of an 'area of peace', consisting of countries not aligned to either group but at the same time friendly to both, in order to 'reduce the chance of war'.[62] Thus, the responsibility for ensuring peace and fostering co-operation lay not only with the superpowers but also with the newly emerging free countries of the world and particularly those in Asia. In this regard, he had provided an early indication in his September 1946 statement (highlighted above) as to how Asia was likely to shape itself and position itself vis-à-vis Cold War politics by noting that 'the future is bound to see a closer union between India and Southeast Asia on the one side, and Afghanistan, Iran, and the Arab world on the other.'[63]

A natural corollary to the imperative of creating an 'area of peace' was India's opposition to all superpower alliances and specifically to the two US-sponsored Cold War alliances in Asia – Southeast Asia Treaty Organization (SEATO) and Central Treaty Organization (CENTO). Nehru simply could not understand the military rationale for alliances between a superpower endowed with enormous capabilities including nuclear weapons and 'a little pigmy of a country'.[64] These small and weak allies which did not possess the bomb could have 'little or no military value' for the superpower from the point of a nuclear war.[65] More importantly, to think of a nuclear war and the inevitable destruction and catastrophe that would result amounted to 'insanity', because wars are fought to achieve specific objectives and 'not to bring ruin on oneself'.[66] Thus, there was no logic to alliances in a nuclear age. Under these circumstances, the only practical alternative was to prevent war and to avoid war.[67]

As the Cold War intensified, the other elements of India's internationalist foreign policy framework began to assume shape, with

---

[61] Nehru made this point in a note that he prepared in September 1948 as guidance for the Indian delegation to the United Nations. Cited in B. R. Nanda, *Three Statesmen: Gokhale, Gandhi, and Nehru* (New Delhi: Oxford University Press, 2004), pp. 232–33.

[62] Nehru, 'Correct Perspective', in *India's Foreign Policy*, p. 67.

[63] Nehru, 'Future Taking Shape', in *India's Foreign Policy*, pp. 2–3.

[64] Nehru, 'Correct Perspective', in *India's Foreign Policy*, p. 66.

[65] Ibid.

[66] Ibid.

[67] Ibid.

each element designed to lower international tensions, foster peace and co-operation and nudge the world towards a true international order centred on the United Nations.

The outbreak of war in the Korean Peninsula and the subsequent conflict in Indo-China brought to the fore India's mediatory role to relax Cold War tensions, localise conflicts, terminate them at the earliest and prevent them from spilling into a world war involving the two superpowers. Thus, while India accepted the initial attack on South Korea as North Korean aggression and supported US military action, it subsequently cautioned the United States against taking the war across the 38th parallel and against attacking targets across the Yalu which would inevitably draw China into the conflict.[68] Nehru saw China's entry into the war as indicative of the world being 'on the very verge of a world war'.[69] To avoid the catastrophe that was bound to result from such a denouement, India advocated the only practical way out: that of peaceful negotiation among parties to the conflict, including China.

Similarly, in the case of Indo-China, India's mediatory role was designed to prevent a square-off between the two Cold War blocs. It first appealed for a ceasefire, followed it up with a proposal for direct negotiations between parties to the dispute and later played a key but unofficial role at the 1954 Geneva Conference, all of which eventually led to the establishment of the International Control Commission under Indian chairmanship.[70] India's important role at Geneva prompted the then French Premier Mendes-France to wittily describe the conference as 'this ten-power conference – nine at the table – and India'.[71] Nehru himself would note in the Indian Parliament that the historic nature of the Geneva conference lay in the fact that it 'was the alternative or the deterrent to what threatened to lead to the third world war'.[72]

One other episode that highlights India's mediatory efforts to ease Cold War tensions and pave the way for peaceful co-operation took

---

[68] For a recent assessment of India's role in the Korean War, see Kim ChanWahn, 'The Role of India in the Korean War', *International Area Studies Review*, 13, 2 (June 2010), pp. 21–37.

[69] Nehru, 'United Nations Action', in *India's Foreign Policy*, p. 418.

[70] Rana, *Imperatives of Nonalignment*, pp. 241–42.

[71] Cited in Nanda, *Three Statesmen*, p. 235.

[72] Nehru, 'The Geneva Agreement', in *India's Foreign Policy*, p. 402.

place at the United Nations in September 1960. On this occasion, Nehru launched what was described as a 'one-man effort to end the Cold War'. In order to gain support for an Indian resolution calling for the re-establishment of contact at the highest level between the two superpowers, on a single day Nehru conferred with several world leaders – US President Eisenhower, British Prime Minister Macmillan, Soviet Premier Khrushchev, the Canadian Prime Minister Diefenbaker, UN Secretary General Hammarskjold, Egyptian President Nasser, and the Ghanaian President Nkrumah – but all to no avail.[73]

The full-blown eruption of the Cold War in the wake of the Korean conflict and the accompanying race for nuclear arms brought to the fore the fourth element of India's internationalist foreign policy framework – its earnest effort to convince the world of the imperative of nuclear disarmament. In 1956, India suggested some initial steps for disarmament and nuclear disarmament in particular: (*a*) suspension of nuclear tests pending their eventual ban, (*b*) dismantling of some nuclear weapons thus reversing the nuclear arms race, (*c*) a public declaration by nuclear weapon powers that they would not manufacture any more nuclear weapons, and (*d*) the publication of military budgets and a commitment not to expand military strength and immediately carry out what reductions could be made.[74] Nehru followed this up a year later with a direct appeal to the two superpowers to stop nuclear tests and proceed towards effective disarmament.[75]

To Nehru, the rationale for disarmament was twofold. First of all, the danger of nuclear weapons use was likely to continuously grow given that it was becoming progressively easier and cheaper to acquire nuclear and even thermonuclear bombs. He even considered that it was only a matter of time before any industrialised country would be able to produce such weapons. If the number of countries with nuclear and thermonuclear bombs were to increase, it would become progressively more difficult to control nuclear weapons. Nehru even thought that a situation might in fact arise where even individuals are able to acquire such weapons and

---

[73] Lefever, 'Nehru, Nasser, and Nkrumah on Neutralism', p. 98.

[74] Nehru, 'Towards Disarmament', in *India's Foreign Policy*, p. 199.

[75] See Nehru's 'Appeal to the U.S.A. and the U.S.S.R.', in *India's Foreign Policy*, p. 202.

'terrorise the world'. Given all this, he contended that it was best to move towards disarmament 'before the danger spreads too much'.[76] Secondly, Nehru thought that disarmament would 'remove fears and apprehensions, hatreds and suspicions' and create 'an atmosphere of co-operation'. Such a co-operative atmosphere would, in turn, enable 'the larger efforts to rid the world of war and the causes of war'. In Nehru's view, peace in the nuclear age was not merely a moral imperative but a practical necessity. For, the choice was between 'utter annihilation' and 'peaceful co-existence between nations'.[77]

This imperative of peaceful co-existence constituted the fifth element of India's internationalist foreign policy framework. Since war was not a practical choice in the nuclear age, it became essential that countries, riven as they were by differing ideologies, beliefs and creeds, had to necessarily co-exist peacefully. Nehru argued that '[t]hey cannot convert each other by force or threats of force', because any such attempt would only result in 'catastrophe for all'.[78] He consequently advocated peaceful co-existence as the only way forward for the world and as a middle path between survival and destruction. The five principles, which came to be known as Panchsheel, that underlay peaceful co-existence were embodied in the agreement that India signed with China in 1954. These were subsequently incorporated into the Bandung Declaration and were even endorsed in a UN General Assembly Resolution passed in December 1957. Nehru was convinced that Panchsheel provided the basis for 'healthy, peaceful and co-operative' relationships between countries, since it rested on equality, mutual respect and peaceful co-existence and ruled out war and interference in internal affairs. In his view, conflicts arose only when 'one country dominates over another or interferes in another's internal affairs'. Therefore, if all countries adopted these five principles, 'peace would be assured everywhere, and co-operation would follow'.[79] The implicit assumption in all this was that peaceful co-operation between countries would lead to a real

---

[76] Nehru, 'Suspension of Nuclear Tests', in *India's Foreign Policy*, p. 197.

[77] Nehru, 'Problems of Peace', in *India's Foreign Policy*, p. 219.

[78] Nehru, 'Appeal to the U.S.A. and the U.S.S.R.', in *India's Foreign Policy*, p. 202.

[79] Nehru, 'The Concept of Panchsheel', in *India's Foreign Policy*, p. 101.

world order and pave the way for the realisation of the ideal of One World.

That all these elements were integral parts of a unified conception of internationalism and of the imperative of nudging the world towards the ideal of One World centred on the United Nations is clearly evident in a speech that Nehru delivered at the General Assembly on December 20, 1956.[80] He began by noting that the very existence of the United Nations was of great significance since it represented the 'world community' and provided a forum to address and attempt to solve the problems of the world. As a result, 'the sense of a world community conferring together' had begun to develop across the world. Nehru expressed the hope that over time each country's representative would begin to think of himself also as a representative of 'the world community'. He, however, cautioned that this cannot happen if countries continued to take a short-term view. What they needed to do was 'to look ahead ... for some kind of a world order, One World, to emerge' and at the same time not do anything that would come in the way of 'the evolution of that order'. An essential prerequisite for looking ahead was international co-operation based on the freedom of nations and of individuals. But unfortunately, the Cold War stood in the way of such co-operation and the emergence of peace. Nehru pointed out that the Cold War has led to the formation of alliances that did not have any military utility and that alliances have only added to the hostility between the two blocs. In his view, if peace were the objective, it necessarily followed that 'we must not have the Cold War', and the Cold War should not be reinforced by 'military establishments and pacts and alliances'. At the same time, the Cold War has also led to an arms race, making disarmament difficult to achieve. Disarmament was necessary to 'lessen the chances of war and the fear of war' and to create 'a climate of peace in the world'.

Thus, putting an end to the Cold War and to its associated elements in the form of an arms race, alliances and interventions that threaten to escalate into a superpower conflict and practising peaceful co-existence would lead to the evolution of a world order and to the internationalist ideal of One World.

---

[80] All quotes in this paragraph are from Nehru, 'Towards a World Community', in *India's Foreign Policy*, pp. 173–79.

Building on Nehru's Legacy

Nehru's internationalist aspiration to engender a new world order could not materialise given the substantial conflicts of interests and the insecurities that drove the policies of the superpowers as well as of regional countries. Consequently, the arms race continued unabated and disarmament became a will-o'-the-wisp. Several Asian countries themselves became members of the two Cold War blocs. While Communist China assumed membership in the Soviet bloc, other countries in Southeast and West Asia became members of the two US-sponsored military alliances, SEATO and CENTO. In the early 1960s, the idea of the enduring friendship between India and China also lay in tatters with the onset of the border conflict, at the root of which lay the Tibet issue. The early 1970s saw a major reconfiguration of the Cold War security calculus, with China and the United States forging a common front. The emergence of the China–Pakistan–United States combination left India with no choice but to enter into a quasi-alliance with the Soviet Union, though New Delhi refused to get drawn into the Cold War per se. The threat from China and the American attempt to coerce India during the 1971 war also compelled New Delhi to demonstrate its nuclear weapons capability in 1974. After the Soviet security guarantee vanished with the collapse of the Soviet Union and given US-led non-proliferation attempts to deny it the nuclear option, India fully entered the nuclear club with a series of nuclear tests in 1998. Thus, India itself began to increasingly adopt a foreign policy impelled more by national security interests rather than internationalist aspirations. It is but inevitable in an anarchical international system, characterised by the security dilemma, for India to cater to its insecurities.

Yet, the fact remains that internationalism continues to inform India's foreign policy to an extent, as evidenced, for instance, by its continued advocacy of universal nuclear disarmament. Instead of fully abandoning its internationalist quest, India needs to build on the Nehruvian legacy by sagaciously pursuing its national interests and simultaneously promoting the international interest as well. As the pledge taken on August 15, 1947 by members of the Constituent Assembly averred, India should not only aim to attain its 'rightful place in the world' but should also make its 'full and willing contribution to the promotion of world peace and the welfare of mankind'.[81] These twin objectives should continue to inform India's approach to international affairs. Such an approach is all the more relevant in a world where Asia is emerging as the new centre of gravity in the international system. India itself is a part of this process of the Return of Asia to the centre stage of the world and thus, unlike in the past, it will have greater power to shape the international system.

---

[81] Nehru, 'A Tryst with Destiny', in *India's Foreign Policy*, pp. 12–13.

6
ECONOMIC MODERNISATION AND THE GROWING INFLUENCE OF NEOLIBERALISM IN INDIA'S STRATEGIC THOUGHT

N. S. Sisodia

The natural effect of commerce is to bring about peace, because two nations which trade together render themselves reciprocally dependent.[1]

Ever since India attained its freedom in 1947, its grand strategic perspectives have been influenced by divergent streams of thinking or visions. Their votaries have been described variously as moralists, Hindu nationalists, strategists and liberals[2] or as Nehruvians, neoliberals and hyperrealists.[3] In the real world, public policies do not necessarily conform to precise theories or schools of thought; they are often an amalgam of various strands of thinking. However, to the extent that we can characterise Indian grand strategy since 1947, it was dominated by Nehruvianism, with non-alignment being its principal feature.[4]

Some minor shifts began to be introduced in the mid-1980s initially in the domestic economy through partial liberalisation.

---

[1] Montesquieu as cited in Albert O. Hirschman, *National Power and the Structure of Foreign Trade* (Berkeley: University of California Press, 1945), p. 10.

[2] Rahul Sagar, 'State of Mind: What Kind of Power Will India Become?', *International Affairs*, 85, 4 (2009), pp. 801–16.

[3] Kanti Bajpai, 'India and the World: The Grand Strategy Debate', in Niraja Jayal and Pratap Bhanu Mehta, eds, *The Oxford Companion to Politics in India* (New Delhi: Oxford University Press, 2010), pp. 521–41.

[4] For a discussion on divergent strands of India's strategic thought, also see Stephen P. Cohen, *India: Emerging Power* (New Delhi: Oxford University Press, 2001), pp. 36–65.

This process was propelled by the balance of payment crisis of 1991 which forced India to physically lift bullion to secure credit. The comprehensive economic reforms initiated in its wake marked a radical shift in India's economic policies, resulting in the state-controlled socialist model of growth giving way to a free market economy. On the external front this led to the abandonment of autarky in favour of an open economy, trade and investment. India's outward orientation, increasing political and economic engagement with key players in the global arena and greater participation in multilateral fora were a natural corollary to economic liberalisation. While India's grand strategy can still be interpreted variously, the dominant influence during the two decades following economic reforms can be traced to neoliberal thinking, both in terms of political economy and international relations.

This chapter argues that the neoliberal influence on India's grand strategy has so far not enhanced her security environment. Divided into four sections, the chapter first discusses neoliberalism at some length. The second section analyses the circumstances that led to a review of India's strategy for economic growth and security. The third section considers empirical evidence of the neoliberal shift in the domain of economic policy and India's international relations. It then briefly demonstrates how the shift in strategy has not succeeded in improving India's security. And finally, the fourth and concluding section explores the factors which impede or can potentially impede achievement of the desired outcomes and suggests possible measures to deal with them.

Neoliberalism: Key Features

In his essay on India's strategic thought, Kanti Bajpai refers to the following key features of neoliberalism: neoliberals concede the general characterisation of international relations as a state of anarchy in which coercion plays a key role.[5] However, neoliberals regard the prospect of mutual gain as a powerful influence on inter-state relations. This is facilitated by interdependence. While neoliberals accept the need for adequate defence, they give primacy to economic strength and well-being. An important aspect of the neoliberal view is that free market policies, which involve free trade, can alone promote economic growth. Further, a sound economy is the

---

[5] Bajpai, 'India and the World', pp. 521–41.

source of robust defence. Neoliberals believe that free trade leads to mutual gain even if the relative gains are asymmetric. Realists focus on relative gains, whereas neoliberals are more concerned with absolute gains.

In essence, neoliberals support the old liberal ideas about the possibility of progress and change, but they reject the latter's idealism. Robert Keohane traces classical liberal theory to three distinct perspectives: first, 'commercial liberalism' which emphasises the pacific effects of trade; second, 'democratic liberalism' which stresses the pacific effects of republican government; third, 'regulatory liberalism' which refers to the pacific effects of international institutions, rules, regimes behaviour, etc.[6] To these Joseph Nye adds a fourth, that is, 'sociological liberalism', which argues that transnational contacts and coalitions can influence national attitudes and help redefine national interest.[7]

Keohane and Nye in fact, propose a theory of what they call 'complex interdependence'.[8] They point out that transnational actors are becoming increasingly important; military force is becoming less useful among interdependent states as compared to economic and institutional instruments; and military security is becoming less important, whereas welfare issues are gaining increasing salience. Three distinct characteristics of 'complex interdependence' have been highlighted by the authors – multiple channels connecting societies; absence of any hierarchy among issues in interstate relations (military security does not consistently dominate the agenda); and military force is not used by a government towards other governments within a region when complex interdependence exists, as the costs of such intervention will outweigh benefits.[9]

Neoliberals, like realists, acknowledge anarchy as the absence of a supra-government, but contend that this perennial aspect of international relations allows a variety of interactions among states.

---

[6] Robert O. Keohane, 'International Liberalism Reconsidered', in John Dunn, ed., *The Economic Limits to Modern Politics* (Cambridge: Cambridge University Press, 1999), pp. 175–82.

[7] Joseph S. Nye, *Power in the Global Information Age: From Realism to Globalization* (New York: Routledge, 2004), p. 29.

[8] Robert O. Keohane and Joseph S. Nye, *Power and Interdependence*, Third Edition (New York: Longman, 2001), pp. 20–32.

[9] Ibid.

Realists and neoliberals share the view that co-operation among states is possible, but the former argue that it is difficult to achieve and harder to maintain. While realists lay stress on relative gains, neoliberals emphasise absolute gains as a more important driver of interstate relations. In general, realists give primacy to military security; for neoliberals, however, economy is the key. While neoliberals emphasise intentions, for realists it is capabilities that matter, as intentions can change. Realists concede that institutions and regimes matter in international relations; however, they assert that neoliberals exaggerate their significance.[10]

The boundaries between the realist and neoliberal schools of thought often get blurred. Nye asserts that '... the sharp disagreement between Realism and Liberalism is overstated. In fact, the two approaches can be complimentary'.[11] He points out that realist theory is better at explaining interactions than interests. 'The more sophisticated variants of Liberal theory', he states, 'is a useful supplement by directing attention to ways in which domestic and international factors interact to change states' definitions of their interests'.[12]

In this chapter, we focus on this variant of neoliberalism which asserts that 'complex interdependence' can help redefine states' interests and promote mutually beneficial interstate co-operation.

The Shift Towards Neoliberalism

From the 1950s to the mid-1980s, the Indian state was dominated by a centrally planned and highly regulated system as a consequence of which its economy stagnated at what is famously known as the Hindu rate of growth of around 3.5 per cent. Over the years, the experience of an insular economy, relying on an inefficient public sector and import substitution, led to widespread disillusionment. As this phase was ending, four key developments deeply influenced policy makers in India. First, India's own disappointing experience with a shackled economy and an autarkic model of growth,

---

[10] For an analysis of the debate between the two schools, see David A. Baldwin, ed., *Neorealism and Neoliberalism: The Contemporary Debate* (New York: Columbia University Press, 1993).

[11] Nye, *Power in the Global Information Age*, pp. 21–33.

[12] Ibid., p. 24.

prompted introspection among experts and policy-makers. The entrepreneurial class felt suffocated under the heavy hand of the state. Despite government's efforts to eliminate poverty, the absolute number of poor people continued to grow. Second, the global paragon of a centrally planned socialist economy, the Soviet Union, collapsed under the weight of its own economic policies and defence expenditure. The state-controlled economies of East Europe were also floundering. Third, the Peoples' Republic of China which embraced the market economy under Deng Xiaoping was surging ahead both economic-ally and as a military power. The East Asian tiger economies of South Korea, Taiwan, Hong Kong and Singapore had achieved impressive economic growth and welfare for their people by pursuing a market-led, export-oriented strategy. Fourth, India's non-alignment was gradually losing its sheen and leading to disappointments in the global arena. The 1991 invasion of Kuwait by Iraq and the response of NAM countries further disillusioned India. Elsewhere, Europe had moved towards a unified economic structure setting aside its historic disputes and divisions, forging co-operative economic institutions and contributing to collective welfare. India itself had to look for new anchors in a world which was no longer bipolar and was now dominated by the US as the lone superpower, enjoying the allegiance of democratic, market economies of the West. As Rothermund observes '... the sudden change in the wake of these unexpected developments left India in a position of a voyager who has lost his compass at sea'.[13]

The ferment in the international system had already led to some rethinking on India's grand strategy during the 1980s. India's youthful Prime Minister Rajiv Gandhi, more modern in his outlook and largely free from the baggage of the past, sought to forge new links with both China and Pakistan. At home, some steps were taken towards deregulating the economy. However, the more fundamental change was precipitated by the Gulf War, spurt in oil prices and the balance of payment crisis of 1991, when India had been left with only a billion dollars of reserves, barely sufficient to cover two weeks of imports. It had to seek recourse to IMF's structural adjustment accommodation. This crisis provided an opportunity for the economist Finance Minister Manmohan Singh to usher in

---

[13] Dietmar Rothermund, *India: The Rise of an Asian Giant* (New Delhi: Stanza, 2008), p. 51.

significant economic reforms. In his budget speech of July 24, 1991 to India's Parliament, he referred to the country being on the edge of a precipice. He talked of the adverse consequences of excessive and indiscriminate protection to domestic industry, the need to 'expose Indian industry to competition from abroad', and for 'the policy regime for direct foreign investment'.[14] These reforms were measured, but wide-ranging and have since included: deregulation of industry; tariff reduction on imports; making the rupee convertible on the current account with assurance to make it convertible on the capital account; encouragement to foreign direct investment; and financial sector and fiscal reforms. The thrust was on opening up the economy, promoting private entrepreneurship, exposing Indian industry to global competition and promoting trade.

While a plethora of official documents and scholarly literature exists on India's economic reforms,[15] there are hardly any authoritative documents which provide a coherent rationale of the shift in the geostrategic perspective.[16] This is partly attributable to the fact that the shift in strategy was not sudden but evolved over several years. The evidence of this change has to be, therefore, pieced together from the texts of political leaders' speeches, important policy changes, some scholarly writings and from the empirical data on the outcomes of this shift.

Some of the key features of this shift over the last two decades can be summarised as follows:

(a) With the collapse of the Soviet Union and demise of the bipolar world, there was a growing recognition of the irrelevance of non-alignment.
(b) The country moved from the initial consensus on developing a socialist society to building a modern capitalist one.

---

[14] Surendra Mishra, ed., *Finance Ministers' Budget Speeches 1947–1996* (New Delhi: Surjeet Publications, 1996).

[15] For an excellent account of the reforms and their impact, see Arvind Pangariiya, *India: The Emerging Giant* (New York: Oxford University Press, 2008).

[16] For a collection of essays on the subject, see Sanjaya Baru, *Strategic Consequences of India's Economic Performance* (New Delhi: Academic Foundation, 2006). C. Raja Mohan also offers a good account of transformation in India's foreign policy in his *Crossing the Rubicon: The Shaping of India's New Foreign Policy* (New Delhi: Viking, 2003).

(c) Economic growth became the national priority; it was to be achieved through liberalisation, emphasis on trade and foreign direct investment; hence economic diplomacy was emphasised.

(d) Free from the constraints of Cold-War politics India imparted a new vitality to its relations with the US, EU, Japan, South Korea, and the Association of Southeast Asian Nation (ASEAN).

(e) It sought strategic partnerships with all the major powers, that is, the US, EU, Russia, Japan, and China.

(f) An attempt was made to strengthen India's ties with its neighbours through a vision of developing South Asia as a common economic space in which borders act as connectors and India as an economic opportunity for the neighbours.

(g) Finally, to ensure that India's deterrence capability is adequate, its nuclear weapons were tested and a nuclear doctrine was announced emphasising its defensive character.

The changing geopolitical environment was signalled first by P. V. Narasimha Rao in September 1991, characteristically without much ceremony. 'Now, the cold war is over', he observed, 'there is an element of co-operation instead of confrontation. It is a new situation. And we have to respond to that also. So, certain policy reorientations will take place to ensure that our national interest does not suffer'.[17] In late 1991 he instructed the foreign office to focus on the economic aspects of India's foreign relations and in his travels abroad he sought political support for India's economic liberalisation policies.[18] A reorientation in India's policies towards neighbours was attempted by I. K. Gujral through his five principles known as the Gujral Doctrine. It recognised the importance of co-operative relations with neighbours and announced that India would not insist on reciprocity in its relationships with neighbours like Bangladesh,

---

[17] The speech was given in New Delhi on September 29, 1991. Cited in Chan Wahn Kim, *Economic Liberalisation and India's Foreign Policy* (New Delhi: Kalpaz Publications, 2006), p. 175.

[18] For an analysis of India's commercial diplomacy after the reforms, see Kripa Sridharan, 'Commercial Diplomacy and Statecraft in the Context of Economic Reform: The Indian Experience', *Diplomacy and Statecraft*, 13, 2 (June 2002), pp. 57–82.

Bhutan, Maldives, Nepal, and Sri Lanka; instead it would follow a policy of liberal accommodation, based on good faith and trust.[19] Prime Minister Vajpayee's tenure was noteworthy for abandoning India's long-standing nuclear ambiguity and going ahead with nuclear tests in May 1998. This was seen to be a realist response to India's security dilemma.[20] At the same time, however, it was accompanied by purposeful engagement with the United States, a historic visit to Lahore and a renewed dialogue with China. To reassure neighbours and major powers that India's nuclear posture was essentially defensive, Vajpayee announced a voluntary moratorium on future tests. Furthermore, India's nuclear doctrine announced in 2003 was based on the principles of non-use against non-weapon states, no-first use and minimum credible deterrence.

With India's accelerating economic growth, increasing integration with the world and nuclear status, more self-confident and bolder foreign policy moves became possible in the first decade of the 21st century. These were accompanied by a growing understanding of an increasingly interdependent world. In a speech delivered on November 11, 2005, at an Indian thinktank, Prime Minister Manmohan Singh outlined the following broad approaches to the nation's security strategy:

(*a*) strengthen India economically and technologically;
(*b*) develop adequate defence capability by making optimal use of modern science and technology; and
(*d*) develop partnerships in the strategic, economic and technological spheres to enlarge policy choices and development options.[21]

Stressing co-operation, he observed: 'we must engage in co-operative, constructive and mutually beneficial relations with all

---

[19] I. K. Gujral, *Matters of Discretion: An Autobiography* (New Delhi: Penguin, 2011).

[20] See Jason A. Kirk, 'The Evolution of India's Nuclear Policies', in Sumit Ganguly, ed., *India's Foreign Policy: Retrospect and Prospect* (New Delhi: Oxford University Press, 2010), pp. 275–300.

[21] 'Prime Minister Manmohan Singh's IDSA Anniversary Speech', November 11, 2005. Available at http://pmindia.nic.in/speech-details.php?nodeid=211, accessed on April 20, 2012.

major powers of the world. Most of all, we must engage in proactively strengthening multilateral mechanisms for financial, economic and political security'.[22]

In a Lok Sabha debate on foreign policy, Dr Singh referred to India's relations with China, advocating 'a more meaningful and inclusive co-operative framework in the region across a range of issues from security to trade and investment'. Speaking on neighbouring countries, he said 'South Asia must work together to emerge as a major powerhouse of economic creativity and enterprise. It is with this perspective that we have extended our hand of friendship and co-operation to all our neighbours'.[23]

Impact of Liberalisation on India's Economy

The story of India's economic liberalisation and its impact is well documented and does not require a detailed discussion here. Following the policy changes of the 1990s, India's GDP has grown rapidly, making it the second fastest growing economy of the world. Its exports have risen from USD 18.14 billion in 1990–91 to USD 185.29 billion in 2008–09.[24] During the same period foreign currency reserves have surged from USD 2.24 billion to USD 241.43 billion; and foreign investment flows from USD 103 million to USD 8.34 billion.[25] India's share of world exports has increased from 0.5 per cent in 1990 to 1.1 per cent in 2008.[26] According to the Planning Commission estimates India's poverty ratio has declined from 36.0 per cent in 1993–94 to 27.5 per cent in 2004–05.[27]

---

[22] 'Prime Minister Manmohan Singh's IDSA Anniversary Speech', November 11, 2005. Available at http://pmindia.nic.in/speech-details.php?nodeid=211, accessed on April 20, 2012.

[23] 'Prime Minister Manmohan Singh's Reply to the Lok Sabha Debate (Rule 193) on Foreign Policy', May 12, 2005. Available at pmindia.nic.in/speech/content4print.asp, accessed on September 19, 2011.

[24] Ministry of Finance, Government of India, Economic Survey 2010–11, pp. A1–2 and Reserve Bank of India, *Handbook of Statistics on Indian Economy*, September 15, 2010. For details, see Table A6.1 at the end of this chapter.

[25] Ministry of Finance, Government of India, *Economic Survey 2010–11*.

[26] United Nations, 2008 International Trade Statistics Year Book, 2009, as cited in Ministry of Finance, Government of India, *Economic Survey 2010–11*, pp. A100–103. For details, see Table A6.2 at the end of this chapter.

[27] Planning Commission, Government of India, *Poverty Estimates for 2004–05*. Available at http://pib.nic.in/release/release.asp?relid=26316&kwd=

Over the past two decades, India has sought to balance its defence outlays with its socio-economic priorities – an approach consistent with neoliberal shift in India's strategy. India's defence expenditure as a share of GDP during the period 1991 to 2010 has generally remained below the global average of 2.5 per cent and significantly less than corresponding figures for China and Pakistan. However, this share must be viewed in the context of India's rapidly growing GDP, which has enabled the government to raise the defence outlay significantly from USD 13.8 billion in 1991 to USD 34.8 billion in 2010.[28] More importantly, India's nuclear arsenal is expected to provide her the ultimate instrument of deterrence.

Following India's economic liberalisation, Indian diplomacy also began to pursue an omnidirectional international engagement, based on the premise that an open, globally connected economy would encourage the free flow of ideas, goods, capital, technology, and people. This, in turn, it was hoped, would create interdependencies, help develop common stakes in stability and security and mitigate the risks of outright conflict.

During the two decades following economic reforms, conscious efforts have been made to improve bilateral relations with key players in the global market place, particularly with the US, EU, UK, Germany, France, the Peoples Republic of China, and the rapidly growing economies of East and South-east Asia. The transformation of India's relations with the US is the most significant development of the post-reform period in India's external relations. Its highpoint is the India–US civil nuclear energy agreement which ends India's nuclear apartheid. But its strategic implications are deeper, as it is likely to open doors for more substantive co-operation in the sphere of high technology.

The efforts to improve trade and investment led to another strategic initiative – India's Look East policy in 1992. Addressing the 16th Asia Society Corporate Conference at Mumbai on March 16, 2006, Prime Minister Manmohan Singh explained the policy's rationale: 'This was not merely an external economic policy, it was also

---

poverty, accessed on September 16, 2011. For details see Table A6.3 at the end of this chapter.

[28] Stockholm International Peace Research Institute (SIPRI), Military Expenditure Database, 'Military Expenditure of India'. Available at http://milexdata.sipri.org/result.php4, accessed on September 22, 2011.

a strategic shift in India's vision of the world and India's place in the evolving global economy'.[29] During the cold war, India was unable to secure the status of a dialogue partner with the ASEAN. Subsequently, trade and economic relations between India and Southeast Asia have grown significantly. India's trade with the ASEAN region has risen from USD 5.8 billion in 1996–97 to USD 43.9 billion in 2009–10.[30] In 1992, India was accorded the status of a sectoral dialogue partner and, by 1995, it became a full dialogue partner. Soon thereafter, India was invited to join the ASEAN Regional Forum, which was meant to serve as a platform for security dialogue in the region. And in December 2005, India was invited to the East Asia Summit, comprising ASEAN countries and India, China, Japan, Australia and New Zealand. A number of trade, Comprehensive Economic Partnership and Economic Co-operation agreements with various countries have been concluded in pursuance of a conscious policy of deeper economic engagement.[31]

Stronger links with West Asia have also been forged not only to promote trade but also in view of India's growing energy requirements and the presence of nearly 5 million Indians in the Gulf region. India imports nearly 75 per cent of its oil from sources abroad, of which three fourths come from the Middle East, in particular the Persian Gulf region. Indians living in this region annually remit around USD 10 billion to India. The region serves as an important market for Indian goods and services. Recognising its importance, India launched a 'Look West' policy in July 2005 to pursue closer

---

[29] 'Prime Minister Dr. Manmohan Singh's Address at the 16th Asian Corporate Conference on 'Driving Global Business : India's New Priorities, Asia's New Realities', Embassy of India, Washington DC, March 18, 2006. Available at http://www.indianembassy.org/prdetail931/--%09--prime-minister-dr.-manmohan-singh's-address-at-the-16th-asian-corporate-conference-driving-global-business-%3A-india's-new-priorities,-asia's-new-realities, accessed on September 20, 2011.

[30] Department of Commerce, Ministry of Commerce and Industry, Government of India, Export-Import Data Bank figures. Available at http://commerce.nic.in/eidb/default.asp, accessed on September 15, 2011. For details see Table A6.6 at the end of this chapter.

[31] Broad list of these on-going engagements or agreements, given in Tables A6.4 and A6.5 provide some idea of the range and depth of India's growing integration with the world.

economic relations with its neighbours in the Gulf. It has also sought to increase its naval contacts in the region keeping in view the need for the safe transit of energy and trade flows.

DIVERSIFICATION IN DEFENCE RELATIONS

The demise of the bipolar world order and India's outward orientation have opened up strategic choices for India. India's defence diplomacy has grown manifold and diversified. During the cold war, India's defence relations were confined mainly to the erstwhile Soviet Union and some countries of East Europe. However, following India's rapid growth, its growing defence budgets and defence modernisation programmes have given impetus to India's defence diplomacy. During the past two decades, India has been able to establish defence co-operation with 47 countries. In 1992, diplomatic relations were established with Israel. Since then, defence co-operation between the two countries in the form of high technology imports, intelligence-sharing and counter-terrorism has flourished. Israel is now the second largest source of defence supplies to India. Such a vibrant defence relationship would have been unthinkable during the Cold War years.

IMPACT ON INDIA'S SECURITY

What has been the impact of the neoliberal shift on India's security environment? Any answer to this question is likely to be contested. Using different lenses and arguments, very diverse conclusions can be reached. This chapter's argument is that, so far, India's neoliberal policies have been ineffective in improving her security environment. Admittedly, this cannot be attributed to India's grand strategy or any one factor alone. International relations have been aptly likened to macro-economics, where many variables are at work simultaneously.

India's neoliberalism has undoubtedly catapulted her into the league of major emerging powers, and it is slated to emerge as the world's third strongest power in a few decades.[32] Its relations

---

[32] National Intelligence Council (NIC), Office of the Director of National Intelligence, 'Global Trends 2025: A Transformed World', November 2008, p. 7. Available at www.dni.gov/nic/NIC_2025_project.html, accessed on September 19, 2011.

with major powers have undergone a transformation, particularly with industrialised democracies like the US, Japan and South Korea. The most noteworthy development is its growing strategic partnership with the US, which had tended to view India as a part of the Soviet bloc just two decades ago. India is active in multilateral fora such as the India, Brazil and South Africa (IBSA); Brazil, Russia, India, China and South Africa (BRICS); ASEAN Regional Forum (ARF); East Asia Summit (EAS); Group of Twenty (G-20); among others. With the India-US civil nuclear deal her nuclear apartheid has ended. Thus, the changing geopolitical environment coupled with India's neoliberal policies have deepened her engagement with key countries and facilitated her integration in a globalising economy.

However, it would be premature to conclude that as a result of this shift in strategy, India's security environment has improved significantly or that the co-operation and interdependence thus developed has minimised her security challenges. India's adversarial relations with Pakistan persist and the latter continues to view India as its principal threat. Despite several bold initiatives on India's part, Pakistan treats Jammu and Kashmir as the Partition's unfinished business; terror has been used relentlessly as an instrument of Pakistan state's policy; and some radical militant outfits in Pakistan continue to pursue a viscerally hostile anti-India agenda. Following the terror attack on India's parliament in 2001, the two countries nearly went to war. The perpetrators of the November 2008 terror attack on Mumbai had links with elements within the Pakistani establishment. Despite call for their removal by India and constant international pressure terrorists' camps continue to be operated on Pakistani territory. The composite dialogue process between the two countries has been held hostage to political differences and has made very limited headway. Despite the large potential, bilateral trade remains minimal (USD 2.23 billion in 2008) and business links weak. Overall, the relations between the two countries remain brittle, the threat of terrorism against India remains and an outbreak of hostilities cannot be ruled out.

The Peoples' Republic of China is the other key neighbour with which India was engaged in a war in 1962. This led to deep distrust which continues to persist. Several initiatives have been taken over the past two decades which include high level political visits, impetus to bilateral trade and investment, cultural exchanges, defence exchanges and people-to-people contact. Between 1990–91 and 2009–10 bilateral trade grew impressively from a mere USD 18.2 million to USD 42.4 billion. With over USD 60 billion worth of trade now, China is among India's largest trading partners.[33] In terms of the number of bilateral agreements, dialogues, ministerial visits and issue of visas, between 1990 and 2006, there has been a significant and progressive increase in interactions.[34] During his visit to China in January 2008, the Indian PM signed a joint vision document with the Chinese PM, which resolved to develop 'strategic and co-operative partnership for peace and prosperity between the two countries'.[35] However, this growing co-operation, particularly in the economic field, has not reduced the trust deficit. The boundary dispute between the two countries remains unresolved despite fifteen rounds of bilateral dialogue. The Chinese Government is perceived to have become more assertive on its claims particularly on Arunachal Pradesh. Visas have been denied to residents of Arunachal Pradesh and stapled visas were for some time issued to people of Jammu and Kashmir. China's 'all-weather friendship' with Pakistan which has included assistance for Gwadar port, nuclear and missile technology and systematic development of strategic infrastructure close to India's northern border have caused grave misgivings in India. Chinese assistance to and presence in Myanmar, Bangladesh, Sri Lanka, and Pakistan have deepened distrust of China among India's strategic community. In a recent study of China and India, Jonathan Holstag has concluded that 'trade and mutual economic gains have not neutralised the military security dilemma between the two countries'.[36]

---

[33] Ministry of External Affairs, Government of India, 'India-China Relations', August 2011, p. 5. Available at http://www.mea.gov.in/mystart.php?id=50042452, accessed on September 21, 2011.

[34] Jonathan Holstag, *China + India, Prospects for Peace* (New York: Columbia University Press, 2009), p. 62.

[35] Ministry of External Affairs, Government of India, 'A Shared Vision for the 21st Century of the Republic of India and the People's Republic of China', January 14, 2008. Available at http://www.mea.gov.in/mystary.php?id=500413515, accessed on September 21, 2011.

[36] Holstag, *China + India,* p. 169.

A key test of India's neoliberal strategy would be its efficacy in India's neighbourhood. As an institution founded in 1985 to promote regional co-operation, the South Asian Association for Regional Co-operation (SAARC) has been described as a 'somnolent and disappointing regional body'.[37] In its initial years, it was seen by India as an effort by her smaller neighbours to 'gang up' against her. However, over time, India's attitude towards her neighbours and SAARC has changed. Speaking to parliamentarians from SAARC countries in June 2007, India's External Affairs Minister Pranab Mukherjee expressed his belief that: 'South Asian countries can work together to emerge as a major powerhouse of economic creativity and enterprise.'[38] He also reiterated that India was ready to accept asymmetrical responsibilities. Prime Minister Manmohan Singh articulated his own neoliberal vision of the neighbourhood through 'greater connectivity in transport, road, rail, and waterways links, communication, transit routes through each other's territory transforming each sub-region of the sub-continent into an interconnected web of economic and commercial links [in order to ...] create mutual dependencies for mutual benefit'.[39] However, India's neighbours see considerable gap between pronouncements and performance. Intra South Asian trade in total trade of South Asian countries remains around an abysmal 5 per cent, rising from 3 per cent in 1991.[40] The 'glacial' progress of SAARC can be attributed to a

---

[37] Rajeev Ranjan Chaturvedy and David M. Malone, 'India and Its South Asian Neighbours', Working Paper No. 100 (November 26, 2009), Institute of South Asian Studies (ISAS), National University of Singapore.

[38] 'Address by External Affairs Minister, Shri Pranab Mukherjee to the Conference of Parliamentarians from SAARC Region on '"Evolving South Asian Fraternity": Calls For Free Movement of People and Goods in the Region', Ministry of External Affairs, Government of India, June 3, 2007. Available at http:www.mea.gov.in/mystrat.php?id=530112877, accessed on September 19, 2011.

[39] 'Speech by Prime Minster Dr Manmohan Singh at India Today Conclave', New Delhi, Ministry of External Affairs, Government of India, February 25, 2005. Available at http://www.mea.gov.in/mystart.php?id=53019055, accessed on September 19, 2011.

[40] International Monetary Fund, 'Direction of Trade Statistic'. Available at http://elibrary-data.imf.org/FindDataReports.aspx?d=33061&e=170921, accessed on September 10, 2010.

variety of factors: (*a*) India's initially lukewarm attitude to SAARC; (*b*) Its continued emphasis on bilateral relations; (*c*) the distrust of India's smaller neighbours; (*d*) India's inability as the largest and pivotal country to provide public goods in the region; (*e*) meagre inter-state economic links; (*f*) Pakistan's intransigence; and (*g*) the role of extra-regional powers.[41] It should be clarified, however, that SAARC is just one aspect of India's neighbourhood policy, and has been briefly discussed here just as a case study of the oldest regional institution in post-colonial South Asia.

Identifying Impediments

Why has the shift in India's grand strategy achieved only modest outcomes and what factors operate as impediments to this approach? At least some tentative conclusions can be reached based on the experience so far. These can promote further debate regarding neoliberal influences on India's grand strategy and on the possible measures for developing 'complex interdependence'.

Such impediments may operate at the geopolitical, regional or bilateral levels. First, among the geopolitical factors it is necessary to consider the adverse consequences of the ongoing economic crisis which has led to widespread unemployment in the US, a deep, persistent recession and calls for protectionist measures. The European Union is also undergoing a similar crisis, with the fear of sovereign default by countries like Greece, unemployment and popular resentment against austerity measures. These developments could lead to serious questions about unfettered, free-market policies and may have global consequences. Already, in India the growth of the Naxalite movement, protests regarding land acquisition and environmental damage caused by large projects is being attributed to neoliberal economic policies. Similar protests have been reported from China. These developments could lead to a backlash and the erosion of popular support for neoliberal policies both domestically and in the international domain. Neoliberal strategies in international relations need to be, therefore, accompanied by domestic policies to address the issues of equity and inclusive growth.

---

[41] Vidya Nadkarni, *Strategic Partnerships in Asia, Balancing Without Alliances* (New York: Routledge, 2010), pp. 187–93.

Second, it would appear that in the current geopolitical environment characterised by greater interactions amongst states, India's relations with the Peoples' Republic of China and Pakistan and her other neighbours cannot be seen in isolation. During the past two decades, India has moved closer both to the US and Japan and its relations with South Korea and Australia are also growing. On the other hand, China's relations with Pakistan have also grown with continuing assistance to the latter in the nuclear sphere. Similarly, China is active amongst India's neighbouring countries, that is, Myanmar, Bangladesh, Sri Lanka, and Nepal. These developments are a source of growing distrust on either side. It is difficult to conceive of 'complex interdependence' just between India and China unless countries like the US and Japan are also seen as supportive of such a partnership and also participate in larger co-operation frameworks in the region. At the very least, the existing distrust will have to be dispelled to facilitate genuine partnership between China and India on the one hand and India and her other neighbours on the other. If India's partnership with the US and Japan is perceived as a countervailing move vis-à-vis China and if China's relations with Pakistan are similarly viewed in India, greater bilateral co-operation and interdependence is unlikely.

Third, as argued by Mearsheimer, political pronouncements regarding constructive co-operation are often rhetorical, made to satisfy domestic or foreign publics.[42] Keohane and Nye also point out that 'Political leaders often use interdependence rhetoric to portray inter-dependence as a natural necessity' and that 'co-operation alone holds the answer to world problems'.[43] Behind closed doors, however, political elites speak the language of power. History is replete with examples in which major powers have unhesitatingly shown their disdain for international institutions, regimes and norms. More recently, while addressing common security challenges, such as security of space, cyber space, nuclear proliferation, terrorism, and climate change, countries have given precedence to national interests over co-operation. These factors are likely to constrain the impulse for co-operation in India's strategic behaviour.

---

[42] John J. Mearsheiner, *The Tragedy of Great Power Politics* (New York: W.W. Norton & Company, 2001).

[43] Keohane and Nye, *Power and Interdependence*, pp. 5–7.

At the regional, bilateral and national levels, there are at least six factors which can impede greater co-operation and interdependence. First, India's trading and economic relationship with all its neighbours is limited. Even with China, despite booming trade, the trade composition does not create the type of interdependence which can work as a safeguard against possible hostilities. It has been pointed out that over time, as India's economy matures, existing complementarities can disappear. Further, there is a risk of competition between the two countries both for consumer markets and raw materials. Hence, the bilateral economic linkages have to be diversified, made deeper and continually dynamic.

Second, societal interactions between India and its neighbours including China are weak. With China, despite long civilisational links, there are cultural and linguistic differences. In contrast, India shares a common language and liberal political values with the US and much greater people-to-people contact, which is reinforced by 2.5 million Indian diaspora there. While India enjoys common historical and cultural bonds with its neighbours, because of the asymmetries in size and strength, she is perceived as hegemonic. A pre-requisite for greater co-operation, therefore, is much greater interaction and communication at the societal level.

Third, the neoliberal orientation in India's external strategy cannot be divorced from domestic politics. Domestic opposition can stymie efforts at reconciliation or interstate co-operation. There is a need to develop popular support for such policies through systematic coalition building amongst stake holders within states and across states. A recent example in which the Chief Minister of West Bengal declined to accompany the Indian Prime Minister on a visit to Bangladesh and, thus, obstructed the conclusion of an agreement for sharing of the Teesta river waters, underscores the need for such coalition building.[44]

Fourth, institutional linkages between India and the countries in her neighbourhood including China remain inadequate. While bilateral agreements, multiple exchanges and dialogue mechanisms do

---

[44] Mohua Chatterjee, 'Mamata Banerjee refuses to go to Dhaka with PM', *The Times of India*, September 5, 2011. Available at http://articles.timesofindia.indiatimes.com/2011-09-05/india/30115583_1_teesta-water-bangladesh-visit-mamata-banerjee, accessed on October 11, 2013.

exist, these do not ensure state behaviour in accordance with agreed norms, procedures or rules. The existing institutions cannot mediate differences and resolve disputes fairly. The absence of strong institutional frameworks thus impedes interdependence.

Fifth, the existence of an overarching threat can facilitate interstate co-operation. The success of the European Union is partly attributed to the American security umbrella and the common Soviet threat. While no such threat exists in the region, there are grave common challenges like terrorism, religious extremism, natural disasters, climate change, environmental degradation, the ongoing global economic crisis and water shortage, which are present or looming on the horizon. These can be met only through transnational co-operative approaches and should provide a strong basis for co-operation. China and India have, with some success, already attempted co-operation in the area of trade and climate change negotiations. These challenges offer potential opportunities for greater co-operation with a larger number of actors in the region and the global community.

Sixth, complex interdependence should enable the concerned states to re-order the inter-se priority of their national interests or even redefine them. The density of such interdependence should be such that the states and societies learn to prefer absolute over relative gains. Issues of military security, territory and sovereignty should be under-emphasised in the inter-se priority of national interests and the greater benefits of co-operation like mutual security, economic prosperity and enhanced capacity to meet common challenges, should receive precedence. Such a stage can be reached when there are multiple levels of contact and communication, genuine economic interdependence and strong enough coalitions of stakeholders, who clearly see the greater benefits of mutual co-operation. Such coalition building efforts with stakeholders will be needed in India, Pakistan, China and among India's other neighbours, failing which traditional perceptions of national interest are likely to stymie co-operation.

In sum, it must be noted that India's strategic initiatives to promote interdependence and co-operation are still at a nascent stage. There is need to learn from her past experience and pursue with greater vigour approaches which promote genuinely complex interdependence.

Conclusion

This chapter has attempted to analyse the circumstances under which India's grand strategy began to be influenced by neoliberal ideas. It would, however, be simplistic to describe India's grand strategy as unalloyed neoliberalism. It remains and will continue to remain an amalgam of various strands of thought. India's strategic reorientation towards neoliberalism has evolved as a consequence of her economic liberalisation and the end of the Cold War. The shift in strategy has benefited India in many ways, particularly in accelerating its economic growth, its deepening engagement with all major powers and its growing integration with the global economy. It has also led to the opening of a new chapter in its relations with its neighbours including Pakistan and the Peoples' Republic of China. However, the strategy has not yet succeeded in significantly improving the security environment in India's neighbourhood and in particular, its relations with Pakistan and China. While this strategy has led to greater exchanges, interactions and trade, it has not succeeded in resolving India's security challenges. To optimise the outcomes of this strategy, there is a need to focus on intensifying societal and commercial interactions and developing stronger institutional mechanisms. The objective should be to establish genuinely 'complex interdependence' which can ensure greater co-operation, mutual gains and mitigate the risks of conflict.

However, none of these efforts will guarantee peace for all times to come and therefore, strategists will do well not to 'ignore the role of military security in an era of peace and economic growth' for that would be 'like forgetting the importance of oxygen to our breathing'.[45]

---

[45] Keohane and Nye, Power and Interdependence, pp. xvii.

Appendix

Table A6.1: External Sector (in USD million)

	1990-91	2000-1	2005-6	2006-7	2007-8	2008-9	
Exports	18,143	44,076	103,091	126,414	163,132	185,295	Exports
Imports	24,075	49,975	149,166	185,735	251,654	303,696	Imports
Foreign Currency Reserves	2,236	39,554	145,108	191,924	299,230	241,426	Foreign Currency Reserves
Foreign Investment Inflows	103	5,862	15,528	14,753	43,326	8,341	Foreign Investment Inflows

Source: Ministry of Finance, Government of India, *Economic Survey 2012–13*, p. A83. Available at http://indiabudget.nic.in/, accessed on August 28, 2013; and Reserve Bank of India, *Handbook of Statistics on Indian Economy*. Available at http://www.rbi.org.in/scripts/AnnualPublications.aspx?head=Handbook%20of%20Statistics%20on%20Indian%20Economy, accessed on August 28, 2013.

Table A6.2: India's Share in World Exports by Commodity Divisions and Groups

Year	World exports (USD million)	India's exports (USD million)	India's share in world exports (%)
1990	3,303,563	18,143	0.5
2000	6,254,511	41,543	0.7
2007	13,800,097	145,898	1.1
2008	15,926,318	181861	1.1

Source: United Nations: 2008 International Trade Statistics Year Book, UN-2009, as cited in Ministry of Finance, Government of India, *Economic Survey 2010–11*, pp. A100–103. Available at http://indiabudget.nic.in/budget2011-2012/es2010-11/estat1.pdf, accessed on April 5, 2011.

Table A6.3: Comparison of India's Poverty Estimates (%)

	1993–94	2004–05
Rural	37.3	28.3
Urban	32.4	25.7
Total	36.0	27.5

Source: Planning Commission, Government of India, *Poverty Estimates for 2004–5*. March 2007. Available at http://pib.nic.in/release/release.asp?relid=26316&kwd=poverty, accessed on September 4, 2010.

Table A6.4: Trade Agreements: India's Current Engagements in RTAs during the Post-1991 Period

India–Sri Lanka Comprehensive Economic Partnership Agreement (CEPA) negotiations
India–Thailand Comprehensive Economic Co-operation Agreement (CECA) negotiations
India–Malaysia Comprehensive Economic Co-operation Agreement (CECA) negotiations
India–Indonesia Comprehensive Economic Co-operation Agreement (CECA) negotiations
Bay of Bengal Initiative for Multi-Sectoral Technical and Economic Co-operation (BIMSTEC) Free Trade Agreement (FTA) negotiations
India–Gulf Co-operation Council (GCC) Free Trade Agreement (FTA) negotiations
India–Mauritius Comprehensive Economic Co-operation and Partnership Agreement (CECPA) negotiations
India–SACU Preferential Trade Agreement (PTA) negotiations
India–Pakistan Trading Arrangement
India–EU Board Based Trade and Investment Agreement negotiations
India European Free Trade Association (EFTA) Negotiations on broad based Bilateral Trade and Investment Agreement
India–Chile Preferential Trade Agreement (PTA) negotiations

Source: Department of Commerce, Ministry of Commerce and Industry, Government of India, 'Trade Agreements'. Available at http://commerce.nic.in/index.asp, accessed on September 6, 2010.

Table A6.5: Agreements Already Concluded

The Agreement on SAARC Preferential Trading Arrangement (SAPTA) signed was in Dhaka on April 11, 1993 between the People's Republic of Bangladesh, the Kingdom of Bhutan, the Republic of India, the Republic of Maldives, the Kingdom of Nepal, the Islamic Republic of Pakistan, and the Democratic Socialist Republic of Sri Lanka.
The India–Sri Lanka Free Trade Agreement (ILFTA) was signed on December 28, 1998.
A Preferential Trade Agreement was signed between India and Afghanistan on March 6, 2003 in New Delhi.
A Framework Agreement was signed between India and MERCOSUR on June 17, 2003 at Asuncion, Paraguay. MERCOSUR is a trading bloc in Latin America comprising Brazil, Argentina, Uruguay and Paraguay, founded in 1991.
India and Thailand a signed a Free Trade Agreement (FTA) on October 9, 2003.

Table A6.5 (Continued)

Table A6.5 (Continued)

- The Agreement on South Asian Free Trade Area (SAFTA) was signed by all the member states of the South Asian Association for Regional Co-operation (SAARC), namely, India, Bangladesh, Bhutan, Maldives, Nepal, Pakistan, and Sri Lanka, during the Twelfth SAARC Summit held in Islamabad on January 4–6, 2004.
- The India–Singapore Comprehensive Economic Co-operation Agreement (CECA) was signed on June 29, 2005, during Prime Minister Lee Hsien Loong's State Visit to India.
- The Bangkok Agreement renamed as Asia Pacific Trade Agreement (APTA) was signed in the first session of the Ministerial Council on November 2, 2005 in Beijing, China. The Agreement is operational among five countries namely, Bangladesh, China PR, India, Republic of Korea, and Sri Lanka.
- The Agreement on Trade and Commerce between India and Bhutan was concluded in January 17, 1972. It has been renewed periodically, with mutually agreed modifications. The current Agreement between the two countries on Trade, Commerce and Transit was renewed on July 28, 2006 and was operational from July 29, 2006 for a period of 10 years.
- India and South Korea signed the Comprehensive Economic Partnership Agreement (CEPA) on August 7, 2009.
- The India–Association of South East Asian Nations (ASEAN) Free Trade Agreement (FTA) was signed was signed on August 13, 2009. India's engagement with the Association of South East Asian Nations (ASEAN) started with its 'Look East Policy' in the year 1991. ASEAN has a membership of 10 countries, namely Brunei Darussalam, Cambodia, Indonesia, Lao PDR, Malaysia, Myanmar, Philippines, Singapore, Thailand, and Vietnam. India became a Sectoral Dialogue Partner of ASEAN in 1992 and Full Dialogue Partner in 1996. In November 2001, the ASEAN–India relationship was upgraded to the summit level.
- India and Nepal signed a new Trade Treaty in October 27, 2009.
- Agreement on Economic Co-operation between India and Finland was signed on March 26, 2010.
- SAARC Agreement on Trade In Services (SATIS) was signed on April 29, 2010 between the Governments of the South Asian Association for Regional Co-operation (SAARC) Member States comprising the Islamic Republic of Afghanistan, People's Republic of Bangladesh, the Kingdom of Bhutan, the Republic of India, the Republic of Maldives, Nepal, the Islamic Republic of Pakistan, and the Democratic Socialist Republic of Sri Lanka.
- The India–Japan Comprehensive Economic Partnership Agreement (CEPA) was signed on February 16, 2011 in Tokyo, Japan. India–Japan CEPA entered into force on August 1, 2011. This is India's 3rd Comprehensive Economic Partnership Agreement (after Singapore and South Korea) and India's first with a developed country.

Source: Department of Commerce, Ministry of Commerce and Industry, Government of India, 'Trade Agreements'. Available at http://commerce.nic.in/index.asp, accessed on September 6, 2010.

Table A6.6: India's Trade with ASEAN (USD billion)

Year	Exports	Imports	Total
1996–97	2.9	2.9	5.8
2005–06	10.4	10.9	21.3
2009–10	18.1	25.8	43.9

Source: Department of Commerce, Ministry of Commerce and Industry, Government of India, *Export–Import Data Bank*. Available at http://commerce.nic.in/eidb/default.asp, accessed on September 4, 2010.

7

AN ELEPHANT WITH A SMALL 'FOOTPRINT'
THE REALIST ROOTS OF INDIA'S STRATEGIC THOUGHT AND POLICIES

Bharat Karnad

India is widely regarded as a would-be great power with a slew of mainstream realist strategic policies. It has not shied away from the use of force nor from coercing its smaller neighbours. But it professes peace and is committed to resolving disputes through negotiation. Characteristically though, India's use of hard power is more evident in domestic politics and in its extended domain, in its relations with the smaller states of the subcontinent that are within the Indian social and cultural orbit, than in its dealings with the more consequential countries. The differences in the premises and presumptions of the two separate sets of policies are at the heart of the country's strategic incoherence and potential irrelevance in the coming years.

India is among the most violent societies in the world today, immersed as it is in the turbulent processes of social reordering and nation-building.[1] In an extremely diverse and politicised milieu where tradition collides with modernity at every turn, and caste is pitted against caste, sub-castes against each other, the haves against the have-nots, the cities against the countryside, the grassroots against the provincial administrations and the states against other states

---

[1] The 2010 Global Peace Index lists India in the 'red' category of the most socially unstable states where violence is endemic, alongside Afghanistan, Pakistan and a few African states, ranking it 128 out of 149 countries examined in the survey. The GPI score for India is available at http://www.visionofhumanity.org/gpi-data/#/2010/conf/IN/detail, accessed on May 17, 2012.

and the federal government, India finds itself in a quasi-Hobbesian situation with each constituent group grabbing political space and forcefully claiming its rights and a larger share of the national pie. Yet abroad, India's image is benign, betraying none of the internal turmoil or the tendency to ready violence. It is, in fact, viewed by Western capitals as a rather soft, loose, if a politically rambunctious, democracy arcing upwards economically (until the recent slowdown) that, fortunately from their point of view, acts reasonably and responsibly, meaning not always against their interests in the international arena.

This chapter will show that the impulses for an upheaving polity and India's punitive and pettifogging attitude towards its South Asian neighbours are traceable to its *realpolitik*-laced ancient statecraft, and its generally low-key approach and status quo orientation when dealing with the superior states, arise from deference to hierarchy and power also embedded in the same statecraft, resulting in an over-cautious strategic mindset fuelled by perceptions of national weakness. International Relations theory-wise, it is offensive realism at work in the first instance, and defensive realism in the second.[2] In either case, it is realist considerations that shape policies, obtaining an India feared by the weaker countries in the region but projecting diffidence in its relations with the bigger powers.[3]

But what constitutes a realist outlook? Theories assume, for instance, that, in a given situation there is a clearly marked out 'realist' path separate from other sub-optimal policy tracks, and that this

---

[2] For a useful critique of the two theories, see Steven E. Lobell, 'Structural Realism/Offensive and Defensive Realism', in Robert Denemark, general editor, *The International Studies Compendium Project* (Oxford: Wiley Blackwell, 2010), pp. 6651–69.

[3] Speaking on June 1, 2010 at the Council on Foreign Relations, New York, on the eve of the first Ministerial-level India–United States Strategic Dialogue in Washington involving the Indian Minister for External Affairs S. M. Krishna and the American Secretary of State Hillary Clinton, the US Under-Secretary of State William Burns said: 'Some Americans worry ... that India sometimes has a hard time realising how far its influence and its interests have taken it beyond its immediate neighbourhood ... that India doesn't see as clearly as others do how vital its own role in Asia is becoming'. The text of this speech, 'India's Rise and the Promise of U.S.–Indian Partnership', is available at http://www.state.gov/p/us/rm/2010/136718.htm, accessed on May 17, 2012.

is discernible to policymakers and the interested public alike. Historical evidence suggests, however, that policy is variable because it is moulded by the leader's threat perception and assessment of the situation, and his risk-averse or risk-acceptant nature. This predisposes him to view the external reality and domestic and other constraints in a certain light, define the goals accordingly and to craft policies to match, all the while being convinced that his chosen policy course is realistic and maximises benefits without compromising vital national interests. And, ultimately, a realist policy judged by its positive outcome.

Nothing illustrates the point better than the saga of Vidkun Quisling. A former Norwegian army major, who staged a short-lived coup in Oslo in 1940 and, two years later, was installed at the head of a friendly 'National Socialist' regime by Hitler. Quisling – an anglophile, actually – very early saw a major war coming and in the 1930s railed against measly military spending which he feared would deny Norway credible means of defence. He espoused neutrality as a way of balancing Britain's maritime dominance of Norway's seaward flank with Germany's land-based ambitions. It is another matter that Quisling eventually acquiesced in the Nazi order as, perhaps, a second-best option and won himself lasting infamy.[4] But to indulge in the what-ifs of history, what if the Axis Powers had won the war and Germany remade Europe and the world in its image? Quisling would have been hailed as a leader who, having correctly gauged the game, did the right thing by Norway. And his methods would have been copied by less well-endowed countries caught up in regional power dynamics.

Indian policies are in a different sort of twilight zone. Anchored at one end culturally and subconsciously in the Hindu hyperrealist strategic thought originating in the Vedas – the four great books and repositories of the wisdom of the Indic civilisation – and at the other, tethered rhetorically, at least, to Mahatma Gandhi's brand of pixilated pacifism[5] and, more substantively, to Jawaharlal Nehru's

---

[4] Hans Fredrik Dahl, *Quisling: a Study in Treachery*, trans. by Anne-Marie Stanton-Ife (Cambridge: Cambridge University Press, 1999), pp. 115–116, 120, 136, 147–49, 157, 171–93.

[5] For a detailed analysis proving that Mahatma Gandhi's *moralpolitik* – the use of morality as a political instrument – was inconsistent and more of a nuisance than an effective political weapon against the British colonial

1950s worldview, Indian strategic policies seem, at once, expedient, archaic and short-sighted. Moreover, burdened in recent years by the excessive international expectations of 'responsible state behaviour', which New Delhi has done everything to stoke, the surprise is that India has had any strategic impact at all. Using a broad-brush analysis, policies relating to Pakistan, China and the United States (US) will be deconstructed in this chapter in terms of the traditional Indian statecraft and Nehruvian logic. The aim specifically is to plumb the extent to which the Vedic postulates of the use of hard power and Prime Minister Manmohan Singh's personal tilt towards soft power, which is mistakenly attributed to Nehruvian thinking that the ruling Congress Party has a stake in, inform the three policy streams.

Vedic Precepts, *Arthashastra*, and Domestic and Subcontinental Politics[6]

The values, principles, postulates, and procedures that animated the ancient Hindu statecraft were catalogued, codified and commented upon in 323 BCE by Kautilya (also known as Chanakya), the advisor to Emperor Chandragupt Maurya – the first of the great rulers to hold sway over what is now most of South Asia, including Afghanistan. The resulting compilation bearing the title *Arthashastra* – translated from Sanskrit literally as the *Science of Material Gain* – contained practical advice to the sovereign on strategies and stratagems of war and peace, on the ways to maintain order in society and safeguard interests, to continually expand and strengthen the realm and effectively

---

regime, see Bharat Karnad, *Nuclear Weapons and Indian Security: The Realist Foundations of Strategy*, 2nd edn (New Delhi: Macmillan India, 2005[2002]), pp. 29–64.

[6] All quotes and references to Vedic texts, information about and insights into the ancient Hindu statecraft reflected in treatises, including the *Arthashastra* and *Sukraniti*, in this chapter are derived from Karnad, *Nuclear Weapons and Indian Security*, pp. 3–19. There is growing appreciation of the traditional Indian statecraft, especially Kautilya, in the West. See Roger Boesche, *The First Great Political Realist: Kautilya and His Arthashastra* (Lanham, MD: Lexington Books, 2003), and Torkel Brekke, 'Wielding the Rod of Punishment: War and Violence in the Political Science of Kautilya', *Journal of Military Ethics*, 3, 1 (March 2004), pp. 40–52.

to manage it for the extraction of maximum benefit. It provides a 'tool-kit' for the conduct of international relations always with an eye to territorial aggrandisement, increasing influence, wealth and power of the state and to attaining predominance. Most of its contents were distilled from the four Vedas – *Rig Veda, Sama Veda, Yajur Veda*, and *Atharva Veda* and what is regarded as the fifth Veda, the Puranas, featuring, among numerous stories, myths and legends, the two great epics – the Mahabharata and the Ramayana, which continue (to this day) to shape the thinking of the people and colour political discourse. Thus, Indian politicians routinely invoke characters from these epics, referring to the values they represent and the principled actions attributed to them in criticising opponents or justifying their own posture and attitude.[7] (The Vedas have been sourced back to two to four millennia; a more precise dating by historians has not been possible.) Considering that India has long been associated with morality, spirituality and pacifistic otherworldliness, the hard-headed, no-nonsense and strictly ends-focused (means be damned!) policy approach, packaged in the ancient texts and updated by Kautilya in his codex, and portrayed even more starkly in the later treatises such as the *Sukraniti*, is astounding in its clarity, suggesting an alternative basis for worldview and policies that could have served the country's interests better in the modern day.

International relations are governed, say the Vedas, by 'the law of the fish', of big fish swallowing the small fish until there remains only the hegemon or *chakravartin*, with a realm extending to 'the very ends uninterrupted (so as to) constitute one state and administration up to the seas'. The *vijigisu* (aspirant) is enjoined by the *Rig Veda*, the most important of the Vedas, to become the *chakravartin* in an ever-enlarging territorial space acquired by 'subjugating' and 'absorbing'

---

[7] In a recent controversy in the Gujarat province run by the opposition Bharatiya Janata Party (BJP) involving an investigation into the alleged involvement of the Chief Minister Narendra Modi and Home Minister Amit Shah in an extra-legal killing of an extortionist, the Congress Party pleaded with the BJP to stop supporting these two leaders, and cited characters and events in the Ramayana to buttress their case. See 'Congress Cites Ramayana, to Ask BJP to Shun Modi, Shah', *DNA*, July 28, 2010. Available at http://www.dnaindia.com/india/report_congress-cites-ramayana-to-ask-bjp-to-shun-modi-shah_1415863, accessed on May 17, 2012.

smaller states, which process is said to usher in peace and stability. In the Vedic geopolitics, the paradigm consists of concentric circles of alternately adversarial and friendly states. By this reckoning, the adjoining set of countries is necessarily adversarial which, in turn, are bounded by the next circle of basically friendly countries and so on whom to befriend. The geopolitical thrust, therefore, is to subdue a progressively larger circle of countries, starting with those in the innermost circle with or without the help of countries in the next outer tier, while allying with states farther off and seeking their help when needed. With the sovereign enjoined to constantly enlarge his kingdom territorially by hook or by crook, the stress in the Vedic system of nation-states (*rajmandala*) is towards large composite entities, which because of their inherent capabilities and strength, are perceived as being more resilient, self-sufficient and survivable as compared to smaller entities that are not.

The collection of peoples, thus, obtained by the would-be hegemon assimilating an ever larger number of proximal states with force when persuasion fails, is *ipso facto* a more heterogeneous mix of faiths, nationalities and ethnicities, where the separate and unique identities of the various peoples the king is urged to respect. In this concept, the large states are seen to be in perpetual conflict pending the emergence, in the latter-day Darwinian sense, of the strongest and the fittest subduing all the others by whatever means and assuming the mantle of the sole hegemonic power.

The primacy accorded force, subversion and military means by the Vedas is reflected in the fact that diplomacy and other relatively peaceful methods are subsumed in the manual of war (*Yuddhakundam*). This manual lays great store by *kutayuddha* or covert war, in which espionage, assassination, poisoning and sowing dissension in enemy ranks are sanctioned as a way of softening up the enemy state as prelude to unleashing 'total war' (*samukhayuddha*) to bring it to its knees. To achieve this, the king is advised to scruple to nothing. Mirroring the nuances of modern-day concepts of nuclear deterrence, the texts suggest that enemy populations, for instance, be terrorised by the threat of use of weapons of mass destruction (WMD), but that the actual use of such weapons be considered only as a last resort. (Numerous WMD and their effects are sketched out in vivid detail, with the ultimate weapon – the *brahmastra*, for example, being described as exploding with the brightness of 'a thousand crore suns'!).[8] According to the Puranas, the causes of war are many: aggression by another state, boundary dispute, actions prejudicial to one's sovereignty, feelings of natural hostility, espionage, violation of treaties and disturbance of the existing *mandala* or balance of power. Morality, in this scheme of things, is a situational variable, not an absolute value. In the Mahabharata, for example, Lord Krishna addresses the wavering and morally conflicted prince, Arjuna, facing his teachers and kinfolk arrayed against him on the battlefield thus: 'When life is in danger ... when one's property is at stake, truth becomes unutterable and so falsehood becomes truth and truth falsehood.' He urges the use of 'unrighteous' means, justifying it by saying that 'When the number of one's foes [becomes] great, their destruction should be effected by [all] contrivances and means.' Lord Krishna's bare-knuckled approach is in the context of the admonition in the *Rig Veda* to 'destroy' those 'unfriendly to us', including 'kindred and unallied'.

For all their apparent bloody-mindedness, however, the emphasis in the Vedic texts is on peaceful means. They warn that war is only the last recourse when *sama* (conciliatory measures), *dana* (gift, aid and assistance of all kinds) and *bheda* (sowing dissension) fail, and only *danda* (punishment, acts of violence, and war) promises the desired result. The reasons for war, declares *Sukraniti*, are the accretion of territory, wealth, power and allies gained by co-opting the defeated countries with political and material inducements. War, moreover, is to be waged only after properly studying the prevailing 'balance of forces' and the 'conjuncture of circumstances' and when victory is certain.

Such principles of the ancient statecraft had two dissimilar consequences for the evolving Indian polity over several millennia. By firing up the hegemonic ambitions of every small and big ruler in the vast subcontinent, by making the realisation of such ambition a kingly 'duty' and by offering each the same plausible game-plan for expansion and goal realisation, they ensured perpetual strife. Thus, a socio-culturally unitary nation existed but in a perpetually politically fractured condition featuring hundreds of small, medium-sized and large kingdoms, princely states and principalities, each of them with their own slightly different ethnic mix and cultural identity and

---

[8] A crore, in numerical terms, equals 10 million.

all of them exhausting themselves in endless intrigue, internecine rivalries and conflicts with each other. The whole was, thereby, rendered vulnerable to the depredations by a string of invaders from Alexander of Macedon in 322 BCE, the Umayyad Caliphate armies in 664 CE to the Mughals coming down from Central Asia and later the British venturing in from the sea.

It is a reflection of the splintered nature of the indigenous polity that in almost every instance the invader was assisted by local rulers who hoped to use the distant power signified by the foreigner to try and tilt the balance in his rivalry with the proximal adversarial state, without foreseeing the perils of this strategy in case the ambitious outsider stayed on to establish himself as the new hegemon. Thus, Alexander the Great was partnered by local Hindu kings (in what is now southern Afghanistan and northern Pakistani Punjab) in defeating the most powerful Indian sovereign in the region King Porus, in the decisive Battle of Hydespas in 326 BCE; the sword-arm of the Mughal empire in its growth stage was provided by the Hindu kings of Rajputana; and the British found local allies among the Indian rulers disaffected with the increasingly decrepit Mughal dispensation to transform a small trading outpost over several centuries into the fabled Raj. The mind of the besieged Indian ruler, in the event, when not tending to collaborationism to escape the excesses of the alien incursionist, gradually turned inward, his worldview becoming narrower, pettier. At the same time though, and notwithstanding the burgeoning diversity and pluralism as waves of invaders settled down alongside of established communities in the Indo-Gangetic heartland and in the peninsular expanse, foreign religions brought in by invaders and traders (such as Islam to the Kerala coast) got Indianised – their rituals and values taking on Hindu traits. Moreover, with masses of native converts, usually from the lower castes who had reason to escape social discrimination, the subcontinental society, with millennial memories of indecisive outcomes of incessant warring, over time subliminally internalised the pragmatic aspects of the ancient strategic methods, where more distant or more powerful nations were concerned. A latter-day manifestation of this tendency is the UPA government's desire to placate Washington by signing the nuclear deal with the US despite some very grave nuclear security concerns. A less accommodative mindset, however, endured when it came to dealing with immediate neighbours. It made for a template of prickly co-existence marred by the occasional flare-up.

Post-1947 and Partition, the newly independent countries and mainland India and Pakistan (and since 1971, the breakaway nation of Bangladesh, previously East Pakistan), shared not just the same social and cultural milieu and overlapping populations with similar ethnic, cultural and religious identities (there are more Muslims now in India than in Pakistan, the state carved out as the homeland for 'the Muslims of India'),[9] but also a unitary governmental, economic and administrative structure and space that was consolidating ever since Ashoka the Great (304–232 BCE) considerably extended the Mauryan empire by the sword, before discovering Buddhism, and the Mughals established their empire in the 16th century with the Timurid sultan, Babar, storming down into India from the Ferghana Valley. That, in this process, the undivided strategic space too was sundered, meant that the security perceptions and the military effort of the two largest successor states, India and Pakistan, turned against each other, their troubled relationship indicative of the sometimes tense relations between Hindus and Muslims in the larger sub-continental society pockmarked by unresolved disputes, frequent exchanges of hot words and fighting rhetoric but, characteristically, infrequent armed hostilities and that too of the tamer variety. When hostilities did break out, the ensuing wars were reduced by historical and socio-cultural predisposition and practice to uniquely controlled conflicts.[10]

This inhibition against decimating the 'brother enemy' was reinforced post-independence by the concept of 'marginal war' that the British academic P. M. S. Blackett, 1948 Physics Nobel Prize winner and an early defence adviser to Jawaharlal Nehru, passed on to the first Indian Prime Minister. Blackett cautioned against wasting scarce financial resources in building up the Indian armed forces

---

[9] The highly-regarded Pakistani columnist, Member of Parliament, and former civil servant, Ayaz Amir, argues that the overly Islamic identity of Pakistan is spurious because, he says, 'Throughout the 800 years of Muslim history in the subcontinent Hinduism felt threatened on occasion, but never Islam. Even when the Mughal empire was in decline and different centres of power and influence were emerging across this vast and varied land, Islam was never in danger'. See his 'Khaki Problem: Poverty of Imagination', *The News*, July 30, 2010.

[10] Karnad, *Nuclear Weapons and Indian Security*, pp. 564–72.

and conceived the concept of 'marginal war' to buttress his case.[11] Whatever India's military prowess, Blackett argued, in a war with a major power, such as the US or Russia, it would lose. On the other hand, however weak its military resources and plans, India would win against smaller neighbouring countries. Therefore, he concluded, India ought optimally to prepare for wars it can afford to fight, namely, 'marginal' wars with limited aims against a like power. After the 1947–48 operations in Kashmir, the like power-mantle was made to fit Pakistan. It is a concept that still animates Indian and Pakistani military planning – not that either country would acknowledge it – notwithstanding the fact that, India, hugely superior using any criteria at the time of Partition, has only added to its heft as a potential great power even as Pakistan lurched towards 'failed state' status. India's strategic vision has remained stuck on Pakistan, however, letting the larger, more potent, threat – China – go largely unaddressed.[12]

In the event, such India–Pakistan conflicts as have occurred have been wars of manoeuvre – in the inter-war German military terminology, *bewegrungskrieg* – except that these have proved to be nowhere as injurious to either side. Nor have they been animated by any grand objective, such as taking France out of the Second World War inside of two-odd weeks, realised by the armoured dash of the Panzer Corps under Von Manstein's Army Group 'A' across the Meuse River and the Ardennes to reach the coast. In the South Asian 'wars', Indian and Pakistani mechanised forces, while massively deployed,[13] have sought manageable counterforce tangles leading to a lot of back and forth along the border, leading in turn to the inevitable impasse in these mainly tactical contests to make at-most small theatre-level gains. These essentially force-on-force engagements may be seen as representing the chivalric code of conduct in the Vedic strategic culture that conceives 'righteous' war as the sum of individual combat

---

[11] Karnad, *Nuclear Weapons and Indian Security*, pp. 130–31.

[12] Ibid., pp. 130–31, 579.

[13] The 1965 India–Pakistan War, for instance, featured the largest concentration of armour since the Allied Eighth Army-Panzer Korps Afrika battles in the Western Desert in the Second World War. Refer to John Keegan and Andrew Wheatcroft, *Zones of Conflict: An Atlas of Future Wars* (New York: Simon & Schuster, 1986), pp. 55–56.

of soldier against soldier, war elephant against war elephant, etc.[14] It is a pattern evidenced in the India–Pakistan conflicts of 1947–48, 1965 and 1971.

These limited conflicts resulted, not surprisingly, in small casualty rates – the total fatalities on both sides being less than the number of deaths from 'police action' in either of the countries in any given year! They have taken place within a restricted geographic ambit – a narrow belt astride the border, have been constrained by time (no war has lasted more than a fortnight) and limited in their intensity (both countries preferring to build capabilities exclusively for fighting small, short duration, counter-force wars). India and Pakistan have eschewed beefing up their respective war wastage reserves and the war stocks to enable prosecution of long duration, decisive wars and used their defence allocations to acquire modern armaments and the veneer of technologically up-to-date military instead. Both sides have also scrupulously avoided civilian targeting, counter-value strikes and aerial bombardment of each other's densely populated cities. Taking all these factors into account, military professionals on both sides concede that the late Indian scholar–soldier, Major General D. K. Palit's description of India–Pakistan clashes as 'communal riots with tanks' in that they resemble riots more than they do wars, is right after all.[15]

Considering that India, owing to its organic links (of kinship and shared religion and culture) with Pakistan and because of domestic political compulsions (with Muslim voters, now wielding the 'swing vote' in almost half of the 523 Lok Sabha – Lower House of Parliament – constituencies, who will look askance at any policy

---

[14] Major General (Retd) G. D. Bakshi, 'War Fighting in Ancient India', in *Indian Way of Warfighting*, edited and compiled by Centre for Joint Warfare Studies (CENJOWS) (New Delhi: CENJOWS, 2008).

[15] For the analysis of India–Pakistan wars along these lines and how and why they resemble 'riots' more than they do hard charging, highly destructive wars of the kind we know in the modern era, see Bharat Karnad, 'Key to Peace in South Asia: Fostering "Social" Links Between the Armies of India and Pakistan', *The Round Table: The Commonwealth Journal of International Affairs*, 338 (April 1996), pp. 205–29. For a more detailed deconstruction, refer to Karnad, *Nuclear Weapons and Indian Security*, pp. 561–77; Bharat Karnad, *India's Nuclear Policy* (Westport, CN, and London: Praeger Security International, 2008), pp. 110–23.

aimed at annihilating Pakistan) has been reluctant to destroy that country by conventional military means, the possibility it will seek to do so using nuclear weapons seems very remote indeed (unless nuclear weapons use is initiated by the Pakistan Army). Besides, the consequences of dismantling would be disastrous for India. It would mean absorbing some 180 odd million Pakistani Muslims, a huge number of them radicalised – a recipe for endless civil strife. Even balkanising Pakistan would have seriously deleterious effects. Instead of one troublesome entity for New Delhi to deal with, it may have several new potentially difficult national entities to contend with, each of them seeking leverage against India by currying favour with some extra-territorial power or the other.

In this context, the Western-inspired hysteria about a 'nuclear flashpoint' in South Asia would appear to be motivated claptrap masquerading as objective research.[16] Besides, if the organic links and the dangerous uncertainties of departing from the established mode of constrained wars will not deter the Pakistan Army from initiating nuclear weapons use against India when the conventional war is being lost on the ground, the prospect of a prohibitive 'exchange ratio' – India's loss of a couple of cities in return for the certain extinction of the Pakistani state and society – surely will.[17] Nevertheless, the flashpoint thesis is propagated with great verve in the West, in Pakistan, and by many Indian analysts, most of the latter either uninformed or taking their cue from the academe in the West, notwithstanding contrary experience and empirical evidence of past wars. Then again, promoting the flashpoint thesis is a matter of survival for many Washington think-tanks and university political science departments in the United States in the business of embroidering

---

[16] For the case that the chances of an India–Pakistan nuclear exchange is improbable and why the usual deterrence theory paradigms do not apply, see Bharat Karnad, 'South Asia: The Irrelevance of Classical Nuclear Deterrence Theory', *India Review*, 4, 2 (April 2005), pp. 173–213; Karnad, *India's Nuclear Policy*, pp. 108–33.

[17] Karnad, 'South Asia: The Irrelevance of Classical Nuclear Deterrence Theory', *India Review*. Also see Bharat Karnad, 'Cold Start and the Nuclear Tripwire'. Paper presented at the International Conference on 'Cold Start: India's New Strategic Doctrine and Its Implications', Center for Contemporary Conflict, US Naval Post-Graduate School, Monterrey, California, May 29–30, 2008.

the American policy line and viewpoints and now even for some Indian institutions, relying on Western-sourced 'research' funding.[18] Further, publicising this line, for instance, allows many of these Western and Indian 'experts' to retain access to Islamabad.[19] On the flip side, even though it knows better, Pakistan frequently sounds the nuclear alarm, less because it actually fears a nuclear war or seeks to inject credibility into its deterrence posture than because it wants to firm up its leverage with its chief patron, the United States, by playing on the latter's worst fears of a nuclear 'Armageddon'[20] and the possibility of being drawn into a 'catalytic' nuclear war.[21]

But Pakistan's use of the asymmetric tool of terrorism is a problem that the Indian government seems unable to muster the will to tackle. Delhi has shown no stomach for imposing a heavy price on

---

[18] Among Indian policy research institutions, for instance, which survive on American funds and generally adhere to the US line on arms control and non-proliferation, are the New Delhi-based Delhi Policy Group and Institute of Peace and Conflict Studies.

[19] A director of a Washington think-tank, for instance, refused to publish as his Centre's monograph a paper I had written in the 1990s about the organic links between India and Pakistan making for extremely restrained war-fighting and for Delhi never contemplating a 'war of annihilation' against Pakistan – not because it did not meet his high academic standards but rather because he feared that 'the gates will close on me in Islamabad'!

[20] An illustration of the kind of fright-mongering by Pakistani officials and the like as a means of getting Washington to approve a 'nuclear deal' like the one India secured, is a recent op/ed piece by Shamshad Ahmed, the former Pakistan Foreign Secretary, who writes that India and Pakistan 'are facing a nuclear precipice with their future remaining hostage to a single accident or one strategic miscalculation', and that an 'Armageddon' may ensue. This can only be avoided, Ahmed argues, though it isn't clear how, by according Pakistan formal nuclear parity with India via a nuclear deal and in other ways! See his 'Need for Even-Handedness', *The News* (Islamabad), June 30, 2010. This 'equality of treatment' theme is the stock in trade of Pakistani government and analysts. See Shuja Nawaz, *Pakistan in the Danger Zone: A Tenuous U.S.-Pakistan Relationship* (Washington DC: Atlantic Council, June 2010). Shuja is brother of the former Pakistan Army chief, 1991–93, the late General Asif Nawaz Janjua.

[21] For the argument that the chances of the US being pulled into a 'catalytic' nuclear war triggered by Pakistani first use are extremely low, see Karnad, *India's Nuclear Policy*, pp. 128–30.

Pakistan by, in effect, laying formal claim to the Pakistan-held portions of Kashmir, helping the Freedom Movements in Baluchistan and the Muhajir Quami Movement spread disaffection in Karachi and the Sindh province, or publicising the automaticity of a punitive conventional military retaliatory strike in case of a terrorist attack (of the 26/11 type),[22] and mounting targeted intelligence operations to indicate how much Pakistan stands to lose if it persists with its policy of cross-border terrorism. It will invalidate the claim by many American and South Asian academics that Pakistan-supported terrorist acts fuel the so-called 'stability–instability paradox' in that such acts leave India no option other than to escalate matters by initiating conventional military hostilities, thereby destabilising the existing situation. It highlights the fact that India's strained forbearance in not reciprocating with like actions, in fact, reflects its policy generally towards troublesome adjoining nations and resembles the central government's attitude vis-à-vis its own sometimes restless provinces on the periphery, some of them suffering from insurgencies (Jammu and Kashmir and Manipur, Assam and Nagaland in the Northeast and the Naxalite Maoist fighters in Central India) where really hard actions to eliminate the rebels are disregarded.

More significantly, such reluctance hews to the recommendation in the Vedas to deal with domestic rebels and weaker but recalcitrant neighbours in a similar manner, with a combination of the mailed fist and generous rewards. Serious disagreements between Delhi and the provincial capitals, especially those ruled by opposition parties, are the norm. However, the internal security problems created by misgovernance and the inability to deliver development, which has resulted in the people taking up arms, have been tackled by the above tried and tested if not always successful method.[23] Thus, alongside the deployment of the army and para-military forces in

---

[22] Bharat Karnad, 'Militancy in Pakistan: Implications and Possible Strategies for India'. Paper presented at the conference on 'Countering Militancy in Pakistan: Domestic, Regional and International Dimensions', Centre for Muslim States and Societies, University of Western Australia, Crawley, August 3–4, 2009.

[23] In a televised press conference on June 30, 2010 to release his Ministry's Monthly Report, Home Minister P. Chidambaram restated this policy. Referring to the problem of tackling militants, he said: 'Political action is taking place along with action by the armed forces'.

counter-insurgency operations, secessionist movements have been quelled by special development programmes, by channelling huge financial subsidies (among all the Indian provinces, Kashmir is the biggest beneficiary of central government subventions[24]) and by offering the rebellious elements political opportunities to enter the mainstream, such as providing the leaders of insurgencies the chance to legitimately rule the states they previously sought to separate from the Union. It is a remedy that simultaneously ends uprisings, serves the desire for autonomy, and draws disaffected peoples into active national politics and the mainstream.

Thus, Lalthanhawla who led the 'freedom fighters' in the northeastern state of Mizoram, for example, was the elected Chief Minister[25] and more recently, after years of futile guerrilla wars waged against the Indian state, the United Liberation Front of Assam (ULFA) and the main Isak Muivah-faction of the militant National Socialist Council of Nagaland are preparing to negotiate peace deals with the Indian government as also their participation in state politics.[26] Insurgencies usually begin on a violent note, but years of facing the draconian provisions of the Armed Forces Special Powers Act induces fatigue all round and saps the will of the people to support the rebellion. The insurgents end up losing popular support and soon enough they sue for peace unless, of course, the insurgency is stoked by a neighbouring country, such as the secessionist–Jihadi

---

[24] Jammu and Kashmir state relies on the Centre for some 60 per cent of its expenditure. Compare this figure with the next eight northeastern states combined, which have also been wracked by insurgencies, but look to the Federal government for subsidies amounting to 49 per cent of their expenditures. See Subodh Varma, 'J&K Dependency on Centre Alarming', *The Times of India*, July 19, 2010.

[25] See Lalthanhawla's speech on 'Peace Processes, Governance and Development' at the seminar on 'The North-East-Challenges of Governance', Centre for North-East Studies, Jamia Milia University, New Delhi, September 14, 2010.

[26] See Lalthanhawla, 'Peace Processes, Governance and Development'. Home Minister P. Chidambaram disclosed that the Assam Chief Minister Tarun Gogoi will decide on the modalities of negotiating peace with ULFA. Regarding Nagaland, see 'Nagas Optimistic About Talks With Centre', *Expressbuzz*, February 28, 2010. Available at http://expressbuzz.com/topic/nagas-optimistic-about-talks-with-centre/152203.html, accessed on May 17, 2012.

groups active inside Kashmir that are plugged into the Pakistan Army's Inter-Services Intelligence Directorate support system.[27]

New Delhi's attitude and policies towards the weaker countries in the 'immediate abroad' exactly mirror and are an extension of its punitive mindset and posture adopted vis-à-vis militant organisations.[28] If the country abutting India takes care not to offend, it gains from New Delhi's largesse. Bhutan has the highest per capita income in South Asia owing to an arrangement whereby India has already built and is in the process of constructing, at its own cost, a series of hydroelectric projects utilising the watershed resources of the small Himalayan kingdom, training Bhutanese personnel to run them, agreeing to pay a royalty and off-taking at commercial rates the electricity produced in excess of the local needs. It has ensured a steady source of large revenue and strengthened Bhutan's stake in an entente with India. New Delhi is trying to entice Nepal with this economic–political model of pacification (involving the potential harvesting of the Mahakali River) that promises its resources for development. Elsewhere, Bangladesh under the friendly National Awami Party regime led by Prime Minister Sheikh Hasina has been rewarded with a billion dollar grant to improve its infrastructure and the renewal of railway traffic in return for letting India use the Monga and Chittagong ports for transshipping goods to the northeastern states, clamping down on anti-India Islamic radicals[29] and denying the ULFA insurgents safe haven in that country.[30]

---

[27] The National Security Adviser Shivshankar Menon believes that the Lashkar-e-Tayyaba terrorist group is 'fused' operationally and ideologically with the Pakistani state. See 'State and Terror One in Pak: Menon', *The Indian Express*, July 21, 2010.

[28] People in the adjoining countries like Indian films, music and cultural artifacts, but fear India. Indeed, a recent public poll by the Pew Research Center in Washington DC, indicated that a majority of Pakistanis polled perceive India as more of a threat (53 per cent) than the Taliban Islamist militant group (23 per cent). See 'Pak Thinks India Bigger Threat than Taliban', *Hindustan Times* (New Delhi), July 31, 2010.

[29] The Bangladesh Supreme Court's recent ruling returning the country to a secular Constitution and banning Islamist parties helps in this cause. See 'Bangla Islamist Parties Face Shutdown After SC Verdict', *The Times of India*, July 30, 2010.

[30] See the text of the Joint Communique issued at the end of the talks that the Bangladesh Prime Minister Sheikh Hasina held with her Indian counterpart,

The Bangladeshi economist Farooq Sobhan has observed that states bordering India and wanting '8–9 percent growth and the status of a middle income country' cannot do without 'regional and sub-regional cooperation' centering on India.[31] Pakistani commentators too are beginning to wonder if their country shouldn't seek similar connectivity with India and benefit from plugging into its giant economy. A senior retired Pakistan military officer, Air Vice Marshal Shahzad Choudhry, opines that Pakistan should open itself up to trade and commerce as a means of gaining 'leverage' with India and attracting Indian investments in order to create jobs and spread prosperity. This will require Pakistan, he says, 'to dump archaic notions of security and access and instead redouble efforts to channel potential in the right direction.'[32] It is a view that meshes with the political vision that Asif Ali Zardari articulated soon after becoming President of Pakistan. He talked of economically developing the swath of land from Gwadar to the Indian border state of Gujarat in order to 'service' what he called 'the central Indian market'. The restoration of the unitary subcontinental economic space is, in any case, an end-state the economist in Prime Minister Manmohan Singh and international financial institutions devoutly desire.[33] It falls within the ambit of the Vedic injunctions (in the sama category) to purchase the loyalty of neighbouring states with generous financial assistance and trade arrangements.

But what if an adjoining state is immune to such blandishments and is undeterred by its comparative weakness? A paper democracy, uncontrolled domestic social and religious turmoil and a Gross Domestic Product (GDP) (USD 169 billion) a quarter of the size of the market capitalisation of the Mumbai (Bombay) Stock

---

Dr Manmohan Singh, in Delhi and carried in full by *The Daily Star* (Dhaka), July 1, 2010. It outlines the array of cooperative and collaborative measures the two governments are committed to implementing.

[31] Dr Rashid Ahmad Khan, 'The Imperatives of Regional Connectivity', *The Daily Times* [Islamabad], June 29, 2010.

[32] See Choudhry, 'Indo-Pak Dialogue: Undertones and Ramifications', *The Daily Times*, June 28, 2010.

[33] See the World Bank sponsored study by Sadiq Ahmed, Saman Kelegama, and Ejaz Ghani, eds, *Promoting Economic Cooperation in South Asia: Beyond SAFTA* (New Delhi: Sage, 2010).

Exchange[34] notwithstanding, Pakistan unrealistically defines itself, not only as a rival to the much larger and more powerful India, but as its literal equal in every way.[35] While the Pakistan Army's survival instinct compels it to commit to a strategy of mutual exhaustion (in Delbruckian terms, *Ermattungsstratgie*), fortunately for it, the Indian army too has a similar outlook apparently because it politically suits the Indian government to do so,[36] Islamabad is not above seriously discomfiting India by utilising the 'all weather' friendship with India's main adversary, China. This friendship has fetched Islamabad nuclear missiles, courtesy generous and continuing transfers of nuclear military technologies, materials and expertise and has kept India strategically off-balance, increased (or so Islamabad believes) Pakistan's regional and international relevance and relatively advantaged China. Islamabad's canoodling with Beijing is just what Kautilya would have ordered for a weak power seeking to make the most of a bad bargaining position. Further, Pakistan, ironically, has proved a far more agile and adept practitioner of kutayuddha or covert war than India. It has cultivated and carefully utilised terrorism as a low cost asymmetric tool of war, using its intelligence assets, including the extremist Islamist groups, such as Lashkar-e-Tayyaba (LeT) staging out of Pakistan and indigenous Indian Islamic militant outfits, such as the Indian Mujahideen and the Students Islamic Movement of India and the Progressive Front of India that have, for instance, communalised the hitherto peaceful province of Kerala.[37]

---

[34] Karnad, *India's Nuclear Policy*, p. 112.

[35] Pakistanis themselves are laceratingly critical of their country. A former Federal Secretary Roedad Khan, for instance, writes that Pakistan is associated with 'military coups, sham democracy, an accidental and powerful president, a sovereign rubber-stamp parliament, and a ceremonial prime minister' and has become 'not just a "rentier state", not just a client state [but] a slave state, ill-governed by a power-hungry junta and a puppet government set up by Washington.' See his 'A Carnival Atop a Volcano', *The News*, July 30, 2010.

[36] Karnad, *India's Nuclear Policy*, p. 110.

[37] Kerala Chief Minister V. S. Achyutanandan has charged that the Muslim-dominated Popular Front of India (PFI) has a programme for converting Hindu and Christian youth to Wahabi Islam with the lure of money and offers of marriage, with the aim of achieving a Muslim majority state and eventual separation from the Indian Union. See C. G. Manog,

It has kept the Indian government and society anxious and unsettled regarding possible Islamic militant strikes in metropolitan areas *a la* the 2008 26/11 Mumbai attack[38] and the Kashmir issue on the boil by orchestrating the protests in the Srinagar Valley.[39] In the circumstances, Delhi, while hoping to peacefully resolve all outstanding disputes with Pakistan, has fallen back on the fail-safe policy of 'trust but verify'[40] reflecting a constant of Vedic thinking and the Nehruvian approach alike – antipathy towards immediate neighbours.

Distrust, driven by history, is seemingly the bedrock of unsettled India–Pakistan relations.[41] But building trust is something Prime Minister Manmohan Singh's Pakistan policy set out to do.[42] It almost worked in 2006 when the Kashmir dispute was all but resolved in negotiations with the then President General Pervez Musharraf. The pity is that both leaders stepped back from the brink that might have fetched lasting peace – having envisaged de-militarisation; the freer movement of peoples, investments, and goods; and a formalisation of the Line of Control, which in effect would have turned it into an international boundary. The Indian leader, in a tipping of the hat to Pakistani sensitivities, also agreed to a joint mechanism ostensibly to 'oversee' the affairs on both sides of the border. These elements

---

'PFI to Make Kerala a "Muslim Country"', says VS', *The Indian Express*, July 25, 2010.

[38] 'LeT Planned More 26/11-like Strikes', *The Economic Times*, July 21, 2010.

[39] See 'State and Terror One in Pak: Menon'.

[40] Manmohan Singh is quoted as saying: 'in dealing with Pakistan, our attitude has to be trust – trust but verify. So only time will tell which way the animal will turn'. See the extracts of the Prime Minister's June 29, 2010 press conference in *The Indian Express*, June 30, 2010.

[41] The introduction of the travel permit/visa regime by the Indian government in 1947 to prevent the reverse migration of masses of Indian Muslims who, having migrated to Pakistan and finding life difficult in their new 'homeland', wanted to return to their homes in India, may have seeded bad feelings. See Vazira Fazila-Yacoobali Zamindar, *The Long Partition and the Making of Modern South Asia: Refugees, Boundaries, Histories* (New York: Columbia University Press, 2007). For the historical reasons for Muslim-Sikh/Hindu animosity, see Haroon Khalid, 'Partition and the Mughals', *The Daily Times*, July 15, 2010.

[42] See the Prime Minister's press interview in *The Indian Express*, June 30, 2010.

could well constitute the core of a final settlement of Kashmir at some point in the future.

But neither Singh nor his advisers seem to have much of a clue about how to take on China and are reduced to following the stock Nehruvian policy that is long past its sell-by date.

Subservience to China

The differences with Pakistan can be resolved given time and some generosity and goodwill on India's part because the basic ingredients for a durable peace are around.[43] How else can one explain that India has never used so seminal a leverage as water against Pakistan and the 1960 Indus Waters Treaty has remained unviolate even during the numerous India–Pakistan conflicts and crises?[44]

The trust deficit with China, however, seems unbridgeable, as much a result of clashing national interests and unresolved border disputes as of irreconcilable interests and mutual incomprehensibility of each other's policy goals. The emergence of both India and China as economic powers and rivals has exacerbated the situation. New Delhi has time and again succumbed to Chinese pressures and reacted mildly to the sustained infringement, over the years, of the disputed border – the Line of Actual Control. Repeated armed intrusions led finally in April 2013 to a military face-off and diplomatic row. Beijing has also shown scant respect for Indian interests which

---

[43] Some 63 years after Partition, it is amazing how often in the Pakistani newspapers the desire is expressed for re-forging old and resilient social and cultural links and having warm relations with India. This sentiment is particularly rife among the influential community of Muslims who moved to Pakistan. For a recent example, refer to Sehar Tariq, 'Searching for Aftab Manzil', *The News* (Islamabad), June 8, 2010.

[44] Eighty per cent of the water in the Indus River system is allocated to Pakistan and yet this has never been used as leverage by India. Even so Pakistani paranoia of being denied water remains. See Lydia Polgreen and Sabrina Tavernise, 'Water Dispute Increases India-Pakistan Tension', *The New York Times*, July 21, 2010. For a Pakistani view on the sharing of the Indus waters and why the peaceable route has helped the two countries surmount potentially difficult problems, see Nauman Asghar, 'Resolving Pak–India Water Dispute', *The Nation* (Islamabad), June 9, 2010, http://www.pkcolumns.com/2010/07/09/resolving-pak-india-water-dispute-by-nauman-asghar/, accessed on May 17, 2012.

are to have (*a*) an 'autonomous' Tibet as a buffer, (*b*) Arunachal Pradesh outside the Chinese claim-line, (*c*) various northeastern rebels in India cut off from Beijing's lifeline and, (*d*) an undammed Yarlung–Tsangpo River in Tibet guaranteeing plentiful supply of water as it becomes the Brahmaputra River on entering India.[45] Other than belatedly acknowledging the China threat,[46] New Delhi has responded gingerly to the comprehensive Chinese military and infrastructure build-up in Tibet and along the nearly 4000 km-long land border and seaward, directly threatening Indian security. Other than two Light Mountain Divisions being raised for offensive warfare purposes – seven divisions short of the strength needed to give the People's Liberation Army pause for thought – and a plan to build a network of border roads that is being implemented very slowly, there has been no matching Indian military build-up and actions and counter-measures.[47] Worse, by putting off resumption of nuclear testing to facilitate the nuclear deal with the United States, far from blunting its thermonuclear edge, India has allowed China to retain it.[48] Instead, New Delhi hopes the rapprochement with America will pay off in terms of strategic security coverage vis-à-vis China. With regard to the geopolitical shoving of India into the corner even in South Asia which Beijing has managed to insulate itself, India has reacted with little more than the usual hand-wringing and waffle.[49]

---

[45] As to how a dammed Yarlung–Tsangpo River could lead to nuclear war, see Karnad, *India's Nuclear Policy*, pp. 146–49.

[46] Addressing the top military commanders, Defence Minister A. K. Antony said: 'We cannot lose sight of the fact that China has been improving its military and physical infrastructure. In fact, there has been an increasing assertiveness on the part of China.' Cited in Manu Pubby, 'Antony Flags China's Rising Military Power', *The Indian Express*, September 14, 2010.

[47] Bharat Karnad, 'India's Future Plans and Defence Requirements', in N.S. Sisodia and C. Uday Bhaskar, eds, *Emerging India: Security and Foreign Policy Perspectives* (New Delhi: IDSA and Promilla & Co. Publishers, 2005).

[48] Bharat Karnad, 'Firming up the Critical Capability Triad: Strategic Muscle, Sub-Conventional Punch and IT-enabled Network Centricity and Electro-Magnetic Warfare Clout', in Lieutenant General (Retd) Vijay Oberoi, *Army 2020: Shape, Size, Structure and General Doctrine for Emerging Challenges* (New Delhi: Centre for Land Warfare Studies and Knowledge World, 2005).

[49] For a take on this policy by an Indian commentator published, interestingly, in a Pakistani newspaper, see Abhishek Parajuli, 'China's Growing

India's acquiescence in the Chinese take-over of the buffer state of Tibet in 1950 and Prime Minister Nehru's deliberately meek response set the tone. Anticipating the move by Communist China to annex Tibet, the Indian Army was for a proactive policy. Following on the Lhasa-based Indian Political Agent's report suggesting military measures to pre-empt China, Lieutenant General Sir Francis Tuker, the last British General Officer Commander-in-Chief of the Eastern Army, advised Nehru in 1947 that 'rather than see a Chinese occupation of Tibet, India should be prepared to occupy the plateau itself.'[50] Such advice was ignored because Nehru had already taken to the appeasement track. Starting in the late 1940s, Nehru advocated China's entry into the United Nations and sought assurances on Formosa (Taiwan) from the United States and the United Kingdom in the expectation that a grateful China would reconsider moving against Tibet.

Once the Chinese Red Army took Lhasa, however, the tocsin was sounded again, this time by Nehru's senior-most cabinet colleague and a stalwart of the Freedom Movement, Home Minister Vallabhbhai Patel, known for his no-nonsense ways. In a famous letter dated November 7, 1950 to Nehru, Patel, among other things, rued the betrayal of the Tibetans' trust and faith in India, pointed out that the Prime Minister's numerous friendly gestures up till then had failed to allay China's 'suspicion' and 'scepticism' about Indian motives, observed the insidious nature of 'Chinese irredentism and Communist imperialism' and noted both the breach in India's security perimeter and the emergence for the first time of a security threat from the north and northeast. On a practical level, he noted the absence of '[c]ontinuous defensive lines' – a fact, Patel correctly predicted, that would result in a 'potentially troublesome frontier' and advocated strengthening of the Indian military on an urgent basis. Aware of Nehru's tendency to play Hamlet, he warned against vacillation and complacency and urged a cabinet discussion on an adequate response on the basis of a thorough intelligence assessment of the internal and external threat posed by China.[51]

Role in South Asia', *The Daily Times* (Islamabad), June 9, 2010, http://www.dailytimes.com.pk/default.asp?page=2010/07/09/story_9-7-2010_pg3_6, accessed on May 18, 2012.

[50] Cited in Charan Shandilya, *India–China Relations* (Ghaziabad: Pandit Sunderlal Institute of Asian Studies and Supriya Art Press, 1999), p. 50.

[51] Ibid.; the text of the Patel letter in Appendix I, pp. 190–93.

Nehru responded 11 days later but not directly to Patel, writing instead a 'Note on China' to the Ministry of External Affairs (with a copy passed on to the Home Minister) laying down the guidelines for a policy that has persisted to this day. After clarifying that India recognised Chinese 'suzerainty', not 'sovereignty', over Tibet, he ruled out the possibility of any 'major attack' by China. Firstly, because it would necessitate, he argued, the thinning out of its forces from its 'main front in the South and the East' facing Taiwan and their redeployment over the harsh Tibetan terrain, which he deemed 'inconceivable'. And secondly, owing to the rivalry between ideological blocs post-1945, he believed that a 'world war' would result should China attack India, which fact would deter Beijing from doing so. 'If we ... had to make full provisions [for such a contingency],' he additionally noted, 'this would cast an intolerable burden on us, financial and otherwise and it would weaken our general defence position.' He added parenthetically that given the economically poor condition the country was in at the time, 'there are limits beyond which we cannot go, at least for some years' and more questionably, that 'a spreading out of our army on distant frontiers would be bad from every military and strategic point of view.' Subsequent Indian governments paid scant attention to his significant qualifier – 'at least for some years' – and invoking Nehru, stuck to the contours of a non-provocative policy long after India stopped being the 90-pound weakling that feared getting sand kicked in its face by Beijing.[52]

But to return to Nehru, he premised his approach on the belief that India championing the Tibetan cause would end in having a 'really hostile China on our doorstep', to obviate which he advocated working 'only' at 'the diplomatic level'. Nehru's stance was reinforced by the kind of advice he was getting from government economists who used the country's impoverished condition to argue that the race with China was primarily in the sphere of economic development; a view endorsed, incidentally, by the US – the principal economic aid-giver at the time.[53] Having thus dismissed the threat from China and expressed his intent to rely mostly on diplomacy to secure the nation's interests, Nehru proceeded to make a mountain out of a molehill of a threat from Pakistan. Incredibly, he rounded on this smaller, weaker, country, until recently a part of India, as a threat

---

[52] Shandilya, *India–China Relations*, Appendix I, pp. 190–93.
[53] Karnad, *Nuclear Weapons and Indian Security*, p. 261.

because of Pakistan's refusal 'to settle the points of issue between us' as desired by New Delhi, which criterion fitted China better. Entirely unmindful of the huge and obvious disparities prevailing even then, Nehru stated that '[O]ur major possible enemy' being Pakistan, it 'compelled us to think of our defence mainly in terms of Pakistan's aggression'. As if to confound his own fairly ridiculous threat perception, which has dogged the Indian Establishment's security outlook ever since, he averred as an after-thought that '[i]f we begin to think of, and prepare for, China's aggression in the same way we would weaken considerably on the Pakistan side' and get caught in 'a pincer movement'.[54] By inverting principles of realism and maintaining that because India was in no position militarily to confront, even less deter, China, its resources would be best spent blunting the weaker claw in the supposed pincer – Pakistan, Nehru achieved precisely the Pakistan–China nexus he apprehended.

In the circumstances that Nehru found himself in, Vedic principles (not dissimilar to the much later Western ideas of *realpolitik*) dictated a three-pronged approach, requiring India speedily to develop credible nuclear and thermonuclear forces to, as the *Rig Veda* puts it, strike terror into the heart of a powerful and seemingly undeterrable enemy; and to enter into military alliances with a strong 'distant power' as also with weaker states in the vicinity in a bid to ring China, the potential regional hegemon and thwart its expansionist plans. Nehru succeeded partially, but brilliantly, with the first prong. He covertly developed a broad-based and versatile nuclear energy programme, securing for the country capability to obtain both thermonuclear weapons and atomic power plants. He faltered, as did his successor, Lal Bahadur Shastri, however, in that he did not muster the will to authorise nuclear weaponisation once the war with China in 1962 and the Chinese atomic test in October 1964 provided pluperfect provocation-qua-justification for doing so.

Indira Gandhi in 1974 and Atal Bihari Vajpayee in 1998 – by not following up the nuclear tests they had ordered with open-ended testing to produce an array of advanced nuclear and thermonuclear weapons designs and by not structuring strategic forces complete with the command and control and downstream facilities, such as

---

[54] The text of Nehru's note on China, dated November 18, 1950, is in Shandilya, *India–China Relations*, Appendix II, pp. 194–97.

dispersed launch sites, silos, and mountain tunnels for invulnerable storage – were just as culpable as Nehru and Shastri for ignoring the military imperative of fielding a safe, proven and reliable thermonuclear arsenal when confronting the Chinese megaton forces. This failure was especially stark in the light of the BJP Deputy Prime Minister, L. K. Advani's reference, presumably with some understanding of its Vedic import, of India now possessing the 'brahmastra'![55]

Nehru was, however, successful in the 1950s in garnering assurances and promises from the United States and Britain of military intervention in case of Chinese attack. The Pentagon, in fact, planned for the 'Defence of India' with prospective deployment of, among other American fighting assets, an airborne division, an aircraft carrier task-force, an expeditionary Marine group with integral air support and a 'composite air strike force' including long range (presumably nuclear) bombers detached from the US Strategic Air Command.[56] In exchange, Nehru did not give up his enormously elastic 'nonalignment' rhetoric and policy that permitted dallying with the Soviet Union or his tendency to preach on a host of international issues (colonialism, racism, disarmament), which drove Washington and London batty but which was tolerated just so India could be counted as part of a worldwide anti-Communist front in the Cold War.[57]

Curiously, Nehru was disinclined to develop the third prong against the Chinese threat: namely, forging military partnerships with Pakistan and Myanmar and drawing Nepal into the architecture, to secure the extended region against common external dangers. The threat posed by China was obvious to leaders in Sri Lanka (Ceylon) and Myanmar (Burma) and also to the Pakistan President, General Ayub Khan, who repeatedly offered India a joint defence pact as late as 1961. Nehru, however, summarily dismissed pleas for collective security arrangements by Sri Lanka and Myanmar[58] and rebuffed Pakistan with sarcastic remarks, such as 'defence against

---

[55] Karnad, *Nuclear Weapons and Indian Security*, Ch. 3, and Karnad, *India's Nuclear Policy*, pp. 35–49.
[56] Karnad, *India's Nuclear Policy*, pp. 140–46.
[57] Ibid., Chapter 2.
[58] Ibid., pp. 70–71.

what?'[59] For all his sagacity in crafting policies in that decade that allowed India, a then weak and impecunious state, to punch way above its weight in the international arena and to enjoy the protection of the Western strategic umbrella without suffering the downside of formal alliance, this rejection of offers of collective security by neighbouring states and particularly Ayub's well-meaning efforts illustrated the fundamental flaw in Nehru's strategic visioning. It presaged events that led in December 1962 to the Pakistan President ceding strategically important real estate in the northern-most part of Pakistan-held Kashmir to China in an accord the *Arthashastra* would have identified as *adistra sandhi*: of land being traded for peace. That agreement led to China's gaining a foothold in the region and its studied cultivation of Pakistan as a staunch and wily ally. Pulling no punches, Beijing proceeded to arm its new friend with nuclear missiles and masses of conventional military hardware, enabling it successfully to fight India to a standstill and successfully stare it down in a crisis (the 2002 'Operation Parakram'). As a Chinese proxy, Pakistan has distracted and 'contained' India to the subcontinent as Beijing had hoped would happen. Islamabad, for its part, has wielded the China card alongside its use of terrorism as an asymmetric tool, to stymie India.

Elsewhere, New Delhi's short-sighted policies have afforded China a role in South Asia. Indian insistence on democracy in Myanmar ended up 'pushing' that military junta-ruled country 'into China's arms'[60], its ambiguity with regard to the independent *eelam* (country) the Jaffna Tamils wanted to carve out of Sri Lanka forced Colombo to seek out China as counterweight[61] and in supporting the *ancien regime* in Nepal, it lost the goodwill of the people hankering for change.[62] In each instance, China gained – up to and until now,

---

[59] Bharat Karnad, 'India's Weak Geopolitics and What To Do About It' in *Future Imperilled: India's Security in the 1990s and Beyond* (New Delhi: Viking, Penguin India, 1994), pp. 25–28.

[60] This was said by the Myanmar Foreign Minister visiting Delhi several years ago, on the sidelines of an Indian Council of World Affairs event, in response to the author's query about what had prompted Myanmar to go over to China.

[61] 'The Colombo Consensus', *The Economist,* July 8, 2010.

[62] Foreign Secretary Shyam Saran in a discussion on 'India and its Neighbourhood', Centre for Policy Research, July 26, 2010. Saran was Ambassador in Kathmandu during Prime Minister Vajpayee's tenure.

when it has penetrated countries that should legitimately comprise an Indian 'sphere of influence'. Worse, India remained passive even when it had opportunities and leverages it could have exploited. China, for instance, could have been stalled in the region by implementing an imaginative combination of sama, dana and bheda. India ought to have long ago strategically armed Vietnam with nuclear missiles in a tit for tat gesture and intensified its military links with countries, such as Taiwan, Japan and the Association of Southeast Asian Nations (ASEAN) states on China's periphery.[63] It should have moved aggressively to win over Myanmar by giving arms aid, thereby playing on its traditional fear of China and offered other states in the vicinity similar military help and generous economic terms – free trade agreements (FTAs) on a bilateral basis if the multilateral South Asian Association of Regional Countries (SAARC) was considered too cumbersome, generous grants-in-aid for infrastructure build-up, technology transfers and technical assistance of all kinds. It could have pushed the Indian private sector into making large cross border investments (as is starting to happen in Bangladesh and Myanmar) and subsidised the sale to all these countries of Indian-manufactured capital industrial equipment as part of its development aid programmes and involved them in joint prestige projects.

The necessity of such actions has been belatedly recognised by New Delhi, which appears to have finally woken up to the inroads made by China over the years in these countries, except that now the Indian assistance programmes are on the recipients' terms.[64] Even so, it has yet to begin encouraging Pakistan's move towards a more neutral position by addressing Islamabad's security concerns – for instance, by unilaterally withdrawing the nuclear capable, short-range, liquid-fuelled Prithvi missiles from its western border (this would not hurt Indian security because all Pakistani targets are within reach of the longer-range Agnis) and by more substantive actions such as restructuring the Indian tank and mechanised forces into a single, largish, armoured corps and the surplus material and manpower used to constitute two additional offensive mountain corps against China. These measures would immediately impact Pakistani perceptions for the better. If they were followed up with,

---

[63] Karnad, *India's Nuclear Policy*, pp. 29–33.

[64] See C. Raja Mohan, 'Myanmar Gen Connects, Plays India and China in New Bay Geopolitics', *The Indian Express*, July 26, 2010.

say, offers of an unconditional and unilateral free trade pact to create stakeholders in Pakistan, Islamabad would find it very difficult to continue in its adversarial mode.[65]

Instead, however, the Indian government remains niggardly and nitpicking, its big-brother attitude offending states and predisposing them favourably towards China. New Delhi's policy is exactly the reverse of what Beijing has done, leading to China's burgeoning economic and political profile in South and South East Asia and its growing military and naval presence in the Indian Ocean region and the littoral. Berthing rights for merchant ships that are perhaps convertible to military use may have been secured by Beijing in Hambantota in Sri Lanka and in the Maldives, Coco Islands in Myanmar and the Gwadar port on Pakistan's Baluchistan coast, enabling the Chinese navy and airborne rapid reaction forces to embark on distant operations in the Indian Ocean area. India did not follow the obvious course that *Arthashastra* and common sense suggest of creating dissension in the enemy ranks by covertly cultivating the Uighur Muslim groups active in Xinjiang and studiously nursing the 'Tibet card' by mobilising recruits from the exile community in India for guerrilla warfare inside Tibet, maintaining an aggressive intelligence presence on the Tibetan plateau and a capacity to mobilise the Tibetan people against the Chinese with the goal of raising the costs to China of occupation. New Delhi, moreover, should by now have begun to question the 'one China' idea and begun championing independence for Tibet in direct response to Beijing's deliberate dithering over the status of the Indian province of Arunachal Pradesh and Indian Kashmir and helping the northeastern rebels. This would have amounted to a substantive payback.[66] It is these sorts of actions that would have riled Beijing into over-reaction and into making mistakes, which could then have been used as a wedge for further exploitation. Tibet is a critical unused leverage, but a wasting asset, considering that the Dalai Lama, who could have in his own inimitable fashion spearheaded this effort, is now 79 years of age.[67]

---

[65] These were ideas first mooted by this author. See Karnad, *Nuclear Weapons and Indian Security*, p. 577.

[66] Rahul Karmakar, 'Naga Rebel Leader Admits China Links', *The Indian Express*, July 27, 2010.

[67] On the use of the 'Tibet card', see Karnad, *India's Nuclear Policy*, pp. 144–45.

In other words, India should have countered the multi-layered Chinese policy of pacifying neighbouring states with economic inducements and transfers of military hardware, drawing an ever-growing circle of South Asian countries into China's orbit, with its own parallel policy, relying on like means. While maintaining high levels of trade and commerce with China and co-operating with it in multilateral forums on issues where interests converge, such as on climate change and the Doha Round, for example, India ought to have transferred strategic armaments to states on the Chinese periphery such as Vietnam, pounced relentlessly on every small military, economic, diplomatic and political Chinese misstep to embarrass and show up China everywhere in the world, but especially in South and Southeast Asia. Loudly professing Sino-Indian friendship while discomfiting China in every way possible should have been (and ought to be in the future) the main Indian foreign and military policy thrust. Instead, Indian governments from Nehru's days have done precious little, permitting Indian interests to erode, in many respects, precipitously.

A passive-defensive approach to China has calcified into the worst manifestation of the over-cautious Nehruvian perspective that the Vedic texts would have excoriated. The picture of India as a Chinese punching bag is reinforced by the neo-colonial pattern of the Sino-Indian trade with Indian raw materials (such as coal, iron ore, other minerals, leather, cotton, and gems among others) constituting the bulk of exports to China in return for mainly Chinese light manufactures and capital goods (such as modern telecommunications equipment) in bilateral trade that touched USD 65 billion by 2011.[68]

Subsidiary Ally of the United States

India's strategic reduction by China can reasonably be sourced to Nehru's pusillanimity. But, easing relations with the United States on American terms is the work of successive governments in recent times. It is a process begun by the Congress Party Prime Minister P. V. Narasimha Rao in the early 1990s as a way of broadening

---

[68] Tang Zhihao and Li Jiabao, 'India and Russia Keen to Make the Most of Debut', *ChinaDaily.com.cn*, August 9, 2011. Available at http://www.chinadaily.com.cn/cndy/2011-09/08/content_13645948.htm, accessed on May 18, 2012.

India's options post-Cold War. The successor Bharatiya Janata Party regime advanced towards this goal in the belief that India could not handle China alone and needed sophisticated technology, trade, and capital from the US to bring India up to speed. Prime Minister Manmohan Singh has pushed these policies to a point where he sees rapprochement with the United States as the answer to India's myriad ills and believes the price India is asked to pay in terms of hobbling its strategic capabilities is bearable.

In the longstanding debate on 'sequencing' in official circles since Indira Gandhi's time, the former economist-bureaucrat Dr Singh has been on the side contending that India ought to first become a meaningful economic power before acquiring matching military muscle.[69] Predictably, he saw in the US an all-purpose solution to achieve not just fast-paced economic growth and technological ad-vancement but also greater international prominence. Manmohan Singh's policy suppositions were for India to prosper, with the now liberalised export-driven Indian economy needing to service the Western markets.[70] As the source of direct and indirect investment capital (through the World Bank and the International Monetary Fund), a well-disposed Washington would help build up economic infrastructure. And US high technology was believed crucial to updating Indian industrial capabilities and spurring economic growth.

While India's geopolitical value as a counterpoise to China in Asia motivated Washington, New Delhi had to be accommodating on the non-proliferation issue for it to get traction in Washington. This last was the ground that first began to be prepared by Narasimha Rao, with nuclear tests in the mid-1990s cancelled when Washington remonstrated. Vajpayee ordered the series of five test explosions in 1998 and to mollify Washington quickly, announced a voluntary suspension of testing, heedless of its consequences on the quality of the Indian thermonuclear deterrent. The hydrogen device tested having proved a dud, what was in fact mandated iterative testing of fusion weapons designs to ensure the country has a consequential strategic arsenal.[71] Be that as it may, America had so long been demonised in India that it was not easy for any of these

---

[69] Karnad, *Nuclear Weapons and Indian Security*, pp. 286–87.
[70] Sanjaya Baru, 'Credibility crunch', *The Indian Express*, August 20, 2013.
[71] Ibid., pp. 398–405.

Indian governments led by various parties to immediately switch plans, reverse gears, and fast-forward relations simultaneously. The 19 rounds of 'strategic dialogue' between Prime Minister Vajpayee's representative, Jaswant Singh, and President Bill Clinton's Deputy Secretary of State, Strobe Talbott, led to better appreciation of each other's systemic constraints and the limits to which either side could be pushed on sensitive strategic issues.[72]

It was Prime Minister Manmohan Singh, however, who acted with surprising alacrity but apparently little concern for national security interests. Motivated by his personal conviction that acquiring economic heft in exchange for curbs on Indian strategic capability was a good bargain, the test for the prime minister was to deliver the civilian nuclear deal, which achieved for the US its long-cherished goal of bringing the Indian nuclear energy programme within the purview of the 1968 Non-Proliferation Treaty (NPT). The Nuclear Suppliers Group approval for imports by India of light water reactors and enriched uranium fuel, supposedly to reduce the energy shortages, followed.

Manmohan Singh's mantra to try and sell the deal in Parliament and to the Indian people, ignoring its high price, was '20,000 megawatts by 2020'. As many of the critics of the nuclear deal had warned, this deal entails diversion of financial and human resources from the original 'Bhabha plan' (relying on the 'plutonium economy' based on the country's abundant thorium reserves – fully 30–40 per cent of the world's stock – and progressing in three stages towards energy sufficiency, from natural uranium reactors, to plutonium breeder reactors, to thorium reactors), to the 'uranium economy' and dependence on imported reactors and fuel. Thermonuclear weaponisation is in limbo because the no-testing predicate of the nuclear deal freezes the quality of the deterrent at the level of a flawed hydrogen weapon design. Further, weapon-grade plutonium production is now limited to just eight pressurised heavy water military use-designated reactors, thereby restricting the surge capacity and the size of the Indian nuclear force. The integrity of the dual-use Indian nuclear energy programme, moreover, is undermined by its separation into civilian and military streams, with facilities in the former going under

---

[72] Strobe Talbott, *Engaging India: Diplomacy, Democracy and the Bomb* (New Delhi: Penguin-Viking, 2004).

international safeguards. By these various means, India's strategic independence and wherewithal have been weakened with little compensation. India's promised recognition as a nuclear weapon state under the NPT has not happened. Moreover, it is unlikely that 20,000 MW of nuclear-sourced electricity will show up in the grid even by 2040 or 2050. Finally, in accordance with the deal, Indian foreign policy now has to conform to America on issues such as Iran, which will hugely limit Indian foreign policy options.[73]

The larger geopolitical imperative, as per the *Arthashastra*, to partner a powerful extra-regional country like the United States to contain the regional hegemon, China, as backdrop for the present Indian policies is all very well. But this deal is not the *swarna sandhi* that the ancient Hindu texts praise as an accord between equals. Neither is it a *karma sandhi* or an agreement for common gain – in this case, containment of China, because the Indian and US governments seem in their different ways to be avoiding conflict with Beijing. It is an aim that Delhi, in any case, appears reluctant to realise by more discriminate and targeted strategic engagement with the US because it is unable to see that Washington's eagerness to retain its predominance and therefore to curtail China's increasing military and economic reach and clout equals (if not) surpasses India's interest in strategically hampering China's rise by whatever means and to whatever extent. This differential in the preferred outcomes endows India with leverage that New Delhi has so far been loath to recognise, let alone exploit. As a result, better terms in the US–India 'global partnership with strategic significance' that National Security Adviser Shivshankar Menon claims is now in place[74] have not been secured and no effort has been made to exacerbate the growing

---

[73] These and many other deficiencies and drawbacks of the deal were pointed out by a few who opposed it all the way from the Joint Statement in July 2005 to the Manmohan Singh government's seeking parliamentary approval for it in mid-2008 and beyond. For writings against the deal by its main critics, see P. K. Iyengar, A. N. Prasad, A. Gopalakrishnan, and Bharat Karnad, *Strategic Sellout: Indian–US Nuclear Deal* (New Delhi: Pentagon Press, 2009).

[74] See Shivshankar Menon, 'A Global Partnership', in N. S. Sisodia, Peter R. Lavoy, Cherian Samuel, and Robin Walker, eds, *India–U.S. Relations: Addressing the Challenges of the 21st Century* (New Delhi: IDSA and Magnum Books, 2008), p. 9.

Sino-American politico-military and economic rifts in order to increase India's strategic leverage with both these states.[75]

Conclusion

China's rise has been 'peaceful' only because it has not been contested by India – the Asian country with the most to lose by not doing so, or by the United States, which now has a genuine peer competitor. The Indian government's mindless preoccupation with Pakistan and its policy of hamstringing the development of its thermonuclear force is short-sighted.

These failures are particularly galling because in the harsh and unforgiving world of international relations, the sharp-edged Vedic *machtpolitik* inhering in the ancient Indian statecraft and in the 'living traditions' offers an alternative, potentially more successful, policy path. Among the many Vedic axioms, the following three are central to India's concerns: (*a*) Never compromise one's interests to serve those of a distant power; (*b*) prevent, by any and all means, the rise of a rival state in the vicinity as *chakravartin* (hegemon) because not doing so will not only hurt the chances of improving one's own relative status but also disturb the existing *rajmandala* (balance of forces in the international system) to one's detriment; and (*c*) win over and co-opt countries in an ever-widening circle by judicial use of hard and soft power and where weaker states are concerned, by generous trade terms, schemes of huge grants-in-aid and unconditional transfers of Indian-manufactured military hardware. This is both to bring down the unit cost of equipment purchased by the Indian Armed Forces and to connect these countries to a reinvigorated Indian defence-industrial complex and Indian security architecture.

The fact that these axioms are not being followed in no way detracts from the salience of the Vedic strategic culture that, perhaps, remains as a pentimento in the South Asian peoples' consciousness subliminally affecting policy-makers – something that may be fleetingly glimpsed in policies and pronouncements by Indian political leaders. But it is true that Vedic thinking has not formally shaped

---

[75] Former Foreign Secretary Shyam Saran has suggested enlarging the proposed East Asia Summit to include the United States and Russia, contrary to what China wants. See Shyam Saran, 'India Needs to Have Sharper Focus', *The Business Standard*, July 16, 2010.

Indian policies, with Prime Ministers from Nehru to Manmohan Singh behaving as if overawed by the country's obvious shortcomings rather than acting on the basis of its burgeoning self-confidence and obvious strengths. This is the result of decades of diffidence and status quo-ist thinking by several generations of political leaders conditioned by the country's past, first as a colonial dependency and post-1947 as a habitual laggard and under-achiever.[76]

Animated by a mixture of lassitude, lack of confidence and an over-cautious and risk-averse calculus, India's counter-productive Pakistan policy when juxtaposed against its deferential attitude towards the United States and China reflects the core failure of its strategic policies. Further, as the only Asian country with the requisite attributes and potentially comprehensive heft and resources to be a credible counterweight to China, India has disappointed smaller Asian states who are understandably apprehensive of rallying to its side because they see New Delhi as a woolly-headed, weak-willed, wimp of a state, incapable of firming up a front and leading it and otherwise taking the fight to the 'big dragon'.

India is an elephant only in size. Owing to its foreign and military policies devoid of strategic visioning and weight and its approach bereft of the rock-hard principles of *realpolitik* in Vedic statecraft, it has contrived for itself a negligible impress – a very small footprint, in the region, in Asia and in the world. Its over-cautious, 'safety first', attitude may have now and then won India respite from immediate tensions and troubles with China and the United States. But it has also pushed back realisation of its entirely legitimate great power ambitions.

---

[76] For a sample commentary that lauds India 'working within its limitations', see Bhanu Pratap Mehta, 'The Great Gameplan', *The Indian Express*, July 22, 2010.

8

'JISKI LATHI, USKI BHAINS'
THE HINDU NATIONALIST VIEW OF INTERNATIONAL POLITICS

*Rahul Sagar**

༄༅

The title of this essay is a transliteration of a rustic Hindi proverb that captures one of the truths of human existence in a way that only a proverb can. Taken literally, the proverb says that 'the one who owns the stick owns the buffalo'. Of course, proverbs are not meant to be taken literally – this particular proverb needs to be understood in the context of rural life in India where disagreements are all too often settled by rough and ready means. Seen from this perspective, the truer meaning of this proverb is that in this world of ours, 'the strong do what they have the power to do and the weak accept what they have to accept'.[1] I have chosen this proverb as the title for this essay because it accurately describes what two intellectual heavyweights of the Hindu nationalist movement, Vinayak Savarkar and Madhav Golwalkar, take the nature of international politics to be. Unfortunately, I cannot take credit for this use of the proverb. I must admit to having borrowed it from Golwalkar, who tells the story of the eminent Indian barrister N. C. Chatterjee declaring the proverb the first principle of international law.[2] Nonetheless,

---

* I am grateful to Kanti Bajpai, Sunil Khilnani, Devesh Kapur, Prasenjit Duara, Srinath Raghavan, C. Raja Mohan, Bharat Karnad, Rahul Mukherji, and Siddharth Mallavarapu for their helpful comments on prior drafts. I am solely responsible for the content of this essay.

[1] Thucydides, *History of the Peloponnesian War*, trans. by Moses I. Finley (London: Penguin, 1972), p. 402.

[2] Madhav S. Golwalkar, *Bunch of Thoughts* (Bangalore: Vikrama Prakashan, 1966), p. 340.

I hope to still earn some credit by explaining why it best describes the Hindu nationalist view of international politics.

Few subjects have occupied students of modern India in the way that Hindu nationalism has. One consequence of this has been a veritable avalanche of publications on the subject. Yet, it is notably the case that barely a handful of these have examined the Hindu nationalist view of international politics. This neglect can be attributed to two factors. The first is context. Over the past three decades, the instability and violence associated with the upsurge in Hindu nationalism have prompted scholars to focus on its implications for domestic politics. The recent spate of works on riots is a case in point.[3] By contrast, the statements and actions of the Bharatiya Janata Party (BJP), the political wing of the Hindu nationalist movement, have not been seen as having introduced significant discontinuities in Indian foreign policy. Hence, there has been relatively little incentive to investigate the Hindu nationalist view of international politics.[4]

The second factor is methodology. The bulk of the research on Hindu nationalism has been oriented toward explanation rather than interpretation. This has led to a wealth of scholar-ship on the extent to which the development and contemporary appeal of Hindu nationalism can be attributed to, among other things, colonial history, the unsuitability of the concept of secularism in the Indian context, organisational features and political tactics of Hindu nationalist groups, the policies of the Congress Party, and hostility toward democracy and Westernisation.[5] But, it has also resulted in

---

[3] For example, see Steven I. Wilkinson, *Votes and Violence: Electoral Competition and Ethnic Riots in India* (New York: Cambridge University Press, 2004); Ashutosh Varshney, *Ethnic Conflict and Civic Life: Hindus and Muslims in India* (New Haven: Yale University Press, 2002).

[4] James Chiriyankandath and Andrew Wyatt, 'The NDA and Indian Foreign Policy', in Katherine Adeny and Lawrence Saez, eds, *Coalition Politics and Hindu Nationalism* (London: Routledge, 2005), p.193. Also see Apurba Kundu, 'The NDA and National Security', in Adney and Saez, *Coalition Politics*, 212–37.

[5] For example see, Partha Chatterjee, *Nationalist Thought and the Colonial World: A Derivative Discourse* (New Delhi: Oxford University Press, 1986); Rajeev Bhargava, ed., *Secularism and Its Critics* (New Delhi: Oxford University Press, 1998); Amrita Basu, 'Mass Movement or Elite Conspiracy: The Puzzle

a paucity of studies on the foundational texts of Hindu nationalist thought.[6]

I noted above that a few publications have in fact discussed the Hindu nationalist view of international politics. Unfortunately, they have cast a very uneven light on the subject. To begin, only one of these, Kanti Bajpai's path-breaking essay on Indian strategic thought, has closely examined the relevant texts.[7] Then there is the broader problem that these publications have tended to interpret Savarkar's and Golwalkar's writings on international politics as little more than expressions of an irrationally assertive nationalism. Bajpai, for example, asserts that the Hindu nationalist view of international relations draws on a 'narrative about the past, present, and future of the Hindu community' that has produced a 'hard-bitten' ethics.[8] This can be seen, for example, in contrasting attitudes toward nuclear weapons, which 'are seen by many Westerners as a tragic necessity',

---

of Hindu Nationalism', in David E. Ludden, ed., *Contesting the Nation* (Philadelphia: University of Pennsylvania Press, 1996); Christophe Jaffrelot, *The Hindu Nationalist Movement in India* (New York: Columbia University Press, 1998); Ashutosh Varshney, 'Contested Meanings: India's National Identity, Hindu Nationalism, and the Politics of Anxiety', *Daedalus*, 122, 3 (1993), pp. 227–61. Thom Blom Hansen, *The Saffron Wave: Democracy and Hindu Nationalism in Modern India* (Princeton: Princeton University Press, 1999).

[6] Recent exceptions are Chetan Bhatt, *Hindu Nationalism: Origins, Ideologies, and Modern Myths* (Oxford: Berg, 2001); Jyotirmaya Sharma, *Hindutva: Exploring the Idea of Hindu Nationalism* (New Delhi: Penguin, 2003). Also see Christophe Jaffrelot, ed., *Hindu Nationalism: A Reader* (Princeton: Princeton University Press, 2007), Part I; Dhananjay Keer, *Veer Savarkar* (Bombay: Popular Prakashan, 1966); B. D. Graham, *Hindu Nationalism and Indian Politics: The Origin and Development of the Bharatiya Jana Sangh* (New York: Cambridge University Press, 1990), Chapter 3.

[7] Kanti Bajpai, 'Indian Conceptions of Order and Justice: Nehruvian, Gandhian, Hindutva, and Neo-Liberal', in Rosemary Foot, John Gaddis and Andrew Hurrell, eds, *Order and Justice in International Relations* (Oxford: Oxford University Press, 2003), pp. 378–81. Also see Sumit Sarkar, *Beyond Nationalist Frames: Postmodernism, Hindu Fundamentalism, History* (Bloomington: Indiana University Press, 2002), Chapter 7; Praful Bidwai and Achin Vanaik, *New Nukes: India, Pakistan, and Global Nuclear Disarmament* (New York: Interlink, 2000), pp. 78–79.

[8] Kanti Bajpai, 'Hinduism and Weapons of Mass Destruction: Pacifist, Prudential, and Political', in Sohail Hashmi and Steven P. Lee, eds, *Ethics and Weapons of Mass Destruction* (New York: Cambridge University Press, 2004), pp. 308, 313.

whereas 'political Hinduism embraces them'.[9] This leads him to the conclusion that Hindu nationalism's 'stance on international relations and the use of violence is not a particularly prudential one'.[10]

In my view, this interpretation misidentifies what is truly distinctive about the Hindu nationalist view. As I outline in the following, Savarkar and Golwalkar see conflict and war as undesirable but inevitable as long as the world comprises selfish individuals and parochially-minded communities. Hence, they recommend that India cultivate the willingness and ability to engage in war and power politics in order to be able to fend off external aggression. In this respect, I argue, their view of international politics bears a family resemblance to realist strains of international relations theory, which lay equal, if not greater, weight on the acquisition of all possible 'capabilities.'[11] But the family resemblance runs only so far, because, unlike theorists in the realist tradition, Savarkar and Golwalkar take the view that national power depends heavily on the cultivation of an assertive and exclusionary nationalism. What explains this striking divergence? It owes, as we shall see, to their belief that only this brand of nationalism can provide India with the martial spirit and social cohesion it needs to defend itself against external aggression.

The benefit of uncovering this relationship between international politics and nationalism in Hindu nationalist thought is that it opens up the possibility of challenging Savarkar and Golwalkar on their own terms by showing that an exclusionary nationalism actually undermines national power. Such a critique, which distinguishes between the relatively less controversial premise that Savarkar and Golwalkar start out with and the highly controversial conclusion they draw from it, will obviously be at variance with traditional critiques of Hindu nationalism, which are averse to casting arguments in the language of national power. But such a critique is worth pursuing because it will likely be more effective in combating any chauvinism that may be provoked by the challenging international environment that India faces in the decades ahead.

---

[9] Bajpai, 'Hinduism and Weapons of Mass Destruction', p. 318.

[10] Ibid., p. 317.

[11] For example, see Hans J. Morgenthau, *Politics Among Nations: The Struggle for Power and Peace*, 5th revised edn (New York: Alfred A. Knopf, 1978); John Mearsheimer, *The Tragedy of Great Power Politics* (New York: Norton, 2001).

Before I elaborate on these claims outlined, I want to preemptively address an important interpretative issue. I recognise that a close focus on Savarkar and Golwalkar may raise questions about the scope of the claims made in this essay. No doubt a full treatment of the Hindu nationalist view of international politics needs to account for the influence of the intellectuals and activists that preceded Savarkar and Golwalkar (including Swami Vivekananda, Swami Dayanand and Aurobindo Ghose in the late 19th century, and Lala Lajpat Rai, Bipin Chandra Pal and Bal Gangadhar Tilak in the early 20th century), and for the transformations wrought by the leaders and statesmen that succeeded them (a list that includes Shyama Prasad Mookherjee, Balraj Madhok, Deendayal Upadhyaya, Atal Behari Vajpayee, Lal Krishna Advani, and Jaswant Singh).[12] Unfortunately, it is not possible to pursue such a thorough examination in the limited space available here. Moreover, it is reasonable to focus on Savarkar and Golwalkar, since they, above all others, offer something approximating a 'theory' of international politics. By contrast, the thinkers and statesmen that have succeeded them appear to have had little inclination or opportunity to put forward a fully developed view of international politics.[13] This is not to suggest that we can, therefore, safely ignore these prominent figures. Rather, it emphasises the fact that while there is much that is missing from this study, it at least has the virtue of focusing on the most developed part of the canon.

A Theory of International Politics

Let me begin with Savarkar's theory of international politics. The starting point of his theory is the premise that a universal state or a worldwide federation constitutes the highest ideal in politics. This claim will likely come as a surprise to those who see Savarkar as fixated on national power and glory, but consider how he describes his political views in a letter written in 1920. He says:

> We believe in an universal state embracing all mankind and wherein all men and women would be citizens working for and enjoying equally the

---

[12] On the former see Bhatt, *Hindu Nationalism*, Chapters 2–3.

[13] An important exception here is Jaswant Singh, *Defending India* (New York: St. Martin's Press, 1999).

fruits of this earth and this sun, this land and this light, which constitute the real Motherland and the Fatherland of man. All other divisions and distinctions are artificial though indispensable.[14]

This is a fascinating passage because it shows Savarkar to be something less than a 'true believer' in the idea of the nation. That is, unlike the 19th-century theorists of nationalism by whom he is said to have been inspired, he does not seem to believe that nations represent genuine racially or ethnically distinct peoples. At the same time, this passage makes clear that Savarkar is no cosmopolitan either, since he clearly does not believe that mankind ought to shed national distinctions. I will explain shortly why he sees these distinctions as 'indispensable'. But first I want to get across the point that Savarkar does not view national distinctions as constituting an inherent source of conflict. On the contrary, he views co-operation between nations as feasible and desirable so long as they treat each other as equals. This is why, he claims, he can 'conscientiously cooperate' with the British if they are willing to grant Indians constitutional rights (a reference to the Montagu–Chelmsford Report of 1918, which promised to gradually expand self-government in India). As 'humanity is higher patriotism', Savarkar writes, 'any Empire or Commonwealth that succeeds in welding numbers of conflicting races and nations in one harmonious, if not homogeneous, whole in such ways as to render each of them better fitted to realise, enrich and enjoy life in all its noble aspects is a distinct step to the realisation of that ideal'.[15] He defends his revolutionary activities against the British on the same basis. 'It was this very principle that humanity was a higher patriotism that made us so restless', he claims, for 'when we saw that a part of it should aggrandise and swell like a virulent cancer in such ways as to threaten the life of the human whole', it 'forced us for want of any other effective remedy to take to the Surgeon's knife'.[16]

It is not unreasonable to be sceptical about the tenor and content of the earlier remarks as they came at a time when Savarkar

---

[14] Vinayak D. Savarkar, *Echoes from Andaman* (Bombay: Veer Savarkar Prakashan, 1984), p. 33.
[15] Ibid., pp. 33–34.
[16] Savarkar, *Echoes from Andaman*, pp. 27, 34.

had been pleading with the British for the commutation of a long prison sentence that had begun in 1910. The circumstances, one might imagine, likely gave Savarkar an incentive to present himself as far more peaceable than he really was.[17] However, it is worth noting that Savarkar appears to have made similar remarks both in the years prior to his imprisonment and in the years following his return to freedom, a fact that suggests that his views on international politics at least cannot be straightforwardly attributed to his circumstances.[18] Consider, for example, his annual address before the Hindu Mahasabha in 1938, where he states that 'the Ideal of Politics itself ought to be a Human state, all mankind for its citizen, the earth for its motherland'.[19] The same point is made with even greater emphasis in an address to the same body, the previous year:

> [W]hen a nation or community treads upon the rights of sister nations or communities and aggressively stands in the way of forming larger associations and aggregates of mankind, its nationalism or communalism becomes condemnable from a human point of view. This is the acid test of distinguishing a justifiable nationalism or communalism from an unjust and harmful one.[20]

Fascinating as these passages are, I want to caution against placing a great deal of weight on them. I cite them only to underscore that Savarkar does not begin his account of international politics with the premise that war or violence between nations is desirable. That said, it is vital to understand that Savarkar believes that conflict between nations is almost inevitable because of the human tendency toward parochialism and selfishness. The former, he writes, 'is responsible for dreadful wars throughout human history'.[21] The latter, he

---

[17] On the controversy surrounding Savarkar's plea, see A.G. Noorani, 'Savarkar and Gandhi', *Frontline*, March 28, 2003; Krishnan Dubey and Venkitesh Ramakrishnan, 'Far from Heroism: The Tale of Veer Savarkar', *Frontline*, April 7, 1995.

[18] See, for example, the defence offered on behalf of revolutionary activity in Vinayak D. Savarkar, *The Indian War of Independence 1857* (Bombay: Phoenix, 1947), pp. 273–74. This work was first published in 1909.

[19] Vinayak D. Savarkar, *Hindu Rashtra Darshan* (Bombay: Veer Savarkar Prakashan, 1984), p. 23. Hereafter HRD.

[20] Ibid., p. 8.

[21] Ibid.

repeatedly observes, is hard to strip away from mankind, a point made most clearly in his critique of Buddhism:

> Buddhism had made the first and yet the greatest attempt to propagate a universal religion. "Go, ye Bhikkus, to all the ten directions of the world and preach the law of Righteousness!" Truly, it was a law of Righteousness. It had no ulterior end in view, no lust for land or lucre quickening its steps; but grand though its achievements were it could not eradicate the seeds of animal passions nor of political ambitions nor of individual aggrandisement in the minds of all men ...[22]

This pessimistic view of mankind leads Savarkar to an operating premise very different from the one we started with, namely, that the human condition is scarred by an incessant 'terrible struggle for existence', which makes 'survival of the fittest' the rule in nature.[23] From this premise Savarkar draws the inference that a willingness to defend oneself using all available means is necessary, and therefore, ultimately, moral. 'Call it a law of nature or the will of God as you like', he says, but 'the iron fact remains that there is no room for absolute non-violence in nature'.[24] The lesson of history, he says, is that

> [N]ations which, other things equal, are superior in military strength are bound to survive, flourish and dominate while those which are militarily weak shall be politically subjected or cease to exist at all. It is idle to say, we shall add a new chapter to history but you cannot add to or take away a syllable from the iron law of Nature itself. Even today if man hands over a blank cheque to the wolf and the tiger to be filled in, with a human pledge of absolute non-violence, no killing of a living being, no armed force to be used, then the wolves and the tigers will lay waste all your mandirs and mosques, culture and cultivation, Aramas and Ashrams-finish man Saint and sinner alike before a dozen years pass by![25]

So far I have been describing Savarkar's chain of thought. I now hasten to add that Golwalkar operates under broadly the same set

---

[22] Vinayak D. Savarkar, *Essentials of Hindutva* (New Delhi: Bharati Sahitya Sadan, 2003), p. 22.
[23] Savarkar, HRD, p. 15. Also see Keer, *Veer Savarkar*, pp. 271–73.
[24] Savarkar, HRD, p. 84.
[25] Ibid., p. 85.

of premises. To start, not unlike Savarkar, Golwalkar claims on the very first page of his *Bunch of Thoughts* that 'the ideal of human unity, of a world free from all traces of conflict and misery, has stirred our hearts since times immemorial'.[26] And, also, like Savarkar, Golwalkar emphasises that the 'hard reality' is quite disheartening. He writes:

> Today, humanity is divided and subdivided into so many small exclusive groups called nations or states, each one of them devoted to its own narrow self-interest. And it is a matter of common experience that wherever there are groups inspired only by self-interest, there is bound to be mutual conflict. Obviously, human unity and welfare is impossible so long as this type of conflict continues.[27]

This deplorable condition, Golwalkar notes, leads to the demand that nationalism 'be rooted out from the minds of men all over the world'.[28] But he demurs on this point. Even more than Savarkar, he takes the view that a strict cosmopolitanism (or what he terms 'internationalism') is neither desirable nor necessary. It is undesirable because nationalism in its own way helps combat self-interest, as it inspires the spirit of real service and sacrifice in the individual'.[29] Since nationalism is instrumentally desirable in this way, 'it cannot and should not be destroyed', according to Golwalkar.[30] Consequently, the problem, he says, 'boils down to one of achieving a synthesis of national aspirations and world welfare'.[31] In this regard Golwalkar readily admits that mankind has long struggled to find a convincing solution to this problem. In his view, past efforts to develop a synthesis between national aspirations and world welfare have failed because they have been attempted by societies that, steeped in materialism, have been unable to sustain a love for mankind. He observes:

> From the materialist point of view we are all gross entities, each separate and exclusive in itself, who can have no bonds of mutual affinity or affection.

---

[26] Golwalkar, *Bunch of Thoughts*, p. 2.
[27] Ibid.
[28] Ibid.
[29] Ibid., p. 3.
[30] Ibid.
[31] Ibid.

There can also be no inner restraint in such beings, which can make them control their selfishness from running amuck, in the interest of the humanity as a whole. After all, any arrangement evolved for achieving world welfare can be fruitful only to the extent the men behind it are inspired by real love for mankind which will enable them to mould their individual and national conduct in tune with the welfare of humanity. Without that supreme urge, any scheme, however good its purpose may be, will only provide one more alluring mask for the aggrandizement of power-drunk nations. That has been the uniform verdict of history right up to the present times.[32]

The only way to defeat this destructive materialism, Golwalkar argues, is to turn to transcendentalism. It is only the 'occasional realisation' of our 'innate oneness', he argues, 'that inspires us to strive for the happiness of others'.[33] Consequently, the search for world unity and human welfare can be realised, he concludes, 'only to the extent mankind realises this common Inner Bond, which alone can subdue the passions and discords stemming from materialism, broaden the horizon of the human mind and harmonise the individual and national aspirations with the welfare of mankind'.[34] Notably, he does not see such transcendentalism as threatening national attachments, because in his view individuals, groups, and nations all have distinct identities that can be expressed in a manner that does not produce conflict or disorder. He writes:

> Needless to say, the idea of creating a stateless condition, of levelling all human beings to one particular plane of physical existence, erasing their individual and group traits, is foreign to us. The World State of our concept will, therefore, evolve out of a federation of autonomous and self-constrained nations under a common centre linking them all.[35]

No doubt Golwalkar's concept of an organic 'World State' raises serious questions, foremost being the concern that it may contain elements of domination (rare indeed is the concept of an organic

---

[32] Golwalkar, *Bunch of Thoughts*, p. 4. A possible source for Golwalkar's analysis is Aurobindo Ghose, *The Ideal of Human Unity* (Madras: Sons of India, 1919).
[33] Golwalkar, *Bunch of Thoughts*, p. 5.
[34] Ibid.
[35] Ibid., p. 6.

order that does not contain elements of domination). This conceptual matter becomes a more distant concern once we see how Golwalkar envisions the world coming to heed transcendentalism. In contrast to Savarkar, who argues that a worldwide federation is desirable, but likely unreachable, Golwalkar argues that it is India's 'destiny' to make the impossible possible on account of Hinduism's rootedness in transcendental philosophy. It is the 'unique national genius' of the Hindu people, he says, 'to realise the dream of world unity and human welfare'.[36] It is not entirely clear as to what this is meant to imply in practice: he refers to both an 'empire of the Spirit', as well as to the 'political empires' of ancient India that expanded quite some distance beyond the subcontinent.[37] At any rate, the point to note is that Golwalkar is quite clear that India cannot fulfill its 'destiny' until and unless it is able to stand up for itself. As he puts it:

> How can a society given to self-derision, weakened by all-round disruption and dissipation, kicked and humiliated at every point by any and every bully in the world, teach the world? How can one, devoid of the urge or the capacity to ennoble one's own life, show the path of greatness to others?[38]

In light of this observation we should not be surprised to find Golwalkar changing tone and counseling Indians to come to terms with power politics and the ever-present threat of war. Thus he warns his readers that 'it is in the nature of predatory nations to overrun, plunder and destroy other weaker countries'.[39] He goes on to say: 'whatever the strategy, the basic rule of relations between nations is the law of the jungle – the strong feeding upon the weak and getting stronger'.[40]

Up to this point I have been trying to show that Savarkar and Golwalkar both believe that a pacific international order constitutes the highest ideal in politics, and that while they differ as to how or even whether this order can come about, they are united in the view

---

[36] Golwalkar, *Bunch of Thoughts*, p. 6.

[37] Ibid., p. 7. Also see Madhav S. Golwalkar, *We or Our Nationhood Defined* (Nagpur: Bharat Prakashan, 1939), p. 76.

[38] Ibid., pp. 8–9; also see pp. 270–71.

[39] Ibid., p. 213; also see pp. 265–66.

[40] Golwalkar, *Bunch of Thoughts*, p. 270.

that in the interim, at least, India faces circumstances not unlike those described by the realist tradition, that is, it needs to engage in 'self-help'.[41] What I want to focus on next is the point where Savarkar's and Golwalkar's inferences and prescriptions diverge from the realist tradition. As will quickly become clear, this divergence constitutes the more controversial aspect of their theory.

From the premise that the international order is characterised by lawlessness, Savarkar and Golwalkar draw a number of inferences familiar to students of international politics. For example, Savarkar advocates entering into alliances and partaking in balance of power politics whenever this is likely to bolster India's position vis-à-vis the threat of the day. 'The sanest policy for us, which practical politics demand', he says, 'is to befriend those who are likely to serve our country's interests in spite of any "ism" they follow for themselves, and to befriend only so long as it serves our purpose'.[42] As evidence, he points to events preceding the outbreak of the Second World War, focusing in particular on the relationship between England and America. He observes:

> Were not these very Americans although her own kith and kin, held up by England before the world as the most faithless and treacherous type of humanity in spite of the fact that they were republicans when they revolted against England and secured their independence? And yet now that a close alliance with America is almost the last refuge guaranteeing any certainty of saving England from a disastrous defeat, what desperate love has locked John Bull and Uncle Sam into an unseparable embrace![43]

Golwalkar makes much the same point. If there is one lesson to be gleaned from the story of the permutations and combinations of the relationships between nations of Europe in the last few centuries, he says, it is that 'nations change their friends and foes as it suits their self-interest'.[44] That being said, Golwalkar keenly emphasises that alliances must not to be considered substitutes for national power since 'the strong do not desire the friendship of the weak except to

---

[41] Kenneth Waltz, *Theory of International Politics* (Reading: Addison-Wesley, 1979), Chap. 6.
[42] HRD, p. 81. Also see Golwalkar, *Bunch of Thoughts*, p. 260.
[43] HRD, p. 81.
[44] Golwalkar, *Bunch of Thoughts*, p. 260.

exploit the latter'.[45] When we read the world correctly, he argues, 'we are forced to arrive at the simple conclusion that the only basis for our free and prosperous national life is invincible national strength – a strength that will strike terror into the hearts of aggressive powers and make other nations seek our friendship'.[46]

Curiously enough, even as Savarkar and Golwalkar make these fairly predictable sorts of inferences, they take what is, to modern minds at least, an unusual view of the sources of national power. In the first place they are firmly united in the belief that national power vitally depends on people having a martial spirit. For example:

> What is that real and inexhaustible source of national strength? It is the consolidated, dedicated and disciplined life of the people as a whole. After all, the various spheres of national life are only so many manifestations of the innate strength of the people. Political power is one such manifestation. Military power is the well-disciplined, intensely patriotic and heroic attitude of the people.[47]

It hardly needs to be pointed out that Golwalkar's view, as stated above, differs from the contemporary realist belief that what ultimately counts in international politics is relative state power, which is usually measured in terms of a well-equipped professional military, an effective bureaucracy, especially in the areas of intelligence and planning, and economic heft. I hasten to add that Golwalkar's view is not necessarily at odds with this view, since cultivating a martial spirit in the people does not preclude the cultivation of state power. Moreover, Golwalkar, I should underscore, is hardly averse to the acquisition of weaponry.[48] Nonetheless, central to his view is the notion that arms by themselves are inadequate in the absence of a martial spirit necessary for their use. 'It is not the gun but the heart behind it that fights', he says. So, 'without a strong patriotic heart no amount of arms and ammunition will save the country'.[49]

It is not difficult to discern the reasons behind Golwalkar's and Savarkar's focus on the martial spirit of the people. In part both

---

[45] Ibid., p. 323. Also see pp. 261–62.
[46] Ibid., p. 262.
[47] Ibid., p. 277.
[48] Ibid., pp. 308–9. On Savarkar's view, see HRD, p. 93.
[49] Golwalkar, *Bunch of Thoughts*, p. 277.

were responding to the belief, widespread since the Hindu Renaissance of the late 19th century, that Hindus were an unmanly race.[50] It is no coincidence then that when Golwalkar proclaims the need for Indians to develop 'strong and healthy bodies', he should quote Swami Vivekananda, the most prominent spokesman of that era, as saying that 'I want men with muscles of iron and nerves of steel'.[51] For much the same reason we find Savarkar celebrating the decision of the British to send Indian soldiers to the battlefields of Europe during World War I:

> It sent a thrill of delight in my heart to hear that the Indian troops were allowed to go to Europe, in their thousands to fight against the best military power in the world and that they had acquainted themselves with such splendour and were covered with military glory. Thank God! Manliness after all is not dead yet in the land![52]

The more immediate factor motivating Savarkar's and Golwalkar's emphasis on cultivating a martial spirit was the need they felt to combat the doctrine of non-violence popularised by Mahatma Gandhi.[53] From their perspective, this 'doctrinal plague', as Savarkar termed it, added insult to the injury because it 'sought to kill the very martial instinct of the Hindu race and had succeeded to an alarming extent in doing so'.[54] Therefore, the need of the hour, as he saw it, was to 'whip up military enthusiasm amongst the Hindus'.[55] Most immediately, this need was met by practical measures such as Savarkar's calls in the late 1930s for Hindus to be drafted into the war effort so that they may 'get themselves re-animated and re-born into a martial race'.[56] But ultimately it was necessary to directly confront the legitimacy of Gandhi's doctrine. Savarkar was only too willing to take up the challenge. 'We denounce your doctrine of absolute non-violence not because we are less saintly but because we are

---

[50] Gyanendra Pandey, 'Which of Us Are Hindus?', in Gyanendra Pandey, ed., *Hindus and Others* (New Delhi: Viking, 1993), pp. 262–64.

[51] Golwalkar, *Bunch of Thoughts*, p. 49.

[52] Savarkar, *Echoes from Andaman*, pp. 12–13.

[53] Anthony Parel, ed., *Gandhi: 'Hind Swaraj' and Other Writings* (New York: Cambridge University Press, 1997), p. 55.

[54] HRD, p. 86.

[55] Ibid.

[56] Ibid., p. 85.

more sensible than you are', he thundered. 'Relative non-violence is our creed', he declared, 'therefore, we worship the defensive sword as the first saviour of man'.[57] This reference to self-defence should not be overlooked. Neither Savarkar nor Golwalkar view the cultivation of martial spiritedness as preparation for the undertaking of expansionary wars. Rather, they appear to have thought that martial spiritedness, by strengthening Indian resolve, would serve to deter potential aggressors. Consider, for example, Golwalkar's statements in the wake of India's defeat to China in 1962. 'The thinking in our country during the last few decades has been one of looking down upon strength as something sinful and reprehensible', he writes. Indeed, 'we have begun to look upon strength as 'violence' and to glorify our weakness'.[58] This line of thought is actually counterproductive, Golwalkar argues, because weakness incites the predatory appetites of other nations, whereas strength provides the foundation for the genuine practice of non-violence. As is so often the case in Golwalkar's writings, the point is made through a parable:

> Suppose a strong man is going in a road and somebody knocks against him. If the strong man says with compassion, 'All right, my dear fellow, I excuse you for the wrong you have done me', then we say that the strong man has practised non-violence. For, though he is capable of giving him a blow and smashing his skull, he has restrained himself. Suppose, a thin, lean man – just a mosquito! – is going and somebody pulls his ears and the 'mosquito' trembling from head to foot says, 'Sir, I excuse you', who will believe him? Who will say that he is practising non-violence?[59]

So far I have been making the case that one aspect of Savarkar's and Golwalkar's understanding of national power is that they see it as depending heavily on the martial spirit of the people. The other aspect of their understanding of national power is that they see it as depending heavily on social cohesion. Consider, for example, the following passage from Golwalkar:

> Let us now look for the source of such a strength. Where does it reside? We say, it lies in the organised life of the people. But, what type of people?

---

[57] HRD, p. 85.
[58] Golwalkar, *Bunch of Thoughts*, p. 271.
[59] Ibid., pp. 271–72.

They should be such as are imbued with unity of mind and thought, bound together with a common code of morality and faith in each other, and filled with absolute loyalty to the nation. Unless they are such, their organised strength is not likely to protect the nation.[60]

In one sense, there is little mystery as to why Savarkar and Golwalkar view social cohesion as a vital component of national power. It is because, like so many of their generation, they attribute the conquest of India by the British to disunity in Indian society, which 'allowed foreigners to come in'.[61] And they attribute the power of these foreigners in turn to the idea of nationalism. 'Europeans, as Nations, are free and strong and progressive', Golwalkar argues, 'for the simple reason that they have cherished and do still foster correct national consciousness'.[62]

Given these premises, it is hardly surprising that both Savarkar and Golwalkar try to foster social cohesion in the Indian context by constructing a national identity that could motivate individuals and communities to present external aggressors with a united front. For both, the first step in this direction is to prove the existence of an Indian nation.[63] This explains their self-consciously creative use of history. Savarkar, in particular, is quite explicit that history ought to be interpreted with a view towards its use. As he writes in the introduction to *The Indian War of Independence*, 'a nation must develop its capacity not only of claiming a past but also of knowing how to use it for the furtherance of its future. The nation ought to be the master and not the slave of its own history'.[64] But, as is well known, this creative process directly leads to the most controversial and unpleasant aspect of Savarkar's and Golwalkar's political theories – the claim that Hindus should be the rulers of India. What explains this turn of events? Why exactly does the search for social cohesion end up leading to an exclusionary nationalism? To see why Savarkar and

---

[60] Golwalkar, *Bunch of Thoughts*, p. 48.
[61] Savarkar, *The Indian War of Independence*, p. 542.
[62] Golwalkar, *We or Our Nationhood Defined*, p. 71. Also see Christophe Jaffrelot, *The Hindu Nationalist Movement and Indian Politics: 1925-1990* (London: Hurst and Company, 1996), p. 52.
[63] Golwalkar, *The We or Our Nationhood Defined*, pp. 18-19.
[64] Savarkar, *Indian War of Independence*, p. xxiii.

Golwalkar think social cohesion depends on exclusion, it is vital to meditate on the following passage from *Essentials of Hindutva*:

> [E]verything that is common in us with our enemies, weakens our power of opposing them. The foe that has nothing in common with us is the foe likely to be most bitterly resisted by us just as a friend that has almost everything in him that we admire and prize in ourselves is likely to be the friend we love most.[65]

I submit that this passage is the single most important in Savarkar's corpus, and by extension in the canon of Hindu nationalist thought. It places before us, quite clearly, the *instrumental* nature of Savarkar's brand of nationalism: its purpose is to provide Indians with a corporate identity sufficient to motivate them to rally in opposition to external aggression. Nowhere is this truer than with regard to the religious aspect of Savarkar's nationalism: he readily assumes that men are most willing to fight when they believe they are defending their religion. History, he says, teaches that 'the necessity of creating a bitter sense of wrong and invoking a power of undying resistance' is accomplished best 'by cutting off even the semblance of a common worship'.[66] Conversely, when such exclusivity is missing, Savarkar argues, history shows that 'the tie of common Holyland has at times proved stronger than the chains of a Motherland', citing as examples not only Muslims in India, but also Jews in Europe, Christians in Turkey, and Germans in America, who, as members of multi-religious, multi-ethnic polities, find 'their love is divided'.[67] With respect to the former, Savarkar infamously says,

> Look at the Mohammedans. Mecca to them is a sterner reality than Delhi or Agra. Some of them do not make any secret of being bound to sacrifice all India if that be to the glory of Islam or could save the city of their prophet.[68]

---

[65] Savarkar, *Essentials of Hindutva*, p. 24.

[66] Ibid., p. 24.

[67] Ibid., pp. 139–40.

[68] Ibid., p. 135. Bear in mind that Savarkar was writing in the wake of the pan-Islamic Khilafat movement. This movement, led by Muslims in India, demanded that the British protect the sovereignty of the Khalifah (the Ottoman Sultan or Caliph) in Turkey following the end of World War I. For more see Francis Robinson, *Separatism Among Indian Muslims:*

It is this logic that explains why Savarkar wants to define a Hindu as one who considers the territory of India 'his Fatherland as well as his Holyland'.[69] As he defensively explains at the close of *Essentials of Hindutva*,

> As long as other communities in India or in the world are not respectively planning India first or mankind first, but all are busy in organizing offensive and defensive alliances and combinations on entirely narrow racial or religious or national basis, so long, at least, so long O Hindus, strengthen if you can those subtle bonds that like nerve threads bind you in one organic social being.[70]

The same instrumental use of an exclusionary nationalism can be seen in Golwalkar's writings. Consider, for example, the following anecdote, which Golwalkar uses to illustrate the dangers of what he terms 'internationalism'. He tells the story of two men once travelling in the same train compartment as he. As the men began to converse, one of them, a military officer, praised his fellow traveller's proficiency in Urdu. The speaker responded by saying that he no longer loved Urdu because its literature referred only to Persia and had nothing to say about India. This statement, Golwalkar reports, provoked the military officer to criticise his fellow traveller as provincial and insular. 'Now the times are such that we should give up thinking in narrow confines of country, nation and so on', the officer said to his fellow traveller. 'Now we have to think in terms of the whole world'.[71] Having narrated the account, Golwalkar appends the following query:

> Suppose such an army officer goes out for war; will he be able to fight with conviction for the protection of his country? At any moment the "world consciousness" in him may revolt and he may feel, "What is all this humbug? Why should I fight? What does it matter if they conquer? After all they are as much human beings as we are!" Then what will be our fate? Will such "world consciousness" save us from annihilation?[72]

The Politics of the United Provinces (Cambridge: Cambridge University Press, 1974), pp. 289–91.
[69] HRD, p. 43.
[70] Savarkar, *Essentials of Hindutva*, p. 141.
[71] Golwalkar, *Bunch of Thoughts*, p. 265.
[72] Ibid., p. 265.

As this passage shows, Golwalkar, like Savarkar, believes that ideas that foster transnational attachments are likely to have a visceral effect on an individual's willingness to make sacrifices on behalf of his nation. Hence, we should not be surprised to find Golwalkar too expressing distrust of the patriotism of Muslims and Christians in India on the grounds that their sympathies can easily drift toward their co-religionists, who live beyond India's borders. By contrast, a Hindu, he claims, can never have any 'any conflict in his mind between *Swadharma* [duty] and *Swadesh* [country]; there has always been identification between the two'.[73]

A Realist Critique of Hindu Nationalism

Thus far I have been outlining Savarkar's and Golwalkar's theory of international politics. I have made the case that their theory starts out from a premise familiar to students of realism, that is, the view that the international arena is characterised by lawlessness and the ever-present threat of war. From this premise Savarkar and Golwalkar draw a number of predictable inferences, the most notable being the idea that anarchy in the international arena makes it rational for polities to cultivate power in order to secure their continued existence. However, Savarkar's and Golwalkar's understanding of what constitutes national power, I have argued, diverges quite substantially from contemporary realist thinking. In their view, national power depends at least as much on martial spiritedness and social cohesiveness as it does on material factors such as economic heft and astute leadership. In this section I want to offer a few critical comments on this aspect of their theory.

There are, broadly speaking, two ways in which one could challenge Savarkar's and Golwalkar's theories of international politics. In the first instance, one could challenge the operational premise they adopt as well as the inferences that follow from it. In the Indian context, such a challenge has long been offered by Nehruvians, who emphasise the potential for international co-operation, and Gandhians, who emphasise the importance of non-violence. The former, as Bajpai has written, have taken the view that 'states can overcome

---

[73] Golwalkar, *Bunch of Thoughts*, p. 170.

the rigours of anarchy and fashion at least seasons and locales of peace and co-operation'.⁷⁴ The latter, as Martha Nussbaum has put it, have argued that 'being a 'real man' is not a matter of being aggressive and bashing others; it is a matter of controlling one's own instincts to aggression and standing up to provocation with only one's human dignity to defend oneself'.⁷⁵ I will not pursue these lines of criticism here in part because other scholars, most notably Bajpai, have already examined them at length.⁷⁶ The more immediate reason though is that I want to draw attention toward an alternative, potentially more effective, way of challenging Savarkar's and Golwalkar's theories of international politics. This is to show that an exclusionary nationalism actually hinders, rather than enhances, national power. As this statement implies, such a critique would start out from a premise that is quite at variance with Nehruvian and Gandhian thinking about international politics. Unlike them, this critique would accept the central tent of realism – that national power is in fact the ultimate arbiter of national fate. But – and this is the point to note – it would disagree sharply with Savarkar's and Golwalkar's view that an exclusionary nationalism contributes to national power. I see three points of disagreement in particular.

The first is that the identity politics fostered by Savarkar's and Golwalkar's nationalism is not likely to be able to secure domestic peace and stability, which are vital components of national power. This is because, as Pratap Bhanu Mehta has warned, striving to attain a singular national identity, particularly in a country as diverse as India, is an 'inherently dangerous' quest that will always leave 'some subset of citizens' at risk of persecution.⁷⁷ Under the circumstances, it is far more preferable for Indians to learn to 'live on the basis of difference'.⁷⁸ The alternative is incomprehensible. Ashutosh Varshney is exactly right when he says that, 'to believe that 110 million Muslims can be beaten into submission is to believe a lie,

---

[74] Bajpai, 'Indian Conceptions of Order and Justice', p. 239.

[75] Martha Nussbaum, 'Fears for Democracy in India', *Chronicle of Higher Education*, 53, 37 (2007), p. B6.

[76] Bajpai, 'Indian Conceptions of Order and Justice.'

[77] Pratap Bhanu Mehta, 'Hinduism and Self-Rule', *Journal of Democracy*, 15, 3 (2004), p. 119.

[78] Ibid.

a most dangerous lie'.[79] Needless to say, a move in this direction would greatly exacerbate the alienation and sense of vulnerability felt by members of this community. It would only invite them to support and indeed take recourse to extremism, thus compelling the state to address internal rather than external challenges to security and order. The evidence here is plentiful; consider, for instance, the upsurge in home-grown terrorism in India following the anti-Muslim pogroms in Gujarat in 2002. The ultimate consequence of all this is enervation. As Baldev Raj Nayar and T. V. Paul have argued, focusing on 'debilitating internal issues – such as building temples on contested sites and suppressing minority rights – is likely to take India away from its central goals of speedily achieving internal cohesion, prosperity, and international status'.[80]

The second way in which an exclusionary nationalism threatens national power is by hampering economic development. This is because the pursuit of such a form of nationalism is invariably accompanied by demands for the maintenance of cultural purity and a corresponding hostility toward the disruptions brought about by modernity, particularly the individualism and materialism encouraged by free enterprise and the cosmopolitanism fostered by interconnectedness. Indeed, we do not have to look too hard to see Golwalkar making complaints of this sort.[81] Yet if India's economy is to develop, these disruptions can hardly be avoided. If there is one lesson to be learnt from contemporary economic history, it is that trade and commerce are essential to economic growth, as evidenced by the incredible rise of China and the 'Asian Tigers'. And if there is a second lesson to be learnt, it is that maintaining economic competitiveness in an era of rapid technological development depends on being able to attract highly skilled migrants, as evidenced by America's leadership in the area of advanced engineering and information technology, which owes in no small measure to the inward flow of talent. It hardly needs to be pointed out that a nation that founds its

---

[79] Varshney, 'Contested Meanings', p. 255.

[80] Baldev Raj Nayar and T.V. Paul, *India in the World Order: Searching for Major Power Status* (Cambridge: Cambridge University Press, 2003), p. 263.

[81] For example see Golwalkar, *Bunch of Thoughts*, p. 242. More generally see Thomas Blom Hansen, 'The Ethics of Hindutva and the Spirit of Capitalism', in Thomas Blom Hansen and Christophe Jaffrelot, eds, *The BJP and the Compulsions of Politics in India* (New Delhi: Oxford University Press, 1998).

identity along racial, ethnic or religious lines is unlikely to be able to be able to attract, much less absorb, talented immigrants.

Finally, it should be noted that pluralism within India constitutes an important power resource in itself. In part, this is because the internal diversity fostered by pluralism creates many more potential channels of contacts with other societies and cultures. The distinctively social character of India's relationship with the United States is a case in point. This relationship has been built on the back of increasingly robust exchanges of peoples, ideas and norms, a development that in turn has served to bolster a deep-seated economic relationship based on cross-investment.[82] An India that is fearful of cultural 'contamination' will be ill-equipped to take advantage of such opportunities. Furthermore, the norms and practices fostered by pluralism improve India's chances of being able to fashion and uphold the principles of co-existence, particularly in Asia. This, in turn, may help make other societies and cultures somewhat less wary of India's increasing power and influence than they otherwise would be. This is not an insubstantial advantage when one considers the enormous cultural barriers and corresponding distrust that China, by comparison, is likely to encounter as it attempts to exert power across the globe.

This is all that I will say for now. The rationale behind this essay has been to illuminate the Hindu nationalist view of international politics, rather than to try to challenge it at length. That being said, let me close by explaining why further study along these lines may prove valuable. Earlier in this essay I noted that few scholars have chosen to examine the Hindu nationalist view of international politics because the BJP did not introduce significant discontinuities in Indian foreign policy during its terms in office. From this record one may conclude that there is little reason to be concerned about Savarkar's and Golwalkar's increasingly distant mutterings. But this, I think, is to take far too narrow a view of the matter. In order to comprehend the continuing relevance of Savarkar and Golwalkar, we need to reflect on the conditions under which their ideas were formed and gained traction. Both lived in the first half of the 20th century, a time when India confronted a whirlpool of anxieties.

---

[82] Rahul Sagar, 'What's In a Name? India and America in the Twenty-First Century', *Survival*, 46, 3 (2004), p. 127.

Now look to the future. Is it possible to envision such circumstances ever returning, thus setting the stage for a revival of Savarkar's and Golwalkar's ideas? I can see at least two such possible openings. For one, it is conceivable that the great powers of the day, the Americans, the Chinese and the Europeans, will respond to India's increasing power and influence with something other than equanimity. Consider, in this respect, their concerted disapproval of India's nuclear tests in 1998.[83] Furthermore, it is hard to imagine that China, with its burgeoning ambition and history of conflict with India, will be able to transition to great power status without stepping on at least a few toes.[84] Given all this, I think it behoves us to consider the effect that such events could have on Indian minds. If world history is any indication of what is possible, it would seem that a renewed sense of inferiority or humiliation will likely unleash a fierce bout of chauvinism, not unlike what occurred in Russia, Japan and Germany in the late 19th and early 20th centuries, where gross perversions followed from what Isaiah Berlin has described as 'the inflamed desire of the insufficiently regarded to count for something among the cultures of the world'.[85] Should the same desire descend on India, it is not unlikely that appeals to the ideas of Nehru, Gandhi and Tagore, will be met by this passage from Golwalkar:

> The world is not prepared to listen to the philosophy, however sublime, of the weak. There is an old incident, which appeared in many of our important papers. Our great national bard Rabindranath Tagore had gone to Japan. He was to address the University students on the greatness of Hindu philosophy. But the lecture hall remained vacant except for a few professors! Thinking that such a poor show would be an insult to the distinguished visitor, one of the professors tried to persuade the students, who were standing far away, to attend the lecture. The students

---

[83] For example, see Ted Galen Carpenter, 'Roiling Asia', *Foreign Affairs*, 77, 6 (1998).

[84] For a survey of the challenges that lie ahead see John W. Garver, *Protracted Conflict: Sino-Indian Rivalry in the Twentieth Century* (Seattle: University of Washington Press, 2001), Chapter 13. Also see essays by Ashley J. Tellis and Sumit Ganguly in Francine R. Frankel and Harry Harding, eds, *The India–China Relationship: What the United States Needs to Know* (New York: Columbia University Press, 2004).

[85] Isaiah Berlin, 'The Bent Twig: A Note on Nationalism', *Foreign Affairs*, 51, 1 (1972), p. 30.

firmly refused saying, "We do not want to listen to the philosophy of a slave nation!"[86]

As such stories of humiliation easily segue into pleas on behalf of an exclusionary nationalism, I think it is important that we become prepared to take on Savarkar's and Golwalkar's ideas on their own terms, that is, to make counterarguments that show how an exclusionary nationalism undermines national power. I suspect that the traditional critics of Hindu nationalism will consider this course of action distasteful. In their view, Indians ought to oppose an exclusionary nationalism because it is intrinsically undesirable. While I am deeply sympathetic to this point of view and obviously condone efforts to foster a liberal public culture in India, I nonetheless fear that if we do not also make the case that an exclusionary nationalism undermines national power, then we face the risk that this dangerous idea will surge to the forefront of public consciousness, if not at the first sign of trouble then surely at the outbreak of hostilities. In the event we will have reason to be doubly sad, because our insistence on challenging this ideal in the old way will in part have contributed to its strength on the day of reckoning.

---

[86] Golwalkar, *Bunch of Thoughts*, p. 270. It seems this episode actually occurred in China: see Sisir Kumar Das, 'The Controversial Guest: Tagore in China', in Madhavi Thampi, ed., *India and China in the Colonial World* (New Delhi: Social Science Press, 2005), p. 117. Tagore's ideas did receive similar treatment in Japan though: see Stephen N. Hay, *Asian Ideas of East and West: Tagore and His Critics in Japan, China, and India* (Cambridge, MA: Harvard University Press, 1970), pp. 121–22.

9

SECURING INDIA
GANDHIAN INTUITIONS

Siddharth Mallavarapu*

Gandhi represents several research puzzles rolled into one. In his own words: 'I make no hobgoblin of consistency. If I am true to myself from moment to moment, I do not mind all the inconsistencies that may be flung in my face.'[1] However, notwithstanding his 'textured interiority' in the midst of real world struggles, *Gandhiana* remains arguably the most enchanting and intellectually rewarding political subject of study.[2] There are several available interpretations of Gandhi's life and work (apart from his own prolific writings) and I can make no special claim to seek your indulgence. However, as Gandhi would have argued each must choose for oneself what might appeal to him or her premised on one's own authentic life experiences. From this vantage point, everybody is entitled to read Gandhi one way or the other. I reside here. However, this is no plea for methodological anarchism. Several scholars have accurately suggested

---

* I would like to express my special gratitude to the Gandhian scholar Thomas Weber and participants at the IFS–IDSA International Conference on 'India's Grand Strategic Thought' held in Oslo, September 8–11, 2010 for their insightful comments. My gratitude also extends to V. Krishnappa for generously sharing his personal collection of the Gandhian oeuvre. The usual disclaimer applies.

[1] Gopalkrishna Gandhi, ed., *The Oxford India Gandhi: Essential Writings* (New Delhi: Oxford University Press, 2008), p. 796.

[2] D. R. Nagaraj, 'Self-Purification versus Self-Respect: On the Roots of the Dalit Movement', in A. Raghuramaraju, ed., *Debating Gandhi: A Reader* (New Delhi: Oxford University Press, 2006), p. 376. See also Nagaraj, *The Flaming Feet and Other Essays: The Dalit Movement in India* (New Delhi: Permanent Black, 2010).

that there remains a discernible core within Gandhi's thought. This is my version of that kernel.

My intent in this essay is limited. I seek to examine Gandhi's reflections on questions which have a bearing on how we conceive of questions of security or, more narrowly, strategy in the context of the newly emerging independent Indian state. More specifically, what did Gandhi have to say about plausible scenarios for any newly formed state such as responding to a foreign invasion, the role of an army and internal policing? How did Gandhi view the Second World War and the turbulence it had generated, a few years prior to the Indian independence? I argue that none of these questions can be satisfactorily addressed without situating it within the overall Gandhian cosmology and its distinctive lexicon of *Ahimsa* (non-violence), truth, *Satyagraha* and *Swaraj*. Gandhi's scathing critique of western civilisation, his understanding of the modern state as an integral part of this legacy and lessons derived (in particular) from a reading of the Indian epic, the Mahabharata (and its constituent, the Gita) gives us vital clues from which to access the complex world he inhabited.

The Map of Gandhian Referents

Gandhi, during the course of his lifetime, evolved a distinct ethico-political vocabulary of his own. Truth, Ahimsa, Satyagraha, and Swaraj were crucial elements of this worldview. While truth and ahimsa remained the ever present backdrop of Gandhi's political engagements, his variant of anti-colonial nationalism was operationalised largely through the practice of Satyagraha and the demand for Swaraj. None of these practices were frozen in stone. Gandhi incessantly through his lifetime interrogated them with an unwavering persistence and often lamented his own inability (as well of his adherents) at moments to live up to these self-defined standards. The process for arriving at these truth claims was itself both an audacious and assiduous process of self-scrutiny and involved varying degrees of self-suffering.

Let me begin with Gandhi's conception of truth. There was a specific flavour that Gandhi lent to the word truth. As A. L. Basham observes:

> [W]e can perhaps find passages in Western literature in various languages, where the word is given so many meanings, but in fact Gandhi's

concept of truth, implying not only factual truth, truthful speech, honesty, and the resolute carrying out of vows, promises, and plans, but also ultimate reality, can scarcely be paralleled outside India.[3]

Truth to Gandhi was certainly not an intellectual construct. It emerged from the intimacy of one's lived life. Partha Chatterjee clarifies:

> [T]o Gandhi ... truth did not lie in history, nor did science have any privileged access to it. Truth was moral: unified, unchanging and transcendental. It was not an object of critical inquiry or philosophical speculation. It could only be found in the experience of one's life, by the unflinching practice of moral living. It could never be correctly expressed with the terms of rational theoretical discourse; its only true expression was lyrical and poetic. The universalist religiosity of this conception is utterly inconsistent with the dominant thematic of post-Enlightenment thought.[4]

Quite evidently, the Gandhian conception of Truth was at odds with the canonical Enlightenment understanding of truth as an objective reality, dispassionate and independent entirely of the observer. To Gandhi, such a conception of truth did not make much sense, especially as it deprived the political subject of any agency in crafting one's own truth.

Closely tethered to Gandhi's conception of truth was the philosophy of ahimsa. Clarifying in response to a question (posed by Sri Narayan) if he still believed in ahimsa, Gandhi remarked,

> I still believe that man not having been given the power of creation does not possess the right of destroying the meanest creature that lives. The prerogative of destruction belongs solely to the Creator of all that lives. I accept the interpretation of *ahimsa*, namely, that it is not merely a negative state of harmlessness but it is a positive state of love, of doing good even to the evil-doer. But it does not mean helping the evil-doer to continue the wrong or tolerating it by passive acquiescence – on the contrary, love, the active state of ahimsa, requires you to resist the

---

[3] A. L. Basham, 'Traditonal Influences on the Thought of Mahatma Gandhi', in A. Raghuramaraju, ed., *Debating Gandhi: A Reader* (New Delhi: Oxford University Press, 2006), p. 25.

[4] Partha Chatterjee, 'The Movement of Manoeuvre: Gandhi and the Critique of Civil Society', in Raghuramaraju, ed., *Debating Gandhi: A Reader*, p. 90.

wrong-doer by dissociating yourself from him even though it may offend him or injure him physically.[5]

Gandhi then, consistent with the logic of truth, goes on to apply this principle to his personal life. He argues,

> [I]f my son lives a life of shame, I may not help him to do so by continuing to support him; on the contrary, my love for him requires me to withdraw all support from him although it may mean even his death. And the same love imposes on me the obligation of welcoming him to my bosom when he repents. But I may not by physical force compel my son to become good – that in my opinion is the moral of the story of the Prodigal Son.[6]

Again, privileging the experiential over the purely theoretical, Gandhi elaborates elsewhere that,

> [A]himsa is no mere theory with me, it is a fact of life based on experience. How can a man who had tasted apples and repeatedly found them sweet be induced to describe them as bitter? Those who say they are bitter have tasted not apples but something looking very much like them.[7]

An equally important domain or strategy of political action that Gandhi evolved during the course of the anti-colonial nationalist movement was Satyagraha. A thread running through all the facets of the Gandhian cosmology is an explicit recognition that 'we cannot and must not cease to be moral subjects'.[8] The satyagrahi must serve as an illuminating illustration of the rigorous application of truth and non-violence to political life. Akeel Bilgrami makes a

---

[5] Mahatma Gandhi, 'Religious Authority for Non-Cooperation', *The Collected Works of Mahatma Gandhi*, Vol. XVIII, The Publications Division, Ministry of Information and Broadcasting, India (Ahmedabad: Navjivan Trust, 1965), p. 195.

[6] Ibid., p. 195.

[7] Mahatma Gandhi, 'Answer to Questions', On the Train, May 9, 1947, *The Collected Works of Mahatma Gandhi*, Vol. LXXVII, The Publications Division, Ministry of Information and Broadcasting, India (Ahmedabad: Navjivan Trust, 1983), p. 441.

[8] Akeel Bilgrami, 'Gandhi's Integrity: The Philosophy Behind the Politics', in Raghuramaraju, ed., *Debating Gandhi: A Reader*, p. 254.

persuasive philosophical claim suggesting that 'the morally purehearted satyagrahi sees no ... connection between moral judgment and moral criticism'.[9] On the contrary '[f]or him conscience and its deliverances, though relevant to others, are not the well-spring of principles. Morals is only about conscience, not at all about principles'.[10] Thus, there is no attempt by Satyagrahis to foist their understanding as a mandatory requirement for all political subjects. Bilgrami notes, '[h]e too wants one's act of conscience to have a universal relevance, so he too thinks one chooses for everyone, but he does not see that as meaning that one generates a principle or imperative for everyone.'[11] In the absence of 'the' principle, the role of an 'exemplar' becomes vital.[12] The satyagrahi is expected to fill in this vacuum and 'provide a wholesale alternative to the concept of principle in moral philosophy'.[13]

Gandhi himself wrote at some length explicating the need and value of satyagraha. In terms of its lineage, while the idea of satyagraha may have originated during his political struggle in South Africa, Gandhi first translated this strategy in the context of the Ahmedabad mill workers' strike in 1919. Psychoanalyst Erik Erikson observes in this connection that 'there is little doubt that Gandhi chose to unfold his whole Satyagraha technique first in a locality and with people who spoke his language and shared his brand of mercantile shrewdness.'[14] It was only after the 'success' of this effort that Gandhi 'a year later ... would command nationwide civil disobedience against the British government.'[15]

It is interesting to also notice in this context that there has been a tendency to view Gandhi through the lens of either the 'saint' or the 'politician'. Rejecting this binary, Erikson complains that he

> for one, sees no reason to decide whether he was a saint or a politician – a differentiation meaningless in the Hindu tradition of combining work

---

[9] Akeel Bilgrami, 'Gandhi's Integrity: The Philosophy Behind the Politics', in Raghuramaraju, ed., *Debating Gandhi: A Reader*, p. 254.

[10] Ibid., p. 257.

[11] Ibid.

[12] Ibid.

[13] Ibid.

[14] Erik H. Erikson, 'On the Nature of Psycho-Historical Evidence: In Search of Gandhi', *Daedalus*, 97, 3, Philosophers and Kings: Studies in Leadership (Summer 1968), p. 715.

[15] Ibid., p. 718.

and renunciation — for his life is characterized by an ability to derive existential strength as well as political power, from the very evasion of all job specifications.[16]

Several of Gandhi's writings on satyagraha have been brought together in an indispensable volume titled *Non-Violent Resistance (Satyagraha)* edited by Bharatan Kumarappa, who makes an important point in his introductory note:

> *Satyagraha* or non-violent resistance, as conceived by Gandhiji, has an important lesson for pacifists and war-resisters of the West. Western pacifists have so far proved ineffective because they have thought that war can be resisted by mere propaganda, conscientious objection, and organization for settling disputes. Gandhiji showed that non-violence to be effective requires constructive effort in every sphere of life, individual, social, economic and political. These spheres have to be organized and refashioned in such a way that the people will have learnt to be non-violent in their daily lives, manage their affairs on a cooperative and non-violent basis, and thus have acquired sufficient strength and resourcefulness to be able to offer non-violent resistance against organized violence. The practice of non-violence in the political sphere is not, therefore, a mere matter of preaching or even of establishing arbitration courts or League of Nations, but involves building up brick by brick with patience and industry a new non-violent social and economic order. It depends ultimately on banishing violence from the heart of the individual, and making of him a transformed disciplined person. Gandhiji's contribution lay in evolving the necessary technique and showing by example how all this can be done.[17]

Another important pillar of the Gandhian cosmology was his conception of Swaraj. In 1909 Gandhi authored *Hind Swaraj*. He wrote it originally in Gujarati and subsequently translated it into English. Stylistically, *Hind Swaraj* is framed as a conversation between the reader and Gandhi who is the editor. This is an interesting exchange on what freedom might bring to the Indian nation and what vision that should translate into. At the base of Gandhi's conception of Swaraj is his diagnosis of imperialism.

> [He] has no doubt in his mind that the source of modern imperialism lies specifically in the system of social production which the countries

---

[16] Ibid., p. 728.
[17] Bharatan Kumarappa, 'Editor's Introduction', in M. K. Gandhi, *Non-Violent Resistance (Satyagraha)* (Mineola, New York: Dover Publications, 2001), p. v.

of the Western world have adopted. It is the limitless desire for ever-increased production and ever-greater consumption, and the spirit of ruthless competitiveness which keeps the entire system going, that impel these countries to seek colonial possessions which can be exploited for economic purposes. Gandhi stated this position quite emphatically as early as in *Hind Swaraj* and held on to it all his life. It was, in fact, in many ways the most crucial theoretical foundation of his entire strategy of winning *swaraj* for India.[18]

Gandhi realised quite early in the day that '[n]ations are not formed in a day; the formation requires years'.[19] He further argued that '[c]ivilisation is like a mouse gnawing while it is soothing us'.[20] Rejecting the idea of Western civilisation, Gandhi attempts to flesh out his conception of civilisation. In this context, he argues,

> [C]ivilisation is that mode of conduct which points out to man the path of duty. Performance of duty and observance of morality are convertible terms. To observe morality is to attain mastery over mind and our passions. So doing, we know ourselves. The Gujarati equivalent for civilisation means "good conduct."[21]

Clearly, Western civilisation did not come anywhere close to this ideal of 'good conduct' as far as Gandhi was concerned.

Gandhi's Reading of the Mahabharata and the Gita

Gandhi claimed that ahimsa predated the Mahabharata (of which the Gita remains an integral part.) An important caveat needs to be introduced here. Gandhi did not recognise the Mahabharata and thereby the Gita as a historical text:

> [E]ven in 1889, when I first became acquainted with the Gita, I felt that it was not a historical work, but that, under the guise of physical warfare, it described the duel that perpetually went on in the hearts of mankind,

---

[18] Chatterjee, 'The Movement of Manoeuvre', p. 78.
[19] Anthony Parel, ed., *Gandhi: 'Hind Swaraj' and Other Writings* (New Delhi: Cambridge University Press, 2009 [1997]), p. 20.
[20] Ibid., p. 43.
[21] Ibid., p. 67.

and that physical warfare was brought in merely to make the description of the internal duel more alluring.²²

As part of the living tradition of Hinduism, Gandhi lent a particular spin to the great epic. What was Gandhi's interpretation of the Mahabharata and the Gita? As evident in the brief quote, Gandhi disagreed particularly with one school of thought which commonly asserted that the Mahabharata affirmed the need to wage war for a righteous end. On the contrary, Gandhi thought of the Mahabharata as representing a contest between right and wrong. Gandhi is willing to concede momentarily that the epic may have drawn on historical events but he is clear that it had no historical veracity. I have reproduced here one of Gandhi's account of the famous battle between the Kauravas (representative of the forces of evil) and Pandavas (representative of the forces of good) and the seer Krishna's advice to Arjuna, a Pandava warrior.

> Arjuna believed in war. He had fought the Kaurava hosts many times before. But he was unnerved when the two armies were drawn up in battle array and when he suddenly realized that he had to fight his nearest kinsmen and revered teachers. It was not love or man or the hatred of war that had actuated the questioner. Krishna could give no answer than he did. The immortal author of Mahabharata, of which the Gita is one – no doubt the brightest – of the many gems contained in that literary mine, has shown to the world *the futility of war by giving the victors an empty glory* ... seven victors alive out of millions said to have been engaged in the fight in which unnameable atrocities were used on either side. But the Mahabharata has a better message even than the demonstration of *war as a delusion and folly*. It is the spiritual history of man considered as an immortal being and has used with a magnifying lens an historical episode considered in his times of moment for the tiny world around him, but in terms of present-day values of no significance. In those days the globe had shrunk to a pinhead, as it has to-day, on which the slightest movement on one spot affects the whole. The *Mahabharata* depicts for all time the eternal struggle that goes on daily between the forces of good and evil in the human breast and in which though good is ever victorious evil does put up a brave show and baffles even the keenest conscience. It shows the only way to right action. (Emphasis added).²³

---

²² Mohandas Gandhi, *Selected Writings* (Mineola, New York: Dover Publications, 2005), p. 35.
²³ Ibid., pp. 66–67.

In another iteration on the same subject, Gandhi adds,

> [T]he author of the *Mahabharata* has not established the necessity of physical warfare; on the contrary he has proved its futility. He has made the victors shed tears of sorrow and repentance, and has left them nothing but a legacy of miseries.[24]

It is not hard to extrapolate from this account what Gandhi envisages as the toll of modern warfare. He referred to the invention of the atomic bomb (in his own lifetime) 'as the most diabolical use of science.'[25] When news broke out of the first instance of atomic use on Hiroshima, Gandhi categorically emphasised that '[u]nless now the world adopts non-violence, it will spell certain suicide for mankind.'[26] It took several decades after the invention of the atomic weapon before Mikhail Gorbachev and Ronald Reagan openly acknowledged in a summit in Iceland that there was no winning a nuclear war. Gandhi opposed nuclearisation unequivocally during his lifetime and, without doubt, would not have approved of the road the world and India specifically has chosen to adopt with regard to its own nuclear programme. It is somewhat perverse to suggest that since Gandhi preferred self-defence to cowardice he would have approved of India's nuclearisation. It is a deliberate and mischievous reading of his cowardice argument to which I shall return later. Gandhi, it is more likely than anyone else, would have made the case for India's unilateral and unconditional rejection of nuclearism in all its manifestations.[27] Gandhi was unambivalently sceptical of any species of the armament race – conventional or nuclear. He observed:

> [W]hether one or many, I must declare my faith that it is better for India to discard violence altogether even for defending her borders. For India to enter into the race of armaments is to court suicide. With the loss of India to non-violence the last hope of the world will be gone. I must give up to the creed I have professed for the last half a century

---

[24] Mohandas Gandhi, *Selected Writings*, p. 35.
[25] Gopalkrishna Gandhi, *The Oxford India Gandhi: Essential Writings*, p. 603.
[26] Ibid.
[27] Praful Bidwai and Achin Vanaik, 'Gandhi's Second Assassination', in *New Nukes: India, Pakistan and Global Nuclear Disarmament* (New York: Interlink Books, 2000), pp. 142–44.

and hope to the last breath that India will make non-violence her creed, preserve man's dignity, and prevent him from reverting to the type from which he is supposed to have raised himself.[28]

Vincent Sheean also reconfirms Gandhi's interpretation of the Gita when he writes,

> [H]e did not agree that the Gita was either in intention or in the sum total an argument in defence of a righteous war. Though the argument of the Gita was presented in a setting of physical warfare, the "righteous war" referred to in it was the eternal duel between right and wrong that is going on within us.[29]

Another leitmotif for Gandhi which he derived from the Gita is the theme of renunciation. He observes in this context that '[r]enunciation means the absence of hankering after fruit. As a matter of fact, he who renounces reaps a thousand fold. The renunciation of the Gita is the acid test of faith.'[30] Gandhi's regime of self-imposed austerity in his own life had owed a good deal to the teachings of the Gita. However, Gandhi's idea of renunciation was not to disengage with the world and depart to the Himalayas for spiritual contemplation, but to live in the world, fulfil one's obligations (neatly defined) and remain detached, if not actively indifferent, to getting one's due.

Thus, the gist of the story is that the Mahabharata and the Gita far from turning Gandhi away from ahimsa doubly re-confirmed his faith in the practice. The tract on warfare was a lesson in the futility of warfare. It was sham to claim that there would be any victors. Gandhi, in his inimitable idiom, called the bluff again and revitalised the ancient epic by compelling it to speak to the modern human condition.

Gandhi's Critique of the Enlightenment

I have already gestured briefly earlier in this piece to Gandhi's deep opposition to the Enlightenment ethic. What was this ethic composed

---

[28] Mahatma Gandhi, 'On Trial' (Segaon, October 10, 1939, *Harijan*, 14-10-1939), *The Collected Works of Mahatma Gandhi*, p. 245.

[29] Interview to Vincent Sheean, New Delhi, January 27/28, 1948, *The Collected Works of Mahatma Gandhi*, p. 512.

[30] Mohandas Gandhi, *Selected Writings*, p. 38.

of and why did Gandhi repudiate its foundational tenets so categorically? Gandhi understood correctly that the Enlightenment ethic above all privileged instrumental reason over all else. As far as Gandhi was concerned this was behind much of the modern human misery. The human conquest of nature was an integral part of this script and is a case in point. European modernity's undiluted emphasis further on modern technology, linear time and science as a panacea for all human ills led Gandhi to be hugely suspicious of its key claims.

However, it is important to clarify some of Gandhi's key positions,

> [F]or Gandhi, it is precisely because Indians were seduced by the glitter of modern civilisation that they became a subject people. And what keeps them in subjection is the acceptance by leading sections of Indians of the supposed benefits of civilization.[31]

In his critique of modern civilisation, Gandhi argues that,

> [W]hat modern civilization does is to make a prisoner of his craving for luxury and self-indulgence, release the forces of unbridled competition, and thereby bring upon society the evils of poverty, disease, war and suffering. It is precisely because modern civilization looks at man as a limitless consumer and thus sets out to open the floodgates of industrial production that it also becomes the source of inequality, oppression, and violence on a scale hitherto unknown in human history.[32]

Gandhi's practice of non-violence is also the antithesis of the Enlightenment ethic. As Akeel Bilgrami claims,

> [N]on-violence was central in his nationalist mobilization against British rule in India. But the concept is also situated in an essentially religious temperament as well as in a thorough-going critique of ideas and ideologies of the Enlightenment and of an intellectual paradigm of perhaps a century earlier than the Enlightenment.[33]

There have been interesting reflections on the Enlightenment modality of writing as well and how Gandhi's eventual willingness

---

[31] Chatterjee, 'The Movement of Manoeuvre: Gandhi and the Critique of Civil Society', p. 76.

[32] Ibid., p. 77.

[33] Bilgrami, 'Gandhi's Integrity: The Philosophy Behind the Politics', p. 249.

to write an autobiography (an Enlightenment modality) also transcended and transgressed the boundaries of the medium. Bhiku Parekh suggests that Gandhi 'distinguished between *jeevanvritanta* (description of life) and *atmakatha* (the story of a soul) and insisted that his autobiography belonged to the second category.'[34] Also dispensing with the conventional chronological narrative, Gandhi evolved a 'distinctly circular time structure'.[35] Therefore, while '[t]he narration of his life was brisk and unilinear, whereas that of his experiments was circular and had an air of timelessness about it.'[36]

Most relevant under this rubric is a discussion of Gandhi's stance on technology. It is accurate to suggest that 'Gandhi rejected technicism, not technology.'[37] More fundamentally, 'Gandhi never accepted either modern science – or its extensions within the various secular theories of liberation – as the baseline for all social criticism. He saw religions and traditions themselves as a means of criticising the existing and challenging the dominant.'[38] Gandhi did not fit neatly into the anti-science paradigm. As Ashis Nandy perceptively argues, '[m]odernity knows how to deal with those who are anti-science or anti-technology; it does not know how to deal with those using plural concepts of science and technology.'[39] This was also coupled with a critical perspective on traditional technologies as well. Gandhi rejected 'many aspects of traditional technology as alienating, dehumanising or as a plain simple bore.'[40]

Gandhi's opposition to the machine was not because of the machine *per se* but because of its exploitative qualities. He recognised that '[t]he machine as capital has already enslaved Western

---

[34] Bhikhu Parekh, 'Indianization of Autobiography', in Raghuramaraju, ed., *Debating Gandhi: A Reader*, p. 162.

[35] Ibid., p. 164.

[36] Ibid.

[37] Ashis Nandy, 'From Outside the Imperium: Gandhi's Cultural Critique of the West', in *Traditions, Tyranny, and Utopias: Essays in the Politics of Awareness* (New Delhi: Oxford University Press, 1992), p. 137.

[38] Ibid., p. 133.

[39] Ibid., p. 137.

[40] Ibid., p. 139.

man.'[41] Modernity in its most stark version has led to the disenfranchisement of select populations:

> [T]here are people whose lives have been brutalised by the complete disorganisation of their social formations by modern technology. They include the peasants, artisans, tribals and women in general. Their knowledge systems, methods of work, organisation of production, work ethic, and social and moral values, everything is in disrepute. The desecration of their epistemic and technical traditions continues through the ideology and practice of modern technology and development.[42]

Swadeshi as far as Gandhi was concerned was also 'a regulative belief, a basis for the incorporation of human values within the body of science and technical practice.'[43]

Most importantly for Gandhi, the balance between man and nature was skewed as a consequence of the Enlightenment ethic that privileged and encouraged human greed through conspicuous patterns of consumption. Gandhi was not persuaded that self-interest alone could be the goad to politics and he rejected lock, stock and barrel the 'modern scientific/positivist divorce of morality from politics'.[44] He was also of the view that such an ethos was harmful to any genuinely inclusive democracy.[45]

Where does this leave us? Gandhi's rejection of the Enlightenment ethic also had significant implications for his overall understanding of the modern state system and the rituals of *Realpolitik*. It also manifests itself in terms of a strong critique of modern weapon systems and its accompanying technological fetishism. Gandhi deciphered the instincts of modernity and quarrelled patiently with its proponents. To him, modernity was built on misplaced premises. It focused on the superficial. A favourite illustration of his point was modern medicine. Notwithstanding its tall claims, it cured the symptom but left the disease untouched. It lays emphasis on specialisation

---

[41] Sunil Sahasrabudhey, 'The Machine', in Raghuramaraju, ed., *Debating Gandhi: A Reader*, p. 178.

[42] Ibid., p. 179.

[43] Ibid., p. 192.

[44] Thomas Pantham, 'Thinking with Mahatma Gandhi: Beyond Liberal Democracy', *Political Theory*, 11, 2 (May 1993), p. 178.

[45] Ibid., p. 176.

and splintering missing an overall sense of the patient. To Gandhi this was another telling instance of missing the forest for the trees. And far more worrying for him was the Indian enthusiasm to board this ship of modernity that was, both in metaphysical and actual terms, predestined to drown (eventually) under the weight of its own contradictions. He firmly believed that India would continue to be enslaved well after independence if it treated the Enlightenment model as the high ideal of economic, social and political life.

Locating the State: Why International Relations (IR) Realists Struggle to Comprehend Gandhi

Consistent with his rejection of the Enlightenment project, Gandhi remained deeply suspicious of the modern State. They were at least four important planks of this opposition. First, Gandhi did not envisage politics as a realm of absent moralities. Morality was intimately connected with politics and to posit these as separable domains was to Gandhi the first error which the language of modernity compelled.[46] Second, politics was not a zero sum game. It could be a win-win game.[47] There was no reason to believe that the dominant idiom of winners and losers was the only possible outcome or indeed the natural outcome of all politics. Third, Gandhi also apprehended the concentration of violence in the State. Weber's classic definition of the state as a form of political community which has a 'legitimate monopoly' in terms of recourse to violence hits the nail on the head.[48] Gandhi expressed his anxiety in unequivocal terms. He wrote that '[t]he state represents violence in a concentrated and organised form. The individual has a soul, but as the state is a soulless machine, it can never be weaned from violence to which it owes its very existence.'[49]

---

[46] Chatterjee, 'The Movement of Manoeuvre: Gandhi and the Critique of Civil Society', pp. 75–128.

[47] Nandy, 'From Outside the Imperium: Gandhi's Cultural Critique of the West', pp. 127–62.

[48] Max Weber, 'Politik als Beruf', in *Gesammelte Politische Schriften* (München: Drei-Masken-Verl, 1921), pp. 396–450; see also Max Weber, 'Politics as a Vocation', in H. H. Gerth and C. Wright Mills, eds, *From Max Weber: Essays in Sociology* (Oxford: Oxford University Press, 1946).

[49] Mohandas Gandhi, *Selected Writings*, p. 244.

Thus, to Gandhi, the constitutive violence which underpinned the State could never be completely erased in its subsequent functioning. Violence remains a reflex borne by habit for the modern state. Finally, he was opposed to the centralisation of political power in the modern State. His entire philosophy of decentralisation was aimed at ensuring stake ownership by the people themselves in whose name state governance was being administered.

Let me develop the Gandhian critique of some of these themes further. The divorce of morality from politics is a staple in contemporary IR realist scholarship. Morgenthau was willing to concede at least minimally that politics demanded a different kind of morality.[50] Subsequent structural or neo-realists such as Kenneth Waltz completely eliminated this possibility through a far more technical understanding of structure predicated on an evaluation of distribution of economic and strategic capabilities.[51] However, in more recent years, the work of scholars such as Terry Nardin has been useful to demonstrate that notwithstanding the denial of Realists that politics has nothing to do with questions of morality, there is actually a privileging of certain normative preferences inherent even in the Realist approach.[52] So, for example, to suggest that material interests matter over all else is itself indicative of a certain moral ordering of what matters more or most in the realm of international politics.[53] The normative dimension has always been present in politics but the unstated though underlying 'ethics' of different theoretical approaches reveal their diverse moral commitments.[54]

Reflecting as far back as 1952, Arnold Wolfers in a classic piece titled 'National Security as an Ambiguous Symbol' argued that even

---

[50] Hans J. Morgenthau, *Politics Among Nations: The Struggle for Power and Peace*, 5th revised edn (New York: Alfred A. Knopf, 1978).

[51] See for instance Robert K. Ashley, 'The Poverty of Neorealism', *International Organization*, 38, 2 (Spring 1984), pp. 225–86.

[52] Terry Nardin, 'International Ethics', in Christian Reus-Smit and Duncan Snidal, eds, *The Oxford Handbook of International Relations* (Oxford: Oxford University Press, 2008), pp. 594–611.

[53] Jack Donnelly, 'The Ethics of Realism', in Reus-Smit and Snidal, eds, *The Oxford Handbook of International Relations*, pp. 150–62.

[54] For a comprehensive account of the underlying ethical commitments of different International Relations theoretical approaches, see Reus-Smit and Snidal, eds, *The Oxford Handbook of International Relations*.

apparently hard decisions involving 'national security' entailed a balancing of competing values and considerations rather than taking political decisions in an amoral vacuum.[55] A part of the Realist incomprehension and dismissal of Gandhi is his complicating of their crassly reductionist picture of politics. Gandhi defied frontally in more ways than one the Realist common sense. Politics in its most naked form may involve brute force but to Gandhi to 'normalize' this paradigm based on assumptions of an irretrievable Hobbesian human nature represented not only a flawed but indeed mischievous reading of the political realm with unsavoury implications.[56] Gandhi vigorously contested and rejected such a vision of politics. As Thomas Pantham suggests,

> Gandhi ... repaired this modern scientific/positivist divorce of morality from politics. He argued that if the stuff of politics is taken to be atomistic, amoral conception of human interests, there would necessarily ensue the vicious circle of mindless competition, hierarchy, overcentralization and violent coercion. In his view, therefore, we cannot escape the inherent contradictions of liberal democracy without abandoning the liberal-individualistic conception of humanity, and the atomistic, amoral conception of its interests. He argued that a promotion of human freedom and fulfilment and the building of a human community depend on our ability and willingness to adopt a new conception of humanity *and* act on the basis of that new conception. That new conception is that humans are essentially social beings, that not all their interests or wants are of equal moral worth, and that they can be educated to discover and pursue their morally justifiable interests.[57]

In terms of his conception of politics, Gandhi again used it as an opportunity to critique what Western civilisation took to be the 'taken for granted' criteria for the conduct of politics:

> [T]hese elements were (1) the image of normal politics as a non-synergic game in which each person's gain is another person's loss; (2) the idea that normal politics of self-interest, if properly managed, contributes to the social good and to humane social arrangements; what Gandhi called

---

[55] Arnold Wolfers, 'National Security as an Ambiguous Symbol', *Political Science Quarterly*, 67, 4 (December 1952), pp. 481–502.
[56] Pantham, 'Thinking with Mahatma Gandhi: Beyond Liberal Democracy', p. 183.
[57] Ibid., p. 178.

the vision of a social structure so perfect that it would obviate the need for personal goodness; (3) the separation of normal politics from the search of self-realization ... and (4) the belief, underlying much of the modern critical tradition, that the 'dirtier' and the crueller is always the more real self of man and that all altruism is, in the final analysis, a social imposition or cultural artefact.[58]

In the context of anti-colonial nationalism, Gandhi's critique of the modern State was also performing an equally important function – which is to help Indians think of what form of political community they may wish to reside in after the successful establishment of Home Rule. Gandhi recognised that '[t]he transition of power would create new possibilities. The national state leadership might decide, as Gandhi dearly wished but could not entirely believe, to abdicate its coercive authority in the field of social development and leave it to popular agencies consisting of trained and committed volunteers to carry out the work of economic reconstruction.'[59] As another commentator astutely remarks, 'Gandhi knew how to use human sense of guilt creatively.'[60]

Securing Independent India

Many of the ideas discussed under various titles here reflect a distinct Gandhian sensibility. These ideas themselves were the product of an unhesitant and deep engagement with the political world and were subject to fine tuning premised on new experiential realities. These organising devices or Gandhian referents were constantly amenable to being honed and applied to specific domains. Security was undoubtedly one such domain. Gandhi was periodically asked to respond to various challenges that the independent Indian nation could be expected to face in the foreseeable future. The contours of the conversation of the means that should be adopted to secure an independent Indian nation assumed a particular urgency in the

---

[58] Nandy, 'From Outside the Imperium: Gandhi's Cultural Critique of the West', p. 145.

[59] Chatterjee, 'The Movement of Manoeuvre: Gandhi and the Critique of Civil Society', pp. 115–16.

[60] Ashis Nandy, 'Final Encounter: The Politics of Assassination of Gandhi', in Raghuramaraju, ed., *Debating Gandhi: A Reader*, p. 66.

context of the Second World War. The demand for Home Rule had gained substantial momentum by now and it appeared more a question of 'when' rather than 'if' independent rule would be conceded by the British.

GANDHI'S RESPONSE TO THE SECOND WORLD WAR

What was Gandhi's response to the Second World War? When posed a question regarding the likely inefficacy of his method of non-violence vis-à-vis a hardened adversary such as Hitler, Gandhi wrote,

> You may be right. History has no record of a nation having adopted non-violent resistance. If Hitler is unaffected by my suffering, it does not matter. For I shall have lost nothing worth [preserving]. My honour is the only thing worth preserving. That is independent of Hitler's pity. But as a believer in non-violence, I may not limit its possibilities. Hitherto he and his likes have built their invaluable experience that men yield to force. Unarmed men, women and children offering non-violent resistance without any bitterness in them will not be a novel experience for them. Who can dare say that it is not in their nature to respond to the higher and finer forces? They have the same soul as I have.[61]

At another juncture, Gandhi claims that non-violence remains the only 'cure' for Nazism.[62]

Offering counsel to the Czech President Dr Benes, Gandhi urged him to recognise '[t]hat there is no bravery greater than a resolute refusal to bend the knee to an earthly power, no matter how great, and that without bitterness of spirit and in the fulness [sic] of faith that the spirit alone lives, nothing else does.'[63] Gandhi's irresolute faith in 'soul force' over arms was constantly reiterated. He also suggested to the Czechs that numbers alone cannot compensate for the

---

[61] Mahatma Gandhi, 'If I Were a Czech' (Peshawar, October 6, 1938, *Harijan*, 15-10-1938), *The Collected Works of Mahatma Gandhi*, Vol. LXVII, p. 405. See also Thomas Weber, 'Gandhi and World Politics', in B. S. Chimni and Siddharth Mallavarapu, eds, *Handbook of International Relations: For the Global South* (New Delhi: Pearson, forthcoming).

[62] Mahatma Gandhi, 'A British Endorsement' (Sevagram, October 16, 1940, *Harijan*, 20-10-1940), *The Collected Works of Mahatma Gandhi*, Vol. LXXIII, p. 108.

[63] Mahatma Gandhi, 'If I Were a Czech', p. 406.

absence of a more thoroughgoing faith in the method of collective non-violence. He observed in this context,

> [W]hen I first launched out on satyagraha, I had no companion. We were thirteen thousand men, women and children against a whole nation capable of crushing the existence out of us. I did not know who would listen to me. It all came in a flash. All the 13,000 did not fight. Many fell back. But the honour of the nation was saved. New history was written by the South African Satyagraha.[64]

Gandhi was also convinced that it was not in India's interest to exploit the war moment and align with the Axis powers to the detriment of the British. He made every effort possible to convince the Indian National Congress of his thinking on the Allied war effort. He observed,

> [W]hilst all violence is bad and must be condemned in the abstract, it is permissible for, it is even the duty of, a believer in *ahimsa* to distinguish between the aggressor and the defender. Having done so, he will side with the defender in a non-violent manner, i.e., give his life in saving him. His intervention is likely to bring a speedier end to the duel and may even result in bringing about peace between the combatants. Applying the argument to the present war, if the Congress actively sides with the Allies in a non-violent way, the Congress assistance will lift the Allied cause to a high moral plane and the Congress influence will be effectively used in the cause of peace. What is more it will be the special business of the Congress to see that, if the war is fought to a finish, no humiliation is heaped upon the vanquished. That is the role I have conceived for the Congress. The declaration of independence has become a necessity. The question having been raised, the Congress cannot help Britain if Britain is secretly fighting for imperialism while it declares to the world that the fight is for saving democracies. For Britain to be in the right a clear definition of her war aim is a necessity, irrespective of Congress policy.[65]

His principal objection to the arms race and the Indian acquisition of these weapons to wage war was that 'to arm India on a large scale is to Europeanise it.'[66] However, if that transpired, '[t]hen her

---

[64] Mahatma Gandhi, 'If I Were a Czech', 405–6.

[65] Mahatma Gandhi, 'A Poser' (Segaon, October 16, 1939, *Harijan*, 21-10-1939), in *The Collected Works of Mahatma Gandhi*, Vol. LXX, pp. 257–58.

[66] Parel, ed., *Gandhi: Hind Swaraj and Other Writings*, p. 77.

condition will be just as pitiable as that of Europe.'⁶⁷ Gandhi was also asked pointedly on more than one occasion how India once independent would respond to a foreign invasion. *The Hindu* (news daily) reported on September 24, 1938 that

> [W]hen asked how non-violence could check foreign aggression, Mahatma Gandhi is reported to have replied that if India had one crore of non-violent volunteers, he was confident that no nation could conquer India. If they failed in their attempt to prevent aggression, then the fault was theirs, not in the philosophy of non-violence.⁶⁸

Gandhi often argued that '[s]trength does not come from physical capacity. It comes from an indomitable will.'⁶⁹ It is here also that Gandhi makes mention of the exceptional circumstances under which violence may be resorted to. Again, by way of personal illustration, Gandhi illuminates the distinction:

> [W]here there is only a choice between cowardice and violence, I would advise violence. Thus when my eldest son asked me what he should have done, had he been present when I was almost fatally assaulted in 1908, whether he should have run away and seen me killed or whether he should have used his physical force which he could and wanted to use, and defended me, I told him it was his duty to defend me even by using violence. Hence it was that I took part in the Boer War, the so called Zulu Rebellion and the late war. Hence also do I advocate training in arms for those who believe in the method of violence. I would rather have India resort to arms in order to defend her honour than she should, in a cowardly manner, become or remain a helpless witness to her own dishonour.⁷⁰

However, this is not the complete story. Gandhi goes on to contextualise and clarify

> [T]hat non-violence is infinitely superior to violence, forgiveness is more manly than punishment. Forgiveness adorns a soldier. But abstinence is forgiveness only when there is power to punish; it is meaningless when

---

⁶⁷ Ibid.
⁶⁸ Mahatma Gandhi to *The Hindu*, September 24, 1938, in *The Collected Works of Mahatma Gandhi*, p. 371.
⁶⁹ Mohandas Gandhi, *Selected Writings*, p. 54.
⁷⁰ Ibid., p. 53.

it pretends to proceed from a helpless creature. A mouse hardly forgives a cat when it allows itself to be torn to pieces by her. I therefore appreciate this sentiment of those who cry out for the condign punishment of General Dyer and his ilk. They would tear him to pieces, if they could. But I do not believe India to be helpless. I do not believe myself to be a helpless creature. Only I want to use India's and my strength for a better purpose.[71]

Gandhi never tired of making the point that non-violence was infinitely superior and demanded qualities of greater strength than violence. The intent was

[E]ntirely to blunt the edge of the tyrant's sword, not by putting up against it a sharper-edged weapon, but by disappointing his expectation that I should be offering physical resistance. The resistance of the soul that I should offer instead would elude him. It would at first dazzle him, and at last compel recognition from him, which recognition would not humiliate him but would uplift him.[72]

Gandhi also drives a wedge between the inherent superiority of forgiveness over vengeance. He suggests that in the ultimate analysis

[V]engeance too is weakness. The desire for vengeance comes out of fear of harm, imaginary or real. A dog barks and bites when it fears. A man who fears no one on earth would consider it too troublesome even to summon up anger against one who is vainly trying to injure him. The sun does not wreak vengeance upon little children who throw dust at him. They only harm themselves in the act.[73]

GANDHI'S THOUGHTS ON AN INDIAN ARMY
POST-INDEPENDENCE

Gandhi was also expected to clarify what role (if any) he envisaged for an army for the new independent Indian state. There is an interesting conversation with General Cariappa which Gopalkrishna Gandhi records in a volume of 'Essential Writings on Gandhi'. The General is distressed by the fact that everybody including Gandhi

---

[71] Mohandas Gandhi, *Selected Writings*, p. 53.
[72] Ibid., p. 59.
[73] Ibid., p. 60.

looks at the army as 'a very violent tribe' and the community is thus 'very much maligned'.[74] Gandhi in a subsequent conversation with the General clarifies that he 'always had the greatest admiration for the discipline in the army and also for the importance ... army people pay to sanitation and hygiene. I tell my people in my talks to them to copy the army in these respects.'[75] However, Gandhi was still evasive and searching in his own mind for a more robust answer to what role the army could potentially play in an independent India.

In 1946, in another dialogue with army men, Gandhi clarifies his stance on the question.

> [I]ndependent India will have need of you. You have had military training. You will give India the benefit of that training. You have learnt the lesson of camaraderie under common danger. It would be a bad day, if the moment the peril is lifted, the lesson is lost. But in free India you won't be pampered as you are today. You won't have these lavish privileges which a foreign Government bribes you at the expense of India's poor. India is destitute. You cannot serve her unless you are prepared to share her destitution ... Unless you are prepared to forego your privileges, you will feel sorry when Independence comes, and sigh for the return of old times and old masters.[76]

Thus, Gandhi was keen to emphasise that the status, pomp and grandeur traditionally associated with modern armies was not worth replicating. It would only impoverish a democracy that already had very limited financial means. However, more than the cost argument or the guns and butter trade-off issue for a poor country, Gandhi was keen to ensure that a new Leviathan is not erected with its corresponding demands for its own pound of political flesh.

Gandhi envisaged at times a core of volunteers who would commit their lives to non-violence. Positing an Indian exceptionalism in the matter, he suggests that

> [I]ndia is the one country which can learn the art of non-violence, that if the test were applied even now, there would be found, perhaps,

---

[74] Gopalkrishna Gandhi, *The Oxford India Gandhi*, p. 673.
[75] Ibid., p. 675.
[76] Ibid., p. 576.

thousands of men and women who would be willing to die without harbouring malice against their persecutors. I have harangued crowds and told them repeatedly that they might suffer much including death by shooting. Did not thousands of men and women brave hardships during the salt campaign equal to any that soldiers are called upon to bear? No different capacity is required from what has already been evinced, if India has to contend against an invader. Only it will have to be on a vaster scale.[77]

However, Gandhi quite clearly envisaged only a skeletal and minimal role if any for the army. He was very sure that it should have nothing to do with administrative affairs of the state and quotidian political life. From this perspective, Gandhi would have wholeheartedly endorsed the Nehruvian civil–military resolution in terms of privileging the civilian over the military in Indian political decision making.

ON INTERNAL POLICING IN AN INDEPENDENT INDIA

Gandhi expected both the army and the police to display exemplary conduct as free citizens. In a speech at a prayer meeting, he remarked that

> [T]he army and the police should be the first to experience the glow and excitement of freedom. Let not the people get a chance to say that good behaviour can be expected of them only under strict discipline imposed on them from above. They have to establish through correct behaviour that they too can become good and ideal citizens of India. If these protectors of law disregard law itself, it would be difficult to carry on administration at all.[78]

He goes on to point out that he lacks 'the courage to declare that we can carry on without a police force [or] ... of an army.[79] In another brief text titled 'My Idea of a Police Force', Gandhi sketches his vision of this force. He observes,

---

[77] Gandhi 'On Trial' (Segaon, October 10, 1939, *Harijan*, 14-10-1939), *The Collected Works of Mahatma Gandhi*, Vol. LXX,), p. 244.

[78] Mahatma Gandhi, 'Speech at a Prayer Meeting', November 19, 1947, *The Collected Works of Mahatma Gandhi*, Vol. XL, p. 74.

[79] Ibid., Vol. LXXII, p. 403.

[t]he police of my conception will, however, be of a wholly different pattern from the present-day force. Its ranks will be composed of believers in non-violence. They will be servants, not masters, of the people. The people will instinctively render them every help, and through mutual co-operation they will easily deal with ever decreasing disturbances. The police force will have some kind of arms, but they will be rarely used, if at all. In fact the policeman will be reformers. Their police work will be confined primarily to robbers and dacoits. Quarrels between labour and capital and strikes will be few and far between in a non-violent state, because the influence of the non-violent majority will be so great as to command the respect of the principal elements in society. Similarly there will be no room for communal disturbances. Then we must remember that when such a Congress Government comes into power the large majority of men and women of 21 years and over will have been enfranchised. The rigid and cramped Constitution of today has of course no place in this picture.[80]

Gandhi's claims for a minimalist police force again stem from his overall philosophy of State scepticism. In fact, Gandhi believed that under ideal circumstances, a police force would be redundant when individuals themselves exercised their own moral judgement and refrained from any crime – petty or large. However, in the absence of such an ideal state of 'enlightened anarchy', Gandhi reluctantly conceded the need for a minimalist police force. Gandhi also envisaged that the police force become the repositories of public trust and contribute to good citizenship. He was against any reproduction of the master–slave dynamic that colonialism had made the natural order of things. Gandhi's deeper anxieties about the excesses of an unaccountable and unresponsive police force appear to ring true several decades after the establishment of the new postcolonial state.

In Lieu of a Conclusion

Having presented in some detail and often in Gandhi's own words, some of his key positions, I will restrain from going over the same ground once more. Eschewing either the stance of a hagiographer or one of outright dismissal, I would like to ask what Gandhian instincts

---

[80] Ibid., pp. 403–4.

are worth both preserving and retrieving, if need be. I merely gesture to two such possibilities for now. This is quite distinct from the brute empirical fact that Gandhi towards the end of his own life was witnessing his marginalisation from the Indian political mainstream. He was not unaware of it. Post-Partition of the subcontinent, Gandhi lamented that the two principal vehicles of attaining Swaraj, truth and ahimsa were no longer in vogue. In fact, he claimed that they were both already 'forgotten'.[81] Behind this lament was a deep sense of frustration at the manner in which politics was unfolding in the recently decolonised Indian state. Gandhi would have in all probability have objected to any claims of successful 'decolonisation.'

There are several elements in the Gandhian worldview that are worth mulling over and, with some wisdom, translating into practice. Foremost among these was his abiding faith in non-violence. As the pre-eminent practitioner of non-violence, Gandhi established the strengths of the method. What he proved most eloquently was that it was not a sign of weakness to be non-violent. In fact, non-violence demanded more courage than violence. Violence that generated counter-violence was locked into a vicious spiral of blood spilling, which would leave nobody untouched and certainly no real victors either. To defuse the scalding heat of a conflict, Gandhi would go to extreme lengths to persuade his adversary of the unlikelihood of success through violence. In fact, Gandhi acknowledged that it was the aggressor who was more in need of healing than the aggressed.[82] For somebody who could douse the violence of the North-Western Frontier Province and win over the support of Khan Abdul Ghafar Khan, Gandhi remained an exemplar of the potentialities of the non-violent method. The United States (US) with all its firepower and technology is at odds when it comes to dealing with Afghanistan or (for that matter) Iraq. Quite evidently there are glaring limitations of the use of force staring us in the face at this very moment in time.

The other part of Gandhi that might be worth retrieving is his eternal suspicion of the facets of modernity. In his own way, Gandhi

---

[81] Mahatma Gandhi, 'Fragment of a Letter', November 19, 1947, *The Collected Works of Mahatma Gandhi*, Vol. XL, p. 71.

[82] Ashis Nandy, *The Intimate Enemy: Loss and Recovery of Self Under Colonialism* (New Delhi: Oxford University Press, 1983).

demonstrated that human greed and consumption created a false need for continued warfare and economic domination. Ecologists have for long recognised Gandhi as prophetic when it came to predicting the costs of man's conquest of nature. Most crucially from the perspective of security and the State, Gandhi's counsel would be against the 'politics of excess'.[83] What this translates into is that states too need to shed flab. Large defence forces and internally unaccountable police forces are no panacea to any of our ills. While it is important to protect our boundaries against foreign invasion and to protect life and property within the nation, the economies of large scale generate hidden and long-term costs (well beyond the purely economic) that might not be worth enduring. Gandhi would have objected to any prevalent national hysteria or boundary fetishism as base impulses generated by the Westphalian model.[84] Perhaps, a part of the paradox emerges from the very nature of the beast, namely the modern State. Gandhi recognised that the State cannot escape violence because of its endogenous prior history. However, in his own way, Gandhi in his vision sought to 'humanise' and dignify the post-colonial State to the extent such an endeavour was possible. A series of checks and balances could serve well to circumscribe the potential abuse of power inherent in these institutions of the state. This was particularly important, Gandhi would have suggested, from the perspective of substantive democracy as well.

If push came to shove, Gandhi would not, perhaps, have objected under very limited conditions to a modicum of force being used to resist attack to protect the boundaries. But this was only after exhausting all other methods including giving non-violence a serious chance. He would further argue that if non-violence was genuinely allowed to breathe it would in all probability pre-empt and eliminate the first possibility altogether. The ball is back in the court of the modern State system now. The real issue hinges on how willing is it

---

[83] Achille Mbeme, *On the Postcolony* (Berkeley: University of California Press, 2001).

[84] For an interesting account of Gandhi's ambivalence surrounding nationalism and differences with Westphalia, see Kanti Bajpai, 'Indian Conceptions of Order/Justice in International Relations: Nehruvian, Gandhian, Hindutva and Neo-Liberal', in V. R. Mehta and Thomas Pantham, eds, *Political Ideas in Modern India: Thematic Explorations* (New Delhi: Sage, 2006), pp. 367–90.

to give non-violence a serious chance. Not much, as we can gather from the record so far. Gandhi saw the writing on the wall with breathtaking clarity, much to the discomfiture of the conventionally mighty, then and even now as I write these lines.

Part III
Grand Strategy: Core Interests and Vital Peripheries

10

INDIAN STRATEGIC CULTURE
THE PAKISTAN DIMENSION

Ali Ahmed

The usual refrain in Indian strategic discourse is that India lacks a strategic culture. This is the self-serving argument of those who want Indian strategy to take a specific turn. In particular, it is the starting point of realists, who by so arguing hope to bring about a realist turn to strategic culture and security policy. Since Pakistan figures high in the thinking of realists, they would like India to adopt a more aggressive, power-oriented prescription in dealing with that country. I argue instead that India's Pakistan policy is already being influenced by a realist-inclined strategic culture. Not only does strategic culture exist, as against the assumptions of realists, it is responsible for India's Pakistan posture. This posture has been informed by realism, despite the lament of realists regarding the ostensible absence of an understanding of power in India. The essay, thus, performs a compensating function in attempting to bring balance back into India's strategic discourse. The problem with the realist understanding is that, were it to carry the day, India is liable to be overly assertive strategically. In the nuclear era, this cannot be without great risk. Therefore, bringing balance back into India's strategy is vitally important.

The essay is laid out in two parts. The first part covers cultural theory and takes a look at India's strategic culture through a theoretical lens. This is to establish that India's strategic culture has tended towards strategic assertion over the past four decades. Strategic assertion over the past two decades has been paralleled by the advent and influence of cultural nationalism in India's political culture. That this has resulted in an offensive orientation towards Pakistan is covered in the second part of the article which looks at India's post-1971 strategic doctrine towards Pakistan. I show that India's has moved from a doctrine of deterrence to one of compellence. Evidence of this can be found in Indian military postures and pronouncements dating from 1971 to the current period.

India's Pakistan problem has resulted from India's exacerbation of Pakistan's security dilemma. The resulting Pakistani actions are taken by realists as necessitating and legitimising ever more power-reliant policies. The findings and conclusion of this essay to the contrary are offered as a corrective to India's dominant strategic discourse. India would do well to take the conciliatory path with Pakistan to its logical fruition. By confronting realist arguments and prescriptions, the essay seeks to provide India with the self-assurance to be more conciliatory and, through conciliation, to safeguard its long-term security.

Strategic Culture and Indian Strategic Culture

Cultural theory suggests that a state's strategic orientation is a function of interactivity across three planes – political, strategic, and organisational. This paper restricts itself to the first two located at the national or 'unit' level of analysis.[1] Alastair Iain Johnston's argument, in his study of Ming China, is illuminating with respect to India's strategic behaviour. Johnston's finding is that there exists a *parabellum* or *hardpolitik* strategic culture. The parabellum or hardpolitik view 'in essence, argues that the best way of dealing with security threats is to eliminate them through the use of force.'[2] His finding is that the 'preference is tempered by one's own capacity ... In other words, the operational strategic culture predisposes those socialized in it to act more coercively against an enemy as relative capabilities become more favourable.'[3] That this inference for Ming China holds true for the contemporary Indian case is sought to be shown in second section of the paper.

---

[1] For the significance of organisational culture, see Elizabeth Kier, *Imagining War: French and Military Doctrine between the Wars* (Princeton: Princeton University Press, 1997); Jeffrey Legro, 'Military Culture and Inadvertent Escalation in World War II', *International Security*, 18, 4 (1994), pp. 108–42.

[2] Alaistair Johnston, *Cultural Realism: Strategic Culture and Grand Strategy in Ming China* (Princeton: Princeton University Press, 1995), p. x.

[3] Ibid.

JOHNSTON'S THEORETICAL FRAMEWORK

Political culture shapes and influences strategic culture. Johnston's view is that culture or political culture 'consists of shared assumptions and decision rules that impose a degree of order on individual and group conceptions of their relationship to their social, organisational or political environment'.[4] Johnston goes on to define 'strategic culture' as

> [A]n integrated system of symbols (e.g., argumentation structures, languages, analogies, metaphors) which acts to establish pervasive and long lasting strategic preferences by formulating concepts of the role and efficacy of military force in interstate political affairs, and by clothing these conceptions with such an aura of factuality that the strategic preferences seem uniquely realistic and efficacious.[5]

Johnston argues that strategic culture has two elements – 'one a symbolic or idealised set of assumptions and ranked preferences, and one an operational set that had a nontrivial effect on strategic choice.'[6] His thesis is:

> [S]trategic culture consists of two basic elements: (a) a central paradigm that supplies answers to three basic, related questions about the nature of conflict in human affairs, the nature of the enemy, and efficacy of violence; and (b) a ranked set of strategic preferences logically derived from these central assumptions.[7]

His finding is that contrary to the acultural and ahistorical realist framework, States are predisposed to the use of force not because of an international system marked by anarchy, but rather because of the underlying parabellum strategic culture.[8]

---

[4] Johnston, *Cultural Realism*, p. 45. 'Strategic culture' is a term attributed to Jack Snyder, *The Soviet Strategic Culture: Implications for Nuclear Options* (Santa Monica: RAND, 1977)), who defined it as 'sum total of ideals, conditional emotional responses, and patterns of habitual behaviour that members of the national strategic community have acquired through instruction or imitation and share with each other with regard to national strategy' (quoted in Johnston, *Cultural Realism*, p. 36).

[5] Johnston, *Cultural Realism*, p. 46.
[6] Ibid., p. x.
[7] Ibid., pp. ix–x.
[8] Ibid., p. 2.

Johnston's theory of cultural realism suggests that change in political–military or strategic culture is a product of changing domestic political contexts.[9] It varies as domestic politics varies. He writes that:

> construction of group identities involves creation of in-group-out-group tensions ... Thus, as in-group identification intensifies, it should be easier to denigrate out-groups and identify them as potential threats ... the greater the intensity and exclusiveness of state identity, the closer a state will be to the high extreme ... States sharing these levels of in-group identification will tend to share strategic cultures which exhibit hard *realpolitik* characteristics. Conversely, states with weak in-group identification, or states which perceive other states as sharing values characteristic of the in-group, are more likely to be influenced by *idealpolitik* strategic cultures.[10]

Johnston's theory is useful on two counts. First, it suggests that India's operational set is explicable in the theoretical frame provided by Johnston. Second, his reflection on the effect of group identities is useful in explaining the effect of cultural nationalism on strategic culture, and, more specifically for our discussion, the effect of cultural nationalism on India's Pakistan policy, with Pakistan as the 'Other' in Indian identity construction.

INDIAN STRATEGIC CULTURE

George K. Tanham's findings on the lack of an Indian strategic culture were carried in his influential essay, 'Indian Strategic Thought: An Interpretive Essay' (1992).[11] The doyen of India's strategic community, K. Subrahmanyam concurred, making this the usual starting point of reflection on strategic culture.[12] For Kanti Bajpai, the view that India lacks a strategic culture is 'not altogether incorrect' because there is no single, dominant view on grand strategy.[13]

---

[9] Johnston, *Cultural Realism*, p. 20.

[10] Alaistair Johnston, 'Thinking About Strategic Culture', *International Security*, 19, 4 (1995), p. 60.

[11] George Tanham, *Indian Strategic Thought: An Interpretive Essay* (Santa Monica: RAND, 1992).

[12] K. Subrahmanyam (with A. Monteiro), *Shedding Shibboleths: India's Evolving Strategic Outlook* (New Delhi: Wordsmiths, 2005), p. i.

[13] Kanti Bajpai, 'Indian Strategic Culture', in Michael Chambers, ed., *South Asia in 2020: Future Strategic Balances and Alliances* (Carlisle: US Army War College, 2002), p. 246.

Pratap Bhanu Mehta also suggests that it is not so much that India lacks strategic thinking; rather, it is that there are '... deep divisions in the country'.[14] Cohen likewise alights on this point: 'The Indian strategic community is an elite divided against itself and within itself'.[15] I suggest that while realists in India – and elsewhere – suggest that India does not have a strategic culture, others argue that India does not have a singular strategic culture but rather different schools of thought or perspectives.

Cultural theory suggests that while there is a dominant culture, multiple cultures exist alongside.[16] India's strategic culture is not monolithic.[17] In Mehta's view, Indian foreign policy has two strands: an idealist ('Ashokan') one; and a realist ('Kautilyan') one.[18] Cohen uses the terms Gandhian and Machiavellian instead.[19] Rajesh Rajagopalan has disaggregated 'hard' power perspectives into three types: hyper-power, national-power, and liberal-power.[20] For Bajpai, 'ever since the end of the Cold War, at least three different streams of thinking are vying for dominance',[21] namely Nehruvianism, Neoliberalism, and Hyperrealism.[22] Their shared features include, first, that at the heart of international relations is the notion of the sovereign state that recognises no higher authority; second, that interests, power, and violence are the staples of international

---

[14] Pratap Mehta, 'Still Under Nehru's Shadow? The Absence of Foreign Policy Frameworks in India', *India Review*, 8, 3 (2009), pp. 209–33, 210.

[15] Stephen Cohen, *India: Emerging Power* (New Delhi: Oxford University Press, 2001), p. 64.

[16] Kier, *Imagining War*, p. 27. Also see, Johnston, 'Thinking About Strategic Culture', pp. 10, 35.

[17] Rodney Jones, 'India's Strategic Culture'. Paper prepared for Defense Threat Reduction Agency Advanced Systems and Concepts Office (Washington DC, 2006), p. 1. Available at http://www.fas.org/irp/agency/dod/dtra/india.pdf, accessed on January 16, 2010.

[18] Mehta, 'Still Under Nehru's Shadow?', p. 210.

[19] Cohen, *India: Emerging Power*, p. 63.

[20] N. Mirilovic, 'Exploring India's Foreign Policy Debates' (Washington DC: Sigur Center for Asian Studies, Policy Brief, 2010), p. 1. Available at http://www.gwu.edu/~power/publications/publicationdocs/indiafp_policybrief.pdf, accessed on May 6, 2010.

[21] Bajpai, 'Indian Strategic Culture', p. 245.

[22] Ibid., p. 251.

relations; and, third, conflict and war are a constant shadow over interstate relations.[23]

Following the two levels to strategic culture identified by Johnston, Bajpai delineates the three perspectives into their respective central strategic paradigms and grand strategic prescriptions. Thus, Nehruvians believe that the state of international anarchy can be mitigated through international laws and institutions, military restraint, negotiations and compromise, co-operation, free intercourse between societies, and regard for the well-being of peoples everywhere. For Nehruvians, arms spending can impoverish societies materially, and balances of power are fragile at best. Neoliberals, on the other hand, argue that economic strength can substitute for military power. In a globalised world of complex interdependence, force has questionable utility. Neoliberals believe that economic well-being furnishes national security in a broader sense. Finally, Hyperrealists think that the surest way of achieving peace and stability is through the accumulation of military power and willingness to use force.[24] Bajpai argues that in the post-Cold War era, 'Indian policy correlates or is congruent with the Neoliberal approach more than either the Nehruvian or Hyperrealist approach.'[25]

Pakistan is viewed quite differently in the three schools of thought.[26] Nehruvians believe that India and Pakistan 'can and will live in peace'.[27] They prefer 'patience and long-run diplomacy'.[28] Their prescription consists of defence, leveraging international law and institutions to bring about a more pacific Pakistan, and weaning away its external supporters and changing its attitudes through contact and communication. Neoliberals expect the promise of mutual gain to make Pakistan more accommodative. A non-threatening force posture and economic development will lead to peace. The Hyperrealist perspective is that Pakistan only understands the language of power and must be dictated to from a position

---

[23] Bajpai, 'Indian Strategic Culture', p. 251.

[24] Ibid., pp. 252–53.

[25] Ibid., p. 249.

[26] Kanti Bajpai, 'Indian Strategic Culture and the Problem of Pakistan', in Swarna Rajagopalan, ed., *Security and South Asia: Ideas, Institutions and Initiatives* (New Delhi: Routledge, 2006), p. 55.

[27] Ibid., p. 67.

[28] Bajpai, 'Indian Strategic Culture and the Problem of Pakistan', p. 68.

of strength.[29] Hyperrealists believe in prevailing over Pakistan by reducing it to a 'permanent state of chaos and debility'.[30] Amitabh Mattoo uses the words *Subedar, Saudagar* and *Sufi* with respect to India's Pakistan policy.[31] His typology is quite similar to Bajpai's.

The nuclear tests of 1998 were crucial in shifting the balance between the different perspectives. While there was a consensus in India on keeping open the option to develop a nuclear weapons programme, exercising that option was a decision taken by those who wanted to shift strategic thinking towards a more assertive India. Rajesh Basrur discerns the impact of the 1998 tests in relation to nuclear doctrine, noting that the 'once predominantly political understanding of nuclear weapons has slowly given way to a more operational conception of those weapons'.[32] In effect, strategic culture, being socially constructed, is constantly subject to change.[33] India has strategic subcultures and their votaries are in constant tussle for the political high ground.

Applying Johnston's Lens

At one level, India's strategic culture has encouraged restraint in the use of force. In the 1947–48 War with Pakistan, India did not proceed with the complete integration of the princely state of Jammu and Kashmir. It took the dispute to the UN instead. It also accepted the ceasefire offer of the Chinese in 1962 and did not continue the fight even after rearming itself with British and American help. New Delhi agreed to a ceasefire in the 1965 War with Pakistan and, at the Tashkent conference in January 1966, it agreed to return territories that it had captured during the war. India also did not take the 1971 War into West Pakistan.[34] Even in internal security operations, its doctrine has been one of considerable restraint in the use of force

---

[29] Bajpai, 'Indian Strategic Culture and the Problem of Pakistan', pp. 68–74.
[30] Ibid., p. 67.
[31] See Mattoo's essay in Amitabh Mattoo, Kapil Kak and H. Jacob, eds, *India and Pakistan: The Pathways Ahead* (New Delhi, Knowledge World, 2007).
[32] Rajesh Basrur, 'Nuclear Weapons and Indian Strategic Culture', *Journal of Peace Research*, 38, 2 (2001), p. 195.
[33] Ibid., p. 184.
[34] Stephen P. Cohen and S. Dasgupta, *Arming without Aiming: India's Military Modernisation* (New Delhi: Penguin Viking 2010), p. 9.

even though the military has expansive powers under the Armed Forces Special Powers Act (AFSPA). It has not employed higher calibreS weapons or air power in internal operations, other than briefly in Mizoram in 1966. In the Kargil conflict in 1999, its forces and air power did not cross the Line of Control, though at a considerable cost in lives. Nor did it use the terror attack on Parliament in December 2001 as a *casus belli* to launch a war against Pakistan. In addition, it maintained a 'strategy of restraint' despite the enormous terrorist provocation during the Mumbai 26/11 attack.[35] Even though it has gone nuclear, it has a 'no first use' (NFU) doctrine, a unilateral moratorium against testing, pursues minimum deterrence, abjures nuclear arms racing, and favours disarmament through a Nuclear Weapons Convention.

At another level, at the level of Johnston's 'operational set', India has a more assertive, parabellum posture. India's parabellum culture can be seen in its use of force or threat of use of force. The first instance was within a few months after Independence. This included military action in integrating the princely states of Junagadh and Jammu and Kashmir. Thereafter, there was the police action against the Nizam's state of Hyderabad in 1948 and eventually the eviction of the Portuguese from Goa in 1961. A 'forward policy' was followed in respect of tackling the Chinese threat across the Himalayas after 1959. This culminated in Nehru ordering the ouster of the Chinese in 1962. India expanded the scope of the 1965 conflict which began in in Kashmir but which New Delhi enlarged to the plains of Punjab. It intervened in the internal conflict in East Pakistan in 1971 and executed a meticulously planned military operation in November–December of that year. It carried out the occupation of the Saltoro heights on the Siachen glacier in 1984 and has maintained its occupation since then. In internal security, it deployed the army in the northeastern states in the 1950s and 1960s and later in Punjab in the 1980s. Its peacekeeping operation in the north and east of Sri Lanka turned into an enforcement action in 1987. It used military exercises to signal its resolve in the 1980s in relation to both Pakistan and China in the form of 'Exercise Brasstacks' and 'Exercise Chequerboard'. The former turned into the crisis of 1987.[36] Through the

---

[35] Cohen and Dasgupta, *Arming without Aiming*, p. 13.
[36] Ibid., p. 11.

1990s, the army was deployed in Kashmir under laws permissive of the use of force. In sum, it is evident that a parabellum strategic culture is present in India as well.

The instances recounted here indicate a predisposition towards force that is not easily explained by the popular understanding of India's pacific credentials. How do we, on the other hand, explain India's record of restraint? The argument here is that decisions and actions indicating restraint can be explained in terms of national aims, power balances, grand strategic constraints, the availability of national resources, etc. India's focus on territorial integrity, preservation of freedom in foreign policy, desire to be recognised as a power of consequence, and the need for economic development can account for its restraint.[37] Mehta describes the resulting foreign policy as one of 'cautious prudence'[38] or the absence of a tradition of thought that takes 'power as an objective' of foreign policy.[39] For him, India's realist framework is constrained more as a consequence of its military, social, and political 'incapacity',[40] since Indian foreign policy has to be 'conducted with the consciousness that the use of force is not readily available as an instrumentality of projecting power'.[41]

Bajpai, likewise, sees the deficiency in power as being the reason for restraint. He writes: 'National interests as articulated by the state, national power, and the ability to coerce are very much part of India's security conception, but so, broadly, are institutional and non-coercive means that aim to accommodate or change through peaceful means the views of enemies and rivals, both external and internal.'[42] There are two reasons for this. One is expediency: deficiency in power or in the ability to use power encourages India to be accommodative. The second interpretation is that accommodation is a function of conviction. In the latter – ideational – interpretation, there exists a norm against power seeking. This too has

---

[37] Mehta, 'Still Under Nehru's Shadow?', p. 227.
[38] Ibid., p. 230.
[39] Ibid., p. 219.
[40] Ibid., p. 212.
[41] Ibid., p. 230.
[42] Kanti Bajpai, 'India: Modified Structuralism', in Muthiah Alagappa, ed., *Asian Security Practice: Material and Ideational Influences* (Stanford: Stanford University Press, 2008), p. 194.

a cost-benefit rationale since the pursuit of power could give rise to an outcome that one seeks to avoid, namely, the security dilemma.[43] The point is that India is defensive not because of a commitment to diplomatic norms and a tradition of non-violence, as realists allege, but rather because of its vulnerabilities and angularities as a state and society.

Change in Strategic Culture

A cultural interpretation would suggest that strategy and strategic culture has less to do with threats and balances of power and more to do with a sense of identity and prestige. Cultural theory explains change in strategic culture as a result of the tendency of political leaders to choose security policies that enhance their domestic power and the nation's international standing.[44] In India's case, we have witnessed the shift in the centre of gravity in politics from the political left to the political right, in the transition from the socialist to the liberalisation era.

C. Raja Mohan refers to the shift in strategic culture figuratively in the title of his book *Crossing the Rubicon*.[45] Tobias Engelmeier notes that 'India has over the years become more realist in its foreign policy'.[46] For Engelmeier, 'Indian foreign policy is becoming increasingly more pragmatic, driven by strategic considerations based on realism'.[47] Nehruvianism had dominated earlier.[48] Now, a new breed of Neoliberals and Hyperrealists comprising 'insurgent'

---

[43] Bajpai, 'India: Modified Structuralism', p. 195.

[44] W. P. S. Sidhu, 'India's Nuclear Use Doctrine', in Peter Lavoy, Scott Sagan and J. Wirtz, eds, *Planning the Unthinkable: How New Powers Will Use Nuclear, Biological, and Chemical Weapons* (Cornell: Cornell University Press, 2000), p. 146.

[45] C. Raja Mohan, *Crossing the Rubicon: The Shaping of India's New Foreign Policy* (New Delhi: Viking 2003).

[46] Tobias Engelmeier, *Nation Building and Foreign Policy in India: An Identity-Strategy Conflict* (New Delhi: Cambridge University Press India Ltd, 2009), p. 29.

[47] Ibid., p. 247.

[48] The ingredients of this were anti-colonialism; Asian solidarity; non-alignment; countervailing external involvement in the region; taking the Himalayan crest as India's security perimeter; and lastly, self-reliance in both the conventional and nuclear fields. See U. S. Bajpai, *India's Security: The Politico-Strategic Environment* (New Delhi: Lancers, 1983), pp. 66–67.

alternatives has grown in influence.[49] Bajpai argues that while Neo-liberalism dominates Indian policy, 'Indian thinking has evolved in a more Hyperrealist direction since September 11 [2001] and particu-larly after December 13 [2001]. The biggest changes are in respect of the utility of force.'[50]

Tobias Engelmeier attributes the change to developments in political culture.[51] He writes: 'In terms of identity, the BJP stood for a different national project, one not based on supra-religious, supra-traditional values, but one based on Hindu culture.'[52] The BJP view is based on 'the assumption that identity can generate political stability and that the less natural a common identity, the more precarious the nation-building process and hence the more urgent the need for ideological politics which will, in turn, impact on strategic culture and foreign policy.'[53] He argues,

> that is not to say however that there is no Indian strategic culture. There is one – but it is not defined by ancient tradition. It is defined, rather by the modern imagining of the Indian nation, by what nationalists have interpreted and institutionalized as Indian political culture. From a diverse cultural legacy, a certain view of Indian strategic culture was constructed by way of emphasis, selection, and interpretation. Strategic culture is the product of the dynamics created by nationalism. Nationalism in turn references aspects of traditional culture.[54]

Stephen Cohen, similarly, believes that the Nehruvian perspective has been credibly challenged by 'a renascent conservative–realist perspective and second a more ideologically driven 'Hindutva' (or revitalist Hindu) viewpoint'.[55] He notes that both groups have found political space in the Bharatiya Janata Party (BJP). He traces the political roots of this to the Swatantra party's challenge of non-alignment and socialism in the 1950s and 1960s. In his view, the inheritors of the centre-right position are realists such as Jaswant Singh and K. C. Pant. However, the major supporter of the BJP is

---

[49] Bajpai, 'Indian Strategic Culture and the Problem of Pakistan', p. 76.
[50] Ibid., p. 291.
[51] Engelmeier, *Nation Building and Foreign Policy in India*, p. 71.
[52] Ibid., p. 29.
[53] Ibid., p. 59.
[54] Ibid., p. 57.
[55] Cohen, *India: Emerging Power*, p. 43.

the Rashtriya Swayamsevak Sangh (RSS) that had earlier lent its support to the Hindu Mahasabha and Jana Sangh.[56] According to Cohen, revitalists subscribe to a culture-driven view of the world. They are inclined to stress the active nature of conflict between civilisations. They think India, being non-aggressive, has been mistakenly regarded as weak and submissive.[57] Much of the inspiration for the strategic vision of revitalists has its origins in domestic politics, in particular 'Indianisation' or 'purification through Hinduisation'.[58]

Both the change and its explanation finds echo in the leftist perspective of Praful Bidwai and Achin Vanaik who write:

> The central motif of this *Hindutva* ideology is the idea of a 'strong India'. To become strong India must be united culturally and politically. This in turn requires recognition and acceptance of its cultural foundations, which are supposedly unambiguously Hindu, and a complete transformation of society.[59]

Cultural nationalists notice internal diversity and see it as weakness. They emphasise a harmonising ideology to strengthen internal unity in the hope of both begetting internal security and creating strength against external threats.

While realists may not have Hindutva ideological inclinations, the work of realists is being appropriated by cultural nationalists. Together, the realists and the cultural nationalists have pushed Indian strategic culture towards the realist end of the continuum of possible strategic postures. In effect, there is a danger that the realists are being co-opted by the cultural nationalists.

In India's early post-independence era, Nehruvianism, which affirmed the efficacy of internationalism and diplomacy rather than narrow definitions of self-interest and the utility of military power, was dominant. It was followed by a more assertive and pragmatic

---

[56] Cohen, *India: Emerging Power*, p. 46; also see, M. Kerttunen, *Nuclear Weapons and Indian Foreign Policy: 'A Responsible Nuclear Weapons Power'* (Helsinki: National Defence University, 2009), pp. 87–88.

[57] Cohen, *India: Emerging Power*, p. 45.

[58] Ibid., p. 47.

[59] Achin Vanaik and Praful Bidwai, *South Asia on a Short Fuse* (New Delhi: Oxford University Press, 1999), p. 95.

strategic paradigm in the form of the 'Indira Doctrine'.[60] The Indira Gandhi period privileged self-interest defined in terms of power. Greater changes in India's political culture can be traced to the early 1980s with the rise of cultural nationalism. The Hindutva philosophy, designed to bring about a unifying, harmonising identity for the denominational majority, had strategic cultural effects. One of those effects was the creation of an out-group in the form of an external 'Other', namely, Pakistan. The creation of Pakistan as an out-group encouraged an assertive strategic doctrine that has, in turn, prompted a change in military doctrine towards the offensive. The persistence of the Pakistani challenge despite this assertive turn has further legitimised an offensive strategic culture. Cultural theory, therefore, has value in explaining the movement in India towards a greater assertion of power.

THE PAKISTAN DIMENSION

As seen in the previous section, India's strategic culture has shifted from Nehruvianism to a more assertive perspective informed in part by the rise of cultural nationalism over the last two decades. This section of the paper traces the effects of the change in strategic doctrine towards Pakistan. The aim is to show that strategic doctrine has moved towards the offensive in fits and starts. It is necessary to show this in order to challenge the dominance of realism that is keeping India's Pakistan policy in a limbo of indecision between power politics and the politics of engagement.

INDIA'S STRATEGIC ORIENTATION

Largely determined by a hard line strategic culture, India's strategic doctrine has moved from a defensive stance to a form of deterrence bordering on compellence.[61] The change has occurred in three phases: the first phase saw a shift from the strategic defensive posture of the 1950s and 1960s to a strategic offensive posture from the early 1970s through the 1980s; the second phase featured a return to the strategic defensive, until the turn of the century; and the third phase has seen India move once again to the strategic offensive.

---

[60] Cohen, *India: Emerging Power*, pp. 137–38.
[61] Rajesh Basrur, *Minimum Deterrence and India's Nuclear Security* (Stanford: Stanford University Press, 2006), pp. 80–101.

By the 1965 War, India had learnt its lesson in terms of a better understanding of military power. Not only did India take the Haji Pir pass during the war, in late August 1965, it also opened up the Punjab front to offset Pakistan's 'Operation Grand Slam' in the Akhnur sector in early September. Yet, India agreed to a ceasefire before any substantial gains could be made and later gave back Haji Pir. The offensive approach was also evident in the 1971 War in which India launched a premeditated attack involving a multi-pronged offensive for the liberation of East Pakistan. Thereafter, as the victor in 1971 War, India was a satisfied regional power.

After an introspective decade in the aftermath of the 1971 War, Pakistan sought to undercut the power asymmetry. Its military, back in power in 1977, tried to avenge itself. In the 1960s, Pakistan had adopted the stance of the strategic offensive to the extent of launching a revisionist proxy war in Punjab and Kashmir.[62] This was in keeping with its practice, ever since independence, of using irregular forces against India, evident, for instance, in its employment of tribal *lashkar*s in 1947.[63] In 'Operation Gibraltar' in 1965,[64] a prelude to the conventional 'Operation Grand Slam',[65] Pakistan once again used the infiltration of irregular forces into Kashmir. In the 1970s and 1980s, its sub-conventional attacks on India were enabled by the strategic opportunity provided by India's mismanagement of its internal security, initially in Punjab[66] and later in Kashmir.[67] Taking advantage of these internal problems, Pakistan attempted to tie down Indian power in manpower-intensive counterinsurgency operations[68] and in holding terrain of marginal strategic importance, as in Siachen[69] and Kargil.[70] With India's regional power ambitions

---

[62] Verghese Koithara, *Crafting Peace in Kashmir: Through a Realist Lens* (New Delhi: Sage, 2004), p. 22.

[63] Ved Marwah, *India in Turmoil: Jammu and Kashmir, the Northeast and Left Extremism* (New Delhi: Rupa, 2009), p. 30.

[64] Brian Cloughley, *A History of the Pakistan Army: Wars and Insurrections* (Karachi: Oxford University Press, 1999), p. 68.

[65] Ibid., p. 72.

[66] Koithara, *Crafting Peace in Kashmir*, p. 41.

[67] Ibid., p. 43.

[68] Ibid., p. 86.

[69] Cloughley, *A History of the Pakistan Army*, p. 291.

[70] P. R. Chari, Stephen Cohen and Pervez Cheema, *Four Crisis and a Peace Process: American Engagement in South Asia New* (New Delhi: Harper Collins, 2008), p. 126.

peaking in the mid-1980s, Pakistan's attempts, through external balancing, to undercut India also continued to rise.

The second phase, beginning in the early 1990s, saw India on the defensive. Beset with coalition era politics and managing a difficult transition to liberalisation in the midst of an emerging world order, India's strategic profile changed. A precipitate drop in the defence budget was brought on by liberalisation.[71] The drop in the defence budget was also due to the diversion of funds into the development of the nuclear deterrent, as revealed by Narasimha Rao to the Kargil Review Committee.[72] A decline in the level of India's conventional deterrence emboldened Islamabad, even though Pakistan was in the midst of economic and political difficulties resulting from the withdrawal of US support at the end of the Cold War and, later, from the imposition of sanctions in the wake of the Chagai nuclear tests.[73] Islamabad's boldness culminated in the Kargil war of 1999 and in the terrorist attack on India's Parliament in December 2001.

The cumulative impact of these two attacks on India, in the circumstance of growing Indian power, expanding defence budgets (as economic growth increased sharply in the late 1990s), and the increasing assertiveness of cultural nationalists, led to the formulation of an offensive strategic doctrine. In response to the attack on parliament, the politically-conservative NDA government mobilised India's forces all along the border with Pakistan and kept them there for seven months. 'Operation Parakram' was an extended act of coercive diplomacy[74] or 'compellence'.[75] The centre-right successor United Progressive Alliance (UPA) government, while cognisant

---

[71] Raju Thomas, 'The Growth of Indian Military Power: From Sufficient Defence to Nuclear Deterrence', in Ross Babbage and Sandy Gordon, eds, *India's Strategic Future: Regional State or Global Power?* (New Delhi: Oxford University Press, 1992), p. 36.

[72] B. G. Verghese, *First Draft: Witness to the Making of Modern India* (New Delhi: Tranquebar Press, 2010), p. 428.

[73] Hussain Haqqani, *Pakistan: Between Mosque and Military* (Washington DC: Carnegie Endowment for International Peace, 2005), p. 247.

[74] Mohan, *Crossing the Rubicon*, pp. 196–203.

[75] Gaurav Kampani, 'India's Compellance Strategy: Calling Pakistan's Nuclear Bluff Over Kashmir', Monterey Institute for International Studies, June 2002. Available at http://cns.miis.edu/stories/020610.htm, accessed on January 6, 2009. Also see, Chari et. al., *Four Crisis and a Peace Process*, pp. 154–55.

of the political value of being strong on defence, has been more prudential. Its response to the Mumbai terrorist attack on November 26, 2008 was quite different to the NDA's response in 2001 and avoided the use of coercive, offensive action.

Military Outcomes

In terms of its location, size, and military power, India is the predominant state in South Asia. Pakistani attempts to redress the asymmetry with India through its association with the US in the Reagan years and through the development of nuclear weapons in the 1970s and 1980s, led to changes in Indian strategic doctrine. As brought out in the last section, it has tended towards the offensive at the conventional level. This section traces the military outcomes of the new strategic doctrine.

The incipient nuclearisation of South Asia in the wake of the 1974 tests and Pakistan's covert reaction to it led India towards mechanisation of its military at the conventional level and, to the extent that the restrictive technology regime permitted, operationalisation of its nuclear capabilities. Mechanisation in the General Sundarji era gave teeth to two strike corps.[76] Military doctrine at this stage was built around the idea of carrying the war into enemy territory through counter-offensives. This was exactly Pakistan's fear during 'Exercise Brasstacks', and Islamabad's response to the exercise led to the 1986–87 crisis. The doctrinal ideas of the Sundarji era were carried over into the budgetary lean periods of the 1990s, with the headquarters of the Indian Peace Keeping Force (IPKF) in Sri Lanka being re-designated as head of a third strike corps.[77] The Navy, through the 1980s, expanded in order to acquire a blue water presence and role. The Air Force was upgraded technologically, in response to the arrival of the F-16s in Pakistan, with the induction of the Jaguars and the new series of MiGs and Mirages. Nuclear developments in Pakistan, including its more or less overt weapons status by 1987, led India to speed up its integrated missile programme (which had been started in 1983). When the Rajiv Gandhi nuclear disarmament

---

[76] For India's doctrinal and organisational development, see Ali Ahmed, 'India's Strategic and Military Doctrines: A Post 1971 Snapshot', *USI Journal*, 126, 578 (January 2010), p. 578.

[77] See Southern Command webpage on Indian Army website. Available at http://indianarmy.nic.in/command.html, accessed on January 16, 2010.

plan of 1988 got little or no international support, New Delhi finally approved the operationalisation of India's nuclear weapons capability. By 1990, a state of 'recessed' nuclear deterrence existed in South Asia.

Pakistan's proxy war and straitened Indian defence budgets in the early 1990s had a debilitating impact on the military, particularly the army. Even though the Indian army had the conventional advantage, this was offset by being bogged down in counterinsurgency operations and intensive patrolling of the 700-km Line of Control (LOC). In addition, India's presence on the Siachen glacier required more than a brigade of troops.[78] The turnover of units from peacetime to field positions, and vice versa, increased stress levels in the army.[79] The idea gained ground that it was the decline in India's conventional deterrence posture that had emboldened Pakistan. Additionally, Pakistan was using nuclear weapons as a cover to go on the offensive at the sub-conventional level.

India's thinking now veered around to changing its strategic doctrine from the defensive to the offensive. With three strike corps, waiting for the enemy to attack before launching India's counter-offensive riposte was no longer essential. Instead, in keeping with the view in organisational theory that militaries prefer offensive doctrines, India moved towards an offensive doctrine.[80] This doctrinal change was still being conceptualised when the Indian government caught its own military and the world by surprise by ordering a series of nuclear tests in May 1998.[81]

The original understanding of India's nuclearisation was that New Delhi would be able to draw down the size of its military and resolve outstanding disputes, particularly with Pakistan, given that nuclear

---

[78] Vasant Raghavan, *Siachen: Conflict without End* (New Delhi: Penguin, 2002).

[79] Shail Singh Arya, 'Stress Management in the Armed Forces', *USI Journal*, 139, 576 (April–June 2009), p. 576.

[80] Scott Sagan, 'The Origins of Military Doctrines and Command and Control Systems', in Peter Lavoy, Scott Sagan and J. Wirtz, eds, *Planning the Unthinkable: How New Powers Will Use Nuclear, Biological and Chemical Weapons* (Cornell: Cornell University Press, 2000), p. 18.

[81] India's nuclear tests were conducted on May 11 and May 13, 1998 and were soon followed by nuclear tests at Chagai by Pakistan on May 28 and May 30, 1998.

weapons made war too risky. This optimistic view did not reckon with the nature of the Pakistani state and the military mind that ran it. In the event, the under-prepared Lahore peace process, begun in 1999, ran aground at Kargil later that year. Being taken by surprise at Kargil only quickened and crystallised India's doctrinal shift. The idea of a limited war in nuclear conditions now made its appearance in Indian army thinking, with the army chief, V. P. Malik, its strongest votary.[82] The doctrine was formalised after the attack on the Parliament in December 2001 and the seeming inability of India to follow through on its conventional advantage during that crisis. The new doctrine came to be known as 'Cold Start'.[83]

Cold Start is considerably more offensive in nature.[84] The doctrine involves limited offensives so as to stay below Pakistani nuclear thresholds.[85] A nuclear doctrine positing massive nuclear retaliation was promulgated in 2003 in order to raise Pakistani nuclear thresholds.[86] The promise of massive retribution exacting unacceptable damage is designed to stop Pakistani nuclear weapons from checking Indian conventional offensives launched under the new doctrine. The introduction of the term 'massive' into doctrinal statements has proved controversial.[87] That Pakistani interference has declined in

---

[82] V. P. Malik, 'Limited War and Escalation Control', Part I and II, IPCS (2004). Available at http://www.ipcs.org/Military_articles2.jsp?action=showView&kValue=1583&keyArticle=1018&status=article&mod=a, accesssed on December 15, 2009.

[83] For an analysis, see Walter Ladwig Jr., 'A Cold Start for Hot Wars? The Indian Army's New Limited War Doctrine', *International Security*, 32, 3 (2007/8), pp. 158–90.

[84] Harinder Singh, 'India's Emerging Land Warfare Doctrines and Capabilities', Working Paper 210 (October 13, 2010), S. Rajaratnam School of International Studies (RSIS), Singapore. Available at http://www.idsa.in/system/files/WP210.pdf, accessed on September 8, 2013.

[85] P. Cotta-Ramusino and Maurizio Martellini, 'Nuclear Safety, Nuclear Stability and Nuclear Strategy in Pakistan: A Concise Report of a Visit by Landau Network – Centro Volta', 2002. Available at http://www.pugwash.org/september11/pakistan-nuclear.htm, accessed on October 10, 2008.

[86] Cabinet Committee on Security, 'Press Release of the Cabinet Committee on Security on Operationalisation of India's Nuclear Doctrine, 04.01.03'. Available at http://meadev.nic.in/news/official/20030104/official.htm, accessed on May 30, 2009.

[87] Ali Ahmed, 'The Need for Clarity in India's Nuclear Doctrine', IDSA, New Delhi, 2008. Available at http://www.idsa.in/publications/stratcomments/AliAhmed111108.htm, accessed on May 30, 2009.

Kashmir since 2003 can be attributed to the success of the new doctrine in some measure. On the other hand, the fact that Pakistan is increasing its production of fissile material faster than any other nuclear power may also have been caused by Indian statements about massive retaliation and escalation dominance arising from nuclear superiority.[88] Over the past decade, Indian attempts to raise the ante with Pakistan militarily in terms of heightening the defence budget have been balanced somewhat by the inflow and diversion of US military aid to Pakistan in the wake of September 11, 2001.

Perspectives in Contention

Pakistan has demonstrated a capacity for balancing India either by external or internal balancing. External balancing has been given effect by gaining access to US largesse, Chinese support, and 'strategic depth' in Afghanistan. Internal balancing has taken the form of leveraging the extremist version of Islam. Pakistan has used terrorism as a strategic asset. Its deployment of terrorism in India has been to reinforce the hard line in India. At the political level, Pakistan nicely fits the image of the 'Other' in the project of national identity construction championed by majoritarian nationalists in India. Indian identity is also being shaped by the construction of an internal 'Other' with links to terrorism and extremism. A conservative-realist nexus has thus formed, bringing about a realist-dominated strategic culture. Though the UPA government is a Neoliberal one, it has only been partially successful in bringing about a more balanced view of strategy. While India seems to have opted for a strategy of restraint at this time, the blowback from Prime Minister Manmohan Singh's meeting with Pakistani Prime Minister Gilani in Sharm el Sheikh indicates that a restrained posture may at best be a holding operation. The unfolding strategy under the UPA seems to signal a shift towards a more realist stance. Indian military spending is accelerating, with Chinese military outlays and the dangers of a 'two front' conflict involving China and Pakistan as the rationale for India's greater defence effort.[89] India seems to be looking at bringing about

---

[88] See 'Pakistan', NTI Country Profiles. Available at http://www.nti.org/country-profiles/pakistan/nuclear/, accessed on May 19, 2012.

[89] Rajat Pandit, 'Army Reworks War Doctrine for Pakistan, China', *The Times of India*, December 30, 2009; Rajat Pandit, 'Future War on Two-and-a-Half Fronts?', *The Times of India*, May 31, 2010.

such an asymmetry with Pakistan that Islamabad can no longer be a strategic challenge.

The rationalist prescription of greater communication, contact and co-operation between adversaries has the merit of trying to address squarely the causes and consequences of an adversarial relationship. Reducing the threat perception of Pakistan would help deprive the Pakistani army of its inflated claim to legitimacy and strengthen forces in Pakistani civil society which are trying to reclaim political space. Since democracies tend not to fight each other, the strengthening of civil society is in India's interest.[90] A rationalist turn to strategic doctrine implies a step back from compellence and a step towards a greater focus on deterrence. Deterrence can be achieved in two ways: by the promise of denial and by the threat of punishment. In the 1970s, India depended on deterrence by denial. In the 1980s, it has moved towards deterrence by punishment. Given that this shift accentuated Pakistan's security dilemma, resulting in three decades of proxy war, deterrence by punishment appears questionable, and deterrence by denial seems preferable. Denial would entail a restructuring of India's armed forces, including a re-assessment of its strike corps. A review of India's posture cannot be done in isolation. It will require a strategic dialogue with Pakistan. In the interim, it is promising that the Indian military is distancing itself from the Cold Start formulation.[91]

Eventually, the scope of relations will be determined by the relative strength of the rationalists and the realists. At present, the realists are dominant in India and Pakistan. Relations between the two countries will likely remain 'normal' in the South Asian sense – a cold, wary standoff. For the relationship to become 'normal' in the warmer sense, the rationalists must come to power on both sides of the border. Since India is the more significant state, it has the power to determine the nature of the relationship. This means that Indian liberals need to capture the policy space.

---

[90] For a useful bibliography on democratic peace theory, see the Democratic Peace Bibliography, Version August, University of Hawaii, 2009. Available at http://www.hawaii.edu/powerkills/DP.BIBLIO.2009.HTML, accessed on April 21, 2011.

[91] Press Trust of India, 'India Has No Cold Start Doctrine: Army Chief'. Available at http://www.ndtv.com/article/wikileaks%20revelations/india-has-no-cold-start-doctrine-army-chief-70159, accessed on January 5, 2011.

Conclusion

The future of the India–Pakistan relationship is dependent on the outcome of the internal contest. India's Pakistan policy must be based on a grand vision, of a developed and prosperous India with its national interests predicated on a stable neighbourhood, on military power for strategic autonomy, on internal cohesion, and on sustained economic growth with equity. This will require a balanced grand strategy to include economic, military, and foreign policy instruments buttressed by soft power. A hard-line strategy that envisages international isolation of Pakistan, covert operations and an aggressive military posture is a not an attractive option. Instead, a balanced posture based on a regional vision that sees South Asia as a single strategic and economic space is essential. This will require political sagacity, military restraint, an economic reaching-out, and openness in societal and cultural interactions as well as internal political and constitutional innovativeness in Kashmir.

Since India's growth trajectory can do without the distraction of internal and external confrontation, determining the Indian national interest in new light is vital. The Neoliberal peace thesis indicates that India should work with a democratic Pakistan. To induce Pakistan to cooperate, India needs to shift from away from a Kautilyan framework to an Ashokan one. Instead of a strategy of coercion or compellence or of covert war, India should adopt a bolder approach. A coercive strategy can only beget the same response from a military-led Pakistan. If Pakistan responds aggressively, then India's hard line will only be reinforced. A vicious circle of strategic responses will make both worse off.

The vicious cycle must be broken. A liberal turn in India is the only way to bring about change. The liberal strain in strategic culture needs to triumph over the realist. This paper is an attempt to instigate change by showing that the realist critique of strategic restraint is unfounded and self-serving. India's policy makers should be wary of allegations of being 'soft' on defence. Instead, they should stick to a policy of self-imposed military and diplomatic restraint and move gradually to resolve the dispute with Pakistan.

11

CHINA, IN THREE AVATARS

Tanvi Madan

Scholars continue to debate whether and to what extent India appears on China's 'radar screen',[1] but China has loomed large for India since independence – not necessarily, however, in one avatar. Contemporary Indian strategic thinking on China is not monolithic. But, then, it never has been. As C. Raja Mohan has noted, even in the first two decades of independent India, while there might have been a dominant view of foreign policy, there was never a consensus view.[2] This was especially true in the case of how Indians viewed the country's largest neighbour and remains the case today. Depending on the lens through which the Indian observer peers, China appears in one of three avatars. This chapter explores

---

[1] The term is in Stephen P. Cohen, *India: Emerging Power* (Washington DC: Brookings Institution Press, 2001), p. 26. Shirk has argued that India does not really feature high in China's priorities. Susan L. Shirk, 'One-Sided Rivalry: China's Perceptions and Policies Towards India', in Francine R. Frankel and Harry Hardling, eds, *The India–China Relationship: What the United States Needs to Know* (New York: Columbia University Press, 2004), p. 75. Tellis, on other hand, has argued, 'Beijing has paid New Delhi more geostrategic attention than it has been willing to publicly admit'; in Ashley Tellis, 'China and India in Asia', in Frankel and Harding, eds, *The India–China Relationship*, p. 140. Ganguly has compared the level of interest in Sumit Ganguly, 'India and China: Border Issues, Domestic Integration, and International Security', in Frankel and Harding, eds, *The India–China Relationship*, p. 104: 'in Indian eyes the long-term Chinese threat is the most serious that India faces, for China the magnitude of the threat from India is relatively smaller'.

[2] C. Raja Mohan, 'The Re-Making of Indian Foreign Policy: Ending the Marginalization of International Relations Community', *International Studies*, 46, 1&2 (2009), p. 149.

these prisms through which the Indian strategic community views China, the perceptions of China and of Sino-Indian relations that emerge through them, and the proposed strategies towards China that flow from those perceptions.

Most analyses of Sino-Indian relations tend to begin with the question of whether China and India's evolving relationship will 'be competitive or cooperative or a mixture of both'.[3] Scholars have been contemplating this question for decades, as have Indian policy-makers. This chapter shows that their answers tend to reflect the prism through which they perceive China and the Sino-Indian relationship. Those prisms lead to different perceptions of China – its capabilities, intentions and behaviour – and, consequently, suggest different appro-aches towards China.

This chapter first briefly looks back at past Indian debates on China, using an exchange over China in 1950 between Indian decision-makers as a device. Building on existing scholarship, the chapter then identifies the three dominant prisms of the Indian strategic community – an optimistic one, a pessimistic one and a pragmatic one.[4] It examines the three avatars of China that appear through those prisms. In a third section, the chapter explores the strategic approaches to China that the optimists, pessimists and pragmatists propose. Finally, it concludes by laying out factors – internal, bilateral, regional and international – that might affect which prisms, perceptions and policies prevail.

Past Prisms, Perceptions and Policies

In independent India, the debate on China can be most explicitly traced to India's first prime minister, Jawaharlal Nehru, and its deputy prime minister, Sardar Vallabhbhai Patel. The contours of

---

[3] Waheguru Pal Singh Sidhu and Jing-dong Yuan, *China and India: Co-operation or Conflict?* (Boulder, CO: Lynne Rienner Publishers, 2003), p. 4; Kanti P. Bajpai and Amitabh Mattoo, eds, *The Peacock and the Dragon: India–China Relations in the 21st Century* (New Delhi: Har-Anand Publications, 2000), p. 7. This is also the theme of many of the chapters in Frankel and Harding, eds, *The India–China Relationship*.

[4] In that community, this essay includes military and civilian policy-makers and scholars, as well as business and labour groups and sections of the media who participate in the debate on China.

that debate are evident in their notes of November 1950, which this section briefly surveys. While such a brief glimpse can hardly do full justice to their positions, it serves to highlight their different perceptions of China, as well as their proposed strategies. Furthermore, it demonstrates that the current Indian debate on China is not entirely new – many of today's perceptions, concerns and proposed policies echo those mentioned in the debate between Nehru and Patel.

In a letter to Nehru, Patel laid out what could be considered a realist view of China. Suspicious of Chinese intentions, Patel argued that China's leaders were hoodwinking their Indian counterparts. Furthermore, he insisted that China did not see India as a friend despite India's recognition of the communist regime and its efforts to facilitate Beijing's seating at the United Nations (UN). Patel argued that it was unlikely that anything India did to convince China of its good intentions would change the minds of the Chinese leadership, which was hostile towards India. Finally, he asserted that China's behaviour suggested that it was a 'potential enemy', which was no longer separated by a Tibetan buffer and had territorial ambitions that included parts of India's northeast and Burma.

Patel was critical of the Indian government's approach and concerned about India's capabilities. Writing in the aftermath of the Chinese invasion of Tibet, he asserted that India had been too placatory and weak in its response. He believed that complacency and vacillation would increase the threat from China. He felt that poor communications and defence lines and unmanned or poorly manned passes were undermining Indian security. India's border areas in the northeast – not the most integrated with India and where there were questionable loyalties – were vulnerable as, potentially, were Bhutan and Nepal. India also had other internal weaknesses, which could worsen if Indian communists gained supplies and access to the international communist movement through China.

Patel's proposed solution was 'enlightened firmness, strength and a clear line of policy'. He called for a threat assessment, analysis of India's existing and needed defence capabilities, reconsideration of India's support for China at the UN, strengthening of India's northeast and of Bhutan, Nepal and Sikkim, internal security measures in India's border states, improvement of transport and communication lines to the border, manning of key border posts, re-assessment of

India's Tibet presence and its position on the McMahon Line and, finally, a re-examination of India's external relations.[5]

The Nehru–Patel debate has sometimes been caricatured, placing Nehru the idealist against Patel the realist. But there continues to be debate about what constitutes a 'Nehruvian' view of China. The traditional interpretation has been that Nehru's vision of China stemmed from idealism.[6] Others have argued that it originated from an amalgam of idealism and liberalism ('idealist internationalism').[7] Yet others have asserted that Nehru was a realist, disguising his belief in *realpolitik* in rhetoric.[8] Most recently, Srinath Raghavan has suggested that while Nehru might have been a liberal idealist in his early years, by the 1930s, liberal realism was a more accurate description of his worldview.[9]

Nehru's note, written a few days after Patel's letter, contains elements of a number of these strands. He saw China as less antagonistic than Patel did, and perceived the lack of a Chinese demand for

---

[5] Letter from Vallabhbhai Patel (Indian Deputy Prime Minister) to Jawaharlal Nehru (Indian Prime Minister), November 7, 1950 in Durga Das, ed., *Sardar Patel's Correspondence, 1945–50, Vol. X* (Ahmedabad, India: Navjivan Publishing House, 1974), pp. 335–41.

[6] See John W. Garver, 'Evolution of India's China Policy', in Sumit Ganguly, *India's Foreign Policy: Retrospect and Prospect* (New Delhi: Oxford University Press, 2010), pp. 85–86. Also see Amitabh Mattoo, 'Imagining China', in Bajpai and Mattoo, eds, *The Peacock and the Dragon*, pp. 16–17.

[7] Shashi Tharoor, *Nehru: The Invention of India* (New York: Arcade Publishing, 2003), pp. 210–12.

[8] A. G. Noorani, 'Balance of Power in South Asia', *Frontline*, 22, 8 (March 12–25, 2005). Available at http://www.hindu.com/fline/fl2208/stories/20050422004507600.htm, accessed on August 23, 2011.

[9] Srinath Raghavan, *War and Peace in Modern India* (Ranikhet: Permanent Black, 2010), p. 14. From Raghavan and others there has recently been more scholarship on other determinants of Nehru's and India's foreign policy. See Rudra Chaudhuri, 'Why Culture Matters? Revisiting the Sino-Indian Border Conflict of 1962', *Journal of Strategic Studies*, 32, 6 (December 2009) for a constructivist view. And for the role of domestic politics, Dinshaw Mistry, 'Diplomacy, Domestic Politics, and the U.S.–India Nuclear Agreement', *Asian Survey*, 46, 5 (September/October 2006), pp. 675–98; Vipin Narang and Paul Staniland, 'Ideologies, Coalitions, and Indian Foreign Policy', Paper Presentation at the International Studies Association Annual Convention, New Orleans, February 19, 2010.

the complete withdrawal of Indian facilities from Tibet as significant. He believed that China desired India's friendship and that India should reciprocate. Nehru stressed the need to keep in mind the long-term perspective – China and its communist regime were there to stay and New Delhi needed to establish a working relationship with Beijing. He argued that there was very little India could do to prevent the takeover of Tibet – India did not have the capacity to act militarily. Even if it did make such an effort, it would likely fail and would lead to Chinese hostility towards India and constant insecurity at India's borders. Instead, Nehru sought a more limited, what he considered feasible, goal – Tibetan autonomy – arguing that India could not help achieve even this if Sino-Indian relations were bad.

As for whether China posed a threat to India, Nehru did not think there would be any 'real' Chinese military invasion of India in the 'foreseeable future'. For one, this would likely spark a world war. Also, China needed to defend its other borders and would hardly be able to divert the troops required for a major attack on India. Nehru did, however, expect 'gradual infiltration' across the border and Chinese occupation of disputed territory. This required improving connectivity to the tribal areas in the northeast, which were not well integrated with the rest of the country.[10] The government also needed to prepare to prevent any Chinese infiltration. Furthermore, India needed to tackle the other real threat from China – the 'infiltration of ... ideas' – with ideas of its own.[11] In practice,

---

[10] This particular thought was expressed a year before when Nehru had predicted that China would invade Tibet, possibly within the year, bringing it to India's doorstep. Letter from Jawaharlal Nehru to CPN Singh (Indian Ambassador in Nepal), New Delhi, September 10, 1949 and Letter from Jawaharlal Nehru to John Matthai (Indian Finance Minister), New Delhi, September 10, 1949 in S. Gopal et al., eds, *Selected Works of Jawaharlal Nehru, Second Series*, Vol. 13 (New Delhi: Jawaharlal Nehru Memorial Fund, 1993), pp. 258–60.

[11] Nehru outlined his views of how the lack of democracy and development could be a breeding ground for communism in a letter responding to the Nepalese king: 'The Communists have succeeded in countries where the masses of the people were poor and, more especially, where the agrarian system was feudal and backward. In Asia it is this backward agrarian system which has been the chief cause of trouble and which has encouraged

he went further, supporting a crackdown on communists within the country.

While Patel called for visible military strengthening, Nehru believed that this was neither desirable nor feasible. Any attempt to build up India's military on the Sino-Indian border would likely reinforce Chinese insecurity and be counterproductive – instead of preparation acting as a deterrent, it would serve as provocation. Furthermore, Nehru asserted that India did not have the financial and military resources to prepare for an unlikely attack. The prime minister asserted that Pakistan was the major potential threat to India and diverting significant resources to the Sino-Indian border would undermine Indian defence on the India–Pakistan fronts. He believed, additionally, that Pakistan would take political or military advantage of tensions in Sino-Indian relations. Even if India enhanced its defence capabilities or looked abroad for military supplies it would then be left in a strategically 'unsound' position with two major enemies.

Nehru did not rule out the possibility that the Chinese communists would be expansionist, but he did not believe this was inevitable. It depended on a number of factors, including the development of both countries and how communist China really became. He felt that Sino-Indian conflict would be destructive to both and allow external actors to take advantage. Given this assessment and the level of India's capabilities, while India should prepare for contingencies, Nehru believed the best approach was reaching 'some kind of understanding' with China, as long as Beijing desired the same.[12]

---

communism. The Chinese National Government has collapsed because of its inability to deal with the agrarian problem. There was no democracy in China. It was a purely authoritarian State. Wherever there was an element of democracy, communism was checked' (Letter from Jawaharlal Nehru to Mohan Shamsher Jung Bahadur Rana [Nepalese prime minister], New Delhi, August 19, 1949 in Gopal et al., eds, *Selected Works of Jawaharlal Nehru*, p. 255). He also stressed that communism could be nipped in the bud if one 'delivered the goods'. (Jawaharlal Nehru, Speech at a Reception given by the UN Correspondents Association, Lake Success, NY, October 19, 1949 in Gopal et al., eds, *Selected Works of Jawaharlal Nehru*, p. 330).

[12] Prime Minister Nehru's Note on China and Tibet, November 18, 1950 in Durga Das, ed., *Sardar Patel's Correspondence*.

Prisms and Perceptions: Interpreting China's Capabilities, Intentions and Actions

Six decades later, there continue to be different Indian perceptions of China and debates about which avatar most accurately represents the real China. Amitabh Mattoo has noted the different constructions of China in the Indian public imagination: 'ancient friend and modern ally; role model; unpredictable adversary and dangerous rival; inscrutable and mysterious'.[13] Others have pointed out that even among India's strategic elite there is no one singular Indian school of thought on China. Breaking down the monolithic 'India', Steven Hoffman has outlined three Indian 'perceptual positions' on China: the 'China is hostile' position, the 'China is not hostile' position and the mainstream position.[14] Sidhu and Yuan have identified China-threat proponents, co-operation proponents and middle-of-the road pragmatists.[15]

Building on that work, this chapter identifies three major strands of Indian strategic thinking about China: that of the optimists, the pessimists and the pragmatists. In the movie *Rashomon*, different observers recall the same incident in their own ways. Similarly, optimists, pessimists and pragmatists see China's past and present attitude and behaviour in distinct ways, ascribing dissimilar motivations and intentions to the same Chinese actions.[16] This section compares the optimists', pessimists' and pragmatists' attitudes towards China, interpretations of Sino-Indian relations in the past and assessments of Chinese behaviour with regard to various issues and regions.[17] The discussion does not aim to be all-encompassing, but, rather, to represent the dominant perceptions among these groups.

---

[13] Mattoo, 'Imagining China'.

[14] Steven A. Hoffman, 'Perceptions and China Policy in India', in Frankel and Harding, eds, *The India–China Relationship*, pp. 39–49.

[15] Sidhu and Yuan, *China and India*, pp. 145–51.

[16] In a book about the different ways Americans, Indians and Pakistanis perceive India-Pakistan crises, the authors used a similar device. See P. R. Chari, Pervaiz Iqbal Cheema and Stephen P. Cohen, *Four Crises and a Peace Process: American Engagement in South Asia* (Washington DC: Brookings Institution Press, 2007).

[17] In these groups, this essay includes both Indians and non-Indians who take active part in the Indian debate on China.

This chapter neither implies that the categories form neat stovepipes nor contends that individuals have unchanging or easily categorised views. Furthermore, though it notes that the dominant view in the Indian government is a pragmatic one, the chapter does not contend that there is a monolithic view of China within the Indian government or even within certain ministries. Finally, while the chapter identifies some of the theoretical frameworks from which the groups' thinking derives, the categorisation is not framed on the basis of these paradigms.

TALE OF THE TWO TIGERS: THE OPTIMISTIC VIEW

General Attitude

Optimists believe that China and India are likely to co-operate in the future. This group includes 'Asia-firsters', idealists, some liberals (in the traditional sense of the term), the left and, ironically given the latter, the corporate lobby. According to Sidhu and Yuan, 'seasoned China scholars, former diplomats, and some members of the leftists parties in India' hold this optimistic view of China and Sino-Indian relations. They also include in this group Indian corporations and industry groups interested in doing business in China or with Chinese companies.[18] Hoffman has identified idealism as the source of the optimists' perception of China.[19] Some optimists' thinking, however, stems more from pan-Asianism. Another set of optimists finds inspiration in communism. Yet another set's thinking derives from a liberal perspective.

The optimists have a benign view of China. Most of them, though not on the left, argue that India's neighbour is no longer revolutionary. They interpret some Chinese actions that other groups perceive as aggressive as defensive. Optimists see China as a status quo power, one that does not use military force until unavoidable. Furthermore, they argue that Beijing has proved that it is a responsible stakeholder, having signed up to a range of constraining multilateral regimes. The liberals among the optimists add that China is too integrated into the global system to play a destabilising role, which would be self-defeating.[20]

---

[18] Sidhu and Yuan, *China and India*, p. 148.
[19] Hoffman, 'Perceptions and China Policy in India', pp. 53–54.
[20] Mattoo, 'Imagining China', pp. 19–20.

Idealists and Asia-firsters see China as an 'ancient friend and modern ally' of India. Mattoo notes that theirs is 'essentially a normative idealised view, rooted in the desire to see India and China emerge as strong allies in the contemporary international system'.[21] This group highlights both countries' ancient civilisations and their past ties. They stress that China takes 'decisions on the basis of ... non-Western criteria'. There is a significant amount of mirror imaging of China and India among these optimists, who highlight China and India's similar experiences, challenges and opportunities.[22] According to them, these shared characteristics, along with past links form the basis for a strong partnership.

This set of optimists tends to emphasise the difference between China and India on the one hand and the west broadly on the other. There can be an element of anti-Westernism in general and anti-Americanism in particular associated with this perspective. Indeed, those who propound these beliefs see the need to counter 'American hegemony' and 'western' discourses as a major reason for a Sino-Indian partnership.[23]

Another set of optimists, with ideas stemming from commercial liberalism, also indulge in mirror imaging – though in this case they emphasise China and India's shared experience as large emerging economies. They see shared interests not just between China and India but also with the rest of the world. They see increased bilateral interaction *and* global integration as the most solid basis for Sino–Indian co-operation.[24]

Overall, those who have an optimistic view emphasise the range of China's and India's intersecting interests and note positively the increasing breadth and depth of interaction between the two countries.[25] Optimists assert that India can learn a lot from China on issues ranging from science and technology development[26] to

---

[21] Ibid., p. 16.

[22] Surjit Mansingh, 'Why China Matters to India', in Bajpai and Mattoo, eds, *The Peacock and the Dragon*, pp. 156–57.

[23] Mattoo, 'Imagining China', p. 18.

[24] Ibid., p. 20.

[25] C. V. Ranganathan, 'India in China's Foreign Policy', *Seminar*, 562 (June 2006). Available at http://www.india-seminar.com/2006/562/562-cv-ranganathan.htm, accessed on August 23, 2011.

[26] Bappaditya Mukherjee, 'China and the RMA', in Bajpai and Mattoo, eds, *The Peacock and the Dragon*, p. 141.

environmental policy[27] to how to deal with countries like the United States.[28] Furthermore, they assert that China does not see India as a threat. Most also play down bilateral differences, considering the 1962 war and Sino-Pakistan relations, for example, as 'aberrations'.[29] Critics, however, call the optimists 'apologists' for China[30] or 'Beijing's Indian cheerleaders'.[31] Others believe this group 'often exaggerate[s] ... both the historical links as well as the space for contemporary co-operation'.[32]

Interpretation of the Past

Robert Jervis has noted, 'observers use other's past behaviour to infer how they will behave in the future'.[33] And, indeed, Indian perceptions of past Chinese actions colour contemporary thinking of China and the future of the Sino-Indian relationship. Among the corporate optimists, there tends to be an emphasis on moving beyond history. Other optimists look back at the history of the relationship and highlight the two countries' shared experiences: China and India's battles against colonialism and imperialism, and their efforts to disengage from superpower entanglements during the Cold War. They see cold war politics as the cause of Sino-Indian tension and 'lost opportunities' in the late 1950s and the 1960s.[34] They assign a significant share of the responsibility for the tension to the superpowers. Chinese actions during the period of Sino-Indian tension are consequently seen as having been anti-American or anti-Soviet, rather than anti-Indian.

Optimists also fault misunderstanding and misperceptions for past strain.[35] They acknowledge China's territorial rights, as well as

---

[27] Betwa Sharma, 'Can Learn from China, says Jairam', *The Indian Express*, September 24, 2009. Available at http://global.factiva.com, accessed on August 23, 2011.

[28] Mansingh, 'Why China Matters to India', p. 163.

[29] Ibid., pp. 18–19.

[30] Ibid., p. 16.

[31] Swapan Dasgupta, 'Of Actual Control', *The Telegraph*, April 8, 2005. Available at http://www.telegraphindia.com/1050408/asp/opinion/story_4586091.asp, accessed on August 23, 2011.

[32] Mattoo, 'Imagining China', p. 16.

[33] Robert Jervis, *Perception and Misperception in International Politics* (Princeton, NJ: Princeton University Press, 1976), p. 9.

[34] Ranganathan, 'India in China's Foreign Policy'.

[35] Ibid.

the contribution of Indian actions in leading to the 1962 Sino-Indian War.[36] They admit that Chinese policymakers did not necessarily correctly assess Indian intentions. But they also fault India's 'intransigence' and Indian decision-makers' lack of knowledge and understanding of China's perspective and imperatives.[37]

The lessons optimists have learned from history are that misperceptions can cause tension and external actors can drag the two countries into their battles. They do not consider the Panchsheel principles of co-existence[38] to be naïve and misguided, as critics contend. Instead, optimists see these principles as the optimal basis for bilateral interaction.[39]

Territorial Issues

Optimists argue that the numerous rounds of bilateral border talks that have taken place show that Beijing is serious about solving this key area of Sino-Indian dispute. There has been progress on this front and, moreover, this has led to improvement in the overall relationship. They believe that New Delhi has assured China by its stance on Tibet and Beijing, on its part, has more or less accepted Sikkim's accession to India. Optimists have also interpreted the principle included in a 2005 agreement as China's acceptance of India's claims on Arunachal Pradesh.[40]

Some optimists downplay or deny any incidents at the border, arguing that reports of Chinese hostility are 'either baseless or highly

---

[36] Hoffman, 'Perceptions and China Policy in India', p. 45.

[37] Mansingh, 'Why China Matters to India', p. 159.

[38] '(1) Mutual respect for each other's territorial integrity and sovereignty; (2) Mutual non-aggression; (3) Mutual non-interference in each other's internal affairs; (4) Equality and mutual benefit: and (5) Peaceful coexistence'. See 'Agreement Between the Republic of India and the People's Republic of China on Trade and Intercourse Between Tibet Region of China and India', April 29, 1954. Available at http://untreaty.un.org/unts/1_60000/9/1/00016004.pdf, accessed on August 23, 2011.

[39] Ranganathan, 'India in China's Foreign Policy'.

[40] The principle stated that 'in reaching a boundary settlement, the two sides shall safeguard due interests of their settled populations in the border areas'. Pranab Dhal Samanta, 'The China Chill', *The Indian Express*, September 24, 2009. Available at http://global.factiva.com, accessed on August 23, 2011.

exaggerated'.[41] Others acknowledge that skirmishes continue along the border but assert, 'both sides are firm on maintaining peace'.[42] They point out that the border has been relatively peaceful and assert that the broader strategic dialogue, high-level visits, a range of confidence-building measures (CBMs) and coordination in multilateral settings have facilitated better understanding between the two countries.[43] Optimists consider these interactions beneficial, not just because they promote official understanding, but also because they prepare the public ground for an eventual broader territorial settlement.[44]

One set of optimists remains concerned that such a settlement will not take place as long as Tibet remains a 'destabilising' factor in Sino-Indian relations.[45] This group argues that critics have misrepresented Chinese actions in Tibet, where the situation is an improvement from the feudal and theocratic system that prevailed before China took over.[46] According to them, further integration with the rest of China will be even more beneficial for Tibetan development.[47] These optimists assert that China has done everything

---

[41] C. G. Manoj, 'View from the Left', *The Indian Express*, October 7, 2009. Also see 'CPM Uneasy, but Doesn't Slam China', *The Indian Express*, October 14, 2009. Available at http://global.factiva.com, accessed on August 23, 2011.

[42] Kanti P. Bajpai, 'India, China and Asian Security', *The Peacock and the Dragon*, p. 38.

[43] Francine Frankel, 'Introduction', in Frankel and Harding, eds, *The India-China Relationship*, p. 10; Bajpai, 'India, China and Asian Security', p. 31.

[44] Ranganathan, 'India in China's Foreign Policy'.

[45] Subramanian Swamy, 'Sino-Indian Relations through the Tibet Prism', *Frontline*, 17, 18 (September 2–15, 2000). Available at http://www.hindu.com/fline/fl1718/17180240.htm, accessed on August 23, 2011.

[46] C. V. Narasimhan, 'Letter to the Editor: Thoughts on Tibet', *Frontline*, 17, 25 (December 9–22, 2000). Available at http://www.hindu.com/fline/fl1725/17251070.htm, accessed on August 23, 2011. The author was a former Under-Secretary General of the UN. Also see N. Ram, 'Celebrating Social Emancipation in Tibet', *The Hindu*, March 28, 2009. Available at http://www.hindu.com/2009/03/28/stories/2009032854911000.htm, accessed on August 23, 2011.

[47] 'Tibet's Development Spells Progress in Human Rights: N. Ram', *The Hindu*, April 23, 2008. Available at http://www.hindu.com/2008/04/23/stories/2008042359671200.htm, accessed on August 23, 2011.

possible to extend a hand to the Dalai Lama, but he has been intransigent. The Tibetans, instigated by western countries, are holding out for independence, despite their protestations otherwise.[48] Overall, these optimists consider the presence of the Dalai Lama in India — and his political activities from Dharamshala — as provocative and harmful to the Sino-Indian relationship.

The Sino-Pakistan Relationship

A former Indian defence secretary called China's relationship with Pakistan 'a strange marriage of convenience'.[49] India's China optimists argue that, instead, this relationship is a natural reaction to China's feeling of encirclement.[50] Furthermore, they assert that critics exaggerate the extent of Chinese support to Pakistan and note that Islamabad has no 'formal guarantee' from Beijing.

Optimists argue that, at times, China has even distanced itself from Pakistan's Kashmir position, moving away from what analysts have called its 'previously unqualified support'.[51] During the Kargil war in 1999, optimists note, 'Beijing was perceptibly sympathetic to the Indian position'. They see this Chinese 'tilt' as stemming from a desire to see 'a peaceful and bilateral resolution of the Kashmir conflict', as well as deriving from Beijing's own 'anxieties over the rising tide of Islamic separatis[m] and fundamentalis[m]'.[52] Related to the latter, optimists point to a shared Chinese and Indian interest in containing the spill over effects of violent Islamic extremism from Pakistan and in encouraging stability within that country.

The Near Abroad

Optimists see China as being a force for good in south and southeast Asia. They see Indian involvement in the Association of South East Asian Nations (ASEAN) and Chinese involvement in the South Asian Association for Regional Co-operation (SAARC) as positive

---

[48] N. Ram, 'The Politics of Tibet: A Reality Check', *The Hindu*, July 5, 2007. Available at http://www.hindu.com/2007/07/05/stories/2007070559671300.htm, accessed on August 23, 2011.

[49] S. S. Khera, *India's Defence Problem* (Bombay: Orient Longmans, 1968), p. 46. Khera was the Indian cabinet secretary from 1962–64.

[50] Hoffman, 'Perceptions and China Policy in India', p. 46.

[51] Tellis, 'China and India in Asia', p. 147.

[52] Bajpai, 'India, China and Asian Security', p. 37.

developments.⁵³ According to them, co-operative schemes like the Kunming initiative, designed to facilitate economic interaction between Bangladesh, China, India and Myanmar, serve as models for regional behaviour.

The New Great Game

In the 19th century, Britain and Russia were seen to play a 'Great Game' vying for economic domination and 'political ascendancy' across 'a vast chessboard' stretching from the Caucasus to Tibet.⁵⁴ Today China and India are seen as indulging in a new great game, seeking resources and influence not just in central Asia but also in Africa, the Middle East and even Latin America. While some on the left reject such 'neo-imperialism', most China optimists see this vast playing field as ripe for Sino-Indian collaboration. They point to instances of successful co-operation in the energy sector, in which Chinese and Indian companies have jointly bid for oil and natural gas assets, as a model for broader co-operation.⁵⁵

The Economic Sphere

Proponents of Sino-Indian co-operation note that the two countries are doing a lot of business together. They welcome the increase in bilateral trade, pointing out how rapidly it has grown overall over the last decade. Optimists highlight Indian businesses' interest in investing in China (and vice versa).⁵⁶ They see the two countries increased economic ties as beneficial and a huge area of opportunity – and potentially what will cause the two countries to reach a political settlement. Some optimists also see the Chinese 'model of development' as one India should consider. Pointing out that China is far ahead of India, they argue that since India cannot beat China, the country should follow its northern neighbour's path.⁵⁷

---

⁵³ Ranganathan, 'India in China's Foreign Policy'.

⁵⁴ Peter Hopkirk, *The Great Game: The Struggle for Empire in Central Asia* (New York: Kodansha International, 1994), p. 2.

⁵⁵ See Mani Shankar Aiyar, 'India and China in Asia's Quest for Energy Security', in Mohan Guruswamy, ed., *Emerging Trends in India–China Relations* (Gurgaon: Hope India Publications, 2006), pp. 15–24.

⁵⁶ Ranganathan, 'India in China's Foreign Policy'.

⁵⁷ Manoj, 'View from the Left'.

Chinese Capabilities

Optimists believe that the expansion of Chinese military capabilities as directed not against India, but as defensive – arising from China's insecurities with regard to other powers. Overall, they tend to place more emphasis on development rather than defence. They see an arms race as a waste of resources and, moreover, dangerous. They worry about the impact of growing Indian capabilities. Most see the Indian nuclear weapons programme as provocative. They identify former Indian Prime Minister Vajpayee's letter stating China as the reason for India going nuclear as especially harmful to the bilateral relationship.[58] Furthermore, optimists see the possibility that India will expand its nuclear programme, as well as enhance and modernise its conventional capabilities, as leading to further tension with China.

Multilateral Fora

Optimists highlight the success of Sino-Indian collaboration in international fora such as the World Trade Organization, as well as in climate change negotiations. Those on the left argue that such collaboration can serve to limit American unilateralism. Others see it as a way to protect China and India's autonomy.[59] Some optimists believe that there are some issues tailor-made for Sino-Indian co-operation; that China and India have 'parallel policy interests' when it comes to issues like humanitarian intervention, human rights, environmental and trade standards, and self-determination.[60] Liberal institutionalists see these fora as sites to promote co-operation between the two countries, as well as others.

The US Role in Asia and the World[61]

The Asia-firsters and the idealists often see the US role as negative and disruptive. They fear that the US could potentially play a

---

[58] Bajpai, 'India, China and Asian Security', pp. 42–43.

[59] Frankel, 'Introduction', pp. 4–6.

[60] James Clad, 'Convergent Chinese and Indian Perspectives on the Global Order', in Frankel and Harding, eds, *The India–China Relationship*, p. 285. Also see Mansingh, 'Why China Matters to India'.

[61] This essay assesses the US role not because it does not think other countries mater but working from the basis of Kumar and Menon's contention that the 'Future of the USA would probably be the scenario defining driver for most countries of the world as it is for India'. Rajiv Kumar and Admiral Raja Menon, *The Long View From Delhi: To Define The Indian Grand Strategy For Foreign Policy* (New Delhi: Academic Foundation, 2010), p. 26.

'de-stabilising role' in Asia.[62] By threatening China, it could cause China to pursue more military capabilities, thus causing India to do the same. Thus, they believe that the US could potentially trigger a conventional and nuclear arms race between China and India.[63] Some on the left go further and see the US role as hostile. They accuse the US and 'pro-US' Indians of trying to 'complicate' Sino-Indian relations.[64] They argue that American policymakers and lobbies are trying to engender Sino-Indian conflict, motivated by a desire to sell arms to India.[65] They see the US–India nuclear deal as anti-China and provocative. The liberals, however, see a more collaborative triangular relationship developing between China, India and the US.

CROUCHING TIGER, HIDDEN DRAGON: THE PESSIMISTIC VIEW

General Attitude

Pessimists foresee competition or even conflict between China and India in the future.[66] They perceive China to be unworthy of trust and view suspiciously its India strategy of 'overt engagement and covert containment'.[67] Pessimists believe China to be an 'unpredictable adversary and dangerous rival ... the greatest potential threat' to India in the medium to long term.[68] They do not think China and India are mirrors, but book-ends: countries that will 'remain competitive' because of 'divergent self-images', 'different political systems', as well as overlapping aspirations in 'Asia and beyond'.[69]

Most pessimists see Chinese strategic culture as steeped in *realpolitik*. They believe China has a 'preference for offensive uses of

---

[62] Bajpai, 'India, China and Asian Security', p. 49.

[63] Ibid., p. 41.

[64] 'CPM Uneasy, but Doesn't Slam China'.

[65] Manoj, 'View from the Left'.

[66] This school of thought is similar to Hoffman's 'China is hostile' category and Sidhu and Yuan's 'China as a threat' category.

[67] Gurmeet Kanwal, 'Countering China's Strategic Encirclement of India', *Bharat Rakshak Monitor*, 3, 3 (November–December 2000). Available at http://www.bharat-rakshak.com/MONITOR/ISSUE3-3/kanwal.html, accessed on August 23, 2011.

[68] Mattoo, 'Imagining China', p. 21. Also see Hoffman, 'Perceptions and China Policy in India', p. 47.

[69] Ganguly, 'India and China', p. 124.

force, mediated by a keen sensitivity to relative capabilities'. This sensitivity causes China to be co-operative right now because the balance of power is not in its favour.[70] The pessimists do not, however, believe that the bonhomie will last. Beijing might feel the 'need to show a benign face to the world' currently but this is a temporary expedient.[71] As 'the armed might of China increases', so will the chance of conflict between China and India.[72]

Critics called the pessimists 'alarmists'.[73] Some call them 'China-baiters'.[74] But, the pessimists argue that they are realistic; that the optimists have their heads stuck in the sand or are fearful of Chinese retaliation, leading them to advocate 'caution and circumspection'. The pessimist believe that the optimistic perception of China, stemming from a 'Nehruvian worldview', 'stalk[s] the corridors of South Block' – where the Indian foreign and defence ministries are housed – and criticise it as naïve, at best, and dangerous, at worst.[75]

According to some observers, the pessimistic view dominates in the 'military and intelligence services [and] in ... some sections of the ... BJP'.[76] Hoffman associates this position with ultra-realists who stress 'the pursuit of power'.[77] Along with the realists, one can also include in this category cultural nationalists, as well as those who support the independence of Tibet and those who are critics of Chinese human rights policies.[78] Another group of pessimists – which might expand in the future – includes local businesses and labour groups wary of a 'China threat' in the economic sphere.

---

[70] Mattoo, 'Imagining China', pp. 22–23.

[71] Arun Shourie, 'Digging our Head Deeper in the Sand', *The Indian Express*, April 7, 2009. Available at http://global.factiva.com, accessed on August 23, 2011.

[72] Kanwal, 'Countering China's Strategic Encirclement of India'.

[73] 'Home Ministry 'alarmist' on China: Jairam Ramesh', *NDTV*, May 10, 2010. Available at http://www.ndtv.com/news/india/home-ministry-alarmist-on-china-jairam-ramesh-24348.php, accessed on August 23, 2011.

[74] Mattoo, 'Imagining China', p. 16. Also see Swamy, 'Sino-Indian Relations through the Tibet Prism'.

[75] Ganguly, 'India and China', p. 126.

[76] Sidhu and Yuan, *China and India*, p. 145. Mattoo notes that this pessimistic view is 'widely supported within the armed forces' Mattoo, 'Imagining China', p. 21.

[77] Hoffman, 'Perceptions and China Policy in India', p. 54.

[78] Shourie, 'Digging our Head Deeper in the Sand'.

Interpretation of the Past

The pessimists' historical narrative highlights the shortcomings of Nehru's perception of and policy towards China.[79] His 'unrealistic assessment' of China led, according to them, to 'conciliation and appeasement'. He did not confront Beijing with regard to Tibet, accepting the Chinese position without demanding a *quid pro quo*. Faulting Nehru for naïveté and misreading China, they often argue that if Patel had been alive for a few more years, India would have taken a more realistic attitude towards China – indeed, Patel is both inspiration and embodiment for many pessimists. Some pessimists also criticise past bureaucrats or military officials as having come up short in assessing and reacting to the China threat.[80]

Overall, pessimists argue that independent India's early China policy showed weakness, as did India's approach towards the border issue. They argue that New Delhi's claim was couched in legalese even though China only respected strength.[81] India should have sought military capabilities and, if necessary, alliances in the first decade of independence. Nehru, pessimists assert, should never have trusted China. In the 1950s, Chinese behaviour in Tibet, during the Korean war and at the Bandung conference should have been seen as warning signs. Even after Indian policymakers sensed trouble, they did not handle expeditiously or effectively the Chinese road-building activities or the border dispute. Pessimists believe that the 1962 war only made evident what Nehru should have recognised before.

For pessimists, the lesson of the past, above all, is that China cannot be trusted. A right-wing newspaper put it bluntly: China '*ke iraade nek nahin hein*' (China's intentions are not noble').[82] Furthermore, Indian weakness invites Chinese aggression. China backs down if

---

[79] Ganguly, 'India and China', p. 106: 'flawed' 'political and strategic choices ... sparked the tensions'.

[80] Bharat Karnad, 'An Ostrich before the Dragon's Roar', *Express Buzz* October 25, 2009. Available at http://expressbuzz.com/Opinion/Op-Ed/an-ostrich-before-the-dragons-roar/114953.html, accessed on August 23, 2011.

[81] Ganguly, 'India and China', p. 111.

[82] Seema Chishti, 'Austerity: At What Cost?', *The Indian Express*, September 25, 2009. Available at http://global.factiva.com, accessed on August 23, 2011.

confronted; this, pessimists argue, was evident from the Sino-Indian skirmishes in 1967 when Chinese soldiers 'test[ed]' India's resolve'[83] and again in 1986–87.[84]

Territorial Issues

Pessimists consider border talks 'fruitless' and as 'playing into China's hands'.[85] Border negotiations are a way for Beijing to buy time to strengthen China economically and militarily and, in particular in the border areas, logistically and diplomatically. Most pessimists believe that China will eventually, through military action or 'coercive diplomacy', seek a territorial solution to its liking. Meanwhile, Beijing's pressure on the border serves to aid Pakistan by keeping Indian resources tied up.[86]

Pessimists further argue that China has displayed little genuine desire to resolve the border issue.[87] Beijing instead blames New Delhi for the lack of progress in negotiations.[88] China's 'intransigence' on territorial issues does not bode well for 'long-term stability' and could lead to a broader conflict.[89] Pessimists acknowledge that the border talks might have helped 'reduce the likelihood of accidental conflict', but argue that the broader Sino-Indian dialogue has not led to 'any fundamental breakthroughs' or 'tangible progress'.[90] India has made 'asymmetric' concessions.[91] Furthermore, China has

---

[83] Kanwal, 'Countering China's Strategic Encirclement of India'.

[84] Karnad, 'An Ostrich before the Dragon's Roar'.

[85] Brahma Chellaney, 'Clueless on China', *The Sunday Guardian*, July 4, 2010. Available at http://chellaney.net/2010/07/03/india-plays-into-chinas-hands-by-staying-engaged-in-useless-border-talks, accessed on August 23, 2011.

[86] Kanwal, 'Countering China's Strategic Encirclement of India'.

[87] Ganguly, 'India and China', p. 103.

[88] 'Indian Hegemony Continues to Harm Relations with Neighbours', *People's Daily Online*, October 14, 2009. Available at http://english.people daily.com.cn/90001/90780/91343/6783357.html, accessed on August 23, 2011.

[89] Kanwal, 'Countering China's Strategic Encirclement of India'.

[90] Ganguly, 'India and China', p. 121. For example, he asserts that talks have not led to any Chinese promises to curtail their sales to Pakistan (p. 123). Also see Kanwal, 'Countering China's Strategic Encirclement of India'.

[91] Kanwal, 'Countering China's Strategic Encirclement of India'. For example, while India has put in place patrolling restrictions in sensitive

delayed implementation of previous agreements.[92] Finally, Beijing has in the past 'violated the letter and spirit' of agreed-upon CBMs on a number of occasions.[93]

Pessimists argue that China's real attitude towards India's territorial integrity can be seen in its not-so-reassuring stances on Sikkim and Arunachal Pradesh.[94] China first resisted Sikkim's integration with India, then refused to recognise it.[95] In recent years, pessimists assert that far from accepting the state's accession to India, China's attitude has been vague and wavering. They emphasise that China has repeatedly transgressed in border areas in Sikkim that India had 'considered settled',[96] and note reports of potential Chinese plans to build roads through these areas.[97]

China behaves similarly, pessimists assert, with regard to Arunachal Pradesh, which China still claims.[98] They point out that a year after a 2005 agreement suggested a change in the Chinese attitude, China's foreign minister asserted that the agreement 'did not mean China had given up its claim on Arunachal Pradesh'.[99]

---

border areas, despite military dissatisfaction, 'China has imposed no such restrictions on its Army'. Pranab Dhal Samanta, 'Army Wants Patrol Curbs along China Border Lifted', *The Indian Express*, September 13, 2009. Available at http://global.factiva.com, accessed on August 23, 2011.

[92] Kanwal, 'Countering China's Strategic Encirclement of India'.

[93] Mattoo, 'Imagining China', p. 23. Most recently, in 2009, they pointed to border violations 'in Arunachal Pradesh, Uttarakhand, Leh and Sikkim'. See Suman K. Jha, 'View from the Right', *The Indian Express*, September 24, 2009. Available at http://global.factiva.com, accessed on August 23, 2011.

[94] Mattoo, 'Imagining China', p. 23.

[95] Ganguly, 'India and China', p. 104 and p. 123, Kanwal, 'Countering China's Strategic Encirclement of India'.

[96] Samanta, 'The China Chill'.

[97] Manu Pubby, 'T-72 Tanks Moved to Remote Sikkim Area after China Tests Indian Defences', *The Indian Express*, July 28, 2009. Available at http://global.factiva.com, accessed on August 23, 2011.

[98] One pessimist notes, 'China still claims that the reunification of Arunachal Pradesh is a sacred duty for its military'. Kanwal, 'Countering China's Strategic Encirclement of India'.

[99] Samanta, 'The China Chill'. Also see Brahma Chellaney's perspective in Madhur Singh, 'Can China and India be Friends?', *Time*, December 21, 2007. Available at http://www.time.com/time/world/article/0,8599,1697595,00.html, accessed on August 23, 2011.

According to pessimists, China has also actively resisted Indian claims. On a number of occasions Beijing has refused to grant visas to politicians and civil servants from Arunachal.[100] Chinese officials have also repeatedly expressed their displeasure when Indian leaders visit the state.[101] In 2009 Beijing even protested the assembly elections in Arunachal.[102] Furthermore, at the Asian Development Bank (ADB) Beijing raised objections to – and eventually effectively blocked – an Indian development plan that included a project in that state.[103]

Some pessimists argue that Beijing has not been content with disputing India's border claims, but has also stirred trouble within India. Beijing's true goal, some pessimists assert, is the 'Balkanisation of India'.[104] They express concern that China's past support to Naga and Mizo separatists[105] could be resumed and extended to groups such as the Maoists.[106] Some point out that there is already an element in China – tolerated by the regime in Beijing – that is sympathetic to the Maoists.[107] Furthermore, pessimists argue that even if

---

[100] Ganguly, 'India and China', p. 125. Also see Samanta, 'The China Chill'.

[101] 'Now China Objects to President Pratibha Patil's Visit to Arunachal', *The Indian Express*, April 7, 2009. Available at http://global.factiva.com, accessed on August 23, 2011.

[102] China went public with its protests regarding the PM's electioneering visit and also vociferously protested the Dalai Lama's visits to the state. Pranab Dhal Samanta, 'China Chooses Election Day to Stir the Arunachal Pot Again', *The Indian Express*, October 14, 2009. Available at http://global.factiva.com, accessed on August 23, 2011.

[103] Pranab Dhal Samanta, 'At ADB, Beijing Blocks India's $60-m Project for Arunachal', *The Indian Express*, April 14, 2009. Available at http://global.factiva.com, accessed on August 23, 2011.

[104] This assertion was fuelled by a report from a 'quasi-official' Chinese think tank that laid out a road map for the 'Balkanisation of India'. 'Break India, says China Think-tank', *The Times of India*, August 13, 2009 at http://articles.timesofindia.indiatimes.com/2009-08-12/india/28195335_1_daibingguo-state-councillor-chinese-website. Also see Reshma Patil, 'Speaking in Two Voices', *Hindustan Times*, August 14, 2009. Available at http://www.hindustantimes.com/Speaking-in-two-voices/Article1-443023.aspx, accessed on August 23, 2011.

[105] Ganguly, 'India and China', p. 120.

[106] Tellis, 'China and India in Asia', p. 138.

[107] D. S. Rajan, 'China: Signs of Ultra-Leftist Support to Maoists of India and Nepal', *South Asia Analysis Group*, Essay 1565, May 10, 2005. Available

China might not be directly supporting insurgents, it is indirectly facilitating the destabilisation of India through the 'large-scale supply of cheap small arms... to regimes inimical to India', which eventually provide them 'to insurgent groups in Jammu and Kashmir and the north-eastern states of India'.[108] They also highlight reports that some criminals or terrorists wanted in India might be based in China.[109]

Pessimists assert that India, on its part, has gone out of its way to allay Chinese insecurities on Tibet, recognising Chinese rights there and banning Tibetan political activity in India. Yet these steps have not reassured Beijing, which is 'paranoid' on Tibet.[110] Some pessimists criticise the Indian government for repeatedly 'shut[ting] its eyes' to what China is doing in Tibet. India should do more, they argue, because 'India's security is inextricably intertwined with the existence and survival of Tibet as a buffer state and to the survival and strengthening of Tibetan culture and religion'.[111] Some base their criticism on strategic grounds; others point to human rights imperatives.[112]

The Sino-Pakistan Relationship

Pessimists see China's relationship with Pakistan as highly problematic. They argue that despite some tactical concessions to India, in recent years the Sino-Pakistan relationship has, at best, remained strong and, at worst, deepened. China has played a major hand in strengthening Pakistan's conventional, missile and nuclear capabilities. They argue that the Pakistani nuclear programme could not have been 'sustained' without China.[113]

---

at http://www.southasiaanalysis.org/essays16/essay1565.html, accessed on August 23, 2011.

[108] Kanwal, 'Countering China's Strategic Encirclement of India'.

[109] 'ATS Arrests 3 with Arms', *The Indian Express*, August 6, 2009. Available at http://global.factiva.com, accessed on August 23, 2011.

[110] Inder Malhotra, 'The Anniversary of Exile', *The Indian Express*, March 6, 2009. Available at http://global.factiva.com, accessed on August 23, 2011.

[111] Shourie, 'Digging our Head Deeper in the Sand'.

[112] See Bhartendu Kumar Singh, 'George Fernandes and Sino-Indian Relations', *IPCS*, Essay 1044, May 27, 2003. Available at http://www.ipcs.org/article/china/george-fernandes-and-sino-indian-relations-1044.html, accessed on August 23, 2011.

[113] While there continues to be debate about the extent, if any, of Chinese aid to the Pakistani missile programme, many pessimists believe that there

On Kashmir, in the pessimists' view, China remains ambivalent. Beijing might not explicitly support Pakistan on Kashmir, but it has not 'endorse[d] India's position either'.[114] In the recent past, China's ambivalence has shown in its issuing of paper visas to Kashmiris with passports issued in Srinagar instead of stamping the visas in passports.[115] It has also been helping Pakistan develop the transport and communications infrastructure in the disputed Northern Areas, where China is also undertaking a number of projects.[116]

Optimists highlight the common interest that China and India have in countering terrorism, but pessimists insist that Chinese co-operation is limited. They point out that when India has attempted to sanction Jamaat-ud-Dawa and Lashkar-e-Taiba leaders at the UN, China has attempted to block these moves in collusion with Pakistan.[117] Indeed, they argue, China has consistently given Pakistan support in various international fora, especially the UN Security Council (UNSC), on a number of issues.

The Sino-Pakistan relationship is here to stay, according to the pessimists. China will not jettison Pakistan. Given the restiveness in Xinjiang province, Beijing needs Islamabad 'more than ever to . . . rein in Islamic zealots'.[118] Furthermore, Pakistan is part of China's 'strategic insurance' policy against India.[119] By strengthening Pakistan's capabilities China can build Pakistan as a 'counterweight' to India.[120]

---

has been co-operation in this realm too. Swaran Singh, 'China's Nuclear Deterrent', in Bajpai and Mattoo, eds, *The Peacock and the Dragon*, pp. 73–74.

[114] Ganguly, 'India and China', p. 125.

[115] Shishir Gupta, 'MEA Alerted Immigration against Chinese Essay Visas in Jan 2009', *The Indian Express*, October 4, 2009. Available at http://global.factiva.com, accessed on August 23, 2011.

[116] 'India Protests Pak's Gilgit Order and China Dam Pact', *The Indian Express*, September 12, 2009. Available at http://global.factiva.com, accessed on August 23, 2011.

[117] Pranab Dhal Samanta, 'Sanctioning Jaish Chief: UK Blinks, China Lone Dissenter', *The Indian Express*, June 25, 2009; Pranab Dhal Samanta, 'India Wants Him, Pak Uses Jaish Chief to Defuse Mosque Tension', *The Indian Express*, June 28, 2009. Available at http://global.factiva.com, accessed on August 23, 2011.

[118] Ganguly, 'India and China', p. 125.

[119] Tellis, 'China and India in Asia', p. 143.

[120] Mattoo, 'Imagining China', p. 23.

It can thus 'keep India tied down in the subcontinent and mired in its continuing conflict with Pakistan'.[121]

The Near Abroad

China is also keeping India preoccupied in South Asia and 'marginalise[d] ... in Asia', pessimists assert, by its actions in India's near abroad.[122] Aiming for the 'strategic encirclement' of India,[123] Beijing is trying to create a 'ring of anti-Indian influences around India' through shuttle diplomacy, military and economic assistance packages, and infrastructure development in India's neighbourhood.[124] Pessimists view China's interactions with Bangladesh, Nepal[125] and Sri Lanka[126] with much concern. Sino-Myanmar co-operation is also a subject of anxiety, given Myanmar's natural resources and geographical position.[127] Chinese involvement in Afghanistan is another source of concern, especially with the impending US drawdown.

China's efforts in this regard are seen as paying off. Pessimists point out that in 2009, for example, almost all the SAARC members backed observer status for China.[128] Pessimists do not see China's involvement in SAARC as benign or its overall activities in South

---

[121] Ganguly, 'India and China', p. 119.

[122] Kanwal, 'Countering China's Strategic Encirclement of India'.

[123] Hoffman, 'Perceptions and China Policy in India', p. 47. Also see Shourie, 'Digging our Head Deeper in the Sand'.

[124] Kanwal, 'Countering China's Strategic Encirclement of India'.

[125] See 'Extend Tibet Railway Line to Kathmandu, Nepal Tells China', *The Indian Express*, October 12, 2009; Yubaraj Ghimire, 'Prachanda's Latest: India and US Planned to Attack China Using Nepal', *The Indian Express*, August 6, 2009; Yubaraj Ghimire, 'Hemmed in at Home, Non-Maoist Nepal Leaders Line Up to Visit India', *The Indian Express*, March 10, 2009; Pranab Dhal Samanta, 'China Warms Up to Nepal Again as Maoists Stoke Anti-India Fires', *The Indian Express*, September 6, 2009. Available at http://global.factiva.com, accessed on August 23, 2011.

[126] See Kiren Rijiju, 'Too Far from Delhi', *The Indian Express*, October 17, 2009 at http://global.factiva.com. Also see Brahma Chellaney, 'Behind the Sri Lankan Bloodbath', *Forbes*, October 9, 2009. Available at http://www.forbes.com/2009/10/08/tamil-tigers-rajiv-gandhi-opinions-contributors-sri-lanka.html, accessed on August 23, 2011.

[127] Ganguly, 'India and China', p. 123.

[128] Rijiju, 'Too Far from Delhi'.

and Southeast Asia as constructive in terms of Sino-Indian relations. Even co-operative ventures like the Kunming initiative are seen as China-led and dominated. Furthermore, some pessimists note that while China is increasingly active in India's neighbourhood, Beijing is actively trying to stem Indian influence in Southeast Asia.[129]

The New Great Game

Pessimists believe that China and India will clash over resources, business and influence even beyond their immediate neighbourhoods.[130] China has been taking '[p]redatory actions' in Africa and beyond to achieve its interests.[131] It is undercutting India, which is falling behind in this new great game because Delhi is not being aggressive enough. This will have repercussions for Indian interests. Pessimists also believe that China's and India's competing goals in these areas 'will significantly limit the prospects of bilateral or trilateral co-operation'.[132]

The Economic Sphere

Besides the two countries' search for energy across the globe, another sign of resource competition, according to pessimists, is the reported Chinese construction on its side of the Brahmaputra river.[133] This construction has been undertaken despite Indian requests that Beijing not continue with the project because of the socio-economic and environmental impact on India.[134] Pessimists argue that Chinese assurances have not been sincere. The scope of the joint mechanism established for information sharing on rivers that run through both countries has been limited.[135] Pessimists also highlight an even

---

[129] Shourie, 'Digging our Head Deeper in the Sand'.

[130] Mattoo, 'Imagining China', p. 22.

[131] Bharat Karnad, *India's Nuclear Policy* (Westport, CT: Praeger, 2008), p. 145.

[132] Ganguly, 'India and China', p. 105.

[133] Shubhajit Roy, 'Govt Underlines: Dalai Lama Free to Visit Arunachal', *The Indian Express*, October 17, 2009. Available at http://global.factiva.com, accessed on August 23, 2011.

[134] 'Significant Impact, Will Check with China on Dam: New Delhi', *The Indian Express*, October 16, 2009. Available at http://global.factiva.com, accessed on August 23, 2011. Also see Rijiju, 'Too Far from Delhi'.

[135] Pranab Dhal Samanta, 'China Begins Building Dam on its Side of the Brahmaputra', *The Indian Express*, October 15, 2009. Available at http://global.factiva.com, accessed on August 23, 2011.

worse possibility: the re-routing of the Brahmaputra.[136] Such a diversion – and competition over natural resources more broadly – is seen as even the potential 'trigger' for a conflict with China.[137] In the short to medium term, it will negatively affect India's internal economic development.

So, some pessimists argue, will other Chinese actions in the economic sphere. They believe that while China undertakes bilateral trade 'where it feels its interests converge with those of India', competition for investment, resources and markets is inevitable.[138] They are concerned about India's trade deficit with China.[139] Pessimists also believe India is getting the short end of the stick when it comes to what is being traded. While India is exporting its raw materials to China, Beijing is 'dumping' finished goods, which is threatening small-scale Indian industry.[140] Pessimists also highlight other irritants in the bilateral economic relationship – for example, complaints from Indian companies about market access and high transaction costs for import of some raw materials from China,[141] and India's brief banning of the import of toys from China.[142] Labour issues have also arisen. Tension between Chinese and local labour led to the Indian government cracking down on the Chinese use of business visas for semi- and un-skilled labour.[143] The Indian government had

---

[136] Brahma Chellaney, 'China's Hydra-Headed Hydropolitics', *Project Syndicate*, August 5, 2009. Available at http://www.project-syndicate.org/commentary/chellaney1/English, accessed on August 23, 2011.

[137] Karnad, *India's Nuclear Policy*, p. 144.

[138] Kanwal, 'Countering China's Strategic Encirclement of India'.

[139] Kartikay Mehrotra, 'India's Chinese Imports 3 Times More than Exports', *The Indian Express*, October 10, 2009 at http://global.factiva.com, accessed on August 23, 2011.

[140] Shishir Gupta, 'NSC Meet Discusses China, Agrees India Needs to Keep an Eye in Long Term', *The Indian Express*, August 3, 2009. Available at http://global.factiva.com, accessed on August 23, 2011.

[141] 'India Seeks Sops for Steel Industry', *The Indian Express*, March 19, 2009. Available at http://global.factiva.com, accessed on August 23, 2011.

[142] Even after it lifted the ban, New Delhi imposed safety standards, which in effect restricted imports from China. 'China Willing to Settle Toy Ban Issue through Talks', *The Indian Express*, March 20, 2009. Available at http://global.factiva.com, accessed on August 23, 2011.

[143] Pranab Dhal Samanta, 'Govt Finds Out: 25K Chinese Entered India on Business Visas but are in Unskilled Jobs', *The Indian Express*, September 14, 2009 at http://global.factiva.com, accessed on August 23, 2011.

also banned Chinese workers from the Indian power industry where Chinese companies have invested in a number of projects.[144]

Moreover, pessimists remain concerned about India falling behind. Even sectors where India was thought to be ahead, such as information technology have become a source of anxiety – a former minister indeed asserted that 'information technology [was] ... a central component of China's 'comprehensive challenge to India'.[145] Finally, while economic interaction is well and good, pessimists believe that if 'strategic animosities remain unaddressed, interdependent commercial ties do not guarantee moderation'.[146]

Chinese Capabilities

The realists among the pessimists pay special attention to Chinese military and intelligence capabilities, specifically their expansion and modernisation. Furthermore, they worry that the gap between Chinese and Indian capabilities is increasing.[147] These pessimists are troubled by the Chinese revolution in military affairs across the board, but note with special concern that China has upgraded its logistics and forces in Tibet, which has 'drastic strategic implication[s] for India'.[148] There is rising concern about cyber warfare, seen as the newest tool in the Chinese arsenal that, pessimists argue, has already been used to attack official Indian networks.[149]

China's naval capabilities have also been enhanced and some defence analysts express 'serious concern' about the Chinese navy's

---

[144] Kartikay Mehrotra, 'Chinese Labourers Banned from Indian Power Sector', *The Indian Express*, September 26, 2009. Available at http://global.factiva.com, accessed on August 23, 2011.

[145] Clad, 'Convergent Chinese and Indian Perspectives on the Global Order', p. 284.

[146] Brahma Chellaney, 'Assessing India's Reactions to China's 'Peaceful Development' Doctrine', 18, 5 (April 2008).

[147] Kanwal, 'Countering China's Strategic Encirclement of India'. Also see 'Now, Air Force Chief Cools the China Heat', *The Indian Express*, September 24, 2009. Available at http://global.factiva.com, accessed on August 23, 2011.

[148] Rijiju, 'Too Far from Delhi'. Also see Kanwal, 'Countering China's Strategic Encirclement of India'.

[149] Manu Pubby, 'In China Cyber Attack, NIC Most Affected, 9 Embassies Hit', *The Indian Express*, March 31, 2009. Also see Manu Pubby, 'Leaked Tibet Info Could Have Led to Deaths: Expert', *The Indian Express*, April 1, 2009. Available at http://global.factiva.com, accessed on August 23, 2011.

'increased activism' in the Indian Ocean. They point to Chinese documents indicating that, in that ocean, Beijing intends to check Indian dominance and take more control of the sea lines of communication and, potentially, the chokepoints.[150] Chinese activism has not been restricted to the waters but extends to 'many of the littoral countries' with which it has forged ties.[151] Of special concern to pessimists has been the leasing of Coco Islands from Myanmar where China reportedly has a signals intelligence facility,[152] and the development of Myanmari ports.[153] Pessimists view with suspicion China's development of Pakistan's Gwadar and Sri Lanka's Hambantota ports.[154] They believe this effort is part of Beijing's 'string of pearls' strategy.[155] They see Chinese assistance in the development of Bangladesh's Chittagong port as the latest evidence of this strategy. While pessimists acknowledge that these ports might serve economic purposes, they assert that Beijing's interest in them is also of a military and strategic nature.[156]

---

[150] Anil Joseph Chandy, 'China's Naval Power', in Bajpai and Mattoo, eds, *The Peacock and the Dragon*, pp. 97–98. This 'activism' includes the PLAN's recent operations in the Gulf of Aden. C. Raja Mohan, 'Maritime CBMs', *The Indian Express*, August 12, 2009. Available at http://global.factiva.com, accessed on August 23, 2011.

[151] Chandy, 'China's Naval Power', p. 98. Also see Amit Kumar, 'China's Island Strategy in the Indian Ocean: Breaching India's Sphere of Influence', *Observer Research Foundation Essay*, September 17, 2009. Available at http://www.orfonline.com/cms/sites/orfonline/modules/analysis/attachments/influence_1253251335478.pdf, accessed on August 23, 2011.

[152] Ganguly, 'India and China', p. 123. Also see Pratap Chakravarty, 'China Bigger Threat to India Than Pakistan: Defence Minister', *Agence France-Press*, May 3, 1998. Available at http://global.factiva.com, accessed on August 23, 2011.

[153] Chandy, 'China's Naval Power', pp. 98–99.

[154] B. Raman, 'Gwadar, Hambantota and Sitwe: China's Strategic Triangle', *South Asia Analysis Group*, Essay 2158, March 6, 2007. Available at http://www.southasiaanalysis.org/essays/essay2158.html, accessed on August 23, 2011.

[155] Arun Kumar Singh, 'The Games at Gwadar', *Deccan Chronicle*, January 29, 2010. Available at http://global.factiva.com, accessed on August 23, 2011. Also see Rijiju, 'Too Far from Delhi'.

[156] Mukul Devichand, 'Is Chittagong One of China's '"String of Pearls"?', *BBC News*, May 17, 2010. Available at http://news.bbc.co.uk/2/hi/business/8687917.stm, accessed on August 23, 2011.

Another concern revolves around changes in Chinese nuclear doctrine and capabilities: 'China's strategic shift ... to a more proactive warfighting' policy; the development and deployment of tactical nuclear weapons; and the development of a triad.[157] Pessimists believe that '[r]ecent trends indicate that China may use its nuclear capabilities to actually blackmail its adversaries'.[158] Furthermore, while China has a no-first-use policy in place, analysts contend that it does not apply to potential use against India.[159] There is special concern about China's stationing of nuclear warheads in Tibet.[160] Some pessimists are convinced that these are aimed at India.[161] Others acknowledge that India might not be their sole target, but argue that the weapons' 'potential political and psychological impact ... during a future conflict cannot be underestimated'.[162]

Multilateral Fora

Pessimists believe that while China might hesitantly accept India as a potential Asian power, its version of multipolarity does not envision India as a global power.[163] They note that while collaborating with India in multilateral settings when convenient for its own interests, Beijing's real attitude towards India's global aspirations are more evident in other activities: its attempts to block Indian membership in ASEAN (and, in the past, in the Asia-Europe Meeting and Asia-Pacific Economic Co-operation[164]), its behind-the-scenes attempt to scuttle Nuclear Suppliers' Group approval of a waiver for

---

[157] Swaran Singh, 'China's Nuclear Deterrent', p. 51.

[158] Ibid., p. 71.

[159] Ibid., p. 65. Chinese statements have noted that disputed areas are not considered to be non-Chinese territory, where NFU applies. Also see Kanwal, 'Countering China's Strategic Encirclement of India'. Kanwal argues that since 'China has not renounced its claim over Arunachal Pradesh, or for that matter is still to recognise Sikkim, it may seriously consider the first use of tactical nuclear weapons during a border conflict with India in the future.'

[160] Pratap Chakravarty, 'China Bigger Threat to India than Pakistan'.

[161] Kanwal, 'Countering China's Strategic Encirclement of India'.

[162] Mattoo, 'Imagining China', p. 24.

[163] Kanwal, 'Countering China's Strategic Encirclement of India'.

[164] Tellis, 'China and India in Asia', pp. 169–170. Harry Harding, 'The Evolution of the Strategic Triangle: China, India, and the United States', in Frankel and Harding, eds, *The India–China Relationship*, p. 341.

India and also its ambivalent-to-negative stance on Indian permanent membership in the UNSC.[165] Overall, Beijing sees New Delhi 'as a competitor for the high table'[166] and wants to prevent India's rise, keep New Delhi's influence limited and establish its own dominance in Asia.[167]

The US Role in Asia and the World

Pessimists do not have a monolithic view of the US role. Some see the US desire to improve relations with India as motivated by China. They believe that improved US–India relations have given India much needed leverage against China. Beijing takes New Delhi more seriously because Washington does. But other pessimists note that Washington acts in its own interests and no one else's and should not necessarily be considered reliable vis-à-vis Beijing.[168]

PRICKLY PORCUPINES OR TANGOING TIGERS?
THE PRAGMATIC VIEW[169]

General Attitude

The pragmatists' response to the co-operate-or-compete question is 'both' or, perhaps more accurately, 'it depends'. A certain uncertainty characterises the pragmatists' view of whether China constitutes a threat. Beijing, pragmatists believe, keeps its options open.[170] In the short term, they do not think of China as a direct antagonist. In the long term, pragmatists believe that China might pose a threat,

---

[165] Samanta, 'The China Chill'. Also see Shourie, 'Digging our Head Deeper in the Sand'.

[166] Shishir Gupta, 'NSC meet discusses China'.

[167] Hoffman, 'Perceptions and China Policy in India', p. 47.

[168] A glimpse of the debate among pessimists on the US role can be found in Martin Sieff, *Shifting Superpowers: The New and Emerging Relationship between the United States, China and India* (Washington DC: Cato Institute, 2009), pp. 159–60.

[169] Assessing forthcoming Sino-Indian military exercises, C. Uday Bhaskar noted, 'The two sides will be like two porcupines facing each other . . . They have had little contact for 40 years, and a negative perception of the other still prevails, more so, perhaps, on the Indian side'. Madhur Singh, 'Can China and India be Friends?'

[170] Hoffman, 'Perceptions and China Policy in India', p. 43.

but this is not inevitable.[171] Furthermore, they do not necessarily consider international politics a zero-sum game, stressing that there is 'ample space' for both China and India's aspirations.[172]

While pragmatists borrow from the other two groups, they do not necessarily just split the difference.[173] They believe that China and India have a number of shared interests: countering terrorism and co-operating in certain multilateral fora, for example. But there are also 'outstanding' issues on which China and India's interests clash, especially China's relations with Pakistan and the border dispute.[174]

Pragmatists believe a desire to focus on internal economic development is at the root of Beijing's cooperative stance. They hold that China's behaviour is pragmatic – not static, but dependent on factors like leadership,[175] internal stability, external power and others' behaviour towards them. Pragmatists thus think that Indian actions can shape Chinese perception and behaviour.

Hoffman has called the pragmatists the mainstream group, who peer through a moderate-realist prism. There are also strains of neo-liberalism in pragmatists' arguments. A few realists sometimes find themselves in this group as well. Pessimists argue that the Indian government tends to behave like optimists; the optimists believe the opposite. In practice, however, overarching government policy has tended to reflect a pragmatic view of China. Scholars have located them in the Ministry of External Affairs and in some sections of the military (especially the China experts) and the two leading political coalitions.[176]

Interpretation of the Past

Pragmatists share some of the optimists' and pessimists' perceptions of the past. Like the optimists, they are wary of the danger

---

[171] Shishir Gupta, 'NSC Meet Discusses China'.

[172] 'PM's Interview to Thai Media', July 30, 2004. Available at http://pmindia.nic.in/visits/content.asp?id=9, accessed on August 23, 2011. Also see Shubhajit Roy, 'Meaningful Talks with Pak Only After it Acts against Terror, says Krishna', *The Indian Express*, August 25, 2009. Available at http://global.factiva.com, accessed on August 23, 2011.

[173] Sidhu and Yuan, *China and India*, p. 150.

[174] Shubhajit Roy, 'Meaningful Talks with Pak'.

[175] There is more recognition that the decision-makers in China are not monolithic. Alka Acharya, 'PRC–India Relations: An Overview', in Bajpai and Mattoo, eds, *The Peacock and the Dragon*, p. 196.

[176] Sidhu and Yuan, *China and India*, pp. 149–50.

of misperception and miscalculation. Like the pessimists, they have learned the importance of building and making evident strength (albeit more subtly). But they also emphasise other lessons. One is that public opinion can get out of hand and constrain India's policy-makers. Nehru and his officials learned this the hard way in 1959 when their release of Sino-Indian correspondence on the border dispute arguably constrained Nehru's available policy options.[177] A second lesson is the importance of understanding the motivations and constraints of Chinese decision-makers. A third lesson – likely stemming from interpretations of India's forward policy in the early 1960s – is the need to calibrate one's goals and actions to one's capabilities and vice versa.

Territorial Issues

Pragmatists believe that China does not want to escalate the border situation beyond a manageable level – it has too much at stake. They see China's claims to Arunachal and Sikkim as instrumental, a tool to gain leverage in negotiations. They see India as having similar leverage with the Tibet issue. Pragmatists, nonetheless, acknowledge Chinese sensitivities on Tibet and recognise that the presence of Tibetans in India and Tibet's status as an international cause makes the situation potentially more explosive.[178]

Pragmatists consider border talks and the broader strategic dialogue as necessary, even while acknowledging the slow progress in border negotiations.[179] The pragmatists see the dialogue as more than a forum for solving disputes; they see it as a mechanism through which to manage Sino-Indian relations. They argue that success must be measured not just in terms of deliverables on the border, but also taking into account how the border talks, strategic dialogue and CBMs have affected the broader bilateral relationship.

While parleying is important, pragmatists acknowledge that preparation, too, is essential – thus they look with favour upon the

---

[177] See Raghavan, *War and Peace in Modern India*, pp. 257–66.

[178] Bajpai, 'India, China and Asian Security', p. 48. Also see Tellis, 'China and India in Asia', p. 141.

[179] While 'progress has been slow, [the two countries] have got some issues out of the way'. Shekhar Gupta, 'Stop Fighting the 1962 War', *The Indian Express*, September 19, 2009. Available at http://global.factiva.com, accessed on August 23, 2011.

approval of the formation of new mountain divisions in Arunachal,[180] the revival of airbases, the movement of forces to strengthen vulnerable areas[181] and the planned construction of roads to improve connectivity to border areas.[182]

Being prepared and alert are critical, but pragmatists insist that overplaying border incidents can be dangerous and lead to overreaction.[183] They reject criticism that they downplay aggressive Chinese behaviour or the China threat scenario. They stress the importance of keeping things in perspective. Violations of airspace or incursions, for example, are not necessarily 'alarming', according to them, but more often than not are 'routine'.[184] Military probes are generally intended 'to test preparedness, find gaps and locate depth of defences, not to start a war'.[185]

The Sino-Pakistan Relationship

Pragmatists believe that Sino-Pakistan collaboration makes it harder to deal with Pakistan on other issues. But, they also believe that New Delhi can use China's desire to maintain positive relations with India as leverage to get Beijing to influence Islamabad positively

---

[180] Rahul Bedi, 'India Seeks to Counter China with Strengthened Border Presence', *Jane's Defence Weekly*, February 15, 2008. Available at http://www.janes.com/products/janes/defence-security-report.aspx?ID=1065926994, accessed on August 23, 2011.

[181] Pranab Dhal Samanta, 'Generals in Charge of China Border Head for Beijing – and Lhasa', *The Indian Express*, August 31, 2009. Available at http://global.factiva.com, accessed on August 23, 2011.

[182] Tannu Sharma, 'Meanwhile, Near LAC: Airfield Takes off, 4 Roads Get SC Green Flag', *The Indian Express*, September 19, 2009. Available at http://global.factiva.com, accessed on August 23, 2011.

[183] 'China Row: 'Paranoid Hallucination of an Individual', says Cong', *The Indian Express*, August 13, 2009; 'MEA Rejects Chinese Analyst's Report', *The Indian Express*, August 12, 2009; 'Now, Air Force Chief Cools the China Heat'. Available at http://global.factiva.com, accessed on August 23, 2011.

[184] 'Army Plays Down Air Space Violation', *The Indian Express*, September 1, 2009. Also see 'India to Boost Air Defence on China Border', *The Indian Express*, September 26, 2009. Available at http://global.factiva.com, accessed on August 23, 2011.

[185] A. I. Nomani, 'Letter to Editor: Don't Panic', *The Indian Express*, September 22, 2009. Available at http://global.factiva.com, accessed on August 23, 2011. The author's unit served on the border in the 1980s.

or even to moderate its relations with Pakistan. They acknowledge that China is unlikely to give up its long-standing relationship with Pakistan, but also believe that China's concern about separatist tendencies on its western extremity give China and India a common area of concern vis-à-vis Pakistan. Nonetheless, they share the pessimists' concern about continued Chinese nuclear collaboration with Pakistan, including, most recently, a proposal to sell more nuclear reactors to Pakistan. One expert bluntly calls 'the Pakistani nuclear-missile threat ... a Chinese contribution'.[186] Pragmatists also watch with care Beijing's vacillating position on Kashmir and note that China often uses its position on Kashmir as retaliation, leverage or a signalling device.[187]

The Near Abroad

Pragmatists watch with discomfort China's growing ties with India's smaller neighbours, but accept it as somewhat inevitable. India, after all, is making inroads in southeast Asia. Thus, both are 'jockeying' for access in each other's backyards.[188] Furthermore, while India might not have the bank balance that China does, it has other advantages. In the case of some countries this is geographic, in others cultural and in yet others, India serves to balance Chinese influence. In some countries such as Myanmar, Indian influence might even be preferred as India has a 'negative' goal: keeping the country free from a dominating external influence rather than seeking to exercise such dominance.[189] Finally, in some countries, pragmatists do not necessarily see China's growing involvement as necessarily a bad thing. For example, if Beijing does not 'let its special relationship with Islamabad come in the way of greater Sino-Indian co-operation in Central Asia and Afghanistan', these areas can be sites of co-operation.[190]

---

[186] K. Subrahmanyam, 'Explosive Disclosures', *The Indian Express*, September 25, 2009. Available at http://global.factiva.com, accessed on August 23, 2011.

[187] After the fracas over the Indian nuclear tests, for example, Xinhua criticised India over Kashmir and the government brought up the UN resolution. Acharya, 'PRC–India Relations', p. 194.

[188] C. Raja Mohan, 'Beijing's NAM', *The Indian Express*, July 15, 2009. Available at http://global.factiva.com, accessed on August 23, 2011.

[189] Tellis, 'China and India in Asia', p. 153.

[190] C. Raja Mohan, 'The Great Game Folio', *The Indian Express*, July 8, 2009. Available at http://global.factiva.com, accessed on August 23, 2011.

The New Great Game

In areas further afield, pragmatists believe that India can neither 'ignore' Chinese efforts in Africa, central Asia, the Middle East, and Latin America, nor 'mimic' them.[191] There is a sense that when it comes to deployed resources – 'boots on the ground', economic and military ties, shuttle diplomacy – India is lagging behind.[192] But also an assertion that India has certain advantages in operating in these regions, which it should exploit.[193] Simultaneously, pragmatists think that India can continue to co-operate with China in some countries and compete with it in others.

The Economic Sphere

Similarly, when it comes to trade and investment, pragmatists believe that there are opportunities, but also that healthy competition between China and India is natural.[194] Pragmatists welcome China's growing economic interaction with India. They also, however, recognise its limits and that it can lead to its own problems. There is scepticism of whether trade and politics can really be considered in a stove-piped fashion. As one scholar noted, 'it is difficult to promote border trade beyond certain levels in a situation where borders are contested and there are geopolitical and other tensions in those areas'.[195] The blurry lines have been evident in the Indian government's limiting of equipment purchases and use from certain Chinese technology companies over security concerns,[196] as well as

---

[191] 'Nearest Continent', *The Indian Express*, October 19, 2009. Available at http://global.factiva.com, accessed on August 23, 2011.

[192] C. Raja Mohan, 'Beijing's NAM'.

[193] Constantino Xavier, 'India's Strategic Advantage over China in Africa', *IDSA Comment*, June 30, 2010. Available at http://www.idsa.in/idsacomments/IndiasstrategicadvantageoverChinainAfrica_cxavier_300610, accessed on August 23, 2011.

[194] Lally Weymouth, 'In the Eye of the Storm', *Newsweek*, November 21, 2009. Available at http://global.factiva.com, accessed on August 23, 2011.

[195] Acharya, 'PRC–India Relations', pp. 197–98.

[196] Bruce Einhorn, 'A Setback for China's Tech Ambitions in India', *Business Week*, May 6, 2010. Available at http://www.businessweek.com/magazine/content/10_20/b4178036082613.htm, accessed on August 23, 2011. Also see 'India Bid to Block Investment will Sour Ties: China', *Zee News*, July 22, 2010. Available at http://zeenews.india.com/news/nation/india-bid-to-block-investment-will-sour-ties-china_642577.html, accessed on

in restrictions on foreign (especially Chinese) investment in supercritical power projects.[197]

Chinese Capabilities

The China pragmatists express concern about growing Chinese capabilities, as well as Chinese-backed Pakistani capabilities.[198] They acknowledge concerns about the gap between China and India's capabilities,[199] but assert that India's capabilities are improving as well – improvement that China, in turn, watches carefully.[200] Concerned about speeding up an arms race that India is currently ill equipped to win, however, they warn against over-reaction.[201]

Multilateral Fora

In multilateral fora, too, pragmatists present limits and possibilities. The Indian policymakers among the pragmatists 'clearly recognize a useful potential for convergent political action' with China.[202] They find common cause with China and other countries on working to limit western trade protectionism, reforming multilateral institutions, negotiating climate change agreements, protecting sovereignty and limiting interference by outsiders in countries' internal affairs.[203]

But pragmatists also realise that Chinese and Indian co-operation in multilateral fora has not been all smooth sailing. On some issues in multilateral trade negotiations, for example, China and India have

---

August 23, 2011.

[197] Kartikay Mehrotra, 'Govt Short-Circuits Chinese, gives Domestic Firms a Leg Up', *The Indian Express*, September 11, 2009. Available at http://global.factiva.com, accessed on August 23, 2011.

[198] Ruchika Talwar, 'Naval Envy', *The Indian Express*, August 1, 2009. Available at http://global.factiva.com, accessed on August 23, 2011.

[199] 'Gorshkov Price to be Fixed in Two Days', *The Indian Express*, August 28, 2009. Available at http://global.factiva.com, accessed August 23, 2011.

[200] C. Raja Mohan, 'Party is State', *The Indian Express*, April 15, 2009. Available at http://global.factiva.com, accessed on August 23, 2011.

[201] K. Subrahmanyam, 'Coping with China', *The Acorn*, August 16, 2009. Available at http://acorn.nationalinterest.in/2009/08/17/k-subrahmanyam-on-admiral-mehtas-speech, accessed on August 23, 2011.

[202] Tellis, 'China and India in Asia', p. 142.

[203] 'Protectionism Threatens Global Recovery: BRIC', *The Indian Express*, September 6, 2009. Also see Pranab Dhal Samanta, 'Will Complete Doha Round by 2010: India Agrees with G8', *The Indian Express*, July 9, 2009. Available at http://global.factiva.com, accessed on August 23, 2011.

found themselves on the opposite side.[204] On climate change negotiations, while India worked successfully with China at the Copenhagen summit, hammering out a position beforehand, there were also signs that Beijing did not necessarily see this as an exclusive, set-in-stone agreement. A Sino-US memorandum of understanding on climate change, for example, caused some concern about a potential rift in Sino-Indian collaboration.[205]

Moreover, pragmatists recognise that China's participation in multilateral fora might not be beneficial for India.[206] They are wary of India, in turn, being left off the invitation list to global governance structures and aware that China might play a major hand in excluding India.[207]

The US Role in Asia and the World

Pragmatists note that there is no monolithic China perspective in the US or vice versa.[208] On the one hand, there has been talk of a G-2 and pragmatists are wary of the 'prospect of a Sino-US strategic convergence',[209] which could have negative repercussions for India interests. On the other hand, there are also continuing signs of tension in the Sino-US relationship, for example, the trade war in September 2009, the fracas at the climate change negotiations and the war of words over American policymakers seeing the

---

[204] 'Impasse breaks in Delhi, Doha trade talks to resume in Geneva, Sept 14', *The Indian Express*, September 5, 2009. Available at http://global.factiva.com, accessed on August 23, 2011.

[205] Neha Sinha, 'Ramesh to Visit China to Forge Common Climate Change Stand', *The Indian Express*, August 23, 2009. Available at http://global.factiva.com, accessed on August 23, 2011.

[206] Shyam Saran, 'Geopolitical Consequences of Current Financial and Economic Crisis: Implications for India', Speech by the PM's Special Envoy, India Habitat Centre, New Delhi, February 28, 2009. Available at http://www.indembassy.be/speeches_statements/february/feb28.html, accessed on August 23, 2011.

[207] Bajpai, 'India, China and Asian Security', p. 29. Also see C. Raja Mohan, 'Now the G-3', *The Indian Express*, July 1, 2009. Available at http://global.factiva.com, accessed on August 23, 2011.

[208] C. Raja Mohan, 'London Duet: Hu and Obama', *The Indian Express*, April 2, 2009. Available at http://global.factiva.com, accessed on August 23, 2011.

[209] Saran, 'Geopolitical Consequences'.

Dalai Lama.[210] However, pragmatists are also wary of assuming US support for India vis-à-vis China, pointing out, for example, that in the past the US has looked the other way on Sino-Pakistani nuclear co-operation because of Washington's need for Beijing and Islamabad's co-operation.[211]

From Prisms and Perceptions to Proposed Policies

Jervis has noted that different perceptions can result in different policy preferences.[212] And, indeed, the three avatars of China that optimists, pessimists and pragmatists perceive lead to their advocating different strategies towards that country. This section explores those approaches.

THE OPTIMISTS: CHINDIA RISING

China optimists invoke Deng Xiaoping's 1992 guidance for Sino-US relations as the best path for Sino-Indian relations: 'increase trust, reduce trouble, promote co-operation, avoid confrontation'.[213] They believe that Beijing can be co-opted and accommodated. If China feels attacked or isolated, it is more likely to behave aggressively. Thus optimists stress that the belligerence they perceive in Indian policy towards China and in the political atmosphere in general needs to be toned down, if not eliminated.

Since the optimists' diagnosis has been that misunderstanding and misperception have caused Sino-Indian tension in the past, the prescription they offer stresses better communication. Conflict is not inevitable. If Chinese and Indian leaders act with 'maturity' to 'achieve a strategic consensus', China and India can acquire power without 'a display of power politics'.[214] That strategic consensus, optimists argue, can only be achieved with increased dialogue. Already, greater interaction 'has helped bring predictability to the relationship'.[215] In this vein, they assert that it is unproductive to

---

[210] C. Raja Mohan, 'Double Whammy', *The Indian Express*, September 16, 2009. Available at http://global.factiva.com, accessed on August 23, 2011.
[211] Subrahmanyam, 'Explosive Disclosures'.
[212] Jervis, *Perception and Misperception*.
[213] Ranganathan, 'India in China's Foreign Policy'.
[214] Ibid.
[215] Bajpai, 'India, China and Asian Security', pp. 38–39.

hold the entire relationship hostage to the border talks. It is also essential for China and India to have a better understanding of each other.[216] This can only be achieved, according to the Asia-firsters, if India does not 'uncritically accept extra-Indian evaluations of China's capabilities and intentions'.[217]

Optimists acknowledge that the Sino-Indian relationship will be more stable if concessions are reciprocal and not merely rhetorical.[218] But there is a tendency to put the onus on New Delhi to reassure Beijing about India's good intentions. Optimists assert that accommodation and understanding need to pervade the handling of every issue, including Tibet. Writing in 2000, an optimist asserted, 'Sino-Indian relations can never become a close, friendly and warm partnership unless India's blind spot on Tibet is removed, and China is reassured'.[219] Optimists acknowledge the Indian government's reassurances to China since then, but argue that more can be done – especially because as long as the Dalai Lama remains in India, those assurances might not be convincing enough.[220] They believe that the Dalai Lama's political activities should be curtailed, if not eliminated. He can and should be encouraged to make peace with Beijing. Furthermore, the Indian government should not use the Tibet card, lest it instigate China to encourage and support Indian separatists.[221]

When it comes to the other major obstacle to better relations – Sino-Pakistan relations – optimists urge recognition of strains in that bilateral relationship.[222] But they do not think that Beijing will 'betray' its ally. Instead, optimists believe India can be reassured that China will continue to 'strive for middle ground'.[223] Other optimists argue that India might not necessarily even want China to jettison Pakistan since Beijing can exercise a stabilising influence

---

[216] Mansingh, 'Why China Matters to India', p. 159.

[217] Ibid., p. 164. Also see Reena Marwah, 'Interview with Mira Sinha Bhattacharjea', April 21, 2008. Available at http://politics.soc.ntu.edu.tw/raec/act/india04.doc, accessed on August 23, 2011.

[218] Ibid., p. 159.

[219] Swamy, 'Sino-Indian Relations through the Tibet Prism'.

[220] N. Ram, 'The Politics of Tibet'.

[221] Narasimhan, 'Thoughts on Tibet'.

[222] Mansingh, 'Why China Matters to India', p. 158.

[223] Bajpai, 'India, China and Asian Security', p. 38.

on Islamabad. Yet others urge Beijing, Islamabad and New Delhi to explore 'common interests'.[224]

Optimists believe that China and India should also work together in the near and far abroad. In their neighbourhood, the governments should encourage co-operation and work on efforts like the Kunming initiative.[225] Optimists see the border sub-regions as bridges rather than barriers between the two countries. Further afield, they reject the great game for 'exclusive access to raw materials and markets'. Instead, they advocate that China and India operate jointly, for example, in the energy sector where their companies can submit joint bids for oil and natural gas assets.[226]

On the broader economic front, optimists assert that China and India's 'greater ... interaction can only enhance their desire for mutual accommodation'. Competition is not inevitable. Commercial liberals especially point out that there is 'considerable scope' for joint ventures and bilateral trade. Furthermore, some argue that the two countries are not necessarily vying for the same type of foreign direct investment.[227] Optimists believe China and India should make the most of their geographical proximity.[228] The countries could increase trade and investment by improving physical links through transport and communication infrastructure upgrades. Optimists also assert that better interaction between the business communities is essential. The government could facilitate this by creating a better visa regime. Furthermore, optimists believe it is crucial to insulate economic ties from the political arena so tension in the latter does not negatively affect the former. Economic disputes should not be allowed to escalate. If New Delhi takes punitive economic measures, Beijing will only retaliate, resulting in a tit-for-tat spiral.[229]

---

[224] Mansingh, 'Why China Matters to India', p. 158.

[225] Gulshan Sachdeva, 'India–China Economic Co-operation in a Growth Quadrangle?', in Bajpai and Mattoo, eds, *The Peacock and the Dragon*, pp. 223–25.

[226] For this train of thought, see Aiyar, 'India and China'.

[227] Anupam Srivastava, 'Re-calibrating India's Relations with China', in Bajpai and Mattoo, eds, *The Peacock and the Dragon*, p. 243.

[228] Shahul Hameed, 'India and China: The Economic Relationship', in Bajpai and Mattoo, eds, *The Peacock and the Dragon*, pp. 210–11.

[229] C. G. Manoj, 'Guess Who's Behind China Chill? US Lobbies, says Karat', *The Indian Express*, October 3, 2009. Available at http://global.factiva.com, accessed on August 23, 2011.

Disputes should be resolved amicably and, some optimists believe, bilaterally.

Optimists contend that, on the global stage, China and India should also work together towards multipolarity. Some on the left see this being achieved by strengthening co-operation between some combination of Brazil, China, India, Russia, and South Africa.[230] The Asia-firsters emphasise co-operation with Asian countries and working towards 'a pan Asian community of interests'.[231] A third group believes that China and India can and should work together with multiple countries in an integrated world. The left and the Asia-firsters also advocate that China and India work to limit the role of external actors, especially the US, in Asia. Furthermore, they assert that Indian policymakers should not allow other bilateral relationships – such as the one with the US – to jeopardise relations with China.[232] Liberals, on the other hand, seek co-operation between China, India and the US to maintain stability and prosperity in the region.

Nothing, optimists argue, could be more harmful to the region than a nuclear or conventional arms race, which China and India should avoid. Some optimists see constraining regimes such as the Comprehensive Test Ban Treaty and the Fissile Material Cut-off Treaty as potentially helpful in this regard. They also believe that the US can help the situation by refraining from pursuing a national missile defence system or a security build-up against China.[233]

The Pessimists: How Do You Solve a Problem Like China?

China pessimists believe that India should work towards containing China and, if and when necessary, be prepared to confront it. Some pessimists suggest a dual-track approach – co-operate and compete – but they do not expect it to work in the medium to long term.[234] Most think that accommodation is futile and 'has not

---

[230] Communist Party of India (Marxist), 'Manifesto for the 15th Lok Sabha Elections', 2009. Available at http://cpim.org/elections/2009ls/manifesto.pdf, accessed on August 23, 2011.
[231] Ranganathan, 'India in China's Foreign Policy'.
[232] Ibid.
[233] Bajpai, 'India, China and Asian Security', p. 42.
[234] Kanwal, 'Countering China's Strategic Encirclement of India'.

inspired any reciprocity from the Chinese'.[235] If there is anyone who should be doing the reassuring, it should be China, which has shown little inclination to do so even though it is the bigger threat.[236]

Pessimists argue that one should look at what Beijing does and not what it says. Furthermore, it is crucial to watch carefully China's capabilities, which are likely to increase. They believe that it is quite possible – some say inevitable – that China will reverse its current policies, creating 'serious problems for India's security'.[237] Conflict is a given or highly likely. Thus preparation is critical and needs to involve assertive diplomacy, military strengthening and the development of alliances, if necessary. Planning and preparation will not just help in the contingency that China threatens India, but will also show strength.

They assert that India should especially stand strong at the border and 'should in no uncertain terms warn our neighbours off our borders'.[238] India should also 'raise [its] voice in the forums of the world' about aggressive Chinese behaviour.[239] If necessary, India should 'exploit' the Tibetan issue to 'pressure China'. New Delhi should not necessarily limit Tibetan political activities or restrict other governments' access to the Dalai Lama in India.[240] Some pessimists even suggest that New Delhi explore stealth democracy promotion efforts in China.[241]

Pessimists argue that a border settlement needs to be sought as soon as possible, while India still has a reasonably favourable military balance.[242] Unless there is agreement on the border issue – the 'core' issue – it is futile to undertake a broader strategic dialogue. Simultaneously, New Delhi needs to focus on improving military capabilities in the border areas. Moreover, India needs to upgrade

---

[235] Tavleen Singh, 'A Foreign Policy for Wimps', *The Indian Express*, September 13, 2009. Available at http://global.factiva.com, accessed on August 23, 2011.
[236] Ganguly, 'India and China', p. 104.
[237] Kanwal, 'Countering China's Strategic Encirclement of India'.
[238] Suman K. Jha, 'View from the Right', *The Indian Express*, September 24, 2009. Available at http://global.factiva.com, accessed on August 23, 2011.
[239] Tavleen Singh, 'A Foreign Policy for Wimps'.
[240] Ganguly, 'India and China', p. 126.
[241] Kanwal, 'Countering China's Strategic Encirclement of India'.
[242] Ibid.

the transportation and communications infrastructure and invest heavily in the economic development of these areas.[243] India also needs to strengthen its naval capabilities in maritime zones,[244] as well as enhance its overall intelligence capabilities.[245] Furthermore, it requires a nuclear weapon posture that is 'credible and effective' to hedge 'against the possibility of a belligerent China in an uncertain anarchic world'.[246] While Indian governments have taken certain measures to improve capabilities, pessimists believe that greater initiative is needed.[247]

On Pakistan, some pessimists think India needs to be more assertive in standing up to Pakistan and acting against the Sino–Pakistan relationship.[248] Other pessimists take a different stance, urging that India work to resolve its issues with its 'relatively small and resource-challenged neighbour' and focus on the real threat, that is, China.[249]

As for India's near abroad, pessimists believe that China's influence has increased because New Delhi has 'lack[ed] a voice' there.[250] India thus needs to reassert itself in south Asia. Furthermore, if China seeks to encircle India, India should do the same to China. It should strengthen military and economic ties with countries in southeast Asia – and do so aggressively.[251] This would serve to warn

---

[243] Rijiju, 'Too Far from Delhi'. Also see Samudra Gupta Kashyap, 'Poll-vaulting Assets: An Arunachal Story', *The Indian Express*, October 8, 2009. Available at http://global.factiva.com, accessed on August 23, 2011.

[244] Chandy, 'China's Naval Power', p. 101.

[245] Kanwal, 'Countering China's Strategic Encirclement of India'.

[246] Mattoo, 'Imagining China', p. 22.

[247] Bharat Karnad, 'Habit of Free-Riding', *Seminar*, 599 (July 2009). Available at http://www.india-seminar.com/2009/599/599_bharat_karnad.htm, accessed on August 23, 2011.

[248] Brahma Chellaney, 'Dangerous Misconceptions', *India Abroad*, August 14, 2009. Available at http://chellaney.net/2009/07/30/the-fallacies-behind-indias-pakistan-policy, accessed on August 23, 2011.

[249] Bharat Karnad, 'Getting it Right on Pakistan', *Mint*, March 18, 2007. Available at http://www.livemint.com/Articles/2007/03/18235352/Getting-it-right-on-Pakistan.html, accessed on August 23, 2011.

[250] 'Time to Strengthen Frontiers: Bhagwat', *The Indian Express*, October 3, 2009. Available at http://global.factiva.com, accessed on August 23, 2011.

[251] Karnad, 'Habit of Free-Riding'. Also, Kanwal, 'Countering China's Strategic Encirclement of India'.

China that it does not have a free rein in India's neighbourhood. The Indian government and companies should also increase their efforts in central Asia and beyond.[252] Furthermore, India should take China 'head-on' in places like Africa and Latin America.[253]

Pessimists see external actors as challenges or opportunities. Some see countries like the US as potential allies and therefore believe that India should, at the very least, seek 'strategic linkages' with them to 'counter' and pressure China.[254] But others think a third party's interests can also complicate India's security. In 1971, for example, Sino-US rapprochement in the midst of the Bangladesh/ East Pakistan crisis complicated India's policy options. Thus, pessimists assert that India should make use of a range of external actors to increase its leverage against China, but not necessarily rely on them.

Overall, pessimists think India needs to be more competitive and less 'apologetic'.[255] Thus, in the economic sphere India should explicitly compete for investment and markets.[256] In multilateral fora, India should be prepared to act in its own interests – China's interests are not always those of India. Furthermore, New Delhi needs to rethink its backing of China's increased power in multilateral organisations.[257] Chinese actions in the ADB – blocking the funding of an Indian development package – should serve as a warning to India, especially as China's clout in other institutions such as the International Monetary Fund and World Bank increases.[258]

---

[252] Kanwal, 'Countering China's Strategic Encirclement of India'.

[253] Karnad, 'Habit of Free-Riding'.

[254] Kanwal, 'Countering China's Strategic Encirclement of India'.

[255] 'BJP Demands All-Party Meeting on China', *The Indian Express*, October 15, 2009. Available at http://global.factiva.com, accessed on August 23, 2011.

[256] Kanwal, 'Countering China's Strategic Encirclement of India'. On the competition over water resources, a BJP leader said the Indian government should pressure China on the Brahmaputra dam dispute 'forc[ing]' it to sign a water treaty. 'Repeat of 1962 Can't be Ruled Out, says Rajnath', *The Indian Express*, October 4, 2009. Available at http://global.factiva.com, accessed on August 23, 2011.

[257] 'Chinese Whispers', *The Indian Express*, April 15, 2009. Available at http://global.factiva.com, accessed on August 23, 2011.

[258] Samanta, 'At ADB, Beijing Blocks India's $60-m Project for Arunachal'.

THE PRAGMATISTS: 'PLAY COOL AND CONTINUE TO DEVELOP CAPABILITIES'[259]

The pragmatists' general approach towards China is co-operate, if possible, and compete, if necessary. They call for a 'pragmatic assessment' of China and a 'differentiated strategy' to deal with it.[260] Pragmatists welcome occasions to build trust and improve communications. They seek mutual reassurance. They see engagement as beneficial for its own sake and also as a form of containment. While hoping and working for the best, however, pragmatists also emphasise the need to plan and prepare for the worst – the possibility that China will emerge as an explicit threat.

This planning and preparation has to be cautious, however, as it can be misinterpreted and exacerbate the security dilemma. Keeping in mind 'the long-term perspective',[261] India should 'continue ... to assess the threat' China might pose.[262] But pragmatists believe that 'demonis[ing]' China and exaggerating the threat is counter-productive.[263] Moreover, such vilification reduces decision-makers' flexibility. Thus, rather than merely react after anti-China fervour builds up, the government needs to be proactive on this front, not letting public discourse over-heat.[264]

Pragmatists call for the bilateral relationship to be 'managed with prudence but firmness'[265] and to be handled with 'nuanced diplomacy'. They believe that it is crucial that the two countries recognise that they have some 'convergent interest[s]', but also 'acknowledge

---

[259] Air Chief Marshal P. V. Naik remarked that when it came to China, India was not 'downplaying the challenges before us. But there is a strategy to handle it. One can either deal with it sternly or play cool and continue to develop capabilities'. 'Now, Air Force Chief Cools the China Heat'.

[260] Srivastava, 'Re-calibrating India's Relations', p. 237.

[261] Shishir Gupta, 'NSC Meet Discusses China'. Also see, 'The China "Threat"', *The Indian Express*, September 21, 2009. Available at http://global.factiva.com, accessed on August 23, 2011.

[262] 'China Row: "Paranoid Hallucination of an Individual", says Cong'; 'MEA Rejects Chinese Analyst's Report'.

[263] Shishir Gupta, 'NSC Meet Discusses China'. Also see, 'The China "Threat"'.

[264] 'Press Charges', *The Indian Express*, September 22, 2009. Available at http://global.factiva.com, accessed on August 23, 2011.

[265] Saran, 'Geopolitical Consequences'.

that there are competitive components in [Sino-Indian] relations'.[266] Pragmatists see the border dispute as one of those components, but assert that the broader relationship has to proceed on parallel tracks. They hope that an improved Sino-Indian relationship will lead to a more conducive atmosphere for border talks. This requires patience.[267] In the meantime, if and when the Chinese military 'moves to test Indian control', the Indian military should not back down.[268] But while preparation is good, provocation – accidental or deliberate – must be avoided. If that requires India to place unilateral restrictions on its troops in sensitive areas, so be it.[269]

Pragmatists assert that India is not without leverage in the border talks and should consider using it.[270] India can reassure China on Tibet, recognising that domestically Beijing might have limited flexibility on the issue. But India should show an increased willingness to play the Tibet card, as it has in the recent past.[271] Some pragmatists suggest that New Delhi could also go further and 'link a final and unequivocal legitimisation of China's sovereignty over Tibet to a settlement of the border dispute'.[272] But, simultaneously, pragmatists add that India should be careful not to overplay its hand, which could result in Chinese retaliation.[273]

Pragmatists see as essential the economic development of India's border areas, especially as China is rapidly developing its side of

---

[266] Saran, 'Geopolitical Consequences'.

[267] Shekhar Gupta, 'Stop Fighting the 1962 war'.

[268] Pubby, 'T-72 Tanks Moved to Remote Sikkim Area after China Tests Indian Defences'.

[269] Samanta, 'Army Wants Patrol Curbs Along China Border Lifted'.

[270] 'After Menon's Visit to China, Nirupama Rao Meets Dalai Lama', *NDTV,* July 11, 2010. Available at http://www.ndtv.com/article/india/after-menon-s-visit-to-china-nirupama-rao-meets-dalai-lama-36796, accessed on August 23, 2011.

[271] Shubhajit Roy, 'Govt Underlines: Dalai Lama Free to Visit Arunachal', *The Indian Express,* October 17, 2009. Available at http://global.factiva.com, accessed on August 23, 2011.

[272] Zorawar Daulet Singh, 'India's Tibet Card', *Hard News,* July 2008. Available at http://www.hardnewsmedia.com/2008/07/2251, accessed on August 23, 2011.

[273] Tellis, 'China and India in Asia', p. 149 and Bajpai, 'India, China and Asian Security', p. 48.

the border.[274] Furthermore, they assert that India should continue to strengthen its logistical position at the border, better integrate its border areas and improve communications and transportation, preferably without a lot of fanfare.[275] On a broader scale, as a hedge and as a signal, pragmatists believe that India also needs to develop a 'modest' nuclear deterrent, undertake conventional force modernisation and invest in defence and technology research and development. Further, it should maintain and enhance its military supply relationships with countries like France, Israel, Russia and the US, which would have the additional benefit of creating pro-India stakeholders in these countries.[276] Some add that in acquiring capabilities, India should 'play to its strengths' rather than get into an all-out arms race with China, which it is unlikely to win in any case and will result in diversion from development needs.[277] Simultaneously, India should continue to encourage not just political but military engagement with China, involving high-level visits, military exercises and broader interaction, so as to avoid miscalculation.[278]

On the relationship between China and Pakistan, some pragmatists suggest encouraging pressure from countries like the US to restrict their nuclear co-operation. Another suggestion involves using China to pressure Pakistan. Others, however, assert the limitations of strategies aiming for Chinese or US pressure on Islamabad.[279]

---

[274] Shishir Gupta, 'NSC Meet Discusses China'. Also see 'CCS Clears Choppers for Navy, Projects in Arunachal', *The Indian Express*, August 7, 2009; Samudra Gupta Kashyap, 'China Won't Wage War: Arunachal CM', *The Indian Express*, September 21, 2009; 'PM Cools Hot Air over China', *The Indian Express*, September 19, 2009; and 'Press Charges'.

[275] Nomani, 'Don't Panic'. Pragmatists thus approve of higher allocations in budgets for upgrading border infrastructure on the grounds that good fences are more likely to make good neighbours. 'With Rs 2,284 cr, Budget Aims to Secure Borders', *The Indian Express*, July 7, 2009. Available at http://global.factiva.com, accessed on August 23, 2011.

[276] Tellis, 'China and India in Asia', pp. 142–43.

[277] C. Raja Mohan, 'Maritime CBMs'. Also see 'At Sea Over Navy Chief', *The Indian Express*, August 17, 2009. Available at http://global.factiva.com, accessed on August 23, 2011.

[278] C. Raja Mohan, 'Party is State'. Also see 'Maritime CBMs' and 'Now the G-3' by the same author.

[279] Zorawar Daulet Singh, 'New Dynamics of an All Weather Friendship', *Pragati*, February 2009. Available at http://pragati.nationalinterest.

Yet others argue that the only way of limiting Sino-Pakistan ties is to 'find peace with Pakistan'.[280]

In India's near abroad and further afield, while India should be aware that it is falling behind in the assistance race,[281] pragmatists argue that analysts should stop seeing every gain for China as a loss for India and overreacting.[282] Pragmatists advocate that the two countries work together wherever possible and where they have shared interests. This co-operation, however, need not be exclusive. Furthermore, while India needs to recognise that it cannot always compete with China,[283] it should not hesitate to compete where it can, using all the resources at its disposal in countries across Asia and beyond.

Thus pragmatists encourage the continued 'revitaliz[ation]' of India's relationships with east and southeast Asian states.[284] This Look East policy 'prevent[s] China from acquiring forward basing and presence' that could be threatening to Indian autonomy; limits Chinese influence so that Beijing cannot 'coerce the local states into supporting Chinese policies aimed at undercutting Indian security'; and allows India to 'operate within the region as required, and to extend support that may be requested by its regional partners'.[285] But pragmatists assert that India needs to act with care and especially consider carefully the level and kind of military assistance it offers in China's backyard, lest this provoke China.

Pragmatists believe that India should increase 'connectivity' and the depth and breadth of engagement with countries across Asia, Africa and Latin America.[286] It should extend military and economic

---

in/2009/02/new-dynamics-of-an-all-weather-friendship, accessed on August 23, 2011.

[280] Shekhar Gupta, 'A New Project Pakistan', *The Indian Express*, August 8, 2009. Available at http://global.factiva.com, accessed on August 23, 2011.

[281] Mohan, 'Maritime CBMs'.

[282] Mohan, 'The Great Game Folio'.

[283] Mini Kapoor, 'India's Help to Tajikistan Linked to Energy Security', *The Indian Express*, September 8, 2009. Available at http://global.factiva.com, accessed on August 23, 2011.

[284] Tellis, 'China and India in Asia', p. 142.

[285] Ibid. p. 163.

[286] Saran, 'Geopolitical Consequences'. Also see 'Project Stilwell', *The Indian Express*, June 26, 2009. Available at http://global.factiva.com, accessed on August 23, 2011.

assistance, as well as political co-operation.²⁸⁷ Furthermore, India should work with the governments that it finds in these countries, even if they are not the governments India would like. If New Delhi appears judgmental about the internal politics of certain countries and isolates them, as it did briefly in Myanmar, this will only push the countries further 'into the arms of China'.²⁸⁸

On the role of the US, pragmatists assert that India cannot take the US for granted as a balancer. Nor can China and India form a balancing coalition against it, as some optimists have suggested. India needs to continue to pursue deeper US–India relations and use that relationship as leverage with China.²⁸⁹ Pragmatists believe that India should not 'underestimate the growing tension between [the US and China's] short-term imperatives to co-operate on a range of global issues and the inevitable long-term rivalry between an America in relative decline and a rapidly rising China'.²⁹⁰ But they do not advocate a US–India alliance. Partnerships or coalitions of the willing are preferred. Not just with the US, but with other countries as well.

International politics is in flux – at different times there have been talks of a G-2 (China, US), a G-3 (China, Japan, US), a China–Russia–India axis and an 'Asian democratic quad' (Australia, India, Japan, US).²⁹¹ When it comes to partnerships, China is 'hedging its bets' and pragmatists believe that India should too.²⁹² Sino-American rapprochement in 1971 and Soviet behaviour during the 1962 War have shown that partners can be unreliable and will place their national interests above that of India. Thus India must diversify its portfolio of partners. Simultaneously, India needs to prepare for the consequences of China's partnerships with a range of other countries, but especially with the US.²⁹³

In multilateral fora, pragmatists believe that China and India could 'build coalitions on different issues of shared concern'.²⁹⁴ They can

---

²⁸⁷ Tellis, 'China and India in Asia', p. 152.
²⁸⁸ Ibid., p. 151.
²⁸⁹ Saran, 'Geopolitical Consequences'.
²⁹⁰ Mohan, 'London Duet'.
²⁹¹ Mohan, 'Now the G-3'.
²⁹² Saran, 'Geopolitical Consequences'.
²⁹³ C. Raja Mohan, 'American Embrace', *The Indian Express*, March 18, 2009. Available at http://global.factiva.com, accessed on August 23, 2011.
²⁹⁴ Saran, 'Geopolitical Consequences'.

find 'common ground in their negotiating positions' on the economic front when their interests coincide, even while they continue to compete for markets and raw materials.[295] But these interests will not always coincide in multilateral settings and thus India needs to attain and maintain its own seat at the high table. Pragmatists assert that India can achieve this by showing that it is 'ready to take up its international responsibilities'.[296]

The Path Ahead

What does the future hold for the Sino-Indian relationship? The scenarios usually outlined reflect the predictions of the three groups: 'deepening competition leading to open rivalry, a turn towards co-operation, and continued quiet competition'.[297] The avatar and approach that will dominate in India's resolve depend on a number of factors. How these factors play out can strengthen the hands of one group or the other. Chinese behaviour in the late 1950s and 1960s, for example, strengthened the position of the hawks on China, weakened that of the doves and created space for those advocating improved relations with the US. A decade or so later Sino-American rapprochement, in conjunction with the Bangladesh/East Pakistan crisis, provided leverage to advocates in New Delhi of an Indo-Soviet treaty.

One set of factors that could influence the outcome is internal. Within this set, a subset involves decision-making: the nature and character of the Chinese and Indian political and bureaucratic leaderships; the identity of the decision-makers; the priorities of the ministries dominating decision-making; the nature of civil-military relations; as the range of sectors across which China and India interact expands and the lines between domestic and foreign policies blurs, the potential role of a broader range of ministries and departments; the impact of the involvement of state governments; the level

---

[295] T. N. Srinivasan, 'Economic Reforms and Global Integration', in Frankel and Harding, eds, *The India–China Relationship*, p. 221.

[296] C. Raja Mohan, 'Before the Chance Fades', *The Indian Express,* July 20, 2009. Available at http://global.factiva.com, accessed on August 23, 2011.

[297] Mark W. Frazier, 'Quiet Competition and the Future of Sino-Indian Relations', in Frankel and Harding, eds, *The India–China Relationship*, p. 296.

and kind of impact of external influences – think tanks, corporate lobbies, human rights activists, labour groups – on decision-making; and the ability of the government to coordinate and implement the various strands of China policy.

Another subset of factors involves politics and public discourse in China and India: domestic politics; the nature of the governments; the influence and use of public opinion; the ability of the governments to manage public discourse; the level of nationalism; and the legacy of history. A third subset of factors involves internal developments: the state and pace of economic development; national priorities; the level of internal stability; and the state of internal movements – for example, the independence movement in Tibet or the Maoist insurgency in India.

On the bilateral front, factors that could impact Indian perceptions and policies could include: China's increasing capabilities; India's growing capabilities; developments in the search for resources (energy, water); the 'healthiness' of Sino-Indian economic competition; the level and kind of bilateral economic interaction; the influence of economics and politics on each other; and progress on the border issue and the strategic dialogue.

A third set of factors is regional: the state of Sino-Pakistan relations; the state of the India–Pakistan relationship; the level of stability in Pakistan; developments in Afghanistan; the nature and level of Chinese and Indian activities in south and southeast Asia and China's and India's perceptions of the same; the willingness and ability of smaller states in Asia to play China and India off against each other; and developments within these regional states.

A final set of factors is international: the reaction of external actors to developments in Sino-Indian relations; the role of key actors especially, but not only, Russia and the US; the state of Sino-US relations; the state of the US–India relationship; developments in the Chinese and Indian global quest for influence, resources and markets; the level and kind of Sino-Indian interaction in multilateral fora; and Chinese reaction to Indian aspirations for global leadership.

This is a representative list, not necessarily a comprehensive one and, as Kumar and Menon have noted, some factors matter more than others.[298] This list, however, highlights the complexity of developing and maintaining a coherent strategy towards China. A grand

---

[298] See Kumar and Menon, *The Long View From Delhi.*

strategic approach would require even more capacity, especially 'the ability to see how all of the parts of a problem relate to one another, and therefore to the whole thing', as John Lewis Gaddis has noted.[299]

There is a lively debate about whether India has a grand strategy and whether one is necessary or possible, as well as outlines of what an Indian grand strategy would look like.[300] Pessimists often argue that India does not have such a strategy. Pragmatists and optimists assert that India already has one, or does not need one. This paper does not enter into that debate. But it concludes with a suggestion that, at the very least, thinking about a grand strategy towards China might be helpful. Doing so would require one to contemplate available means and ends, the interaction of multiple actors and the interplay of multiple factors, action, reaction and anticipation, politics and priorities, capabilities and intentions, coordination and implementation, consequences and contingencies and, most of all, not just what is desirable vis-à-vis China, but also what is feasible.

---

[299] John Lewis Gaddis, 'What Is Grand Strategy?'. Speech delivered at Duke University, Durham, NC, February 26, 2008.

[300] See Harsh V. Pant, *Contemporary Debates in Indian Foreign and Security Policy: India Negotiates its Rise in the International System* (New York: Palgrave Macmillan, 2008); Srinath Raghavan, 'Virtues of Being Vague', *Deccan Chronicle*, January 7, 2010; Sunil Khilnani, 'Delhi's Grand Strategy', *Newsweek*, July 18, 2009 at http://global.factiva.com, accessed on August 23, 2011; Amitabh Mattoo, 'India's International Relations: The Search for Stability, Space, and Strength', in Alyssa Ayres & Philip Oldenburg, eds, *India Briefing; Takeoff at Last?* (New York: ME Sharpe, 2005).

12

ABERRANT CONVERSATIONALISTS
INDIA AND THE UNITED STATES SINCE 1947

Rudra Chaudhuri

That India's relationship with the United States (US) has been transformed for the better might well be considered a given.[1] Whether it be the subtler aspects of deepening cultural and societal exchanges, strengthened by the large diaspora of 'Asian Indians' – a legislative term introduced as early as 1980 – living inside the US,[2] the more material issue of constantly rising trade levels, or the much vaunted subject of defence co-operation,[3] there is little doubt that the present state of affairs is, at the very least, more positive and indicative of co-operation than at any point in the past.

Indeed, books, articles and chapters on the US and India do not fail to highlight the sharp contrast between the somewhat peevish attitudes of Indian elites in the post-independence period with elite celebration, even self-congratulation surrounding exchanges and compacts in the contemporary times.[4] Reluctance to engage with the

---

[1] Paul Kapur and Sumit Ganguly, 'The Transformation of US–India Relations: An Explanation for the Rapprochement and Prospects for the Future', *Asian Survey* 47, 4 (July/August 2007), pp. 642–56.

[2] Vinay Lal, *The Other Indians: A Political and Cultural History of South Asian in America* (New Delhi: Harper Collins, 2008), p xi.

[3] For a detailed analysis of rising trade levels, see US Census Bureau, 'Foreign Trade' at http://www.census.gov/foreign-trade/balance/c5330.html, accessed on May 18, 2012. For a substantial note on expanding defence co-operation see Raymond E. Vickery Jr, *The Eagle and the Elephant: Strategic Aspects of US–India Economic Engagement* (Baltimore: Johns Hopkins University Press, 2011), Chapter 1.

[4] For example see David Malone, *Does the Elephant Dance? Contemporary Indian Foreign Policy* (London: Oxford University Press, 2011), pp. 153–54.

US has given way to pragmatism. Arguably, the shadow of colonialism and neo-colonialism has been eclipsed by a considerable measure of forthrightness.[5] The rhetoric chosen and initiatives adopted by national principals would suggest that the days of 'estrangement' have been replaced by an era of engagement. Take, for instance, President Obama's celebrated speech to the joint session of the Indian Parliament in November 2010 where he spoke of 'shared prosperity' and the promise of India and the US as 'indispensable partners in meeting the challenges of our time'.[6]

Yet, and notwithstanding cheering expressions of intent, few works extrapolate to what this transformation means for India, the US or for the lines and curves that underlie global security concerns such as international terrorism and troublesome regimes. Key questions remain under explored: how exactly has India changed, and to what extent have Indian elites shed the darker memories of India–US relations for the lighter contours of what might be called an unfastened alliance with the US? This essay approaches the question of change by focusing on three cases or crises: the Korean War in 1950, the Iraq War in 2003 and, finally, the predicaments linked to the present conflict in Afghanistan.

Hence, rather than providing a substantive narrative or simply repeating the well-known historiography of US–India relations, it traces the push and pull tensions that mark this uneasy partnership.[7] Further, it approaches the cases from the perspective of Indian elites, all the while delineating what their actions and eventual decisions mean for both US–India relations and the study of Indian strategic behaviour. Indeed, the cases demonstrate how and why these 'natural allies' convergent language to define broad common interests, but, in most cases, adopt altogether different scripts to interpret

---

[5] C. Raja Mohan, 'India and the Balance of Power', *Foreign Affairs*, 85, 4 (July–August 2006), pp. 17–32.

[6] 'See Full Text of Obama's Parliament Speech', November 8, 2010 at http://ibnlive.in.com/news/full-text-of-obamas-parliament-address/134649-3.html, accessed on May 18, 2012.

[7] For example see Dennis Kux, *India and the United States: Estranged Democracies* (Washington: National Defence University Press, 1993); Teresita C. Schaffer, *India and the United States in the 21st Century: Reinventing Partnership* (New Delhi: India Research Press, 2010).

narrower ends and means. In many ways, this is a select account of a less-than-natural exchange between aberrant conversationalists.

The Korean War

American interest in India grew considerably at the turn of the 20th century. Whether through the teachings of Swami Vivekananda – a delegate at the Parliament of Religions in Chicago in 1893 – or the writings of Rabindranath Tagore, who visited the US five times in the first three decades of the 1900s, the philosophical ideas of India were soon popularised in the minds of American elites. By the 1930s, resolutions introduced in the US Senate condemned 'British repression in India'.[8] In 1945, President Franklin Roosevelt made a case, although with restraint, for Indian independence. His successor, President Harry S. Truman invited Prime Minister Jawaharlal Nehru to Washington shortly after independence.

For much of the late 1940s, discussions between Indian and American officials revolved around the thorny issues of economic aid and military assistance. In short, whilst Indian representatives looked at ways to secure material support, the government, and the Prime Minister in particular, made clear that nothing would compromise India's new found freedom. For most American interlocutors, the reality of independent India – as a tough negotiator – soon obscured the miasma surrounding the value-laden judgments about Indian democracy. American views of India were complicated by its foreign policy of non-alignment: an approach to international politics quite distinct from the highly-polarising policy design of the US during the Cold War. The question of India's allegiance to one camp or the other dominated almost any conversation between official and non-official representatives of the two countries. Finally, in 1950, the impending conflict on the Korean peninsula laid bare the differences on international relations.

On June 25, 1950, North Korean forces invaded South Korea. Almost immediately, the US drafted a resolution demanding the removal of all North Korean forces from the South. The resolution

---

[8] For an excellent introduction to the US's interest in India, see Kenton J. Clymer, *Quest for Freedom: The United States and India* (New York: Columbia University Press, 1995), pp. 2–10.

passed in the United Nations (UN) Security Council and was supported by India.[9] This was important. Members of the US National Security Council (NSC), representatives in the State Department and officers in the Department of Defence made clear that, potentially, India had 'tremendous influence in Asia'.[10] India's vote was thought to help secure much needed legitimacy in the east. Further, strategists argued that Indian support could ensure 'military rights in South Asia as the US government may determine to be essential'.[11]

Yet, on June 27, 1950, India abstained from a vote to furnish armed support to South Korea.[12] Prime Minister Jawaharlal Nehru's thinking was clearly outlined in a series of letters to his Chief Ministers, to whom he wrote every other fortnight. On July 2, 1950, he emphasised that 'there could be no doubt that the North Korean Government had committed aggression on a large scale on South Korea'. Hence, it was reasonable for India to support the UN resolution condemning North Korea. However, given that the war may well expand into other parts of Asia, Indian military support in a US-led initiative risked drawing India into the Cold War on the US's side. Nehru argued that as he understood it, President Truman saw the Korean War as an extension of the Cold War, whereas India did not.[13]

---

[9] For details see Robert McMahon, *The Cold War on the Periphery: The United States, India, and Pakistan* (New York: Columbia University Press, 1994), pp. 82–83.

[10] Anita Inder Singh, *The Limits of British Influence: South Asia and the Anglo-American Relationship 1947–56* (London: Pinter, 1993), p. 72.

[11] 'Draft Statement of Policy Proposed by the National Security Council on South Asia', enclosure to NSC 98/1, 22 January, 1951, FRUS VI Part II (United States Government and Printing Office, Washington, 1977), pp. 1651–52.

[12] 'The resolution asked for the cessation of all hostilities, withdrawal of all North Korean forces from South Korea, military support to be furnished to South Korea by all UN member states. The primary objective of the resolution was to 'repel the armed attack and to restore international peace and security'. Nehru to Chief Ministers, New Delhi, July 2, 1950 in G. Parthasarthi, ed., *Jawaharlal Nehru: Letters to Chief Ministers*, Volume 1, 1947 (London: Jawaharlal Nehru Memorial Fund and Oxford University Press 1985), p.118.

[13] Ibid.

India's nuanced position of condemning North Korea but unwilling to contribute troops, did little for the relationship with the US, and Truman in particular.[14] For Nehru, it was important to engage in dialogue with the recently formed People's Republic of China (PRC). This was, of course, rejected by all major Western powers. On July 7, 1950, when the United Kingdom's (UK) Permanent Representative tabled a resolution in the UN to create a unified command structure under American leadership, India abstained from the vote.[15] By September 1950, US–India strategic relations had reached breaking point.

In the beginning of September, there was discussion about UN forces, under the command of General Douglas Macarthur, crossing the 38th parallel into North Korea.[16] The Chinese premier – Chou En Lai – sent a message to the Indian ambassador in China, K. M. Panikkar; he argued that China was not obligated to honour UN resolutions as it was not yet a member state. Chou also told Panikkar that if UN forces crossed the Yalu River and the 38th parallel, the People's Liberation Army (PLA) would enter the war on the side of North Korea.[17] Panikkar passed Chou's message to Nehru, who communicated the warning to the US administration.[18]

In some ways, Nehru saw India's role as a bridge between the two powers that might help clear up the misperceptions that dogged Sino-American relations. Yet, with little attention paid to India's counsel, US officials prepared the diplomatic ground for crossing the 38th parallel. Warren Austin, the US representative to the UN, forcefully argued for the removal of 'opportunities of new acts of aggression' by denying 'aggressor forces' any 'refuge behind an imaginary line'.[19] On October 7, India voted against a resolution to

---

[14] Parthasarthy, *Jawaharlal Nehru*, p. 118.

[15] Ibid., p. 227.

[16] The 38th parallel is the imaginary circle of latitude that divides Korea into the north and the south. In 1945, following the end of the Second World War, the parallel was recognised as the frontier between the Soviet occupied north and the American occupied south.

[17] Nehru to Chief Ministers, New Delhi, February 1, 1951, Parthasarthy, *Jawaharlal Nehru*, p. 32.

[18] Inder Singh, *Limits of British Influence*, p. 83.

[19] Nehru to Chief Ministers, New Delhi, October 1, 1950, Parthasarthy, *Jawaharlal Nehru*, pp. 217–18.

unify Korea.[20] India even refused to brand China as the aggressor in the Korean War,[21] a position that was diametrically opposite to that of the US and most of the Western world.[22] This was 'India's great crime in American eyes'.[23] Indeed, at the tail end of the war, Truman was alleged to have said that 'Nehru has sold us [the US] down the Hudson. His attitude has been responsible for our losing the war in Korea'.[24] Nehru was called a 'hypersensitive egoist', branded as a 'socialist' with 'deep-rooted suspicions of our [American] capitalist economy and its intentions in Asia'.[25]

The Korean affair reveals two points of detail that are worth noting. First, for Nehru, the Korean War served as a turning point. India's failed attempts to persuade the Truman administration to back down convinced Indian leaders that the US was not willing to deal with India on an equal footing. In many ways, this served to re-enforce the appeals of being non-aligned, rather than having to choose sides in the early years of the Cold War. Freedom rather than dependency, even when the latter may have afforded security guarantees and military assistance, was more attractive to a newly-independent state.

The normative base underlying India's emerging strategic outlook was reinforced by political concerns. Unimpressed by the Truman administration as a whole, Nehru was wary about contributing troops to a mission that might well have spilled beyond Near East Asia. What would the Soviets do? Most importantly, what would happen to Sino-Indian relations if China decided to intervene? After all, India could hardly risk sparking a war on its border by aggravating a newly-formed Communist China. Hence, material considerations and strategic realities necessitated treading cautiously in this time of crises.

Second, Indian elites were concerned about the impact that joining the war might have on its international standing in the eastern

---

[20] The resolution however, was passed in the UN General Assembly. See McMahon, *Cold War*, p. 86.

[21] Nehru to Chief Ministers, New Delhi, February 18, 1951, Parthasarthy, *Jawaharlal Nehru*, p. 331.

[22] Ibid., October 14, 1950, Parthasarthy, *Jawaharlal Nehru*, Vol. 1, p. 227.

[23] Vincent Sheean, 'The Case for India', *Foreign Affairs* 30 (1951–52), p. 82.

[24] Kux, *Estranged Democracies*, p. 74.

[25] Stated by McGhee in McMahon, *Cold War*, pp. 88–89.

hemisphere. A rule-based international society required that the considerations of eastern states were as important as those in the West. India could not join an alliance that was selective in its construction of legitimacy. Indeed, while the Korean War was legitimised by the UN Security Council, India grew distrustful of a UN system monopolised by the victor powers of the Second World War.

The misgivings that took root in the early 1950s informed India's approach to the US for much of the Cold War, or at least till the late 1970s. Yet, such reservations were accompanied by an ever-present conversation about intent and motivation. Whether it was Nehru's discomfort with the US' efforts to ally with Pakistan in 1954, Prime Minister Indira Gandhi's condemnation of the US' interventionist policies in South East Asia in the 1960s, President Gerald Ford's fury following India's nuclear tests in 1974 or President Jimmy Carter's disappointment in India's initial support for Soviet intervention in Afghanistan, the underlining frustration was constantly communicated between the two governments and societies. By design or otherwise, the conversations sustained the most comprehensive relationship between India and another nation state, a point that is so often missed in assessments of India–US relations.

The 2003 Iraq War

To an extent, the intellectual crevice that once divided Indian and American elites in their respective approaches to potent questions of state and security had begun to close even before the collapse of the Soviet Union. Indira Gandhi's visit to Washington in 1982 was nothing short of historic. Sixty-four years old, the Prime Minister made it her mission to induce Washington to look beyond the differences and tension points between the two countries. Whilst the US' aid to Pakistan and the ambiguity of nuclear non-proliferation remained irritants, both Prime Minister Indira Gandhi and President Ronald Reagan understood that the US–India relationship was far too important to be subsumed by slighter, essentially bureaucratic matters.[26]

This momentum was sustained in the mid 1990s. The economic reforms introduced by, perhaps, the most consequential Finance Minister in Indian history, Manmohan Singh – later (and currently)

---

[26] For details, see Kux, *Estranged Democracies*, pp. 390–95.

the Prime Minister – revised India's standing in Washington. Further, India survived the Cold War. Indeed, and at the risk of irritating sceptics – of which there are a few too many – of 'Nehruvian India', non-alignment worked. Unlike Pakistan, India resisted dependence. Distinct from western Europe and parts of the Middle East and South East Asia, India was not reliant on any other state for its security or survival. A sense of resilience coupled with imagination energised Indian foreign policy and its relationship with the US.

The changes in India's policies in the 1990s, paralleling the economic reforms, did not amount to the replacement of non-alignment by what the Bharatiya Janata Party (BJP) – the majority party in the National Democratic Alliance (NDA) government – called engagement. Rather than being 'marginalised', non-alignment was moulded, bent and recast.[27] Alliances remained taboo, but this did not mean that India could or would not entertain a conversation on alignment. By the end of the 1990s, the BJPs chief foreign policy aim of 'engaging with all major powers' had gained wide acceptance within both the legislature and Indian civil society.[28] Yet, the complexities underlying this refreshingly innovative approach were fully revealed in 2003 when India was asked to join the so-called 'Coalition of the Willing' to militarily intervene in Iraq.

From the outset, and notwithstanding three invitations to play a role in Iraq from President Bush,[29] Prime Minister A. B. Vajpayee asserted that India would 'take a decision in case of outbreak of war', thus giving his government more time to think about the issue at hand.[30] Within India, there was wide consensus that the 'neat', supposedly predictable and positive consequences of intervention were 'completely bogus'. India's role would be in the aftermath of major

---

[27] C. Raja Mohan, *Crossing the Rubicon: The Shaping of India's New Foreign Policy* (New Delhi: Penguin–Viking, 2003), p. xxi.

[28] Author's interview with Brajesh Mishra, New Delhi, August 11, 2008. Mishra was National Security Advisor and Principal Secretary to the Indian Prime Minister from 1998–2004. Also see C. Raja Mohan, 'India and the Balance of Power'.

[29] Amitabh Srivastava, 'I Refused to Help Bush: Vajpayee', *Hindustan Times*, March 28, 2003.

[30] Mahendra Ved, 'India Not to Back War, Says PM', *The Times of India*, February 26, 2003.

operations, when the 'internal structures of governance and order will collapse'.[31]

Subsequent to the commencement of operations against Iraq on March 20, the government adopted a somewhat curious position. It had 'chosen to adopt the middle path over Iraq to ensure that the government's carefully nurtured relationship with the US is not destroyed'.[32] Labelled a 'pragmatic approach', the Prime Minister argued that 'whatever the rights and wrongs of the Iraq situation, our [India's] relationship with others [presumably the US] cannot be defined by a single issue.' Many analysts agreed. They argued that it was alright to 'criticise' the US but not 'condemn' its actions. India needed to 'tread softly' on the Iraq war.[33] According to C. Raja Mohan, the well-informed strategic analyst, '[t]empered by realism', the 'middle-path' reflected 'the new pragmatic strain that ha[d] taken root in India's foreign policy'.[34] Following fiery debates in parliament, all parties agreed to use the Hindi word *ninda* (deplore) to articulate India's official response to the US-led intervention.[35]

The BJP's moderate view on the Iraq intervention could well be considered a major departure from past policy. However, at the same time, Vajpayee suggested that sending troops under US command would potentially impact India's independent approach to foreign policy.[36] He argued that India was 'following an honest non-aligned policy'.[37] The non-aligned narrative, lamented for being 'meaningless' and 'a matter of history', was still making its way into public discourse.[38]

---

[31] Editorial, 'Wait Watchers' Club', *Outlook*, February 10, 2003.

[32] Aunohita Mojumdar, 'India Won't Jeopardise Relations with US Over Iraq', *The Times of India*, March 21, 2003.

[33] K. Subramanyam, 'Criticise, Not Condemn: India Must Tread Softly on Iraq War', *The Times of India*, April 7, 2003.

[34] C. Raja Mohan, 'India and the Iraq War', *The Hindu*, March 27, 2003.

[35] 'Opposition is Politicising the Issue: BJP', *Hindustan Times*, April 8, 2003.

[36] Jyothi Malhotra, 'India Won't Be a Lackey', *The Indian Express*, June 3, 2003.

[37] Manoj Joshi, 'India is Still Non-aligned, Says PM', *The Times of India*, June 3, 2003.

[38] Thomas P. Thornton, 'India Adrift: The Search for Moorings in a New World Order', *Asian Survey*, 32, 12 (December 1992), p. 1067.

The US had asked for one Indian division to be sent to Iraq after Baghdad fell.[39] It was later revealed that the VI division was earmarked for deployment under the command of a two-star General.[40] On record, the US Secretary of Defence Donald Rumsfeld claimed, 'I never publicly pressured countries to do anything, I talked privately to them about what they might do ... I did not want them to feel as though the United States had dragged them kicking and screaming into it, that's not the kind of thing we wanted'.[41] Nevertheless, the Bush administration lobbied hard to include India in the Coalition. As one former diplomat closely associated with the negotiations put it, 'there was a lot of pressure to consider the troops option'.[42] Rumsfeld concedes that the US was 'interested in help'.[43]

India's response post April 2003 validates these assessments. In May, the Cabinet Committee on Security (CCS), the highest policy decision-making body in the country, met to discuss options in Iraq. The Cabinet asked the Ministry of External Affairs to 'obtain clarifications' from the UN Special Advisor to Iraq, Rafeeuddin Ahmed, about the legalities of how troop deployments would work. Unease was not restricted to the CCS. The Indian Army was uncomfortable with the issue of a US-led command structure. It could not be seen reporting directly to US military authority. The Army, as well as India's political elite, insisted that if India was to be given a sector in Iraq, then the division commander would be his own boss in that sector.[44]

Finally, India's trepidations about an adequate UN mandate and an acceptable command structure led the Bush administration to send a delegation to India led by Peter Rodman, the US Assistant Secretary of Defence for International Security Affairs. This visit gave those Indian analysts and commentators in favour of sending troops

---

[39] Author's interview with Brig. Gurmeet Kanwal, August 2, 2007, New Delhi.
[40] Vishal Thapar, 'Army Was All Dressed Up to Go to Iraq', *Hindustan Times*, July 15, 2003.
[41] Author's interview with Donald Rumsfeld, November 13, 2008.
[42] Author's interview with former Indian diplomat, London, March 2010. (Exact date withheld)
[43] Author's interview with Donald Rumsfeld, November 13, 2008.
[44] V. Sudarshan, 'Keeping America's Peace', *Outlook*, June 2, 2003.

a window of opportunity in which to make their case. Proponents argued that 'sending a division-sized force to Iraq would significantly raise New Delhi's military profile in the Persian Gulf and lay the foundations for long term security co-operation with Washington in the Indian Ocean region'.[45]

This notwithstanding, by June it had become increasingly clear that the stabilisation of Iraq would also mean war-fighting under US command. This was a big stumbling block, not the least because the 'shooting war' would be fought by those not wearing blue helmets. Ultimately, the CCS turned down what many thought was India's opportunity to make its mark on the global stage. India would not contribute troops.

Yet, and aside from New Delhi's eventual decision, the change in 'attitude' in India was unmistakable. Claudio Lilienfeld, a key member of Rodman's team, was surprised that India was giving the issue such serious attention. It was a 'strategic moment' for India, and despite the eventual result, the tensions underlying this moment indicated to the US decision-makers that they were dealing with a 'changing India'.[46]

India's approach to the US dovetailed with a renewed sense of directness – a point that was not lost on a Republican administration that had tried hard to capitalise on Indian diplomatic activism. The newly-elected Congress-led United Progressive Alliance (UPA) government recognised the conceptual changes in Indian foreign policy initiated in the 1980s and reinitiated at the turn of the twentieth century. In June 2005, India and the US agreed on a programme of defence collaboration including an expanded partnership in missile defence. Titled the 'New Framework for US–India Defence Partnership for the Next Ten Years', the accord substantiated the existing spirit of entente.

Three years later, the bugbear of non-proliferation that once haunted bureaucratic co-operation between India and the US was addressed. In September 2008, the US Congress authorised President Bush to sign into law a bill that permitted the US government

---

[45] C. Raja Mohan, 'Indo-US Talks on Iraq Today', *The Hindu*, June 16, 2003.

[46] Author's interview with Claudio Lilienfeld, Washington DC, September 24, 2008.

to enter into nuclear-related trade with India. Described as the 'deal of the century', the so-called US–India Nuclear Deal (or the N-Deal for short), had for the first time in history paved the way for the US to engage in nuclear-related trade with a country that had not signed the Nuclear Non-Proliferation Treaty (NPT).[47]

Interestingly, neither the fervour surrounding the deal nor the deal itself caused India to lose its sense of identity and autonomy. This was far from an alliance, a point that has become increasingly clear to Washington insiders who track Indian policies in Afghanistan. Despite pressure from the US to curtail Indian involvement on the ground in Afghanistan – an American stance designed to appease Pakistan – the Indian Mission in Afghanistan has engaged local leaders and pursued its own course in the country. New Delhi's Afghan policy is a clear example of its determination to maintain an independent foreign policy.

The last case in this essay shows how India deals with US pressures in a theatre where India's growing influence is not necessarily or always encouraged.

India, the US and the Afghan Conflict

During the US election campaign in 2008, then Senator Barack Obama argued that India and Pakistan should 'try to resolve the Kashmir crisis so that [Pakistan] can stay focused not on India, but on the situation with those militants [camped on the border with Afghanistan]'.[48] The logic, at least for this US administration, seemed fairly simple. If India began a series of discussions on Kashmir, Pakistan would feel more confident about relocating a bulk of its troop formations from the border with India to that with Afghanistan. This, no doubt, was one of Pakistan's demands.[49]

---

[47] For a background analysis see C. Raja Mohan, *Impossible Allies: Nuclear India, the United States, and the Global Order* (New Delhi: India Research Press 2006), pp. 1–10.

[48] Quoted in C. Raja Mohan, 'Barack Obama's Kashmir Thesis', *The Indian Express*, November 3, 2008. Also see Barack Obama, 'Renewing American Leadership', *Foreign Affairs*, (July/August 2007). Available at http://www.foreignaffairs.com/articles/62636/barack-obama/renewing-american-leadership, accessed on November 25, 2013.

[49] For a comprehensive review see: Stephen P. Cohen, C. Christine Fair, Sumit Ganguly, Shaun Gregory, Aqil Shah, and Ashley J. Tellis, 'What's

Between November 2008 and January 2009, the transition period for the new US administration, Washington insiders indicated that Richard Holbrooke, the erstwhile envoy to the Balkans, was being considered to serve the new President as Special Envoy to Afghanistan and Pakistan. His brief was to include India and to induce it to parley with Pakistan with regard to the Kashmir dispute. According to diplomatic sources, 'when the Indian government learned Holbrooke was going to do [Pakistan]–India, they swung into action and lobbied to have India excluded from his purview ... and they succeeded. Holbrooke's account officially does [did] not include India'.[50] Daniel Markey, having spoken to Indian officials, suggests that the Indians 'freaked out' over the possibility of a special envoy whose remit would include Kashmir. Markey adds that India had a 'fairly effective lobbying machine' in Washington.[51]

The merits and demerits of US policy interests notwithstanding, the Indian government's response to the Obama approach provides an indication of how India manages relations with the US after having entered into the nuclear deal.[52] Importantly, India's chosen approach on the ground in Afghanistan underscores the importance and benefits of an alliance-free approach to international politics.

Unlike in Iraq, India was not a welcome party in Afghanistan. As Rumsfeld put it, 'India was an enormously important country in terms of its geopolitical position, but in terms of Afghanistan, the fact India had a reasonably good relationship with the Northern Alliance was a complicating factor because of our [US] need to get co-operation from Pakistan'.[53] Indeed, in a report prepared by General Stanley McChrystal, the former Commander of the US-led International Security Assistance Forces (ISAF) – replaced by General David Patraeus in the summer of 2010 – India's close relationship

---

the Problem with Pakistan?', *Foreign Affairs*, March 2009. Also see John R. Schmidt, 'The Unravelling of Pakistan', *Survival*, 51, 3 (June–July 2009), pp. 29–54.

[50] 'India's Stealth Lobbying Against Holbrooke Brief', *Foreign Policy Magazine: The Cable*, January 23, 2009.

[51] Ibid.

[52] For an analysis see Daniel Markey, 'From AFPAK to PAKAF: A Response to the New US Strategy in South Asia', *Council for Foreign Relations*, Policy Options Paper, April 2009.

[53] Author's interview with Donald Rumsfeld, November 13, 2008.

with the Karzai government and growing goodwill on the streets of Afghanistan was a matter of concern for the US. The US was, after all, required to work closely with a peeved and ever-sensitive Pakistani military leadership.[54] For its part, India chartered its own course in Afghanistan, crafting strategies independent of the wishes and desires of the US and ISAF.

Whether it is the streets of Kabul or within the many offices at ISAF Headquarters, India's contribution to rebuilding the Afghan state has not gone unnoticed.[55] The difference between India and the many other contributing nations is one of intent. For ISAF, development goes hand-in-hand with what is famously called counter-insurgency (COIN)-contracting.[56] Development monies, sometimes hundreds of millions of dollars, are distributed depending on whether the receiving party can alter the political dynamics. For instance, certain tribal groupings might be preferred to others if they serve to increase stability in a particular locale. Contracts-in-exchange-for-stability is a commonly held view amongst most NATO nations.[57]

While a lot of the development funds are used to construct key infrastructure,[58] the politics of fund disbursement has gone some way in convincing local Afghans that the US and ISAF, with an eye to a timely withdrawal, are more interested in political deals with key ISAF-friendly parties than they are interested in funding development per se.[59] On the other hand, India's advantage is that, on the ground, it has refused to work with or even engage either ISAF or the US. Despite the many meetings and seminars with US and British officials in Washington, London, and New Delhi, India is steering its own course in Afghanistan.

---

[54] General Stanley McChrystal, Commander's Initial Assessment, August 30, 2009, pp. 2–10. Available at http://media.washingtonpost.com/wp-srv/politics/documents/Assessment_Redacted_092109.pdf, accessed on May 18, 2012.

[55] These observations are based on the author's personal interactions with both local Afghan's as well as senior ISAF officers, Kabul, August, 2010.

[56] Author's interview with a very senior British officer, Regional Command (South), Kandahar, August 2010.

[57] Author's interview with development expert, Kabul, August 2010.

[58] This observation is based on an extensive study of planning documents at ISAF HQ and RC (S) HQ, August 2010.

[59] Author's interview with the head of a local media company, Kabul, August 2010.

Afghanistan illustrates the fact that as India's power metric (economic or political) rises, and its ability to actively engage in neighbouring nations increases, it is most comfortable following its own path. As one senior US intelligence official put it, 'in Afghanistan, India demonstrates the archetype of remaining non-aligned yet relevant'.[60] Distrustful of Western designs and scheming, India's rise is increasingly marked by a keen sense of independence and the ability to judge events on its merits and demerits. Working with the US on the top-end of policy – military-to-military contacts and nuclear legislation – but maintaining a distance on matters of 'ground-policy' is a rarity in international relations. Indeed, as representatives of any ISAF-member state in Afghanistan will admit, policy initiatives within the coalition are often hijacked by the massive influence brought to bear by the US. One only has to turn to Pakistan to appreciate how a model of dependency can severely impact the ability of a government to say no to the US.

Conclusion

There is little doubt that India's approach to the US has transformed in the past 60 or so years. Unlike the first thirty years following Indian independence, the last thirty have been marked by attempts to build a strong diplomatic relationship between the world's oldest and largest democracies. Yet, the hard work of deepening (in terms of enlarging the remit of discussions) and substantiating the dialogue (by way of realising groundbreaking agreements) has by no means stifled India's ability to independently make key foreign policy decisions.

Equality rather than disproportion defines this burgeoning relationship, where the power disparity has been transcended by the need for real engagement. No doubt serious differences exist. This is clear in the incongruent views expressed by representatives of the two governments in multilateral forums. Whether it is the case of climate change, the lending practices of the International Monetary Fund (IMF), intervention in Libya, or the issue of Palestinian membership in the UN, it is obvious that India and the US do not necessarily agree on all the pressing questions in international politics.

---

[60] Author's interview with senior US intelligence official, ISAF HQ, Kabul, August 2010.

However, the India–US divergence is not new. Over time, disagreement has actually strengthened a relationship marked by tough, sometimes bitter, but ultimately enduring exchanges between two aberrant conversationalists. In the years to come, calls for India–US co-operation based on shared interests will undoubtedly be subjected to hard-headed negotiations. India has historically maintained a policy stance in support of key national objectives, whether in Korea, Iraq or Afghanistan. It has always rebuffed suggestions to join alliances or act like an ally. Looking to the future, there is a greater need to develop the existing India–US conversation rather than insist right away on convergence and the need for co-operation.

13

INDIA, AFGHANISTAN AND THE 'END GAME'?

Shanthie Mariet D'Souza*

India's role in post-9/11 Afghanistan has been a subject of intense internal policy deliberations. On one hand, India is seen as needing to play a critical role in the reconstruction of the war-ravaged country; on the other hand, India's growing influence in Afghanistan as a result of its aid diplomacy is thought to have increased Pakistan's real or imagined concerns of encirclement in what it perceives to be its 'strategic backyard'. This apparently 'zero-sum' geopolitical rivalry between India and Pakistan, dubbed by Western analysts as the 'new great game', is a source of further instability.

India's interests in post-9/11 Afghanistan have centred on the support for a democratic and pluralistic government, creating the economic, political, and social conditions in which extremism and terrorism will be reduced, helping connect Afghanistan as a land bridge that would yield economic benefits to the region. To achieve these objectives, India has adopted a 'soft power' approach consisting of developmental aid, civilian capacity building, revival of its cultural and historical linkages with Afghanistan, and working for the trade and energy integration of the war-ravaged country with South and Central Asia. This role, which has been well received by the Afghans, has important lessons for the international community for the long-term stabilisation of Afghanistan. However, as the discourse on the 'end game' gains momentum, whether India's interests can be defended and its role in Afghanistan can be sustained or even expanded, is a subject of growing importance in the strategic debate in New Delhi.

---

* This chapter is a revised version of an earlier working paper – 'India, Afghanistan and the "End Game?"', Working Paper No. 124 (March 14, 2011), Institute of South Asian Studies (ISAS), National University of Singapore.

India, Afghanistan and the Cold War

Most of the commentators on India's foreign policy bemoan the absence of a 'grand strategy'[1] as a factor which has impeded India's rise as a major power on the global stage. Contrary to such perceptions, a brief survey of India's relations with Afghanistan indicates that there has been a constant search for 'the right balance between force and diplomacy, functional and political criteria'.[2] Peace and stability in Afghanistan have remained important foreign policy objectives for India. Being members of the Non-Aligned Movement (NAM), both countries maintained a posture of 'neutrality' during the Cold War. Afghanistan's neutrality was expressed as adherence to its traditional policy of *bi-tarafi*,[3] an effort to balance its relations with the great powers, India's in non-alignment. The signing of a friendship treaty in 1950 between India and Afghanistan paved the way for development of New Delhi's links with King Zahir Shah's regime which continued till the late 1970s.

The Soviet intervention in Afghanistan, which brought the Cold War to India's doorsteps, spurred immense diplomatic activity in New Delhi. According to a well-known commentator, 'Never before in the history of Indian diplomacy was there so much groping for ideas and directions. Never before was India's foreign policy an act of sterner choice'.[4] There were serious worries over great power confrontation and militarisation in the region, especially with US arms supplied to Pakistan after the Soviet intervention. J. N. Dixit, former Indian Ambassador to Afghanistan, noted that Indian Prime

---

[1] George K. Tanham, *Indian Strategic Thought: An Interpretive Essay* (Santa Monica: RAND, 1992). Available at http://www.rand.org/pubs/reports/2007/R4207.pdf, accessed on August 20, 2010.

[2] Srinath Raghavan, Virtues of Being Vague', *Asian Age,* January 7, 2010. Available at http://www.deccanchronicle.com/dc-comment/virtues-being-vague-973, accessed on August 20, 2010.

[3] For much of the 20th century, the rulers of Afghanistan highlighted the approach of neutrality, as expressed by King Nadir Shah in 1931: 'The best and most fruitful policy that one can imagine for Afghanistan is a policy of neutrality. Afghanistan must give its neighbours assurances of its friendly attitudes while safeguarding the right of reciprocity.'

[4] Bhabani Sen Gupta, *The Afghan Syndrome: How to Live with Soviet Power* (New Delhi: Vikas Publishing House, 1982), p. 106.

Minister Indira Gandhi's 'reservations about the Soviet intervention in Afghanistan in December 1979 was tempered by the valid perception that this intervention had taken place only because Pakistan and Saudi Arabia, backed by the US, were trying to subvert a critical exercise being undertaken by a segment of Afghan society to transform their country from its semi-medieval predicament into a modern society'.[5]

Historical anecdotes suggest that despite India's muted public opposition to the Soviet intervention in Afghanistan, India did register its displeasure at various private forums.[6] According to former Foreign Secretary, M.K. Rasgotra, 'There was no international support for the Soviet intervention. In fact, Moscow's intentions and motives were suspect even in friendly countries ... Indira Gandhi [told] Brezhnev in Moscow in October 1982 that he should withdraw Russian troops from Afghanistan; the sooner the better'.[7] India's ambivalent public posture, however, dented its international credibility and cost it good will amongst the Afghan people.[8]

---

[5] Author's discussion with former Indian Ambassadors to Afghanistan, Ambassador J. N. Dixit in New Delhi (October 2001) and Ambassador I. P. Khosla in New Delhi (January 2011). Also see J. N. Dixit, *India's Foreign Policy 1947–2003* (New Delhi: Picus Books, 2003), p. 137; J. N. Dixit, *An Afghan Diary: Zahir Shah to Taliban* (New Delhi: Konark Publishers, 2000); I. P. Khosla, 'India and Afghanistan,' in Atish Sinha and Madhup Mohta, eds, *Indian Foreign Policy: Challenges and Opportunities* (New Delhi: Academic Foundation, 2007).

[6] G. S. Bhargava, *South Asian Security after Afghanistan* (Lexington: Lexington Books, 1983).

[7] In response, according to Mr Rasgotra, Brezhnev had said Taraki had been asking him for 10,000 Russian troops, that for a time he had repeatedly rejected the request but finally sent ten thousand troops and now there were one hundred thousand of them there. He added, 'I do not know what they are doing there, I want to get out of Afghanistan, you know the area better, show me a way'. Indira Gandhi had responded, 'Mr Secretary General, the way out is the same as the way in'. See Maharajakrishna Rasgotra, 'Afghanistan: The Way Out; Give Guarantees for its Neutrality', *The Tribune*, December 31, 2009. Available at http://www.tribuneindia.com/2009/20091231/edit.htm#4, accessed on August 25, 2010. Maharajakrishna Rasgotra, 'Afghanistan: The March of Folly', *The Hindu*, June 11, 2010.

[8] Surjit Mansingh, *India's Search for Power: Indira Gandhi's Foreign Policy 1966–1982* (New Delhi: Sage, 1984) p. 158; P. S. Ghosh and R. Panda,

During the Soviet intervention, ensuring peace and stability in Afghanistan remained an important foreign policy objective for India. Criticising the external powers for jeopardising peace and development in the region, Indian Prime Minister Rajiv Gandhi, at a joint session of Congress in June 1985, said: 'Outside interference and intervention have put in jeopardy the stability, security and progress of the region. We stand for a political settlement in Afghanistan that ensures sovereignty, integrity, independence and non-aligned status, and enables the refugees to return their homes in safety and honour.'[9] He asserted, 'India could not remain indifferent to the developments which had brought the confrontation of major powers to its doorstep'.[10]

Despite the deterioration of the political situation in the region, relations between India and Afghanistan, especially on trade, banking, industry, sports, education and cultural exchanges, continued uninterrupted. The signing of an agreement on February 20, 1984 in Kabul between the two countries envisaged several 'measures for expanding and diversifying bilateral trade and for establishing direct contacts between the banks of the two countries'.[11] A cultural exchange programme planned for 1985–87 between the two countries was signed in New Delhi on August 7, 1985. India agreed to provide scholarships to Afghan nationals for doctoral studies and fellowships for visiting scholars for training in public co-operation and child development. India also agreed to impart training to Afghan nationals in the repair and preservation of historical monuments and rare manuscripts. Further, both countries agreed to undertake joint research and teaching programmes. India promised to strengthen the programme of Afghan studies, hold film weeks, and

---

'Domestic Support for Mrs. Gandhi's Afghanistan Policy: The Soviet Factor in Indian Politics', *Asian Survey*, 23, 3, pp. 261–63.

[9] Quoted in Shelton U. Kodikara, 'Role of Extra-Regional Powers and South Asian Security', in Sridhar K. Khatri, ed., *Regional Security in South Asia* (Kathmandu: Centre for Nepal and Asian Studies, Tribhuvan University, 1987), p. 50.

[10] Satish Kumar, ed., *Yearbook on India's Foreign Policy 1989* (New Delhi: Sage, 1990), p. 31.

[11] Satish Kumar, 'India and the World: Trends and Events', in Satish Kumar, ed., *Yearbook on India's Foreign Policy 1983–84* (New Delhi: Sage, 1986), p. 25.

supply textbooks.¹² It also agreed to assist Afghanistan in the expansion of its health institutions and provide equipment worth INR 2 million, which included setting up a 300-bed maternity hospital and expanding the India-aided Institute of Child Health in Kabul. India promised to supply medicine worth INR 200,000 every year and to add ten more sheds to an industrial estate in Kabul.¹³

As political reconciliation began to take place in Afghanistan, Foreign Minister Abdul Wakil visited New Delhi on February 7, 1987 and briefed Indian leaders including Prime Minister Rajiv Gandhi on the reconciliation moves.¹⁴ Three months later, in May 1987, the eighth session of the Indo-Afghan Joint Commission was held in Kabul. Both countries decided to establish direct banking arrangements, closer co-operation between trading organisations and intensify industrial co-operation. In addition, India also agreed to set up a cultural centre in the Indian Embassy in Kabul.¹⁵ The Afghan Government endorsed India's role as an important stakeholder in conflict resolution. On March 3, 1989, Afghanistan's Ambassador to the UN, Shah Mohammad Dost, said in his address to the press at the UN, 'India is a leading country of the region and has a vital stake in what happens there. It has an important role in ensuring that the problems of the region are resolved'.¹⁶

Following the Soviet withdrawal from Afghanistan, India continued to support the Soviet-backed Najibullah Government in Afghanistan.¹⁷ On 4 May 1989, Afghan President Najibullah visited India and held discussions on the Geneva Accords with Prime Minister Rajiv Gandhi, culminating in the call for the implementation of the Geneva Accords. On September 5, 1989, an agreement

---

¹² 'Cultural Exchanges with Afghanistan', *Asian Recorder*, 31, 44 (29 October–4 November 1985), p. 18580.

¹³ Ibid.

¹⁴ Ministry of External Affairs, New Delhi, *Annual Report 1986–87*, p. 9.

¹⁵ Satish Kumar, 'India and the World: Survey of Events', in Satish Kumar, ed., *Yearbook on India's Foreign Policy 1987/1988* (New Delhi: Sage, 1988), p. 45.

¹⁶ Kumar, ed., *Yearbook on India's Foreign Policy 1989*, p. 31.

¹⁷ Barbara Crossette, 'India to Provide Aid to Government in Afghanistan', *The New York Times*, March 7, 1989. Available at www.nytimes.com/1989/03/07/world/india-to-provide-aid-to-government-in-afghanistan.html, accessed on August 12, 2010.

to establish a Joint Business Council was signed between the Federation of Indian Chambers of Commerce and Industry (FICCI) and the Afghan Chamber of Commerce and Industry (ACCI) with a view 'to provide for an institutional framework for augmenting India's trade with Afghanistan'.[18]

Regular high-level exchange visits between India and Afghanistan continued throughout the 1990s. Agreements signed between the two countries included co-operation between agricultural institutes, telecommunications and cultural exchanges, and the prevention of trafficking in narcotics drugs and psychotropic substances.[19] With the objective of rebuilding the social and economic fibre of war-ravaged Afghanistan, India announced a slew of new projects, such as the construction of a 300-bed gynaecological and obstetrics hospital, and additional industrial sheds together with enhanced co-operation in agriculture, cartography, meteorology, and tourism.[20]

The increased bonhomie between the two countries continued until the entry of the Taliban onto the Afghan political scene. Following the fall of the communist government in Kabul, Prime Minister Narasimha Rao attempted to engage the warring mujahidin and moderate the differences between New Delhi and various Afghan power-brokers.[21] This policy recalibration continued until the Taliban captured power in 1996. In September that year, India shut down its diplomatic mission in Kabul after the embassy was vandalised. Like most countries, India did not recognise the Taliban. Only Saudi Arabia, Pakistan, and the United Arab Emirates recognised the new regime. After the Taliban consolidated its hold on Afghanistan, India maintained minimal contact with the country, mostly through support to the internationally recognised United Islamic Front (UIF), popularly known as the Northern Alliance.[22]

---

[18] Kumar, ed., *Yearbook on India's Foreign Policy 1989*, pp. 31–32.
[19] Ibid., p. iv.
[20] Ibid., p. 75.
[21] Prime Minister Manmohan Singh's visit to Kabul in May 2011 is seen to have reset India's Afghan policy to its pristine moorings. M. K. Bhadrakumar, 'Manmohan Singh Resets Afghan Policy', *The Hindu*, May 16, 2011.
[22] The United Islamic Front (UIF) included forces and leaders from different political backgrounds as well as from all Afghan ethnicities including Tajiks, Pashtuns, Uzbeks, Hazaras or Turkmens. From the Taliban conquest

India's brief interaction with the Taliban during the hijacking of Indian Airlines Flight IC 814 on December 24, 1999, which had landed in Kandahar after taking off from Kathmandu, left behind painful memories. The ensuing eight-day saga of hostage swap negotiations was made contingent on the release of three Pakistani terrorists held in Indian prisons. The protracted negotiations ended with Indian Foreign Minister Jaswant Singh personally delivering the three terrorists in exchange for the passengers.[23] Within days, the terrorists were roaming free in Pakistan. One of the released terrorists, Maulana Masood Azhar, went on to establish the Jaish-e-Mohammad (JeM). The JeM has been identified as being involved in several terrorist strikes in Jammu and Kashmir and beyond, including the attack on Indian Parliament in December 2001.[24] India's opposition to the Taliban stems not just from its links to Pakistan but also the support it provided to terrorism in India.

India in Afghanistan after 9/11

India's interests in Afghanistan after the terror strikes of September 11, 2001 need to be viewed in the context of its concerns over terrorism emanating from the extremely volatile Pakistan–Afghanistan border and spilling into India. A strong, stable, and democratic Afghanistan would reduce the dangers of extremist violence and terrorism destabilising the region. New Delhi's worries are linked to its view that Pakistan's objective in Afghanistan is to assure itself of 'strategic depth' by reinstalling a pliant Taliban regime.

---

in 1996 until November 2001, the UIF controlled roughly 30 per cent of Afghanistan's population. For further details on the rationale behind India's support to the Northern Alliance, see H. M. Ansari, 'Afghanistan', in Jyotindra N. Dixit and Shailendra K. Singh, eds, *External Affairs: Cross-border Relations* (New Delhi: Roli Books, 2005), p. 183; C. Christine Fair, 'India in Afghanistan and Beyond: Opportunities and Constraints' A Century Foundation Report, 2010. Available at http://tcf.org/publications/2010/9/india-in-afghanistan-and-beyond-opportunities-and-constraints/pdf, accessed on January 11, 2011.

[23] John Cherian, 'Failure of Diplomacy', *Frontline*, 17, 1, January 8–21, 2000.

[24] Praveen Swami, 'Terrorism in Jammu and Kashmir in Theory and Practice', *India Review*, 2, 3 (July 2003), pp. 55–88.

Following the ouster of the Taliban in 2001, India renewed its diplomatic ties with Kabul and reopened its mission and four consulates in Mazar-e-Sharif, Jalalabad, Kandahar and Herat. India adopted a 'soft power approach' in the reconstruction process of Afghanistan.[25] Steering clear of a military role, India concentrated on developmental aid, civilian and administrative capacity building, the re-establishment of cultural and historical links, and, for the longer term, trying to position its relationship with Afghanistan in the context of its energy and trade interests in Central Asia.

With the establishment of an interim government in Afghanistan under President Hamid Karzai and following India's well-received role in the Bonn Conference of 2001, India announced USD100 million in reconstruction aid to Afghanistan.[26] Then Indian Prime Minister Atal Bihari Vajpayee told the Indian Parliament that India's goal was to have a 'maximum possible' role in the establishment of a broad-based, non-aligned and fully representative post-Taliban regime in Afghanistan.[27]

In December 2001, India moved in with humanitarian assistance by reopening the Indira Gandhi Children's Hospital in Kabul and sending in medical missions to assist in humanitarian work, donating three Airbus aircraft to enable the state run airline, Ariana, to resume operations and also donating hundreds of city buses for public transit facilities. Subsequently, India expanded its aid coverage to other crucial areas through both short- and long-term projects including in the educational field. Thus, India has provided 675 annual long-term university scholarships sponsored by the Indian Council for Cultural Relations (ICCR) for under-graduate and post-graduate studies in India. Similarly, it has granted an additional 675

---

[25] Shashi Tharoor, 'Indian Strategic Power: Soft', *The Huffington Post*, May 26, 2009. Available at http://www.huffingtonpost.com/shashi-tharoor/indian-strategic-power-so_b_207785.html, accessed on June 24, 2010.

[26] Author's discussions with Ambassador Satinder K. Lambah, Prime Minister of India's Special Envoy on Afghanistan, New Delhi, October 2010. See also, 'India Seeks Larger Role', *Asia Times Online*, November 28, 2001. Available at http://www.atimes.com/ind-pak/CK28Df03.html, accessed on September 12, 2010.

[27] 'India Seeks Larger Role', *Asia Times Online*, November 28, 2001. Available at http://www.atimes.com/ind-pak/CK28Df03.html, accessed on April 1, 2012.

annual short-term India Technical and Educational Co-operation (ITEC) training scholarships. These are targeted at Afghan public servants who are interested in enrolling in Indian technical and professional institutions.[28]

India's developmental involvement in Afghanistan has been costly but has generated tremendous goodwill locally.[29] Unlike other international donors, who have relied on their own agencies and subcontracting, thereby creating parallel structures of governance while doing little to extend the writ of the Afghan Government, most of India's aid is currently channelled through the Afghan Government and works in conjunction with local needs. In contrast, Western aid resources have returned to the donor countries, a classic example of 'phantom' aid. Whether it is high-visibility infrastructure projects in the north and west of Afghanistan or the small-scale, low-visibility projects in the south and east, the emphasis has been on local participation and capacity building. India's wide-ranging assistance programme, provided directly to the Afghan Government, is designed to maximise Afghan participation both at the government and community levels while maintaining a low visibility. For example, India has actively provided assistance to women's groups through self-employment generation schemes as well as health and capacity building in Kabul and the western province of Herat. As a long-term stakeholder in rebuilding the social and economic

---

[28] 'India–Afghanistan Relations', Ministry of External Affairs, Government of India, January 2011. Available at http://meaindia.nic.in/meaxpsite/pressrelease/2011/01/bilateralafganistan.pdf, accessed on April 1, 2012.

[29] Author's interviews and discussions with the Afghan Government officials and locals in various Afghan provinces (May–June 2007, October 2010, March 2011, May–June 2011, October 2011, and January–February 2012) indicated an appreciation of India's role in rebuilding their country. Opinion polls consistently reveal that Afghans rate India as the most favourable foreign presence in their country. Shubhajit Roy, 'With Thumbs Up from Afghans, India Explores More Areas of Aid', *The Indian Express*, January 5, 2010; Tom A. Peter, 'India Outdoes US Aid Efforts in Afghanistan', *Global Post*, September 9, 2010. Available at http://www.globalpost.com/dispatch/afghanistan/100908/india-outdoes-us-aid-efforts-afghanistan, accessed on September 12, 2010; Shanthie Mariet D'Souza, 'Change the Pattern of Aid to Afghanistan', *IDSA Strategic Comments*, June 28, 2007. Available at http://www.idsa.in/profile/smdsouza?q=taxonomy/term/57, accessed on August 10, 2010.

fabric, India has found aid delivery through women's groups and tribal organisations to be effective.

In the difficult and insurgency prone Pushtun areas of the south and east, India is investing in small development projects (SDPs) in support of local needs, thereby ensuring greater local participation and ownership. This method of aid delivery has its roots in the Gandhian way of doing things at a community level. India's assistance has broad acceptance given the way aid is delivered, sensitive to the shared history, culture, and traditions of the two societies. In addition, unlike the Western countries, India avoids taking a judgmental or normative stance on domestic issues such as corruption, nepotism, cronyism, or the ineffectiveness of the Afghan government. A decade later, while the international community's involvement has come under scrutiny, the prudence of India's method of engagement has increasingly been understood, even emulated.[30]

Not all of India's aid is developmental; it is also dedicated to building or rebuilding infrastructure. India's strategic interests lie in the long-term stabilisation of Afghanistan. As part of a long-term strategy, India has invested substantially in infrastructure projects, in particular, power generation and roads. One of the most visible projects to be completed is the 218 km-long Zaranj-Delaram highway which connects landlocked Afghanistan to the Iranian Port of Chabahar. The road reduces Afghanistan's dependence on Pakistan by providing a potential alternate route linking Iran to Central Asia. Other large-scale, high-visibility infrastructure projects, primarily in the relatively stable north and west, include the installation of a transmission line bringing power to Kabul from the northern grid, the construction of a large hydro-electric dam in the province of Herat, and the construction of a new Afghan parliament building.[31]

Beyond developmental/infrastructural aid, India has invested heavily in administrative and civilain capacity building. Thus, during

---

[30] Shanthie Mariet D'Souza, 'India's Stake in Afghanistan', *The Journal of International Security Affairs*, 20 (Spring/Summer 2011), pp. 131–32.

[31] See Indian Ministry of External Affairs, 'India and Afghanistan: A Development Partnership', Public Diplomacy Division, Ministry of External Affairs, Government of India. Available at http://meaindia.nic.in or http://meakabul.nic.in, accessed on September 17, 2011.

the two-day visit to Kabul in August 2005, by Indian Prime Minister Manmohan Singh, leaders of both countries reiterated their commitment to building a new partnership for the 21st century. This included expanding bilateral co-operation to wide-ranging areas such as development, education, energy, trade, defence, fighting terrorism, and working towards the greater economic and cultural integration of South Asia. Probably the highlight of the visit, though, was the foundation-laying ceremony of the Afghan Parliament building to be built by India – a symbol of New Delhi's desire to play a catalysing role in the rebuilding of Afghanistan's democracy. Over the years, India has invested in addition in training and capacity building, working with legislators, parliamentary staff, and diplomats to develop the political sector. In addition to regular parliamentarian visits to India, more than twenty Indian civil servants served as coaches and mentors under the Capacity for Afghan Public Administration programme supported by the UNDP and the governments of Afghanistan and India.[32]

Over time, India has been active in reviving the historical and cultural ties with Afghanistan. As part of its cultural diplomacy, Indian musicians have been training young Afghans in musical instruments such as the tabla and the sitar. Joint musical performances have been organised both in Kabul and Jalalabad, cementing the cultural ties and historical traditions of the region.[33] Another way of engaging ordinary Afghans has been through sporting relations, particularly in cricket and football.[34]

Finally, as a major regional and economic power, with ambitions of extending its influence beyond its immediate neighbourhood, India has worked towards reviving the role of Afghanistan as a land bridge connecting South Asia with Central Asia to tap energy resources and augment trade. India has also promoted economic

---

[32] 'India–Afghanistan Relations', Ministry of External Affairs, Government of India.

[33] Author's interview with Gul Agha Sherzai, Governor of Nangarhar Province, and interactions with locals at the India–Afghan musical concert (Jalalabad, October 12, 2010).

[34] 'Subroto Cup: Afghan Girls in Fray; Prize Money Increased', *The Times of India*, November 2, 2011. Afghanistan sent one team each for the under-17 years boys, under-14 years boys, and under-17 years girls Subroto Cup Football Tournament in New Delhi in November 2011.

integration with Afghanistan through SAARC.³⁵ Through the Agreement on Strategic Partnership (ASP) of 2011 both countries have committed 'to deepening and diversifying co-operation in sectors such as agriculture, rural development, mining, industry, energy, information technology, communications, transport, including civil aviation.' The Agreement is a reiteration of India's commitment to Afghanistan's economic progress and also its development as a bridge between South Asia and Central Asia. Two Memoranda of Understanding (MoUs) were signed for the development of minerals and natural gas in Afghanistan, which is said to hold mineral deposits worth USD 1 trillion. A consortium led by state-run Steel Authority of India (SAIL) could invest up to USD 6 billion in the Hajigak mines in the province of Bamiyan.³⁶ The product of the Turkmenistan–Afghanistan–Pakistan–India (TAPI) pipeline would be sold not just to India but would benefit other countries as well including Pakistan – an indication that India's role in Afghanistan may have collateral benefits for Pakistan and that not everything in zero-sum as between Indian and Pakistani involvement in that troubled country. A Preferential Trade Agreement was signed between India and Afghanistan in 2003, reducing customs duty on a range of goods. Bilateral trade has increased considerably as a result, worth over USD 600 million in 2011, with Indian markets absorbing the largest share of Afghan exports.³⁷

---

³⁵ These views and perceptions were gathered from interactions and discussions with senior Indian government officials in New Delhi and Kabul in October 2010. Also see, Gautam Mukhopadhaya, 'India', in Ashley J. Tellis and Aroop Mukharji, eds, *Is a Regional Strategy Viable in Afghanistan?* (Washington, D.C.: Carnegie Endowment for International Peace, 2010). Available at http://carnegieendowment.org/files/regional_approach.pdf, accessed on July 23, 2010; C. Christine Fair, 'India in Afghanistan and Beyond: Opportunities and Constraints', A Century Foundation Report, 2010. Available at http://tcf.org/publications/2010/9/india-in-afghanistan-and-beyond-opportunities-and-constraints/pdf, accessed on January 11, 2011.

³⁶ Sanjeev Miglani, 'Indian Firms Eye Huge Mining Investment in Afghanistan', *Reuters*, September 14, 2011. Available at http://www.reuters.com/article/2011/09/14/afghanistan-india-idUSL3E7KB02A20110914?feedType=RSS&feedName=everything&virtualBrandChannel=11563, accessed on October 11, 2011.

³⁷ See Press Trust of India, 'Afghanistan Seeks Indian Investment to Boost its Agri Sector', *Business Standard*, December 3, 2010. See also Asian

A crucial focus for India has been the development of a southern trade corridor linking India with Iran, Afghanistan, Central Asia, and Russia. The establishment of a bilateral trade and transit agreement between Tehran and Kabul, leading to the creation of the Chabahar Free Zone Authority (CFZA) in 2002, was an important benchmark for the southern trade corridor. While the 218 km Zaranj-Delaram road provides economic opportunities for India in those countries, it also provides Afghanistan with an alternative in reducing its dependence on Pakistan for transit facilities. This is of particular significance given the difficult trade and transit arrangements and bilateral relations between Afghanistan and Pakistan.[38] Additionally, it provides the international community with an alternative supply route through the northern distribution network (NDN), as the present routes through Pakistan are increasingly targeted by the insurgents.

To meet India's burgeoning energy needs, there is a view that it is vital to connect Afghanistan to energy-rich Central Asia. With this objective, India has been pursuing better relations with the Central Asian states. It has provided a USD17 million grant for the modernisation of a hydropower plant in Tajikistan and has signed a memorandum of understanding with Turkmenistan for a natural gas pipeline that will pass through Afghanistan and Pakistan.[39] Similarly several commercial ventures have been started. A Gas Pipeline Framework Agreement was signed by Turkmenistan, Afghanistan, Pakistan, and India in 2008 which envisages over a thousand miles

---

Development Bank, 'Key Indicators for Asia and the Pacific 2011,' p. 4. Available at http://www2.adb.org/Documents/Books/Key_Indicators/2011/pdf/AFG.pdf, accessed on March 29, 2012.

[38] The recognition of the Durand Line has remained problematic between Afghanistan and Pakistan. See Ralph H. Magnus and Eden Naby, *Afghanistan: Mullah, Marx and Mujahid* (Boulder, Co.: Westview Press, 2002); Barnett Rubin, *The Fragmentation of Afghanistan* (New Haven: Yale University Press, 2002); Mohib Ullah Durani and Ashraf Khan, 'Pakistan–Afghan Relations: Historic Mirror', *The Dialogue*, IV, 1 (Winter 2009) at http://www.qurtuba.edu.pk/thedialogue/The%20Dialogue/4_1/02_ashraf.pdf, accessed on August 18, 2010.

[39] Jayshree Bajoria, 'India-Afghanistan Relations', Backgrounder, *Council on Foreign Relations*, (July 22, 2009). Available at http:// www.cfr.org/publication/17474/indiaafghanistan_relations.html, accessed on August 25, 2010.

of pipe connecting Turkmenistan's natural gas fields with energy-deficient South Asia.[40] Importantly, it could have the effect of binding the conflicting countries in a mutually interdependent security-economic relationship.

In sum, since 2001, India has been the 'fifth or sixth largest'[41] bilateral donor country, having pledged USD 2 billion and invested in diverse areas including healthcare, education, infrastructure, social welfare, the training of politicians, diplomats and policemen, and institution building.

Challenges to India's Role in Afghanistan: Pakistan and the Taliban

Geopolitical rivalry continues to shape Pakistan's response to the increasing bonhomie between India and Afghanistan. While Afghanistan looks towards India for greater co-operation, Pakistan appears determined to stop the relationship from deepening and is continually in search of ways and means to regain its 'strategic depth'. It typically sees the Indian presence as inimical to its interests and India's developmental assistance and the goodwill it has generated among Afghans with a suspicion bordering on paranoia.[42]

---

[40] John Foster, 'Afghanistan, the TAPI Pipeline, and Energy Geopolitics', *The Journal of Energy Security*, March 23, 2010. Available at http://www.ensec.org/index.php?option=com_content&view=article&id=233:afghanistan-the-tapi-pipeline-and-energy-geopolitics&catid=103:energysecurityissuecontent&Itemid=358, accessed on April 2, 2012.

[41] Statement in the Parliament by the Minister of State in the Ministry of External Affairs, Government of India, on December 7, 2011. Available at http://mea.gov.in/mystart.php?id=100518693, accessed on March 29, 2012.

[42] Gautam Mukhopadhaya, 'India'. Sumit Ganguly and Nicholas Howenstein, 'India Pakistan Rivalry in Afghanistan', *Journal of International Affairs*, 63, 1 (Fall/Winter 2009), pp. 127–40. Available at http://jia.sipa.columbia.edu/files/jia/Ganguly_Howenstein.pdf, accessed on July 21, 2010. Also see Fahmida Ashraf, 'India–Afghanistan Relations: Post-9/11', *Strategic Studies*, 27, 2 (2007), pp. 90–102. Available at http://catalogo.casd.difesa.it/GEIDEFile/INDIA%C3%90AFGHANISTAN_RELATIONS_POST-9-11.HTM?Archive=191494691967&File=INDIA%ADAFGHANISTAN+RELATIONS+POST-9-11_HTM, accessed on November 8, 2010.

Pakistan's military and intelligence establishment has approached the various wars in and around Afghanistan as a function of its main institutional and national security interests, 'first and foremost, balancing India'.[43] For Pakistan, a pliant regime in Afghanistan under Pakistani influence, or at least a benign Afghanistan, is a matter of overriding strategic importance.[44] Fearing increased Indian influence in Afghanistan and beyond, Islamabad has denied India an overland trade and transit facilities, thereby compelling India to rely on the Iranian alternative.

The confidential report by General Stanley McChrystal, the former commander of US forces in Afghanistan, noted that 'Indian political and economic influence is increasing in Afghanistan, including significant development efforts and financial investment.' While acknowledging, 'Indian activities largely benefit the Afghan people', the report pointed out 'increasing Indian influence in Afghanistan is likely to exacerbate regional tensions and encourage Pakistani countermeasures in Afghanistan or India'.[45] This line of thinking finds resonance among Western analysts, who posit that 'the road to peace in Afghanistan runs not just through Kabul and Islamabad, but Delhi as well.'[46] This, in turn, feeds Pakistani threat perceptions

---

[43] Barnett R. Rubin, 'Saving Afghanistan', *Foreign Affairs*, (January/February 2007), pp. 57–78.

[44] George Friedman, 'WikiLeaks and the Afghan War', *STRATFOR*, July 27, 2010. Available at http://www.stratfor.com/weekly/20100726_wikileaks_and_afghan_war, accessed on August 25, 2010.

[45] Stanley A. McChrystal, 'COMISAF Initial Assessment' (Kabul: ISAF Headquarters, August 30, 2009). Available at http://www.globalsecurity.org/military/library/report/2009/090830-afghan-assessment/090830-afghan-assessment.pdf, accessed on August 25, 2010.

[46] Pakistan is trying to actively project the Indian threat to the coalition through private and public diplomacy and linking the Afghan issue with India–Pakistan relations and the issue of Jammu and Kashmir. See C. Christine Fair, 'India in Afghanistan and Beyond: Opportunities and Constraints', A Century Foundation Report, 2010. Available at http://tcf.org/publications/2010/9/india-in-afghanistan-and-beyond-opportunities-and-constraints/pdf, accessed on January 11, 2010. Also see Jeremy Kahn, 'India is Key Player in Afghan Conflict', *Newsweek*, October 19, 2009. Available at www.newsweek.com/blogs/wealth-of-nations/2009/10/19/india-is-key-player-in-afghan-conflict.html, accessed on August 25, 2010.

to the effect that India's presence in Afghanistan is intended to encircle Pakistan.

A dominant view in India is that Indian and Pakistani interests and actions in Afghanistan amount to a 'zero-sum' game. Pakistan's quest for 'strategic depth' in the 1970s, its role in the Taliban's advance to power in the 1990s, and its desire to regain its lost 'strategic depth' in the 2000s by providing sanctuary to the Afghan Taliban leadership are all seen by Indian analysts as part of Pakistan's desire to control what happens in Afghanistan as part of a larger India–Pakistan game. Islamabad's attempts to broker talks between the Afghan Government and sections of the Taliban to ensure a pro-Pakistan dispensation in Kabul after the withdrawal of the Western coalition forces has compounded Indian fears of Pakistani intentions.

Beyond Pakistan, the recurring attacks by the Taliban and its affiliates on Indian personnel pose a major challenge for India. Investing in large developmental projects in the insurgency-affected provinces in south and east Afghanistan has become hugely risky. The killing of Kasula Suryanarayana, an Indian telecommunications engineer in Zabul Province in April 2006, and, earlier, the killing of Maniappan Kutty, a driver working with the Border Roads Organisation (BRO) project on the Zaranj-Delaram Highway in 2005, have dramatised the risks. Although such incidents have only been sporadic, they continue to raise concerns about the safety of Indians working on reconstruction projects in Afghanistan.[47]

The gruesome and high profile symbolic attacks on the Indian Embassy in Afghanistan, in July 2008 and October 2009 continue to highlight India's vulnerabilities in Afghanistan.[48] Intended as a

---

[47] According to the Ministry of External Affairs estimates (in 2007), there are approximately 3,500 Indian nationals working in various private and public sector projects in Afghanistan. See Statement of the External Affairs Minister Pranab Mukherjee in Rajya Sabha on May 15, 2007. Available at http://mea.gov.in/mystart.php?id=100512642, accessed on April 13, 2012.

[48] The growing bonhomie between New Delhi and Kabul, coupled with the increased presence of India's development projects in Afghanistan, remains the target of the Taliban-led insurgency, which includes a huge array of insurgent and anti-government forces operating in tandem beyond south and east Afghanistan. While the Taliban-affiliated Haqqani network, aided by Pakistan's Inter-Services Intelligence (ISI), was blamed for the

warning to India to downsize its role, these attacks are aimed at raising the costs of the hearts-and-minds policy. After a brief hiatus, India resumed its much-acclaimed medical mission in Afghanistan which was scaled down following the February 2010 terror attack in Kabul that left nine Indians dead.[49]

After the ouster of the Taliban regime in 2001, Pakistan has repeatedly questioned India's growing profile in Afghanistan and has launched a diplomatic campaign aimed at reducing New Delhi's influence. Mindful of the difficulties of doing so and of the possible reactions of Islamabad and Washington, India has steered clear of any military involvement in Afghanistan, in spite of Afghan interest in Indian help.

Since 9/11, New Delhi's policy has broadly been in congruence with the US goal of destroying the Taliban-Al Qaeda combine and instituting a democratic regime in Kabul. However, nine years later, the Taliban has been able to regroup and resurge, in addition to further intensifying its linkages with anti-India groups based in Pakistan. A worrisome development has been expansion of the Lashkar-e-Taiba's (LeT) activities beyond Kunar and Nooristan provinces to other parts of Afghanistan, which could emerge as a centre of anti-Indian and anti-Western operations.[50] Thus, one stream of Indian

---

July 2008 attack on the Indian Embassy, the Taliban claimed responsibility for the October 2009 attack. See Shanthie Mariet D'Souza, 'Securing India's Interests in Afghanistan', *The Hindu*, October 23, 2009; Emily Wax, 'India's Eager Courtship of Afghanistan Comes at a Steep Price', *The Washington Post*, April 3, 2010. Available at http://www.washingtonpost.com/wp-dyn/content/article/2010/04/02/AR2010040204313.html, accessed on September 2, 2010.

[49] India launched the medical missions in Afghanistan in 2001–02 and was operating five such missions in Kabul, Herat, Kandahar, Jalalabad and Mazar-e-Sharif. These missions reportedly have treated over 300,000 patients for free, mostly women and children. Though the Mazar-e-Sharif medical mission is functioning normally, the other four missions spread around war-torn Afghanistan have been temporarily suspended. The Taliban suicide attacks in two Kabul hotels killed six doctors of the 11-member medical team of these missions in February 2010. 'India to Resume Medical Mission Work in Afghanistan', *The Times of India*, July 20, 2010.

[50] As military operations and drone attacks intensify in Pakistan's tribal areas, these groups increasingly operate from other parts of Afghanistan. Based on author's discussions with officials and locals from Nuristan province during a field visit to Afghanistan, October 2010.

thinking emphasises the need for India to use military and diplomatic tools to secure its 'outer periphery' or 'extended neighbourhood'.[51]

Thus, in April 2008, Afghanistan's Defence Minister, General Abdul Rahim Wardak visited New Delhi and met with his Indian counterpart, A. K. Antony, to discuss possible military co-operation.[52] Three years later, Wardak, who indicated that military supplies from India are under consideration, said in Delhi in June 2011 that his country 'will welcome any co-operation' in the field of 'training and helping' Afghan National Security Forces 'to be able to defend their country'.[53] Indian Defence Minister A. K. Antony confirmed India's commitment to building the capabilities of the Afghan National Security Forces (ANSF), composed of the Afghan National Army (ANA) and Afghan National Police (ANP), a commitment that found expression in the 2011 Strategic Partnership agreement.[54]

India has been particularly involved in assisting the ANP. This emphasis on police training is significant if the security situation in Afghanistan deteriorates considerably and the project of building a large Afghan army becomes infeasible or indeed if the army splinters.[55] Given that recruiting and sustaining a large Afghan army is an economically unviable project, a capable police force is essential. Not surprisingly, Afghanistan has repeatedly requested trainers,

---

[51] This stream of thinking is evident in the writings of K. Subrahmanyam, Brajesh Mishra, Ambassador G. Parathasarthy, Brigadier Gurmeet Kanwal, and others.

[52] Wardak also visited the headquarters of the Indian Army's 15th Corps located in Srinagar. STRATFOR reported that Wardak was seeking India's assistance in maintaining the Soviet-era helicopter gunships'. Afghanistan: Why India's Co-operation is a Problem for Pakistan', *STRATFOR*, April 11, 2008. Available at http://www.stratfor.com/memberships/114567/analysis/afghanistan_why_india_s_co-operation_problem_pakistan, accessed on January 15, 2010.

[53] 'India to Help Strengthen Afghan Security Forces', *Defence News*, June 3, 2011. Available at http://www.defencenews.in/defence-news-internal.asp?get=new&id=510 or 'India to Help Strengthen Afghan Security Forces', *Daily Outlook Afghanistan*, June 2, 2011.

[54] 'India Committed to Building the Capabilities of Afghan Security Forces', *The Hindu*, June 2, 2011.

[55] Anatol Lieven, 'Afghanistan: The Best Way to Peace', *The New York Review of Books*, February 9, 2012.

equipment, and capacity building for its police force.[56] In the south, there are requests for India's assistance in training Special Forces and in teaching techniques of community policing and police sensitisation programmes.[57]

India's involvement in Afghanistan has generated a fair amount of domestic debate, especially in the light of the vulnerabilities of Indian aid projects and personnel in Afghanistan. While some advocate the need to put 'boots on ground', others propound a continuation of the present aid policy vis-à-vis those who call for downsizing in case the US withdraws. A complete US withdrawal would not be in India's interest, but an outright Indian military response, say, of troop deployments, apart from its limited utility, would only confirm the propaganda of the Taliban and dissipate the goodwill that India has earned so far. Having steered clear of the military option and provided huge developmental assistance instead, India is seen as a friendly and neutral country with no ethnic affinities, unlike the neighbouring countries which have actively exploited ethnic ties and waged proxy wars in Afghanistan.

As talk of the end game in Afghanistan intensifies, there have been calls from various quarters for India to play a more active role.[58] Afghanistan is in some ways the test case of the extent to which India is willing to use its hard power to advance its strategic and commercial interests. Rahul Roy-Choudhury of the International Institute for Strategic Studies, London says: 'As India's influence grows it will become increasingly involved in the local politics of a foreign country. It cannot afford to see itself as an innocent bystander anymore.'[59] Similarly, former Indian diplomat Rajiv Sikri, criticising India's soft power approach, notes: 'Although India's security remains deeply

---

[56] Discussion with Sediq Sediqqi, Spokesman, Director of Communication, Ministry of Interior Affairs, Islamic Republic of Afghanistan, Kabul, October 8, 2011.

[57] Interview with General Abdul Raziq Achikzai, Chief of Police in Kandahar province, Kandahar, October 5, 2011.

[58] Frank Schell, 'The U.S. Needs a New Af-Pak Strategy', *Far East Economic Review*, November 10, 2009. Available at http://www.feer.com/international-relations/20098/november53/The-U.S.-Needs-a-New-Af-Pak-Strategy, accessed on January 11, 2011.

[59] Quoted in Somini Sengupta, 'Afghan Bombing Sends Stark Message to India', *The New York Times*, July 9, 2008.

affected by what happens in Afghanistan, India's disadvantage is that it is not involved in Afghanistan's security in any meaningful way.'[60]

The Agreement on Strategic Partnership (ASP) signed between the two countries in 2011 has provided a much-needed institutional mechanism in terms of 'regular foreign office consultations and strategic dialogue' to sustain the engagement beyond 2014, the cut off year for the drawdown of American forces.[61] The signing of the Strategic Partnership is a step in the direction of being more active on security. It was the first country to sign such an agreement.[62] The Agreement is a sign of India's risk-taking ability and to that extent can be seen as a sign of the maturing of India's foreign policy. In the past few years there has been a gradual realisation that South Asia and the immediate neighbourhood is vital, and India has moved ahead with several initiatives in Bangladesh, Myanmar and Sri Lanka. The Strategic Partnership with distant Afghanistan has signalled that New Delhi is ready to work closely with countries even in adverse and difficult conditions.

At the other end of the spectrum, there are those who warn that India may fall into a 'reputation trap' and be susceptible to overstretch in a region which is perceived as Pakistan's backyard. Western analysts who have internalised Pakistan's concerns call for a downsizing of India's presence to assuage Pakistan's fear and concerns.[63]

---

[60] Quoted in Tim Sullivan, 'India's Afghan Endgame – and What it Means for the U.S.', *Centre for Defense Studies*, April 19, 2010. Available at http://www.defensestudies.org/cds/india%E2%80%99s-afghan-endgame-and-what-it-means-for-the-u-s/, accessed on April 13, 2012.

[61] 'Text of Agreement on Strategic Partnership between the Republic of India and the Islamic Republic of Afghanistan', Ministry of External Affairs, Government of India, October 4, 2011. Available at http://www.mea.gov.in/mystart.php?id=100018343&pid=2339, accessed on October 5, 2011; Shanthie Mariet D'Souza, 'Indian-Afghan Strategic Partnership: Perceptions from the Ground', *The Af-Pak Channel, Foreign Policy*, October 26, 2011. Available at http://afpak.foreignpolicy.com/posts/2011/10/26/indian_afghan_strategic_partnership_perceptions_from_the_ground, accessed on October 27, 2011.

[62] India's partnership agreement came ahead of agreements with the US, UK, EU, France and others. Discussions with senior diplomats in New Delhi and Kabul, October 2011.

[63] Barnett R. Rubin and Ahmed Rashid, 'From Great Game to Grand Bargain: Ending Chaos in Afghanistan and Pakistan', *Foreign Affairs*,

In Indian diplomatic circles, there is a view that India's presence in Afghanistan is of questionable utility given that Pakistan will continue its proxy war against India from Afghanistan. There are those who therefore call for a redefinition of India's interests in Afghanistan, of a need to engage Pakistan, and of using various forms of 'leverage' to elicit responsible behaviour from Islamabad.[64] In the wake of the conclusion of the ASP, strategic thinkers like C. Raja Mohan forewarn that the partnership agreement 'is bound to add a new layer of complexity to the triangular relationship between New Delhi, Rawalpindi and Kabul.' He says, 'The big challenge for the prime minister is to signal India's determination to do all it can to strengthen Kabul's capacity to preserve its independence while dispelling the widespread perception that Delhi is eager to compete with Rawalpindi in Afghanistan'.[65]

Perhaps the last word should go to Prime Minister Manmohan Singh. For the Prime Minister, Afghanistan features heavily in his view of the future of regional economic integration, which he sees as benefiting Afghanistan, Pakistan, and India alike. In 2007, Singh spelled out his vision statement for the region when he said: 'I dream of a day, while retaining our respective national identities, one can have breakfast in Amritsar, lunch in Lahore and dinner in Kabul. That is how my forefathers lived. That is how I want our grandchildren to live'.[66]

In Search of a Political Solution: Reintegration and Reconciliation

As instability and violence in Afghanistan intensify and calls for a Western exit gather momentum, the Afghan Government and

---

(November–December 2008). Available at http://www.vfp143.org/lit/Afghanistan/ForeignAffairs-From_Great_Game_to_Grand_Bargain.pdf, accessed on April 13, 2012.

[64] Author's discussions with senior Indian officials, New Delhi, October 2010.

[65] C. Raja Mohan, 'Kabul Gameplan', *The Indian Express*, October 4, 2011.

[66] Sudhir Chadda, 'Manmohan's Dream Breakfast in Amritsar, Lunch in Lahore and Dinner in Kabul a Real Possibility', *India Daily*, January 8, 2007. Available at http://www.indiadaily.com/editorial/15067.asp, accessed on September 24, 2010.

international community have initiated parallel efforts at negotiations with the Taliban. While there has been a lack of clarity in the international community's attempts at finding a political solution to the Afghan war, New Delhi has indicated support for the Afghan-led reintegration process. In an interview with the Wall Street Journal on the sidelines of the UN General Assembly in New York in September 2009, Indian External Affairs Minister, S. M. Krishna said India did 'not believe that war can solve any problem and that applies to Afghanistan too.'[67] This line of thinking is indicative of New Delhi's recognition of the Afghan Government's efforts to build an inclusive political order much as the Indian government over the years has been involved in various such dialogues, negotiations, and reintegration mechanisms in dealing with its own insurgencies.

There have also been indications recently that New Delhi is supportive of President Karzai's reintegration overtures towards the tribal fighters. India's Foreign Secretary Nirupama Rao, addressing a closed door international seminar on Afghanistan in October 2009, declared that India would support the process of reintegrating individuals into the national mainstream – that is, India would back a dialogue with the moderate Taliban who agree to renounce violence. The Foreign Secretary stated, 'We support the Afghan Government's determination to integrate those willing to abjure violence and live and work within the parameters of the Afghan constitution.'[68] This change in stance, however, came with a qualification. Pakistan, which is widely believed to support the Taliban and provide shelter in Quetta to its leaders, would need to cease assistance to the Taliban. The concerns of New Delhi stem from the fact that the Pakistan military's continued support to the Afghan Taliban leadership, as a 'strategic asset', would make any meaningful reconciliation an exercise in futility.

In contrast to those favouring talks with the Taliban, following the February 2010 attack on Indians in Kabul, thinkers like the Indian Vice President Hamid Ansari, Pakistan–Afghanistan envoy Satinder Lambah and former diplomat Chinmay Gharekhan have

---

[67] 'Indian Minister Urges Afghan Political Settlement', *Wall Street Journal*, September 23, 2009. Available at http://online.wsj.com/article/SB125364105273431343.html, accessed on September 2, 2010.

[68] Ajai Shukla, 'India Supports Reconciliation with Taliban', *Business Standard*, October 8, 2009.

urged India to adopt a neutral position in Afghanistan. Former Foreign Secretary M. K. Rasgotra favours steering clear of India being involved in any reintegration efforts. 'Wisdom demands that this task of reintegration be left to President Hamid Karzai,' advises Rasgotra.[69] This line of thinking advocates staying out of internal Afghan politics and carrying on with the development effort.

New Delhi is keeping its door open with respect to a reconciliation effort involving various elements of the Taliban-led insurgency and is said to have reached out to a faction of Gulbuddin Hekmatyar's Hezb-e-Islami (HIG).[70] Given that many HIG members are now part of the Afghan Government, such gestures might not be entirely misplaced. New Delhi is attempting to revive its traditional relations with Pushtuns in the south by engaging second generation Pushtun leaders like Nangarhar Governor Gul Agha Sherzai and former Northern Alliance leaders like Marshal Fahim, Karim Khalili, and Mohammed Mohaqiq. India's expansion of SDPs in the insurgency prone south and east speaks volumes about the success of these local initiatives and the at least grudging assent of the local Taliban.[71]

As the possibility of negotiations with the Taliban gained momentum, New Delhi has continued to adjust its posture. In a significant shift of thinking, Prime Minister Manmohan Singh expressed support for Kabul's decision to begin an Afghan-led process of negotiation and reconciliation with the Taliban.[72] There is a growing

---

[69] Maharajakrishna Rasgotra, 'Afghanistan: The March of Folly', *The Hindu*, June 11, 2010.

[70] For further details on the Taliban insurgency, see Seth Jones, 'Counterinsurgency in Afghanistan', *RAND Counterinsurgency Study* 4 (Arlington, VA: RAND, 2008); Antonio Giustozzi, *Koran, Kalashnikov and Laptop: The Neo-Taliban Insurgency in Afghanistan* (New York: Columbia University Press, 2008); Ahmed Rashid, *Descent into Chaos: How the War Against Islamic Extremism is Being Lost in Pakistan, Afghanistan and Central Asia* (London: Penguin, 2008), pp. 240–61; C. Christine Fair and Seth G. Jones, 'Securing Afghanistan: Getting on Track', *United States Institute of Peace*, Working Paper , January 23, 2009. Available at http://library.usip.org/articles/1012068.1022/1.PDF, accessed on January 11, 2011.

[71] Taliban spokesman, Zabihullah Mujahid claimed the organization did not want India out of Afghanistan. See 'Taliban Say They Can "Reconcile" with India,' *The Times of India*, March 26, 2010.

[72] It should be noted that New Delhi emphasises 'Afghan led'. New Delhi does not support the involvement of other countries, individuals, and secret

recognition in New Delhi that negotiations with the Taliban will occur, as the West's desire to exit mounts. New Delhi's more flexible approach is reminiscent of the policy it adopted following Soviet withdrawal in 1989, when Prime Minister Rao committed India to deal with whosoever rose to power in Kabul, providing it with the flexibility to engage with various stakeholders in the future.

The Af-Pak Strategy, Transition, and Conditional Withdrawal/Drawdown of Forces

The Obama Administration's 'Af-Pak strategy' heightened expectations in Afghanistan of a renewed American commitment to stabilise the war-ravaged country. Its stated goal of 'disrupt, dismantle and destroy' the terrorist infrastructure was also seen as a positive turn by the Indian strategic community.

While India supports the effort at stabilisation in Afghanistan, it is clear that 'stability' continues to elude Afghanistan after a decade of a US involvement. There is universal acknowledgement now that security in Afghanistan is at its worst since 2001 even as the Western countries move towards disengagement. As a result, 'beyond a general commitment against terrorism, the US notion of "stability" would look very different from that envisaged by India'.[73]

There is a broad congruence in Indian and American interests in Afghanistan, but the US dependence on Pakistan continues to be a constant source of irritation in the relationship.[74] For instance, Brahma Chellaney warns, 'The US can never win in Afghanistan without first dismantling the Pakistani military's sanctuaries and sustenance infrastructure for the Taliban. The proposed surge could help the already-entrenched Taliban sharpen its claws while strengthening US logistics dependence on the Pakistani military,

---

negotiations. See MEA Statements, 'Address by Prime Minister to the Joint Session of the Parliament of Afghanistan', Ministry of External Affairs, May 13, 2011. Available at http://www.mea.gov.in/outgoing-visit-detail.htm?354/Address+by+Prime+Minister+to+the+Joint+Session+of+the+Parliament+of+Afghanistan, accessed on November 1, 2013.

[73] Aunohita Mojumdar, 'India's Role in Afghanistan: Narrow Vision Returns Meagre Gains', *The Times of India*, April 17, 2010.

[74] Sumit Ganguly and Nicholas Howenstein, 'India-Pakistan Rivalry in Afghanistan'. Available at http://jia.sipa.columbia.edu/files/jia/Ganguly_Howenstein.pdf, accessed on July 21, 2010.

which fathered that Islamist militia and LeT'.[75] On a rather ominous note, Chellaney warns that 'Unless the US reverses course on Pakistan, it will begin losing the war in Afghanistan'.[76] He underlines the futility of the US effort in Afghanistan 'without a fundamental shift in US policy on Pakistan and recognition in Washington that the path to success in Afghanistan lies through Pakistan.'[77] Bharat Karnad, critiquing India's piggy backing on the US Af-Pak policy states, 'Free-riding offers relatively poor and weak countries or states, unwilling adequately to invest in their own defence, security without sweat, but it is something a would-be great power, such as India, should eschew.'[78]

As Pakistan seeks reaffirmation of its crucial role in the war on terror, the Obama administration has grappled with how to conceive of India's role in Afghanistan. Washington is clearly feeling the heat from Pakistan on India's role in Afghanistan.[79] At the same time, the US has recognised India's positive contribution to the 'build and transfer component' of the US counter-insurgency strategy of clear, hold, build and transfer. Indeed, there have been calls for India to expand its developmental role.[80] In the first Indo-US Strategic Dialogue in June 2010, Afghanistan topped the agenda. The need to work together in building an inclusive architecture

---

[75] Brahma Chellaney, 'An Afghanistan "Surge" is a Losing Battle: So Why is Mr Obama Betting on It?', *Wall Street Journal*, January 9, 2009.

[76] Brahma Chellaney, 'Stop Pampering Pakistan's Military!', *Christian Science Monitor*, December 12, 2008.

[77] Brahma Chellaney, 'Success in Afghanistan lies through Pakistan', *The Hindu*, January 31, 2009.

[78] Bharat Karnad, 'Habit of Free-Riding', *Seminar*, 599, July 2009. Available at http://www.india-seminar.com/2009/599/599_bharat_karnad.htm, accessed on March 30, 2012.

[79] Emily Wax, 'India's Eager Courtship of Afghanistan Comes at a Steep Price', *The Washington Post*, April 3, 2010. Available at www.washingtonpost.com/wp-dyn/content/article/2010/04/02/AR2010040204313.html, accessed on September 2, 2010.

[80] Author's discussions with senior US government officials and diplomats in Washington DC, April 2010. Also see Assistant Secretary Robert O. Blake, Jr., 'The Obama Administration's Priorities in South and Central Asia' Rice University, Houston, Texas, January 19, 2011. Available at http://www.state.gov/p/sca/rls/rmks/2011/155002.htm, accessed on March 3, 2012.

and rebuilding Afghanistan was reiterated by American Secretary of State Hillary Clinton and Indian External Affairs Minister S. M. Krishna.[81]

During the visit of President Obama to New Delhi in November 2010, there was a reaffirmation of India's positive role. President Obama lauded India's enormous contribution to Afghanistan's development and welcomed greater Indian assistance. The two sides committed to intensify consultation, co-operation and coordination to promote a stable, democratic, prosperous and independent Afghanistan. They also resolved to pursue joint development projects with the Afghan Government in capacity building, agriculture and women's empowerment.

However, US recognition of India's helpful role came with a caveat. Thus, the US President underlined that all the countries of the region, including Pakistan, had to share the responsibility of bringing about stability in that nation: 'Pakistan has to be a partner in this process [of bringing about stability in Afghanistan] ... We don't think that we can do this alone', he said, asserting 'a stable Afghanistan is achievable'.[82] The US dependence on Pakistan has remained a roadblock in the way of deepening India-US co-operation in Afghanistan.

Though India's development assistance has complemented the civilian (hold, build and transfer) component of international military's counter insurgency (COIN) effort and though the US now wants to work with India on developmental projects, India has maintained a distance. New Delhi's worry is that India could be overly identified both in Afghanistan and in neighbouring countries with the Western campaign. The US nevertheless continues to show

---

[81] Secretary Clinton welcomed India's vital contribution to reconstruction, capacity building, and development efforts in Afghanistan and its offer to enhance efforts in this direction. Both sides pledged to explore opportunities for coordination on civilian assistance projects that advance Afghan self-sufficiency and build civilian capacity. See 'US–India Strategic Dia-logue Joint Statement', Office of the Spokesman, US Department of State, Washington DC, June 3, 2010. Available at http://www.state.gov/r/pa/prs/ps/2010/06/142645.htm, accessed on August 21, 2010.

[82] 'Obama Appreciates India's Role in Afghanistan', *The Hindu*, November 7, 2010. Available at http://www.thehindu.com/news/national/article872842.ece, accessed on November 9, 2010.

an interest in collaborating on various projects and programmes.[83] The possibility of joint projects in agriculture, education, and women's empowerment has been explored since President Obama's visit to India last year, but nothing has materialised thus far. While USAID wants to partner India in the widely popular scholarships programme and work with women's groups, Indians, both official and non-official, remain hesitant. Women's groups, like the Self Employed Women's Association (SEWA), have preferred to work alone or in a SAARC framework. There are some sectoral initiatives that have been taken by USAID in co-operation with Indian institutions, without the involvement of the Indian government, including sending Afghan agricultural science students to Indian agricultural universities at their own expense.[84] On the whole, though, the possibility of India and US governments working together in Afghanistan remains a distant possibility, the prospects of commercial venture collaboration seems more probable.

The End Game in Afghanistan?

As consideration of an exit intensifies in the West, the search for an Afghan end game has intensified. In his 1 December 2009 speech at the US Naval Academy at West Point, President Barack Obama underlined his commitment to the war by increasing troop numbers. At the same time, he set a deadline of July 2011 for the conditional drawdown of forces. This seemingly arbitrary timetable, however, evoked regional scepticism and concern in the Karzai government and amongst various sections of Afghan opinion. In the event of a withdrawal or drawdown of forces, with declining public support in the West for the war, and the deterioration in security in Afghanistan, there has been growing worry in New Delhi of a spillover into India.

---

[83] See: White House document, 'The US–India Partnership: The Fact Sheets', White House website, November 2010. Available at http://www.whitehouse.gov/the-press-office/2010/11/08/us-india-partnership-fact-sheets, accessed on April 13, 2012.

[84] Author's interview with senior government officials and policy makers in New Delhi, October 2011. Also see Shanthie Mariet D'Souza, 'India-US Strategic Dialogue: Can India and US Be Partners in Afghanistan?', *Al Arabiya*, July 19, 2011. Available at http://www.alarabiya.net/articles/2011/07/19/158285.html, accessed on July 20, 2011.

In Indian policymaking circles, debates on post-US exit strategies have gained momentum. Concerns abound that India's USD 2 billion aid package, which has been the source of tremendous goodwill, may not be enough to sustain reconstruction and development activities, if Western troops withdraw prematurely. New Delhi's bigger worry is that Pakistan's military might play a major role in reconciliation moves in a post-US negotiated settlement.[85] Without a clear, coordinated, Afghan-led reconciliation policy and adherence to various red lines, the danger is that the Karzai government will be quickly overrun by radical elements.

Conservative strategic analysts caution against the return of the Taliban and of civil war-like conditions as in the early 1990s. According to former National Security Adviser Brajesh Mishra:

> India will be one of the biggest losers if Taliban-isation grips Afghanistan and extremism spreads through Pakistan. Therefore, it is imperative that India ramps up its defence preparedness, which has been hopelessly neglected since the end of the Cold War. India should also expect more terror attacks from Pakistan-based groups if the Taliban finds a high enough space in Kabul. In the Afghanistan game, India stands to be the big loser and Pakistan the big gainer. India will need to think ahead to reverse that situation.[86]

Similarly, K. Subrahmanyam indicates, 'The war in Afghanistan is crucial from the point of view of Indian national security. If the Americans withdraw and jihadis emerge with a sense of triumphalism, India will face increasing onslaughts of terrorism. The LeT Chief has already declared his goal is to break up India. A US withdrawal will make them feel that they have defeated two superpowers and therefore they can take on India'.[87] Indian diplomacy

---

[85] Pakistan has been positioning itself as a serious interlocutor in the power-sharing arrangement in a post-US Afghanistan. Shanthie Mariet D'Souza, 'Great Game's Endgame?', *Business Standard*, October 31, 2010. Available at http://www.business-standard.com/india/news/shanthie-Mariett-d%5 Csouza-great-game%5Cs-endgame/413240/, accessed on November 1, 2010.

[86] 'Talibanization of Afghanistan Will Hit India Hard: Brajesh', *The Times of India*, March 13, 2010.

[87] K. Subrahmanyam, 'War in Afghanistan', *National Maritime Foundation*, September 6, 2009. Available at http://www.maritimeindia.org/pdfs/ksub 6sep.pdf, accessed on August 21, 2010.

wants to avoid such an eventuality by seeking a long-term international commitment in Afghanistan and strengthening the hands of the Afghan Government that would prevent the Taliban from returning to power.

The downsizing of the US troop presence, however, has caused some sections of India's security community to think it prudent to wind up India's development activities. There has been scathing criticism of India's aid diplomacy and soft power approach whenever India's embassy or Indian personnel are targeted. At these times, there is much talk of sending in the Indian Army and 'putting boots on ground'. Thinkers like Gurmeet Kanwal are not averse to putting boots on the ground to retaliate and prevent further attacks. Kanwal has written: 'I wouldn't use the expression, 'flex its muscles'. I would say the time has come to live up to our responsibility. If it involves military intervention, so be it'.[88]

In addition to sending troops there are increased calls for training Afghan troops in order to retain India's influence in the security sector. According to C. Raja Mohan:

> Instead of debating whether we should send troops to Afghanistan, Delhi should look at a range of other ways it can help Kabul and Washington make the Afghan National Army a credible and effective fighting force. The best contribution that India could make might be in the areas of combat training and creating capacities in logistics and communications. India could also perhaps help the Afghans in re-building their Air Force.[89]

Some are also urging training and rearming the former Northern Alliance, who were India's allies during the Taliban interregnum in Afghanistan. If the Taliban looks to return to power, it is not unlikely that India will use its 'northern card'.[90] There is also the thought that New Delhi should revive its traditional and historical linkages among the Pushtuns as a way of balancing the Taliban and protecting its developments projects in the south and east.[91] For example,

---

[88] Somini Sengupta, 'Afghan Bombing Sends Stark Message to India', *The New York Times*, July 9, 2008.

[89] C. Raja Mohan, 'Debating India's Stand on Military Aid to Afghanistan', *The Indian Express*, July 7, 2009.

[90] Jayanth Jacob, 'India Shuffles its Northern Card', *Hindustan Times*, August 9, 2010.

[91] Author's discussions with senior Indian officials, New Delhi, October 2010.

C. Raja Mohan who has urged New Delhi to think boldly in its policy towards Kabul, states:

> Central to any restructuring of India's policy must be a decision to intensify the engagement with the Pashtun leaders on both sides of the Durand Line that divides Pakistan and Afghanistan. India can no longer deny itself the option of engaging the Pashtuns, including the Afghan Taliban, who hold most of the aces in the unfolding battle for the lands between the Indus and the Hindu Kush.[92]

Talking to the Taliban

Critics in India have been quick to point out that fixing an arbitrary timeframe for the drawdown of US forces runs the danger of working to the advantage of the insurgents.[93] New Delhi is concerned that amongst the ramifications of a possible US troop drawdown has been an acceleration of the Afghan Government's efforts at reconciliation with the Taliban and America's inordinate hurry to hand over the running of Afghanistan to the Karzai administration. India worries that Washington is moving too fast and leaving the door open for Pakistan military's to install a pliant regime.

The need to painstakingly stick to President Obama's promise of a 'conditions-based process' for leaving Afghanistan is compelling the US to take extraordinary steps to engage the Taliban. US Af-Pak envoy Ambassador Richard Holbrooke travelled to New York on July 6, 2010 specifically to negotiate the removal of select Taliban members from the UN anti-terror blacklist. Former National Security Advisor Brajesh Mishra observed, 'The worry [about US withdrawal] is caused by a feeling in the policy establishment that the US wants to get out [of Afghanistan] as soon as possible ... Pakistan

---

[92] C. Raja Mohan, 'To Rawalpindi, Via Kabul', *The Indian Express*, July 20, 2010.

[93] In the Indian context, counter-insurgency campaigns are carried out over a long period of time under a liberal democratic constitutional framework where the state is ready to 'bleed' to let the insurgent groups engage the state through various dialogue mechanisms and in some cases even political representation. The successful end of the Mizo insurgency in India's northeast is a case in point. See Shanthie Mariet D'Souza, 'Obama's Afghan Strategy: Regional Perspectives', *Atlantic Review*, December 10, 2009.

wants to broker a deal. The worry is that would lead us back to the 1990s'.[94]

The Pakistani military is clearly positioning itself as a serious interlocutor in the present reconciliation effort. Media reports have indicated that in June 2010 secret talks took place between the Afghan President and a Taliban affiliate, Sirajuddin Haqqani.[95] The fact that Pakistan has successfully resisted the attempts of individual Taliban leaders in Pakistan to open talks directly with the Afghan Government, since the arrest of Taliban commander Mullah Baradar in Karachi in February 2010, has not gone unnoticed in Kabul. Karzai, seemingly out of desperation, appears amenable to shake hands with Pakistan.[96]

While some commentators in India argue that the warmth between Afghanistan and Pakistan will not be at India's cost, it remains a fact that in recent times Karzai has tried to sideline the Northern Alliance, a group that remains opposed to any form of peace with the Taliban. Karzai's dismissal of Interior Minister Hanif Atmar, belonging to the People's Democratic Party of Afghanistan (PDPA), and National Security Chief Amrullah Saleh, belonging to the Northern Alliance, citing security lapses has been interpreted as an attempt to remove internal hurdles to the reconciliation plan.[97]

The release of 90,000 classified US military documents related to the Afghan war by the whistleblower website WikiLeaks vindicated New Delhi's charge that Pakistan's intelligence agency, the ISI, has been playing a double-game in Afghanistan by providing both

---

[94] Alistair Scrutton, 'In Afghan End-game, India Gets that Sinking Feeling', *Reuters*, March 29, 2010. Available at http://www.alertnet.org/thenews/newsdesk/SGE62B0F9.htm,accessed on March 30, 2010.

[95] 'Karzai "Holds Talks" With Haqqani', *AlJazeera*, June 28, 2010. Available at http://english.aljazeera.net/news/asia/2010/06/20106277582708497.html, accessed on September 6, 2010.

[96] Both countries have signed a series of pacts seeking political, strategic, and trade co-operation. 'Afghanistan and Pakistan Agree Key Trade Agreement', *BBC News*, July 19, 2010. Available at http://www.bbc.co.uk/news/world-south-asia-10679464, accessed on August 12, 2010.

[97] Discussions with Hanif Atmar, Kabul, October 8, 2011. Also see Ernesto Londoño, 'Karzai Removes Afghan Interior Minister and Spy Chief', *The Washington Post*, June 7, 2010. Available at http://www.washingtonpost.com/wp-dyn/content/article/2010/06/06/AR2010060600714.html, accessed on August 12, 2010.

supplies and sanctuary to Taliban fighters.⁹⁸ The documents, now in the public domain, substantiates the view that the ISI continues to maintain liaisons with and support for the Taliban despite claims by the Pakistani Government that ISI was swept clean of pro-Taliban officers years ago. The document reveal that General Hamid Gul, ISI's Director-General from 1987 to 1989, still informally serves the agency and works to promote Taliban activities.⁹⁹

However, it is highly unlikely that these revelations will bring about dramatic changes in US–Pakistan counter-terrorism co-operation. While Pakistan remains a key ally for the US in anti-Taliban operations in Afghanistan, the Pakistani military stands to benefit from the huge financial and military aid it accrues as a beneficiary of such co-operation. US officials privately admit the deep complicity of the Pakistan army and the ISI in maintaining links with top levels of the Afghan Taliban leadership. Yet, they are unwilling to publicly admit to Pakistan's role or delink from co-operation. In view of Pakistan's complicity and lack of co-operation in bringing the Taliban leadership (the Quetta shura) to the negotiating table, there are those who argue for India to initiate a dialogue with the Taliban. For example, Ajai Shukla argues 'while the US-led coalition is tied up in day-to-day fire fighting, New Delhi can afford to take a longer-term view. From that perspective, Mullah Omar and the Quetta Shoora provide a dominant Pashtun leadership, and India must begin the process of engaging with that group'.¹⁰⁰

Reverting to the Traditional Alliance: Iran and Russia

The possibility of US and NATO withdrawal from Afghanistan and the accommodation of the Taliban without strengthening the

---

⁹⁸ Robert Winnett and Andy Bloxham, 'Afghanistan War Logs: 90,000 Classified Documents Revealed by Wikileaks', *The Telegraph,* July 26, 2010. Available at http://www.telegraph.co.uk/news/worldnews/asia/afghanistan/7909742/Afghanistan-war-logs-90000-classified-documents-revealed-by-Wikileaks.html, accessed on July 28, 2010.

⁹⁹ 'WikiLeaks Vindicates India's Charge of ISI Terror Network', *The Economic Times,* July 28, 2010.

¹⁰⁰ Ajai Shukla, 'Time to Talk to the Taliban?', *Aspen Institute India,* Policy Paper No. 3. Available at http://www.aspenindia.org/pdf/taliban.pdf, accessed on March 30, 2012.

Afghan Government could compel India to work towards a coalition with Iran and Russia. This 'self-interested coalition'[101] in the longer run could also include several Central Asian states that fear a Taliban return to Kabul. While the Taliban remain an anathema for Iran, Russia, and India, who believe that the extremists pose significant risks to the region, it was Russia's opposition that stalled US moves to remove Taliban from the UN blacklist. Moscow repeated its stand at the Kabul conference in 2010 to the effect that any move to rehabilitate an unrepentant Taliban must be resisted.

After years of chill between India and Iran, since the days when India voted with the US in the IAEA against Iran's nuclear programme, a new warming between both countries is perceptible. In the first week of August 2010, Iranian Deputy Foreign Minister Mohammad Ali Fathollahi visited India on a three-day tour to discuss wide-ranging issues including efforts to stabilise Afghanistan. This was the second ministerial visit from Iran to India in less than a month. It followed the 9 July 2010 Joint Commission meeting at which both countries had discussed expediting the expansion of Chabahar Port in Iran, a move that could deepen India's reach in both Afghanistan and Central Asia, bypassing Pakistan. This came at a time when India's rights to trade and transit through Pakistan's territory were again denied at the recently concluded Afghanistan-Pakistan Trade and Transit Agreement (APTTA).

India and Iran have also decided to hold structured and regular consultations with regards to closer co-operation in Afghanistan. Both have been seen as inching closer in their assessments of the Afghan quagmire and both seem to perceive a strategic advantage in coordinating efforts against the Taliban. In late 2011, Indian Foreign Secretary, Ranjan Mathai, called on the international community to 'add Iran to the list of countries needing to be discussed' when looking at 'the prospects for stability in Asia in connection with Afghanistan'.[102] In the days leading to the ouster of the Taliban

---

[101] Tim Sullivan, 'India, Pakistan Face Off in Afghanistan: Neighbours' Heated Rivalry Will Have a Major Impact on U.S. Plans to Deal with Taliban and Get Out', *Associated Press*, May 1, 2010. Available at http://www.statesman.com/opinion/insight/india-pakistan-face-off-in-afghanistan-657210.html, accessed on August 15, 2010.

[102] Ranjan Mathai, 'Forging Stability in Asia: Keynote Address at MEA-IISS-IDSA Dialogue', Institute for Defence and Security Analyses, New Delhi, November 21, 2011.

regime in 2001, both India and Iran backed the Northern Alliance. However, with Iran blocking the transit of fuel into Afghanistan, US–Iran relations and India–Iran relations have a deadlocked quality. Most recently, Iran-India relationship has been troubled further by an oil payments problem. Moreover, with India signing an agreement for the TAPI gas pipeline in Ashgabat in December 2010, the 2,300 km Iran-Pakistan-India gas (IPI) pipeline has been put on a backburner. US backing for the TAPI project and attempts to wean India away from the IPI pipeline are seen as moves to further isolate Iran. Notwithstanding Washington's opposition, Delhi and Tehran are now engaged in structured consultations on Afghanistan.[103]

During the first week of August 2010, the then Indian Foreign Secretary Nirupama Rao visited Russia and held talks with her Russian counterpart, First Deputy Foreign Minister Andrei Denisov, as well as Deputy Foreign Minister Alexei Borodavkin who reiterated Moscow's continued emphasis on the red lines for reconciliation with the Taliban, (the red lines had been drawn at the London Conference on Afghanistan). The security situation in Afghanistan and the need to develop a coordinated strategy between the two countries were discussed during foreign office consultations in Moscow. Russia, which allowed the US to transport weapons across its territory to Afghanistan in 2009, has been wary of the Taliban insurgency's destabilising effects on Central Asia and the spillover effects into its Caucasus region. During Russian President Dmitry Medvedev's visit to New Delhi in 2010, both sides agreed to further step up their co-operation for peace and stability in Afghanistan.

Conclusion

Following President Obama's speech at West Point in December 2009 announcing the troop surge and a tentative date for the drawdown of forces, as also promises of withdrawal by other NATO countries, concerns abound in Afghanistan and the region regarding the commitment of the international community to stabilise Afghanistan. Though there has been a subsequent toning down of the withdrawal discourse since then, there is clearly a desire to bring the Afghan

---

[103] Harsh V. Pant, 'India's Relations with Iran: Much Ado About Nothing', *The Washington Quarterly* (Winter 2011), p. 65.

involvement of these countries to an end. The rush to exit has been complicated by a lack of consensus amongst the US and its allies on the timeline of withdrawal and on defining an 'end state', as witnessed during the NATO Lisbon Summit in November 2010. This lack of unified vision and effort in the international community has contributed to a further dissipation of the war effort. Every actor is interested in imposing its own 'end state' on Afghanistan, as seen through its national agenda, with little or no attempt at understanding of Afghan priorities and interests. The transitional and exit strategy of the Obama US administration, with its arbitrary timetables and the lack of a coherent stabilisation strategy, has only added to the complexities and anxieties in Afghanistan.

These developments pose fresh challenges for Indian policy in Afghanistan. These continue to give rise to serious concerns about whether India can sustain its present 'aid only' policy under the shrinking US security umbrella.[104] If the West in a rush to exit leaves the door open for a Taliban take over, there is little doubt that India's options will be severely constrained. Even in the most likely scenario beyond 2014, which envisions a limited US troop presence in strategic bases, leaving the countryside open to Taliban influence, India will have to minimise its presence and restrict its developmental activities to key cities.

Indian investments in Afghanistan, which have generated a significant amount of good will amongst Afghans, could evaporate if not translated into long-term influence. This calls for a recalibration of policy until 2014. The high-visibility infrastructure projects have essentially involved building an asset and handing it over to the Afghan authorities. While this has given New Delhi prestige and a measure of gratitude, it is unlikely to give India enduring influence. The SDPs, though successful in the south and east, need constant monitoring and evaluation, which could be difficult in the days ahead. What India needs is a shift from asset creation to programme delivery. By designing and running large development programmes in the context of poverty, illiteracy, and systemic administrative dysfunction, India can fill a critical gap in rebuilding the economic, social, and political capital of Afghanistan and thus sustain an enduring channel of influence.

---

[104] C. Christine Fair, 'Under the Shrinking US Security Umbrella: India's End Game in Afghanistan?', *The Washington Quarterly* (Spring 2011), p. 181.

India will have to take a lead in preventing a new civil and proxy war in Afghanistan as the West exits the country. In all likelihood, this will involve forging a regional consensus on Afghan governance and security. The Strategic Partnership is the basis for greater mutual interdependence and co-operation. New Delhi can secure both its primary and secondary interests in the long-term through a regional framework. In addition, talks with Pakistan, will remain crucial to allay concerns and devise joint strategies. In chalking out a regional strategy, India will have to reach out to its extended neighbourhood and assume more leadership.

14

COLLATERAL DAMAGE
IRAN IN A RECONFIGURED INDIAN GRAND STRATEGY

Sarang Shidore*

The best of friends must part – Persian proverb

India and Iran have been two great proximate civilisations in history. In modern times, they share many similarities – both are civilisational, multi-ethnic states, both have extra-regional ambitions, both have had a strong attachment to an independent foreign policy for several decades. However, as India emerges as a high-growth economy and regional, possibly global power, and as Iran's conflicts with the West sharpen, the relationship between the two is subject to complex pulls and pressures, convergences and divergences. How their relationship develops could be critical for major questions of war and peace in the region, besides being of major import to global dimensions of trade and energy.

In this chapter, I propose an explanation for the shifts in the India–Iran relationship in the post-Cold War period in the context of the evolution of India's strategic culture and grand strategy. As India's relationship with the United States (of which the Indo-US nuclear deal was an important part) played a critical role in influencing its ties to Iran, I dwell at some length on the US factor. However, to the extent this is engaged, its focus is to delineate how this factor, by influencing the evolution of India's grand strategy, significantly impinged on India's policy towards Iran.

I begin by foregrounding the chapter in a materially-oriented estimation of Iran's salience in India's energy and security interests. I then provide an empirical narrative of the India–Iran relationship, with a particular focus on the critical period of 2005–10, through a detailed examination of Indian media archives.

---

* The author wishes to acknowledge Dr Rahul Rao for his valuable feedback and many useful suggestions.

I then show that a material–structural lens cannot fully explain India's choices in its Iran policy during this critical period. A deeper understanding can only be gained if we examine the evolution of India's strategic culture, the associated identity shift, and consequent state preferences. I use discourse analysis as a tool to analyse discourses in the Indian state, media, and scholarship, showing that domestic and diaspora-related factors created a predisposition among Indian elites towards privileging a partnership with the United States. The consequence was a process of reorientation of Indian identity and a distancing of Iran.

Iran's Role in India's Energy and Security Interests

As a fast-growing economy situated in a difficult neighbourhood, India faces a number of major challenges on the energy and security front. Iran's geography, material advantages, and security interests lead to a substantial convergence with India's priorities in the region. In this section, I shall examine two key areas in which this convergence is particularly strong – energy and security.

Energy

India's rapid economic growth in recent years has led to increasing energy consumption, with a projected annual growth rate of 3.5 per cent through 2030.[1] A serious problem remains a chronic shortfall in electricity, with only two-thirds of all households with access.

Coal is the mainstay of India's energy profile accounting for the bulk of its power generation.[2] However, demand is outstripping supply, and India is now a coal importer with imports growing at 7 per cent per year.[3] Coal is also associated with high emission of greenhouse gases and other pollutants.

Oil faces the problems of being an inefficient source for power generation. Hydroelectric projects have major potential, but environmental factors have stalled a number of these projects. In any case, hydroelectric power cannot by itself meet India's projected

---

[1] International Energy Agency (IEA), World Energy Outlook, (2008), p. 108. Available at http://www.iea.org/textbase/nppdf/free/2008/weo2008.pdf, accessed on August 31, 2010.

[2] S. Pandian, 'Energy Trade as a Confidence-Building Measure between India and Pakistan: A Study of the Indo-Iran Trans-Pakistan Project', *Contemporary South Asia*, 14, 3 (2005), pp. 307–20.

[3] International Energy Agency, World Energy Outlook, p. 108.

demands. Reliance on renewable energy such as wind and solar is projected to increase, but these technologies are unlikely to be scalable in the medium-term.[4]

Although the Indo-US nuclear deal is expected to yield up to 20,000 MW of energy from nuclear plants by 2020, this represents only about 8 per cent of India's projected energy needs.[5] Also, the long gestation periods, high capital and insurance costs, and safety issues especially in the wake of the 2011 Fukushima disaster mean that even these projections are probably highly optimistic.[6]

This leaves natural gas as a highly competitive alternative. Gas production is far from peak and will continue to increase for several decades,[7] especially with recent technology-enabled breakthroughs auch as shale gas. Gas prices have generally been historically lower[8] compared to oil.[9] The post-2008 economic crisis has greatly increased this spread, as cartelised oil prices stay high, and non-cartelised gas prices fall.[10] Gas prices are projected to remain low

---

[4] Tanvi Madan, The Brookings Foreign Policy Studies Energy Security Series: India, The Brookings Institution, 2006. Available at http://www.brookings.edu/~/media/Files/rc/reports/2006/11india_fixauthorname/2006india.pdf, accessed on August 31, 2010. Also see Tanvi Madan, 'India's International Quest for Oil and Natural Gas: Fueling Foreign Policy?', *India Review*, 9, 1 (2010), pp. 2–37.

[5] Praful Bidwai, 'Clean' Nuclear Energy and a Nuclear Renaissance: Hype and Hyperbole', *Third World Resurgence* 235 (March 2010). Available at http://www.twnside.org.sg/title2/resurgence/2010/235/cover01.htm, accessed on August 25, 2010.

[6] Praful Bidwai and M. V. Ramana, 'Home, Next to N-Reactor', *Tehelka*, September 4, 2010. Available at http://www.tehelka.com/story_main31.asp?filename=Ne230607home_next_SR.asp, accessed on September 4, 2010.

[7] G. Dietl, 'Gas Pipelines: Politics and Possibilities', in I.P. Khosla, ed. *Energy and Diplomacy* (New Delhi: Konark Publishers, 2005).

[8] 'Oil Soars, and Natural Gas Slips', The New York Times, November 9, 2007. Available at http://www.nytimes.com/imagepages/2007/11/09/business/20071110_CHARTS_GRAPHIC.html, accessed on August 25, 2010.

[9] Assuming 1 barrel of oil is equivalent to 5.8 MBTU of natural gas.

[10] Unlike in the Americas, gas prices in Asia are linked to oil price benchmarks due to historical reasons. This linkage is however under considerable pressure.

for the 'foreseeable future'.[11] Natural gas also emits about half the level of greenhouse gases as compared to coal. Gas-fed power generation is highly efficient with recent combined-cycle gas turbines[12]. These factors explain why gas is already the fastest-growing source of electricity generation in developing countries,[13] and gas demand has risen rapidly in India in recent years.[14]

The one disadvantage of natural gas is its relatively high transportation cost, especially in LNG form. Thus geographic proximity of consumers to gas sources is critical. India is fortunate in this regard in terms of being geographically close to the site of the world's largest gas source – the Persian Gulf, Iran and Qatar together possess 30 per cent of the conventional global gas reserves,[15] and therefore are clear proximate choices,[16] for India for sourcing scaled-up volumes of gas at reasonable prices.[17]

India has an ongoing and successful LNG supply arrangement with Qatar for 7.5 million tonnes per year. An argument can be made that India should continue to rely on Qatar for most of its growing gas needs. However, Qatari gas can only be imported as more expensive LNG, as a deep-sea pipeline across the Arabian Sea presents major challenges. Also, any further expansion of supplies from Qatar is uncertain, due to a moratorium[18] imposed on gas production by the emirate due to extraction issues, and resource nationalism due to growing domestic demand. These factors make Iran's role important in India's energy strategy.

The IPI pipeline and LNG supply projects with Iran were planned with these imperatives in mind. However, as these projects have stalled, India is being forced to make spot LNG purchases of

---

[11] 'Natural Gas Tumbles on Ample Stockpile, Lack of Storm Threat in U.S. Gulf', *Bloomberg News*, August 31, 2010.

[12] International Energy Agency, World Energy Outlook, p. 113.

[13] Ibid., p. 144.

[14] S. Pandian, 'Energy Trade as a Confidence-Building Measure', p. 310.

[15] G. Dietl, 'Gas Pipelines: Politics and Possibilities'.

[16] Pipelines proposed from Turkmenistan and Myanmar to India have been long stymied due to the intractable Afghanistan war and the Myanmar junta's preference for China.

[17] 'China Pips India to Sign Gas Sales Agreement with Daewoo', *The Hindu*, December 30, 2008.

[18] 'The Coming Gas Supply Shock in the Gulf', *Khaleej Times*, July 24, 2008.

gas at much higher prices to cover its nearly 40 per cent supply shortfall.[19] Though there has been an increase in domestic gas finds, they are not sufficient to make up the fast-growing demand. Alternative sources of natural gas, such as shale gas, are transforming the US energy landscape, but remain saddled with significant and unresolved environmental and health concerns.[20] Moreover, the export of large volumes of US unconventional gas to India is still uncertain, and there are many constraints to exploiting domestic Indian shale reserves.

Security

Several reasons motivate a particularly strong Indo-Iranian cooperation on security matters. These include factors related to Afghanistan, Pakistan, and Central Asia.

India perceives Pakistan as its most important security threat, the two states having fought four wars since 1947. A key development related to these tensions was the rise of the Pakistan-backed Taliban militia in Afghanistan. The Taliban played a supportive role in the December 1999 hijack of an Indian Airlines plane by Pakistan-backed militants. The Taliban, with their militant Wahhabi ideology, also massacred thousands among Afghanistan's Shia Hazara minority and killed several Iranian diplomats based in Mazar-e-Sharif.[21] The Islamism of the Iranian regime, though at times virulent and directed outwards, rarely, if ever, posited India as its target, as contrasted with Islamism emanating from the Saudi state and Pakistan.

Thus there was a strong convergence of material security interests of India and Iran in Afghanistan. Consequently, India, Iran, Tajikistan and Russia provided military assistance to the Tajik-led Northern Alliance in their war against the Pakistani-backed Taliban in the 1990s.[22]

---

[19] 'India Lures LNG Spot Cargoes as Asia, Europe Cut Imports', *Financial Express*, April 23, 2009.

[20] The documentary *Gasland* (Sundance, Dir. Josh Fox, 2010) investigates this issue. Also see the report by European Parliament Committee on Environment, Public Health, and Food Safety, 'Impacts of Shale Gas and Shale Oil Extraction on the Environment and on Human Health', 2011.

[21] Amin Saikal, 'Iran's Turbulent Neighbour: The Challenge of the Taliban', *Global Dialogue*, 3, 2–3 (2001), pp. 93–103.

[22] Christine Fair, 'India and Iran: New Delhi's Balancing Act', *The Washington Quarterly*, 30, 3 (2007), pp. 145–59.

Another factor is the complexity of Iranian–Pakistani relations.[23] The nuclear proliferation network of Pakistani scientist AQ Khan sold nuclear technology to Iran.[24] However, from the 1980s onwards, Pakistani ruling elites increasingly sympathised with Saudi Arabia, Iran's rival in the region. Within Pakistan, Sunni extremist groups began a violent campaign against the Shia minority in the 1980s.[25] Iran accuses Pakistan of harbouring Sunni militants that have staged several recent attacks in the Iranian province of Sistan-Balochistan.[26] Iran is also wary of the substantial US military presence in Pakistan's borderlands. The Iran–Pakistan relationship therefore has come under appreciable strain in recent years.

Finally, China, historically Pakistan's closest ally, has embarked upon major infrastructural projects[27] that have military implications with respect to India. China's development of the Gwadar port[28] provides a relatively sheltered base for the Pakistani navy as compared to Karachi. Iran's geographic location gives India a route to countering joint Sino-Pakistani moves. Iran's Chahbahar port, close to Gwadar, could provide the Indian navy with an invaluable base to monitor Pakistani naval movements. Iran is also India's only practical land route into Afghanistan, the terrain for intense India–Pakistan rivalry since the fall of the Taliban. Moreover, an India–Iran partnership also gives India access to Tajikistan, a close Persian-speaking ally of Iran. Tajikistan has already facilitated India's building of an airbase on its soil.[29]

Iran's significantly deeper economic links with China as compared to India also motivates an Indian hedging strategy of building strong ties with Iran to prevent the emergence of a future China–Pakistan–Iran axis. Such an axis could develop, if for example,

---

[23] S. Alam, 'Iran–Pakistan Relations: Political and Strategic Dimensions', *Strategic Analysis*, 28, 4 (2004), pp. 526–45.

[24] Ibid., p. 541.

[25] Ibid., p. 533.

[26] 'Iran Accuses Pakistan Over Attack', *BBC*, October 19, 2009.

[27] Selig Harrison, 'China's Discreet Hold on Pakistan's Northern Borderlands', *The New York Times*, August 26, 2010.

[28] Robert Wirsing, 'In India's Lengthening Shadow: The US–Pakistan Strategic Alliance and the War in Afghanistan', *Asian Affairs*, 34, 4 (2008), pp. 235–40.

[29] Sudha Ramachandran, 'India's Foray into Central Asia', *Asia Times*, August 12, 2006.

US–Pakistani and US–Chinese relations sour, in the wake of the planned US withdrawal from Afghanistan. A weaker version of this scenario is simply an Iran hostile to Indian interests in the region, which by itself can present unacceptable costs to Indian regional policies.

The India–Iran Relationship: An Empirical Narrative

I now locate key shifts and inflection points in the India–Iran relationship through a detailed examination of its chronology as evidenced through media archives.

The Cold War Period

India and Iran have had ancient ties for millennia.[30] In modern times, the Indian freedom struggle from British colonial rule was generally covered sympathetically be the Iranian press.[31] However, the Cold War created a rift between Iran, which allied itself with the United States, and India, which declared a policy of non-alignment opposed to military alliances. Iran supported Pakistan in the 1965 and 1971 India–Pakistan wars. However, it did not cut off oil exports to India at any time,[32] and even backed India in its war against China in 1962.[33]

The 1979 revolution in Iran overthrew the Pahlavi monarchy and ushered in an Islamist government. India welcomed the revolution, seeing it as a 'reflection of Iran's quest for identity and national self-assertion'. India sent an unofficial delegation to Tehran to congratulate the new government.[34] India expected Iran to align itself with the principles of non-alignment. However, Iran's non-alignment had

---

[30] A. Jorfi, 'Iran and India: Age Old Friendship', *India Quarterly*, 50, 4 (1994), pp. 65–92.

[31] A. Ahanchi, 'Reflections of the Indian Independence Movement in the Iranian Press', *Iranian Studies*, 42, 3 (2009), pp. 423–43.

[32] E. Yazdani, 'The Dynamics of India's Relations with Iran in the Post-Cold War Era: A Geopolitical Analysis', *South Asia: A Journal of South Asian Studies*, 30, 2 (2007), pp. 351–68.

[33] Farah Naaz, 'Indo-Iranian Relations 1947-2000', *Strategic Analysis*, 24, 10 (2001), pp. 1911–26.

[34] Naaz, 'Indo-Iranian Relations 1947–2000', p. 1918.

a strongly Islamist character to it.[35] Consequently, the new Iranian government began stressing self-determination for Muslims in Kashmir. The Muslim United Front, a Kashmiri Islamist bloc that led opposition to Indian rule in the 1980s, may have been partly funded by Iran.[36] Iran condemned the demolition of the Babri mosque by Hindu militants in 1992 and Iranian president Rafsanjani backed self-determination for Kashmir during a visit to Pakistan.[37]

THE POST-COLD WAR PERIOD UNTIL 2004

However, with the end of the Cold War and the death of Ayatollah Khomeini, Iran's foreign policy began undergoing a substantial shift under President Rafsanjani.[38] The first significant movement in its relations with India came in 1989, when an Iranian diplomat and an Indian scientist proposed an overland gas pipeline to India through Pakistan,[39] which came to be known as the Iran–India–Pakistan (IPI) pipeline. It was also dubbed the 'peace pipeline' due to its promise of creating irreversible economic dependencies between India and Pakistan, aiding peace. A Memorandum of Understanding (MoU) on the IPI pipeline was signed between India and Iran during Indian Prime Minister Rao's visit to Tehran in 1993.

Another key shift was visible in 1994, when Iran used its clout to persuade Pakistan to drop a resolution in the UN Human Rights Commission strongly condemning Indian actions in Kashmir.[40] However, the Islamist lens in Iranian foreign policy towards India continued to persist to some degree throughout the 1990s. Iran's Supreme Leader Khamenei cited Kashmir[41] in his opening remarks

---

[35] Mohammed Reza Saidabadi., 'Islam and Foreign Policy in the Contemporary Secular World: The Case of Post-revolutionary Iran', *Global Change, Peace and Security*, 8, 2 (1996), pp. 32–44.

[36] Farah Naaz, 'Indo-Iranian Relations: Vital Factors in the 1990s', *Strategic Analysis*, 25, 2 (2001), pp. 227–41.

[37] Naaz, 'Indo-Iranian Relations: Vital Factors in the 1990s', p. 238.

[38] John Calabrese, *Revolutionary Horizons: Regional Foreign Policy in Post-Khomeini Iran* (New York: St. Martin's Press, 1994). Also see Arshin Adib-Moghaddam, *Iran in World Politics: The Question of the Islamic Republic* (New York: Columbia University Press, 2008).

[39] Ali Shams Ardekani and Rajendra Pachauri, respectively.

[40] Naaz, 'Indo-Iranian Relations: Vital Factors in the 1990s', p. 238.

[41] Final Communique of the 8th Islamic Summit of the OIC. Available at http://www.oic-oci.org/english/conf/is/8/8th-is-summits.htm#FINAL%20%20COMMUNIQUE, accessed on August 23, 2010.

to the OIC conference in Tehran in 1997 and Iran expressed its support for the Kashmir cause during the Pakistani foreign secretary's visit to Tehran in 1999.[42]

Rao's visit was reciprocated by President Rafsanjani in 1995, which was followed by a number of reciprocal visits by top officials of both states. These marked a steady improvement of Indo-Iranian ties. India, Iran and Russia signed a key trade agreement with the creation of the North-South Transportation Corridor for enhanced trade with Central Asia.[43] Not much progress was made in the IPI pipeline during this period however, due to consistent opposition from Pakistan.[44]

The coming to power of the Taliban in Afghanistan with its anti-Shia and anti-India agendas[45] provided a powerful incentive for Indo-Iranian cooperation, and Indo-Iranian relations began to improve dramatically.[46] Afghanistan was a focus in Indian foreign minister Jaswant Singh's visit to Tehran in 2000.[47]

The visit of Indian Prime Minister Vajpayee to Tehran in 2001 marked the movement of the India–Iran relationship into a strategic plane. The visit culminated in the Tehran Declaration. While lauding the 'civilizational affinities and historical links' between the two countries, the declaration condemned states that 'aid, abet, and directly support international terrorism' and directly cited Afghanistan in expressing 'their deep concern over the growth of extremism'.[48]

Indo-Iranian ties peaked following Iranian president Mohammed Khatami's visit to New Delhi in 2003 during which he was the chief

---

[42] Naaz, 'Indo-Iranian Relations: Vital Factors in the 1990s'.

[43] Harsh Pant, 'India and Iran: An Axis in the Making?', *Asian Survey*, 44, 3 (2004), pp. 369–83. Also by the same author, see 'India and Iran: Too close for comfort', in Harsh Pant, ed., *Contemporary Debates in Indian Foreign and Security Policy: India Negotiates its Rise in the International System* (New York: Palgrave Macmillan, 2008).

[44] M. N. Khan, 'Vajpayee's Visit to Iran: Indo-Iranian Relations and Prospects of Bilateral Cooperation', *Strategic Analysis*, 25, 6 (2001), pp. 765–779.

[45] M. Ayoob, 'Southwest Asia after the Taliban', *Survival*, 44, 1 (2002), pp. 51–68.

[46] 'Pragmatic Turn', *Economic and Political Weekly*, 36, 16 (2001), p. 1273.

[47] Naaz, 'Indo-Iranian Relations: 1947–2000', p. 1922.

[48] Ministry of External Affairs, Government of India, 'Tehran Declaration', April 10, 2011. Available at at http://www.mea.gov.in/other.htm?dtl/20048/Tehran+Declaration, accessed on August 20, 2010.

guest at India's annual Republic Day parade, a significant honour. The two sides issued the joint New Delhi Declaration[49] which called for 'controlling the re-emergence of terrorist forces' in Afghanistan, decided to 'explore opportunities for cooperation in defense', announced a proposal for the supply of Iranian Liquefied Natural Gas (LNG) to India, and called for a peaceful solution to the growing crisis in Iraq. The Indian prime minister standing next to the president of Iran, a member of George Bush's 'axis of evil', and opposing a war on Iraq was seen as a symbol of India's independent foreign policy in the region. The emerging defense relationship between the two states was another major development. India and Iran held joint naval exercises in the Arabian Sea in March 2003.[50] There were also reports that Iran had agreed to allow India use of its military bases in the event of an India-Pakistan war.[51] Driven by convergent interests, the prospects for a deepening India–Iran partnership appeared bright.

The LNG proposal initially envisaged a competitive price of approximately USD 2 per Million British Thermal Units (MBTU) and an Indian stake in the South Pars gas field[52] with a linkage of LNG price to that of the Brent crude oil. Negotiations over the IPI pipeline also intensified after Indian Prime Minister Manmohan Singh's statement expressing willingness to go forward with the project provided Pakistan gave adequate security guarantees.[53] This appeared to be a reversal of a previous position by the Vajpayee government, which had linked the pipeline to a broader trade opening with Pakistan.[54]

The LNG talks ran into difficulties when India began to demand a much lower price for the gas. Iran offered a price of USD 2.22 per MBTU, but India insisted on a price of USD 1.72 per MBTU,[55] in spite of the fact that Iran's offer also included a sweetener of 20 per cent stake in the Kushk–Husseineh oilfield.

---

[49] 'Tehran Declaration', April 10, 2011
[50] Pant, 'India and Iran: An Axis in the Making?'
[51] 'Strategic Shift in South Asia', *Jane's Foreign Report*, January 30, 2003.
[52] 'Iran Offers Cheaper LNG Than RasGas', *Financial Express*, April 15, 2004.
[53] 'Changing Tack on the Gas Pipeline', *The Hindu*, June 7, 2004.
[54] 'Pipedreaming Again', *Financial Express*, June 9, 2004.
[55] 'Iran, India Fail to Cut Gas Deal', *Times of India*, July 1, 2004.

Even as discussions continued, the price of oil in international markets began to rise substantially. In another crucial development, China entered the market for Iran's gas.[56] Iran began insisting on a higher price, reportedly USD 4 per MBTU.[57] In early 2005, the two countries seriously discussed a variable price linked to Brent crude, capped at USD 3.21 per MBTU.[58] The protracted negotiation phase concluded successfully, when a major agreement worth USD 22 billion for an annual supply of 5 million tonnes of LNG for 25 years was signed in June 2005, with India agreeing to pay an effective price of USD 3.51 per MBTU.[59] The signing of the LNG agreement marked a major achievement in the India–Iran relationship.

The Indian and Pakistani governments had begun a serious peace process in 2003, which facilitated an intensification of negotiations over the IPI pipeline. However, the talks stalled when Pakistan reportedly linked progress on the project to a resolution of the Kashmir issue.[60] India in turn revived its earlier demands of linking the pipeline project to a broad opening of trade, and also added transit rights for its goods bound for Central Asia and Iran as a new condition.[61]

As bilateral India–Pakistan ties continued to improve, Pakistan dropped its stance of linking the pipeline to Kashmir[62] and strongly argued that the pipeline ought to be seen as creating mutual dependencies that could enable a broader peace with India.[63] Meanwhile, Iran extended its security assurances on the pipeline by proposing to take responsibility for delivery of gas to India at the Pakistani rather

---

[56] 'Sustainability of Iran LNG Imports Questioned', *Economic Times*, December 7, 2004.

[57] 'Indo-Iran LNG Deal Hits Hurdle', *The Indian Express*, December 7, 2004.

[58] 'Oil Diplomacy Pays Off, India Signs Mega LNG Import Deal with Iran', *The Indian Express*, January 8, 2005.

[59] 'Welcome LNG Agreement', *Hindu Business Line*, June 15, 2005.

[60] 'India Puts Pipeline Talks on Slow Burner', *The Indian Express*, September 14, 2004.

[61] 'On Aiyar's Table for Aziz: Give us Our MFN, Then Iran Gas Pipeline Can Run Through Pak', *The Indian Express*, November 22, 2004.

[62] 'Kasuri Offers Guarantees on Gas Line to India', *The Hindu*, December 29, 2004.

[63] 'Gas Project is a Win-Win for India, Pakistan', *The Hindu*, November 25, 2004.

than the Iranian border.[64] Thus, though a final agreement was as yet elusive, the three parties appeared to be engaging seriously on the pipeline project.

POST-NUCLEAR DEAL PERIOD, 2005–10

The United States took a public interest in the IPI pipeline project for the first time in early 2005. US Secretary of State Condoleezza Rice, during her visit to India, expressed 'concerns about gas pipeline cooperation between Iran and India', adding that 'those concerns are well known to the Indian government'.[65] On the same day, Indian Petroleum Minister Mani Shankar Aiyar argued that Iran ought to reduce the price further for such a large deal.[66] India specifically demanded a price no greater than USD 2.25 per MBTU for the piped gas,[67] even as Iran continued to press for the project's implementation by 2006.[68] India's objections however, may have reflected a genuinely different point of view on the acceptable price.

On July 18, 2005 India and the United States issued a joint statement[69] announcing a proposal for an Indo-US civil nuclear agreement.[70] Under its terms, India agreed to put some of its reactors under IAEA safeguards, participate in US-led initiatives on non-proliferation and counter-proliferation, and provide a de facto commitment to a test ban. In return, the US agreed to persuade the Nuclear Suppliers Group and the US Congress to lift all international and US sanctions imposed on India after its nuclear tests, and enable the supply of US nuclear technology for India's expanding

---

[64] 'Iran Agrees to Deliver Gas at Indian Border', *The Indian Express*, February 16, 2005.

[65] Radio Free Europe report, March 18, 2005. Available at http://www.rferl.org/content/article/1058030.html, accessed on August 5, 2010.

[66] 'India Threatens to Pull Out of Iran Pipeline', *Financial Express*, March 16, 2005.

[67] 'India Sets Stiff Terms for Iran Pipeline Gas', *Financial Express*, May 2, 2005.

[68] 'Iran Asks India to Walk its Talk on Pipeline', *Financial Express*, August 3, 2005.

[69] Government of India, Joint Statement on 'Indo-US civil nuclear agreement', July 18, 2005

[70] An excellent empirical summary of the events surrounding the nuclear deal can be found in Dinshaw Mistry, 'Diplomacy, Domestic Politics, and the US-India Nuclear Agreement', *Asian Survey*, 46, 5 (2006), pp. 675–98.

energy needs.[71] This development was to have a major impact on the India–Iran relationship. I explore this linkage further in the next section.

Meanwhile discussions at the International Atomic Energy Agency (IAEA) were moving towards a censure of Iran's nuclear activities for alleged transgressions of the Non-Proliferation Treaty (NPT). The US and its allies declared their intention to find Iran in violation of its international obligations. A divisive vote appeared to loom ahead at the IAEA meeting in September 2005. The India–Iran relationship became a prominent focus of talks between the Indian prime minister and President Bush, in which India assured the US that it would 'work constructively' on the Iran nuclear issue.[72]

In September 2005, India voted at the IAEA for a resolution finding Iran in violation of its NPT commitments. Though an actual referral was deferred, the purview of the UN Security Council was invoked for the first time. The resolution's citation of Article III.B.4 of the IAEA Statute was particularly serious, as it invoked the Security Council's responsibilities for maintaining international peace and security, thereby opening the door to future international sanctions and even military action.[73] In casting the vote, India sided with the US and European states and broke ranks with practically all the members of the Non-Aligned Movement (NAM) as well as Russia and China on the IAEA Board, who either abstained or voted against the resolution.

In voting for the resolution, India also effectively contradicted its long-stated position on the Iran nuclear issue. This position was that Iran should not possess nuclear weapons, but the dispute ought to be resolved through negotiations within the IAEA Board, and no punitive actions should be undertaken. However, India justified the vote by arguing that 'the resolution does not refer the matter to the Security Council and has agreed that outstanding issues be dealt

---

[71] C. Raja Mohan, 'India and the Emerging Non-Proliferation Order: The Second Nuclear Age', in Harsh Pant, ed., *Indian Foreign Policy in a Unipolar World* (London: Routledge, 2009), pp. 43–72.

[72] 'Iran Figures in PM-Bush Talks', *Financial Express*, September 14, 2005.

[73] Siddharth Varadarajan, 'The Unraveling of India's Persian Puzzle', *The Hindu*, September 27, 2005.

with under the aegis of the IAEA itself'.[74], a position that one noted analyst characterised as one of 'extraordinary naivety and even double-speak'.[75]

Iran reacted negatively to the Indian vote, stating it was 'very disturbed' by India's stance,[76] and threatened to 'reconsider ties' to those countries which had voted against Iran.[77] The Iranian envoy at the IAEA informed his Indian counterpart that the LNG agreement signed earlier that year was no longer valid. However, India maintained that it had received no official word from the Iranian ambassador in New Delhi on an impact on its ties with Iran. A few weeks after this assertion, Iran again linked negotiations on its energy deals with India with India's vote at the IAEA.[78]

In February 2006, India again voted against Iran at the IAEA over a resolution that referred Iran to the UN Security Council. Significantly, India justified this vote in terms of national security interests by referring to nuclear proliferation to Iran from the network of Pakistani scientist A. Q. Khan.[79] In a sharp reversal, Iran formally informed India a few weeks after this vote that the bilateral LNG agreement signed in June 2005 was no longer valid, as the price agreed to had not been ratified.[80] India disputed this decision, and insisted that the LNG agreement was a legally binding document that could not be abrogated unilaterally. The matter remains under dispute,[81] though India has refrained from taking legal action as a follow-up to its claims.[82] Simultaneously, the pipeline talks ran into new obstacles when Iran increased its asking price for the pipeline

---

[74] 'India's IAEA Vote was Decided in Advance', *The Hindu*, September 26, 2005.

[75] Varadarajan, 'The Unraveling of India's Persian Puzzle'.

[76] 'Iran Upset at India's Stance', *The Hindu*, September 28, 2005.

[77] 'No Indication from Iran to Review Ties', *Economic Times*, September 28, 2005.

[78] 'Iran's Armtwisting Begins: Fix Vienna Mistake or Else', *The Indian Express*, November 13, 2005.

[79] 'Govt Took Right Decision on Iran: PM', *Financial Express*, February 17, 2006.

[80] 'India-Iran LNG Deal in Peril', *The Indian Express*, May 3, 2006.

[81] 'MEA Annual Report 2007', p. 43. Available at http://meaindia.nic.in/, accessed on August 1, 2010.

[82] 'India Won't Take Iran to Court for LNG Deal Back-Out', *Financial Express*, December 12, 2006.

project to USD 7.20 per MBTU,[83] and also reversed its earlier commitment to guarantee the security of gas supplies up to the Indian border.

The circumstantial link between Iranian actions and India's IAEA votes appears strong. However, other factors may also have played a role in Iran's responses. Crude oil prices were indeed increasing substantially throughout this period. The enduring mistrust between India and Pakistan was also a major factor in the breakdown of the pipeline talks. Iran's reneging on the signed LNG supply agreement without consulting India was, however, a serious and unusual development that is difficult to explain as simply an opportunistic move in response to changing market conditions.

The IPI pipeline talks remained stalled well into 2007, with Iran adding additional conditions for periodic reviews of any agreed price in the future.[84] The three parties agreed to appoint an independent consultant to resolve the dispute;[85] Iran stated it did not consider itself bound by the consultant's opinion. However, Iran and Pakistan proceeded with their negotiations and recently concluded a bilateral agreement to build a pipeline without India's participation.[86]

In January 2008, India launched an Israeli spy satellite, the purpose of which was reportedly to conduct surveillance over Iran.[87] The satellite may have been designed to aid an attack on Iran, which could explain the secrecy behind the launch. Iran criticised the launch with its ambassador expressing the hope that 'wise and independent countries like India do not give their space technologies to launch spying operations against Iran'.[88]

---

[83] Siddharth Srivastav, 'Price Imbroglio Stymies Iran Pipeline', *Asia Times*, July 27, 2006.

[84] Kaveh Afrasiabi, 'Blockage in the Peace Pipeline', *Asia Times*, July 10, 2007.

[85] 'Iran Cuts LNG Offer Price by 8%', *The Indian Express*, November 18, 2006.

[86] 'India Out of "Peace Pipeline" as Iran, Pakistan Seal Gas Deal', *Times of India*, June 14, 2010.

[87] 'India Launches Israeli Satellite', *BBC*, January 21, 2008.

[88] Ninan Koshy, 'India and Israel Eye Iran', *Foreign Policy in Focus*, February 12, 2008. Available at http://www.fpif.org/articles/india_and_israel_eye_iran, accessed on September 1, 2010.

President Ahmadinejad visited India briefly in April 2008, during which both states spoke glowingly of their ties to each other.[89] However no breakthroughs were achieved on the stalled energy negotiations. In September 2008, India hosted the visit of the Israeli army chief Avi Mizrahi to Kashmir,[90] an event which provoked sharp comments in the Iranian media. In the wake of the devastating Mumbai terrorist attacks in November, carried out by Pakistan-based militants, Iranian president Ahmadinejad implied that the attackers had no links to Pakistan.[91] The Iranian daily *Kayhan*, whose views often mirror those of the Iranian Supreme Leader, alleged that India, US and Israel had secretly staged the attacks.[92] Iran also refused overflight permission to Indian jets on their way to the US to take part in a joint military exercise.[93]

As international tensions over the Iranian nuclear program escalated, India voted against Iran for the third time at the IAEA in 2009.[94] In March 2010, Indian Prime Minister Manmohan Singh and Saudi King Abdullah issued the joint Riyadh Declaration[95] in which the two leaders 'encouraged Iran to ... remove regional and international doubts about its nuclear program'. India's criticism of Iran's nuclear program in a joint statement with Saudi Arabia on Saudi soil was unprecedented, and indicated a new prioritisation of the Gulf states over Iran.[96]

---

[89] 'Iranian President's Visit a Test for India', *The New York Times*, April 30, 2008.

[90] Vijay Prashad, 'India's Reckless Road To Washington Through Tel Aviv', *Counterpunch*, December 26, 2008.

[91] 'How West Asia Views Mumbai Attacks', *The Hindu*, December 17, 2008.

[92] 'How West Asia Views Mumbai Attacks', The Hindu.

[93] Q. 1719, Indian Parliament Q&A. Available at http://meaindia.nic.in/, accessed on September 3, 2010.

[94] 'India Votes Against Iran in IAEA', *Times of India*, November 27, 2009.

[95] 'Riyadh Declaration: A New Era of Strategic Partnership', Press Information Bureau, Government of India. Available at http://pib.nic.in/release/release.asp?relid=58617, accessed on September 3, 2010.

[96] Harsh Pant, 'Looking Beyond Tehran', *Outlook Magazine*, March 17, 2010.

However, prospects of a possible NATO withdrawal from Afghanistan and reported US-backed moves to allow the Taliban to share power in Kabul unnerved India, and contributed to an attempt to re-engage Iran on regional security.[97] India also came out strongly against the latest round of UN sanctions against Iran, and the US and EU imposition of even tougher unilateral measures.[98] On its part, Iran appeared to be showing a revived interest in the Chahbahar port project.[99] The joint Zaranj–Delaram highway project in Afghanistan was implemented successfully by India in 2009.[100] This key highway now allows Indian aid to reach Afghanistan via Iran, and is a major contributor to the Indian presence in the region.

Nevertheless, as the year 2010 progressed, the India–Iran relationship worsened substantially. India banned the Iranian news channel Press TV in Kashmir,[101] after its coverage allegedly incited protests in the valley against Indian rule. Iranian Supreme Leader Khamenei publicly criticised Indian actions in Kashmir three times, and referred to the disputed territory as a 'nation'.[102] This was a significant development in the relationship, ending a decade-long refusal by Iran to criticise India's control of Kashmir. A furious India summoned the Iranian ambassador in protest, and explicitly linked Khamenei's comments to India's abstention on a vote against Iran in the UN Human Rights Council.

As the year drew to a close, the Indian central bank announced that it would no longer use the UN-established Asian Clearing Union mechanism to settle payments to Iran for oil imports.[103] This drew a sharp reaction from Tehran. As this chapter is being written, the two

---

[97] 'India Moves Closer to Iran Over Afghan Concerns', *Live Mint*, July 12, 2010; 'In Scramble for Afghanistan India Looks to Iran', *Reuters*, July 6, 2010.

[98] 'India, China Denounce Unilateral Sanctions on Iran', *Tehran Times*, July 7, 2010.

[99] 'India–Iran JV Comes Under UN Sanctions List; Crude Ferries Hit', *Financial Express*, July 10, 2010.

[100] 'India Hands Over Afghan Road', *The Indian Express*, January 23, 2009.

[101] 'Iran's Press TV Banned in J&K after Clips Spark Violence', *Asian Age*, September 14, 2010.

[102] 'A Persian Gulf', *Outlook*, December 6, 2010.

[103] 'RBI Stifles Iran Oil Imports', *Business Standard*, December 25, 2010.

sides are in intense negotiations to resolve the issue, with Iran reportedly refusing to sell oil to India if a satisfactory solution cannot be found. In the meantime, India has formally joined the Turkmenistan–Afghanistan–Pakistan (TAPI) pipeline project. Washington has consistently pushed the TAPI pipeline, in strong preference to the IPI pipeline, as a solution to South Asia's natural gas needs.

The US Factor and India's Strategic Choice

There is substantial evidence pointing to a link between the India's evolving ties with the United States and the sharp change in India's stance towards Iran around 2005. In this section, I establish this link by examining the discourses in the United States and India during the crucial period when the nuclear agreement was being negotiated using media archives. I also argue that the change in the approach towards Iran was not inevitable, but represented a strategic choice made by India.

There were indications of US interference in the IPI pipeline project months before the nuclear deal announcement.[104] Only days after the announcement, Indian Prime Minister Manmohan Singh appeared to back away from the pipeline negotiations by questioning whether 'any international consortium of bankers would underwrite this project',[105] although in objective terms there were few doubts that India's strong macroeconomic situation almost guaranteed such financing.[106] Before the September IAEA vote, Congressman Tom Lantos, the senior most Democrat in the Congressional committee required to approve the nuclear deal, indicated 'great displeasure' with India's policy towards Iran and demanded that India vote with the US at the IAEA.[107] Subsequent to the vote, Lantos stated that it

---

[104] M. K. Bhadrakumar, 'India, Pakistan, and the Peace Pipeline', *Asia Times*, September 15, 2004. Available at http://www.atimes.com/atimes/South_Asia/FI15Df03.html, accessed on August 28, 2010.

[105] 'Interview: Indian Prime Minister Singh', *The Washington Post*, July 20, 2005.

[106] P. Kumaraswamy, 'Delhi: Between Tehran and Washington', *Middle East Quarterly* 15, 1 (2008), pp. 41–48.

[107] 'US Offer Changed India's Iran Policy', *Dawn*, September 29, 2005.

was this threat that caused a change in India's prior decision to vote against the resolution at the IAEA.

Top Bush administration officials had three rounds of intense talks with India that linked the nuclear deal with India's Iran policy.[108] Congressman Joseph Crowley linked progress on the Indo-US nuclear agreement to both India's Iran vote and the IPI pipeline.[109] A prominent Indian news magazine cited an anonymous Congressional source's statement that the nuclear deal would be 'dead' if India did not back the US against Iran.[110]

Before the February vote, US ambassador to India David Mulford explicitly threatened that an Indian backing for Iran at the IAEA would be 'devastating' for the Indo-US nuclear agreement,[111] though vociferous protests in India[112] forced Washington to subsequently backtrack.[113] Only weeks before the February vote, the United States imposed sanctions on two Indian firms under the Iran Proliferation Act for allegedly supplying chemicals to Iran,[114] allegations which India strongly denied.

Perhaps most significantly Stephen Rademaker, who was US Assistant Secretary for Nonproliferation and International Security during the IAEA voting period, stated (after he had left office) that the Indian votes at the IAEA were 'coerced' by the United States.[115] He also added that 'more is going to be required [of India] because the problems of Iran and North Korea have not been solved'.

Pressure from Washington on India to downgrade its relationship with Iran continued after the IAEA votes, as the US–India nuclear agreement was being formalised in the US Congress. Concerns were raised in India[116] when the Hyde Act, the embodiment of the nuclear agreement under US law, explicitly required India to 'dissuade,

---

[108] 'The Iran Hiccup', *India Today*, October 3, 2005.
[109] 'When in Doubt Shut Up', *Outlook Magazine*, February 13, 2006.
[110] Ibid.
[111] 'N-deal Dies if India Doesn't Vote Against Iran: Mulford', *The Indian Express*, January 25, 2006.
[112] 'Mulford Remark Outrageous', *The Indian Express*, January 26, 2006.
[113] 'David as Goliath', *The Indian Express*, January 26, 2006.
[114] E. Yazdani, 'The Dynamics of India's Relations with Iran', p. 366.
[115] 'India's Anti-Iran Votes Were Coerced, Says Former US Official', *The Hindu*, February 16, 2007.
[116] 'Iran Clause a Stumbling Block', *Hindustan Times*, December 7, 2006.

isolate, and, if necessary, sanction and contain Iran'.[117] Secretary Rice told a Senate panel debating the nuclear agreement that the US had made it 'very clear to India that we have concerns about their relationship with Iran [and] about the pipeline'.[118]

US Energy Secretary Samuel Bodman, in India to negotiate the nuclear deal, stated that the IPI pipeline needed to be stopped as it could help Iran develop nuclear weapons.[119] US preferences also led India to shy away from a deeper engagement with Iran on Afghanistan,[120] and US pressure was allegedly a major factor in the recent Indian central bank decision to stifle Iranian oil payments.[121]

Thus available evidence strongly points to India bending to US demands to downgrade its ties to Iran and take a harder line on the Iranian nuclear issue in exchange for a successful conclusion of the Indo-US nuclear agreement.

Some analysts, adopting a material-structural framework, have argued that the tangible gains from a strategic alliance with the United States far outweigh the losses from any damage done to India–Iran ties.[122] They see the Indian votes against Iran as the inevitable choice of a rational, systemic cost-benefit analysis.

There is no question that there were real or anticipated material gains from the rapidly converging India–US relationship. However,

---

[117] House Report 5682, United States Congress. Available at http://frwebgate.access.gpo.gov/cgi-bin/getdoc.cgi?dbname=109_cong_bills&docid=f:h5682enr.txt.pdf, accessed on September 5, 2010.

[118] 'US Concerned Over India-Iran Ties: Rice', *Agence France Presse*, April 5, 2006.

[119] 'We Need to Stop Pipeline Says Bodman', *The Hindu*, March 23, 2007.

[120] M. K. Bhadrakumar, 'India Seeks a 'Velvet Divorce' From Iran', *Asia Times*, November 4, 2008. Available at http://www.atimes.com/atimes/South_Asia/JK05Df01.html, accessed on August 28, 2010.

[121] 'Slippery Slope', *Deccan Herald,* January 11, 2010.

[122] K. Subrahmanyam,' Indo-US Relations in a Changing World', *Air Power* 2, 3 (2005). Available at http://www.aerospaceindia.org/Journals/Monsoon%202005/Indo-US%20Relations%20in%20a%20Changing%20World.pdf, accessed on September 3, 2010. Also see by the same author, 'No American Can Treat India Like a Pet', *Rediff,* October 11, 2005. Available at http://www.rediff.com/news/2005/oct/11inter.htm, accessed on September 3, 2010.

the argument that rationalist-structural factors of the international system by themselves determined India's behaviour towards Iran is unconvincing. As I shall argue in a subsequent section, key domestic factors and their associated constructions led to a shift in the Indian state's identity, with a strong predisposition among Indian elites in favor of a partnership with the US.

Moreover, the contrast with the behavior of other states is revealing. Pakistan, Malaysia and Egypt chose to abstain at the critical September IAEA vote. Pakistan also successfully concluded the gas pipeline deal with Iran, defying repeated US warnings.[123] South Korea has maintained strong economic ties to Iran, rebuffing US pressure.[124] China's major energy deals with Iran have been concluded successfully.[125] China's trade with Iran, most of it energy-related, has doubled since 2004,[126] and China has invested USD 40 billion in Iran's energy sector.[127] Brazil and Turkey struck a strongly pro-active, independent stance recently with their proposal for a compromise resolution on Iranian enrichment, in spite of adverse US pressure.[128] Subsequent to the proposal's almost offhand dismissal by the Obama administration,[129] both states voted against the US-backed punitive sanctions resolution in the UNSC.

Each of these states has deep structural dependencies with the United States in military, economic, or strategic arenas; some much deeper than India does. Yet each made the choice of a more balanced foreign policy with Iran in key areas. India's actions in distancing itself from Iran were not driven solely by structural-material

---

[123] 'Pakistan Resolute on Iran Gas Deal', *Boston Globe*, June 23, 2010.

[124] R. Weitz, 'Will Asia Nix Iran Sanctions?', *The Diplomat*, August 10, 2010. Available at http://the-diplomat.com/2010/08/10/will-asia-nix-iran-sanctions/, accessed on September 2, 2010.

[125] M. K. Bhadrakumar, 'China Leaves the US and India Trailing', *Asia Times*, December 14, 2007.

[126] M. Richardson, 'Iran will test U.S.-China ties', *The Japan Times*, August 14, 2010. Available at http://search.japantimes.co.jp/cgi-bin/eo20100814mr.html, accessed on September 2, 2010.

[127] R. Weitz, 'Will Asia Nix Iran Sanctions?'

[128] 'Brazil, Turkey Engineer Breakthrough on Iran', *The Nation*, May 18, 2010.

[129] Ibid.

imperatives. India exercised agency and made a strategic choice in posing to itself an either-or question on the US and Iran. As Indian Foreign Secretary Shyam Saran himself admitted:

> long-term trends would probably have brought India and the United States much closer in any case over a period of time. However, *through the exercise of policy choices on both sides*, this gradual and somewhat measured transformation was significantly accelerated over the last year. (emphasis added).[130]

This then raises the important question as to what explains India's choice. Before answering this question, I shall briefly review the framework of strategic culture in the existing literature. I shall then analyse the evolution of India's grand strategy in the post-Cold War era, and show that this provides a more complete explanation for India's choices and their consequent effects on ties with Iran.

Strategic Culture and State Identity

The concept of strategic culture in the field of international relations can be traced to Snyder[131] and Posen.[132] Both scholars saw military doctrine as originating from the structure of the international system. In this they largely aligned themselves with the structural realist tradition. Subsequent scholars – such as Gray[133] and Kier[134] – departing from structural realism, introduced autonomous political–military cultural factors as independent variables.

---

[130] Shyam Saran, 'Transforming India–US Relations: Forging a Strategic Partnership', address at the Carnegie Endowment for International Peace, December 25, 2005. Available at http://www.carnegieendowment.org/files/indianfsdec21.pdf, accessed on September 5, 2010.

[131] Jack Snyder, 'The Soviet Strategic Culture: Implications for Nuclear Options', R-2154-AF, Santa Monica: Rand Corporation, 1977.

[132] Barry R. Posen, *Sources of Military Doctrine: France, Britain And Germany Between The World Wars* (Ithaca: Cornell University Press, 1984).

[133] Colin Gray, 'National Styles', in Carl G. Jacobsen, ed., *Strategic Power: USA/USSR* (London: St. Martin's Press, 1990).

[134] Elizabeth Kier, 'Culture and French Military Doctrine Before World War II', in Peter Katzenstein, ed., *The Culture of National Security: Norms and Identity in World Politics* (New York: Columbia University Press, 1996).

Johnston, in his seminal analysis of Chinese military doctrine, supplied a working definition of strategic culture that will serve as a methodological starting point for this chapter's core arguments:

> Strategic culture is an integrated system of symbols (i.e. argumentation structures, languages, analogies, metaphors, etc.) that acts to establish pervasive and long-lasting grand strategic preferences by formulating concepts of the role and efficacy of force in interstate political affairs.[135]

The symbolic and linguistic element in strategic culture is key, as these are the means through which meaning and preferences are communicated across spans of time, and contribute to its persistent effects.

Johnston divides strategic culture into two levels. First is the central strategic paradigm, embodying core assumptions about orderliness in the world. This includes the role of war, efficacy of the use of force, and the nature of an adversary. The second level is that of grand strategy, which embodies the operationalisation of the central strategic paradigm. Grand strategy springs from fundamental axioms that constitute the central strategic paradigm, and translates into policy preferences (e.g., offense over defence) that mark a state's behaviour.

Johnston further argues that the effect of an ideational variable such as strategic culture on policy can be segregated from the effect of material factors.[136] Therefore, testable hypotheses can be developed that attempt to isolate the effects of strategic culture as an independent variable on behaviour treated as a dependent variable.

Taking issue with whom he labels 'first-generation' theorists such as Gray, Johnston sees core weaknesses in their approach which fails to distinguish cause from effect, leading to a tautological equation of behaviour with culture.

In response, Gray argues that attaching causality to a complex phenomenon such as strategic culture provides little analytical value, as culture provides context to policy rather than acting as an

---

[135] Alastair Iain Johnston, *Cultural Realism: Strategic Culture and Grand Strategy in Chinese History* (Princeton: Princeton University Press, 1995), p. 36.

[136] Alastair Iain Johnston, 'Thinking about Strategic Culture', *International Security*, 19, 4 (1995), pp. 32–64. Also by the same author, 'Strategic Cultures Revisited: Reply to Colin Gray', *Review of International Studies*, 25 (1999), pp. 519–23.

independent variable. This is because 'if there is cause in the effect, how can cause be assessed for its effect?'[137] In other words, strategic culture is not an independent variable that can be separated from material factors – the two embed each other and together provide context that drives policy actions.

Poore, in reviewing the debate between the first and later generation theorists, agrees with the former that culture is a conditioning factor rather than a separate and separable variable against which material variables can be tested.[138] According to this argument, analyses that account for strategic culture must necessarily be non-positivistic, and seek to understand how strategic culture gives meaning to the material factors encountered by states.

Johnston, Gray, Kier and others heavily emphasised war and military strategy in their definition of strategic culture. Bajpai[139] however, expands the concept to include not just military strategy but a wider range of strategic policies states use towards other state actors – 'economic, cultural and other non-military instruments of grand strategy'.[140] I employ Bajpai's more comprehensive approach in this chapter.

The framework of strategic culture is substantially informed by constructivist approaches in international relations theory that place ideational factors, specifically state identity, at the heart of their state behavior. Constructivists argue that interests of states are not a given, rather they are prefigured by the identity of states. Identity is not seen in essentialist terms; rather it is constructed through an interaction between the state and its international environment.[141] Identity,

---

[137] Colin Gray, 'Strategic Culture as Context: the First Generation of Theory Strikes Back', *Review of International Studies*, 25 (1999), pp. 49–69.

[138] Stuart Poore, 'What is the Context? A Reply to the Gray-Johnston Debate on Strategic Culture', *Review of International Studies*, 29 (2003), pp. 279–84.

[139] Kanti Bajpai, 'Indian Strategic Culture', in M. R. Chambers, ed., *South Asia in 2020: Future Strategic Balances and Alliances* (Pennsylvania: Strategic Studies Institute, 2002), pp. 245–303.

[140] Ibid., p. 248.

[141] Ron Jepperson, Alexander Wendt, and Peter Katzenstein, 'Norms, Identity, and Culture in National Security', in Peter Katzenstein, ed., *The Culture of National Security: Norms and Identity in World Politics* (New York: Columbia University Press, 1996).

once constructed, has real effects, though identity itself can change over time, leading to a corresponding shift in perceived interests.

The debate between first and later generation strategic culture theorists also embeds key ontological differences. Whereas some ('thin') constructivists accept the rationalist approach of falsifiability, cause-and-effect, and testable hypotheses, other ('thick') constructivists argue in the vein of Gray and Poore, that ideational factors act as interpretive lenses that condition the perception of material factors. Ideational drivers do not cause behavior in a linear fashion; rather both are mutually and intersubjectively constituted. Instead of a positivist approach researchers should rely on thick descriptions and narratives on the role of identity, norms, and culture in how they shape behaviour and policy.

The analytical approach favoured by thick constructivists to derive the interactions of identity and policy is discourse analysis.[142] Discourse analysis in international relations, with roots in the ideas of Foucault,[143] involves 'investigating empirically the constructions of identity and the formulation of policy within a given debate'.[144] Identities are constructed through context and differentiation, and seek to delineate a Self from one or multiple Others.[145] This differentiation could operate in various degrees for different Others. The identity of Self itself can undergo temporal transformations, leading to multiple Selves over a time period. The understanding of these identity shifts then leads to a deeper understanding of policy shifts.

The investigation of identity is heavily reliant on textual analysis[146] – a tool to understand and delineate identities and policies spawned by various discourses. I employ this approach in the chapter by citing and analysing discourses present at three levels – state, mainstream media, and scholarship – in order to shed light on the Indian state's identity shift in the post-Cold War era.

A key question that arises in employing strategic culture as a theoretical tool is the possible instrumentality of state discourse. In other

---

[142] Lene Hansen, *Security as Practice: Discourse Analysis and the Bosnian War* (New York: Routledge, 2006).

[143] Michel Foucault, *The Archaeology of Knowledge* (London: Tavistock Publications, 1974).

[144] Hansen, *Security as Practice*, p. 30.

[145] Ibid., p. 6.

[146] Hansen, *Security as Practice*, p. 55.

words, how can we tell whether the articulations that inform us about the content of the strategic culture of a given state are sincere? Could they simply be instrumentalised, and therefore describe behaviour rather than identity or cause?[147] Thus, any study employing this concept must show that the strategic culture of the state in question is deployed consistently in multiple situations and is articulated by a range of actors.

India's Post-Cold War Identity Shift

I now apply the theoretical framework of strategic culture and, with discourse analysis as one tool, explain India's privileging of an alliance with the US and the consequent distancing itself from Iran. I do so by first delineating key aspects of the strategic culture of India. I then argue that the post-Cold War period – but particularly the last decade – marked a distinct transformation in India's strategic culture that resulted in a reinterpretation of its strategic environment. The result was an identity shift of the Indian state, with direct implications for reconfiguring the United States as an 'aspirational Other', favouring a 'natural' Indo-US alliance,[148] and a consequent distancing of Iran.

INDIA'S STRATEGIC CULTURE

Two prior studies on India's strategic culture are worth noting. Ollapally[149] examines India's nuclear policies through a lens of strategic culture and detects clear and persistent elements within this culture that contributed to India's maintenance of nuclear ambiguity for as many as 34 years after a clear material threat emerged in its neighbourhood with the overt Chinese weaponisation in 1964. She describes 'strategic ambiguity' that allows multiple options to remain

---

[147] Some scholars in the Gramscian tradition (e.g., Klein, 1988) have argued that strategic culture is always instrumentalised.

[148] The phrase was – then controversially – first used by Indian leader Vajpayee during a 1998 trip to New York when Vajpayee attended the UN General Assembly. See C. Raja Mohan, *Crossing the Rubicon: The Shaping of India's New Foreign Policy* (New Delhi; New York: Penguin, 2005), p. 50.

[149] Deepa Ollapally, 'Mixed Motives in India's Search for Nuclear Status', *Asian Survey*, 41, 6 (2001), pp. 925–42.

open, and 'a streak of ambivalence and historical reticence against irrevocable decisions ... and a tolerance for contradictions'.[150]

Bajpai,[151] in his perceptive analysis of Indian strategic culture, labels this stream of thinking 'Nehruvian'. He contrasts this approach to two other streams of Indian strategic thought that he identifies – the neoliberals and the hyper-realists. While Nehruvians are mainly distinguished by an emphasis on communication and contact as a means of transforming adversaries into allies, and a strong commitment to anti-imperialism, non-alignment and keeping great powers out of the affairs of the subcontinent, neoliberals see trade and economic liberalisation as a means to pragmatically improve (or at least contain) conflictual relations with neighbours, and most importantly, welcome the role of one particular great power – the United States – as an Indian ally, aiding India's rise on the global stage. Hyper-realists take the most nationalistic stance of the three, believing that force and balance-of-power have a significant role in Indian foreign policy, and India should ultimately aim to become a great power itself through a conscious process of militarisation and assertion of its national interests.

In the companion essay in this volume, Bajpai explores three other streams of Indian strategic thought – Marxist, Hindutva and Gandhian. He argues that the first two particularly have important adherents in India. All three propose an idealistic normative view of the world that is in conflict with a system of nation-states. Each expresses distinct suspicions of the United States, though the logic of each is very different.

INDIA'S IDENTITY SHIFT

During the Cold War period, the Indian state had constructed a Self with a predominant identity of Nehruvian non-alignment, Third World solidarity and an independent foreign policy. This Self was differentiated against two Others[152] – the two superpower blocs. This differentiation process had two aspects. The West, with its identity of liberal capitalism, imperialism, and anti-communism, was posited as an adversarial Other. On the other hand, non-alignment was also

---

[150] Ollapally, 'Mixed Motives', p. 942.

[151] Bajpai, 'Indian Strategic Culture', pp. 245–302.

[152] Pakistan, created out of the subcontinent's partition, was also posited as an Other.

articulated as a bridge ideology that could bring reason and dialogue to bear upon a world plagued by an existential enmity between the East and West. The Eastern bloc, without a capitalist, colonial past, was steadily posited as a less adversarial Other; by the late 1970s, the mildly adversarial construction of the East had almost disappeared.

The collapse of the Warsaw Pact and the resultant unipolar world of the 1990s created a crisis in the Indian identity. The decade marked a time of transition, as India attempted to articulate a new central strategic paradigm. Meanwhile, a major identity shift was underway on the domestic front, when India began replacing the *dirigiste* state with a neoliberal market paradigm. The Indian economy had shown steady growth since about 1980[153] in the wake of the state's shift to a pro-capital stance.[154] The 1991 liberalisation process sustained the expansion,[155] and was given most of the credit for India's growth story.

By the mid-1990s, the Indian state was substantially neoliberal in economic policy, seeking integration into the global trading regime. Not so in the foreign policy arena, however. In an age of a normative discourse of human rights and humanitarian intervention in the West, India emphasised a 'multipolar world' and an adherence to norms of sovereignty,[156] along with a fierce rejection of US pressures on non-proliferation and human rights.[157] Indian discourse continued to posit the West as an adversarial Other,[158] and India actively explored Asian partnerships as a facet of its grand strategy.

President Clinton's tilt towards India during the 1999 Kargil war with Pakistan was the first indication of a qualitative change in

---

[153] Deepak Nayyar, 'India's Unfinished Journey: Transforming Growth into Development', *Modern Asian Studies*, 40, 3 (2006), pp. 797–832.

[154] Atul Kohli, 'State, Business, and Economic Growth in India', *Studies in Comparative International Development*, 42 (2007), pp. 87–114.

[155] Arvind Panagariya, 'Growth and Reforms During the 1980s and 1990s', *Economic and Political Weekly*, 39, 25 (2004), pp. 2581–94.

[156] For an Indian viewpoint emphasising sovereignty in the context of the NATO attack on Serbia, see J. N. Dixit, 'Strikes Against Sovereignty', *The Indian Express*, April 15, 1999; 'NATO Air Strikes Cause Anxiety, Says Govt', *The Indian Express*, March 26, 1999.

[157] Sumit Ganguly and Manjit Pardesi, 'Explaining Sixty Years of India's Foreign Policy', *India Review*, 8, 1 (2009), pp. 4–19.

[158] K. Subrahmanyam, 'Clear and Present Danger: US Path to Unipolar Hegemony', *The Times of India*, May 3, 1999.

the India–US relationship.[159] Then, a strategic decision by the new Bush administration of enhancing ties to India[160] led to quick and major advances[161] – India's backing for the controversial US missile defence proposal, its offer to the US of all its military bases after the September 11 attacks, accelerating joint military exercises, and the Indo–US Defence Framework Agreement. The nuclear deal essentially capped this trend.

The above developments mark a major change in the Indo-US relationship, but do not explain its cause. On the Indian side, the core cause was the re-articulation of the Indian central strategic paradigm, in turn driven by a shift in identity of the Indian state. This shift consisted of a change in its definition of the Other of the West, with the 'Third World' practically excluded by being reduced mostly to a site of trade narratives. The West – more accurately, the United States – previously an adversarial Other, was steadily and radically reconfigured as an 'aspirational Other', a term I introduce.

An 'aspirational Other' is an Other that the Self constructs as a site of emulation; in some crude sense also as a superior. Yet, the substantial gulf that separates the aspirational Other from Self also creates a degree of tension and hypersensitivity in the relationship. The example of Turkey is illustrative – the Kemalist creation of the Turkish republic constructed a positivist, rationalist Europe as an 'aspirational Other', seeing it as a standard-bearer of 'contemporary civilization'. Ataturk took the ideational step of privileging secularism as a means to close the perceived gap with the 'aspirational Other' of the West. As a corollary, the Ottoman-era Muslim identity of Turkey was constructed as an existential threat to state and society.

Unlike Turkey in the 1920s however, the shift in India's state identity was more of a bottom-up process. At the heart of it was the emergence of a large and articulate Indian urban middle class with

---

[159] Mohan, *Crossing the Rubicon*, pp. 98–108.

[160] Condoleezza Rice, 'Campaign 2000: Promoting the National Interest', *Foreign Affairs*, 79, 1 (2000), pp. 45–62.

[161] A detailed, empirical narrative of these developments is outside the scope of this chapter, but can be found in C. Raja Mohan, *Impossible Allies: Nuclear India, the United States, and the Global Order* (New Delhi: India Research Press, 2006); Prakash Karat, *Subordinate Ally: The Nuclear Deal and India-US Strategic Relations* (New Delhi: Left Word Books, 2007).

consumerist tendencies. Many of India's foreign policy elites, media commentators, and corporate professionals drew from this class – a class which increasingly identified itself with the aspirations of the American model of society.[162]

The 1980s and 90s also witnessed a huge increase in the Indian diaspora in the United States, most of which drew from the urban educated middle class. It is estimated that 25 per cent of the Indian elite and 30 per cent of India's retired generals have relatives in the US.[163] Indians are also among the highest-earning immigrants in the US.[164] The diaspora's role in altering the perception of India among US elites was critical.[165] Equally, the transmittal of American investment capital, ideas, and neoliberal norms back to India also greatly influenced the Indian state's identity shift. A Pew poll across 24 countries on attitudes towards the US found large majorities of urban Indians having strongly favourable impressions of the United States, including higher levels of support for George W. Bush than Americans themselves.[166] Manmohan Singh himself acknowledged diasporic and corporate influences as being a major driver of strategic ties between the India and the US:

> ... an acceleration of people-to-people contact and the consequent business-to-business interaction has forged closer State-to-State relations. Shared values and growing economic links have enabled a closer strategic engagement.[167]

These factors were crucial in creating a predisposition for a partnership with the US among elite and middle-class Indians. When US attitudes towards India changed under the Bush administration, it

---

[162] Christophe Jaffrelot, 'The India-US Rapprochement: State-Driven or Middle Class Driven?', *India Quarterly*, 65, 1 (2009), pp. 1–14.

[163] Arthur G. Rubinoff, 'The Diaspora as a Factor in U.S.-India Relations', *Asian Affairs*, 32, 3 (2005), pp. 169–187.

[164] Jaffrelot, 'The India-US Rapprochement'.

[165] Rubinoff, 'The Diaspora as a Factor'.

[166] The poll results can be found at http://pewglobal.org/2008/12/18/global-public-opinion-in-the-bush-years-2001-2008/, accessed on August 28, 2010.

[167] Manmohan Singh, 'Address to the India Today Conclave, 2005'. Available at http://pmindia.nic.in/speech/content.asp?id=78, accessed on August 27, 2010.

did not take much persuading for Indian policymakers to respond eagerly.

STATE DISCOURSE

State discourse provides important insights as to how the Indian state has increasingly constructed an identity of Self as a 'liberal democracy' as a means to bridge the perceived gap with the 'aspirational Other' of the United States, and explicitly linked it with its new orientation in global society. In recent years, India has practiced two levels of state discourse. At formal multilateral forums, Indian discourse tends to emphasise themes of equitable development, and underplay themes of liberal democracy.[168] This contrasts with state discourse in bilateral forums and informal settings consisting of mixed audiences. Here Indian state discourse more directly asserts its identity as a 'liberal democracy', and more than hints of a partnership with similar states. The Indian state's actions, and India's media and scholarly discourse (see here), have tended to be more in line with the latter, especially in strategic and security arenas. This suggests that Indian discourse in multilateral gatherings may be largely instrumental in nature, and also designed to pursue a shift in grand strategy covertly, in order to minimise damage to India's interests.

For example, Prime Minister Manmohan Singh argued to an Indian and international audience in New Delhi:

> If there is an 'idea of India' by which India should be defined, it is the idea of an inclusive, open, multi-cultural, multi-ethnic, multi-lingual society... Liberal democracy is the natural order of political organization in today's world... *We should be proud to identify with those who defend the values of liberal democracy and secularism across the world.*[169] (emphasis added)

---

[168] Manmohan Singh, 'Full Text of Manmohan Singh's Speech to UN General Assembly', *Hindustan Times*, September 27, 2008. Available at http://www.hindustantimes.com/Full-text-of-Manmohan-Singh-s-speech-at-UN-General-Assembly/Article1-340789.aspx, accessed on September 4, 2010.

[169] Manmohan Singh, 'Address to the India Today Conclave, 2005'. Also see Sanjaya Baru, 'India and the World: Economics and Politics of the Manmohan Singh Doctrine in Foreign Policy', Institute of South Asian Studies, Working Paper No. 46, November 14, 2008. Available at http://www.isasnus.org/events/activities/20081008%20-%20Prof%20Sanjaya%20Baru.pdf, accessed on August 27, 2010.

The Indo-US joint announcement of 2005 on the nuclear deal heavily emphasised 'democratic values' and a commitment 'to strengthen democratic practices in societies which wish to become more open and pluralistic' as a key driver in the partnership. Indian Foreign Secretary Nirupama Rao heavily stressed similar themes in a recent speech.[170]

Foreign Secretary Shyam Saran's 2005 address focused on a change in India's non-proliferation stance.[171] He indicated that India was no longer opposing the NPT at its core; what it sought was an 'India exception' and inclusion into the existing framework. Significantly, he also linked this evolution with a harder line on Iran. In 2009, Prime Minister Singh made this shift explicit, by demanding that India be allowed to join the NPT as a nuclear weapons state.[172]

In making these statements, Indian leaders were not only describing an organisational principle of the Indian state; they were also communicating a set of symbols that made up a reconstituted Indian central strategic paradigm and asserting the accompanying identity shift to that of a 'liberal democracy', along the lines of the 'aspirational Other' of the United States. In a world where the US was the dominant formulator of global norms, this also implied that India was no longer challenging the core global normative structure on the basis of non-alignment or even a 'multipolar world'. Rather, it was now seeking to enter and endorse the norm-setting club as an insider.

A direct consequence of this was the construction of Iran as a 'distant Other', a term I introduce. A 'distant Other' is perceived neither as an actual or potential ally, nor as an enemy who must be combated or contained. The 'distant Other' occupies a secondary priority in the Self's universe, and is often viewed with a degree of wariness.

---

[170] Nirupama Rao, 'Two Democracies: Defining the Essence of India-US Partnership', address by Indian Foreign Secretary at the Woodrow Wilson Center, March 15, 2009. Available at http://www.wilsoncenter.org/news/docs/Rao%20prepared%20remarks.pdf, accessed on August 31, 2010.

[171] Shyam Saran, 'Transforming India-U.S. Relations'.

[172] Sumit Ganguly, 'Singh's Shrewd Move', *Newsweek*, December 4, 2009.

Media Discourse

Indian media discourse almost overwhelmingly welcomed the nuclear deal[173] and its ramifications of a close partnership with the US. Much of the debate engaged minimally with the technical aspects of energy security or a serious contemplation of the costs of India's strategic choice. Rather the media discourse became a somewhat exultant celebration about India's supposed emergence as a major power aided by the US. It also centered too much on attacking the Indian leftist parties who were opposing the deal in Parliament.[174] Either way, it provided an insightful glimpse of elite India's identity shift.

NDTV's Barkha Dutt, among the most influential media personalities in India, while making a startling admission that most of the details of the nuclear agreement were technical 'gobbledygook' to her, argued:

> Indians know how to distinguish between Bush and the country he governs. And the fact is that many of us have aspirations that take us westwards. It may be our children who go to university in the United States ... it may be our own classmates who work on Wall Street. For many Indians, their future as global players is linked to the American dream.[175]

And again 'language, cultural affinities and the fact that we are both democracies would make us choose America any day over China or Russia'.[176]

Dutt's interventions are revealing because they say much not only about the aspirational and ideational leanings of influential Indian foreign policy commentary, but also reflect the narrow professional and business class character of the project.

---

[173] 'Indian Media Hails Nuclear Deal', *BBC*, March 3, 2006.

[174] Rajdeep Sardesai, 'Karat and Stick', *CNN-IBN*, August 17, 2007. Available at http://ibnlive.in.com/blogs/rajdeepsardesai/1/2315/karat-and-stick.html, accessed on August 28, 2010.

[175] Barkha Dutt, 'Left in a Time Warp', *Hindustan Times*, August 17, 2007. Available at http://www.hindustantimes.com/Left-in-a-time-warp/Article1-243001.aspx, accessed on August 25, 2010.

[176] Barkha Dutt, 'Us and Them', *Hindustan Times*, August 25, 2007. Available at http://www.hindustantimes.com/US-and-them/Article1-244315.aspx, accessed on August 28, 2010.

Other top media analysts made similar arguments. For instance, Shekhar Gupta, editor of *Indian Express* and among India's most prominent journalists, struck a strong aspirational note in launching a frontal attack on non-alignment and arguing that the nuclear deal presented India with an opportunity of a 'breakout from the 'lower middle class' status in the community of nations',[177] while claiming there was no cost to be paid in terms of an independent foreign policy. Sagarika Ghose, Senior Editor at news channel *CNN-IBN*, wrote of a 'massively pro-American middle class' adopting 'America as a subconscious role model' in the context of her support for the nuclear deal.[178]

Other commentators, while attempting to address the costs of the Indo-US partnership, framed the US as an Other of a realpolitik ally, while Iran was constructed as an adversary. Pramit Pal Chaudhuri, foreign editor at *Hindustan Times*, strongly backed India's actions against Iran, because 'a nuclear Iran rebounds in Pakistan's favor'. In contrast, the nuclear deal was highly desirable as it gave India 'nuclear club membership'. Veteran commentator Prem Shankar Jha backed the nuclear deal, but conceded that it was not for free, and required India 'to assume some of the responsibility for maintaining order in an increasingly chaotic world'.[179] Although Jha did not specifically state it, presumably this 'responsibility' also included aligning with the US approach on containing Iran.

Scholarly Discourse

The Indian English-language media's rallying around the nuclear agreement represented the popularisation of arguments that were already being made by key Indian foreign policy academics on the imperatives of a close Indo-US alliance as India's overarching

---

[177] Shekhar Gupta, 'New Pitch, Front Foot Forward', *The Indian Express*, March 4, 2006. Available at http://www.expressindia.com/news/columnists/full_column.php?content_id=88925, accessed on August, 28, 2010.

[178] Sagarika Ghose, 'Howdy Partner', *Hindustan Times*, September 9, 2008. Available at http://www.hindustantimes.com/News-Feed/Columns/Howdy-pardner/Article1-336797.aspx, accessed on August 29, 2010.

[179] Prem Shankar Jha, 'Left With Megawhats?', *Hindustan Times*, August 24, 2007. Available at http://www.hindustantimes.com/editorial-views-on/BigIdea/Left-with-megawhats/Article1-244118.aspx, accessed on August 28, 2010.

foreign policy goal. Underlying this discourse was the assumption that the world was unipolar, and likely to stay that way.[180] The arguments from scholars were situated both within neorealist and neoliberal frameworks.

For example, C. Raja Mohan, among the most prominent Indian foreign affairs analysts, argued that India shared with the US and the West the 'basic ideas of the European enlightenment... values of reason, cosmopolitanism, scientific progress, individual freedom' which provide the 'long-term bond between India and the West'.[181] Thus allying with the US was a 'historic choice' that India must make.[182]

More recently Raja Mohan has also argued that India–Iran relationship is of a much more secondary importance to India's relationship with the Arab Gulf states, which he argues, are hostile to Iran.[183] This is essentially an interests-based argument that merits some attention. India's trade with the GCC (Gulf Cooperation Council) countries indeed eclipses that with Iran. The Gulf is also home to 5.5 million Indian expatriates who remit USD 35 billion to India each year. In comparison, the number of Indians living in Iran is negligible.

However, there is not necessarily a contradiction between a strong India–GCC relationship and durable ties with Iran. After all, India has evolved a much closer strategic relationship with Israel, which Gulf Arab states do not even recognise. Also, the GCC does not speak with one voice on Iran. Although King Abdullah's alleged backing for a war on Iran was recently highlighted by US media, an alternative interpretation[184] of Wikileaks cables argues for a much more nuanced understanding of the Arab–Persian rivalry. Other leaked cables clearly show that many Arab Gulf states are uneasy about the worsening US–Iran relationship, recognising that a conflict in the region can only harm their interests.[185]

---

[180] As evidenced by titles such as Harsh Pant, *Indian Foreign Policy in a Unipolar World* (London: Routledge, 2009).

[181] Raja Mohan, *Crossing the Rubicon*, pp. 57–58.

[182] Ibid., p. 81.

[183] Address to IDSA workshop on India's National Strategy, Institute of Defence Studies and Analyses, New Delhi, December 23, 2010.

[184] Gareth Porter and Jim Lobe, 'Gulf War Cries Over Iran Exaggerated', *Asia Times*, December 8, 2010. Available at http://www.atimes.com/atimes/Middle_East/LL08Ak01.html, accessed on September 3, 2010.

[185] Gareth Porter and Jim Lobe, 'Gulf War Cries'.

K. Subrahmanyam, arguably the most influential strategic thinker in modern India, backed both India's votes against Iran and the nuclear deal with the US from a balance-of-power perspective.[186] However, he struck a distinctly values-based note recently by arguing that India's vital interests are served by an 'international system in which the preeminent power is a pluralist democracy and not a totalitarian one-party state', in explaining his preference an Indian tilt towards the US to balance China.[187]

The construction of a 'natural' alliance between India and the US at least partially built upon a commonality of an identity of 'liberal democracy' leads to certain policy implications. States such as Iran, seen to resist the globally dominant liberal order, are by inference constructed, at the minimum, as 'distant Others', and, at the maximum, as adversaries. The future of the Indo-Iranian relationship will be subject to the prevalence of such constructions. The more the identity of the Indian state evolves in a direction towards that of a 'liberal democracy' to the exclusion of other identities, the greater will be the tensions in the India–Iran relationship.

Conclusion

This chapter aimed to gain a deeper understanding of the Indo-Iranian relationship, using Indian strategic culture as a guiding framework. I began by presenting an empirical narrative of the relationship at a level of detail beyond existing literature, with a particular focus on the critical period of 2005–10. Next, I showed how the US role, in the context of the Indo-US nuclear deal and the broader strategic partnership it represented, was a major factor in India making a strategic choice of distancing itself from Iran.

I then applied the framework to the evolution of Indian foreign policy in the post-Cold War period. India transited from an identity of Nehruvian Third World solidarity in the Cold War era, to a state articulating a 'multipolar world' in the 1990s, and then finally to an increasing articulation of an identity as a 'liberal democracy'; a

---

[186] Subrahmanyam, 'No American Can Treat India Like a Pet'.

[187] Subrahmanyam, 'Partnering with the US: Yes We Can!', *Business Standard*, November 18, 2009. Available at http://www.business-standard.com/india/news/k-subrahmanyam-partneringthe-us-yes-we-can/376773/, accessed on August 28, 2010.

process which is still underway. Key drivers of this identity shift were the effects of the Indian diaspora in the US, deepening Indo–US business ties, and an aspirational construction of the United States by the Indian urban middle class, from which most of its policy elites originated.

The result was a reconfiguration of the US from an adversarial Other to an 'aspirational Other', privileging the desirability of a strategic partnership with the United States, and implying a strengthening rather than challenging of existing global norms. This had a direct impact on India's construction of Iran, which shifted from a partner, aiding the formation of a 'multipolar world', to a 'distant Other'. By making a different choice, as states with similar or greater dependence on the US have done, India could have maintained a closer relationship with Iran with enhanced benefits on energy and security, precluded the emergence of a potentially adversarial Tehran, and still retained a durable, multifaceted relationship with the United States.

More fundamentally, the trajectory of the India–Iran relationship in the post-Cold War era is a fascinating window into what is essentially a growing tension between India's identity and its interests in its neighbourhood. A certain degree of such a tension is inevitable for a complex, continental-sized entity such as India. Nevertheless, if India's re-articulation of its identity does not yield commensurate benefits in terms of its vital and proximate interests, then a space will be created for other challenger identities to re-emerge in the national discourse.

15

REDEFINING INDIA'S GRAND STRATEGY?
THE EVOLVING NATURE OF INDIA'S ISRAEL POLICY

Nicolas Blarel

In September 1950, after two years of intense debates, Indian Prime Minister Jawaharlal Nehru decided to recognise the newly created state of Israel while deferring the establishment of full diplomatic relations.[1] It was not however until January 1992 that India became the last major non-Arab and non-Islamic State to establish full and normal diplomatic relations with Israel.[2] The absence of any substantial exchanges during 42 years is surprising as both countries lacked any direct conflict of interest. Paradoxically, there was no major reappraisal of India's neutral and sometimes even unfavourable posture towards Israel. For the past two decades, India and Israel have developed cooperation in agriculture, culture, tourism and most especially trade and military exchanges. This fast burgeoning relationship demonstrates that there had always been a potential for fruitful and complementary cooperation between the two nations.

How have Indo-Israeli relations moved from almost naught to a rapid and substantial development in certain sensitive sectors like defence cooperation and, in particular, high-tech weaponry in only a few years? What was the strategic thinking behind the foreign policy decisions taken in 1950 and 1992 to first recognise and then to finally establish full diplomatic relations with Israel? How can this apparently contradictory and constantly changing policy

---

[1] K. P. Misra, *India's Policy of Recognition of States and Government* (New Delhi: Allied Publishers, New Delhi, 1966), pp. 50–60.

[2] P. R. Kumaraswamy, 'India and Israel: Prelude to Normalization', *Journal of South-Asian and Middle Eastern Studies*, 19, 2 (1995).

vis-à-vis Israel be understood in light of India's broader strategic objectives?

In these two cases, the Indian leadership apparently took two completely opposing strategic directions. In the early 1950s, India followed a moralistic and anti-imperialistic stance by refusing to establish diplomatic relations with Israel. By contrast, India decided in 1992 to reassess its West Asia policy in a more pragmatic and self-interested light.[3] This paper however argues that the general strategic logic guiding Indian leaders in these two periods was in fact very similar. What differed in these two contexts were firstly international and domestic factors which constrained India in the implementation of its external policies. Secondly, different leaders also had diverging perceptions of the strategic means available to them to attain their objectives.[4] To better understand how specific decisions were taken in different contexts, it is therefore necessary to use a theoretical framework capable of incorporating circumstantial as well as ideational and cognitive variables in a more systematic manner as well as evaluating the constant interaction between these different variables. The grand strategy framework could be an interesting theoretical tool as it concentrates on both the central strategic aims but also on the strategic means and the operational policy that follows from the main assumptions.[5] The emerging literature on grand strategy becomes relevant in this case. This paper will argue that New Delhi's Israel policy can be understood in the more general orientations that have historically been guiding India's strategic behaviour.

This paper proceeds in four parts. In a first section, it is necessary to briefly review the existing literature on grand strategy theories and how it can be applied to the history of Indo-Israeli relations.

---

[3] Rejecting the Eurocentric terms 'Near East' or 'Middle-East', Prime Minister Jawaharlal Nehru had an Asiacentric worldview and therefore referred to this region as 'West Asia'.

[4] David Mitchell, 'Determining Indian Foreign Policy: An Examination of Prime Ministerial Leadership Styles', *India Review*, 6, 4, 2007 and Pratap Bhanu Mehta, 'Still Under Nehru's Shadow? The Absence of Foreign Policy Frameworks in India', *India Review*, 8, 3 (2009).

[5] Alastair Iain Johnston, *Cultural Realism: Strategic Culture and Grand Strategy in Chinese History* (Princeton: Princeton University Press, 1995).

Secondly, this paper concentrates on two historical decisions taken by the Indian leadership vis-à-vis Israel (in September 1950 and January 1992) to trace and compare the decision-making processes leading to these two diverging outcomes. Basing itself on the conclusions from these case-studies, this paper then attempts to delineate the main determinants of India's Israel policy and how they relate to India's grand strategic thought. Finally, this paper will assess the future of Indo–Israeli relations as well as the empirical and theoretical applicability of the grand strategy methodology to study this particular aspect of India's foreign policy.

Relevance of the Grand Strategy Framework to India's Foreign Policy

Over the past two decades, different analytical frameworks have been used to study and evaluate India's strategic thinking.[6] Some scholars have argued that in the last 60 years, some competing 'visions' of India's place in the international system have successively or concurrently shaped the formulation of India's foreign policy.[7] While none of these 'schools' have completely dominated India's decision-making apparatus, the standard view was that India's foreign policy was first dominated by a Nehruvian or moralist school inherited from the freedom movement and shaped by India's first Prime Minister Nehru which was later contested by more realist, Neoliberal and even Hindu nationalist perceptions of international politics. Building on these works, other scholars have interpreted new and bold strategic initiatives in the post-Cold War era in a stylised and almost caricatured 'idealistic vs. pragmatic' foreign policy debate.[8] From this perspective, India's strategic policy underwent a profound shift during the 1990s from a high minded, pious but ultimately ineffective idealism to a sober and more self-interested pragmatism.

---

[6] Mehta, 'Still Under Nehru's Shadow?'
[7] Kanti Bajpai, 'Indian Strategic Culture', in Michael R. chambers, ed., *South Asia in 2020: Future Strategic Balances and Alliances* (Carlisle: Strategic Studies Institute, US Army War College, 2002) and Rahul Sagar 'State of Mind: What Kind of Power will India Become?', *International Affairs*, 85, 4 (2009).
[8] See for example C. Raja Mohan, *Crossing the Rubicon: The Shaping of India's Foreign Policy* (London: Penguin, 2005).

These frameworks have regularly been used to explain India's decision to neglect Israel after 1948 on anti-imperialistic and moral grounds.[9] From this viewpoint, Indian nationalists did not support the Zionist movement, which they considered as a movement exclusively based on religion which was at variance with India's professed secular form of nationalism. Indian leaders like Nehru and Gandhi also saw the Jewish national movement as backed by imperialist forces to create a neo-colonial state at the expense of Arab nationalism.[10] By contrast, India's decision to establish full diplomatic relations with Israel in 1992 was interpreted as a pragmatic redirection of India's ineffective West Asia policy.[11] The 1992 decision was read as a reaction to the lack of reciprocity in India's relations with Arab and Muslim countries in the region. However these one-dimensional interpretations of India's foreign policy tended to simplify more complex and long-term debates within India's strategic community over its position vis-à-vis the region and often overlooked international, regional and domestic constraints which also shaped India's Israel policy. It is equally possible to explain India's Israel policy as a reaction to structural factors such as the end of the Cold War and the disappearance of the Soviet Union.[12] That is why some scholars have argued that India's strategic behaviour could be better explained by theories of grand strategy.[13]

---

[9] Richard Kozicki, 'India and Israel: A Problem in Asian Politics', *Middle Eastern Affairs*, 9, 5 (1958), Leonard Gordon, 'Indian Nationalist Ideas about Palestine and Israel', *Jewish Social Studies*, 37 (1975); B. R. Nanda, *Indian Foreign Policy: The Nehru Years* (New Delhi: Vikas Publishing House, 1976), pp. 74–77.

[10] Government of India, *India and Palestine: The Evolution of a Policy* (New Delhi: External Publicity Division of the Ministry of External Affairs, Government of India, 1968), pp. 69–70.

[11] Sreeram S. Chaulia, 'BJP, India's Foreign Policy and the 'Realist Alter-native' to the Nehruvian Tradition', *International Politics*, 39, 2 (2002); P. R. Kumaraswamy, 'Israel–India Relations: Seeking Balance and Realism', in E. Karsh, ed., *Israel: The First Hundred Years: Israel in the International Arena* (London: Frank Cass, 2004), pp. 254–73.

[12] For such an argument comparing and evaluating different levels of analysis, read Nicolas Blarel, 'Indo-Israeli Relations: Emergence of a Strategic Partnership', in Sumit Ganguly, ed., *India's Foreign Policy: Retrospect and Prospect* (New Delhi: Oxford University Press, 2009).

[13] See for example Kanti Bajpai, 'India: Modified Structuralism', in Muthiah Alagappa, ed., *Asian Security Practice: Material and Ideational Influences*

While there are different conceptualisations of grand strategy, there is a consensus in the theoretical literature that studying grand strategy takes into account not just the strategic orientations but also the means available to attain these objectives. In fact, it concentrates on the relation between the strategic goals and means.[14] It is difficult to identify any clear strategic goals in the Indian context. Some scholars like George Tanham have even concluded that India's policy has been characterised by an absence of grand strategy.[15] However, these scholars have often confused the lack of any evident strategic planning in India's foreign policy decision-making apparatus with the absence of strategic culture. In response, other scholars have rightly observed that a grand strategy does not have to be transparent and declaratory and that it can also be deduced from India's history of military, economic and diplomatic behaviour.[16] Even Tanham recognised there were some long-standing cultural principles dictating India's strategic behaviour.[17]

In spite of competing visions of India's role in world politics, it is possible to delineate at least three traditional and imperative strategic objectives from the literature on Indian strategic culture. These strategic preferences are either rooted in the formative stages of the state or can be influenced to some degree by the philosophical, political, cultural and cognitive characteristics of the state and its elites.[18]

(Stanford, CA: Stanford University Press, 1998); Bajpai, 'Indian Strategic Culture'; Manjeet S. Pardesi, 'Deducing India's Grand Strategy of Regional Hegemony from Historical and Conceptual Perspectives', Working Paper No. 76 (April 2005), Institute of Defence and Strategic Studies (IDSS), Singapore.

[14] Barry R. Posen, *The Sources of Military Doctrine* (New York: Cornell University press, 1984); Paul Kennedy, *Grand Strategies in War and Peace* (New Haven: Yale University Press 1992), Johnston, *Cultural Realism*.

[15] George Tanham, *Indian Strategic Thought: An Interpretive Essay* (Santa Monica, California: RAND Corporation, 1992); Stephen P. Cohen, *India: Emerging Power* (New Delhi: Oxford University Press, 2001); C. Raja Mohan, *Crossing the Rubicon*; Harsh Pant, ed., *Indian Foreign Policy in a Unipolar World* (New Delhi: Routledge, 2009).

[16] Bajpai, 'Indian Strategic Culture', p. 246 and Pardesi, 'Deducing India's Grand Strategy', p. 5.

[17] For instance, Tanham emphasised India's 'non-aggressive' and 'non-dependence' tradition in *Indian Strategic Thought*, p. 230.

[18] See Alastair Johnston, 'Thinking About Strategic Culture', *International Security* 19, 4 (1995) and Bajpai, 'India: Modified Structuralism', pp. 158–65.

Firstly, in an anarchical international system, survival and security have always been major strategic objectives for the Indian state. Depending on different strategists in India, security and survival can involve either protecting the South Asian subcontinent from external power involvement and/or the relatively more modest goal of preserving the Indian state's territorial integrity.[19] Secondly, as India was a newly independent State emerging from colonial rule in the context of the Cold War where nations needed to opt for one of the two emerging ideological blocks, Indian leaders since Nehru have also pressed for a free and independent foreign policy as a strategic priority.[20] Thirdly, some have argued that strategic goals should go beyond security and also encompass economic development.[21] While Nehru already believed that domestic economic development was key to the society's welfare and to preserve internal security 60 years ago, today all schools of strategic thinking in India understand economic development in a broader sense. Economic development is now not only a strategic concern for internal purposes but also for India to become a great commercial power recognised by other established great powers. Its external policies are now also directed towards ensuring access to resources and markets.[22]

How do these main strategic goals relate to Indo-Israeli relations? Israel is a relatively new and small state, which only developed substantial relations with India in the past two decades. Israel is also a distant country and has not been directly integrated in India's regional security policies. Lastly, India has never publicly expressed any long-term policy in direction of Israel. As a result, it seems complicated to integrate India's Israel policy or even its West Asia policy within a discussion on India's grand strategy and more specifically within what Alastair Johnson called a 'central strategic paradigm'.[23] The strategic paradigm only indicates the general predispositions of strategic thinkers. Discussions of grand strategy mostly involve broad

---

[19] Bajpai 'India: Modified Structuralism', pp. 165–72.

[20] Ibid., pp. 173–81; 'Sagar, What Kind of Power', pp. 803–6.

[21] See Bajpai, 'Indian Strategic Culture', pp. 252–54; Sagar, 'What Kind of Power', p. 813.

[22] Bajpai, 'Indian Strategic Culture', p. 186; Sagar, 'What Kind of Power', pp. 813–16.

[23] Johnston, *Cultural Realism*; Bajpai, 'Indian Strategic Culture', p. 247.

strategic aims like security and strategic autonomy in the pursuit of foreign affairs and rarely involve bilateral relations with small powers. Relations or non-relations with Israel must not be interpreted as a strategic end in itself but as an indirect way for India to achieve the grand strategic objectives discussed previously.

The grand strategy analytical framework does not only concentrate on the strategic ends but also looks at the operationalisation of the instruments used to achieve these strategic goals. Kanti Bajpai describes this secondary level of a grand strategy as 'assumptions at a more operational level about what strategic options are the most efficacious for dealing with the threat environment'.[24] India's Israel policy becomes relevant in the second part of the grand strategy methodology which looks at the operational policy.[25] India's strategies for coping with threats and vulnerabilities to ensure its main strategic goals are indeed diverse and numerous. Depending on international and domestic constraints and on leaders' perceptions of their strategic needs and operational challenges to the fulfillment of their main strategic goals, the opportunity of establishing relations with Israel and of developing certain type of relations with Israel will vary. While India's basic assumptions about its position in the international order do not evolve, the instruments at its disposal such as military, economic and/or diplomatic strength change. India's Israel policy is therefore dependent on leaders' operationalisation of India's strategic policy in different historical phases.

From Limited Recognition to Full Engagement: Comparing the 1950 and 1992 Decisions

This next section compares two different decisions the Indian leadership took vis-à-vis Israel which have defined India's policy in the region for the past 60 years. In 1950, India reluctantly decided to recognise Israel but also postponed establishing diplomatic relations. This 'limited relationship policy' was the result of two years of debates and careful consideration of the benefits and disadvantages of establishing relations with Tel Aviv. Similarly, the 1992 decision to normalise relations with Israel was the result of a progressive

---

[24] Bajpai, 'Indian Strategic Culture'.
[25] Ibid., pp. 247, 256.

reassessment of India's West Asia policy and the prospect of furthering relations with Israel in a new international context. These two foreign policy debates are illustrative case-studies of the strategic thinking that occurred prior to India's decisions. Tracing and comparing the processes leading to these two divergent outcomes helps tease out some key determinants of India's Israel policy and help explain how these determinants evolved in light of international, national and individual-level changes over 40 years.

ORIGINS OF INDIA'S ISRAEL POLICY

Contrary to popular belief, moral considerations have never been a decisive factor in the formulation of India's Israel policy. The policy of limited recognition with deferment of diplomatic relations and then the normalisation of relations in the 1990s were indicative of careful pragmatism and diplomatic prudence on India's part. To understand the strategic thinking linked to the September 1950 decision to maintain a limited relationship with Israel, it is necessary to go back to the origins of India's West Asia policy.

India's interest in West Asian affairs had existed prior to independence as some of the freedom movement's first foreign policy initiatives were linked to the region. There was first the active support of the Indian National Congress (INC) to the Khalifat movement in the 1910s. INC leaders such as Gandhi read this foreign issue as a way of forging unity between the Hindus and the Muslims in the subcontinent.[26] The INC seemed therefore ready to compromise on its secular agenda by supporting a purely religious movement in order to ensure the unity of the Indian freedom movement. Although this issue quickly became irrelevant when the pan-Islamic movement was abolished with the creation of the Republic of Turkey in 1923, it was the first demonstration of the indirect effect of India's national interests on its West Asia policy. Following this first foreign policy statement, the Arab struggle against both British imperialism and Zionism was to be linked by some Indian leaders such as Nehru to India's own struggle against British tactics of 'divide and rule'.[27]

---

[26] Rajendra M. Abhyankar, 'Introduction', in Rajendra M. Abhyankar, ed., *West Asia and the Region*: Defining India's Role (New Delhi: Academic Foundation, 2008), pp. 30–31.

[27] Jawaharlal Nehru, *Glimpses of World History*, 6th impression (New Delhi: Oxford University Press, 1989), pp. 763–65, 789.

It was through this shared opposition to British imperialism that the first political links were established between Indian and Arab leaders. Nehru held discussions with Arab nationalists in various anti-imperialist forums and associations such as the 1927 Brussels Conference of Oppressed Nationalities.[28] Although both Gandhi and Nehru had also expressed sentiments of sympathy towards Jewish grievances, they categorically rejected the idea of a Jewish National home.[29] The INC decided to give its full support for an Independent Palestinian State in 1938.[30]

It is possible to read a principled conviction in the INC's position that the demand for a Jewish home was the 'child of British Imperialism',[31] but it is equally important to evaluate this policy in relation with the rise of the Muslim League in domestic politics and the emerging prospect of partition. When India opposed the idea of a Jewish state, it was also out of INC leaders' consideration for the Muslim community at home. Indian leaders could not agree to the question of partitioning a State from their own experience. As a result, the Jewish problem was a minority problem and Nehru envisaged a single Palestinian state based on federal principles, a solution which was consistent with his own domestic position in regard to the Muslim League's demand for Pakistan.[32] When the question of the partition of Palestine became an issue at the United Nations (UN), New Delhi, along with the rest of the newly independent countries members of the UN Special Committee on Palestine (UNSCOP), rejected the 'two nation' theory and instead supported an alternative plan envisaging a federal Palestine with an autonomous status for the Jewish population. Regardless of this initiative, the UN General Assembly approved by a large majority the plan creating the State of Israel on November 29, 1947.

---

[28] Najma Heptulla, *Indo-West Asian Relations: The Nehru Era* (New Delhi: South Asia Books, 1992), p. 38.

[29] Nehru, *Glimpses of World History*, pp. 762–63; Gandhi quoted in D. G. Tendulkar, *Mahatma*, Vol. IV (New Delhi: The Publications Division, 1961), pp. 311–12.

[30] Syed Barakat Ahmad, 'India and Palestine 1896–1947: The Genesis of a Foreign Policy', in Verinder Grover, ed., *West Asia* And *India's* Foreign Policy (New Delhi: Deep & Deep Publications, 1992), pp. 379–80.

[31] Nehru, *Glimpses of World History*, p. 763.

[32] The Prime Minister's position is cited in *India and Palestine: The Evolution of a Policy*, pp. 69–70.

As a result, India had to deal with two new political realities after independence: the partition of the South Asian subcontinent and the creation of Israel in West Asia. India refused to recognise Israel in 1948, despite repeated requests from the latter.[33] Nevertheless, on September 17, 1950, India did ultimately recognise the State of Israel after two years of existence, including UN membership.[34] This decision was unprecedented as recognition was not accompanied by the establishment of diplomatic relations. India seemed to have taken a weighted decision dissociating the legal act of recognition which became inevitable as Israel had become a *fait accompli* (recognised by a large number of states, of which some had an important Muslim population like Iran and Indonesia)[35] from the political act of starting diplomatic relations with the new Jewish state.[36] It is necessary to review the different factors and the strategic thinking that shaped this compromised outcome.

Again, India did not immediately recognise Israel not because of its ideological attachment to the Palestinian cause but because it preferred to monitor the evolving situation in the region as well as to debate the long-term implications of according recognition to the new Jewish state. Consequently, India's delayed recognition of Israel continued to be influenced by national interests. Nehru indicated that:

> Any action that we may take must be *guided not only by idealistic considerations but also a realistic appraisal of the situation. Our general policy in the past has been favourable to the Arabs, at the same time not hostile to the Jews.* That policy continues. For the present, we have said that we are not recognising Israel. But this is not *an irrevocable decision* and the matter will no doubt he considered afresh in view of subsequent developments.[37] (emphasis added)

---

[33] Walter Eytan, *The First Ten Years: A Diplomatic History of Israel* (London: Weidenfeld and Nicolson, 1958).

[34] P. R. Kumaraswamy, 'India's Recognition of Israel, September 1950', *Middle Eastern Studies* 31, 1 (1995).

[35] Constituent Assembly of India Debates Part 1, Vol. 1, No. 18 (New Delhi: Parliamentary Publications, 1950).

[36] K. P. Misra, *India's Policy of Recognition*, p. 60.

[37] Nehru is quoted in G. Parthasarathi, ed., *Jawaharlal Nehru: Letters to Chief Ministers 1947–1964*, Volume 1: 1947–1949 (New Delhi: Oxford University Press, 1985), pp. 127–28.

It became evident that the Indian government wanted to wait until the settlements of both the first Arab–Israeli conflict and the Kashmir dispute to recognise Israel in a less divisive international environment.[38] India was indeed very careful about the impact its Israel policy would have both on the sentiments of Indian Muslims and on its relations with Arab states. For Indian leaders such as Nehru and especially Maulana Abdul Kalam Azad, India's Israel policy had direct implications for internal order and territorial integrity.[39] Some scholars have for instance argued that Azad had warned Nehru that any step towards establishing relations with Israel could have been misinterpreted by the remaining Muslim population in India which had yet to recover from the trauma of partition.[40] It is possible Indian leaders feared a pro-Israel stance would have encouraged further distrust in the Indian state and fuelled more communal violence. In the same period, the Kashmir issue was referred to the UN and the support of the newly independent Arab states became crucial for India. The Arabs had 13 votes at the UN whereas Israel had only one.[41] In different public statements (notably in response to concerned Muslim members of the Constituent Assembly), Nehru indirectly recognised that the friendship of Arab states was the main factor justifying the delay in recognising Israel.[42] Concurrently,

---

[38] Kumaraswamy, 'India's Recognition of Israel, September 1950'.

[39] After leading the Khalifat movement in the 1910s, Azad became one of the main leaders of the Indian Freedom movement. After Independence he was appointed as India's first Minister for Education and served in the Constituent Assembly. Azad remained a close confidante, supporter and advisor to Prime Minister Nehru and played an important role in framing national and international policies.

[40] This is an argument Michael Brecher made in his book *The New States of Asia: A Political Analysis* (London: Oxford University Press, 1963), pp. 129–30.

[41] The Kashmir conflict erupted in 1947 because of competing projects of nation building between India and Pakistan. New Delhi insisted on holding on to Kashmir in order to show that the Muslim Province could thrive in a secular state. In opposition, Islamabad believed that Kashmir, whose population is mostly Muslim, belonged in Pakistan, homeland of the Muslims of South Asia. For more on the Kashmir conflict, see Sumit Ganguly, *The Crisis in Kashmir: Portents of War, Hopes of Peace* (Cambridge: Cambridge University Press, 1997).

[42] Constituent Assembly of India Debates Part 1, Vol. 4, No. 7 (New Delhi: Parliamentary Publications, 1950), pp. 233–34.

Pakistan was actively courting Arab and Muslim support for its position on the Kashmir dispute.[43] In the context of heated UN debates regarding the Kashmir issue, Indian leaders did not see any strategic benefits in immediately engaging Israel.[44]

Since India's Israel policy was not solely based on moral considerations, it was possible for India to recognise Israel in 1950 after it had become a durable political reality. Already in 1949, Nehru had implied that recognition of Israel could not be 'indefinitely deferred' and had even invited a Jewish delegation at the first Asian Relations Conference which met in Delhi in 1947.[45] In 1950, some factors gave India a new strategic leeway in the region: the Israeli–Arab conflict had lost of its sensitivity, Pakistan's efforts to use exploit pan-Islamism in the Kashmir issue proved to be unsuccessful[46] and two Muslim states, Turkey and Iran, had already taken steps towards recognition of the Jewish state.[47] In this new international context, delaying recognition would have become strategically unsound as the international community (including the US and USSR) had acknowledged the existence of Israel. India could not also risk damaging relations with countries like the US (whose financial aid was very important for its first five years plan) by refusing to accept Israel.[48] India was also prudent in its rapprochement with Israel as it made official reassurances to Arab states that recognition did not mean it was endorsing Israeli positions regarding the boundaries and the inalienable rights of the Palestinians to return to their homeland.[49] India also decided to delay the exchange of diplomatic missions until the regional situation stabilised.

This desire to keep all diplomatic options open is consistent with India's strategic goal of preserving foreign policy autonomy. In Nehru's mindset, the limited recognition policy instituted in the

---

[43] Nanda, *Indian Foreign Policy*, p. 75.

[44] Brecher, *The New States of Asia*.

[45] Upendra N. Mishra, 'India's Policy towards the Palestinian Question', *International Studies*, 21 (1982).

[46] Noor Ahmad Baba, 'OIC and Pakistan's Foreign Policy: The Indian Dimension', in Rajendra N. Abhyankar, ed., *West Asia and the Region: Defining India's Role* (New Delhi: Academic Foundation, 2008), pp. 669–73.

[47] *The Hindu*, September 18, 1950.

[48] Mishra, 'India's Policy towards the Palestinian Question'.

[49] *India and Palestine: The Evolution of a Policy*, p. 31.

early 1950s was a satisfactory compromise for India to have good relations with both Arab and Western states. Nehru had indeed said that India's attitude towards Israel 'was adopted after a *careful consideration of the balance of factors. It is not a matter of high principle* but it is based on how we could best serve and be helpful in that area [...] After careful thought, we felt that *while recognizing Israel as an entity, we need not at this stage exchange diplomatic personnel*'[50] (emphasis added). India never expressed a definitive policy towards Israel and kept the option of extending relations.[51] Although, the Indian government invoked financial problems to explain the absence of diplomatic exchanges, it was actually waiting to see how the regional situation would evolve.[52] In the early 1950s, as regional tensions cooled down, India apparently made steps to normalise relations by permitting Israel to open a consulate in Bombay in 1952 and by inviting Israel to the Bandung Conference in 1955,[53] However, the political environment deteriorated after the Suez crisis of 1956 and India ruled out diplomatic relations for many more years.[54] India also hoped its pro-Arab policy could ensure diplomatic support against regional threats like Pakistan (and potentially China).

As a result, the recognition and no-relationship policy was actually a very strategically weighted decision which took in account India's security (territorial integrity with the Kashmir issue, boundary disputes with Pakistan) and the continuation of its independent foreign policy (open-ended policy to further relations with both Arab states and Israel and its international partners like the US). This policy did help India to meet the challenges of the time and to satisfy India's national interests. For example, by refusing to directly engage Israel,

---

[50] Jawaharlal Nehru, statement at press conference, New Delhi, August 7, 1958, quoted in Jawaharlal Nehru, *India's Foreign Policy: Selected Speeches, September 1946–April 1961* (New Delhi: Publications Division, Government of India, 1961), pp. 414–15.

[51] Brecher, *The New States of Asia*, pp. 78–79.

[52] Ministry of External Affairs Annual Report 1951–1952 (New Delhi: MEA Publications, 1952), p. 10.

[53] R. Sreekantan Nair, 'India's Israel Policy: Changing Dimensions', in Rajen Harshe and K.M. Seethi, eds, *Engaging with the World: Critical Reflections on India's Foreign Policy* (New Delhi: Orient Longman, 2005), pp. 430–35.

[54] Michael Brecher, *India and World Politics: Krishna Menon's View of The World* (London: Oxford University Press, 1968), pp. 80–81.

India successfully managed to counter Pakistan's attempts to exploit pan-Islamism in the Kashmir dispute. Nehru was very careful when he justified India's attitude towards Israel because of political developments in West Asia. Nehru had always aimed to maintain, in form if not in substance, a semblance of balance in its West Asia policy. Both Nehru and his close adviser Krishna Menon wanted to keep diplomatic options open with both Arab states and Israel.[55]

However, Nehru's successors followed his Israel policy without considering how international and regional changes could negatively affect India's strategic position. It quickly became apparent that Indo-Arab relations were only one-way as the unambiguous Indian support against Israel in 1956 and in the crises of 1967 and 1973 was never reciprocated by the Arab states, which failed to back India in its regional conflicts against China in 1962 and against Pakistan in 1965 and 1971.[56] It is also true that India's Israel policy was shaped by its growing energy needs. India had to import 70 per cent of its crude oil and was therefore strongly dependent on Gulf energy exports.[57] To meet these challenges, Prime Minister Indira Gandhi decided to further strengthen political links with Arab states, supporting their diplomatic positions against Israel but also by offering engineering services and manpower.[58] As a consequence, India's West Asia policy did bring some relief to India's energy dilemma but failed to guarantee its national security as well as its strategic autonomy as successive Indian leaders constantly and unconditionally supported Arab initiatives until the late 1980s.

REASSESSMENT OF INDIA'S ISRAEL POLICY

Similarly to the decision-making process leading to the 1950 decision, there was a progressive and intense discussion on the long term impact of New Delhi's Israel policy. Although India's official

---

[55] See Menon's opinion in his interview with Michael Brecher, *India and World Politics*, pp. 80–81.

[56] Arthur G. Rubinoff, 'Normalization of India-Israel Relations: Stillborn for Forty Years', *Asian Survey* 35, 5 (1995), pp. 495–98.

[57] 'Does India Need Strategic Oil Reserve', *Business Standard*, November 13, 2002.

[58] Gulshan Dietl, 'The Security of Supply Issue: The Growing Dependence on the Middle East', in Pierre Audinet, P. R. Shukla and Frederic Grare, eds, *India's Energy: Essays on Sustainable Development* (New Delhi: Manohar, 2000).

position towards Israel did not change until January 1992, there had already been an early and important domestic debate regarding the strategic benefits and drawbacks of New Delhi's traditional West Asia policy. The lack of reciprocity in Indo-Arab relations which became evident after the Sino-Indian border dispute of 1962 and the Indo-Pakistani war of 1965 was progressively criticised not only by various opposition parties like the Jana Sangh or the Swatantra party but also by members of the Congress party itself.[59] Disappointed by the Arab states' neutral (if not unfavorable) position towards India during these conflicts, these critics even supported the establishment of Indo-Israeli relations. They did not understand how India could maintain relations with openly hostile nations such as China and Pakistan but not with Israel with whom India never had any direct conflict of interest.[60] India's pro-Arab policy was again condemned after the bad experience at the OIC Rabat conference in 1969 and Arab indifference towards India during the 1971 Bangladesh crisis.[61] Many Indian newspapers also began to denounce India's categorical support to Arab states against Israel in the conflicts of 1967 and 1973.[62] Paradoxically, these decisions seriously narrowed India's strategic leverage in the region.

Before 1992, there had already been some progressive attempts to revise India's Israel policy. Some reports suggested Israeli military assistance had been given to India during the Sino–Indian

---

[59] B. K. Srivastava, 'Indo-Israeli relations: Pulls and Pressures', *Mainstream* (New Delhi) (1967), pp. 17–19.

[60] Rubinoff, 'Normalization of India-Israel Relations', pp. 496–97.

[61] With the third largest Muslim population at that time after Indonesia and Pakistan and with a repeated and unambiguous support to the Palestinian cause during the Arab–Israeli wars, India hoped it had a legitimate right participate at the first meeting of the Organization of the Islamic Conference (OIC) in Rabat in September 1969. As this conference was summoned to condemn Israel's destruction of the holy shrine, India felt its important domestic Muslim population was as concerned with the Palestinian situation as any other Muslim country. Although India was officially invited to the conference, opposition from Pakistan kept the Indian delegation from participating in the conference. This was a serious blow to the Indian Government.

[62] See Girilal Jain, 'Disillusionment with the Arabs: A Shift in Indian Opinion', *Round Table* (1967), pp. 433–38 and Joseph Hadass, 'Evolution of the Relations Between India and Israel', *India Quarterly*, 58, 2 (2002).

conflict in 1962 and the Indo-Pakistani wars of 1965 and 1971.[63] However, these limited informal contacts did not mark any long-term strategic shift. After 30 years of uninterrupted Congress rule, the Janata government came to power in 1977 with the ambition of developing diplomatic relations with Israel. Prime Minister Morarji Desai even secretly invited Israeli Defence Minister Moshe Dayan in 1977.[64] Despite talks of exchanging military technology, these contacts were a failure as the politically fragile coalition led by the Janata party finally decided it could not break with the traditional pro-Arab policy.[65]

Rajiv Gandhi's government in the 1980s was probably the first administration to really understand the need for a different Israel policy which would be more in connection with its main strategic objectives. Unlike his predecessors, Rajiv Gandhi encouraged contacts and interactions with Israeli leaders as well as with pro-Israeli elements in the US. Gandhi knew that India's diplomatic posture towards Israel had alienated many of India's ardent supporters in the US Congress. As a result, the Indian Prime Minister held much publicised meetings with his Israeli counterpart Shimon Peres at a UN session in New York in 1985 and with a leading Jewish lobbyist on US Congressman Stephen Solarz's request in 1988.[66] Again in 1988, a high level Israeli Foreign Ministry official Joseph Hadass was invited by the Indian authorities and a delegation of the American Jewish Anti-Defamation league also met with the Minister for External Affairs Narasimha Rao.[67] These visits were presented as the highest level meetings on Indian soil after Moshe Dayan's visit 10 years earlier. In the new West Asian context of the late 1980s, the Rajiv Gandhi government felt it needed to expand its diplomatic and strategic options by opening up to Israel. Rajiv Gandhi understood that any rapprochement with the US would first involve normalising

---

[63] Rubinoff, op. cit.

[64] Moshe Dayan, *Breakthrough: A Personal Account of the Egypt-Israel Peace Negotiations* (New Delhi: Vikas Publishing House, 1978), p. 26.

[65] J. N. Dixit, *India's Foreign Policy 1947–2003* (New Delhi: Picus Books, 2003), pp. 132–33.

[66] P. R. Kumaraswamy, 'India, Israel and the Davis Cup Tie 1987', *Journal of Indo-Judaic Studies*, 23 (2002).

[67] Farah Naaz, *West Asia and India: Changing Perspectives* (New Delhi: Shipra Publications, 2005), pp. 98–99.

relations with Israel.[68] This incremental approach initiated by Rajiv Gandhi paved the way for normalisation of relations by his successors in January 1992.

As Foreign and Defence Minister in the Indira and Rajiv Gandhi governments in the 1970s and 1980s, Rao had already been involved in India's foreign policy decision-making process. What changed in 1991 is the fragile and divided situation of the ruling Congress party which pushed an uncharismatic Rao to the Prime Minister position. Because he was heading an apparently weak government of transition, Rao did not feel constrained by the Congress' long-established ideological positions and by traditional domestic voting constituencies such as the Muslim vote. As a consequence of this greater flexibility, he gradually pushed for a reformist foreign policy agenda in West Asia.[69]

The end of the Cold War left Indian decision-makers facing a completely uncertain strategic situation where the parameters of a new emerging global order were still undefined. Rao's response was to discern some broad directions of the transformations taking place. In response to these projections, Rao sought to redirect India's strategic and security priorities. Taking advantage of this greater political uncertainty at the international and domestic levels, Prime Minister Rao reoriented New Delhi's West Asia policy in order to better guarantee its strategic goals. In fact, foreign Secretary Jyotindra Nath Dixit explained that the normalisation of relations with Israel was a calibrated move 'after a very careful assessment of our national interests'.[70] Three key factors were taken in consideration.

First, regional and domestic developments in the early 1990 had permitted India to expand its diplomatic options in West Asia and to obtain an unprecedented strategic margin. At the regional level, the Kuwait crisis of 1990–91 and its consequences modified Israel's status vis-à-vis Arab states. Internal opposition within the Arab world and widespread criticism regarding the Palestine Liberation Organisation's (PLO) support of Iraq during the war limited the negative implications of opening up to Israel. The Iraqi intrusion into Kuwait

---

[68] Kumaraswamy, 'India and Israel: Prelude to Normalization'.

[69] K. Shankar Bajpai, 'India in 1991: New Beginnings', *Asian Survey*, 32, 2 (February 1992).

[70] Quoted in *The Statesman*, December 30, 1991.

diverted attention from Israel as the Saddam Hussein regime became the new source of concern in the region.[71] India no longer needed to systematically condemn Israel to obtain Arab sympathies. Following the Gulf war, where Israel showed military restraint in spite of Iraqi attacks, many countries from the region even sought new ties with the Jewish state. A series of West Asian peace initiatives such as the Madrid Conference of October 1991 created a new era in the region where coexistence and negotiations with Israel was possible.[72] Lastly, India's progressive diplomatic rapprochement with Israel was indirectly supported by Yasser Arafat in January 1992 when he declared that 'exchange of ambassadors and recognition are acts of sovereignty on which I cannot interfere ... I respect any choice of the Indian government'.[73] These regional transformations created a window of opportunity for India to develop a strategic partnership with Israel while maintaining relations with other West Asian countries.

At the national level, events in Kashmir in the late 1980s seriously deteriorated relations with its West Asian partners. The Kashmir issue was rarely raised by Pakistan in the early years of the OIC's existence. However, from 1990 onwards, the rise of militancy and of a pro-independence insurrection in Kashmir encouraged a debate on the issue within the OIC. Pakistan exploited the ongoing unrest and reports of human rights violations in the Kashmir valley to mobilise support for its position.[74] Kashmir became one of the leading issues discussed in the different meetings and the OIC regularly passed resolutions condemning India.[75] The negative response of unfailing friends of India within the OIC such as the United Arab Emirates and Iran to back India's counter-insurgency struggle in Kashmir in 1990 put an end to India's expectations of reciprocal support on Kashmir in exchange for its pro-Palestine stance.[76] It became evident that an unconditional pro-Arab policy did not provide India

---

[71] P. R. Kumaraswamy, 'Israel's New Arch of Friendship: India, Russia and Turkey', Gulf Research Center (Dubai), Research Papers, 2005.

[72] P. R. Kumaraswamy, 'India and Israel: Prelude to Normalization'.

[73] *The Indian Express*, January 20, 1992.

[74] Baba, 'OIC and Pakistan's Foreign Policy', pp. 676–79.

[75] Ibid., p. 279.

[76] Prithvi Ram Mudiam in *India and the Middle East* (London: British Academic Press, 1994), pp. 173–74.

any strategic leverage in its efforts to cope with threats to its unity and territorial integrity. These OIC resolutions lead to a strong diplomatic response from the Rao government which asserted that Kashmir was an integral part of India. The government also initiated important diplomatic efforts to counter anti-India propaganda within the Muslim world.[77] In parallel, Prime Minister Rao and Foreign Secretary Dixit also openly expressed their frustration with the lack of support from their Arab partners in regards to the Kashmir issue and decided that establishing diplomatic relations with Israel was a way to indirectly warn its traditional West Asian partners that India's diplomatic support could not be taken for granted.[78] This new diplomatic initiative was more successful to preserve India's security as some of the more influential Muslim countries in the region refused to be partisan in the India-Pakistan dispute.[79] During the Kargil crisis, the OIC did not openly support Pakistan and Saudi Arabia even played a quiet but decisive role in encouraging Islamabad to give up on its territorial aspirations.[80] None of these countries wanted to let the Kashmir (or even the Israel) issues become insurmountable obstacles to developing relations with an emerging power like India.[81] In fact, countries like Saudi Arabia have been actively seeking political and economic ties with India over the two last decades.[82]

Second, the disappearance of the Cold War military blocs, the irrelevance of Non-Alignment in the emerging world order and India's economic crisis led Rao to encourage better relations with the US. In fact, the success of Rao's development strategy based on market reforms depended greatly upon investment and technological assistance from the West, the World Bank, the IMF and especially the US. With economic development and growth becoming main strategic concerns for Indian leaders in the early 1990s, attracting

---

[77] Baba, 'OIC and Pakistan's Foreign Policy', p. 680.
[78] Sumit Ganguly, 'India's Foreign Policy Grows Up', *World Policy Journal*, 20, 4 (Winter 2003–04) and P. R. Kumaraswamy, 'Israel-India Relations: Seeking Balance and Realism'.
[79] A. K. Pasha, 'India and the Gulf States: Challenges and Opportunities', in Harshe and Seethi, eds, *Engaging with the World*, pp. 419–21.
[80] C. Raja Mohan 'Kargil diplomacy', *The Hindu*, August 3, 2000.
[81] Abhyankar, ed., *West Asia and the Region*, pp. 48–49.
[82] Ibid., p. 43.

foreign investment became a priority.[83] As Washington had been pressuring New Delhi to adjust its Israel policy since 1948, Rao was conscious that good relations with the Jewish state were a prerequisite to the easing of prevailing Indo-US tensions. Consequently, India decided to join in the move to revoke the UN General Assembly Resolution 3379 equating Zionism with Racism in December 1991.[84] On January 9, 1992, top officials of both India and Israel met in Washington to discuss the establishment of full diplomatic ties.[85] Symbolically, Narasimha Rao announced the establishment of diplomatic relations with Israel on the eve of a visit to the UN in New York to speak with George H.W. Bush on January 30, 1992.[86]

Finally, after the fall of the USSR, New Delhi's new foreign policy priorities also included ensuring India's defence capabilities.[87] The USSR had been India's largest arms supplier since the early 1960s and in 1991, 70 per cent of India's military equipment was of Soviet origin.[88] Almost overnight, India had to deal with a military industry that was dispersed in 15 countries that emerged from the USSR collapse and with less favourable financial conditions offered by the Russian Federation. As a consequence, India sought assistance from all countries that could help to improve its precarious regional and international security situation threatened by a nuclear Pakistan and a rising China. The strategic rapprochement with Israel became logical as the Israeli military–industrial complex had the capacity to modernise and upgrade the obsolete Soviet military equipment that India had purchased. In addition, the deteriorating internal security situation in Kashmir also pushed India to look for technical assistance from countries which experienced similar terrorist and insurgency problems like Israel.

Consequently, emerging Indo-Israeli relations had a strong security dimension. The question of defence cooperation was first raised

---

[83] Bajpai 'India: Modified Structuralism', pp. 186–89; Jagdish Bhagwati, *India in Transition: Freeing the Economy* (New York: Clarendon, 1993).

[84] Edward Gargan, 'Indian Announces Full Israeli Ties', *The New York Times*, January 30, 1992.

[85] *Times of India*, January 11, 1992.

[86] *Times of India*, January 30, 1992.

[87] Dixit, *India's Foreign Policy 1947–2003*, pp. 225–26.

[88] Amit Gupta, 'Determining India's Force Structure and Military Doctrine', *Asian Survey*, 35, 5 (1995).

by Dixit during his March 1993 visit to Israel.[89] In its rationale for improving relations with Israel, the Rao government also expressed a strong interest in Israel's expertise in counter-terrorism operations.[90] Only a month after the establishment of full diplomatic relations, Rao publicly confirmed India's interest in learning from Israeli's experience in dealing with terrorism.[91] However, despite successive rounds of talks on defence matters, India hesitated to buy weapons from Israel until the late 1990s. Israel's prompt and positive response to Indian requests for military assistance during the Kargil crisis in the end convinced Indian leaders of the strategic benefits of a military partnership.[92] From 1999 onwards, military technology imports have boosted to the point that today Israel is India's second largest military supplier (with sales representing roughly 1.5 billion dollars in 2006[93]) after its abiding partner – Russia.[94]

There were strong strategic reasons for India to look for Israeli assistance. After 1992, the India military was indeed in search of new solutions to fill the qualitative gap it has over overt regional threats like Pakistan and China. Israel, which had developed a domestic high-technology military industry capable of rivalling the Western powers,[95] offered some advantages to India's domestic military industry. For instance, India sought Israeli expertise on many ambitious strategic weapons programs such as the Light Combat Aircraft (LCA) which was expected to replace the ageing MiGs in the Indian Air Force (IAF), the Arjun tank prototype, to replace the obsolete Vijayanta and in the development of its indigenous ballistic missile program.[96] India purchased technologically advanced

---

[89] *Jane's Defense Weekly*, November 13, 1993.

[90] P. R. Kumaraswamy, 'India and Israel: Evolving Strategic Partnership', *Mideast Security and Policy Studies*, 40 (1998).

[91] Ibid.

[92] P. R. Kumaraswamy, *Israel's New Arch of Friendship*.

[93] Bruce Riedel, 'Israel and India: New Allies', *Middle East Bulletin*, Brookings Institute, April 1, 2008.

[94] Josy Joseph, 'Israel May Emerge Top Arms Supplier', *Daily News and Analysis*, February 20, 2008; Josy Joseph, 'India, Israel to Ramp up Military Ties', *Times of India*, December 10, 2009.

[95] Amit Gupta, *Building an Arsenal: The Evolution of Regional Power Force Structures* (Westport: Praeger Publishers, 1997), pp. 173–74.

[96] Stephen Blank, 'Arms Sales and Technology Transfer in Indo-Israeli Relations', *The Journal of East Asian Affairs*, 19, 1 (2005); Nicolas Blarel,

defensive systems which could ensure the protection of its territory from both Pakistani and Chinese attacks. There was for example the highly publicised purchase of the Israeli airborne early-warning and control (AEW&C) Phalcon systems in 2003 which gave India a more effective instrument of surveillance against potential airborne attacks.[97] India also acquired Unmanned Aerial Vehicles (UAVs) from Israel to boost its air surveillance arm.[98] Finally, India has closely been cooperating with Israel in the field of Missile defence. India has signed its biggest defence deal with Israel in February 2009 for the purchase of an advanced air defence (AAD) system (at a cost of USD 1.4 billion) which will become part of India's anti-ballistic missile shield. Under the terms of this deal, Israel will develop and manufacture seaborne and shore-based systems against missile attacks on India.[99]

Today, almost all Indian parties (with the exception maybe of the Communist Party of India (Marxist)[100] understand the strategic benefits of cooperation with Israel and encouraged this new orientation of India's West Asia policy. This relationship has become so strategically crucial for India that the traditionally pro-Palestinian Congress party pursued negotiations with Tel Aviv when it returned to power in 2004. There were initial doubts about the endurance of this new privileged partnership as the United Progressive Alliance[101] electoral program had evoked a new beginning in relations with West Asia with a confirmation of India's support of the Palestinian

---

Inde et Israel: Le Rapprochement Stratégique, Pragmatisme et complémentarité (Paris: L'Harmattan, 2006), pp. 73–89.

[97] 'India Receives Second AWACS, to be Deployed in Agra', *Outlook India*, March 25, 2010; Blarel, *Inde et Israel: Le Rapprochement Stratégique*, pp. 90–94.

[98] Yakoov Katz, 'Israel Eyeing Big Defense Contracts in India', *The Jerusalem Post*, March 14, 2010.

[99] Josy Joseph, 'UPA Govt Signs Rs10,000 cr Israel Missile Deal on the Sly', *Daily News and Analysis*, March 25, 2009; 'India, Israel Sign $1.4 bn Deal for Air Defence System', *The Indian Express*, March 27, 2009.

[100] 'Snap the Growing Ties with Israel, Says Karat', *Rediff India Abroad*, March 5, 2008.

[101] United Progressive Alliance (UPA) is the ruling coalition of political parties that has been heading the government of India since the elections of June 2004. The coalition is led by the Indian National Congress (INC).

cause.[102] However, comparably to the Nehru and Rao governments previously, the current UPA government is aware of the need to diversify its alliances in the region engaging important Western partners like Israel and the US alongside with its traditional Arab and Muslim partners.[103]

India's Israel Policy in Light of its Grand Strategic Goals

As discussed previously, there seems to be a scholarly consensus around at least three important cultural principles dictating India's strategic behaviour over the long term. These values were survival and security (territorial integrity and coping with regional threats), foreign policy autonomy and economic development (progressively considered less as internal development and more as 'economic strength'[104]). Judging from the 1950 and 1992 decisions which dictated India's Israel policy over the last 60 years, these broad strategic aims have partially influenced India's strategic thinking. By concentrating on India's grand strategic orientations, it is equally possible to anticipate the broad contours of future Indo-Israeli relations.

INDIAN SECURITY AND SURVIVAL

Strategic considerations of security, internal order and territorial integrity have always influenced India's Israel policy. Nehru's limited recognition policy was shaped by considerations of domestic political consolidation. Nehru decided to limit diplomatic relations with Israel in order to reassure the Muslim minority and to preserve a fragile internal order in the post-partition years. The non-establishment of diplomatic relations was also a way to comfort Arab allies in order to get their support in the Kashmir territorial issue. The Nehru government almost certainly equally expected Arab support in border disputes with external threats like Pakistan and China. This policy was not definitive and was predestined to evolve if it did not meet India's security concerns.

---

[102] P. R. Kumaraswamy, 'Uncertainties about Indo-Israeli Ties', *The Deccan Herald,* June 15, 2004.

[103] P. R. Kumaraswamy, 'Indo-Israeli Ties: The Post-Arafat Shift', *The Power and Interest News Report (PINR)*, March 2005.

[104] Bajpai, 'India: Modified Structuralism'.

As a result, security was again a major driver for the 1992 decision to normalise relations with Israel. India's precarious security situation in the early 1990s led the Rao government to reassess its Israel policy. In the context of the disappearance of its traditional soviet ally and military supplier and concurrently of emerging threats at the national level (Kashmir) and at the regional level (Pakistan and China), India strongly needed military aid and Israel became an attractive partner to upgrade and modernise India's outdated military equipment. In the early 1990s context, military preparedness became a key strategic concern which could be ensured by Israeli assistance. It is also important to note that India's military exchanges with Israel in the past 15 years have been consistent with India's traditional emphasis on defensive military capacities. India is not an overtly expansionist power and one of the main guiding principles of its security policy is to maintain its territorial integrity. The acquisitions of the Phalcon radar system and anti-missile defensive systems are examples of this particular strategic orientation.

As long as Israel will meet India's crucial strategic needs in surveillance and preventive security mechanisms, Indo-Israeli exchanges will remain important. Similarly, India's goal of self-reliance in its military industry has been one of the main factor encouraging military cooperation with Israel. Israel has had a very positive experience in developing a largely indigenous and self-sufficient military-industrial complex capable of competing with Western powers. The Israeli experience could be an interesting example for emerging Indian indigenous programs. Israel also remained a reliable partner in cases of military embargoes such as the one following the 1998 nuclear tests.[105] These different factors encouraged the current Congress government to pursue its military relations with Israel, although in a more discrete manner.[106]

INDIA'S FOREIGN POLICY AUTONOMY

India's Israel policy has also been governed by the ambition to maintain strategic leeway in the region and to obtain assistance from both Arab nations and Israel and its international partners like the US. Nehru's open-ended policy recognising Israel as a political reality

---

[105] Abhyankar, ed., *West Asia and the Region*, pp. 63–64.
[106] Kumaraswamy, 'Indo-Israeli Ties: The Post-Arafat Shift'.

and envisaging the possibility of furthering diplomatic relations in the close future in 1950 was a way to satisfy its Western partners without alienating its regional Arab allies. Nehru hoped such a progressive and balanced position could have helped India's strategic autonomy in the region. The 1992 decision to normalise relations with Israel was also taken with similar strategic considerations. India's traditional no-relationship policy was indeed progressively perceived as limiting India's strategic independence as it was regularly supporting Arab and Muslim positions without receiving much diplomatic support from its regional partners in exchange. Consequently, the Narasimha Rao government decided to diversify its regional partnerships by establishing diplomatic relations with Israel which had always supported India's position in territorial disputes with Pakistan. This decision was equally meant to signal India's Arab states that its diplomatic support was not unconditional. As New Delhi also expanded economic relations with other Gulf States in parallel, this new Israel policy must be interpreted as a broader strategy aimed at mobilising all political, strategic, economic and cultural resources from the region.

India's foreign policy autonomy in the regional context will mainly depend on how well it manages its relations with both Israel and other Muslim countries in the region like Iran. For some time now, Israel has expressed its concerns regarding the increasing military ties between India and Iran. In October 2003, these qualms were made public by Ariel Sharon, who threatened to put an end to military technology transfer to India that could be redirected towards Tehran.[107] India's aspiration to engage very diverse allies like Iran or Israel was a vital trait of its new balanced foreign policy in regards to West Asia. Motivated by a concern for maintaining its own foreign policy autonomy, India has always tried not to be entangled in military and political alliances.[108] As a result, India will therefore only negotiate strategic partnerships mostly directed by

---

[107] P. R. Kumaraswamy, 'Indo-Iranian Ties: The Israeli Dimension', in 'The "Strategic Partnership" Between India and Iran', Asia Program Special Report, Woodrow Wilson International Center for Scholars, April 2004, p. 28.
[108] Sagar, 'What Kind of Power', p. 804.

contingent factors rather than broader structural or ideological motivations.[109] Israel and Iran are perfect examples of these issue-based alliances for an emerging power like India. Israel has been a reliable military partner for the last 15 years and Iran was a crucial partner to ensure India's energy security.[110] This diversification of partnerships in the region will help preserve India's strategic leverage.

Economic Development

Economic development has been another strategic concern for Indian leaders when thinking about Israel after the security prerequisite was satisfied. Although there were already questions about trade relations with Arab States in the 1950s, economic concerns remained secondary when Nehru initially formulated India's Israel policy. Economic development became a strategic priority in India's relations with the region for Nehru's successors. India's pro-Arab policy was progressively shaped by its growing energy needs in the 1970s and 1980s. India was indeed strongly dependent on Gulf energy exports and repeatedly supported Gulf States' diplomatic positions against Israel.[111] In discussions with Arab states, India equally took into account the presence and well-being of its growing Indian expatriate community in West Asia.[112]

Economic considerations have also weighted in the 1992 decision to establish diplomatic relations with Israel. The liberalisation of the Indian economy and the need for US investment encouraged the reorientation of Indian policy towards Washington which was the main actor within the international financial institutions. Good relations with the Jewish state seemed to be a prerequisite to the easing of prevailing Indo-US tensions. Israeli industries have also been

---

[109] Mehta, 'Still Under Nehru's Shadow', pp. 221–22.

[110] C. Christine Fair, 'Indo-Iranian Relations: What Prospects for Transformation?', in Sumit Ganguly, ed., *India's Foreign Policy*.

[111] 'Does India Need Strategic Oil Reserve', *Business Standard*, November 13, 2002.

[112] These immigrants, ranging from labourers to skilled technicians, employed in the Arab states, have increased tremendously since the 1970's, going from 123,000 in 1975 to approximately 3.5 million today. For more information, see Prakash Jain, 'Indian Diaspora in West Asia', in Abhyankar, ed., *West Asia and the Region*.

able to meet crucial Indian needs in the niche fields of agriculture and technology. In fact, Indo-Israeli relations have now diversified to include knowledge-intensive sectors like IT and software, space research, medical technology and biotechnology and India's quest for improving production and productivity in its agricultural sector has also created space for cooperation in this vital sector of its economy.[113] Indian companies have for example sought Israeli expertise in agriculture and most especially in irrigation and soil management equipment and techniques.[114] Lastly, in its search for new markets and resources, India is currently negotiating a free trade agreement with Israel.[115] As long as Israeli expertise in niche fields proves useful to Indian interests, Indo-Israeli economic relations will continue to prosper.

Conclusion and the Future of India's Israel Policy

Looking at Indo-Israeli relations through the prism of grand strategy helps understand what long-term strategic objectives influenced the 1950 and 1992 decisions regarding Israel. If similar goals guided the Indian leaders in these different periods, the operationalisation of India's Israel policy was different. The timing and nature of the Indo-Israeli partnership is partly due to varying international, regional and domestic environments. At the structural level, the end of the Cold War fundamentally altered India's strategic calculus and made it opportune for New Delhi to engage Israel. At the regional level, non-reciprocity in Indo-Arab relations and the beginnings of a peace process equally encouraged India to reassess its traditional West Asia policy. At the domestic level, there were strategic complementarities between India's growing military market in search of new solutions to replace the traditional Soviet supplier and Israel's

---

[113] During his visit to Israel in November 2005, the Indian Minister for Commerce and Industries established a Joint Study Group (JSG) in order to boost bilateral trade. See 'Israel-India: Final Report of the Joint Study Group', November 10, 2005.

[114] 'India, Israel Planning Joint Fund for Agri Research', *The Financial Express*, March 27, 2006.

[115] James Lamont and Martin Wolf, 'India to Launch Trade Talks with Israel', *Financial Times*, February 11, 2010.

prominent military industry looking for resources to maintain a technological edge. Individual leaders' perceptions of India's national interests are equally decisive to explain differences in India's Israel policy between 1950 and 1992. It is important to highlight the role of the Nehru and Rao governments in devising an Israeli policy which they measured as contextually adequate to respond to their strategic needs given their available instruments.

The grand strategy framework also gives some indications of the future of Indo-Israeli relations. The nature and importance of relations with India's relations with Israel will ultimately depend on its strategic needs. While recognising Israel in 1950, Nehru did not feel it was in India's interest to further engage the Jewish State given the international and regional contexts, especially after the Suez crisis of 1956.[116] In 1992, Rao and his foreign policy advisers came to the conclusion that India should not worry about its Arab and Muslim allies' sensitivities at the cost of direct and indirect benefits of closer relations with Israel. In addition, both in 1950 and in 1992, the decisions taken vis-à-vis Israel were not definitive and remained open to revision in light of changes in India's strategic environment. While Hindu nationalist might have argued the new Indo-Israeli rapprochement could transform itself into a 'natural alliance' collaborating against Islamic fundamentalism in the post-9/11 environment,[117] there are important limits to such a partnership. For example, cooperation on counter-terrorism and intelligence-sharing efforts can only be limited as both countries are not directly fighting the same enemy. India cannot totally identify with Israel's definition of terrorism and India does not focus on the same kind of coercive apparatus Israel has advocated. In addition, Indian decision-makers are equally conscious that Israeli tactics of building walls and waging punitive wars have no proved to be successful over the past years.[118]

---

[116] Brecher, *India and World Politics*, pp. 80–81.

[117] See for example Ilan Berman, 'Israel, India and Turkey: Triple Entente?', *Middle East Quarterly*, Fall 2002, pp. 33–40; Christophe Jaffrelot, 'Inde-Israël, le Nouvel Elément-Clé de l'Axe du Bien?', *Critique Internationale*, No. 21, October 2003. For a review, see Blarel, *Inde et Israël: Le Rapprochement Stratégique*, pp. 31–50.

[118] See Rushda Siddiqui, 'India and Israel's Counter-Terrorism Policy', in Abhyankar, ed., *West Asia and the Region*.

As a result, Indo-Israeli relations can more accurately be described as a selective partnership or a contingent rapprochement in the context of the operationalisation of India's grand strategy. If India aims to be a great power in the coming years, it has to diversify its partnerships and to be open to engaging all countries. In West Asia, a rising India has to be able to 'manage' relations with both Arab countries and Israel in order to mobilise all resources, whether military or energetic, from the region.[119] Although, it is difficult to clearly envisage the impact of future regional events (such as the attack on Nariman House, the Jewish community centre in Mumbai in November 2008) on the evolution of Indo-Israeli relations, it seems improbable that it could put an end to a very prolific and now institutionalised strategic cooperation between the two nations. The only changes for the Indian leadership would be rhetorical in order to not affect long-standing relations with Arab states. While intensifying relations with Israel, India has indeed kept an official pro-Palestinian position in international forums.[120] Because India has a strategic priority of assuring the security of its territory and population, it will accept military aid from any partner, including Israel.

At the methodological level, there are important limits to the applicability of the grand strategy framework to analysing the evolution of Indo-Israeli relations. The grand strategy framework does not help explain India's anomalous Israel policy of the 1970 and 1980s. During this period, India's policies towards West Asia in these two decades were apparently still based on Nehru's original interpretation of the political situation in the region. The problem is that this path-dependent and unproductive policy was not sensible to international and regional changes and was never reassessed. At one point, these policies even appeared in contradiction with what the literature identified as India's traditional strategic goals. The third section of this paper already pointed out the enduring domestic debate that existed on India's Israel policy in the 1970s and 1980s. Paradoxically, there were no changes at the policy-making level. Who then defines the national interest? How are perceptions of leaders, elites

---

[119] Abhyankar, ed., *West Asia and the Region*, p. 52.

[120] Dhiraj Nayyar, 'India Slams Israeli Attack on Gaza Aid Flotilla', *The Indian Express*, June 9, 2010.

and/or of coalitions of the national interest shaping the operationalisation of a policy? Further research informed by recent scholarship on the formulation and execution of Grand Strategic aims could concentrate on this period of India's West Asia policy.[121]

---

[121] See for example Jack Snyder, *Myths of Empire: Domestic Politics and International Ambition* (Ithaca, NY: Cornell University Press, 1991), Jeffrey Legro, *Rethinking the World: Great Power Strategies and International Order* (Ithaca: Cornell University Press, 2005), Kevin Narizny, The Political Economy of Grand Strategy (Ithaca: Cornell University Press, 2007), and Peter Trubowitz, *Politics and Strategy: Partisan Ambition and American Statecraft* (Princeton, NJ: Princeton University Press, 2011).

16

THE INSTITUTIONAL ORIGINS AND DETERMINANTS OF INDIA'S AFRICA POLICY

*Constantino Xavier**

India's re-engagement with Africa in its post-reform period has earned it a lot of attention. Together with China, India seems to have suddenly emerged as a major 'competitor' in Africa, bidding for important resource and infrastructure projects, launching new lines of credit and tariff cuts, expanding its diplomatic network, and increasing its military presence on the continent and across its shores. Different reports have thus emerged to describe India's relations with Africa in great detail across different sub-regions and sectors, mostly from an economic angle.[1] Most of these studies are empirically rich, but tend to club 'the dragon and the elephant' together, offering little space for the exploration of potential differences between the Chinese and Indian models of engagement with Africa.[2]

---

* This chapter is based on research conducted in June–August 2010 as a visiting fellow at the Institute of Defence Studies and Analyses, New Delhi. I am thankful to the institute, to all interviewees, and to several people who have offered comments on draft versions, including Walter K. Andersen, Kanti Bajpai, Ruchita Beri, Sumit Ganguly, C. Raja Mohan, and Anit Mukherjee.

[1] For a general perspective on India in Africa across a variety of sectors and regions, see Sushant K. Singh, 'India and West Africa: A Burgeoning Relationship', Chatham House Asia Programme Briefing Paper, London, 2007; E. Mawdsley and G. McCann, 'The Elephant in the Corner? Reviewing India–Africa Relations in the New Millennium', *Geography Compass*, 4, 2, February 2010, pp. 81–93; Peter Kragelund, 'India's African Engagement', ARI 10/2010, January 2010, Madrid, Real Instituto El Cano; J. Peter Pham, 'India's Expanding Relations with Africa and Their Implications for U.S. Interests,' *American Foreign Policy Interests*, 29, 5, 2007, pp. 341–52.

[2] Such comparative studies include C. H. Broadman's *Africa's Silk Road: China and India's New Economic Frontier* (Washington DC: World Bank,

Contrasting with this relatively sophisticated body of literature on 'India in Africa', there has been, however, surprisingly little research on 'Africa in India'. Assuming India's interests in Africa to be fixed, most analysts therefore neglect the larger institutional and intellectual environment that influences India's forays into Africa. The most popular (and convenient) simplification has flourished under the idea of a monolithic 'Indian Africa policy', giving the impression that India's re-engagement with the continent is now institutionalised as a consensual and coherent set of economic and strategic objectives.[3]

This essay seeks to dig deeper and excavate the contours of the larger infrastructure that supports India's supposed 'Africa policy'. What domestic institutions and actors share expertise and experience on Africa, and what are their sources? How do they relate to each other, and do they influence the decision-making process, both in terms of public policy and in the private sector? How has the image and relative priority of Africa changed over recent years in the Indian lens? Even if non-institutionalised, is there an implicit consensus or policy framework that sets out long-term objectives?

These are the main questions that guide this research essay. Rather than evaluating India's changing profile in Africa, or critically comparing it to other actual or potential competitors, it assumes the role of an in-depth case study on India's foreign-policy making process. It thus contributes to the emerging line of policy-oriented research that surveys the environment that supports India's intensifying and widening scope of external engagement.[4]

The choice of Africa as a case is based on two factors that give it a comparative advantage. First, while North Africa is often excluded for political reasons, there is nevertheless a strong consensus on the geographical delimitation of Africa across different time periods, as

---

2007); Fantu Cheru and Cyril Obi, eds, *The Rise of China and India in Africa: Challenges, Opportunities and Critical Interventions* (London: Zed Books, London, 2010).

[3] A notable exception is Sanusha Naidu, 'India's Growing African Strategy', *Review of African Political Economy*, 35, 115, pp. 116–28.

[4] Several articles addressing this larger foreign policy infrastructure in two recent special journal issues deserve a mention here. First, the January/April 2009 issue (46, 1–2) of *International Studies*, New Delhi, entitled 'International Studies in India'. Second, the July 2009 issue (8, 3) of *India Review*, entitled 'Future Issues in India's Foreign Policy: Ideas, Interests and Values'.

reflected, for example, in relative stable membership of the African Union. Second, India–Africa relations have undergone fundamental change over the last decades, from an ideational to a material emphasis, thus potentially allowing one to measure how these shifting priorities have impacted (or not) India's institutional and intellectual 'Africa apparatus'.

This chapter is organised in three sections. A first part offers a brief historical background to India–Africa relations, tracing their development over time and identifying the main drivers of India's re-engagement with the continent. A second part then maps the Indian expertise on Africa, locating and describing the main institutions and actors involved with Africa on the diplomatic, security, academic, business and civil society fronts. The third and main section, mainly based on interviews and other primary sources, then sets out to identify the main tensions, problems and challenges faced by and between the concerned actors and institutions.

A short note on the method: beyond secondary sources and a year-long weekly clipping of close to one thousand India–Africa news items, I conducted a total of 17 semi-structured, one- to two-hour long interviews between July 7 and August 5, 2010, in New Delhi, Mumbai and Goa.[5] They include eight acting or retired government officials (mostly diplomats), four representatives of the private sector (involved in the trade and investment sectors), four researchers (at universities or research institutes), and one journalist. All are actively involved with Africa, though often on multiple fronts (e.g. retired diplomats now working in the corporate sector or at a research institute). Given the small population of 'Indian Africanists' and the sensitivity of some of the issues addressed by the sample, I have chosen to preserve their anonymity, identifying each interview by a single number and date.

India–Africa Relations across Time

South Asia has been culturally linked to Africa for millennia, in particular with its Eastern shores, through the medium of active trade

---

[5] I compiled these for the weekly *Lisbon India Monitor* e-newsletter I edited for the Portuguese Institute of International Relations between March 2009 and June 2010. Partial archives available at http://www.ipri.pt/artigos/artigo.php?ida=374, accessed on June 2, 2010.

relations and migratory flows. The colonial era intensified these relations, first with the Portuguese and then with the British, with a large Indian diaspora settling across southern and eastern Africa. This Indian proximity and intimacy with Africa is identifiable in several sectors, but is perhaps best reflected in Sugata Bose's study on the Western Indian Ocean as a 'region'.[6] Mahatma Gandhi's presence and political activities in South Africa further strengthened these links in the 20th century, with Africa assuming a pioneering role in India's freedom struggle, both in geographical and rhetorical terms, with several visits by Indian leaders to Kenya, Uganda, and South Africa and Nehru's commitment to embed India's struggle within a wider 'Afro-Asian solidarity' movement.[7]

India's independence then allowed it to expand its leadership and influence in Africa by actively supporting the anti-colonial freedom movements there. This included inviting African representatives to the Asian relations conference held in New Delhi, in 1947, and establishing diplomatic representations in several African countries that were still under formal colonial rule. As a leader of the Non-Aligned Movement and the Group of 77, India also assumed a leading position in the crystallisation of the influential Afro-Asian block that dominated the United Nations' General Assembly well into the 1960s.[8]

With African countries achieving independence and often becoming entangled as 'hot' proxy front wars during the Cold War, India maintained its reputation with the African leadership, but progressively moved off the strategic radar, both uninter-ested and unable to intervene in any significant way in this new frontline of bipolar power politics. Instead of bringing about change, the post-reform era in the 1990s actually intensified this disengagement from Africa.

Facing a radically changed strategic environment and a difficult period of structural economic adjustment, India's policy focus shifted

---

[6] Sugata Bose, *A Hundred Horizons: The Indian Ocean in the Age of Global Empire* (Cambridge, MA: Harvard University Press: 2006).

[7] For an overview of this period, see Richard L. Park, 'Indian–African Relations', *Asian Survey*, 5, 7 (July 1965), pp. 350–58.

[8] Amitav Acharya offers a superb introduction to the dilemmas surrounding India's adoption of non-alignment as a central stance in its foreign policy in *Whose Ideas Matter? Agency and Power in Asian Regionalism* (London: Cornell University Press, 2009).

to redesign its strategic map: while its 'Gujral Doctrine' focused on improving strained relations with the neighbours in South Asia, the 'Look East policy' emerged as a first consolidated attempt of economic policy towards Southeast and East Asian countries as sources of much needed foreign investment.[9] At the same time, with the collapse of its sole 'proto-ally', the Soviet Union, New Delhi was also forced to re-engage the United States and the European Union, even while defying the international community when it went overtly nuclear in May 1998.

It is in this extremely competitive context that Africa naturally suffered a relative decline in terms of strategic importance to India's interest. No longer important to legitimise Delhi's non-aligned stance, it also did not offer any substantial economic benefits for India. It is therefore not surprising that the 1990s are often described as the nadir of modern India-African relations. Barring a few initiatives on the diplomatic front, as during the campaign to overcome the international sanctions imposed after the 1998 tests, India disengaged from the continent. Trade often dropped in both absolute and relative terms, and several diplomatic missions were closed because of lack of funds or strategic interests.[10] In the words of one diplomat, India thus 'lost some of the capital' it had accumulated in Africa during the earlier decades, while others prefer to refer to it as a 'period of adaptation and transition' given increasingly divergent interests.[11]

While there is no precise date or symbolic initiative, it is consensual that the current re-engagement period began somewhere after 2000. The fundamental change that followed is often described as the 'emergence of India's new Africa policy', but the transformation was *practical* and *material*, rather than ideational or programmatic. While India had 'committed rhetorically to Africa since 1947, it now

---

[9] On India's strategic reorientation, see C. Raja Mohan, *Crossing the Rubicon: The Shaping of India's New Foreign Policy* (New Delhi: Viking Books, 2003). On India's 'Look East policy', see Christophe Jaffrelot, 'India's Look East Strategy: An Asianist Strategy in Perspective', *India Review*, 2, 2 (April 2003), pp. 35–68.

[10] This was the case of the missions in Malawi and the Democratic Republic of Congo.

[11] Author's interviews no. 4 and 5, July 14 and 22, 2010.

was, for the first time, able to match these with actual capabilities', according to one former diplomat.[12]

India–Africa relations intensified across the spectrum of political, diplomatic, cultural, and defense relations, but were essentially economically motivated. Bilateral trade figures grew exponentially subsequent to a dramatic increase in official visits. India became a member of the African Union Capacity Building Foundation. Seeking to correct its relative weak presence in Western Africa, India announced in 2004 the Techno-Economic Approach for Africa-India Movement (TEAM-9) with 500 million USD, involving eight, mostly francophone and lusophone countries.[13] In 2005, the Confederation of Indian Industries (CII) started to host an annual business conclave, whose sixth edition on 'India Africa Project Partnership' took place in New Delhi, in 2010, in partnership with the Exim Bank.

On its side, the Federation of Indian Chambers of Commerce and Industry (FICCI) increased the number of Joint Business Councils by signing agreements with at least a dozen more African counterparts. In 2009 it hosted the first India-Africa Hydrocarbons Conference in partnership with the Ministry of Petroleum and Natural Gas, and in 2010 it organised the 'Namaskar Africa' program, a unique business delegation and fair to promote Indian interests in Nigeria and West Africa.

The year 2008, however, marks the culmination of the efforts started during the first half of the decade, with New Delhi hosting the first India–Africa summit in partnership with the African Union, attended by hundreds of official delegates and representatives of 14 African countries, including several heads of state and ministers. Inspired by the Chinese initiative held two years earlier in Beijing, the Indian effort led to the adoption of a common declaration and an action plan that have, since then, structured the larger terms of the relations and are often referred to as the genesis of India's Africa policy.[14] The approved action plan sets out clear targets and puts a

---

[12] Author's interview no. 8, July 27, 2010.

[13] See 'India Pledges $500m to West African Nations', *The Hindu*, March 2, 2004. Available at http://www.hinduonnet.com/2004/03/02/stories/2004030202791200.htm, accessed on June 2, 2010.

[14] For more information and the summit's outcomes, see http://meaindia.nic.in/indiaafricasummit/, accessed on June 2, 2010.

clear emphasis on the issues of training and education, which are referred to in each of the seven areas of privileged co-operation, including the dialogue on peace and security.[15] This focus on the 'softer' dimensions of co-operation has, since then, influenced various fronts.

On the co-operation side, the slots for African countries within the Indian Technical and Co-operation (ITEC) program were increased in 2008 from 1100 to 1600. The Ministry of Agriculture will offer 75 MSc and PhD scholarships to African students each year, while the C. V. Raman scholarships announced in 2010 will seek to attract the brightest African researchers in the field of science and technology. Other initiatives include an Afro-Indian climate change initiative in collaboration with The Energy Resources Institute (TERI), as well as New Delhi playing host in 2010 to a meeting with several leaders of African regional and multilateral organisations.[16] Several others projects envisioned in the 2008 action plan were announced during the second summit that took place in Ethiopia, in May 2011.[17]

The analysis suggests that the economic factor played a determinant role in the intensification of India–Africa relations over the last decade. But the economic factor itself is far from monolithic, integrating different sectors, from the exploration of natural resources to an attractive new investment destination. From a current perspective, however, most explanations for this sudden re-engagement in the 2000s tend to converge around seven different dimensions that drive and determine India's interests in Africa.

The search for natural resources represents one of India's most important stakes in Africa. Fuelled by unprecedented growth rates and domestic consumption demands, India's oil, gas and coal companies were forced to diversify their import basket. Following an almost exclusive concentration on the Middle East supply until the 1990s, Africa thus emerged as the prime alternative destination. Public companies such as ONGC and OIL, but also increasingly

---

[15] The Joint Action Plan is available at http://www.indianembassy.gov.et/download/Joint%20Plan%20of%20Action.doc, accessed on June 2, 2010.

[16] Author's interview no. 12, July 28, 2010.

[17] For the full Summit declaration, see http://pib.nic.in/newsite/erelease.aspx?relid=72319, accessed on May 25, 2012.

private actors such as Tata and Essar have been actively involved in securing these energy resources now in African countries as well.

A second driver relates to Africa as a new investment destination for the increasing global profile of India's multinational corporate sector. Infrastructure development, such as railways, ports, communication networks and housing, often attached to larger projects of natural resources extraction, has been the sector of greatest activity, though investment in the African services sector (banking, education and health) has also attracted increasing Indian capital. The pharmaceutical, diamonds and machinery sectors have absorbed most of Indian investments on the industrial front.

A third driver is more prospective, and places the African countries as long-term high-growth markets with a specific demand for Indian goods and services. While seeking to avoid the trap of being identified as just one more 'neo-colonial' predatory and mercantilist player on the continent, or being accused (as the Chinese often are) of dumping and swamping African countries with low-quality good that stifle local productivity, Delhi's focus has been on the 'softer' sectors of education, skilling and training, and health services. In parallel to Indian consumer and industrial goods, from rice to heavy machinery, these sectors are believed to offer public and private Indian investments valuable inroads into these emerging markets.

A fourth driver relates to the security front, representing a dramatic shift from earlier decades in which the focus was mostly on Africa as a partner in securing India's diplomatic agenda for disarmament and zones of peace. India now has defense agreements or military co-operation and training agreements with more than fifteen African countries[18] and some have expressed their interest in purchasing India's defence equipment.[19] By 2008, India had emerged as the largest contributor to UN mandated operations in Africa.[20]

---

[18] Arvind Dutta, 'Indo-African Defence Co-operation: Need For Enhanced Thrust', *Journal of Defence Studies*, 2, 2 (Winter 2007), pp. 170–77.

[19] This is the case of at least the Dhruv light helicopter, from Hindustan Aeronautics Limited. In this context, one interviewee (author's interview no. 9, July 28, 2010) underlined the importance of supplying defence equipments as incentives, or 'toys', that guarantee privileged access and benefits on other bilateral fronts.

[20] Ruchita Beri, 'India's Role in Keeping Peace in Africa', *Strategic Analysis*, 32, 2 (2008), pp. 197–221.

The increasing piracy threat along the Somali coast, have also encouraged the Indian Navy to develop new security stakes along the East African coast, from the Gulf of Aden to the Mozambique Channel.

Another determinant of India's relations with Africa resides in the diplomatic weight Africa enjoys in several international institutions and that has been rising over the last years. As an aspiring leader of the 'Global South', India seeks to capitalise on its historical role during the Cold War and ensure the African countries' support for its various diplomatic initiatives. This includes its campaign for a permanent and a non-permanent (2011–12) seat in the United Nations' Security Council, the recent acquisition of its special nuclear status under the Non-Proliferation Treaty and Nuclear Suppliers Group, and several other issues, from trade to climate change and the global financial architecture, on which its success largely depends on the votes of African countries.[21]

A sixth driver relates to the large Indian diaspora on the African continent. A 2001 estimate identified close to one hundred thousand Indian citizens residing in Africa, with more than half in eastern and southern Africa. On top of this more recent immigrant community, there are more than 1 million people of Indian origin who have settled in Africa for many generations (close to one million in South Africa; 25,000 in Madagascar; 15,000 in Zimbabwe; and 8,000 in Nigeria).[22] Many still have close links with India, and their privileged position and contacts with the African leadership offer New Delhi a valuable asset to foster its economic and strategic interests. At the same time, such a large population also represents a significant burden for consular structures and a potential security challenge.[23]

---

[21] On the UN campaign, see the specific references about Africa in 'India confident of 150 votes in Security Council bid'. Available at http://www.hindustantimes.com/India-confident-of-150-votes-in-Security-Council-bid/Article1-587487.aspx, accessed on August 16, 2010.

[22] Estimates by the High Level Committee on the Indian Diaspora, whose 2002 report is available at http://www.indiandiaspora.nic.in/contents.htm, accessed on June 2, 2010.

[23] One former intelligence official noted that the Research and Analysis Wing's main tasks in Africa during the 1980s consisted in monitoring the Indian diaspora there, especially their involvement in separatist and criminal networks (author's interview no. 10, July 28, 2010).

A final driver behind India's re-engagement with Africa relates to New Delhi's self-perception and long-term great power ambitions.[24] Fuelled by Chinese forays and the competitive logic behind the 'scramble for Africa', many argue for India's presence on the continent through a mere power projection paradigm. In this view, India's presence in Africa should not be merely linked to specific material interests: as a new forefront of the global arena, Africa should therefore be a crucial ground for India to project its capabilities and influence in order to gain its rightful recognition as an extra-regional power. Beyond natural interests in securing energy and commercial supply routes in the Western Indian Ocean, a significant dimension of India's efforts at securing a predominant strategic position along the East African coast is often legitimised on these lines.

Africa in India: Mapping the Stakeholders and Expertise

This short section attempts to offer a brief survey of the main institutions and actors that relate to Africa, shape India's Africa expertise, or directly influence and shape India–Africa relations. Mapping an area of expertise and institutional responsibilities has its necessary limitations: there is little scope to incorporate change over time, biasing the exercise towards the present while the outcome is generally influenced by the primary sources one relies on. Taking this limitation into consideration, it is possible to distinguish at least four different types of stakeholders: diplomacy, defense and security, academia and research, and business and corporate.

Other actors involved in or with Africa include journalists (such as Manish Chand, of the Indo-Asian News Service, or Renu Malhotra, editor of the recently launched Afro-Asian Business Chronicle), various private bilateral friendship societies (such as the Indo-African Society), or the federal representatives that sit on the various parliamentary friendship committees with African countries. These are, however, very limited in their scope of activities and influence,

---

[24] For a closer analysis on this driver, see 'New Delhi's great power ambition', *Watershed*. Available at http://www.watershed.com.br/article/176/new-delhi%E2%80%99s-great-power-ambition.aspx, accessed on June 2, 2010.

and will thus not be analysed here, but referred to in the following section.

First, at the official level, the bulk of Africa-related work is channelled through the Ministry of External Affairs (MEA), who is responsible for the promotion of India's political, economic and cultural interests abroad. On Africa, the MEA cooperates and consults on a wide range of issues with other ministries, mainly those of Trade, Industry and Commerce, Defence, and Overseas Indian Affairs. Unlike in some other countries, these have no formal representation offices abroad and depend on the MEA. This therefore puts a vast burden on the MEA's Africa Division, which oversees bilateral relations across the spectrum of functional sectors with 53 countries and several multilateral and regional organisations, from the African Union to the Southern African Development Community (SADC).

There are three Joint Secretaries, one each for West Asia and North Africa (WANA, with five African countries), West Africa (WA, 25 countries) and East and South Africa (ESA, 24 countries). The two former ones are the result of a bifurcation in 2003, until which the entire Sub-Saharan Africa was under the sole responsibility of one joint secretary. Cultural matters, including study scholarships and exchange programs are managed through the MEA's Indian Council of Cultural Relations (ICCR). While relations with the African Union are co-managed by the JS ESA, the JS WA co-manages the Pan-African E-Network initiative that includes 47 countries and has its regional hub in Senegal.

These three joint secretaries are in direct contact with the Indian diplomatic representations in Africa, which include 27 embassies or high commissions (five being located in North Africa), five consulate generals and fifteen local honorary consulates.[25] Larger missions are located in South Africa, Egypt, and Mauritius (each with more than 10 diplomats or attachés), closely followed by other significant representations in Nigeria, Kenya, Tanzania, Angola, Sudan, and Ethiopia (from five to nine officials in each mission). This excludes a large number of supporting staff, composed of both Indians and foreigners hired locally.

African diplomatic missions in New Delhi are also important stakeholders in India-Africa relations. While serving their national

---

[25] Compilation of data accessed on the MEA's official website. Available at http://meaindia.nic.in/onmouse/mission.htm, accessed on July 17, 2010.

interests, they also serve as important sources of information and advice for both Indian businessmen and scholars. In total, 42 African countries are represented in the Indian capital, 36 are represented in New Delhi through an embassy or high commission, while six others have established honorary consulates. There are close to twenty more African consulates or honorary consulates in Mumbai, Kolkata and Chennai.[26]

Operating formally within the diplomatic missions, but independently from the MEA, are the intelligence and military attachés. There are around five intelligence officers from the Research and Analysis Wing, India's external intelligence agency, posted in Africa.[27] On the security dimension, India has defense attachés in Egypt, Kenya and Nigeria, and the Indian military can boast of a wide experience on Africa, where it has emerged as one of the largest contributor for UN peacekeeping missions. There is thus a large number of high-ranking Indian army officials with an impressive ground experience on African conflicts. This played an important role in setting up the United Nations Center for Peacekeeping, in New Delhi, whose training courses have been so far attended by 138 officials from 21 African countries.[28]

Beyond the official corridors, where else is Africa engaged and studied in India? Academia plays an important role in this regard, with three full-fledged departments or centers of African Studies.[29] The first department of African Studies was set up at Delhi University, in 1954, at the personal initiative of Jawaharlal Nehru. It has the largest number of faculty slots (15), albeit nine remain vacant, and hosts several study units, a Swahili language programme, and a University Grants Commission-sponsored Africa research centre. On average, six students join every year for the MPhil and three to four students for the PhD degree.[30]

---

[26] Compilation of data accessed on the MEA's official protocol website. Available at http://meaprotocol.nic.in/, accessed on July 17, 2010.

[27] Author's interview no. 10, July 28, 2010.

[28] According to information on its website, Available at http://www.usiofindia.org/CUNP_International%20Linkage.HTM, accessed on July 27, 2010.

[29] Also, the National Eligibility Test (NET, which is compulsory for those wishing to teach at universities or colleges) offers a subject on African Studies within the Politics module. Available at http://www.ugc.ac.in/inside/syllabus.html, accessed on July 27, 2010.

[30] Author's interview no. 5, July 22, 2010.

The African studies division at Jawaharlal Nehru University originated in the vibrant area studies programme initiated at the School of International Studies, in the 1960s, under the leadership of Arjun Appadurai. It operated as an autonomous division under the larger Center for West Asian and African Studies, until finally being upgraded to a full-fledged Center of African Studies in 2009. Its five faculty members supervise around forty students, half of which are PhD students.[31] Its recognition as a 'critical' area studies programme by the UGC has allowed it to access important public funding and thus finance research projects and doctoral fieldwork trips.[32]

The Center also hosts the secretariat of the African Studies Association (ASA), an initiative launched in 2000 to congregate all Indian *Africanists*.[33] The Association has emerged as the apex body for African studies in India, organising several international seminars and talks, and publishes two journals (*Africa Insight* and *Africa Review*) to which most Africa scholars contribute, independently of academic affiliation. ASA cooperates closely with the MEA and African diplomatic missions, and its activities are partially funded by a Ford Foundation grant.[34]

The University of Mumbai hosts the third Department of African Studies in India, established in 1971–71 as the Centre for African Studies. With a faculty strength of just three (six sanctioned positions), it offers a unique MA on Africa since 1986, as well as an MPhil (since 2007) and PhD (1985) degree in African studies. It published the biannual journal *African Currents* and in 2006–07 its annual report registers five MA and one PhD student.[35] Smaller course offerings, faculty and research units specialising on African studies are located at the Jamia Millia Islamia's Academy of Third World Studies, in New Delhi, as well as at the universities of Jadavpur (Kolkata), Allahabad and Hyderabad.[36]

---

[31] Ambassador Shashank, a former Foreign Secretary at the MEA, was expected in 2011 to join as a visiting professor.

[32] Author's interview no. 17, August 5, 2010.

[33] Replacing the earlier African Studies Society, active until the early 1990s.

[34] Author's interview no. 17, August 5, 2010.

[35] Data based on author's interview no. 2, July 13, 2010 and on the department's official website, available at http://www.mu.ac.in/arts/social_science/african_studies/Annual%20Report.html, accessed on July 30, 2010.

[36] For a more detailed perspective on African studies at Indian universities, see Aparajita Biswas, 'African Studies in India', in P.T. Zeleza, ed., *The Study*

Besides formal academia, India is witnessing the emergence of an increasingly vibrant 'think tank industry'. The Institute of Defence Studies and Analyses, funded by the Ministry of Defence and ranked as one of Asia's top think tanks, has an active cluster with at least one senior research associate working exclusively on Africa.[37] The privately-funded Observer Research Foundation, has also hosted seminars and co-published a book on Africa. The historical Indian Council for World Affairs, under the tutelage of the MEA, has hosted several events on Africa and plans to develop its own Africa research expertise in the near future. Overall, the number of seminars and talks on Africa has increased dramatically over the last years, attracting also a number of international scholars, collaborative projects and retired Indian diplomats keen in sharing their ground experience.

As an increasing number of Indian private companies develop their experience in terms of projects and investments in Africa, the corporate sector has also gathered a significant expertise on the continent. Information on specific countries and sectors is still scarce and valuable, and therefore only reluctantly shared. Under the umbrella of India's two industrial and commercial chambers, the Confederation of Indian Industries (CII) and the Federation of Indian Chambers of Commerce and Industry (FICCI), several companies have, however, taken a leading position in pushing for more expertise on Africa. The Tata and Kirloskar groups, for example, have presided over CII's Africa Committee, an apex body whose 34 corporate members are involved in or interested in getting involved in Africa.[38]

The heads of the Africa desks at both CII and FICCI have been in their jobs for around ten years, playing a vital role in facilitating contacts between the government and the business sector. While CII seems to be in closer relation with the MEA, FICCI tends to act as a consultative body to the Ministry of Commerce and Industry, especially in terms of bilateral trade and commercial sectors that

---

of Africa: Global and Transational Engagements, Vol. 2 (London: African Books Collective, 2007), pp. 305–14.

[37] Ruchita Beri, senior research associate, has led initiatives in this area for more than twenty years, coordinating several international conferences and book publications. The institute also regularly hosts visiting fellows on issues related to Africa.

[38] Author's interview no. 15, August 2, 2010.

could affect specific economic interests of its regional members. On the other hand, the smaller Indo-African Chamber of Commerce and Industry (IACCI), established in Mumbai since 1985, has also played an influential role in assisting the expansion of smaller and medium Indian companies to Africa, from visa issues to facilitation of contacts. It hosts the annual 'Africa Day', to which it has successfully attracted several ministers and diplomats from Africa and New Delhi.[39]

Sources of Inter-Institutional Tension and Complex Policy-Making

How do the various stakeholders and actors relate to each other within this complex institutional and ideational infrastructure that supports India's policy-making processes on Africa? Where do the main sources of tension, dispute and challenge reside? To what extent does limited co-operation translate into complex decision-making?

This section seeks to answer these crucial questions by adopting two levels of analysis; one at the *intra*-institutional and the second at the *inter*-institutional. The first level dissects the internal strengths and shortcomings of the MEA, the academic and business communities in terms of their respective Africa expertise and policy-making. The second level then brings these actors into relation, analysing the sources of tension between diplomacy and academia, diplomacy and business, and diplomacy and other stakeholders (civil society, with a particular focus on the role of public diplomacy).

MINISTRY OF EXTERNAL AFFAIRS

On the structural side, does the MEA have the adequate resources to respond to the increasing workload arising from India's reengagement with Africa? Most of the interviewees disagreed, pointing out to several shortcomings: with less than 10 officials, its Africa Division suffers from 'chronic understaffing', a problem that also affects many of the missions in Africa, often in the hands of only two or three diplomats.[40] Others refer to an urgent need in expanding the

---

[39] Author's interview no. 3, July 13, 2010.
[40] Author's interview no. 11, July 28, 2010.

number of embassies and high commissions in Africa, welcoming the recent opening of new missions in Mali, the Democratic Republic of Congo and Niger.[41]

In terms of human resources, while Indian Foreign Service officials all undergo foreign language training for at least one year abroad, very few master French and Portuguese, which is seen as a major impediment to engage with at least a dozen African countries that are crucial to Indian interests.[42] At the same time, Africa is often still seen as a 'punishment posting' for many, although this is slowly changing, with younger generation of diplomats, usually in their forties, expressing an increasing interest in serving in southern and eastern Africa.[43] For one retired diplomat, the persisting lack of interest is not related to financial issues or the recently revised allowances system, but caused by the archaic image of Africa, difficult living conditions faced by the accompanying family, crime and insecurity, and also the language barrier.[44]

Most problems on the diplomatic front seem to originate in a different understanding on the MEA's primary role and responsibility. On the one hand, some interviewees underlined the lack of specialisation amongst Indian diplomats, as reflected in the insufficient language training and the disincentives to focus on one region. On the other hand, others share a more 'generalist' understanding of the MEA as a bureaucratic apparatus that faces an increasingly number of complex and specialised issues that cannot be resolved solely in South Block. In this sense, one former diplomat notes that the traditional 'policy of protecting (the) empire is increasingly unsustainable' as the Ministry now interacts and competes with other actors in a free information society.[45] There is therefore 'no more time to wait

---

[41] On all of these and subsequent issues relating to the MEA's diplomatic structure and manpower, see the detailed analysis offered in Kishan S. Rana, *Inside Diplomacy* (New Delhi: Manas, 2000). For a comparative perspective, see his book on *Asian Diplomacy: The Foreign Ministries of China, India, Japan, Singapore, and Thailand* (Oxford: Oxford University Press, 2008).

[42] Young diplomats are generally posted as third secretaries in Lisbon to attend Portuguese language courses, and then often transferred to Brazil, Angola or Mozambique. French language training is generally offered in Brussels. Author's interview no. 11, July 28, 2010.

[43] Author's interview no. 4, July 14, 2010.

[44] Author's interview no. 11, July 28, 2010.

[45] Author's interview no. 9, July 28, 2010.

for the arrival of the weekly or fortnightly diplomatic bag' and an urgent need to start working in collaboration with outside experts.[46]

Finally, still on the diplomatic front, while one former high-ranking government official observes that Africa has now been upgraded to a 'small priority', most interviewees recognise shortcomings in the larger policy planning and strategic framework that guides this reengagement.[47] There are three levels of criticism. First, there seems to be very little 'bureaucratic memory' with a constant repetition and overlapping of responsibilities. Most concur that there is a lack in policy continuation and follow-up that stems from an excessive dependence on individuals. The recent positive 'spurts' in India's relations with Africa are thus almost invariably attributed to the personal efforts of two or three diplomats, and not to the larger institutional context (divisions, embassies, etc.) that hosted them.

Second, policy planning imperatives and preoccupations often *do* play an influential role, but tend to be discussed informally and circumstantially, at the personal level, or 'over tea' in the words of one observer.[48] This lack of institutionalisation in MEA's thinking capacity is exemplified by the recent marginalisation of its Policy, Planning and Research Division. Describing it as a 'backwater' or 'parking ground' for many diplomats, one interviewee thus laments the Ministry's difficulty in encouraging analytical, prospective and critical thinking.[49] One recurrent example given by interviewees is the excessive focus on large, southern and eastern, or English-speaking African countries, contrasting with the relative neglect of smaller, western and northern, or French- and Portuguese-speaking African countries.

A third recurrent issue relates to the lack of inter-institutional horizontal interaction and collaboration. Many underline the positive experience of the first conclave of Indian ambassadors and high commissioners in Africa, held in 2007 in Ethiopia.[50] However,

---

[46] Author's interview no. 11, July 28, 2010.
[47] Author's interview no. 1, July 8, 2010.
[48] Author's interview no. 6, July 23, 2010.
[49] Author's interview no. 8, July 27, 2010.
[50] Besides the 2007 pan-African conclave in Addis Ababa, there are also occasional informal meetings between heads of mission in a particular sub-region. South Africa has in recent years hosted twice such meetings for the heads of mission in Eastern and Southern Africa.

horizontal contact between the various missions in Africa and an excessive vertical dependence on the central structures in New Delhi still hampers long-term information collection, decision-making and establishment of concrete targets.[51]

ACADEMIA

'We live in an ivory tower', is the frank assessment of a leading Indian scholar in African studies.[52] Interviewees in this area point out to several factors responsible for their relative detachment of from reality.

First, most concede that work in this area is only rarely based on substantial fieldwork and ground experience.[53] At two of the three departments of African Studies, fieldwork at the doctoral level is still an exception. Interestingly, however, none adhere to the popular and conventional explanation of lack of funds. In their view, the problem resides rather in safety concerns of students and their families, lacking encouragement from academic supervisors, and a general absence of interest in accessing primary sources and data.[54] This translates into a wider research culture that is averse to the collection of original materials and to a direct familiarisation with the country or region of study in Africa. African embassies in New Delhi, Indian companies operating in Africa, or the MEA and other government institutions are thus the only sources of information not only for doctoral students, but often also for established scholars, who rarely visit their countries of expertise.[55] Language training is extremely rare, with an almost non-existent interest in French and Portuguese contrasting with persisting optional Swahili language programmes.[56]

---

[51] Author's interview no. 11, July 28, 2010.
[52] Author's interview no. 17, August 5, 2010.
[53] Author's interview no. 17, August 5, 2010.
[54] Author's interview no. 17, August 5, 2010.
[55] However, India's increasing economic engagement, as well as the development of university education and research opportunities in Africa (in particular in South and East Africa), has offered Indian scholars with an unprecedented number of opportunities to travel to Africa to participate in seminars or assume visiting fellowships.
[56] Swahili, and very occasionally also another African language, is offered as an optional course at all three universities. Jawaharlal Nehru University (JNU), New Delhi, has a full-fledged School of International Studies, where

It is thus no surprise that these shortcomings often lead to what one observer called a 'regurgitation of content and data'.[57] For most of the students in African studies, academics are seen as 'the last resort', after the exhaustion of all other options in the public and private job market, where an MA degree is often sufficient and an MPhil or PhD hardly valued outside academia and research.[58] Many attribute these negative developments to the dramatic increase in student numbers and the consequent lowering of academic standards, as well as to an increasing lack of interest in the social sciences and African area studies in particular.[59] While the emergence of the African Studies Association is welcomed by all interviewees, independently of their academic affiliation, there is also a sense that, as a research community, *Africanists* in India still suffer from a 'crab mentality', 'excessive politics' and an overall 'claustrophobic institutional space' in which innovation and change are almost impossible.[60]

BUSINESS AND CORPORATE SECTOR

With the emergence of new Indian corporate stakeholders in Africa, the business sector has also been developing its own research capacities and clout on the continent. What is striking, however, is their isolation from the other stakeholders, perhaps arising from its specific needs, overall profit-oriented dynamics and aversion to the slower-moving bureaucracy and academia. The Indo-African Chamber of Commerce and Industry, for example, has eight in-house researchers and eighteen freelance consultants.[61] The same applies to the Africa desks at CII and FICCI, which normally hire research assistants to work on specific projects.

At the same time, however, interviewees in this sector recognised that most business operations depend excessively on informal contacts, often facilitated by CII or FICCI, and that there is an overall

---

students have the option to enroll in additional language courses.

[57] Author's interview no. 7, July 24, 2010.

[58] Author's interviews no. 2, July 13, 2010, and no. 5, July 22, 2010.

[59] Most interviewees thus also speak with a sense of nostalgia about the first and second generation of Indian Africanists, under whose supervision many have studied. These include, among others, Professors Vijay Gupta, R. R. Ramchandani, Anirudh Dasgupta, and Rajen Harshe.

[60] Author's interviews no. 6, July 23, and no. 2, July 13, 2010.

[61] Author's interview no. 3, July 13, 2010.

need to develop research capabilities to follow up on such initial business contacts and assess the actual potential of investment plans.[62] One corporate representative involved in Africa thus conceded that there is an 'urgent need for experts' to complement the insufficient in-house capacities and an excessive dependence on Indian and foreign consultants with a generalist background and no specific expertise on Africa.[63] The development of political risk analysis and long-term economic scenarios are high on the agenda and generally identified as a potential area for collaboration with Indian academia and diplomacy.[64]

Relations Between MEA and Academia

One interviewee's description of the relationship as a constant 'tussle' between bureaucrats and scholars is perhaps the most apt description.[65] Incompatibility and differing priorities on Africa are natural between different stakeholders, but the problem seems to lie in a persistent inability to, at least punctually, integrate efforts in a mutually beneficial way to improve policy-making processes.

On the ministerial side, there is the recurrent complaint (similar to that from the business sector) that 'scholars (working on Africa) focus excessively on archaic and abstract research topics such as the Non-Aligned Movement and the Cold War period', and thus offer 'very little expertise relevant to MEA'.[66] Reflecting the earlier analysis on the shortcomings in methodology, fieldwork and training at university departments, diplomats also point to the scholars' lacking analytical skills and detachment from ground realities in Africa. One scholar observed that this bureaucracy-academia gap could stem from diverging ideological inclinations after 1990, when Africanist scholars started to be seen by other stakeholders as 'outcasts' persisting in a Marxist and Third-World paradigm that was longer perceived to be in the interest of India's new economic priorities.[67]

From the academic perspective, there are equivalent complaints. Most interviewed scholars are regularly invited to attend official

---

[62] Author's interview no. 16, August 2, 2010.
[63] Author's interview no. 14, August 2, 2010.
[64] Author's interview no. 15, August 2, 2010.
[65] Author's interview no. 9, July 28, 2010.
[66] Author's interview no. 4, July 14, 2010.
[67] Author's interview no. 2, July 13, 2010.

functions organised by the MEA, CII and FICCI, but their critical views on co-operation (or the lack of it) are unanimous: the MEA does reach out to academia, but without any purpose or specific objectives. Various interviewees attended closed meetings conveyed by the Africa and other MEA divisions in 2000, 2003, 2007 and 2010, but lamented the lack of any 'structured interaction' and an overall 'patronizing and condescending' bureaucratic disposition.[68] Other 'formalistic rituals' include the periodic organisation of collaborative seminars and workshops at various universities and research institutes, in which the academic or civil society partner is often 'subservient to' and dependent on the ministerial budget and agenda-setting in terms of topics and speakers.[69]

The underlying reason for such ineffectual events seems to reside in the ministerial need to fulfill budgetary requirements and spend allocated funds for consultations and discussions with civil society; in the expectations about the bureaucracy's ideational permeability, transparency and accountability; in the need to appease various political and economic stakeholders; and, at the same time, a certain compulsion to control the larger environment in which any democratic policy-making is necessarily embedded.[70] One scholar thus noted that there is a tendency in government to use academia as a 'fifth column', giving the example of how the MEA, in the context of the 2008 summit, approached a university department to organise a last-minute international conference 'at any cost'.[71]

The bottom line, shared by all scholars and by some retired diplomats, is that academia and research institutes are mere bureaucratic 'extensions', 'remaining at the margin' of policy-making processes regarding Africa.[72] Reasons for this peripheral influence include a 'lack of (MEA) tradition to ask for external inputs', an overall obsession and commitment to 'consensual thinking' and consequent aversion to critical debates with an inclusive set of stakeholders.[73]

Positive examples do not abound, but include one senior diplomat's proposal to have embassies host doctoral students for certain

---

[68] Author's interview no. 17, August 5, 2010.
[69] Author's interview no. 17, August 5, 2010.
[70] Author's interview no. 6, July 23, 2010.
[71] Author's interview no. 17, August 5, 2010.
[72] Ibid. Also author's interview no. 6, July 23, 2010.
[73] Author's interview no. 2, July 13, 2010.

periods of time in a collaborative project, as well as an increasing number of retired diplomats who have recently joined the corporate sector, academia or research institutes to share their expertise on Africa.[74] One other exception to this rather dim picture of largely ineffectual bureaucracy-academia collaboration is that of one senior scholar who occasionally is requested to brief an incoming minister or outgoing ambassador on Africa.[75]

RELATIONS BETWEEN MEA AND BUSINESS

Beyond the intellectual corridors of academia, the dynamic Indian corporate sector has its own complains about the MEA's African hard- and software. The unanimous view among the interviewees is that of a 'ridiculously slow' bureaucracy, the most popular example relating to the new soft loans for African projects to be executed by Indian companies.[76] In the view of one interviewee, 'too many institutions (are) involved in the clearance, from the Indian diplomatic mission to the Ministry of Finance and the EXIM bank', often dragging out the process for several years.[77] In the perspective of one former diplomat, this is due to Africa lagging chronically behind in the MEA's efforts to shift from an emphasis on political to economic diplomacy.[78]

Describing the MEA's activities on Africa as a 'firefighting' exercise, one retired diplomat notes that many files and projects are persistently sidelined until a contingency or emergency arises, but then often too late for a positive or optimal outcome.[79] Recognising this obstacle, another former diplomat identifies this inefficient delivery capacity as one of the main reasons why India is 'a more frustrating partner for African countries'.[80] A recent report on the actual state of the Indian TEAM-9 investments, for example, identi-

---

[74] This is the aforementioned case of Ambassador Shashank, who is also the Chairperson of the African Studies Association, and of Ambassador H. H. S. Viswanathan, who joined the Observer Research Foundation in May 2010 as a distinguished fellow.
[75] Author's interview no. 17, August 5, 2010.
[76] Author's interview no. 15, August 2, 2010.
[77] Author's interview no. 14, August 2, 2010.
[78] Author's interview no. 15, August 2, 2010.
[79] Author's interview no. 14, August 2, 2010.
[80] Author's interview no. 4, July 14, 2010.

fies several grey areas in which projects are suffering chronic delays and indicate symptoms of corruption and nepotism.[81]

This ad hoc and excessively circumstantial, short-term approach poses a tremendous obstacle to Indian business interests that are often confronted with a lacking long-term strategy and sectoral or regional focus from the ministerial side (which also includes the Ministry of Commerce and Industry). This is where a 'strategy' is most missed. Thus, for one interviewee in the corporate sector, 'people have not yet seen the bigger picture (about Africa's long-term importance), and are too busy with current and immediate issues', failing to plan ahead and establish a road map anchored in specific targets, such as the number of official visits and delegations to Africa or a specific trade volume.[82]

A final criticism relates to the excessive dependence on the bureaucracy and centrality of New Delhi while conducting business relations with Africa, hampering regional initiatives located in Mumbai and other smaller economic poles. In the views of one interviewee, there thus is an excessive 'mannerism and protocol' and a 'bureaucratic compulsion' to interfere and put up obstacles to smaller and medium enterprises that wish to explore Africa without succumbing to the 'Delhi model of doing business with Africa'.[83]

Yet, contrasting with the rather crisp tone marking the bureaucratic-academic axis, India's business houses seem to enjoy a rather privileged relation with official actors and structures. The increasing number of retired diplomats who now serve as consultants on Africa play a crucial role in bridging this gap and ensuring a regular, albeit rather informal link that is not always transparent. Thus, beyond institutional relations, 'what matters are personal relations' to the officers who are in charge of Africa at the MEA and can help on a variety of fronts, from identifying new investment opportunities to ensure that investments are cleared in time, or profits repatriated.[84] In many African countries where economic fraud is widespread and where there are very few references, most interviewees note that Indian diplomatic missions play a crucial role in assisting companies to identify valuable local partners and run background checks.

---

[81] Author's interview no. 17, August 5, 2010.
[82] Author's interview no. 15, August 2, 2010.
[83] Author's interview no. 2, July 13, 2010.
[84] Author's interview no. 2, July 13, 2010.

While one corporate representative underlined the importance of having the MEA acting as 'a hand behind you in case something goes wrong', the reality is that Indian companies do not shy away from looking for any possible assistance and even financial support from the MEA to study the business terrain and promote their products in Africa.[85] At the same time, institutions like CII and FICCI also represent an important asset to the MEA, in that they facilitate contacts with the private sector and assume a significant burden in terms of policy execution (for example by co-organising various summits, conclaves and delegations), while also contributing occasionally in terms of policy-making recommendations.[86]

PUBLIC DIPLOMACY: BRANDING INDIA IN AFRICA

A final area in which different Indian stakeholders converge in regard to Africa is the relation between the MEA and Indian civil society and the international context. Here, the unanimous perspective among all interviewees is that of a persisting negative image of Africa that affects transformative efforts on all fronts – from diplomats' posting preferences, to students' dissertation topic choices and foreign investment preferences. The gravity of the situation is perhaps best indicated by the absence of any full-time Indian media correspondent in Africa (between the 1960s and 2012), Indian newspapers and television broadcasters therefore depending on stringers and freelancers to offer original content on any of the 53 African countries.[87] At the same time, none of the Africa scholar experts interviewed has ever been contacted for a comment on Africa by an India media outlet.

It is therefore no surprise that the continent is still seen as a 'high-risk' destination plagued by various threats that marked its international image in the 1980s and 1990s.[88] Most interviewees with

---

[85] Author's interview no. 15, August 2, 2010. One scholar expressed his 'shock' at the companies' insistence in having the MEA finance their delegations and exhibits to Africa (Author's interview no. 17, August 5, 2010).

[86] Federation of Indian Chambers of Commerce and Industry (FICCI), for example, consults regularly with its members on issues related to Africa and on-going trade negotiations. In 2008, it also prepared a report with several recommendations on economic policy towards Africa for the Ministry of Commerce and Industry (Author's interview no. 16, August 2, 2010).

[87] Author's interview no. 7, July 24, 2010.

[88] Author's interview no. 2, July 13, 2010.

direct experience in Africa observed that the huge potential of 'brand India', reflected in the large African interest and emotional attachment to India, remained undeveloped. On the business front, one representative observed that there is a failure in 'marketing ourselves' across the spectrum, in collaborative projects that would integrate both government and corporate efforts in a single public campaign.[89] At the same time, many interviewees also noted the unexplored capital that India holds with thousands of African students that have, since the 1950s, studied and trained in India under various ITEC, ICCR and defence agreements.

Recent initiatives seem to indicate a slow change in that direction. For example, in 2005, the former peer-reviewed journal *Africa Quarterly* was revamped in content and design to attract a larger readership beyond academics. This was followed, in 2009, by the launch of the web portal *IndiaAfricaConnect.com* by the Minister of External Affairs. Both initiatives were executed by the MEA (including the ICCR, and the Africa, External Publicity, and Public Diplomacy divisions) in collaboration with a private news agency. The main objective, in the words of its chief editor, is to 'package India's Africa policy', 'develop an Indian discourse on Africa' and a type of 'Delhi consensus' to combat the 'Western bias' in existing media content.[90]

The creation of the Public Diplomacy division at MEA, in 2006, further reflects an increasing preoccupation in making Indian diplomacy more 'extrovert', most notably by reaching out to the public and increasing institutional transparency and inter-institutional co-operation and synergies. On Africa, for example, the focus is to identify and publicise concrete areas in which original Indian initiatives have flourished in a mutually beneficial way.[91]

Conclusion

This essay has offered a detailed analysis on the origins, development and strategic determinants of India's relations with Africa; on the actors that share expertise and experience on Africa; on the various intra- and inter-institutional levels of relation between

---

[89] Author's interview no. 15, August 2, 2010.
[90] Author's interview no. 7, July 24, 2010.
[91] Author's interview no. 9, July 28, 2010.

the various Indian stakeholders; and on the sources of tension and sub-optimal policy-making towards Africa. We are perhaps now in the position to revisit our primary question regarding the nature of India's 'Africa policy'.

On the one hand, if India's Africa policy is construed as a coherent, consensual and institutionalised set of long-term guidelines and targets for India's engagement with the continent, there is certainly very limited scope to refer to an Africa policy in India. The consequence, for some, is an urgent need for such a clear document, failing which India will continue to engage Africa at sub-optimal levels.[92] In this perspective, unless the policy is formally institutionalised at the official level and made public, policy-making will therefore remain hostage to contingencies and ad hoc decisions.

On the other hand, for those who see an Indian Africa policy as being already in existence, there are three questions that arise. First, *when* did the supposed policy originate? For one key diplomat on Africa, the efforts are 'at least three thousand years old', with the present policy 'emerging in the 1960s'.[93] Some interviewees, however, defend the view that the policy was established gradually after 2000, which one scholar describes as a clear 'line of division'.[94] Others identify the 2003–5 period. The most popular view is that the policy was set up in 2008, in parallel to the preparation for the Delhi summit.

Second, where did the supposed policy originate? Here, besides an overall consensus on the centrality of economic interests, repeated references are made to two specific individuals, Navdeep Suri and Gurjit Singh, who, in 2006, were respectively joint secretary for West Africa and Ambassador to Ethiopia. In co-operation with other colleagues, they prepared a series of notes and proposals for the Prime Minister's office, focusing on the need to open more diplomatic mission in Africa, to use the African Union as a privileged partner to engage with Africa, to concentrate on the 'softer' and long-term

---

[92] Ambassador Rajiv Bhatia, for example, thus notes that 'if you look for a document on "India's Africa Policy" on our Ministry website, you are unlikely to succeed', in 'India's Africa Policy: Can We Do Better?', *The Hindu*, July 15, 2010. Available at http://www.hindu.com/2010/07/15/stories/2010071554411000.htm, accessed on August 3, 2010.

[93] Author's interview no. 12, July 28, 2010.

[94] Author's interview no. 5, July 22, 2010.

dimensions of economic co-operation such as the Pan-African E-Network, and to hold a major summit in New Delhi.[95]

Finally, what is the exact *nature* of the supposed policy? Once again, while most refer to the 2008 Delhi Declaration and Joint Action Plan, there are differing views on the precise substance of an 'Indian model' of co-operation with Africa. This lacking consensus seems paradoxical at first sight, but finds explanation in the widely popular view that India's strategy for Africa is precisely one of *not* having a strategy for Africa. This finds echo in one of the leading diplomats on Africa: 'we started the Chinese way, (but) then recognised this was not possible or adequate'. In his view, the 2008 summit was held at the explicit request of the African Union, who first approached the MEA to study such a possibility. Implicitly suggesting that no policy is the best policy for India, he therefore underlines that 'our policy is consultative, request-based, and not prescriptive' indicating a perennial ad hoc posture.[96]

While confusing and contradictory, this is indicative of an overall aversion to the idea of strategy, which tends to be equated by many of the interviewees with an inflexible and aggressive (read Chinese) posture that is not only undesirable, as well as impossible in the case of a 'complex' and 'democratic' India. One commentator to this essay, for example, thus noted that 'we are not like the Yangtze (river in China), simple, fast and furious; our Ganges is slow, has many curves and is complex.'[97]

This idea of a 'policy that is no policy' makes sense as longer as one adopts a looser definition of 'policy'. It is further legitimised with arguments such as India's comparative difference and democratic complexity – in the words of one retired diplomat, 'our strength (in Africa) lies precisely in our difference with China'.[98] India's disputed, diffuse, slow and non-institutionalised 'framework of co-operation' for Africa (another popular equivalent for 'policy' or 'strategy') is thus understood as a unique function of India's complex democratic regime, foreign policy posture, historical relations with Africa, among other particularistic factors.

---

[95] Author's interview no. 4, July 14, 2010.

[96] Author's interview no. 13, July 28, 2010.

[97] During a research seminar at which a draft of this essay was presented at the Institute for Defence Studies and Analyses, New Delhi, on August 20, 2010.

[98] Author's interview no. 8, July 27, 2010.

Beyond the debate about the existence of an Africa policy in India, little doubt remains, however, that several domestic factors play a key role in shaping the Indian policy-making processes on Africa and lead to complex outcomes. For the foreign scholar, the natural temptation will be to search for culturalist explanations in Indian history and society. This has to be avoided: most, if not all, of the various problems, tensions and shortcomings identified in India's foreign policy environment are more or less present in other countries with the same trajectory.

The line of inquiry adopted in this essay would, therefore, benefit much more if developed in a comparative framework. How do these research findings compare to other regional and functional sectors in Indian foreign policy? And, in order to escape the rather popular deterministic approach that identifies India as being 'unique', to what extent are the findings in this and other Indian cases also identifiable in other countries' foreign policy infrastructures?

BIBLIOGRAPHY

Archival Sources

All Parties Conference, Report of the Committee Appointed by the Conference to Determine the Principles of the Constitution of India. Allahabad: General Secretary, All India Congress Committee, 1928.
Esher Committee Report, 1919–20, L/MIL/17/5/1762, Asia Pacific & Africa Collections (APAC), British Library, London.
Government of India, March 22, 1919, L/MIL/3/1118, APAC.
Military Requirements Committee, 1921, L/MIL/17/5/1773, APAC.
Proceedings of 1885 and 1886, File No. 1/1885–1920, All India Congress Committee Committee Papers, Nehru Memorial Museum and Library (NMML), New Delhi.
Report of Sub-Committee on Indian Military Requirements, 1922, CID 125-D, CAB 6/4, The National Archives (TNA), London.
Resolutions on Esher Committee, CID 119-D, CAB 6/4, The National Archives (TNA), London.

Secondary Sources

'A Carnival Atop a Volcano', *The News*, 30 July 2010.
'A Persian Gulf', *Outlook*, December 6, 2010. Available at http://www.outlookindia.com/article.aspx?268210, accessed on May 15, 2012.
Abhyankar, Rajendra M., 'Introduction', in Rajendra M. Abhyankar, ed., *West Asia and the Region: Defining India's Role*. New Delhi: Academic Foundation, 2008, pp. 27–65.
Acharya, Amitav, *Whose Ideas Matter? Agency and Power in Asian Regionalism*. London: Cornell University Press, 2009.
Adib-Moghaddam, Arshin, *Iran in World Politics: The Question of the Islamic Republic*. New York: Columbia University Press, 2008.
Admiral Menon, Raja and Rajiv Kumar, *The Long View From New Delhi: To Define the Indian Grand Strategy for Foreign Policy*. New Delhi: Academic Foundation, 2010.
'Afghanistan and Pakistan Agree Key Trade Agreement', *BBC News*, July 19, 2010. Available at http://www.bbc.co.uk/news/world-south-asia-10679464, accessed on August 12, 2010.
'Afghanistan Seeks Indian Investment to Boost its Agri Sector', *Business Standard*, December 3, 2010. Available at http://www.business-standard.

com/article/markets/afghanistan-seeks-indian-investment-to-boost-itsagri-sector-110120300194_1.html, accessed on August 19, 2011.

Afrasiabi, Kaveh 'Blockage in the Peace Pipeline', *Asia Times*, July 10, 2007. Available at http://www.atimes.com/atimes/South_Asia/IG10Df01.html, accessed on May 15, 2012.

'After Menon's Visit to China, Nirupama Rao Meets Dalai Lama', *NDTV*, July 11, 2010. Available at http://www.ndtv.com/article/india/after menon-s-visit-to-china-nirupama-rao-meets-dalai-lama-36796, accessed on August 23, 2011.

Afzal, M. Rafique, ed., *Selected Speeches and Statements of the Quaid-i-Azam Mohammed Ali.* Lahore: Research Society of Pakistan, 1966.

Ahanchi, A., 'Reflections of the Indian Independence Movement in the Iranian Press', *Iranian Studies*, 42, 3 (2009), pp. 423–43.

Ahmad, Syed Barakat, 'India and Palestine 1896–1947: The Genesis of foreign Policy', in Verinder Grover ed., *West Asia* and *India's Foreign Policy*. New Delhi: Deep & Deep Publications, 1992, pp. 373–84.

Ahmed, Ali, 'The Need for Clarity in India's Nuclear Doctrine', *IDSA COMMENT*, Institute for Defence Studies and Analyses (IDSA), New Delhi, 2008. Available at http://www.idsa.in/idsastrategiccomments/TheNeedForClarityInIndiaSNuclearDoctrine_AAhmed_111108, accessed on September 8, 2013.,

———, 'India's Strategic and Military Doctrines: A Post 1971 Snapshot', *USI Journal*, 126, 578 (January 2010). Available at http://www.usiofindia.org/Article/?pub=Journal&pubno=578&ano=4, accessed on September 8, 2013.

Aiyar, Mani Shankar, 'India and China in Asia's Quest for Energy Security', in Mohan Guruswamy, ed., *Emerging Trends in India-China Relations.* Gurgaon: Hope India Publications, 2006, pp. 15–24.

Alam, Muzaffar, 'Akhlaqi Norms and Mughal Governance', in Muzaffar Alam, Francoise Nalini Delvoye and Marc Gaborieau, eds, *The Making of Indo-Persian Culture: Indian and French Studies*. New Delhi: Manohar, 2000, pp. 67–91.

Alamgir, Alena, '"The Learned Brahmen, Who Assists Me": Changing Colonial Relationships in the 18th and 19th Century India', *Journal of Historical Sociology*, 19, 4 (2006), pp. 419–46.

Amir, Ayaz, 'Khaki Problem: Poverty of Imagination', *The News*, July 30, 2010.

Anadkat, Nalin, *International Political Thought of Gandhi, Nehru and Lohia.* New Delhi: Bharatiya Kala Prakashan, 2000.

Aneja, Atul, 'How West Asia Views Mumbai Attacks', *The Hindu*, December 17, 2008. Available at http://www.hindu.com/2008/12/17/stories/2008121752001000.htm, accessed on May 10, 2012.

Ansari, H. M., 'Afghanistan' in Jyotindra N. Dixit and Shailendra K. Singh, eds, *External Affairs: Cross-border Relations*. New Delhi: Roli Books, 2005.

'Army Plays Down Air Space Violation', *The Indian Express*, September 1, 2009. Available at http://www.indianexpress.com/news/army-playsdown-air-space-violation/509765/, accessed on October 3, 2013.

Aron, Raymond, 'The Evolution of Modern Strategic Thought', *Adelphi Series*, 9, 54 (1969), pp. 1–17

Arya, Shail Singh, 'Stress Management in the Armed Forces', *USI Journal*, 139, 576 (April–June 2009), pp. 168–201.

Ashley, Robert K., 'The Poverty of Neorealism', *International Organization*, 38, 2 (Spring 1984), pp. 225–86.

Ashraf, Fahmida, 'India–Afghanistan Relations: Post-9/11', *Strategic Studies*, 27, 2 (2007), pp. 90–102. Available at http://catalogo.casd.difesa.it/GEIDEFile/INDIA%C3%90AFGHANISTAN_RELATIONS_POST-9-11.HTM?Archive=191494691967&File=INDIA%ADAFGHANISTAN+RELATIONS+POST-9-11_HTM, accessed on November 8, 2010.

Asian Development Bank, 'Key Indicators for Asia and the Pacific 2011'. Available at http://www2.adb.org/Documents/Books/Key_Indicators/2011/pdf/AFG.pdf, accessed on March 29, 2012.

'At Sea Over Navy Chief', *The Indian Express*, August 17, 2009. Available at http://www.indianexpress.com/news/at-sea-over-navy-chief/502923/, accessed on October 3, 2013.

'ATS Arrests 3 with Arms', *The Indian Express*, August 6, 2009. Available at http://global.factiva.com, accessed on August 23, 2011. Available at http://www.indianexpress.com/news/ats-arrests-3-with-arms/498454/, accessed on October 3, 2013.

Ayoob, M., 'Southwest Asia after the Taliban', *Survival*, 44, 1 (2002), pp. 51–68.

Baba, Noor Ahmad, 'OIC and Pakistan's Foreign Policy: The Indian Dimension', in Rajendra N. Abhyankar, ed., *West Asia and the Region: Defining India's Role*. New Delhi: Academic Foundation, 2008, pp. 669–73.

Babbage, Ross and Sandy Gordon, eds, *India's Strategic Future: Regional State or Global Power?*. New Delhi: Oxford University Press, 1992.

Badauni, *Muntakhabut Tawarikh*, trans. by George Ranking, Vol. 1. Patna: Academica Asiatica, 1898, reprinted 1973.

Bajoria, Jayshree, 'India–Afghanistan Relations', Backgrounder, *Council on Foreign Relations*, July 22, 2009. Available at http://www.cfr.org/publication/17474/indiaafghanistan_relations.html, accessed on August 25, 2010.

Bajpai, Kanti P. and Amitabh Mattoo, eds, *The Peacock and the Dragon: India–China Relations in the 21st Century*. New Delhi: Har-Anand Publications, 2000.

Bajpai, Kanti, 'India: Modified Structuralism', in Alagappa Muthiah, ed., *Asian Security Practice: Material and Ideational Influences.* Stanford: Stanford University Press, 1998, pp. 157–97.

———, 'Indian Conceptions of Order and Justice: Nehruvian, Gandhian, Hindutva, and Neoliberal', in Rosemary Foot, John Lewis Gaddis and Andrew Hurrell, eds, *Order and Justice in International Relations.* Oxford: Oxford University Press, 2003.

———, 'Indian Strategic Culture', in Michael R. Chambers, ed., *South Asia in 2020: Future Strategic Balances and Alliances.* Carlisle, PA: Strategic Studies Institute, US Army War College, 2003, pp. 245–304.

———, 'Hinduism and Weapons of Mass Destruction: Pacifist, Prudential, and Political', in Sohail Hashmi, ed., *Ethics and Weapons of Mass Destruction.* New York: Cambridge University Press, 2004, pp. 308–20.

———, 'Indian Conceptions of Order/Justice in International Relations: Nehruvian, Gandhian, Hindutva and Neo-Liberal', in V. R. Mehta and Thomas Pantham, eds, *Political Ideas in Modern India: Thematic Explorations.* New Delhi: Sage, 2006, pp. 367–90.

———, 'Indian Strategic Culture and the Problem of Pakistan', in Swarna Rajagopalan, ed., *Security and South Asia: Ideas, Institutions and Initiatives.* New Delhi: Routledge, 2006, pp. 54–79.

———, 'India and the World: The Grand Strategy Debate', in Niraja Jayal and Pratap Bhanu Mehta, eds, *The Oxford Companion to Politics in India.* New Delhi: Oxford University Press, New Delhi 2010, pp. 521–41.

Bajpai, Rochana, *Debating Difference: Group Rights and Liberal Democracy in India.* New Delhi: Oxford University Press, 2011.

Bajpai, Shankar K., 'India in 1991: New Beginnings', *Asian Survey,* 32, 2 (February 1992), pp. 207–16.

Bajpai, U. S., *India's Security: The Politico-Strategic Environment.* New Delhi: Lancers, 1983.

Baldwin, David A., ed., *Neorealism and Neoliberalism: The Contemporary Debate.* New York: Columbia University Press, 1993.

———, 'The Concept of Security', *Review of International Studies,* 23, 1 (1997), pp. 5–26.

'Bangla Islamist Parties Face Shutdown After SC Verdict', *The Times of India,* July 30, 2010.

Barkawi, Tarak and Mark Laffey, 'Retrieving the Imperial: Empire and International Relations', *Millennium,* 31, 1 (2002), pp. 109–27.

Bartholomees, Jr., J. Boone, 'A Survey of Strategic Thought', in J. Boone Bartholomees, Jr., ed., *U.S. Army War College Guide to National Security Policy and Strategy.* Carlisle, PA: Strategic Studies Institute, US Army War College, 2004, pp. 79–100.

Baru, Sanjaya, 'Economic Diplomacy', *Seminar*, 461 (January 1998), pp. 66–69.

———, 'The Economic Dimensions of India's Foreign Policy', *World Affairs*, 2, 2 (April–June 1998), pp. 90–91.

———, *Strategic Consequences of India's Economic Performance*. New Delhi: Academic Foundation, 2006.

———, 'National Security in An Open Economy', in Sanjaya Baru, *Strategic Consequences of India's Economic Performance*. New Delhi: Academic Foundation, 2006, pp. 88–90.

———, 'India and the World: Economics and Politics of the Manmohan Singh Doctrine in Foreign Policy', *Institute of South Asian Studies*, Working Paper No. 46, November 14, 2008. Available at http://www.isasnus.org/events/activities/20081008%20-%20Prof%20Sanjaya%20Baru.pdf, accessed August 27, 2010.

Baruah, Amit, 'India's IAEA Vote was Decided in Advance', *The Hindu*, September 26, 2005. Available at http://www.hindu.com/2005/09/26/stories/2005092606971100.htm, accessed on September 10, 2010.

Basham., A. L., *The Wonder That Was India*. Calcutta: Rupa, 1967.

———, 'Traditional Influences on the Thought of Mahatma Gandhi', in A. Raghuramaraju, ed., *Debating Gandhi: A Reader*. New Delhi: Oxford University Press, 2006, pp. 19–44.

Basrur, Rajesh, 'Nuclear Weapons and Indian Strategic Culture', *Journal of Peace Research*, 38, 2 (2001), pp. 181–98.

———, *Minimum Deterrence and India's Nuclear Security*. Stanford: Stanford University Press, 2006.

Basu, Amrita, 'Mass Movement or Elite Conspiracy: The Puzzle of Hindu Nationalism', in David E. Ludden, ed., *Contesting the Nation*. Philadelphia: University of Pennsylvania Press, 1996.

Bayly, Christopher, 'The Pre-history of "Communalism": Religious Conflict in India, 1700–1860', *Modern Asian Studies*, 19, 2 (1985), pp. 177–203.

———, 'Rammohan Roy and the Advent of Constitutional Liberalism in India, 1800–30', in Shruti Kapila, ed., *An Intellectual History for India*. Cambridge: Cambridge University Press, 2010, pp. 18–34.

———, *Recovering Liberties: Indian Thought in the Age of Liberalism and Empire*. Cambridge: Cambridge University Press, 2011.

Bedi, Rahul 'India Seeks to Counter China with Strengthened Border Presence', *Jane's Defence Weekly*, February 15, 2008. Available at http://www.janes.com/products/janes/defence-security-report.aspx?ID=1065926994, accessed on August 23, 2011.

Beri, Ruchita, 'India's Role in Keeping Peace in Africa,' *Strategic Analysis*, 32, 2 (2008), pp. 197–221.

Berlin, Isaiah. 'The Bent Twig: A Note on Nationalism', *Foreign Affairs*, 51, 1 (1972), pp. 11–30.

Berman, Ilan, 'Israel, India and Turkey: Triple Entente?', *Middle East Quarterly* (Fall 2002), pp. 33–40
Betts, Richard K., 'Should Strategic Studies Survive?', *World Politics*, 50, 1 (1997), pp. 7–33.
Bhadrakumar, M. K., 'Should Strategic Studies Survive', *Asia Times*, September 15 2004. Available at http://www.atimes.com/atimes/South_Asia/FI15Df03.html, accessed on August 28, 2010.
——, 'China Leaves the US and India Trailing', *Asia Times*, December 14, 2007. Available at http://www.atimes.com/atimes/China/IL15Ad01.html, accessed on May 15, 2012.
——, 'India Seeks a "Velvet Divorce" From Iran', *Asia Times*, November 4, 2008. Available at http://www.atimes.com/atimes/South_Asia/JK05Df01.html, accessed on August 28, 2010.
Bhagawan, Manu, 'A New Hope: India, the United Nations and the Making of the Universal Declaration of Human Rights', *Modern Asian Studies*, 44, 2 (2010), pp. 311–47.
Bhagwati, Jagdish, *India in Transition: Freeing the Economy*. New York: Clarendon, 1993.
Blank, Stephen, 'Arms Sales and Technology Transfer in Indo-Israeli Relations, *The Journal of East Asian Affairs*, 19, 1 (2005), pp. 200–41.
Bhargava, G. S., *South Asian Security after Afghanistan*. Lexington: Lexington Books, 1983.
Bhargava, Rajeev, ed., *Secularism and Its Critics*. New Delhi: Oxford University Press, 1998.
Bhatt, Chetan, *Hindu Nationalism: Origins, Ideologies, and Modern Myths*. Oxford: Berg, 2001.
Bidwai, Praful, '"Clean" Nuclear Energy and a Nuclear Renaissance: Hype and Hyperbole', *Third World Resurgence*, 235 (March 2010). Available at http://www.twnside.org.sg/title2/resurgence/2010/235/cover01.htm, accessed on August 25, 2010.
Bidwai, Praful and Achin Vanaik, *New Nukes: India, Pakistan, and Global Nuclear Disarmament*. New York: Interlink, 2000.
——, 'Gandhi's Second Assassination', in *New Nukes: India, Pakistan and Global Nuclear Disarmament*. New York: Interlink Books, 2000, pp. 142–44.
Bidwai, Praful and M. V. Ramana, 'Home, Next to N-Reactor', *Tehelka*, September 4, 2010. Available at http://www.tehelka.com/story_main31.asp?filename=Ne230607home_next_SR.asp, accessed on September 4, 2010.
Bilgrami, Akeel, 'Gandhi's Integrity: The Philosophy Behind the Politics', in A. Raghuramaraju, ed., *Debating Gandhi: A Reader*. New Delhi: Oxford University Press, 2006, pp. 248–66.

Biswas, Aparajita, 'African Studies in India', in P. T. Zeleza, ed., *The Study of Africa Vol. 2: Global and Transnational Engagements*. London: African Books Collective, 2007, pp. 305–14.

'BJP Demands All-Party Meeting on China', *The Indian Express*, October 15, 2009. Available at http://www.indianexpress.com/news/bjp-demands allparty-meeting-on-china/529195/, accessed on October 3, 2013.

Blarel, Nicolas, *Inde et Israel: Le Rapprochement Stratégique, Pragmatisme et Complémentarité*. Paris: L'Harmattan, 2006, pp. 73–89.

———, 'Indo-Israeli Relations: Emergence of a Strategic Partnership', in Sumit Ganguly ed., *India's Foreign Policy: Retrospect and Prospect*. New Delhi: Oxford University Press, 2009, pp. 155–74.

Boesche, Roger, *The First Great Political Realist: Kautilya and His Arthashastra*. Lanham, MD: Lexington Books, 2003.

Booth, Ken, 'The Concept of Strategic Culture Affirmed', in Carl Jacobsen, ed., *Strategic Power USA/USSR*. London: Palgrave Macmillan, 1990, pp. 121–30.

Bose, Sugata, *A Hundred Horizons: The Indian Ocean in the Age of Global Empire*. Cambridge, MA: Harvard University Press, 2006.

Bozeman, Adda, *Politics and Culture in International History*. Princeton, NJ: Princeton University Press, 1960.

'Break India, says China Think-tank', *The Times of India*, August 13, 2009. Available at http://articles.timesofindia.indiatimes.com/2009-08-12/india/28195335_1_dai-bingguo-state-councillor-chinese-website, accessed on August 23, 2011.

Brecher, Michael, *The New States of Asia: A Political Analysis*. London: Oxford University Press, 1963.

———, *India and World Politics: Krishna Menon's View of The World*. London: Oxford University Press, 1968.

Brekke, Torkel, 'Wielding the Rod of Punishment: War and Violence in the Political Science of Kautilya', *Journal of Military Ethics*, 3, 1 (March 2004), pp. 4–52.

———, 'Between Prudence and Heroism: Ethics of War in the Hindu Tradition', in Torkel Brekke, ed., *The Ethics of War in Asian Civilisations: A Comparative Perspective*. Abingdon, Oxon: Routledge, 2006, pp. 113–44.

Brewster, David, 'Indian Strategic Thinking about East Asia', *Journal of Strategic Studies*, 34, 6 (December 2011), pp. 825–52.

Brimnes, Niels, 'Globalization and Indian Civilization: Questionable Continuities', in Mehdi Mozaffari, ed., *Globalization and Civilizations*. London: Routledge, 2002, pp. 242–63.

Brittlebank, Kate, *Tipu Sultan's Search for Legitimacy: Islam and Kingship in a Hindu Domain*. New Delhi: Oxford University Press, 1997.

Broadman, C. H., *Africa's Silk Road: China and India's New Economic Frontier*. Washington DC: World Bank, 2007.

Brown, Judith M., ed., *Mahatma Gandhi: The Essential Writings*. Oxford: Oxford University Press, 2008.
Burns, William, 'India's Rise and the Promise of U.S.–Indian Partnership'. Available at http://www.state.gov/p/us/rm/2010/136718.htm, accessed on May 17, 2012.
'Business, Not Politics', Editorial, *The Indian Express*, January 11, 2001. Available at http://www.indianexpress.com/Storyold/168606/, accessed on August 31, 2001.
Buzan, Barry and Richard Little, *International Systems in World History: Remaking the Study of International Relations*. Oxford: Oxford University Press, 2000.
Cabinet Committee on Security, 'Press Release of the Cabinet Committee on Security on Operationalisation of India's Nuclear Doctrine, 04.01.03'. Available at http://meadev.nic.in/news/official/20030104/official.htm, accessed on May 30, 2009.
Calabrese, John, *Revolutionary Horizons: Regional Foreign Policy in Post-Khomeini Iran*. New York: St. Martin's Press, 1994.
Carpenter, Ted Galen, 'Roiling Asia', *Foreign Affairs*, 77, 6 (1998), pp. 2–6.
'CCS Clears Choppers for Navy, Projects in Arunachal', *The Indian Express*, August 7, 2009. Available at http://www.indianexpress.com/news/ccsclears-choppers-for-navy-projects-in-arunachal/499192/, accessed on October 3, 2013.
Centre for Policy Research, *Policy for India in the Twenty First Century*. A report issued by the Centre for Policy Research, New Delhi. Available at http://www.cprindia.org/workingpapers/3844-nonalignment-20-foreign-and-strategic-policyindia-twenty-first-century, accessed on March 23, 2012.
Chadda, Sudhir, 'Manmohan's Dream Breakfast in Amritsar, Lunch in Lahore and Dinner in Kabul a Real Possibility', *India Daily*, January 8, 2007. Available at http://www.indiadaily.com/editorial/15067.asp, accessed on September 24, 2010.
Chakravarty, Pratap, 'China Bigger Threat to India Than Pakistan: Defence Minister', *Agence France-Press*, May 3, 1998. Available at http://global.factiva.com, accessed on August 23, 2011.
Chandra, Bipan, *The Rise and Growth of Economic Nationalism in India*. New Delhi: People's Publishing House, 1966.
Chandra, Bipan, Mridula Mukherjee, Aditya Mukherjee, Sucheta Mahajan, and K. N. Panikkar, *India's Struggle for Independence 1857–1947*. New Delhi: Penguin, 1989.
'Changing Tack on the Gas Pipeline', *The Hindu*, June 7, 2004.
Chari, P. R., Pervaiz Iqbal Cheema and Stephen P. Cohen, *Four Crises and Peace Process: American Engagement in South Asia*. Washington DC: Brookings Institution Press, 2007.
———, *Four Crises and a Peace Process: American Engagement in South Asia New*. New Delhi: Harper Collins, 2008.

Chatterjee, Partha, *Nationalist Thought and the Colonial World: A Derivative Discourse*. London: Zed Books, 1986.
———, *Nationalist Thought and the Colonial World: A Derivative Discourse*. New Delhi: Oxford University Press, 1986.
Chatterjee, Partha, 'The Movement of Manoeuvre: Gandhi and the Critique of Civil Society', in A. Raghuramaraju, ed., *Debating Gandhi: A Reader*. New Delhi: Oxford University Press, 2006, pp. 75–128.
Chaturvedy, Rajeev Ranjan and David M. Malone, 'India and Its South Asian Neighbours', Working Paper No. 100, (November 26, 2009), Institute of South Asian Studies (ISAS), National University of Singapore.
Chaudhuri, Nirad C., *Thy Hand Great Anarch!*. London: Chatto Windus, 1987.
Chaudhuri, Rudra, 'Why Culture Matters? Revisiting the Sino-Indian Border Conflict of 1962', *Journal of Strategic Studies* 32, 6 (December 2009), pp. 841–69.
Chaulia, Sreeram S., 'BJP, India's Foreign Policy and the "Realist Alternative" to the Nehruvian Tradition', *International Politics*, 39, 2 (2002), pp. 215–34.
Chellaney, Brahma, 'Challenges to India's National Security', in Brahma Chellaney, ed., *Securing India's Future in the New Millennium*. New Delhi: Orient Longman and the Centre for Policy Research, 1999, pp. 527–95.
———, 'Preface', in Brahma Chellaney, ed., *Securing India's Future in the New Millennium*. New Delhi: Orient Longman and the Centre for Policy Research, 1999, pp. xvii–xxii.
———, 'Assessing India's Reactions to China's "Peaceful Development" Doctrine', *NBR Analysis* 18, 5 (April 2008), pp. 23–36.
———, 'Stop Pampering Pakistan's Military!', *Christian Science Monitor*, December 12, 2008. Available at http://www.csmonitor.com/Commentary/Opinion/2008/1212/p09s01-coop.html, accessed on June 12, 2011.
———, 'An Afghanistan "Surge" is a Losing Battle: So Why is Mr Obama Betting on It?', *Wall Street Journal*, January 9, 2009. Available at http://online.wsj.com/article/SB123143672297764875.html, accessed on June 29, 2012.
———, 'Success in Afghanistan lies through Pakistan', *The Hindu*, January 31, 2009. Available at http://www.hindu.com/2009/01/31/stories/2009013151861100.htm, accessed on August 24, 2012.
———, 'China's Hydra-Headed Hydropolitics', *Project Syndicate*, August 5, 2009. Available at http://www.project-syndicate.org/commentary/chellaney1/English, accessed on August 23, 2011.
———, 'Dangerous Misconceptions', *India Abroad*, August 14, 2009. Available at http://chellaney.net/2009/07/30/the-fallacies-behind-indias-pakistan policy, accessed on August 23, 2011.

Chellaney, Brahma, 'Behind the Sri Lankan Bloodbath', *Forbes*, October 9, 2009. Avail-able at http://www.forbes.com/2009/10/08/tamil-tigers-rajiv-gandhi-opinionscontributors-sri-lanka.html, accessed on October 3, 2013.

———, 'Clueless on China', *The Sunday Guardian*, July 4, 2010. Available at http://chellaney.net/2010/07/03/india-plays-into-chinashands-by-staying-engaged-in-useless-border-talks, accessed on August 23, 2011.

Cherian, John 'Failure of Diplomacy', *Frontline*, 17, 1 (January 8–21, 2000). Available at http://www.hindu.com/fline/fl1701/17010200.htm, accessed on August 17, 2012.

Cheru, Fantu and Cyril Obi, eds, *The Rise of China and India in Africa: Challenges, Opportunities and Critical Interventions*. London: Zed Books, 2010.

'China Pips India to Sign Gas Sales Agreement with Daewoo', *The Hindu*, December 30, 2008.

'China Row: "Paranoid Hallucination of an Individual", says Cong', *The Indian Express*, August 13, 2009. Available at http://www.indianexpress.com/news/china-row--paranoid-hallucination-of-an-individual--sayscong/501562/, accessed on October 3, 2013.

'China Willing to Settle Toy Ban Issue through Talks', *The Indian Express*, March 20, 2009. Available at http://www.indianexpress.com/news/china-willing-to-settle-toy-ban-issue-through-talks/436765/, accessed on October 3, 2013.

'Chinese Whispers', *The Indian Express*, April 15, 2009. Available at http://www.indianexpress.com/news/chinese-whispers/447116/, accessed on October 3, 2013.

Chiriyankandath, James and Andrew Wyatt, 'The NDA and Indian Foreign Policy', in Katherine Adeny and Lawrence Saez, eds, *Coalition Politics and Hindu Nationalism*. London: Routledge, 2005.

Chishti, Seema, 'Austerity: At What Cost?', *The Indian Express*, September 25, 2009. Available at http://www.indianexpress.com/news/austerityat-what-cost-/521436/, accessed on October 3, 2013.

Chowdhry, Geeta and Sheila Nair, eds, *Power, Postcolonialism and International Relations: Reading Race, Gender and Class*. London: Routledge, 2002.

Cloughley, Brian, *A History of the Pakistan Army: Wars and Insurrections*. Karachi: Oxford University Press, 1999.

Clymer, Kenton J., *Quest for Freedom: The United States and India*. New York: Columbia University Press, 1995.

Cohen, Eliot, *Citizens and Soldiers: The Dilemmas of Military Service*. Ithaca: Cornell University Press, 1985.

Cohen, Stephen P., *The Indian Army and its Contribution to the Development of a Nation*. New Delhi: Oxford University Press, 1990.

———, *India: Emerging Power*. Washington DC: Brookings Institution Press, 2001.

———, *India: Emerging Power*. New Delhi: Oxford University Press, 2002.

Cohen, Stephen P., Christine C. Fair, Sumit Ganguly, Shaun Gregory, Aqil Shah, and Ashley J. Tellis, 'What's the Problem with Pakistan?', *Foreign Affairs*, (March 2009). Available at http://www.foreignaffairs.com/discussions/roundtables/whats-the-problem-with-pakistan, accessed on November 25, 2013.

Cohen, Stephen and S. Dasgupta, *Arming without Aiming: India's Military Modernisation*. New Delhi: Penguin–Viking, 2010.

Collected Works of Mahatma Gandhi Online, Vol. 29. Available at http://www.gandhiserve.org/cwmg/VOL029.PDF, accessed on August 30, 2010.

Collected Works of Mahatma Gandhi Online, Vol. 32. Available at http://www.gandhiserve.org/cwmg/VOL032.PDF, accessed on August 30, 2010.

Collected Works of Mahatma Gandhi Online, Vol. 86. Available at http://www.gandhiserve.org/cwmg/VOL086.PDF, accessed on July 14, 2010.

Communist Party of India (Marxist), 'Manifesto for the 15th Lok Sabha Elections', 2009. Available at http://cpim.org/elections/2009ls/manifesto.pdf, accessed on August 23, 2011.

'Congress Cites Ramayana, to Ask BJP to Shun Modi, Shah', *DNA*, July 28, 2010. Available at http://www.dnaindia.com/india/report_congress cites-ramayana-to-ask-bjp-to-shun-modi-shah_1415863, accessed on May 17, 2012.

Constituent Assembly of India Debates, Part 1, Vol. 1, No. 18. New Delhi: Parliamentary Publications, 1950.

———, Part 1, Vol. 4, No. 7. New Delhi: Parliamentary Publications, 1950.

Cotta-Ramusino, P. and Maurizio Martellini, 'Nuclear Safety, Nuclear Stability and Nuclear Strategy in Pakistan: A Concise Report of a Visit by Landau Network – Centro Volta', January 21, 2002. Available at http://www.pugwash.org/september11/pakistan-nuclear.htm, accessed on October 10, 2008.

'CPM Uneasy, but Doesn't Slam China', *The Indian Express*, October 14, 2009. Available at http://www.indianexpress.com/news/cpm-uneasybut-doesn-t-slam-china/528701/, accessed on October 3, 2013.

Crossette, Barbara, 'India to Provide Aid to Government in Afghanistan', *The New York Times*, March 7, 1989. Available at http://www.nytimes.com/1989/03/07/world/india-to-provide-aid-to-government-in-afghanistan.html, accessed on August 12, 2010.

'Cultural Exchanges with Afghanistan', *Asian Recorder*, 31, 44, (October 29–November 4, 1985).

D'Souza, Shanthie Mariet, 'Change the Pattern of Aid to Afghanistan', *IDSA Strategic Comments*, June 28, 2007. Available at http://www.idsa.in/profile/smdsouza?q=taxonomy/term/57, accessed on August 10, 2010.

———, 'Obama's Afghan Strategy: Regional Perspectives', *Atlantic Review*, December 10, 2009. Available at http://www.atlanticreview.org/archives/1351-Obamas-Afghan-Strategy-Regional-Perspectives.html, accessed on August 23, 2010.

D'Souza, Shanthie Mariet, 'Securing India's Interests in Afghanistan', *The Hindu*, October 23, 2009.

———, 'Great Game's Endgame?', *Business Standard*, October 31, 2010. Available at www.business-standard.com/india/news/shanthie-Mariett-d%5Csouza-great-game%5Cs-endgame/413240/, accessed on November 1, 2010.

———, 'India's Stake in Afghanistan', *The Journal of International Security Affairs*, 20 (Spring/Summer 2011), pp. 131–32. Available at http://www.securityaffairs.org/issues/2011/20/d'souza.php, accessed on August 17, 2011.

———, 'Indian–Afghan Strategic Partnership: Perceptions from the Ground', *The Af-Pak Channel, Foreign Policy*, October 26, 2011. Available at http://afpak.foreignpolicy.com/posts/2011/10/26/indian_afghan_strategic_partnership_perceptions_from_the_ground, accessed on October 27, 2011.

———, 'India–US Strategic Dialogue: Can India and US Be Partners in Afghanistan?', *Al Arabiya*, July 19, 2011. Available at http://www.alarabiya.net/articles/2011/07/19/158285.html, accessed on July 20, 2011.

Dahl, Hans Frederik, *Quisling: A Study in Treachery*, trans. by Anne-Marie Stanton-Ife. Cambridge: Cambridge University Press, 1999.

Darby, Phillip, *The Fiction of Imperialism: Reading between International Relations and Postcolonialism*. London: Cassell, 1998.

Das, Durga, ed., *Sardar Patel's Correspondence, 1945–50*, Vol. X. Ahmedabad, India: Navjivan Publishing House, 1974.

Das, Sisir Kumar, 'The Controversial Guest: Tagore in China,' in Madhavi Thampi, ed., *India and China in the Colonial World*. New Delhi: Social Science Press, 2005, pp. 85–124.

Dasgupta, Swapan, 'Of Actual Control', *The Telegraph*, April 8, 2005. Available at http://www.telegraphindia.com/1050408/asp/opinion/story_4586091.asp, accessed on August 23, 2011.

'David as Goliath', *The Indian Express*, January 26, 2006.

Dayan, Moshe, *Breakthrough: A Personal Account of the Egypt–Israel Peace Negotiations*. New Delhi: Vikas Publishing House, 1978.

Democratic Peace Bibliography, Version August, University of Hawaii, 2009. Available at http://www.hawaii.edu/powerkills/DP.BIBLIO.2009.HTML, accessed on April 21, 2011.

Deshpande, Anirudh, *British Military Policy in India: Colonial Constraints and Declining Power*. New Delhi: Manohar, 2005.

Devichand, Mukul, 'Is Chittagong One of China's "String of Pearls"?' *BBC News*, May 17, 2010. Available at http://news.bbc.co.uk/2/hi/business/8687917.stm, accessed on August 23, 2011.

Dietl, Gulshan, 'The Security of Supply Issue: The Growing Dependence on the Middle East', in Pierre Audinet, P. R. Shukla and Frederic Grare, eds, *India's Energy: Essays on Sustainable Development*. New Delhi: Manohar, 2000, pp. 209–24.

———, 'Gas Pipelines: Politics and Possibilities', in I. P. Khosla, ed., *Energy and Diplomacy*. New Delhi: Konark Publishers, 2005.

Dikshitar, V. R. Ramachandra, *War in Ancient India*. New Delhi: Motilal Banarsidass, 1987.

Dirks, Nicholas, 'Castes of Mind', *Representations*, 37 (1992), pp. 56–78.

Dixit, J. N., 'NATO Air Strikes Cause Anxiety, Says Govt', *The Indian Express*, March 26, 1999.

———, 'Strikes Against Sovereignty', *The Indian Express*, April 15, 1999.

———, *An Afghan Diary: Zahir Shah to Taliban*. New Delhi: Konark Publishers, 2000.

———, *India's Foreign Policy 1947–2003*. New Delhi: Picus Books, 2003.

'Does India Need Strategic Oil Reserves', *Business Standard*, November 13, 2002.

Donnelly, Jack, 'The Ethics of Realism', in Reus-Smit and Snidal, eds, *The Oxford Handbook of International Relations*. Oxford: Oxford University Press, 2010, pp. 150–62.

Dr Khan, Rashid Ahmad, 'The Imperatives of Regional Connectivity', *The Daily Times*, Islamabad, June 29, 2010.

'Draft Statement of Policy Proposed by the National Security Council on South Asia'. Enclosure to NSC 98/1, January 22, 1951, in *Foreign Relations of the United States*, VI Part II. Washington DC: United States Government and Printing Office, 1977, pp. 1651–52.

Dreyfuss, Bob, 'Brazil, Turkey Engineer Breakthrough on Iran', *The Nation*, May 18, 2010. Available at http://www.thenation.com/blog/brazil-turkeyengineer-breakthrough-iran, accessed on May 15, 2012.

Duara, Prasenjit, 'The Discourse of Civilization and Pan-Asianism', *Journal of World History*, 12, 1 (2001), pp. 99–130.

Dubey, Krishnan and Venkitesh Ramakrishnan, 'Far from Heroism: The Tale of Veer Savarkar', *Frontline*, April 7, 1995.

Dubey, Muchkund, 'India's Foreign Policy: Aims and Strategies', in Nancy Jetly, ed., *India's Foreign Policy: Challenges and Prospects*. New Delhi: Vikas, 1999.

Durani, Mohib Ullah and Ashraf Khan, 'Pakistan–Afghan Relations: Historic Mirror', *The Dialogue*, IV, 1 (Winter 2009). Available at www.qurtuba.edu.pk/thedialogue/The%20Dialogue/4_1/02_ashraf.pdf, accessed on August 18, 2010.

Dutt, Barkha, 'Left in a Time Warp', *Hindustan Times*, August 17, 2007. Available at http://www.hindustantimes.com/Left-in-a-time-warp/Article1-243001.aspx, accessed on August 25, 2010.

Dutt, Barkha, 'Us and Them', *Hindustan Times*, August 25, 2007. Available at http://www.hindustantimes.com/US-and-them/Article1-244315.aspx, accessed on August 28, 2010.

Dutta, Arvind, 'Indo-African Defence Cooperation: Need For Enhanced Thrust', *Journal of Defence Studies*, 2, 2 (Winter 2007), pp. 170–77.

Einhorn, Bruce, 'A Setback for China's Tech Ambitions in India', *Business Week*, May 6, 2010. Available at http://www.businessweek.com/magazine/content/10_20/b4178036082613.htm, accessed on August 23, 2011.

Elias, Norbert, *The Court Society*, trans. by Edmund Jephcott. Oxford: Basil Blackwell, 1983.

Engelmeier, Tobias, *Nation-Building and Foreign Policy in India: An Identity-Strategy Conflict*. New Delhi: Cambridge University Press, 2009.

Erikson, Erik H., 'On the Nature of Psycho-Historical Evidence: In Search of Gandhi', *Daedalus*, 97, 3, Philosophers and Kings: Studies in Leadership (Summer 1968), pp. 695–730.

European Parliament Committee on Environment, Public Health, and Food Safety, Report on 'Impacts of Shale Gas and Shale Oil Extraction on the Environment and on Human Health', 2011. Available at http://www.europarl.europa.eu/document/activities/cont/201107/20110715ATT24183/20110715ATT24183EN.pdf, accessed on May 15, 2012

'Extend Tibet Railway Line to Kathmandu, Nepal Tells China', *The Indian Express*, October 12, 2009. Available at http://www.indianexpress.com/news/extend-tibet-railway-line-to-kathmandu-nepal-tells-china/527936/, accessed on October 3, 2013.

Extracts of the Prime Minister's press conference, June 29, 2010, *The Indian Express*, June 30, 2010.

Eytan, Walter, *The First Ten Years: A Diplomatic History of Israel*. London: Weidenfeld and Nicolson, 1958.

Fair, C. Christine, 'India and Iran: New Delhi's Balancing Act', *The Washington Quarterly*, 30, 3 (2007), pp. 145–59.

———, *India in Afghanistan and Beyond: Opportunities and Constraints*. A Century Foundation Report, 2010. Available at http://tcf.org/publications/2010/9/india-in-afghanistan-and-beyond-opportunitiesand-constraints/pdf, accessed on January 11, 2011.

———, 'Under the Shrinking US Security Umbrella: India's End Game in Afghanistan?', *The Washington Quarterly*, 34 (Spring 2011), pp. 179–192. Available at http://csis.org/files/publication/twq11springfair.pdf, accessed on August 17, 2012.

'Final Communique of the 8th Islamic Summit of the OIC'. Available at http://www.oic-oci.org/english/conf/is/8/8th-is-summits.htm#FINAL%20%20COMMUNIQUE, accessed on August 23, 2010.

Foster, John, 'Afghanistan, the TAPI Pipeline, and Energy Geopolitics,' *The Journal of Energy Security*, March 23, 2010. Available at http://www.ensec.org/index.php?option=com_content&view=article&id=233:afghanistan-the-tapi-pipeline-and-energy-geopolitics&catid=103:energysecurityissuecontent&Itemid=358, accessed on April 2, 2012.

Foucault, Michel, *The Archaeology of Knowledge*. London: Tavistock Publications, 1974.

Frankel, Francine R. and Harry Harding, eds, *The India–China Relationship: What the United States Needs to Know*. New York: Columbia University Press, 2004.

Friedman, George, 'WikiLeaks and the Afghan War', *STRATFOR*, July 27, 2010. Available at http://www.stratfor.com/weekly/20100726_wikileaks_and_afghan_war, accessed on August 25, 2010.

Friedmann, Yohannan, 'Islamic Thought in Relation to the Indian Context', in Richard Eaton, ed., *India's Islamic Traditions: 711–1750*. New Delhi: Oxford University Press, 2003, pp. 50–63.

'Full Text of Obama's Parliament Speech', November 8, 2010. Available at http://ibnlive.in.com/news/full-text-of-obamas-parliament-address/134649-3.html, accessed on May 18, 2012.

Gandhi, Gopalkrishna, ed., *The Oxford India Gandhi: Essential Writings*. New Delhi: Oxford University Press, 2008.

Gandhi, Mohandas, *Selected Writings*. Mineola, New York: Dover Publications, 2005.

Ganguli, Kisari Mohan, *The Mahabharata*, 4 Vols. New Delhi: Munshiram Manoharlal, 4th impression, paperback edn, 2008[1883–96].

Ganguly, Sumit, *The Crisis in Kashmir: Portents of War, Hopes of Peace*. Cambridge: Cambridge University Press, 1997.

———, 'India's Foreign Policy Grows Up', *World Policy Journal*, 20, 4 (Winter 2003–4), pp. 41–47.

———, 'India and China: Border Issues, Domestic Integration, and International Security', in Francine R. Frankel and Harry Harding, eds, *The India–China Relationship: What the United States Needs to Know*. New York: Columbia University Press, 2004, pp. 103–33.

———, 'Singh's Shrewd Move', *Newsweek*, December 4, 2009.

Ganguly, Sumit and Manjit Pardesi, 'Explaining Sixty Years of India's Foreign Policy', *India Review*, 8, 1 (2009), pp. 4–19.

Ganguly, Sumit and Nicholas Howenstein, 'India Pakistan Rivalry in Afghanistan', *Journal of International Affairs* 63, 1 (Fall/Winter 2009), pp. 127–140. Available at http://jia.sipa.columbia.edu/files/jia/Ganguly_Howenstein.pdf, accessed on July 21, 2010.

Gargan, Edward, 'Indian Announces Full Israeli Ties', *The New York Times*, January 30, 1992. Available at http://www.nytimes.com/1992/01/30/world/indiaannounces-full-israeli-ties.html, accessed on September 19, 2013.

Garver, John W., *Protracted Conflict: Sino-Indian Rivalry in the Twentieth Century*. Seattle: University of Washington Press, 2001.

———, 'Evolution of India's China Policy', in Sumit Ganguly, ed., *India's Foreign Policy: Retrospect and Prospect*. New Delhi: Oxford University Press, 2010, pp. 83–105.

'Gas Project is a Win-Win for India, Pakistan', *The Hindu*, November 25, 2004. Available at http://www.hindu.com/2004/11/25/stories/2004 112513461100.htm, accessed on September 10, 2010.

General Malik, V. P., 'Limited War and Escalation Control', Part I and II. New Delhi: Institute of Peace and Conflict Studies (IPCS), 2004. Available at http://www.ipcs.org/Military_articles2.jsp?action=showView&kValue=1583&keyArticle=1018&status=article&mod=a, accessed on December 15, 2009.

General McChrystal, Stanley, 'Commander's Initial Assessment', *Washington Post*, August 30, 2009, pp. 2–10. Available at http://media.washingtonpost.com/wp-srv/politics/documents/Assessment_Redacted_092109.pdf, accessed on May 18, 2012.

Ghimire, Yubaraj, 'Hemmed in at Home, Non-Maoist Nepal Leaders Line Up to Visit India', *The Indian Express*, March 10, 2009. Available at http://www.indianexpress.com/news/hemmed-in-at-home-nonmaoist nepal-leaders-line-up-to-visit-india/433038/, accessed on October 3, 2013.

———, 'Prachanda's Latest: India and US Planned to Attack China Using Nepal', *The Indian Express*, August 6, 2009. Available at http://express india.indianexpress.com/story.php?storyId=498655, accessed on October 3, 2013.

Ghose, Aurobindo, *The Ideal of Human Unity*. Madras: Sons of India, 1919.

Ghose, Sagarika, 'Howdy Partner', *Hindustan Times*, September 9, 2008. Available at http://www.hindustantimes.com/News-Feed/Columns/Howdy-pardner/Article1-336797.aspx, accessed on August 29, 2010.

Ghosh, P. S. and R. Panda, 'Domestic Support for Mrs. Gandhi's Afghanistan Policy: The Soviet Factor in Indian Politics', *Asian Survey*, 23, 3, pp. 261–63.

Ghoshal, U. N., *A History of Indian Political Ideas*. London: Oxford University Press, 1959.

Gilmour, David, *Curzon: Imperial Statesman 1859–1925*. London: John Murray, 1994.

Gilroy, Paul, *The Black Atlantic: Modernity and Double Consciousness*. Cambridge: Harvard University Press, 1993.

Giustozzi, Antonio, *Koran, Kalashnikov and Laptop: The Neo-Taliban Insurgency in Afghanistan*. New York: Columbia University Press, 2008.

Goldstein, Avery, *Rising to the Challenge: China's Grand Strategy and International Security*. Stanford: Stanford University Press, 2005.

Golwalkar, Madhav S., *We or Our Nationhood Defined.* Nagpur: Bharat Prakashan, 1939.
——, *Bunch of Thoughts.* Bangalore: Vikrama Prakashan, 1966.
——, *Bunch of Thoughts*, 3rd edn. Bangalore: Sahitya Sindhu Prakashana, 1996.
Gommans, Jos, *Mughal Warfare: Indian Frontiers and High Roads to Empire 1500–1700.* London: Routledge, 2002.
Gopal Krishna, 'India and International Order: Retreat from Idealism', in Hedley Bull and Adam Watson, eds, *The Expansion of International Society.* Oxford: Clarendon Press, 1984, pp. 269–87.
Gopal, S., ed., *Selected Works of Jawaharlal Nehru. First Series*, Vol. 2. New Delhi: Orient Longman, 1975.
——, *Selected Works of Jawaharlal Nehru, Second Series*, Vols 1 & 13. New Delhi: Jawaharlal Nehru Memorial Fund, 1993.
Gordon, Leonard, 'Indian Nationalist Ideas about Palestine and Israel', *Jewish Social Studies*, 37 (1975), pp. 221–34.
'Gorshkov Price to be Fixed in Two Days', *The Indian Express*, August 28, 2009. Available at http://www.indianexpress.com/news/-gorshkovprice-to-be-fixed-in-two-days-/508136/, accessed on October 3, 2013.
'Govt Took Right Decision on Iran: PM', *The Financial Express*, February 17, 2006.
Government of India, *India and Palestine: The Evolution of a Policy.* New Delhi: External Publicity Division of the Ministry of External Affairs, 1968.
——, Joint Statement on 'Indo-US Civil Nuclear Agreement', July 18, 2005. Available at http://dae.nic.in/?q=node/61, accessed on May 20, 2012.
Graham, B. D., *Hindu Nationalism and Indian Politics: The Origin and Development of the Bharatiya Jana Sangh.* New York: Cambridge University Press, 1990.
Gray, Colin, 'National Styles', in Carl G. Jacobsen, ed., *Strategic Power: USA/USSR.* London: St. Martin's Press, 1990.
——, 'Strategic Culture as Context: The First Generation of Theory Strikes Back', *Review of International Studies* 25, 1 (January 2004), pp. 49–69.
Guha, Ramachandra, *India after Gandhi: A History of the World's Largest Democracy.* New Delhi: Picador India, 2007.
Gujral, I. K., *Matters of Discretion: An Autobiography.* New Delhi: Penguin, 2011.
Gupta, Amit, 'Determining India's Force Structure and Military Doctrine', *Asian Survey*, 35, 5 (1995), pp. 441–58.
——, *Building an Arsenal: The Evolution of Regional Power Force Structures.* Westport: Praeger Publishers, 1997.
Gupta, Shekhar, 'The Real Battle Will be for the Market', *The Indian Express*, January 13, 2001. Available at http://www.indianexpress.com/ie/daily/20010115/shekhar.htm, accessed on August 31, 2011.

Gupta, Shekhar, 'New Pitch, Front Foot Forward', *The Indian Express*, March 4, 2006. Available at http://www.expressindia.com/news/columnists/full_column.php?content_id=88925, accessed on August 28, 2010.

———, 'A New Project Pakistan', *The Indian Express*, August 8, 2009. Available at http://www.indianexpress.com/news/a-new-projectpakistan/499501/0, accessed on October 3, 2013.

———, 'Stop Fighting the 1962 War', *The Indian Express*, September 19, 2009. Available at http://www.indianexpress.com/news/stop-fighting-the-1962-war/518975/, accessed on October 3, 2013.

Gupta, Shishir, 'NSC Meet Discusses China, Agrees India Needs to Keep an Eye in Long Term', *The Indian Express*, August 3, 2009. Available at http://www.indianexpress.com/news/nsc-meet-discusses-chinaagrees-india-needs-to-keep-an-eye-in-long-term/497332/, accessed on October 3, 2013.

———, 'MEA Alerted Immigration against Chinese Paper Visas in Jan 2009', *The Indian Express*, October 4, 2009. Available at http://www.indianexpress.com/news/mea-alerted-immigration-against-chinesepaper-visas-in-jan-2009/524745/, accessed on October 3, 2013.

Hadass, Joseph, 'Evolution of the Relations Between India and Israel', *India Quarterly*, 58, 2 (2002), pp. 15–32.

Hall, Catherine, ed., *Cultures of Empire: Colonizers in Britain and the Empire in the Nineteenth and Twentieth Centuries*. Manchester: Manchester University Press, 2000.

Halliday, Fred, 'Three Concepts of Internationalism', *International Affairs*, 64, 2 (Spring 1988), pp. 187–98.

Hansen, Lene, *Security as Practice: Discourse Analysis and the Bosnian War*. New York: Routledge, 2006.

Hansen, Thomas Blom, 'The Ethics of Hindutva and the Spirit of Capitalism', in Thomas Blom Hansen and Christophe Jaffrelot, eds, *The BJP and the Compulsions of Politics in India*. New Delhi: Oxford University Press, 1998, pp. 291–314.

———, *The Saffron Wave: Democracy and Hindu Nationalism in Modern India*. Princeton: Princeton University Press, 1999.

Haqqani, Hussain, *Pakistan: Between Mosque and Military*. Washington DC: Carnegie Endowment for International Peace, 2005.

Haroon Khalid, 'Partition and the Mughals', *The Daily Times*, July 15, 2010.

Harrison, Selig, 'China's Discreet Hold on Pakistan's Northern Borderlands', *The New York Times*, August 26, 2010. Available at http://www.nytimes.com/2010/08/27/opinion/27iht-edharrison.html, accessed on May 22, 2012.

Hart, Basil Liddell, *Strategy*, 2nd rev. edn. Toronto: Meridian, 1991.

Hay, Stephen N., *Asian Ideas of East and West: Tagore and His Critics in Japan, China, and India*. Cambridge, MA: Harvard University Press, 1970.

Heptulla, Najma, *Indo-West Asian Relations: The Nehru Era*. New Delhi: South Asia Books, 1992.
Hirschman, Albert O., *National Power and the Structure of Foreign Trade*. Berkeley: University of California Press, 1945.
Holstag, Jonathan, *China + India, Prospects for Peace*. New York: Columbia University Press, 2009.
'Home Ministry "alarmist" on China: Jairam Ramesh', *NDTV*, May 10, 2010. Available at http://www.ndtv.com/news/india/home-ministry-alarmiston-china-jairam-ramesh-24348.php, accessed on August 23, 2011.
Hopkirk, Peter, *The Great Game: The Struggle for Empire in Central Asia*. New York: Kodansha International, 1994.
Howard, Michael, *Grand Strategy*, Vol. 4. London: The Stationery Office Books, 1972.
———, *War in European History*. Oxford: Oxford University Press, 1976.
Hudson, Valerie, ed., *Culture and Foreign Policy*. Boulder: Lynne Rienner, 1997.
'Impasse Breaks in Delhi, Doha Trade Talks to Resume in Geneva, Sept 14', *The Indian Express*, September 5, 2009. Available at http://www.indianexpress.com/news/impasse-breaks-in-delhi-doha-trade-talks-toresume-in-geneva-sept-14/513215/, accessed on October 3, 2013.
'In Scramble for Afghanistan India Looks to Iran', *Reuters*, July 6, 2010. Available at http://blogs.reuters.com/pakistan/2010/07/06/in-scrambleforafghanistan-india-looks-to-iran/, accessed on August 20, 2010.
'India Bid to Block Investment will Sour Ties: China', *Zee News*, July 22, 2010. Available at http://zeenews.india.com/news/nation/india-bidtoblock-investment-will-sour-ties-china_642577.html, accessed on August 23, 2011.
'India, China Denounce Unilateral Sanctions on Iran', *Tehran Times*, July 7, 2010.
'India Committed to Building the Capabilities of Afghan Security Forces', *The Hindu*, June 2, 2011. Available at http://www.thehindu.com/news/national/india-committed-to-building-the-capabilities-of-afghansecurity-forces/article2068619.ece, accessed on July 17, 2011.
'India Confident of 150 Votes in Security Council Bid', *Hindustan Times*, August 16, 2010. Available at http://www.hindustantimes.com/Indiaconfident-of-150-votes-in-Security-Council-bid/Article1-587487.aspx, accessed on August 16, 2010.
'India Hands Over Afghan Road', *The Indian Express*, January 23, 2009.
'India, Israel Planning Joint Fund for Agri Research', *The Financial Express*, March 27, 2006. Available at http://www.financialexpress.com/news/india-israel-planning-joint-fund-for-agri-research/129817, accessed on September 19, 2013.

'India, Israel Sign $1.4 bn Deal for Air Defence System', *The Indian Express*, March 27, 2009.
'India, Israel to Ramp up Military Ties', *The Times of India*, December 10, 2009. Available at http://articles.timesofindia.indiatimes.com/2009-12-10/india/28069386_1_second-largest-defence-supplier-admiralnirmal-verma-anti-missile-defence-systems, accessed on September 19, 2013.
'India Launches Israeli Satellite', *BBC*, January 21, 2008. Available at http://news.bbc.co.uk/2/hi/world/south_asia/7199736.stm, accessed on May 22, 2012.
'India Lures LNG Spot Cargoes as Asia, Europe Cut Imports', *The Financial Express*, April 23, 2009. Available at http://www.financialexpress.com/news/India-lures-LNG-spot-cargoes-as-Asia-Europe-cut-imports/450091, accessed on August 30, 2010.
'India Moves Closer to Iran Over Afghan Concerns', *LiveMint*, July 12, 2010. Available at http://www.livemint.com/Politics/vcnwgmP2Trpj KCmhFlKJDO/India-moves-closer-to-Iran-over-Afghan-concerns.html, accessed on August 30, 2010.
'India Out of "Peace Pipeline" as Iran, Pakistan Seal Gas Deal', *The Times of India*, June 14, 2010.
'India Pledges $500m to West African Nations', *The Hindu*, March 2, 2004. Available at http://www.hinduonnet.com/2004/03/02/stories/2004030202791200.htm, accessed on June 2, 2010.
'India Protests Pak's Gilgit Order and China Dam Pact', *The Indian Express*, September 12, 2009. Available at http://www.indianexpress.com/news/india-protests-pak-s-gilgit-order-and-china-dam-pact/516291/, accessed on October 3, 2013.
'India Puts Pipeline Talks on Slow Burner', *The Indian Express*, September 14, 2004.
'India Receives Second AWACS, to be Deployed in Agra', *Outlook*, March 25, 2010, Available at http://news.outlookindia.com/items.aspx?artid=677861, accessed on September 19, 2013.
'India Seeks Larger Role', *Asia Times Online*, November 28, 2001. Available at http://www.atimes.com/ind-pak/CK28Df03.html, accessed on September 12, 2010.
'India Seeks Sops for Steel Industry', *The Indian Express*, March 19, 2009. Available at http://www.indianexpress.com/news/india-seeks-sops-forsteel-industry/436313/, accessed on October 3, 2013.
'India Sets Stiff Terms for Iran Pipeline Gas', *The Financial Express*, May 2, 2005.
'India Threatens to Pull Out of Iran Pipeline', *The Financial Express*, March 16, 2005. Available at http://www.financialexpress.com/news/india-threatens-topull-out-of-iran-pipeline...-/109330/3, accessed on September 5, 2010.

'India to Boost Air Defence on China Border', *The Indian Express*, September 26, 2009. Available at http://www.indianexpress.com/news/india-to-boost-air-defence-on-china-border/521856/, accessed on October 3, 2013.

'India to Help Strengthen Afghan Security Forces', *Defence News*, June 3, 2011. Available at http://www.defencenews.in/defence-news-internal. asp?get=new&id=510, accessed on September 17, 2011.

'India to Resume Medical Mission Work in Afghanistan', *The Times of India*, July 20, 2010. Available at http://articles.timesofindia.indiatimes. com/2010-07-20/india/28307741_1_11-member-medical-team-medicalmission-afghanistan, accessed on May 17, 2011.

'India Votes Against Iran in IAEA', *The Times of India*, November 27, 2009.

'India Won't Take Iran to Court for LNG Deal Back-Out', *The Financial Express*, December 12, 2006. Available at http://www.financialexpress. com/news/india-won-t-take-iran-to-court-for-lng-deal-backout/186159, accessed on August 31, 2010.

'India's Africa Policy: Can We Do Better?', *The Hindu*, July 15, 2010. Available at http://www.hindu.com/2010/07/15/stories/2010071554411000. htm, accessed on August 3, 2010.

'India's Stealth Lobbying Against Holbrooke Brief', *Foreign Policy Magazine: The Cable*, January 23, 2009. Available at http://thecable.foreignpolicy. com/posts/2009/01/23/india_s_stealth_lobbying_against_holbrooke, accessed on November 29, 2013.

'India–Afghanistan Relations', Ministry of External Affairs, Government of India, January 2011. Available at http://meaindia.nic.in/meaxpsite/ pressrelease/2011/01/bilateralafganistan.pdf, accessed on April 1, 2012.

'India–Iran JV Comes Under UN Sanctions List; Crude Ferries Hit', *The Financial Express*, July 10, 2010. Available at http://www.financial express.com/news/indiairan-jv-comes-under-un-sanctions-list-crude-ferrieshit/644545, accessed on September 10, 2010.

'India–Iran LNG Deal in Peril', *The Indian Express*, May 3, 2006.

'Indian Hegemony Continues to Harm Relations with Neighbours', *People's Daily Online*, October 14, 2009. Available at http://english.peopledaily. com.cn/90001/90780/91343/6783357.html, accessed on August 23, 2011.

'Indian Media Hails Nuclear Deal', *BBC*, March 3, 2006. Available at http:// news.bbc.co.uk/2/hi/south_asia/4769424.stm, accessed on August 25, 2010.

'Indo–Iran LNG Deal Hits Hurdle', *The Indian Express*, December 7, 2004.

International Energy Agency (IEA), 'World Energy Outlook 2008'. Available at http://www.iea.org/textbase/nppdf/free/2008/weo2008.pdf, accessed on August 31, 2010.

'Interview: Indian Prime Minister Singh', *The Washington Post*, July 20, 2005. Available at http://www.washingtonpost.com/wp-dyn/content/article/2005/07/20/AR2005072001916.html, accessed on September 1, 2010.

'Iran Accuses Pakistan Over Attack', *BBC*, October 19, 2009. Available at http://news.bbc.co.uk/2/hi/8313625.stm, accessed on September 10, 2010.

'Iran Agrees to Deliver Gas at Indian Border', *The Indian Express*, February 16, 2005.

'Iran Asks India to Walk its Talk on Pipeline', *The Financial Express*, August 3, 2005. Available at http://www.financialexpress.com/news/iran-asksindia-to-walk-its-talk-on-pipeline/138581, accessed on August 31, 2010.

'Iran Clause a Stumbling Block', *Hindustan Times*, December 7, 2006. Available at http://www.hindustantimes.com/News-Feed/NM20/Iranclause-a-stumbling-block/Article1-182693.aspx, accessed on September 10, 2010.

'Iran Cuts LNG Offer Price by 8%', *The Indian Express*, November 18, 2006.

'Iran Figures in PM-Bush Talks', *The Financial Express*, September 14, 2005. Available at http://www.financialexpress.com/news/story/144753, accessed on August 30, 2010.

'Iran Offers Cheaper LNG Than RasGas', *The Financial Express*, April 15, 2004. Available at http://www.financialexpress.com/news/story/104486, accessed on September 10, 2010.

'Iran Upset at India's Stance', *The Hindu*, September 28, 2005. Available at http://www.hindu.com/2005/09/28/stories/2005092812460100.htm, accessed on August 30, 2010.

'Iran, India Fail to Cut Gas Deal', *The Times of India*, July 1, 2004.

'Iran's Armtwisting Begins: Fix Vienna Mistake or Else', *The Indian Express*, November 13, 2005. Available at http://www.indianexpress.com/story Old.php?storyId=81875, accessed on September 10, 2010.

'Iran's Press TV Banned in J&K after Clips Spark Violence', *Asian Age*, September 14, 2010.

'Iranian President's Visit a Test for India', *The New York Times*, April 30, 2008. Available at http://www.nytimes.com/2008/04/30/world/asia/30india.html, accessed on August 30, 2010.

'Israel–India: Final Report of the Joint Study Group', November 10, 2005. Available at https://www.google.com/url?sa=t&rct=j&q=&esrc=s&source=web&cd=1&ved=0CCsQFjAA&url=ftp per cent3A per cent2 Fper cent2Fftp.sni.technion.ac.il per cent2Fevents per cent2FINDIA ISRAEL per cent2Fsources per cent2520of per cent2520informationper cent2FIndia per cent2520Israel per cent2520JSG per cent2520Finalper cent2520Report.pdf&ei=vBY7UrXuMcSHqwHKzoHAAg&usg=AFQ jCNGMM5WqKjKDgvhpM16Iwc9xiV-QZg, accessed on September 19, 2013.

Iyengar, P. K., A. N. Prasad, A. Gopalakrishnan, and Bharat Karnad, *Strategic Sellout: Indian–US Nuclear Deal.* New Delhi: Pentagon Press, 2009.

Jacob, Jayanth, 'India Shuffles its Northern Card', *Hindustan Times*, August 9, 2010. Available at http://www.hindustantimes.com/India-news/NewDelhi/India-shuffles-its-Northern-card/Article1-584429.aspx, accessed on September 7, 2011.

Jaffrelot, Christophe, *The Hindu Nationalist Movement and Indian Politics: 1925–1990.* London: Hurst and Company, 1996.

———, *The Hindu Nationalist Movement in India.* New York: Columbia University Press, 1998.

———, 'India's Look East Policy: An Asianist Strategy in Perspective', *India Review*, 2, 2 (April 2003), pp. 35–68.

———, 'Inde-Israel, le Nouvel Element-Cle de l'Axe du Bien?', *Critique Internationale*, 21 (October 2003), pp. 24–32.

———, *Hindu Nationalism: A Reader.* Princeton, NJ: Princeton University Press, 2007.

———, 'The India-US Rapprochement: State-Driven or Middle Class Driven?', *India Quarterly*, 65, 1 (2009), pp. 1–14.

Jain, Girilal, 'Disillusionment with the Arabs: A Shift in Indian Opinion', *Round Table*, 228 (1967), pp. 433–38.

Jepperson, Ron, Alexander Wendt and Peter Katzenstein, 'Norms, Identity, and Culture in National Security', in Peter Katzenstein, ed., *The Culture of National Security: Norms and Identity in World Politics.* New York: Columbia University Press, 1996, pp. 33–78.

Jervis, Robert, *Perception and Misperception in International Politics.* Princeton, NJ: Princeton University Press, 1976.

Jha, Prem Shankar, 'Left With Megawhats?', *Hindustan Times*, August 24, 2007. Available at http://www.hindustantimes.com/editorial-views-on/BigIdea/Left-with-megawhats/Article1-244118.aspx, accessed on August 28, 2010.

Jha, Suman K. 'View from the Right', *The Indian Express*, September 24, 2009. Available at http://www.indianexpress.com/news/view-from-theright/543348/, accessed on October 3, 2013.

Jisi, Wang, 'China's Search for a Grand Strategy: A Rising Great Power Finds Its Way', *Foreign Affairs*, 90, 2 (March/April 2011), pp. 68–79

Johnson, Robert, *British Imperialism.* Hampshire: Palgrave Macmillan, 2003.

Johnston, Alaistair Iain, 'Thinking About Strategic Culture', *International Security*, 19, 4 (Spring 1995), pp. 32–64.

Johnston, Alaistair Iain, *Cultural Realism: Strategic Culture and Grand Strategy in Chinese History*. Princeton: Princeton University Press, 1995.

——, 'Strategic Cultures Revisited: Reply to Colin Gray', *Review of International Studies*, 25 (1999), pp. 519–23.

Jones, Rodney, 'India's Strategic Culture'. Washington DC: Defense Threat Reduction Agency Advanced Systems and Concepts Office, 2006. Available at https://fas.org/irp/agency/dod/dtra/india.pdf, accessed on September 8, 2013.

Jorfi, A., 'Iran and India: Age Old Friendship', *India Quarterly*, 50, 4 (1994), pp. 65–92.

Joseph, Josy, 'Israel May Emerge Top Arms Supplier', *Daily News and Analysis*, February 20, 2008. Available at http://www.dnaindia.com/india/1151923/report-israel-may-emerge-top-arms-supplier, accessed on September 19, 2013.

——, 'UPA Govt Signs Rs 10,000 cr Israel Missile Deal on the Sly', *Daily News and Analysis*, March 25, 2009. Available at http://www.dnaindia.com/india/1242337/report-upa-govt-signs-rs10000-cr-israelmissile-deal-on-the-sly, accessed on September 19, 2013.

Joshi, Manoj, 'India is Still Non-aligned, Says PM', *The Times of India*, June 3, 2003.

K. Subramanyam, 'Criticise, Not Condemn: India Must Tread Softly on Iraq War', *The Times of India*, April 7, 2003.

Kahn, Jeremy, 'India is Key Player in Afghan Conflict', *Newsweek*, October 19, 2009. Available at http://www.newsweek.com/blogs/wealth-ofnations/2009/10/19/india-is-key-player-in-afghan-conflict.html, accessed on August 25, 2010.

Kak, Kapil, ed., *Comprehensive Security for an Emerging India*. New Delhi: Knowledge World, 2010.

——, ed., *Comprehensive Security for an Emerging India*. New Delhi: Centre for Air Power Studies and Knowledge World Publishers, 2012.

Kampani, Gaurav, 'India's Compellance Strategy: Calling Pakistan's Nuclear Bluff Over Kashmir', *Monterey Institute for International Studies*, June 2002. Available at http://cns.miis.edu/stories/020610.htm, accessed on January 6, 2009.

Kanwal, Gurmeet, 'Countering China's Strategic Encirclement of India', *Bharat Rakshak Monitor*, 3, 3 (November–December 2000). Available at http://www.bharat-rakshak.com/MONITOR/ISSUE3-3/kanwal.html, accessed on August 23, 2011.

Kapoor, Mini, 'India's Help to Tajikistan Linked to Energy Security', *The Indian Express*, September 8, 2009. Available at http://www.indianexpress.com/news/india-s-help-to-tajikistan-linked-to-energy-security/514314/, accessed on October 3, 2013.

Kapur, Paul and Sumit Ganguly, 'The Transformation of US–India Relations: An Explanation for the Rapprochement and Prospects for the Future', *Asian Survey*, 47, 4 (July/August 2007), pp. 642–56.

Karat, Prakash, *Subordinate Ally: The Nuclear Deal and India–US Strategic Relations*. New Delhi: LeftWord Books, 2007.

———, *Politics and Policies: A Marxist Perspective*. Hyderabad: Prajashakti Book House, 2008.

Karmakar, Rahul, 'Naga Rebel Leader Admits China Links', *The Indian Express*, July 27, 2010.

Karnad, Bharat, 'Introduction', in Bharat Karnad, ed., *Future Imperilled: India's Security in the 1990s and Beyond*. New Delhi: Viking, 1994, pp. 1–15.

———, 'India's Weak Geopolitics and What To Do About It', in Bharat Karnad, ed., *Future Imperilled: India's Security in the 1990s and Beyond*. New Delhi: Viking, 1994, pp. 25–28.

———, *Nuclear Weapons and Indian Security: The Realist Foundations of Strategy*. New Delhi: Macmillan, 2002.

———, *Nuclear Weapons and Indian Security: The Realist Foundations of Strategy*, 2nd edn. New Delhi: Macmillan India, 2005[2002].

———, 'Firming up the Critical Capability Triad: Strategic Muscle, Sub-Conventional Punch and IT-enabled Network Centricity and Electro-Magnetic Warfare Clout', in Lieutenant General (Retd). Vijay Oberoi, ed., *Army 2020: Shape, Size, Structure and General Doctrine for Emerging Challenges*. New Delhi: Centre for Land Warfare Studies and Knowledge World, 2005, pp. 235–54.

———, 'India's Future Plans and Defence Requirements', in N. S. Sisodia and C. Uday Bhaskar, eds, *Emerging India: Security and Foreign Policy Perspectives*. New Delhi: IDSA and Promilla & Co. Publishers, 2005, pp. 61–76.

———, 'South Asia: The Irrelevance of Classical Nuclear Deterrence Theory', *India Review*, 4, 2 (April 2005), pp. 173–213.

———, 'Getting it Right on Pakistan', *LiveMint*, March 18, 2007. Available at http://www.livemint.com/Articles/2007/03/18235352/Getting-it-right-on-Pakistan.html, accessed on August 23, 2011.

———, 'Cold Start and the Nuclear Tripwire'. Paper presented at the International Conference on 'Cold Start: India's New Strategic Doctrine and Its Implications', Center for Contemporary Conflict, US Naval Post-Graduate School, Monterey, California, May 29–30, 2008.

———, *India's Nuclear Policy*. Westport, CN, and London: Praeger Security International, 2008.

———, 'Habit of Free-Riding', *Seminar*, 599 (July 2009). Available at http://www.india-seminar.com/2009/599/599_bharat_karnad.htm, accessed on August 23, 2011.

Karnad, Bharat, 'Militancy in Pakistan: Implications and Possible Strategies for India'. Paper presented at the conference on 'Countering Militancy in Pakistan: Domestic, Regional and International Dimensions', Centre for Muslim States and Societies, University of Western Australia, Crawley, August 3–4, 2009.

———, 'An Ostrich before the Dragon's Roar', *Express Buzz*, October 25, 2009. Available at http://expressbuzz.com/Opinion/Op-Ed/an-ostrich-before-the-dragons-roar/114953.html, accessed on August 23, 2011.

'Karzai "Holds Talks" With Haqqani', *Al Jazeera*, June 28, 2010. Available at http://english.aljazeera.net/news/asia/2010/06/20106277582708497.html, accessed on September 6, 2010.

Kashyap, Samudra Gupta, 'China Won't Wage War: Arunachal CM', *The Indian Express*, September 21, 2009. Available at http://www.indianexpress.com/news/china-won-t-wage-war-arunachal-cm/519630/, accessed on October 3, 2013.

———, 'Poll-vaulting Assets: An Arunachal Story', *The Indian Express*, October 8, 2009. Available at http://www.indianexpress.com/news/pollvaulting assets-an-arunachal-story/526376/, accessed on October 3, 2013.

'Kasuri Offers Guarantees on Gas Line to India', *The Hindu*, December 29, 2004. Available at http://www.hindu.com/thehindu/thscrip/print.pl?file=2004122914061300.htm&date=2004/12/29/&prd=th&, accessed on August 28, 2010.

Katz, Yakoov, 'Israel Eyeing Big Defense Contracts in India', *The Jerusalem Post*, March 14, 2010. Available at http://www.jpost.com/Israel/Israeleyeing-big-defense-contracts-in-India, accessed on September 19, 2013.

Katzenstein, Peter, ed., *The Culture of National Security: Norms and Identity in World Politics*. New York: Columbia University Press, 1996.

Kautilya, *The Arthashastra*, trans. by L. N. Rangarajan. New Delhi: Penguin, 1987.

Kautilya, *The Arthashastra*, ed. by L. N. Rangarajan. New Delhi: Penguin, 1992.

Lantis, Jeffrey S., 'Strategic Culture and National Security Policy', *International Studies Review*, 4, 3 (Autumn 2002), pp. 87–113.

Keegan, John and Andrew Wheatcroft, *Zones of Conflict: An Atlas of Future Wars*. New York: Simon & Schuster, 1986.

Keenleyside, T. A. 'The Inception of Indian Foreign Policy: The Non-Nehru Contribution', *South Asia: Journal of South Asian Studies*, 4, 2 (1981), pp. 63–78.

———, 'Nationalist Indian Attitudes Towards Asia: A Troublesome Legacy for Post-Independence Indian Foreign Policy', *Pacific Affairs*, 55, 2 (Summer 1982), pp. 210–30.

Keer, Dhananjay, *Veer Savarkar*. Bombay: Popular Prakashan, 1966.

Kennan, George F., *American Diplomacy*. Chicago: University of Chicago Press, 1984.
Kennedy, Paul, ed., *Grand Strategies in War and Peace*. New Haven: Yale University Press, 1991.
——, *Grand Strategies in War and Peace*. New Haven: Yale University Press 1992.
Keohane, Robert O., 'International Liberalism Reconsidered', in John Dunn, ed., *The Economic Limits to Modern Politics*. Cambridge: Cambridge University Press, 1990, pp. 175–82.
Keohane, Robert O. and Joseph S. Nye, *Power and Interdependence*, 3rd edn. New York: Longman, 2001.
——, *Power and Interdependence*, 4th edn. New York: Longman, 2011.
Kerttunen, M., *Nuclear Weapons and Indian Foreign Policy: 'A Responsible Nuclear Weapons Power'*. Helsinki: National Defence University, 2009.
Khan, Iqtidar Alam, 'Akbar's Personality Traits and World Outlook: Critical Appraisal', *Social Scientist*, 20, 9–10 (1992), pp. 16–30.
Khan, M. N., 'Vajpayee's Visit to Iran: Indo-Iranian Relations and Prospects of Bilateral Cooperation', *Strategic Analysis*, 25, 6 (2001), pp. 765–79.
Khera, S. S., *India's Defence Problem*. Bombay: Orient Longman, 1968.
Khilnani, Sunil, *The Idea of India*. New Delhi: Penguin India, 1998.
——, 'Delhi's Grand Strategy', *Newsweek*, July 18, 2009. Available at http://mag.newsweek.com/2009/07/17/delhi-s-grand-strategy.html, accessed on October 3, 2013.
Khilnani, Sunil, Rajiv Kumar, Pratap Bhanu Mehta, Lt. Gen. (Retd.) Prakash Menon, Nandan Nilekani, Srinath Raghavan, Shyam Saran, and Siddharth Vardarajan, *Non-alignment 2.0: A Foreign and Strategic Policy for India in the 21st Century*. New Delhi: Centre for Policy Research, 2012.
Khosla, I. P., 'India and Afghanistan', in Atish Sinha and Madhup Mohta, eds, *Indian Foreign Policy: Challenges and Opportunities*. New Delhi: Academic Foundation, 2007.
Kier, Elizabeth, 'Culture and French Military Doctrine Before World War II', in Peter Katzenstein, ed., *The Culture of National Security: Norms and Identity in World Politics*. New York: Columbia University Press, 1996, pp. 186–216.
——, *Imagining War: French and Military Doctrine between the Wars*. Princeton, NJ: Princeton University Press, 1997.
Kim, Chan Wahn, *Economic Liberalisation and India's Foreign Policy*. New Delhi: Kalpaz Publications, 2006.
Kirk, Jason A., 'The Evolution of India's Nuclear Policies', in Sumit Ganguly, ed., *India's Foreign Policy: Retrospect and Prospect*. New Delhi: Oxford University Press, 2010, pp. 275–300.

Kodikara, Shelton U., 'Role of Extra-Regional Powers and South Asian Security', in Sridhar K. Khatri, ed., *Regional Security in South Asia*. Kathmandu: Centre for Nepal and Asian Studies, Tribhuvan University, 1987.

Kohli, Atul, 'State, Business, and Economic Growth in India', *Studies in Comparative International Development* 42 (2007), pp. 87-114.

Koithara, Verghese, *Crafting Peace in Kashmir: Through a Realist Lens*. New Delhi: Sage, 2004.

Kolff, Dirk, *Naukar, Rajput and Sepoy: The Ethnohistory of the Military Labour Market in Hindustan, 1450-1850*. Cambridge: Cambridge University Press, 1990.

Koshy, Ninan, 'India and Israel Eye Iran', *Foreign Policy in Focus*, February 12, 2008. Available at http://www.fpif.org/articles/india_and_israel_eye_iran, accessed on September 1, 2010.

Kozicki, Richard, 'India and Israel: A Problem in Asian Politics', *Middle Eastern Affairs*, 9, 5 (1958), pp. 162-72.

Kragelund, Peter, 'India's African Engagement', *Analysis of the Real Instituto El Cano (ARI)* 10/2010, January 2010, Madrid.

Krishnaswami, Sridhar, 'India, US Sign Framework for Defence Co-operation', *The Hindu*, June 30, 2005.

Kulke, Hermann and Dietmar Rothermund, *A History of India*. London: Routledge, 1998.

Kumar, Amit, 'China's Island Strategy in the Indian Ocean: Breaching India's Sphere of Influence', *Observer Research Foundation Paper*, September 17, 2009. Available at http://www.orfonline.com/cms/sites/orfonline/modules/analysis/attachments/influence_1253251335478.pdf, accessed on August 23, 2011.

Kumar, Rajiv and Admiral Raja Menon, *The Long View From Delhi: To Define The Indian Grand Strategy For Foreign Policy*. New Delhi: Academic Foundation, 2010.

Kumar, Ravinder and Hari Dev Sharma, eds, *Selected Works of Motilal Nehru*, Vol. 4. New Delhi: Vikas Publishing House, 1986, pp. 418-21.

Kumar, Rajiv and Santosh Kumar, *In the National Interest: A Strategic Foreign Policy for India*. New Delhi: Business Standard Books, 2010.

Kumar, Satish, ed., *Yearbook on India's Foreign Policy 1983-84*. New Delhi: Sage, 1986.

——, 'India and the World: Survey of Events', in Satish Kumar, ed., *Yearbook on India's Foreign Policy 1987/1988*. New Delhi: Sage, 1988.

——, *Yearbook on India's Foreign Policy 1989*. New Delhi: Sage, 1990.

Kumarappa, Bharatan, 'Editor's Introduction', in M. K. Gandhi, *Non-Violent Resistance. Satyagraha*. Mineola, New York: Dover Publications, 2001.

Kumaraswamy, P. R., 'India and Israel: Prelude to Normalization'. *The Indian Express*, January 20, 1992.

——, 'India and Israel: Prelude to Normalization', *Journal of South-Asian and Middle Eastern Studies*, 19, 2 (1995), pp. 53–66.

——, 'India's Recognition of Israel, September 1950', *Middle Eastern Studies*, 31, 1 (1995), pp. 235–42.

——, 'India and Israel: Evolving Strategic Partnership', *Mideast Security and Policy Studies*, 40 (1998). Available at http://www.biu.ac.il/SOC/besa/books/40pub.html, accessed on September 19, 2013.

——, 'India, Israel and the Davis Cup Tie 1987', *Journal of Indo-Judaic Studies*, 23 (2002), pp. 29–39.

——, 'Indo-Iranian Ties: The Israeli Dimension', in 'The "Strategic Partnership" Between India and Iran', Asia Program Special Report, Woodrow Wilson International Center for Scholars, April 2004.

——, 'Israel–India Relations: Seeking Balance and Realism', in E. Karsh, ed., *Israel: The First Hundred Years: Israel in the International Arena*. London: Frank Cass, 2004, pp. 254–73.

——, 'Indo-Israeli Ties: The Post-Arafat Shift', *The Power and Interest News Report (PINR)*, March 2005.

——, 'Israel's New Arch of Friendship: India, Russia and Turkey', Gulf Research Center. Dubai, Research Papers, 2005.

——, 'Uncertainties about Indo-Israeli Ties', *The Deccan Herald*, June 15, 2004. Available at http://archive.deccanherald.com/Deccanherald/jun152004/edst.asp, accessed on September 19, 2013.

——, 'Delhi: Between Tehran and Washington', *Middle East Quarterly*, 15, 1 (2008), pp. 41–48.

Kundu, Apurba, 'The NDA and National Security', in Katherine Adeny and Lawrence Saez, eds, *Coalition Politics and Hindu Nationalism*. London: Routledge, 2005, pp. 212–37.

Kux, Dennis, *India and the United States: Estranged Democracies*. Washington: National Defence University Press, 1993.

Ladwig Jr, Walter C., 'A Cold Start for Hot Wars? The Indian Army's New Limited War Doctrine', *International Security*, 32, 3 (2007/8), pp. 158–90.

——, 'Delhi's Pacific Ambition: Naval Power, "Look East," and India's Emerging Influence in the Asia-Pacific', *Asian Security*, 5, 2 (2009), pp. 87–113.

Lal, Vinay, *The Other Indians: A Political and Cultural History of South Asian in America*. New Delhi: Harper Collins, 2008.

Lalthanhawla Pu, Speech on 'Peace Processes, Governance and Development' at the seminar on 'The North-East-Challenges of Governance', Centre for North-East Studies, Jamia Millia Islamia University, New Delhi, September 14, 2010.

Lamont, James, and Martin Wolf, 'India to Launch Trade Talks with Israel', *Financial Times*, February 11, 2010. Available at http://www.ft.com/intl/cms/s/0/9df7546a-16d2-11df-afcf-00144feab49a.html, accessed on September 19, 2013.

Lantis, Jeffrey, 'Strategic Culture and National Security Policy', *International Studies Review*, 4, 3 (2002), pp. 87–113.

Lauria, Joe, 'Indian Minister Urges Afghan Political Settlement', *Wall Street Journal*, September 23, 2009. Available at http://online.wsj.com/article/SB125364105273431343.html, accessed on April 27, 2011.

Lefever, Ernest W., 'Nehru, Nasser, and Nkrumah on Neutralism', in Laurence W. Martin, ed., *Neutralism and Nonalignment: The New States in World Affairs*. Westport, Connecticut: Greenwood Press Publishers, 1962, pp. 93–120.

Legro, Jeffrey, 'Military Culture and Inadvertent Escalation in World War II', *International Security*, 18, 4 (1994), pp. 108–42.

———, *Rethinking the World: Great Power Strategies and International Order*. Ithaca: Cornell University Press, 2005.

'LeT Planned More 26/11-like Strikes', *The Economic Times*, July 21, 2010.

Lieven, Anatol, 'Afghanistan: The Best Way to Peace', *The New York Review of Books*, February 9, 2012.

Lobell, Steven E., 'Structural Realism/Offensive and Defensive Realism', in Robert Denemark, General Editor, *The International Studies Compendium Project*. Oxford: Wiley-Blackwell, 2010.

Londono, Ernesto, 'Karzai Removes Afghan Interior Minister and Spy Chief', *The Washington Post*, June 7, 2010. Available at http://www.washingtonpost.com/wp-dyn/content/article/2010/06/06/AR2010060600714.html, accessed on August 12, 2010.

Luttwak, Edward, *The Grand Strategy of the Roman Empire: From the First Century A.D. to the Third Century*. Baltimore: Johns Hopkins University Press, 1979.

———, *The Grand Strategy of the Soviet Union*. New York: St. Martin's Press, 1984.

———, *Integration of the Indian States*. Hyderabad: Orient Longman Ltd, 1997.

———, *The Grand Strategy of the Byzantine Empire*. Cambridge, Mass.: Belknap Press of Harvard University Press, 2011.

Madan, Tanvi, 'The Brookings Foreign Policy Studies Energy Security Series: India', The Brookings Institution, Washington DC, 2006. Available at http://www.brookings.edu/~/media/Files/rc/reports/2006/11india_fixauthorname/2006india.pdf, accessed on August 31, 2010.

———, 'India's International Quest for Oil and Natural Gas: Fueling Foreign Policy?', *India Review*, 9, 1 (2010), pp. 2–37.

Magnus, Ralph H. and Eden Naby, *Afghanistan: Mullah, Marx and Mujahid*. Boulder, CO: Westview Press, 2002.

Mahatma Gandhi, 'Religious Authority for Non-Cooperation', *The Collected Works of Mahatma Gandhi*, Vol. XVIII, July–November 1920. New Delhi: The Publications Division, Ministry of Information and Broadcasting, India, 1965; Ahmedabad: Navjivan Trust, 1965.

———, 'Interview to *The Hindu*, September 24, 1938', in *The Collected Works of Mahatma Gandhi*. New Delhi: The Publications Division, Ministry of Information and Broadcasting, India; Ahmedabad: Navjivan Trust, 1976.

———, *The Collected Works of Mahatma Gandhi*, Vol. LXX, July 16–November 30, 1939. New Delhi: The Publications Division, Ministry of Information and Broadcasting, India, 1977.

———, 'If I Were a Czech', (Peshawar, October 6, 1938; *Harijan*, October 10, 1938), in *The Collected Works of Mahatma Gandhi*, Vol. LXVII, April 1–October 14, 1938. New Delhi: The Publications Division, Ministry of Information and Broadcasting, India, 1976; Ahmedabad: NavjivanTrust, 1977.

———, 'On Trial', (Segaon, October 10, 1939; *Harijan*, October 14, 1939), in *The Collected Works of Mahatma Gandhi*, Vol. LXX. New Delhi: The Publications Division, Ministry of Information and Broadcasting, India, 1977; Ahmedabad: Navjivan Trust, 1977.

———, 'A Poser', (Segaon, October 16, 1939; *Harijan*, October 21, 1939), in *The Collected Works of Mahatma Gandhi*, Vol. LXX. New Delhi: The Publications Division, Ministry of Information and Broadcasting, India; Ahmedabad: Navjivan Trust, 1977.

———, 'A British Endorsement', (Sevagram, October 16, 1940; *Harijan*, October, 1940), in *The Collected Works of Mahatma Gandhi*, Vol. LXXIII. New Delhi: The Publications Division, Ministry of Information and Broadcasting, India; Ahmedabad: Navjivan Trust, 1978.

———, 'My Idea of a Police Force', (Sevagram, August 20, 1940), in *The Collected Works of Mahatma Gandhi*, Vol. LXXII. New Delhi: The Publications Division, Ministry of Information and Broadcasting, India; Ahmedabad: Navjivan Trust, 1978.

———, 'Answer to Questions', (On the Train, May 9, 1947), *The Collected Works of Mahatma Gandhi*, Vol. LXXVII. New Delhi: The Publications Division, Ministry of Information and Broadcasting, India; Ahmedabad: Navjivan Trust, 1983.

———, 'Fragment of a Letter', (November 19, 1947), in *The Collected Works of Mahatma Gandhi*, Vol. XL. New Delhi: The Publications Division, Ministry of Information and Broadcasting, India; Ahmedabad: Navjivan Trust, 1984.

———, 'Speech at a Prayer Meeting', (November 19, 1947), in *The Collected Works of Mahatma Gandhi*, Vol. XL. New Delhi: The Publications Division, Ministry of Information and Broadcasting, India; Ahmedabad: Navjivan Trust, 1984.

Mahatma Gandhi, 'Interview to Vincent Sheean, New Delhi, January 27/28, 1948', in *The Collected Works of Mahatma Gandhi*. New Delhi: The Publications Division, Ministry of Information and Broadcasting, India.

Major General (Retd.) G. D. Bakshi, 'War Fighting in Ancient India', in Centre for Joint Warfare Studies (CENJOWS) ed., *Indian Way of Warfighting*. New Delhi: CENJOWS, 2008.

Malhotra, Inder, 'The Anniversary of Exile', *The Indian Express*, March 6, 2009. Available at http://www.indianexpress.com/news/the-anniversaryof-exile/431440/, accessed on October 3, 2013.

Malhotra, Jyothi, 'India Won't Be a Lackey', *The Indian Express*, June 3, 2003.

Malik, J. Mohan, 'Eyeing the Dragon: India's China Debate', *Asia-Pacific Center for Security Studies (APCSS)*, December 2003. Available at http://www.apcss.org/Publications/SAS/ChinaDebate_Malik.pdf, accessed on September 6, 2010.

Malone, David, *Does the Elephant Dance? Contemporary Indian Foreign Policy*. Oxford: Oxford University Press, 2011.

Manoj, C. G., 'Guess Who's Behind China Chill? US Lobbies, says Karat', *The Indian Express*, October 3, 2009. Available at http://www.indianexpress.com/news/guess-who-s-behind-china-chill--us-lobbies-says-karat/524475/, accessed on October 3, 2013.

———, 'View from the Left', *The Indian Express*, October 7, 2009. Available at http://www.indianexpress.com/news/view-from-the-left/548743/, accessed on October 3, 2013.

———, 'PFI to Make Kerala a "Muslim Country"', says VS', *The Indian Express*, July 25, 2010.

Mansergh, Nicholas, ed., *Constitutional Relations between Britain and India. The Transfer of Power 1942–7: Vol. II: 'Quit India' 30 April–21 September 1942*. London: Her Majesty's Stationery Office, 1971.

Mansingh, Surjit, *India's Search for Power: Indira Gandhi's Foreign Policy 1966–1982*. New Delhi: Sage, 1984.

Markey, Daniel, 'From AFPAK to PAKAF: A Response to the New US Strategy in South Asia', *Council for Foreign Relations*, Policy Options Paper, April 2009. Available at http://www.cfr.org/pakistan/afpakpakaf-response-new-us-strategy-south-asia/p19125, accessed on November 29, 2013.

Marwah, Reena, 'Interview with Mira Sinha Bhattacharjea', April 21, 2008. Available at http://politics.soc.ntu.edu.tw/raec/act/india04.doc, accessed on August 23, 2011.

Marwah, Ved, *India in Turmoil: Jammu and Kashmir, the Northeast and Left Extremism*. New Delhi: Rupa, 2009.

Masani, R. P. *Dadabhai Naoroji: The Grand Old Man of India*. London: George, Allen & Unwin, 1939.

Mathai, Ranjan, 'Forging Stability in Asia: Keynote Address at MEA-IISSIDSA Dialogue', Institute for Defence and Security Analyses, New Delhi, November 21, 2011. Available at http://www.idsa.in/KeynoteAddress/ForgingStabilityinAsia_RanjanMathai, accessed on December 17, 2011.

Mattoo, Amitabh, 'India's International Relations: The Search for Stability, Space, and Strength', in Alyssa Ayres & Philip Oldenburg, eds, *India Briefing: Take off at Last?*. New York: ME Sharpe, 2005, pp. 81–105.

———, 'India–Pakistan Relations: Towards a Grand Reconciliation',in Amitabh Mattoo, Kapil Kak and H. Jacob, eds, *India and Pakistan: The Pathways Ahead*. New Delhi: Knowledge World, 2007.

Mawdsley, E. and G. McCann, 'The Elephant in the Corner? Reviewing India–Africa Relations in the New Millennium', *Geography Compass*, 4, 2 (February 2010), pp. 81–93.

Mbeme, Achille, *On the Postcolony*. Berkeley: University of California Press, 2001.

McChrystal, Stanley A., 'COMISAF Initial Assessment'. Kabul: ISAF Headquarters, August 30, 2009. Available at http://www.globalsecurity.org/military/library/report/2009/090830-afghan-assessment/090830-afghan-assessment.pdf, accessed on August 25, 2010.

McMahon, Robert, *The Cold War on the Periphery: The United States, India, and Pakistan*. New York: Columbia University Press, 1994.

Mearsheimer, John, *The Tragedy of Great Power Politics*. New York: W. W. Norton & Company, 2001.

Mehrotra, Kartikay, 'Govt Short-Circuits Chinese, gives Domestic Firms a Leg Up', *The Indian Express*, September 11, 2009. Available at http://www.indianexpress.com/news/govt-shortcircuits-chinese-givesdomestic-firms-a-leg-up/515659/, accessed on October 3, 2013.

———, 'Chinese Labourers Banned from Indian Power Sector', *The Indian Express*, September 26, 2009. Available at http://www.indianexpress.com/news/chinese-labourers-banned-from-indian-power-sector/521778/, accessed on October 3, 2013.

———, 'India's Chinese Imports 3 Times More than Exports', *The Indian Express*, October 10, 2009. Available at http://www.indianexpress.com/news/india-s-chinese-imports-3-times-more-than-exports/527377/, accessed on October 3, 2013.

Mehta, Pratap Bhanu, 'Hinduism and Self-Rule', *Journal of Democracy*, 15, 3 (2004), pp. 108–21.

———, 'Still Under Nehru's Shadow? The Absence of Foreign Policy Frameworks in India', *India Review*, 8, 3 (July–September, 2009), pp. 209–33.

———, 'The Great Gameplan', *The Indian Express*, July 22, 2010.

Menon, Ramesh, *The Mahabharata*, Vol. 1. New Delhi: Rupa, 2004.

Menon, Shivshankar, 'A Global Partnership', in N. S. Sisodia, Peter R. Lavoy, Cherian Samuel, and Robin Walker, eds, *India–U.S. Relations: Addressing the Challenges of the 21st Century*. New Delhi: IDSA and Magnum Books, 2008.

———, 'State and Terror One in Pak: Menon', *The Indian Express*, July 21, 2010.

Menon, V. P., *The Transfer of Power in India*. Princeton, NJ: Princeton University Press, 1957.

Metcalf, Barbara and Thomas Metcalf, *A Concise History of India*. Cambridge: Cambridge University Press, 2002.

Miglani, Sanjeev, 'Indian Firms Eye Huge Mining Investment in Afghanistan', *Reuters*, September 14, 2011. Available at http://www.reuters.com/article/2011/09/14/afghanistan-india-idUSL3E7KB02A20110914?feedType=RSS&feedName=everything&virtualBrandChannel=11563, accessed on October 11, 2011.

Ministry of Commerce and Industry, 'Export–Import Data Bank Figures', Department of Commerce, Government of India. Available at http://commerce.nic.in/eidb/default.asp, accessed on September 15, 2011.

'MEA Rejects Chinese Analyst's Report', *The Indian Express*, August 12, 2009. Available at http://www.indianexpress.com/news/mea-rejectschinese-analyst-s-report/501026/, accessed on October 3, 2013.

Ministry of External Affairs (MEA), *Annual Report 1951–1952*. New Delhi: MEA Publications, 1952.

———, *Annual Report 1986–87*. New Delhi: Government of India. Available at http://mealib.nic.in/?2026#India's Neighbours, accessed on August 29, 2011.

———, *Annual Report 2007*. Available at http://meaindia.nic.in/, accessed on August 1, 2010.

———, Compilation of Data from Protocol Website. Available at http://meaprotocol.nic.in/, accessed on July 17, 2010.

———, Compilation of Data from Official Website. Available at http://meaindia.nic.in/onmouse/mission.htm, accessed on July 17, 2010.

———, 'Tehran Declaration', April 10, 2011. Available at http://www.mea.gov.in/other.htm?dtl/20048/Tehran+Declaration, accessed on August 20, 2010.

———, 'Address by Prime Minister to the Joint Session of the Parliament of Afghanistan,' May 13, 2011. Available at http://www.mea.gov.in/outgoing-visit-detail.htm?354/Address+by+Prime+Minister+to+the+Joint+Session+of+the+Parliament+of+Afghanistan, accessed on November 1, 2013.

———, 'India and Afghanistan: A Development Partnership,' Public Diplomacy Division, MEA, Government of India. Available at http://meakabul.nic.in/pdfs/partnership.pdf, accessed on September 17, 2011.

MEA, 'India–Afghanistan Relations', MEA, Government of India. Available at http://mea.gov.in/Portal/ForeignRelation/afghanistan-aug-2012.pdf, accessed on January 19, 2012.

——, 'India–China Relations', Government of India, August 2011. Available at http://www.mea.gov.in/mystart.php?id=50042452, accessed on September 21, 2011.

——, 'Text of Agreement on Strategic Partnership between the Republic of India and the Islamic Republic of Afghanistan', Government of India, October 4, 2011. Available at http://www.mea.gov.in/mystart.php?id=100018343&pid=2339, accessed on October 5, 2011.

Ministry of Finance, Government of India, *Economic Survey 2010–11*. Available at http://indiabudget.nic.in/budget2011-2012/es2010-11/estat1.pdf, accessed on April 5, 2011.

——, *Economic Survey 2012–13*. Available at http://indiabudget.nic.in/, accessed on August 28, 2013.

Mirilovic, N., 'Exploring India's Foreign Policy Debates', Sigur Center for Asian Studies, Policy Brief, 2010. Available at http://www.gwu.edu/~power/publications/publicationdocs/indiafp_policybrief.pdf, accessed on May 6, 2010.

Mishra, Surendra, ed., *Finance Ministers' Budget Speeches 1947–1996*. New Delhi: Surjeet Publications, 1996.

Mishra, Upendra N., 'India's Policy towards the Palestinian Question', *International Studies*, 21 (1982), pp. 101–15.

Misra, K. P., *India's Policy of Recognition of States and Government*. New Delhi: Allied Publishers, New Delhi, 1966.

Mistry, Dinshaw 'Diplomacy, Domestic Politics, and the US–India Nuclear Agreement', *Asian Survey* 46, 5 (September/October 2006), pp. 675–98.

Mitchell, David, 'Determining Indian Foreign Policy: An Examination of Prime Ministerial Leadership Styles', *India Review*, 6, 4 (2007), pp. 251–87.

Modelski, George, 'Kautilya: Foreign Policy and International System in the Ancient Hindu World', *American Political Science Review*, 58, 3 (September 1964), pp. 549–60.

Mohan, C. Raja, 'Kargil Diplomacy', *The Hindu*, August 3, 2000. Available at http://hindu.com/2000/08/03/stories/05032523.htm, accessed on September 19, 2013.

——, 'Trade as Strategy: Chinese Lessons', *The Hindu*, August 16, 2001.

——, 'India and the Iraq War', *The Hindu*, March 27, 2003.

——, 'Indo–US Talks on Iraq Today', *The Hindu*, June 16, 2003.

——, *Crossing the Rubicon: The Shaping of India's Foreign Policy*. New Delhi; New York: Viking, 2003.

Mohan, C. Raja, *Crossing the Rubicon: The Shaping of India's New Foreign Policy.* New Delhi; New York: Penguin, 2005.

——, 'India and the Balance of Power', *Foreign Affairs*, 85, 4 (July–August 2006), pp. 17–32.

——, *Impossible Allies: Nuclear India, the United States, and the Global Order.* New Delhi: India Research Press, 2006.

——, 'Barack Obama's Kashmir Thesis', *The Indian Express*, November 3, 2008.

——, 'American Embrace', *The Indian Express*, March 18, 2009. Available at http://www.indianexpress.com/news/american-embrace/435807/, accessed on October 3, 2013.

——, 'London Duet: Hu and Obama', *The Indian Express*, April 2, 2009. Available at http://www.indianexpress.com/news/london-duet-hu-andobama/441902/, accessed on October 3, 2013.

——, 'Party is State', *The Indian Express*, April 15, 2009. Available at http://www.indianexpress.com/news/party-is-state/447126/, accessed on October 3, 2013.

——, 'Now the G-3', *The Indian Express*, July 1, 2009. Available at http://www.indianexpress.com/news/the-g3-of-3g/504210/, accessed on October 3, 2013.

——, 'Debating India's Stand on Military Aid to Afghanistan', *The Indian Express*, July 7, 2009. Available at http://www.indianexpress.com/news/debating-indias-stand-on-military-aid-to-afghanistan/486099/, accessed on July 9, 2011.

——, 'The Great Game Folio', *The Indian Express*, July 8, 2009. Available at http://www.indianexpress.com/news/the-great-game-folio/1139743/, accessed on October 3, 2013.

——, 'Beijing's NAM', *The Indian Express*, July 15, 2009. Available at http://www.indianexpress.com/news/beijing-s-nam/489386/, accessed on October 3, 2013.

——, 'Before the Chance Fades', *The Indian Express*, July 20, 2009. Available at http://www.indianexpress.com/news/before-the-chance fades/491442/, accessed on October 3, 2013.

——, 'Maritime CBMs', *The Indian Express*, August 12, 2009. Available at http://www.indianexpress.com/news/maritime-cbms/500995/, accessed on October 3, 2013.

——, 'Chinese Takeaway', *The Indian Express*, September 16, 2009. Available at http://www.indianexpress.com/news/chinese-takeaway/517628/, accessed on October 3, 2013.

——, 'The Re-Making of Indian Foreign Policy: Ending the Marginalization of International Relations Community', *International Studies*, 46, 1&2 (2009), pp. 147–63.

Mohan, C. Raja, 'India and the Emerging Non-Proliferation Order: The Second Nuclear Age', in Harsh Pant, ed., *Indian Foreign Policy in a Unipolar World*. London: Routledge, 2009, pp. 43–72.

———, 'To Rawalpindi, Via Kabul', *The Indian Express*, July 20, 2010. Available at http://www.indianexpress.com/news/to-rawalpindi-via-kabul/649091/, accessed on August 23, 2010.

———, 'Myanmar Gen Connects, Plays India and China in New Bay Geopolitics', *The Indian Express*, July 26, 2010.

———, 'Kabul Gameplan', *The Indian Express*, October 4, 2011. Available at http://www.indianexpress.com/news/kabul-gameplan/855373/, accessed on October 5, 2011.

Mojumdar, Aunohita, 'India Won't Jeopardise Relations with US Over Iraq', *The Times of India*, March 21, 2003.

———, 'India's Role in Afghanistan: Narrow Vision Returns Meagre Gains', *The Times of India*, April 17, 2010. Available at http://articles.times ofindia.indiatimes.com/2010-04-17/india/28144375_1_indian-role-strategic-interests-foreign-policy, accessed on April 19, 2011.

Mor, Ben D., 'Public Diplomacy in Grand Strategy', *Foreign Policy Analysis*, 2 (2006), pp. 157–76.

Morgenthau, Hans J., *Politics Among Nations: The Struggle for Power and Peace*, 4th edn. New York: A. A. Knopf, 1967.

———, *Politics Among Nations: The Struggle for Power and Peace*, 5th revised edn. New York: A. A. Knopf, 1978.

Mudiam, Prithvi Ram, *India and the Middle East*. London: British Academic Press, 1994.

Mujawar, W. R., ed., *Speeches and Writings of Gopal Krishna Gokhale*, Vol. 1. New Delhi: Mangalam Publications, 2009.

Mukherjee, Pranab, '"Evolving South Asian Fraternity:" Calls For Free Movement of People and Goods in the Region', Ministry of External Affairs, Government of India, June 3, 2007. Available at http://www.mea.gov.in/mystrat.php?id=530112877, accessed on September 19, 2011.

Mukhopadhaya, Gautam, 'India', in Ashley J. Tellis and Aroop Mukharji, eds, *Is a Regional Strategy Viable in Afghanistan?*. Washington DC: Carnegie Endowment for International Peace, 2010, pp. 27–38. Available at http://carnegieendowment.org/files/regional_approach.pdf, accessed on July 23, 2010.

———, 'Indo-Iranian Relations 1947–2000', *Strategic Analysis*, 24, 10 (2001), pp.1911–26.

Mukhopadhaya, Gautam, 'Indo-Iranian Relations: Vital Factors in the 1990s', *Strategic Analysis*, 25, 2 (2001), pp. 227–41.

———, *West Asia and India: Changing Perspectives*. New Delhi: Shipra Publications, 2005.

'Mulford Remark Outrageous', *The Indian Express*, January 26, 2006.
Nadkarni, Vidya, *Strategic Partnerships in Asia, Balancing Without Alliances*. New York: Routledge, 2010.
Nag, Kalidas, *Greater India*. Bombay: The Book Centre Private Ltd., 1960.
Nagaraj, D. R., 'Self-Purification versus Self-Respect: On the Roots of the Dalit Movement', in A. Raghuramaraju, ed., *Debating Gandhi: A Reader*. New Delhi: Oxford University Press, 2006, pp. 359–88.
———, *The Flaming Feet and Other Essays: The Dalit Movement in India*. New Delhi: Permanent Black, 2010.
'Nagas Optimistic About Talks With Centre', *Expressbuzz*, February 28, 2010. Available at http://expressbuzz.com/topic/nagas-optimistic-abouttalks-with-centre/152203.html, accessed on May 17, 2012.
Naidu, Sanusha, 'India's Growing African Strategy', *Review of African Political Economy*, 35 (2008), pp. 116–28.
Nair, R. Sreekantan, 'India's Israel Policy: Changing Dimensions', in Rajen Harshe and K. M. Seethi, eds, *Engaging with the World: Critical Reflections on India's Foreign Policy*. New Delhi: Orient Longman, 2005, pp. 430–35.
Nanda, B. R., *Indian Foreign Policy: The Nehru Years*. New Delhi: Vikas Publishing House, 1976.
———, *Three Statesmen: Gokhale, Gandhi, and Nehru*. New Delhi: Oxford University Press, 2004.
Nandy, Ashis, *The Intimate Enemy: Loss and Recovery of Self Under Colonialism*. New Delhi: Oxford University Press, 1983.
———, 'From Outside the Imperium: Gandhi's Cultural Critique of the West', in *Traditions, Tyranny, and Utopias: Essays in the Politics of Awareness*. New Delhi: Oxford University Press, 1992.
———, 'Final Encounter: The Politics of Assassination of Gandhi', in A. Raghuramaraju, ed., *Debating Gandhi: A Reader*. New Delhi: Oxford University Press, 2006, pp. 45–72.
Narang, Vipin and Paul Staniland, 'Ideologies, Coalitions, and Indian Foreign Policy'. Paper presented at the Annual Convention of the International Studies Association, New Orleans, February 19, 2010.
Narasimhan, C. V., 'Letter to the Editor: Thoughts on Tibet', *Frontline* 17, 25 (December 9–22, 2000). Available at http://www.hindu.com/fline/fl1725/17251070.htm, accessed on August 23, 2011.
Nardin, Terry, 'International Ethics', in Christian Reus-Smit and Duncan Snidal, eds, *The Oxford Handbook of International Relations*. Oxford: Oxford University Press, 2008, pp. 594–611.
Narizny, Kevin, *The Political Economy of Grand Strategy*. Ithaca: Cornell University Press, 2007.
National Intelligence Council (NIC), Office of the Director of National Intelligence, 'Global Trends 2025: A Transformed World', November

2008. Available at http://www.dni.gov/nic/NIC_2025_project.html, accessed on September 19, 2011.

'Natural Gas Tumbles on Ample Stockpile, Lack of Storm Threat in U.S. Gulf', *Bloomberg News*, August 31, 2010.

Nauman Asghar, 'Resolving Pak-India Water Dispute', *The Nation*, June 9, 2010, Islamabad. Available at http://www.pkcolumns.com/2010/07/09/resolving-pak-india-water-dispute-by-nauman-asghar/, accessed on May 17, 2012.

Nayar, Baldev Raj and T. V. Paul, *India in the World Order: Searching for Major Power Status*. Cambridge: Cambridge University Press, 2003.

Nayyar, Deepak, 'India's Unfinished Journey: Transforming Growth into Development', *Modern Asian Studies*, 40, 3 (2006), pp. 797–832.

Nayyar, Dhiraj, 'India Slams Israeli Attack on Gaza Aid Flotilla', *The Indian Express*, June 9, 2010. Available at http://www.indianexpress.com/news/india-slams-israeli-attack-on-gaza-aid-flotilla/631252/, accessed on September 19, 2013.

N-deal Dies if India Doesn't Vote Against Iran: Mulford', *The Indian Express*, January 25, 2006.

'Nearest Continent', *The Indian Express*, October 19, 2009. Available at http://www.indianexpress.com/news/nearest-continent/530383/, accessed on October 3, 2013.

Nehru, Jawaharlal, *India's Foreign Policy, Selected Speeches: September 1946–April 1961*. New Delhi: The Publications Division, Ministry of Information and Broadcasting, Government of India, 1961.

———, *An Autobiography*. New Delhi: Oxford University Press, 1980.

———, *Glimpses of World History*. New Delhi: Oxford University Press, 1982.

———, *Glimpses of World History*, 6th impression. New Delhi: Oxford University Press, 1989.

———, *The Discovery of India*. New Delhi: The Jawaharlal Nehru Memorial Fund and Oxford University Press, 1981[1946].

———, *The Discovery of India*. New Delhi: Penguin, 2004.

'New Delhi's Great Power Ambition', *Watershed*. Available at http://www.watershed.com.br/article/176/new-delhi%E2%80%99s-great-powerambition.aspx, accessed on June 2, 2010.

Nomani, A. I., 'Letter to Editor: Don't Panic', *The Indian Express*, September 22, 2009. Available at http://www.indianexpress.com/news/don-t-panic/519976/, accessed on October 3, 2013.

'No Indication from Iran to Review Ties', *The Economic Times*, September 28, 2005.

Noorani, A. G., 'Savarkar and Gandhi', *Frontline*, March 28, 2003.

———, 'Balance of Power in South Asia', *Frontline* 22, 8, March 12–25, 2005. Available at http://www.hindu.com/fline/fl2208/stories/20050422004507600.htm, accessed on August 23, 2011.

'Now China Objects to President Pratibha Patil's Visit to Arunachal', *The Indian Express*, April 7, 2009. Available at http://global.factiva.com, accessed on August 23, 2011.

'Now, Air Force Chief Cools the China Heat', *The Indian Express*, September 24, 2009. Available at http://www.indianexpress.com/news/nowair-force-chief-cools-the-china-heat/520977/, accessed on October 3, 2013.

Nussbaum, Martha, 'Fears for Democracy in India', *Chronicle of Higher Education*, 53, 37 (2007), p. B6.

Nuclear Threat Initiative (NTI) Country Profiles, 'Pakistan'. Available at http://www.nti.org/country-profiles/pakistan/nuclear/, accessed on May 19, 2012.

Nye, Joseph S., *Power in the Global Information Age: From Realism to Globalization*. New York: Routledge, 2004.

'Obama Appreciates India's Role in Afghanistan', *The Hindu*, November 7, 2010. Available at http://www.thehindu.com/news/national/article 872842.ece, accessed on November 9, 2010.

Obama, Barack, 'Renewing American Leadership', *Foreign Affairs* (July/August 2007). Available at http://www.foreignaffairs.com/articles/62636/barack-obama/renewing-american-leadership, accessed on November 25, 2013.

'Oil Diplomacy Pays Off, India Signs Mega LNG Import Deal with Iran', *The Indian Express*, January 8, 2005.

'Oil Soars, and Natural Gas Slips', *The New York Times*, November 9, 2007. Available at http://www.nytimes.com/imagepages/2007/11/09/business/20071110_CHARTS_GRAPHIC.html, accessed on August 25, 2010.

Ollapally, Deepa, 'Mixed Motives in India's Search for Nuclear Status', *Asian Survey*, 41, 6 (2001), pp. 925–42.

Ollapally, Deepa and Rajesh Rajagopalan, 'The Pragmatic Challenge to Indian Foreign Policy', *Washington Quarterly*, 34, 2 (Spring 2011), pp. 145–62.

Omissi, David, *The Sepoy and the Raj: The Indian Army, 1860–1940*. London: Macmillan, 1994.

——, *Recovering Liberties: Indian Thought in the Age of Liberalism and Empire*. Cambridge: Cambridge University Press, 2011.

'On Aiyar's Table for Aziz: Give us Our MFN, Then Iran Gas Pipeline Can Run Through Pak', *The Indian Express*, November 22, 2004.

'Opposition is Politicising the Issue: BJP', *Hindustan Times*, April 8, 2003.

United States (US) Census Bureau, 'Foreign Trade'. Available at http://www.census.gov/foreign-trade/balance/c5330.html, accessed on May 18, 2012.

'Pak Thinks India Bigger Threat than Taliban', *Hindustan Times* (New Delhi), July 31, 2010.

Panagariya, Arvind, 'Growth and Reforms during the 1980s and 1990s', *Economic and Political Weekly*, 39, 25 (2004), pp. 2581–94.

Pandey, Gyanendra, 'Which Of Us Are Hindus?', in Gyanendra Pandey, ed., *Hindus and Others*. New Delhi: Viking, 1993, pp. 262–64.

———, *Memory, History and the Question of Violence: Reflections on the Reconstruction of Partition*. Calcutta: K. P. Bagchi and Company, 1999.

Pandian, S. G., 'Energy Trade as a Confidence-Building Measure between India and Pakistan: A Study of the Indo-Iran Trans-Pakistan Project', *Contemporary South Asia*, 14, 3 (2005), pp. 307–20.

Pandit, Rajat, 'Army Reworks War Doctrine for Pakistan, China', *The Times of India*, December 30, 2009. Available at http://articles.timesofindia.indiatimes.com/2009-12-30/india/28104699_1_war-doctrine-new doctrine-entire-western-front, accessed on September 8, 2013.

———, 'Future War on Two-and-a-Half Fronts?', *The Times of India*, May 31, 2010. Available at http://articles.timesofindia.indiatimes.com/2010-03-31/india/28115544_1_war-doctrine-western-front-mmrca-deal, accessed on September 8, 2013.

Pangariiya, Arvind, *India: The Emerging Giant*. New York: Oxford University Press, 2008.

Pant, Harsh V., 'India and Iran: An Axis in the Making?', *Asian Survey*, 44, 3 (2004), pp. 369–83.

———, 'India and Iran: Too Close for Comfort,' in Harsh Pant, ed., *Contemporary Debates in Indian Foreign and Security Policy: India Negotiates its Rise in the International System*. New York: Palgrave Macmillan, 2008.

———, *Contemporary Debates in Indian Foreign and Security Policy: India Negotiates its Rise in the International System*. New York: Palgrave Macmillan, 2008.

———, *Indian Foreign Policy in a Unipolar World*. London: Routledge, 2009.

———, 'India's Relations with Iran: Much Ado About Nothing', *The Washington Quarterly*, 34, 1 (Winter 2011), pp. 61–74.

———, 'Looking Beyond Tehran', *Outlook*, March 17, 2010. Available at http://www.outlookindia.com/article.aspx?264729, accessed on May 25, 2012.

Pantham, Thomas, 'Thinking with Mahatma Gandhi: Beyond Liberal Democracy', *Political Theory*, 11, 2 (May 1993), pp. 165–88.

Parajuli, Abhishek, 'China's Growing Role in South Asia', *The Daily Times*, June 9, 2010, Islamabad. Available at http://www.dailytimes.com.pk/default.asp?page=2010/07/09/story_9-7-2010_pg3_6, accessed on May 18, 2012.

Pardesi, Manjeet S., 'Deducing India's Grand Strategy of Regional Hegemony from Historical and Conceptual Perspectives', Working Paper No. 76 (April 2005), Institute of Defence and Strategic Studies (IDSS), Singapore.

Parekh, Bhikhu, *Gandhi: A Very Short Introduction*. Oxford: Oxford University Press, 2001.

———, 'Indianization of Autobiography', in A. Raghuramaraju, ed., *Debating Gandhi: A Reader*. New Delhi: Oxford University Press, 2006, pp. 151–71.

Parel, Anthony, ed., *Gandhi: 'Hindi Swaraj' and Other Writings*. New York: Cambridge University Press, 1997.

———, *Gandhi: 'Hind Swaraj' and Other Writings*. New Delhi: Cambridge University Press, 2009 [1997].

Park, Richard L., 'Indian–African Relations', *Asian Survey*, 5, 7 (July 1965), pp. 350–58.

Parthasarthi, G., ed., *Jawaharlal Nehru: Letters to Chief Ministers, Vol. 1, 1947*. London: Jawaharlal Nehru Memorial Fund and Oxford University Press, 1985.

———, *Jawaharlal Nehru: Letters to Chief Ministers 1947–1964, Vol.1: 1947–1949*. New Delhi: Oxford University Press, 1985.

Pasha, A. K., 'India and the Gulf States: Challenges and Opportunities', in Rajen Harshe and K. M. Seethi, eds, *Engaging with the World: Critical Reflections on India's Foreign Policy*. New Delhi: Orient Blackswan, 2005, pp. 419–21.

Patil, Reshma, 'Speaking in Two Voices', *Hindustan Times*, August 14, 2009. Available at http://www.hindustantimes.com/Speaking-in-two-voices/Article1-443023.aspx, accessed on August 23, 2011.

Peter, Tom A., 'India Outdoes US Aid Efforts in Afghanistan', *Global Post*, September 9, 2010. Available at http://www.globalpost.com/dispatch/afghanistan/100908/india-outdoes-us-aid-efforts-afghanistan, accessed on September 12, 2010.

Pham, J. Peter, 'India's Expanding Relations with Africa and Their Implications for U.S. Interests', *American Foreign Policy Interests*, 29, 5 (2007), pp. 341–52.

'Pipedreaming Again', *The Financial Express*, June 9, 2004. Available at http://www.financialexpress.com/news/pipedreaming-again/107498, accessed on September 3, 2010.

Planning Commission, Government of India, *Poverty Estimates for 2004–05*. Available at http://pib.nic.in/release/release.asp?relid=26316&kwd=poverty, accessed on 16 September, 2011.

'PM Cools Hot Air over China', *The Indian Express*, September 19, 2009. Available at http://www.indianexpress.com/news/pm-cools-hot-airover-china/519022/, accessed on October 3, 2013.

Polgreen, Lydia and Sabrina Tavernise, 'Water Dispute Increases India-Pakistan Tension', *The New York Times*, July 21, 2010.

Poore, Stuart, 'What is the Context? A Reply to the Gray–Johnston Debate on Strategic Culture', *Review of International Studies*, 29 (2003), pp. 279–84.

Porter, Gareth and Lobe, Jim, 'Gulf War Cries Over Iran Exaggerated', *Asia Times*, December 8, 2010. Available at http://www.atimes.com/atimes/Middle_East/LL08Ak01.html, accessed on September 3, 2010.

Posen, Barry R., *Sources of Military Doctrine: France, Britain and Germany Between The World Wars*. Ithaca, NY: Cornell University Press, 1984.

———, *Sources of Military Doctrine*. New York: Cornell University Press, 1984.

Prasad, Bimla, *The Origins of Indian Foreign Policy: The Indian National Congress and World Affairs, 1885–1947*. Calcutta: Bookland Private Ltd., 1960.

Prashad, Vijay 'India's Reckless Road To Washington Through Tel Aviv', *Counterpunch*, December 26, 2008. Available at http://www.counterpunch.org/2008/12/23/india-s-reckless-road-to-washington/, accessed on May 20, 2012.

'Pragmatic Turn', *Economic and Political Weekly*, 36, 16 (2001). Available at http://www.epw.in/editorials/india-iran-relations-pragmatic-turn.html, accessed on May 10, 2012.

'Press Charges', *The Indian Express*, September 22, 2009. Available at http://www.indianexpress.com/news/press-charges/519972/, accessed on October 3, 2013.

Press Information Bureau, Government of India, 'Riyadh Declaration: A New Era of Strategic Partnership'. Available at http://pib.nic.in/release/release.asp?relid=58617, accessed on September 3, 2010.

Press Trust of India, 'India Has No Cold Start Doctrine: Army Chief'. Available at http://www.ndtv.com/article/wikileaks%20revelations/india-has-no-cold-start-doctrine-army-chief-70159, accessed on January 5, 2011.

'Prime Minister Manmohan Singh's Reply to the Lok Sabha Debate (Rule193) on Foreign Policy, May 12, 2005. Available at http://pmindia.nic.in/speech/content4print.asp, accessed on September 19, 2011.

'Prime Minister Manmohan Singh's Address at the 16th Asian Corporate Conference on "Driving Global Business: India's New Priorities, Asia's New Realities"', Embassy of India, Washington DC, March 18, 2006. Available at http://www.indianembassy.org/prdetail931/--%09--prime minister-dr.-manmohan-singh's-address-at-the-16th-asian-corporate conference-driving-global-business-%3A-india's-new-priorities,-asia's new-realities, accessed on September 20, 2011.

'Prime Minister Manmohan Singh's IDSA Anniversary Speech', November 11, 2005. Available at http://pmindia.nic.in/speech-details.php?nodeid=211, accessed on April 20, 2012.

'Project Stilwell', *The Indian Express*, June 26, 2009. Available at http://www.indianexpress.com/news/project-stilwell/481581/, accessed on October 3, 2013.

'Protectionism Threatens Global Recovery: BRIC', *The Indian Express*, September 6, 2009. Available at http://www.indianexpress.com/news/protectionism-threatens-global-recovery-bric/513429/, accessed on October 3, 2013.

Pubby, Manu, 'In China Cyber Attack, NIC Most Affected, 9 Embassies Hit', *The Indian Express*, March 31, 2009. Available at http://www.indianexpress.com/news/china-cyber-attack-nic-most-affected-9-embassies-hit/441134/, accessed on October 3, 2013.

———, 'Leaked Tibet Info Could Have Led to Deaths: Expert', *The Indian Express*, April 1, 2009. Available at http://www.indianexpress.com/news/leaked-tibet-info-could-have-led-to-deaths-expert/441553/, accessed on October 3, 2013.

———, 'T-72 Tanks Moved to Remote Sikkim Area after China Tests Indian Defences', *The Indian Express*, July 28, 2009. Available at http://www.indianexpress.com/news/t72-tanks-moved-to-remote-sikkim-area-afterchina-tests-indian-defences/494964/, accessed on October 3, 2009.

———, 'Antony Flags China's Rising Military Power', *The Indian Express*, September 14, 2010.

Radhakrishnan, S., *The Bhagavadgita*. Noida: Harper Collins/Indus, 1993.

'Radio Free Europe Report'. Available at http://www.rferl.org/content/article/1058030.html, March 18, 2005, accessed on August 5, 2010.

Raghavan, Srinath, 'Virtues of Being Vague', *Asian Age*, January 7, 2010. Available at http://www.deccanchronicle.com/dc-comment/virtues-beingvague-973, accessed on August 20, 2010.

———, 'Virtues of Being Vague', *Deccan Chronicle*, January 7, 2010.

———, *War and Peace in Modern India: A Strategic History of the Nehru Years*. Ranikhet: Permanent Black, 2010.

———, *War and Peace in Modern India: A Strategic History of the Nehru Years*. New Delhi: Orient Blackswan, 2013.

Raghavan, Vasant, *Siachen: Conflict without End*. New Delhi: Penguin, 2002.

Rajagopalan, Swarna, 'Securing Rama's World', in Swarna Rajagopalan, ed., *Security and South Asia: Ideas, Institutions and Initiatives*. New Delhi: Routledge, 2006, pp. 24–53.

———, 'Reconciliation in the Indian Epics', *Peace Prints, South Asian Journal of Peacebuilding*, 1, 1 (Spring 2008). Available at http://www.wiscomp.org/pp-v1/Swarna_Rajagopalan.pdf, accessed on May 16, 2012.

Rajan, D.S., 'China: Signs of Ultra-Leftist Support to Maoists of India and Nepal', *South Asia Analysis Group*, Paper 1565, May 10, 2005. Available at http://www.southasiaanalysis.org/papers16/paper1565.html, accessed on August 23, 2011.

Ram, N., 'The Politics of Tibet: A Reality Check', *The Hindu*, July 5, 2007. Available at http://www.hindu.com/2007/07/05/stories/2007070559671300.htm, accessed on August 23, 2011.

Ram, N., 'Celebrating Social Emancipation in Tibet', *The Hindu*, March 28, 2009. Available at http://www.hindu.com/2009/03/28/stories/2009032854911000.htm, accessed on August 23, 2011.

Ramachandran, Sudha, 'India's Foray into Central Asia', *Asia Times*, August 12, 2006. Available at http://www.atimes.com/atimes/South_Asia/HH12Df01.html, accessed on May 15, 2012.

Raman, B., 'Gwadar, Hambantota and Sitwe: China's Strategic Triangle', *South Asia Analysis Group*, Paper 2158, March 6, 2007. Available at http://www.southasiaanalysis.org/papers/paper2158.html, accessed on August 23, 2011.

Ramesh, Jairam, '"Yankee Go Home, But Take Me With You:" Yet Another Perspective on Indo-American Relations', *Economic and Political Weekly*, 34, 50 (December 11, 1999), pp. 3532–34.

Rana, A. P., *The Imperatives of Nonalignment: Conceptual Study of India's Foreign Policy Strategy in the Nehru Period*. New Delhi: Macmillan, 1976.

Rana, Kishan S., *Asian Diplomacy: The Foreign Ministries of China, India, Japan, Singapore, and Thailand*. Oxford: Oxford University Press, 2008.

———, *Inside Diplomacy*. New Delhi: Manas, 2000.

Ranganathan, C. V., 'India in China's Foreign Policy', *Seminar*, 562 (June 2006). Available at http://www.india-seminar.com/2006/562/562-cvranganathan.htm, accessed on August 23, 2011.

Rao, Nirupama, 'Two Democracies: Defining the Essence of India-US Partnership'. Address by Indian Foreign Secretary at the Woodrow Wilson Center, March 15, 2009. Available at http://www.wilsoncenter.org/news/docs/Rao%20prepared%20remarks.pdf, accessed on August 31, 2010.

Rasgotra, Maharajakrishna, 'Afghanistan: The Way Out; Give Guarantees for its Neutrality', *The Tribune*, December 31, 2009. Available at http://www.tribuneindia.com/2009/20091231/edit.htm#4, accessed on August 25, 2010.

———, 'Afghanistan: The March of Folly', *The Hindu*, June 11, 2010. Available at http://www.thehindu.com/opinion/lead/afghanistan-the-march-of-folly/article453206.ece, accessed on June 19, 2010.

Rashid, Ahmed, *Descent into Chaos: How the War Against Islamic Extremism is Being Lost in Pakistan, Afghanistan and Central Asia*. London: Penguin, 2008.

'RBI Stifles Iran Oil Imports', *Business Standard*, December 25, 2010.

Reeves, Julie, *Culture and International Relations: Narratives, Natives and Tourists*. London: Routledge, 2004.

'Repeat of 1962 Can't be Ruled Out, says Rajnath', *The Indian Express*, October 4, 2009. Available at http://www.indianexpress.com/news/repeat-of-1962-can-t-be-ruled-out-says-rajnath/524743/, accessed on October 3, 2013.

Reserve Bank of India (RBI), *Handbook of Statistics on Indian Economy*, September 14, 2012. Available at http://www.rbi.org.in/scripts/Annual Publications.aspx?head=Handbook%20of%20Statistics%20on%20 Indian%20Economy, accessed on August 28, 2013.

Rice, Condoleezza, 'Campaign 2000: Promoting the National Interest', *Foreign Affairs*, 79, 1 (2000), pp. 45–62.

Richards, J. F., 'Norms of Comportment Among Imperial Mughal Officers', in Barbara Metcalf, ed., *Moral Conduct and Authority: The Place of Adab in South Asian Islam*. London: University of California Press, 1984.

———, *Power, Administration and Finance in Mughal India*. Hampshire: Variorum, 1993.

Richardson, M., 'Iran will test U.S.–China ties', *The Japan Times*, August 14, 2010. Available at http://search.japantimes.co.jp/cgi-bin/eo2010 0814mr.html, accessed on September 2, 2010.

Riedel, Bruce, 'Israel and India: New Allies', *Middle East Bulletin*, April 1, 2008, Brookings Institute, Washington DC. Available at http://www.brookings.edu/research/opinions/2008/03/21-india-riedel, accessed on September 19, 2013.

Rijiju, Kiren, 'Too Far from Delhi', *The Indian Express*, October 17, 2009. Available at http://www.indianexpress.com/news/too-far-from-delhi/530051/, accessed on October 3, 2013.

Robinson, Francis, *Separatism Among Indian Muslims: The Politics of the United Provinces*. Cambridge: Cambridge University Press, 1974.

Rosen, Stephen Peter, *Societies and Military Power: India and Its Armies*. Ithaca, NY: Cornell University Press, 1996.

Rothermund, Dietmar, *India: The Rise of an Asian Giant*. New Delhi: Stanza Publications, 2008.

Roy, Shubhajit, 'Meaningful Talks with Pak Only After it Acts against Terror, says Krishna', *The Indian Express*, August 25, 2009. Available at http://www.indianexpress.com/news/meaningful-talks-with-pak-onlyafter-it-acts-against-terror-says-krishna/506758/, accessed on October 3, 2013.

———, 'With Thumbs Up from Afghans, India Explores More Areas of Aid', *The Indian Express*, January 5, 2010. Available at http://www.indianexpress.com/news/with-thumbsup-from-afghans-indiaexplores-more-areas-of-aid/563545/, accessed on January 9, 2010.

———, 'Govt Underlines: Dalai Lama Free to Visit Arunachal', *The Indian Express*, October 17, 2009. Available at http://www.indianexpress.com/news/govt-underlines-dalai-lama-free-to-visit-arunachal/530152/, accessed on October 3, 2013.

Rubin, Barnett R. and Ahmed Rashid, 'From Great Game to Grand Bargain: Ending Chaos in Afghanistan and Pakistan', *Foreign Affairs* (November–December 2008). Available at http://www.vfp143.org/lit/Afghanistan/

ForeignAffairs-From_Great_Game_to_Grand_Bargain.pdf, accessed on April 13, 2012.

Rubin, Barnett R., *The Fragmentation of Afghanistan*. New Haven: Yale University Press, 2002.

———, 'Saving Afghanistan', *Foreign Affairs* (January/February 2007), pp. 57–78. Available at http://www.foreignaffairs.com/articles/62270/barnett-rubin/saving-afghanistan, accessed on January 19, 2010.

Rubinoff, Arthur G., 'Normalization of India-Israel Relations: Stillborn for Forty Years', *Asian Survey*, 35, 5 (1995), pp. 495–98.

———, 'The Diaspora as a Factor in US–India Relations', *Asian Affairs*, 32, 3 (2005), pp. 169–87.

Rudolph, Susanne Hoeber, 'Presidential Address: State Formation in Asia-Prolegomenon to a Comparative Study', *Journal of Asian Studies*, 46, 4 (1987), pp. 731–46.

S. Alam, 'Iran–Pakistan Relations: Political and Strategic Dimensions', *Strategic Analysis*, 28, 4 (2004), pp. 526–45.

Sadiq Ahmed, Saman Kelegama and Ejaz Ghani, eds, *Promoting Economic Cooperation in South Asia: Beyond SAFTA*. New Delhi: Sage, 2010.

Sagan, Scott, 'The Origins of Military Doctrines and Command and Control Systems', in Peter Lavoy, Scott Sagan and J. Wirtz, eds, *Planning the Unthinkable: How New Powers Will Use Nuclear, Biological and Chemical Weapons*. Cornell: Cornell University Press, 2000, pp. 16–46.

Sagar, Rahul, 'What's In a Name? India and America in the Twenty-First Century', *Survival*, 46, 3 (2004), pp. 115–35.

———, 'State of Mind: What Kind of Power Will India Become?', *International Affairs*, 85, 4 (2009), pp. 801–16.

Sahasrabudhey, Sunil, 'The Machine', in A. Raghuramaraju, ed., *Debating Gandhi: A Reader*. New Delhi: Oxford University Press, 2006, pp. 175–94.

Saidabadi, Mohammed Reza, 'Islam and Foreign Policy in the Contemporary Secular World: the Case of Post-revolutionary Iran', *Global Change, Peace and Security*, 8, 2 (1996), pp. 32–44.

Saikal, Amin, 'Iran's Turbulent Neighbour: The Challenge of the Taliban', *Global Dialogue*, 3, 2–3 (2001), pp. 93–103.

Samanta, Pranab Dhal, 'At ADB, Beijing Blocks India's $60-m Project for Arunachal', *The Indian Express*, April 14, 2009. Available at http://www.indianexpress.com/news/at-adb-beijing-blocks-india-s--60m-projectfor-arunachal/446709/, accessed on October 3, 2013.23, 2011.

———, 'Sanctioning Jaish Chief: UK Blinks, China Lone Dissenter', *The Indian Express*, June 25, 2009. Available at http://www.indianexpress.com/news/sanctioning-jaish-chief-uk-blinks-china-lone-dissenter/481115/, accessed on October 3, 2013.

Samanta, Pranab Dhal, 'India Wants Him, Pak Uses Jaish Chief to Defuse Mosque Tension', *The Indian Express*, June 28, 2009. Available at http://www.indianexpress.com/news/india-wants-him-pak-uses-jaish-chief-to-defuse--mosquetension/482266/, accessed on October 3, 2013.

———, 'Will Complete Doha Round by 2010: India Agrees with G8', *The Indian Express*, July 9, 2009. Available at http://www.indianexpress.com/news/will-complete-doha-round-by-2010-indiaagrees-with-g8/487156/, accessed on October 3, 2013.

———, 'Generals in Charge of China Border Head for Beijing – and Lhasa', *The Indian Express*, August 31, 2009. Available at http://www.indianexpress.com/news/generals-in-charge-of-china-border-head-for-beijing---andlhasa/509263/, accessed on October 3, 2013.

———, 'China Warms Up to Nepal Again as Maoists Stoke Anti-India Fires', *The Indian Express*, September 6, 2009. Available at http://www.indianexpress.com/news/china-warms-up-to-nepal-again-as-maoists stoke-antiindia-fires/513476/, accessed on October 3, 2013.

———, 'Army Wants Patrol Curbs along China Border Lifted', *The Indian Express*, September 13, 2009. Available at http://www.indianexpress.com/news/army-wants-patrol-curbs-along-china-border-lifted/516468/, accessed on October 3, 2013.

———, 'Govt Finds Out: 25K Chinese Entered India on Business Visas but are in Unskilled Jobs', *The Indian Express*, September 14, 2009. Available at http://www.indianexpress.com/news/govt-finds-out-25k-chineseentered-india-on-biz-visas-but-are-in-unskilled-jobs/516740/, accessed on October 3, 2013.

———, 'The China Chill', *The Indian Express*, September 24, 2009. Available at http://www.indianexpress.com/news/the-china-chill/520884/, accessed on October 3, 2013.

———, 'China Chooses Election Day to Stir the Arunachal Pot Again', *The Indian Express*, October 14, 2009. Available at http://www.indianexpress.com/news/china-chooses-election-day-to-stir-the-arunachal-potagain/528880/, accessed on October 3, 2013.

———, 'China Begins Building Dam on its Side of the Brahmaputra', *The Indian Express*, October 15, 2009. Available at http://www.indianexpress.com/news/china-begins-building-dam-on-its-side-of-the-brahmaputra/529244/ accessed on October 3, 2013.

Sapru, Tej Bahadur, 'The Problem of India's Aspirations', *The Contemporary Review* (November 1923), reproduced in K. N. Raina and K. V. Gopala Ratnam, eds, *Tej Bahadur Sapru: Profiles and Tributes*. Allahabad: Tej Bahadur Sapru Commemoration Volume Committee, 1972.

Saran, Shyam, 'Transforming India–U.S. Relations: Forging a Strategic Partnership'. Address at the Carnegie Endowment for International Peace, December 25, 2005. Available at http://www.carnegieendowment.org/files/indianfsdec21.pdf, accessed on September 5, 2010.

Saran, Shyam, 'Geopolitical Consequences of Current Financial and Economic Crisis: Implications for India', Speech by the PM's Special Envoy, India Habitat Centre, New Delhi, February 28, 2009. Available at http://www.indembassy.be/speeches_statements/february/feb28.html, accessed on August 23, 2011.

———, 'India Needs to Have Sharper Focus', *The Business Standard*, July 16, 2010.

Sardesai, Rajdeep, 'Karat and Stick', *CNN-IBN*, August 17, 2007. Available at http://ibnlive.in.com/blogs/rajdeepsardesai/1/2315/karat-and-stick.html, accessed on August 28, 2010.

Sarkar, Sumit, *Beyond Nationalist Frames: Postmodernism, Hindu Fundamentalism, History*. Bloomington: Indiana University Press, 2002.

Sarvepalli Gopal, ed., *Selected Works of Jawaharlal Nehru*, 1st Series, Vol. 2. New Delhi: Orient Longman, 1972.

———, *Selected Works of Jawaharlal Nehru*, 1st Series, Vol. 8. New Delhi: Orient Longman, 1976.

———, *Selected Works of Jawaharlal Nehru*, 1st Series, Vol. 11. New Delhi: Orient Longman, 1978.

Savarkar, Vinayak D., *The Indian War of Independence 1857*. Bombay: Phoenix, 1947.

———, *Hindu Rashtra Darshan*. Bombay: Veer Savarkar Prakashan, 1984.

———, *Echoes from Andaman*. Bombay: Veer Savarkar Prakashan, 1984.

———, *Essentials of Hindutva*. New Delhi: Bharati Sahitya Sadan, 2003.

Schaffer, Teresita C., *India and the United States in the 21st Century: Reinventing Partnership*. New Delhi: India Research Press, 2010.

Schell, Frank 'The U.S. Needs a New Af-Pak Strategy', *Far East Economic Review*, November 10, 2009. Available at www.feer.com/international relations/20098/november53/The-U.S.-Needs-a-New-Af-Pak-Strategy, accessed on January 11, 2011.

Schmidt, John R., 'The Unravelling of Pakistan', *Survival*, 51, 3 (June–July 2009), pp. 29–54.

Scrutton, Alistair, 'In Afghan End-game, India Gets that Sinking Feeling', *Reuters*, March 29, 2010. Available at http://www.alertnet.org/thenews/newsdesk/SGE62B0F9.htm, accessed on March 30, 2010.

Sengupta, Somini, 'Afghan Bombing Sends Stark Message to India', *The New York Times*, July 9, 2008. Available at http://www.nytimes.com/2008/07/09/world/asia/09india.html?_r=0, accessed on July 19, 2011.

Sen Gupta, Bhabani, *The Afghan Syndrome: How to Live with Soviet Power*. New Delhi: Vikas Publishing House, 1982.

Sen, Ashish Kumar, 'When in Doubt Shut Up', *Outlook*, February 13, 2006. Available at http://www.outlookindia.com/article.aspx?230207, accessed on May 25, 2012.

Shamshad, Ahmed, 'Need for Even-Handedness', *The News*, Islamabad, June 30, 2010.
Shandilya, Charan, *India-China Relations*. Ghaziabad: Pandit Sunderlal Institute of Asian Studies and Supriya Art Press, 1999.
Sharma, Betwa, 'Can Learn from China, says Jairam', *The Indian Express*, September 24, 2009. Available at http://www.indianexpress.com/news/can-learn-from-china-says-jairam/520914/, accessed on October 3, 2013.
Sharma, Gautam, *Nationalisation of the Indian Army, 1885-1947*. New Delhi: Allied Publishers, 1996.
Sharma, Jyotirmaya, *Hindutva: Exploring the Idea of Hindu Nationalism*. New Delhi: Penguin, 2003.
Sharma, Tannu, 'Meanwhile, Near LAC: Airfield Takes off, 4 Roads Get SC Green Flag', *The Indian Express*, September 19, 2009. Available at http://www.indianexpress.com/news/meanwhile-near-lac-airfield-takes-off--4-roads-get-sc-green-flag/519021/, accessed on October 3, 2013.
Shaw, Martin, 'Post-Imperial and Quasi-Imperial: State and Empire in the Global Era', *Millennium*, 31, 2 (2002), pp. 327-36.
Sheean, Vincent, 'The Case for India', *Foreign Affairs*, 30 (1951-52), pp. 77-90.
Shiva Rao, B., 'The Vicious Circle in India', *Foreign Affairs*, 19, 4 (July 1941), pp. 842-51.
Shourie, Arun, 'Digging our Head Deeper in the Sand', *The Indian Express*, April 7, 2009. Available at http://www.indianexpress.com/news/diggingour-head-deeper-in-the-sand/443896/, accessed on October 3, 2013.
Shuja Nawaz, *Pakistan in the Danger Zone: A Tenuous U.S.-Pakistan Relationship*. Washington DC: Atlantic Council, 2010.
Shukla, Ajai, 'India Supports Reconciliation with Taliban', *Business Standard*, October 8, 2009. Available at http://www.business-standard.com/article/economy-policy/india-supports-reconciliation-with-taliban-109100800098_1.html, accessed on August 29, 2010.
———, 'Time to Talk to the Taliban?', *Aspen Institute India*, Policy Paper No. 3. Available at http://www.aspenindia.org/pdf/taliban.pdf, accessed on March 30, 2012.
Siddiqui, Iqtidar Husain, *Mughal Relations with the Indian Ruling Elite*. New Delhi: Munshiram Manoharlal, 1983.
Sidhu, Waheguru Pal Singh, 'India's Nuclear Use Doctrine', in Peter Lavoy, Scott Sagan and J. Wirtz, eds, *Planning the Unthinkable: How New Powers Will Use Nuclear, Biological, and Chemical Weapons*. Cornell: Cornell University Press, 2000, pp. 125-57.

Sidhu, Waheguru Pal Singh and Jing-dong Yuan, *China and India: Co-operation or Conflict?*. Boulder, CO: Lynne Rienner Publishers, 2003.

Sieff, Martin, *Shifting Superpowers: The New and Emerging Relationship between the United States, China and India*. Washington DC: Cato Institute, 2009.

'Significant Impact, Will Check with China on Dam: New Delhi', *The Indian Express*, October 16, 2009. Available at http://www.indianexpress.com/news/significant-impact-will-check-with-china-on-dam-new-delhi/529798/, accessed on October 3, 2013.

Singh, Anita Inder, *The Limits of British Influence: South Asia and the Anglo-American Relationship 1947–56*. London: Pinter, 1993.

Singh, Arun Kumar, 'The Games at Gwadar', *Deccan Chronicle*, January 29, 2010. Available at http://global.factiva.com, accessed on August 23, 2011.

Singh, Bhartendu Kumar, 'George Fernandes and Sino-Indian Relations', Paper No. 1044 (May 27, 2003), Institute of Peace and Conflict Studies (IPCS), New Delhi. Available at http://www.ipcs.org/article/china/george-fernandes-and-sino-indian-relations-1044.html, accessed on August 23, 2011.

Singh, Harinder, 'India's Emerging Land Warfare Doctrines and Capabilities', Working Paper 210 (Ocotber 13, 2010), S. Rajaratnam School of International Studies (RSIS), Singapore. Available at http://www.idsa.in/system/files/WP210.pdf, accessed on September 8, 2013.

Singh, Jaswant, *Defending India*. New York: St. Martin's Press, 1999.

Singh, Madhur, 'Can China and India be Friends?', *Time*, December 21, 2007. Available at http://www.time.com/time/world/article/0,8599,1697595,00.html, accessed on August 23, 2011.

Singh, Mahendra Prasad, 'Indian State: Historical Context and Change', *The Indian Historical Review*, 21, 1–2 (1995), pp. 37–56.

Singh, Manmohan, 'Address to the India Today Conclave, 2005'. Available at http://pmindia.nic.in/speech/content.asp?id=78, accessed on August 27, 2010.

——, 'Full Text of Manmohan Singh's Speech to UN General Assembly', *Hindustan Times*, September 27, 2008. Available at http://www.hindustantimes.com/Full-text-of-Manmohan-Singh-s-speech-at-UN General-Assembly/Article1-340789.aspx, accessed on September 4, 2010.

Singh, Sushant K., 'India and West Africa: A Burgeoning Relationship', *Chatham House Asia*, Programme Briefing Essay, London, 2007.

Singh, Tavleen, 'A Foreign Policy for Wimps', *The Indian Express*, September 13, 2009. Available at http://www.indianexpress.com/news/a-foreign policy-for-wimps/516390/, accessed on October 3, 2013.

Singh, Zorawar Daulet, 'India's Tibet Card', *Hard News*, July 2008. Available at http://www.hardnewsmedia.com/2008/07/2251, accessed on August 23, 2011.

———, 'New Dynamics of an All Weather Friendship', *Pragati*, February 2009. Available at http://pragati.nationalinterest.in/2009/02/new-dynamics-of-an-all-weather-friendship, accessed on August 23, 2011.

Sinha, Neha, 'Ramesh to Visit China to Forge Common Climate Change Stand', *The Indian Express*, August 23, 2009. Available at http://global.factiva.com, accessed on August 23, 2011.

Skinner, Quentin, *Visions of Politics: Regarding Method*, Vol. 1. Cambridge: Cambridge University Press, 2002.

'Slippery Slope', *Deccan Herald*, January 11, 2010.

'Snap the Growing Ties with Israel, Says Karat', *Rediff India Abroad*, March 5, 2008. Available at http://www.rediff.com/news/report/karat/20080305.htm, accessed on September 19, 2013.

Snyder, Jack, 'The Soviet Strategic Culture: Implications for Nuclear Options', R-2154-AF. Santa Monica: Rand Corporation, 1977. Available at http://130.154.3.14/content/dam/rand/pubs/reports/2005/R2154.pdf, accessed on May 10, 2012.

———, *The Soviet Strategic Culture: Implications for Nuclear Options*. Santa Monica: RAND, 1977.

———, *Myths of Empire: Domestic Politics and International Ambition*. Ithaca, NY: Cornell University Press, 1991.

'Speech by Prime Minister Manmohan Singh at the India Today Conclave', February 25, 2005, Ministry of External Affairs, Government of India, New Delhi. Available at http://www.mea.gov.in/mystart.php?id=53019055, accessed on September 19, 2011.

Southern Command Official Webpage. Available at http://indianarmy.nic.in/command.html, accessed on January 16, 2010.

Sridharan, Kripa, 'Commercial Diplomacy and Statecraft in the Context of Economic Reform: The Indian Experience', *Diplomacy and Statecraft*, 13, 2 (June 2002), pp. 57–82.

Srimad Valmiki-Ramayana, 2 Vols. Gorakhpur: Gita Press, 6th edn, 2001 [1969].

Srivastav, Siddharth, 'Price Imbroglio Stymies Iran Pipeline', *Asia Times*, July 27, 2006. Available at http://www.atimes.com/atimes/South_Asia/HG27Df02.html, accessed on May 25, 2012.

Srivastava, Amitabh, 'I Refused to Help Bush: Vajpayee', *Hindustan Times*, March 28, 2003.

Srivastava, B. K., 'Indo-Israeli Relations: Pulls and Pressures', *Mainstream* (New Delhi 1967), pp. 17–19.

Stein, Burton, 'The State and the Agrarian Order in Medieval South India: A Historiographical Critique', in Burton Stein, ed., *Essays on South India*. Hawaii: The University Press of Hawaii, 1975, pp. 64–91.

Stockholm International Peace Research Institute (SIPRI), 'Military Expenditure of India'. Available at http://milexdata.sipri.org/result.php4, accessed on September 22, 2011.

'Strategic Shift in South Asia', *Jane's Foreign Report*, January 30, 2003.

Streusand, Douglas, *The Formation of the Mughal Empire*. New Delhi: Oxford University Press, 1989.

Subrahmanyam, K., 'Clear and Present Danger: US Path to Unipolar Hegemony', *The Times of India*, May 3, 1999.

———, 'Asia's Security Concerns in the 21st Century', in Jasjit Singh, ed., *Asian Security Concerns in the 21st Century*. New Delhi: Knowledge World, 1999, pp. 7–23.

———, 'Does India Have a Strategic Perspective?', in K. Subrahmanyam with Arthur Monteiro, *Shedding Shibboleths: India's Evolving Strategic Outlook*. New Delhi: Wordsmiths, 2005, pp. 3–17.

———, 'Indo-US Relations in a Changing World', *Air Power*, 2, 3 (2005). Available at http://www.aerospaceindia.org/Journals/Monsoon%202005/Indo-US%20Relations%20in%20a%20Changing%20World.pdf, accessed on September 3, 2010.

———, 'No American Can Treat India Like a Pet', *Rediff*, October 11, 2005. Available at http://www.rediff.com/news/2005/oct/11inter.htm, accessed on September 3, 2010.

———, 'Coping with China', *The Acorn*, August 16, 2009. Available at http://acorn.nationalinterest.in/2009/08/17/k-subrahmanyamon-admiral-mehtas-speech, accessed on August 23, 2011.

———, 'War in Afghanistan', *National Maritime Foundation*, September 6, 2009. Available at http://www.maritimeindia.org/pdfs/ksub6sep.pdf, accessed on August 21, 2010.

———, 'Explosive Disclosures', *The Indian Express*, September 25, 2009. Available at http://global.factiva.com, accessed on August 23, 2011.

———, 'Partnering with the US: Yes We Can!', *Business Standard*, November 18, 2009. Available at http://www.business-standard.com/india/news/k-subrahmanyam-partneringthe-us-yes-we-can/376773/, accessed on August 28, 2010.

Subrahmanyam, K. with Arthur Monteiro, *Shedding Shibboleths: India's Evolving Strategic Outlook*. New Delhi: Wordsmiths, 2005.

Subrahmanyam, Sanjay, 'A Tale of Three Empires: Mughals, Ottomans, and Habsburgs in a Comparative Context', *Common Knowledge*, 12, 1 (2006), pp. 66–92.

Subramanian, Arvind, *Eclipse: Living in the Shadow of China's Economic Dominance*. New Delhi: Viva Books with the Petersen Institute for International Economics, 2011.

'Subroto Cup: Afghan Girls in Fray; Prize Money Increased', *The Times of India*, November 2, 2011. Available at http://topnews.in/sports/

subroto-cup-afghan-girls-fray-prize-money-increased-222865, accessed on November 3, 2011.

Sullivan, Tim, 'India's Afghan Endgame – and What it Means for the U.S.', *Centre for Defense Studies*, April 19, 2010. Available at http://www.defensestudies.org/cds/india%E2%80%99s-afghan-endgame-and-whatit-means-for-the-u-s/, accessed on April 13, 2012.

——, 'India, Pakistan Face Off in Afghanistan: Neighbours' Heated Rivalry Will Have a Major Impact on U.S. Plans to Deal with Taliban and Get Out', *Associated Press*, May 1, 2010. Available at http://www.statesman.com/opinion/insight/india-pakistan-face-off-in-afghanistan-657210.html, accessed on August 15, 2010.

Sundaram, Chandar, 'Grudging Concessions: The Officer Corps and its Indianization, 1817–1940', in Daniel Marston and Chandar Sundaram, eds, *A Military History of India and South Asia: From the East India Company to the Nuclear Era*. Westport: Praeger Security International, 2007, pp. 88–103.

'Sustainability of Iran LNG Imports Questioned', *The Economic Times*, December 7, 2004.

Swaine, Michael and Ashley Tellis, *Interpreting China's Grand Strategy*. Santa Monica, CA: RAND, 2000.

Swami, Praveen 'Terrorism in Jammu and Kashmir in Theory and Practice', *India Review*, 2, 3 (July 2003), pp. 55–88.

Swamy, Subramanian, 'Sino-Indian Relations through the Tibet Prism', *Frontline* 17,18 (September 2–15, 2000). Available at http://www.hindu.com/fline/fl1718/17180240.htm, accessed on August 23, 2011.

Tagore, Rabindranath, *Nationalism*. New Delhi: Penguin, 2009.

Talbott, Strobe, *Engaging India: Diplomacy, Democracy and the Bomb*. New Delhi: Penguin–Viking, 2004.

'Talibanization of Afghanistan Will Hit India Hard: Brajesh', *The Times of India*, March 13, 2010. Available at http://articles.timesofindia.indiatimes.com/2010-03-13/india/28116780_1_pakistan-indianinterests-military-growth, accessed on March 14, 2010.

Talwar, Ruchika, 'Naval Envy', *The Indian Express*, August 1, 2009. Available at http://www.indianexpress.com/news/naval-envy/496757/, accessed on October 3, 2013.

Tang, Zhihao and Li Jiabao, 'India and Russia Keen to Make the Most of Debut', *ChinaDaily.com.cn*, August 9, 2011. Available at http://www.chinadaily.com.cn/cndy/2011-09/08/content_13645948.htm, accessed on May 18, 2012.

Tanham, George K., *Indian Strategic Thought: An Interpretive Essay*. Santa Monica, CA: RAND, 1992. Available at http://www.rand.org/pubs/reports/2007/R4207.pdf, accessed on August 20, 2010.

Tariq, Sehar, 'Searching for Aftab Manzil', *The News*, Islamabad, June 8, 2010.
Tellis, Ashley J., 'China and India in Asia', in Francine R. Frankel and Harry Harding, eds, *The India–China Relationship: What the United States Needs to Know*. New York: Columbia University Press, 2004, pp. 134–77.
Tendulkar, D. G., *Mahatma*, Vol. IV. New Delhi: The Publications Division, 1961.
Thapar, Vishal, 'Army Was All Dressed Up to Go to Iraq', *Hindustan Times*, July 15, 2003.
Tharoor, Shashi, *Nehru: The Invention of India*. New York: Arcade Publishing, 2003.
———, 'Indian Strategic Power: Soft', *The Huffington Post*, May 26, 2009. Available at http://www.huffingtonpost.com/shashi-tharoor/indian strategic-power-so_b_207785.html, accessed on June 24, 2010.
'The China 'Threat'', *The Indian Express*, September 21, 2009. Available at http://www.indianexpress.com/news/the-china--threat-/519638/, accessed on October 3, 2013.
'The Colombo Consensus', *The Economist*, July 8, 2010.
'The Iran Hiccup', *India Today*, October 3, 2005. Available at http://india today.intoday.in/story/under-pressure-india-tells-us-it-is-opposedin-principle-to-iran-nuclear-programme/1/192951.html, accessed on May 20, 2012.
The Text of the Joint Communique. *The Daily Star*. Dhaka, July 1, 2010. Available at http://archive.thedailystar.net/newDesign/news-details.php?nid=121706, accessed on December 3, 2013.
The 2010 Global Peace Index. The GPI score for India is available at http://www.visionofhumanity.org/gpi-data/#/2010/conf/IN/detail, accessed on May 17, 2012.
Thomas, Raju, 'The Growth of Indian Military Power: From Sufficient Defence to Nuclear Deterrence', in B. G. Verghese, *First Draft: Witness to the Making of Modern India*. New Delhi: Tranquebar Press, 2010.
Thornton, Thomas P. 'India Adrift: The Search for Moorings in a New World Order', *Asian Survey*, 32, 12 (December 1992), pp. 1063–77.
Thucydides, *History of the Peloponnesian War*, trans. by Moses I. Finley. London: Penguin, 1972.
'Tibet's Development Spells Progress in Human Rights: N. Ram', *The Hindu*, April 23, 2008. Available at http://www.hindu.com/2008/04/23/stories/2008042359671200.htm, accessed on August 23, 2011.
'Time to Strengthen Frontiers: Bhagwat', *The Indian Express*, October 3, 2009. Available at http://www.indianexpress.com/news/time-to-strengthenfrontiers-bhagwat/524455/, accessed on October 3, 2013.
Trubowitz, Peter, *Politics and Strategy: Partisan Ambition and American Statecraft*. Princeton, NJ: Princeton University Press, 2011.

'US Concerned Over India–Iran Ties: Rice', *Agence France Presse*, April 5, 2006.

'US Offer Changed India's Iran Policy', *Dawn*, September 29, 2005. Available at http://beta.dawn.com/news/158853/us-offer-changed-india-s-iranpolicy, accessed on May 15, 2012.

United States Congress, *House Report 5682*. Available at http://frwebgate.access.gpo.gov/cgi-bin/getdoc.cgi?dbname=109_cong_bills&docid=f:h5682enr.txt.pdf, accessed on September 5, 2010.

V. Sudarshan, 'Keeping America's Peace', *Outlook*, June 2, 2003.

Vanaik, Achin and Praful Bidwai, *South Asia on a Short Fuse*. New Delhi: Oxford University Press, 1999.

Varadarajan, Siddharth, 'The Unraveling of India's Persian Puzzle', *The Hindu*, September 27, 2005. Available at http://hindu.com/2005/09/27/stories/2005092703011000.htm, accessed on May 10, 2012.

———, 'India's Anti-Iran Votes Were Coerced, Says Former US Official', *The Hindu*, February 16, 2007. Available at http://www.hindu.com/2007/02/16/stories/2007021605671200.htm, accessed on May 12, 2012.

Varma, Subodh, 'J&K Dependency on Centre Alarming', *The Times of India*, July 19, 2010.

Varshney, Ashutosh 'Contested Meanings: India's National Identity, Hindu Nationalism, and the Politics of Anxiety', *Daedalus*, 122 (1993), pp. 22–61.

———, *Ethnic Conflict and Civic Life: Hindus and Muslims in India*. New Haven: Yale University Press, 2002.

Vazira, Fazila-Yacoobali Zamindar, *The Long Partition and the Making of Modern South Asia: Refugees, Boundaries, Histories*. New York: Columbia University Press, 2007.

Ved, Mahendra, 'India Not to Back War, Says PM', *The Times of India*, February, 26, 2003.

Venkatshamy, Krishnappa and Princy George, eds, *Grand Strategy for India: 2020 and Beyond*. New Delhi: Pentagon Publishers, 2012.

Vice Marshal Choudhry, Shahzad, 'Indo-Pak Dialogue: Undertones and Ramifications', *The Daily Times*, June 28, 2010.

Vickery Jr, Raymond E., *The Eagle and the Elephant: Strategic Aspects of US–India Economic Engagement*. Baltimore: Johns Hopkins University Press, 2011.

Vijay, Tarun, *India Battles to Win*. New Delhi: Rupa, 2009.

Vivekanandan, Jayashree, *Interrogating International Relations: India's Strategic Practice and the Return of History*. New Delhi; London: Routledge, 2011.

'Wait Watchers' Club', Editorial, *Outlook*, February 10, 2003.

Waltz, Kenneth N., *Theory of International Politics*. New York: McGraw Hill, 1979.
——, *Theory of International Politics*. Reading, Mass.: Addison–Wesley Pub. Co., 1979.
Wax, Emily, 'India's Eager Courtship of Afghanistan Comes at a Steep Price', *The Washington Post*, April 3, 2010. Available at http://www.washingtonpost.com/wp-dyn/content/article/2010/04/02/AR2010040204313.html, accessed on September 2, 2010.
'We Need to Stop Pipeline Says Bodman', *The Hindu*, March 23, 2007. Available at http://www.thehindu.com/todays-paper/tp-international/we-need-to-stop-pipeline-says-bodman/article1814874.ece, accessed on May 22, 2012.
Weber, Max, 'Politik als Beruf', in *Gesammelte Politische Schriften*. München: Drei-Masken-Verlag, 1921, pp. 396–450.
——, 'Politics as a Vocation', in H. H. Gerth and C. Wright Mill, eds, *From Max Weber: Essays in Sociology*. Oxford: Oxford University Press, 1946.
Weber, Thomas, 'Gandhi and World Politics', in B. S. Chimni and Siddharth Mallavarapu, eds, *Handbook of International Relations: For the Global South*. New Delhi: Pearson, 2012, pp. 434–49.
Weitz, R., 'Will Asia Nix Iran Sanctions?', *The Diplomat*, August 10, 2010. Available at http://the-diplomat.com/2010/08/10/will-asia-nix-iran sanctions/, accessed on September 2, 2010.
'Welcome LNG Agreement', *Hindu Business Line*, June 15, 2005.
Weymouth, Lally, 'In the Eye of the Storm', *Newsweek*, November 21, 2009. Available at http://mag.newsweek.com/2009/11/20/in-the-eye-of-thestorm.html, accessed on October 3, 2013.
White House document, 'The US–India Partnership: The Fact Sheets', November 2010. Available at http://www.whitehouse.gov/the-press-office/2010/11/08/us-india-partnership-factsheets, accessed on April 13, 2012.
'WikiLeaks Vindicates India's Charge of ISI Terror Network', *The Economic Times*, July 28, 2010. Available at http://articles.economictimes.indiatimes.com/2010-07-28/news/27609828_1_taliban-fighters-hamid-gulafghan-pakistani-border, accessed on July 29, 2010.
Wilkinson, Steven I., *Votes and Violence: Electoral Competition and Ethnic Riots in India*. New York: Cambridge University Press, 2004.
Winnett, Robert and Andy Bloxham, 'Afghanistan War Logs: 90,000 Classified Documents Revealed by Wikileaks', *The Telegraph*, July 26, 2010. Available at http://www.telegraph.co.uk/news/worldnews/asia/afghanistan/7909742/Afghanistan-war-logs-90000-classified-documents-revealedby-Wikileaks.html, accessed on July 28, 2010.

Wirsing, Robert, 'In India's Lengthening Shadow: The US–Pakistan Strategic Alliance and the War in Afghanistan', *Asian Affairs*, 34, 4 (2008), pp. 235–40.

'With Rs 2,284 cr, Budget Aims to Secure Borders', *The Indian Express*, July 7, 2009. Available at http://www.indianexpress.com/news/with-rs-2284-cr-budget-aims-to-secure-borders/485945/, accessed on October 3, 2013.

Wolfers, Arnold, 'National Security as an Ambiguous Symbol', *Political Science Quarterly*, 67, 4 (December 1952), pp. 481–502.

Xavier, Constantino, 'India's Strategic Advantage over China in Africa', *IDSA Comment*, June 30, 2010. Available at http://www.idsa.in/idsacomments/IndiasstrategicadvantageoverChinainAfrica_cxavier_300610, accessed on August 23, 2011.

Yazdani, E., 'The Dynamics of India's Relations with Iran in the Post-Cold War Era: A Geopolitical Analysis', *South Asia: A Journal of South Asian Studies*, 30, 2 (2007), pp. 351–68.

Yechury, Sitaram, *Socialism in a Changing World*. Hyderabad: Prajashakti Book House, 2008.

About the Editors

Kanti Bajpai is currently Professor and Vice Dean (Research), Lee Kuan Yew School of Public Policy, National University of Singapore, Singapore. His current research focuses on India–China relations and on Indian strategic thought. He was former Professor, International Politics, Jawaharlal Nehru University, New Delhi, and Professor, Politics and International Relations of South Asia, Oxford University. He was also Headmaster (2003–9), The Doon School, India. Most recently, he was Distinguished Fellow, Institute for Defence Studies and Analyses (IDSA), New Delhi. He writes a regular column for *The Times of India* (New Delhi).

Saira Basit is Research Fellow, Norwegian Institute for Defence Studies (IFS), Oslo. She is part of the IFS Centre for Asian Security Studies and PhD candidate at the Department of Political Science, University of Oslo/IFS. She was a Visiting Scholar at the IDSA, New Delhi (November–December 2008) and co-led the IFS–IDSA project *India's Grand Strategic Thought and Practice*. Her research focuses around energy and security policy issues in Iran, Pakistan and India. Her current interests are Pakistan's security and foreign policy vis-à-vis its neighbours.

V. Krishnappa is Director, Futurestrat Learning Systems Private Limited, New Delhi. Formerly, he was Research Fellow at the IDSA, New Delhi (2004–13). His research and consulting is in the areas of strategic thinking and practice, change management, defence policy, and India's grand strategy. He is co-editor (with Princy Marin George) of *India's Grand Strategy: 2020 and Beyond* (2012) and (with N. S. Sisodia) of *Global Power Shifts and Strategic Transition in Asia* (2009).

NOTES ON CONTRIBUTORS

Ali Ahmed, PhD, has been a research fellow at the Institute for Defence Studies and Analyses (IDSA), New Delhi, and has taught at the Nelson Mandela Centre for Peace and Conflict Resolution, Jamia Millia Islamia, New Delhi.

Nicolas Blarel is a doctoral candidate, Department of Political Science, Indiana University, Bloomington. His main areas of interest are international relations and comparative politics, and he is particularly interested by security issues in South Asia. He published his Master's thesis on Indo-Israeli strategic relations and has written prolifically on India's foreign and security policies.

Rudra Chaudhuri is Lecturer, Strategic Studies and South Asian Security, Department of War Studies and the India Institute, King's College London. He is the author of *Forged in Crisis: India and the United States Since 1947* (2013).

Shanthie Mariet D'Souza is Research Fellow, Institute of South Asian Studies (ISAS), National University of Singapore (NUS). She is currently working on issues of transition and long term stabilisation of Afghanistan.

S. Kalyanaraman is Research Fellow, IDSA, New Delhi. His areas of research include India's foreign policy, defence policy, and the challenges of terrorism and insurgency.

Bharat Karnad is Senior Fellow, National Security Studies, Centre for Policy Research, New Delhi. He is also the author of *India's Rise: Why It's Not a Great Power* (2013), *India's Nuclear Policy* (2008), and *Nuclear Weapons and Indian Security: Realist Foundations of Strategy* (2005 [2002]).

Tanvi Madan is Fellow, Foreign Policy programme, and Director, The India Project, Brookings Institution, Washington DC. Her work explores Indian foreign policy, focusing in particular on India's relations with China and the United States. She also researches the inter-section between Indian energy policies and its foreign and security policies.

Siddharth Mallavarapu is currently Associate Professor and Chairperson, Department of International Relations, South Asian University, New Delhi. He is co-editor (with B. S. Chimni) of *International Relations: Perspectives for the Global South* (2012).

Srinath Raghavan is Senior Fellow, Centre for Policy Research, New Delhi. He is the author of *War and Peace in Modern India: A Strategic History of the Nehru Years* (2010).

Swarna Rajagopalan is a political scientist and works as an independent scholar and consultant.

Rahul Sagar is Assistant Professor, Politics, Princeton University, New Jersey. He has published several essays on Indian strategic thought in edited volumes and journals. He is currently working on a manuscript (co-authored with Devesh Kapur), entitled *How To Be Great? India's Quest to Find Its Place in the World,* which examines Indian views on foreign relations from the nineteenth century to the present.

N. S. Sisodia is former Secretary, Ministry of Defence, Government of India, Vice-Chancellor, University of Udaipur, and Director General, IDSA, New Delhi. He has co-edited 12 books and writes prolifically for journals and newspapers on international relations and defence-related issues.

Sarang Shidore is currently an independent researcher and consultant, and was most recently with the IDSA, New Delhi. His areas of research interest include energy security, India's relations with emerging geographies, and ideational influences in international security.

Jayashree Vivekanandan is Assistant Professor, Department of International Relations, South Asian University, New Delhi. She is the author of *Interrogating International Relations: India's Strategic Practice and the Return of History* (2011).

Constantino Xavier is a doctoral candidate, South Asian Studies, Paul H. Nitze School of Advanced International Studies, Johns Hopkins University, Washington DC, where he researches on India's foreign policy and interventions. A Fulbright scholar and grantee of the Portuguese Ministry for Science, Technology and Higher Education, he has previously worked and researched at the Brookings Institution, Washington DC; IDSA, New Delhi; and the Portuguese Institute for International Relations, Lisbon.

INDEX

adharmik 40–41, 44–47, 53
adistra sandhi (land being traded for peace) 225
Advani, L. K. 224, 238
Afghan Chamber of Commerce and Industry (ACCI) 381
Afghanistan: Af–Pak strategy 399–402; *bi-tarafi*, policy of 377; Durand Line 388n38, 405; end game in 402–5; Indian Airlines Flight IC 814, hijacking of 382; Indo–Afghan Joint Commission 380; Joint Business Council 381; Najibullah, President 380; NATO withdrawal from 407, 428; Northern Alliance 372, 381, 382n22, 406, 409, 416; People's Democratic Party of Afghanistan (PDPA) 406; relations with India *see* India–Afghan relationship; King Zahir 377; Soviet intervention in 366, 377–79; Soviet withdrawal from 380, 399; talking to the Taliban 405–7; traditional alliance, Iran and Russia 407–9; United Islamic Front (UIF) 381, 381n22; US withdrawal from 394, 403, 405, 418
Afghanistan–Pakistan Trade and Transit Agreement (APTTA) 408
Afghan National Army (ANA) 393, 404
Afghan National Police (ANP) 393
Afghan National Security Forces (ANSF) 393
African Studies Association (ASA) 491, 497
African Union 481, 484, 489, 504–5; Capacity Building Foundation 484
Afro–Asian Business Chronicle 488
ahimsa (non-violence), philosophy of 19, 260–61, 264, 267, 276, 282

Ahmadinejad, President 427
Ahmedabad mill workers' strike (1919) 262
Akhlaq-i Humayuni (Ikhtiyar-al-Husaini) 73
Akhlaq-i Jahangiri (Nur ud-Din Qazi) 74
Akhlaq-i Nasiri (Nasir-al Din Tusi) 73
akhlaq (literature) 72–74
Alexander of Macedon 207
anarchy: condition of 117; fear of 93, 41–42
ancient India: fragmented territories 81; political climate in 80; sovereignty in 80
anti-colonial nationalism 259, 274
anti-Muslim pogroms, Gujarat (2002) 254
Antony, A. K. 220n46, 393
Appadurai, Arjun 15, 491
Arab–Israeli conflict 459–60
Arab–Persian rivalry 446
Arafat, Yasser 466
'area of peace' 153–54, 153n5, 169
Armed Forces Special Powers Act (AFSPA), India 214, 294
arms race 173–74, 276, 322, 343, 348, 354
Arthashastra (Kautilya) 10, 84n47, 203–19, 225, 227, 231
Asana 53–54
ASEAN Regional Forum (ARF) 186, 188
Ashoka the Great (304–232 BCE) 208
Ashvamedha (yajna) 48–51
Asian democratic quad 356
Asian Development Bank (ADB) 328, 351
Asian identity (Asianism) 156, 162

Asian Relations Conference (1947) 164, 166, 460, 482
Asian Tigers 254
Asia Society Corporate Conference (2006) 185
Asiatic Federation of Nations 166
Association of Southeast Asian Nation (ASEAN) 182, 186, 226, 320, 336; *see* ASEAN Regional Forum (ARF)
Atharva Veda 204
axis of evil 421
Axis Powers 161, 202, 276
Azad, Maulana Abdul Kalam 459,
Azhar, Maulana Masood 382

Babri mosque, demolition of (1992) 419
balance of power 14, 16, 26, 118, 120, 123, 146, 155, 206, 245, 324, 438, 447
Bandung Declaration 154, 172
Basham, A. L. 259
Basrur, Rajesh 293
Bhabha plan 230
Bhagavad Gita 10, 40, 44; Gandhi's reading of 264–67
Bharatiya Janata Party (BJP) 114, 129, 133, 133n44, 140, 143n72, 204n7, 224, 229, 235, 255, 297, 351n256, 367–68
bheda (dissension) 51–52, 206, 226
Bidwai, Praful 298
Bilgrami, Akeel 261–62, 268
Blackett, P. M. S. 208–9
Bonn Conference (2001) 383
*brahmana*s 40, 46, 50
brahmastra 205, 224
BRICS (Brazil, Russia, India, China, and South Africa) countries 188
British imperialism 151, 157, 158, 159, 163, 456, 457
British Raj 13, 88, 107
Brussels Conference of Oppressed Nationalities (1927) 457
Buddhism 143, 163, 208, 241

Bunch of Thoughts (Madhav Golwalker) 242
Bush, George W. 367, 370, 421, 424; Bush administration 369, 430, 440, 441

Cabinet Committee on Security (CCS) 369
Carter, Jimmy 366
Central Treaty Organization (CENTO) 169, 174
chakravartin 204, 232
Chandragupt Maurya, Emperor 203
Chatterjee, N. C. 234
Chatterjee, Partha 260
Chaudhuri, Nirad 106
Chaudhuri, Pramit Pal 445
Chellaney, Brahma 399–400
China 7, –9, 14, 17–18, 20–22, 25–27, 39n7, 109, 116, 124n31, 125, 128, 133–35, 134n46, 139, 140, 144, 140–45, 148, 149; acceptance of India's claims on Arunachal Pradesh 318; attitude towards India's global aspirations 336; attitude towards India's territorial integrity 327; 'Balkanisation of India' 328; claims to Arunachal and Sikkim 339; hostility towards India 312; Kunming initiative 321, 332, 347; legitimisation of sovereignty over Tibet 353; model of development 321; occupation of Tibet 221; People's Liberation Army (PLA) 220, 364; 244; relation with India *see* India–China relationship; Sino–India war (1962); relation with Pakistan *see* Sino–Pakistani relationship; relation with USA *see* Sino–US relationship; resistance to Sikkim's integration with India 327; 'string of pearls' strategy 335; support to Naga and Mizo separatists 328; Tibet card 327, 346, 353; trade with Iran 432; Uighur Muslim groups 227; use of Pakistan as a

Index ❖ 571

'counterweight' to India 330–31; Xinjiang province 227, 330
Chou En Lai (Chinese Premier Zhou Enlai) 364
Christian missionaries 136, 146
civil–military relations 13, 38n7, 92, 94, 99–100, 105, 108, 357
climate change 192, 194, 228, 322, 343–44, 374, 485, 487
Clinton, Bill 242, 230
Clinton, Hillary 201, 401
coercive diplomacy 301, 326
co-existence, principles of 255, 318
Cohen, Stephen 297–98
'Cold Start' doctrine 21, 304–5
Cold War (and post-Cold War) 8, 17, 20, 23 25, 82, 113, 115–16, 132, 135, 153, 154, 168–71, 173, 174, 182, 186, 187, 195, 224, 229, 291–92, 301, 317, 362–63, 365–67, 377–82, 412, 418–23, 433, 436–38, 447–48, 451–52, 454, 465, 467, 475, 482, 487, 498
commercial liberalism 178, 316
Communist Party of India (Marxist) 8, 128, 470
'community of democracies' 142, 142n71
Comprehensive Test Ban Treaty (CTBT) 8, 140, 142, 348
Confederation of Indian Industries (CII) 484, 492
Congress of Vienna 32
counter insurgency (COIN) 373, 401, 405n93
cross-border terrorism 213
Crossing the Rubicon (C. Raja Mohan) 296
cultural nationalism 287, 290, 299
Curzon, Lord 11, 92–94, 96

Dalai Lama 227, 320, 328, 345, 346, 349
dana (gift-giving) 51–52, 206, 226
dandaniti 52
Delhi Sultanate 69

democratic liberalism 178
Deng, Xiaoping 180, 345
Department of African Studies, India 490–91
Desai, Morarji 464
dharma 11–12, 32, 36, 38, 39–48, 52–53, 56–58, 80, 252
Dixit, J. N. 377, 465, 467, 469
'drain of wealth,' idea of 88
Durand Line 388n38, 405
Dutt, Barkha 444
dvaidibhava (duplicity) 53–54

East Asian tiger economies 180
East Asia Summit (EAS) 186, 188, 232n75
economic nationalism 88
economics, power of 120, 125
engagement, rules of 54–56, 57
Engelmeier, Tobias 114, 296–97
Enlightenment 446; Gandhi's critique of 267–71
Erikson, Erik 262–63
Esher Committee Report 98, 100
Essentials of Hindutva (Vinayak D. Savarkar) 250–51
European Union 17, 191, 194, 483
Exercise Brasstacks 294, 302
Exercise Chequerboard 294
Exim Bank, India 484, 500

fascism, rise of 151, 158
Fathollahi, Mohammad Ali 408
Federation of Indian Chambers of Commerce and Industry (FICCI) 381, 484, 492, 497, 499, 502, 502n86
Fissile Material Cut-off Treaty 348
foreign policy *see* India's foreign policy
free market policies 119, 177, 191
free trade: economic theory of 88; free trade agreements (FTAs) 226
French Revolution 32, 64n3
Fukushima disaster (2011) 414

Gandhians, views of: on dealing with Pakistan, China, and USA 145–46;

on greatest threat to India 136, 145; on image of international life 138–39; on importance of non-violence 253; on India's security 16; on individual conscience 129, 135; on industrial civilisational values 146; on national armies 147; opposition to nuclear weapons programme 148; opposition to the use of organised violence 137–138, 147; on violence and use of force 137, 138–39
Gandhi, Gopalkrishna 278
Gandhi, Indira 15, 223,229, 299, 366, 378, 378n7, 383, 462; Indira Doctrine 21, 299
Gandhi, Mahatma 176, 214, 512, 542; *ahimsa* (non-violence), philosophy of 19, 260–61, 264, 267, 276, 282; conception of truth 259–60; critique of the Enlightenment 267–71; critique of western civilisation 259, 264, 273–74; Gandhian referents, map of 259–64; *Hind Swaraj* 263–64; idea of renunciation 267; on internal policing in an independent India 259, 280–81; modern State, view on 271–72; need and value of satyagraha 19, 259, 261–63; 85; reading of *Mahabharata* and *Gita* 264–67; response to Second World War 259, 275–78; Swaraj, concept of 19, 259, 263–64, 382; thoughts on Indian Army post-independence 259, 278–80
Gandhi, Rajiv 180, 302, 331, 379 380, 464 465
Geneva Accords (1954) 380
Ghafar Khan, Khan Abdul 282
Ghose, Aurobindo 15, 238
Ghose, Sagarika 445
global capitalism 57, 132, 133, 142, 146
globalisation 41, 122, 123, 125, 132, 134, 141, 142, 148, 150, 152

'Global South' 487
Gokhale, Gopal Krishna 90–92, 94, 95, 96, 102, 108
Golwalker, Madhav 18, 133n44, 138n54, 234; *Bunch of Thoughts* 242; concept of an organic 'World State' 243–44; distrust of the patriotism of Muslims and Christians 252; emphasis on cultivating a martial spirit 247; international politics, theory of 234, 242–46; realist critique of Hindu nationalism 68–71; statements in wake of India's defeat to China (1962) 248; understanding of national power 248, 252–54
Government of India Act (1919) 98
grand strategy of India: core interests and vital peripheries 20–25; in history 10–13; Indian epics and 31–34, 56–58; Marxist, Hindutva, and Gandhian 128–475; in modern times 13–20; Nehruvian, Neoliberal and Hyperrealist 116–28
Greater India, idea of 173
greenhouse gases 413, 415
Gross Domestic Product (GDP) 184, 185, 216
Group of 77 (G-77) 482
Group of Twenty (G-20) countries 27, 188
Gujral Doctrine 182, 483
Gulf Cooperation Council (GCC) 446
Gulf War (1991) 180, 466
Gupta, Shekhar 445

Habsburg empire 65, 77
Haqqani, Sirajuddin 406
Hasina, Sheikh 215, 215n30
Hazare, Anna 114
Hekmatyar, Gulbuddin 398
Hezb-e-Islami (HIG) 398
Hind Swaraj (Mahatma Gandhi) 263–64
Hindu Mahasabha 240, 298

Hindu nationalism 16, 18, 26, 235, 237; realist critique of 252–257; Hindu nationalist movement 234–35
Hindu Renaissance 247
Hindutva 16, 18–20, 26, 114, 116, 128–31; on dealing with Pakistan, China, and USA 143–45; on security threats to India 132–37; use of organised violence 138; view of the West 135–36
Hoffman, Steven 314, 315, 324, 338
Holbrooke, Richard 372, 405
Holstag, Jonathan 189
Home Rule 97, 274, 275
human rights violations 47, 153n4, 466
Hussein, Saddam 466
Hydespas, Battle of (326 BCE) 207

IBSA (India, Brazil and South Africa) countries 198
India: adversarial relations with Pakistan *see* India–Pakistan conflicts; Afghan policy *see* India–Afghan relations; Africa policy *see* India–Africa relationship; battles against colonialism and imperialism 155, 162, 317; defence relation with Israel *see* India–Israel relationship; foreign policy 115n4, 154, 158, 162, 167, 168, 174, 311n9, 368, 377, 441, 451–55, 465, 473, 503; grand strategy *see* grand strategy of India; policy towards Iran *see* India–Iran relationship; posture on Pakistan *see* India–Pakistan relationship; as subsidiary ally of United States *see* India–US relationship
India–Afghan relationship: administrative and civilian capacity building 23, 376, 385–86; after 9/11 attack 22, 376, 382–89; Agreement on Strategic Partnership (ASP) 387; aid diplomacy and soft power approach 23, 376, 383, 394, 404; attacks on the Indian Embassy 391, 391n48; Capacity for Afghan Public Administration programme 386; Chabahar Free Zone Authority (CFZA) 388; contribution to rebuilding the Afghan state 373; developmental/infrastructural aid 385; Indian Airlines Flight IC 814, hijacking of 382; Indira Gandhi Children's Hospital 383; Indo-Afghan Joint Commission 380; Institute of Child Health 980; joint research and teaching programmes 379; northern distribution network (NDN) 388; political solution 369–99; Preferential Trade Agreement 387; self-employment generation schemes 388; small development projects (SDP) 385; southern trade corridor 388; Strategic Partnership 393, 395, 411; TAPI *see* Turkmenistan–Afghanistan–Pakistan–India (TAPI) pipeline; Zaranj-Delaram highway 385, 388, 391, 428
India–Africa relationship: in academic sector 496–97; Africa Day 493; African studies division at Jawaharlal Nehru University 491; 'Afro-Asian solidarity' movement 482; Afro-Indian climate change initiative 485; anti-colonial freedom movements 482; bilateral trade 544; in business and corporate sector 497–98; C. V. Raman scholarships 485; Delhi Declaration and Joint Action Plan (2008) 505; Department of African Studies, India 505; India–Africa Hydrocarbons Conference 484; India–Africa summit 25, 484; Joint Business Councils 484; between MEA and academia 498–500; between MEA and business 500–2; Ministry of External Affairs (MEA) 493–96; models of engagement 479; piracy threat

along the Somali coast 487; public diplomacy 502–3; 'punishment posting' 494; Swahili language programme 490, 496
India after Gandhi (Ramachandra Guha) 115
India–China relationship 21–22, 308–09, 1962 war *see* Sino–India war (1962); armed intrusions 219; bilateral relationships 309, 316, 318, 321, 322, 332, 333, 339, 346, 347, 348, 352, 358; border areas, economic development of 350, 353; border disputes 219; border settlement 349; Chindia rising, optimists views on 22,314–23; Chinese military capabilities 322, 323, 325, 349; on climate change negotiations 322, 344; coercive diplomacy 326; confidence-building measures (CBMs) 319; construction of dam on Brahmaputra river 220,332; cooperation in Central Asia and Afghanistan 341; Crouching Tiger, Hidden Dragon 323–37; economic competition 358; as economic powers and rivals 219; in economic sphere 321 332–33, 342, 351; future prospects of 357–59; general attitude 315–17, 323–24; 'Great Game' (New Great Game) 321, 332, 347; import of toys from China 333; influence and use of public opinion on 358; interpretation of China's capabilities, intentions and actions 314–15; labour issues 333–34; on leasing of Coco Islands from Myanmar 335; Line of Actual Control (LAC) 219; McMahon Line 311; military face-off and diplomatic row 219; naval capabilities 334, 350; Past Prisms, Perceptions and Policies 309–14; pessimists views 348–52; Prickly Porcupines or Tangoing Tigers 337–45; pragmatists view 352–57; Sino–Indian friendship 228; Sino–Pakistan relationship, impact of 320, 329, 331, 340; 'string of pearls' strategy 335; subservience to 219–28; Tale of the Two Tigers 315–23; Tibet, issue *see* Tibet; trust deficit 189, 219

India–Iran relationship 23–24, 26, 27, 166, 169, 231, 385, 388, 390, 407–9; Asian Clearing Union 428–29; during Cold War (and after) 418–23; on demolition of the Babri mosque in India 419; IAEA voting 24, 26, 408, 423–25, 426, 427, 429, 430; during India–Pakistan wars 417, 418, 421; during Sino–India war 418; Iranian news channel, banning of 428; IPI pipeline *see* India–Pakistan–Iran (IPI) pipeline; Jaswant Singh's visit to Tehran (2000) 420; joint naval exercises 421; launching of Israeli spy satellite 426; Liquefied Natural Gas (LNG) 415, 421, 422, 425, 426; Mohammed Khatami's visit to New Delhi (2003) 420–21; nuclear issue 424, 431; Prime Minister Vaypayee's visit to Tehran (2001) 420; post-nuclear deal 423–29; security matters 416–18; Tehran Declaration 420; TAPI *see* Turkmenistan–Afghanistan–Pakistan–India (TAPI) pipeline; US factor and India's strategy 429–33

India–Israel relationship 24; advanced air defence (AAD) system 470; airborne early-warning and control (AEW&C) Phalcon systems 470; Arjun tank 469; collaborating against Islamic fundamentalism 476; in counter-terrorism operations 469; 471–74; diplomatic relations 24, 187 471, 473, 474; for economic development 474–75; factors considered in developing 465–68; future of 451, 475–78; history of 450, 452; on India's foreign policy

autonomy 473–74; India's Israel policy, reassessment of 462–71; and India's pro-Arab policy 463, 474; Light Combat Aircraft (LCA) project 469; from limited recognition to full engagement 455–56; 'limited relationship policy' 455; military assistance during India's war with China and Pakistan 463–64; military assistance during the Kargil crisis 469; military technology transfer 464, 473; modernisation of obsolete Soviet military equipment 468; and origins of India's Israel policy 456–62; recognition and no-relationship policy 461; relevance of the grand strategy framework to 451–55; replacement of ageing MiGs aircrafts 302; security and military co-operation 468–70; Unmanned Aerial Vehicles (UAVs) 470
Indian Commissioned Officers (ICOs) 107
Indian Council for Cultural Relations (ICCR) 383, 489, 503
Indian Council for World Affairs 492
Indian epics: core values 39; for creating security 49–58; *dharma*, notion of 41–43; fear of anarchy 43–44; grand strategic thought *see* grand strategy; political ideas 40; searching for strategic insights 40–58; self, other and diversity 44–49; *see also* Mahabharata; Ramayana
Indian Foreign Service 494
Indian internationalism 151, 162; origins of 155–158
Indian military system 95; Army in India Committee 98; contribution to the Allied war effort 97; Europeanisation of the Army 104; force requirements 128; future of 98; Indian Military College (IMC) 107; Indian Territorial Force 101; integrated missile programme 302; military responsibilities overseas 98; military training schools and colleges 106; nationalisation, issue of 99, 100; nuclear programme 134
Indian National Congress 87, 89, 97, 151, 155, 456, 470; Calcutta session (1928) 165; expression of nationalism 151; vision of future of international system 161
Indian nationalism 151, 155, 157, 159–60, 168
Indian nuclear energy programme 230
Indian Peace Keeping Force (IPKF) 302
Indian Sandhurst Committee 103
Indian Strategic Thought: An Interpretive Essay (1994) 6, 236, 290
Indian Technical and Co-operation (ITEC) program 485
Indian Territorial Force 101
India–Pakistan conflicts: 1947–48 war 14, 209–10, 293; 1965 war 209, 210, 293,294, 300, 418, 462, 463, 464; 1971 war 174, 210, 293, 294, 300, 418, 462, 463, 464; Kargil war (1999) 8, 139–40, 301, 320, 439; Operation Gibraltar 300; Operation Grand Slam 300; Operation Parakram (2002) 225, 301; Siachen glacier conflict (1984) 294, 300, 303
India–Pakistan–Iran (IPI) pipeline 23–24, 409, 415, 419–23, 426, 429, 431
India–Pakistan relationship: future of 307; India's Pakistan policy 287, 290, 293, 299, 307; Indus Waters Treaty (1960) 219; Tashkent conference (1966) 293; terror attacks on India 8, 213, 218, 294, 301, 302, 427; wars *see* India–Pakistan conflicts
India–US relations: during Afghan conflict (2008) 371–74; during the

Cold War 362, 363, 365, 366, 367; co-operation based on shared interests 375; defence co-operation 360, 370, 372; Defence Framework Agreement 440; economic aid 222; on foreign policy 362, 367, 368, 374; during Iraq war *see* Iraq war; during Kargil war *see* Kargil war; during Korean war *see* Korean war; as leverage with China 356; media discourse on nuclear deal 444–45; missile defence proposal 440; 'New Framework for US-India Defence Partnership for the Next Ten Years' 370; scholarly discourse 445–47-93; social character of 255; Strategic Dialogue (June 2010) 201n3, 230, 400
Indo-Afghan Joint Commission 380
Indo-Arab relations 462, 463, 475; during Indo-Pakistani war 463, 464; during Sino-Indian border dispute 463
Indo-Soviet treaty 357
indrajala (strategem) 51, 53
Indus Waters Treaty (1960) 219
Institute of Defence Studies and Analyses, India 492
internal security, concept of 1–3, 11, 90, 293, 294, 298, 300, 310, 454
International Atomic Energy Agency (IAEA) 24, 26, 423,424, 425, 426, 427, 429, 430, 432
International Control Commission 170
International Monetary Fund (IMF) 27, 141, 180, 229, 351, 374, 467
international politics, theory of 238–253
international relations (IR), 58, 63, 64, 117, 118, 119, 120, 123, 124, 125, 130, 152; characterisation of 118, 177; discourse analysis in 436; Gandhi's views on 290–93; Hindu nationalist view of 234–38, 255; 'the law of the fish' 204; role of military and economic power in 118

Iran: China's trade with 432; foreign policy towards India 419; IPI pipeline *see* India–Pakistan–Iran (IPI) pipeline; Islamic Revolution (1979) 418; Jaswant Singh's visit 420; North–South Transportation Corridor 420; nuclear programme 24, 408; OIC conference (1997) 420; oil payments problem with India 409; Pahlavi monarchy 418; Proliferation Act 430; relation with India *see* India–Iran relationship; relation with Pakistan *see* Pakistan–Iran relationship; relation with USA 409, 418, 421 support for the Kashmir cause 23, 419–20, 428; TAPI *see* Turkmenistan–Afghanistan–Pakistan–India (TAPI) pipeline
Iraq war (2003) 22, 361, 366–371

Jaffna Tamils 225
*jagir*s 70
Jaish-e-Mohammad (JeM) 382
Jamaat-ud-Dawa 330
Jamia Millia Islamia's Academy of Third World Studies, New Delhi 491
Jana Sangh 298, 463
Japanese militarism in Asia 158
jeevanvritanta (description of life) 269
Jervis, Robert 317, 345
Jinnah, Mohammed Ali 15, 87, 102–06, 108
Johnston, Alastair Iain 288; cultural realism, theory of 290; political culture, theory of 289–90

Kabul conference (2010) 408
Kanwal, Gurmeet 404
Kargil Review Committee 301
Kargil war (1999) 8, 139–40, 301, 320, 439
karma sandhi 231
Karzai, Hamid 373, 383, 397–98, 402, 403, 405, 406

Kashmir (valley): dispute between India and Pakistan on 218–19; financial subsidies 214; human rights violations 466; India's counter-insurgency struggle in 214, 466; as integral part of India 467; jihadi groups active inside 214–15; Kashmir war (1947–48) 14, 209–10, 293; self-determination for Muslims in 419; stapled visas 189; terrorist attacks 8
Kautilya's 'circle of kings' 80
Keohane, Robert 188, 202
Khalifat movement 456, 459n39
Khan, A. Q. 463, 471
Khanwa, battle of (1527) 66
Khatami, Mohammed 420
Khomeini, Ayatollah 419
Kitchener, Lord 92–94
Korean war (1950) 22, 154, 179, 325, 361, 362–63, 364–65
Krishna, S. M. 213n3, 436, 440
*kshatriya*s 40, 52, 54
Kumarappa, Bharatan 263
kutayuddha (covert war) 205, 217
Kuwait crisis (1990–1) 465

Lahore declaration 8
Lantos, Tom 475–76
Lashkar-e-Tayyaba/Lashkar-e-Taiba (LeT) 215n27, 217, 330, 392
League against Imperialism and for National Independence 157
League of Nations 148n86, 263
'legacy of conflict' 167
light water reactors 230
Lilienfeld, Claudio 370
Line of Actual Control (LAC) 219
Line of Control (LOC) 139, 218, 294, 303
Liquefied Natural Gas (LNG) 415, 421, 422, 425, 426
Lisbon Summit (2010) 410
Lodi Afghans 69
Look East policy (1992), India 185, 355, 483

Look West policy (2005), India 186
Lucknow Pact (1916) 97

Macarthur, Douglas 364
McChrystal, Stanley 372, 390
McMahon Line 311
Madrid Conference (October 1991) 466
Mahabharata 9, 11, 31, 36–38, 204, 206, 259; engagement, rules of 54–56; Gandhi's reading of 264–67; Krishna, character of 37, 42, 43, 45, 47, 48, 49 52, 53, 56, 58; policy instruments and approaches 51–54; political ideas 34; sovereignty, rituals of 48–51; versions of 37–38
Malaviya, Pandit Krishna Kant 165
mansabdari system (1573–74) 12, 69
manual of war (*Yuddhakundam*) 205
Maoist insurgency in India 328, 358
marginal war, concept of 208–09
martial races 95, 98, 100, 106
Marxism (Marxist theory) 16, 114, 128–30; dealing with Pakistan, China, and USA 139–42; grand strategy based on 114
maryada purushottama 45
mass civil disobedience 165
Mathai, Ranjan 447
matsyanyaya 41–42, 52
Mauryan empire 208
maya (illusion and deceit) 51, 53
Mehta, Pratap Bhanu 253, 291, 295
Menon, Krishna 462
Menon, Shivshankar 23
military institutions, in colonial era: Commander-in-Chief 92–93, 98–99, 102, 106; in early liberal thought 87–91; eight units scheme of Indianisation of 101–2; Imperial Cadet Corps (ICC) 96, 103; Imperial Service Troops 96; Indian Cadet College, Indore 97; King's Commissioned Indian Officers (KCIOs) 101, 104, 106 –07; King's

Commissioned Officers (KCOs) 95; military expenditure 89–90, 92, 94, 99; Military Member 98–99; Prince of Wales Royal Indian Military College, Dehradun 101, 104; reforms after the Great War 96–101; Royal Military College, Sandhurst 97, 98, 100, 101; towards an Indian Sandhurst 101–7; Viceroy's Commissioned Officers (VCOs) 95, 97, 103, 104, 107
military labour market 68–69, 79
military resources of India 99
Million British Thermal Units (MBTU) 421–23, 426
Ministry of Defence, India 492
Ministry of External Affairs (MEA), India 549–50, 553–56, 559; Policy, Planning and Research Division 555; policy planning imperatives and preoccupations 555; primary role and responsibility 554
Ministry of Petroleum and Natural Gas, India 484
Mishra, Brajesh 442, 444
Mohan, C. Raja 318, 334, 443–44, 492
Montagu–Chelmsford Report (1918) 97–98, 239
Montagu, Edwin 97
moral superiority, notion of 163
Motilal Nehru Report (August 1928) 105
Mughal empire, strategic tradition of 65–71, 71–79
Muhajir Quami Movement 213
Mukherjee, Pranab 190
Mulford, David 430
Mumbai terrorist attacks (2008) 427
Musharraf, Pervez 218
Muslim League 87, 97, 102; demand for Pakistan 457

Naga tribes 14
'Namaskar Africa' program, India 484
Nandy, Ashis 269

Naoroji, Dadabhai 88, 90, 94, 108
Napoleonic wars 32
National Democratic Alliance (NDA) 367
nationalism, Gandhian view of 131
national power 19, 237, 238, 245–49, 252–54, 257
national security 1, 2, 8, 14, 119, 174, 215n27, 230–31, 272, 273, 292, 425, 462
National Socialist Council of Nagaland 214
national values, threats to 3
nation-states: Gandhian view of 131; Westphalian international system of 131
natural gas 321, 347, 387, 388–89, 414, 414–16, 429
Naxalite movement *see* Maoist insurgency in India
Nazi Germany 160
Nazism 151, 158–59, 275
Nehru, Jawaharlal 14, 24, 113–14, 141, 214, 220, 245, 335, 399–402, 504, 509, 512–14; 'A Foreign Policy for India' report 166; foreign policy framework 161–64, 176–82; *Panchsheel* principles 163, 181; reconciling nationalism and internationalism 167–71; response to Chinese aggression 233–37; strategic visioning 237; vision of China 337
Nehru, Motilal 103–05, 108
Nehruvianism 16–20, 113, 114, 117, 128, 132, 149, 176, 291, 296, 298, 299
neoliberalism: 16–20, 113, 114, 116, 128, 132, 149, 291, 297, 338; impact on India's economy 194–97; impact on India's security 184–87; key features of 177–79; shift towards 179–84
nitishastra 80
'no first use' (NFU) doctrine 294, 336n159

Non-Aligned Movement (NAM) 141, 377, 424, 482, 498
non-alignment, policy of 168, 362, 418
non-violence, Gandhi's doctrine of 263
Non-Violent Resistance (Satyagraha) 263
North-South Transportation Corridor 420
North-Western Frontier Province 282
nuanced diplomacy 352
nuclear apartheid 185, 188
nuclear deterrence, concept of 148, 205, 211n16
nuclear doctrine of India 183
'nuclear flashpoint' in South Asia 211
nuclearisation of South Asia 302
Nuclear Non-Proliferation Treaty (NPT) 142, 230, 231, 371, 424, 443
nuclear-sourced electricity 231
Nuclear Suppliers Group 230, 336, 423, 487
nuclear weapons programme 18, 148, 293, 322,
Nussbaum, Martha 253
Nye, Joseph 178-79, 192

Obama, Barack (President) 145n85, 361, 371, 372, 401, 402
Observer Research Foundation 492, 500n74
OIC Rabat conference (1969) 463
One World, notion of 153-55, 167-68, 173
Operation Gibraltar (1965) 300
Operation Grand Slam (1965) 300
Operation Parakram (2002) 225, 301
Ottoman empire 77
Pakistan 14; anti-India agenda *see* India-Pakistan conflicts; Chagai nuclear tests 301; deployment of terrorism in India 305; as failed state 209; Freedom Movements in Baluchistan 213; on India's role in Afghanistan 387, 389-96, 400; international isolation of 307; IPI pipeline *see* India-Pakistan-Iran (IPI) pipeline; Kashmir issue *see* Kashmir (valley); military outcomes 301-5; Muhajir Quami Movement 213; nuclear proliferation to Iran 417, 425; policy of cross-border terrorism 213; proxy war against India 21, 300, 303, 306, 396; relation with China *see* Sino-Pakistani relationship; relation with India *see* India-Pakistan relationship; relation with Iran *see* Pakistan-Iran relationship; 'stability-instability paradox' 213; terror attacks on India 8, 213, 218, 294, 301, 302, 427
Pakistan-Iran relationship 417-18
Palit, D. K. 15, 210
Panchsheel (Panchashila) 16, 154, 172, 318
Panikkar, K. M. 15, 364
Panipat, battles of (1526 and 1556) 66
Pantham, Thomas 273
Pant, K. C. 297
Parekh, Bhiku 269
Parliament of Religions in Chicago (1893) 362
Patel, Vallabhbhai 221, 309; Nehru-Patel debate 311-13; realist view of China 310; threat assessment 310
Peres, Shimon 464
performance of duties 47-48
plutonium breeder reactors 230
power politics 17-18, 153, 164, 168, 237, 299, 244, 245, 345, 482
Progressive Front of India 217

Quisling, Vidkun 202
Quit India Resolution 151, 160, 160n28, 162, 167

Rademaker, Stephen 430
Radhakrishnan, Sarvepalli 15, 165
Rafsanjani, President 419-20
Rajagopalan, Rajesh 114, 291
Rajasuya 48-50, 52
rajmandala 205, 232

Ramayana 9, 11, 31, 34–36, 204, 204n7; engagement, rules of 54–56; killing of Vali and Shambuka 45, 46, 54; policy instruments and approaches 51–54; and ramarajya 36; *Ramcharitmanas* (Tulsidas) 36; sovereignty, rituals of 48–51; Valmiki 36, 45
Rao, Nirupama 397, 409, 443
Rao, P. V. Narasimha 182, 228, 229, 301, 381, 464, 468, 473
Rasgotra, M. K. 378, 378n7, 398
Rashtriya Swayamsevak Sangh (RSS) 114, 133n44, 134n46, 298
Rawlinson, General 100
Reagan, Ronald (President) 266, 366
realpolitik 18, 19, 201, 223, 233, 270, 311, 323, 445;
Research and Analysis Wing 487n23, 490
Rice, Condoleezza 423
Rig Veda 204, 206, 223
ritual sovereignty, notion of 78, 78n32
Riyadh Declaration 427
Rodman, Peter 369–70
Roosevelt, Franklin (President) 362
Rosen, Stephen 38n7, 84
Round Table conference (October 1930) 106
Roy, Rammohan 88
Rumsfeld, Donald 369, 372
Russia 90, 92, 128, 149, 156, 157, 182, 188, 209, 232n75, 256, 321, 348, 354, 356, 358, 378, 378n7, 388, 407–9, 416, 420, 424, 444, 469; *see* Soviet Union

Saleh, Amrullah 406
sama (conciliation) 51–2, 206, 216, 226
Sama Veda 204
samshraya (alliance) 53, 54
samukhayuddha (total war) 205
sandhi (peace) 53; *adistra sandhi* 25; *karma sandhi* 231; *swarna sandhi* 231

Sapru, Tej Bahadur 15, 98, 101, 105, 106, 108
Saran, Shyam 225n62, 433, 443
satyagraha 19, 259, 261–3
Savarkar, Vinayak 14, 18, 19; balance of power politics 245; 'doctrinal plague' 247; emphasis on cultivating a martial spirit 247; *Indian War of Independence, The* 249; international politics, theory of 234, 238–41; political theory 265; realist critique of Hindu nationalism 268–71; understanding of national power 248, 252–54
Science of Material Gain see *Arthashastra* (Kautilya)
shadgunyam 53
Sharia 72
Sharon, Ariel 73
Shastri, Lal Bahadur 233–24
Sheean, Vincent 267
Sherzai, Gul Agha 398
Siachen glacier 294, 303
Simon Commission 105
Singh, Jaswant 230, 238, 297, 382, 420
Singh, Manmohan (Prime Minister; government) 25, 180, 183, 186, 190, 203, 216, 218, 229–30, 231n73, 233, 305, 366, 381n21, 386, 396, 398, 427, 429, 441, 442
Sinha, Satyendra 97
Sino–India war (1962) 13, 317–18 325, 356418, 462, 463, 464,
Sino–Pakistani relationship 21, 345, 417; assistance for Gwadar port 189;
Sino–US relationship 232, 344, 345, 364; memorandum of understanding on climate change 344; rapprochement in 1971 351, 356, 357; strategic convergence 344
Sivaswamy Aiyer Resolutions 98–100, 101
Skeen, Andrew 103
social militarisation in India, levels of 67–68

sociological liberalism 178
South Asian Association for Regional Co-operation (SAARC) 190–91, 226, 320, 331, 387, 402
Southeast Asia Treaty Organization (SEATO) 169, 174
Southern African Development Community (SADC) 489
Soviet Union 4, 8, 14, 17, 130, 180, 187, 227, 452; during Cold War *see* Cold War; collapse of 8, 174, 181, 366; defence relation with India 187; as India's largest arms supplier 468; intervention in Afghanistan 366, 377–78; quasi-alliance with India 174; Warsaw Pact 439; withdrawal from Afghanistan 380
Statutory Commission 105
Steel Authority of India (SAIL) 387
strategic culture: *hardpolitik* 288; Johnston's theoretical framework on 289–90; *parabellum* 288–89; state identity and 433–37
Students Islamic Movement of India 217
Subrahmanyam, K. 6, 15, 113, 447
Suez crisis of 1956 461, 476
Sukraniti (Kautilya) 204, 206
Sulh-i kul (absolute peace) 76–77
Sundarji, General 15, 302
swadeshi 270
swaraj 19, 259, 263–64, 382

Tagore, Rabindranath 15, 162–63, 256, 362
Talbott, Strobe 230
Taliban 23, 26, 215n28, 381–82, 381n22, 383, 391–92, 391n48, 394, 397–99, 403–5, 405–7, 408–10, 416, 417, 420, 428
Tanham, George K. 6, 38n7, 84, 113, 290, 453
Tashkent conference (1966) 293
Techno-Economic Approach for Africa-India Movement (TEAM-9) 484

The Soviet Strategic Culture: Implications for Nuclear Options (Jack Snyder) 82, 289n4
The Indian War of Independence (Vinayak D. Savarkar) 249
thermonuclear weaponisation 230
Tibet 11, 14, 22, 163, 183, 232–34, 239, 336–38, 344–47, 350–51, 355, 360, 362, 365, 372, 375, 379, 384
Tibetan refugees in India 144
Tilak, Bal Gangadhar 97, 238
Truman, Harry S. (President) 362–65
Turkey (Republic of) 250, 250n68, 432, 440, 456, 460
Turkmenistan–Afghanistan–Pakistan–India (TAPI) pipeline 387, 409, 429

Umayyad Caliphate armies 207
Union of Soviet Socialist Republic (USSR) *see* Soviet Union
United Arab Emirates 381, 466
United Kingdom 221, 364
United Liberation Front of Assam (ULFA) 214
United Nations (UN) 42, 142n70, 153, 153n4, 155, 160, 161, 167, 169n61, 170, 171, 173, 221, 310, 363, 457, 482, 487, 490
United Progressive Alliance (UPA) 21, 115, 301, 370, 470, 470n101
United States of America (USA): Af-Pak strategy 399–402; dealing with Afghanistan and Iraq 282, 361 371–74; 'Defence of India' programme 236; Department of Defence 400; Hyde Act 476; Iraq War (2003) 22, 361, 366–71; Korean War 22, 154, 179, 325, 361, 362–63, 364–65; National Security Council (NSC) 363; nuclear technology for India 423–24; relation with England 245; on role in Asia and the world 322–323, 337, 344–45; Taliban 405–7
University Training Corps 101

upeksha (indifference) 51, 53
USAID 402

Vajapeya sacrifice 49
Vajpayee, Atal Bihari (Prime Minister) 183, 223, 225n62, 229, 230, 238, 322, 367, 368, 383, 420, 421, 437n148
Vanaik, Achin 298
varna 39–40, 45
varnashramadharma 39, 41
Varshney, Ashutosh 253
Vedas 1074, 202, 204–5, 213
Venkatapatiraju, B. 103
Vietnam 226, 228
vigraha (war) 53–54
violence and force, role of 137–39
Vivekananda, Swami 238, 247, 362

Wahhabi Islamic forces 23
War and Peace in Modern India: A Strategic History of the Nehru Years (Srinath Raghavan) 15
war, causes of 206

Warsaw Pact 439
weapon-grade plutonium production 230
weapons of mass destruction (WMD) 142, 205
West Asia and North Africa (WANA) 489
West Asian peace initiatives 466
Western colonialism 135, 151, 162
WikiLeaks 406, 446
Wolfers, Arnold 272
World Bank 27, 229, 351, 467
World Trade Organization 322
World War: first (Great War) 247, 250n68; second 3, 17, 107, 165, 209, 209n13, 245, 259, 275, 364n16, 366; Gandhi's response to 275–78

Yajur Veda 204
yana (attack) 53–54

*zamindar*s 68, 69
Zardari, Asif Ali 216
Zionist movement 452